# House and Home in Modern Japan

Harvard East Asian Monographs, 223

# House and Home in Modern Japan

## Architecture, Domestic Space and Bourgeois Culture 1880–1930

Jordan Sand

Published by the Harvard University Asia Center
and distributed by Harvard University Press
Cambridge (Massachusetts) and London 2003

Printed in the United States of America

The Harvard University Asia Center publishes a monograph series and, in coordination with the Fairbank Center for East Asian Research, the Korea Institute, the Reischauer Institute of Japanese Studies, and other faculties and institutes, administers research projects designed to further scholarly understanding of China, Japan, Vietnam, Korea, and other Asian countries. The Center also sponsors projects addressing multidisciplinary and regional issues in Asia.

Library of Congress Cataloging-in-Publication Data

Sand, Jordan, 1960–

House and home in modern Japan : architecture, domestic space, and bourgeois culture, 1880–1930 / Jordan Sand.

p. cm. -- (Harvard East Asian monographs ; 223)

Includes bibliographical references and index.

ISBN 0-674-01218-6 (cloth : alk. paper)

1. Architecture, Domestic--Japan. 2. Japan--Social life and customs--1868–1912. 3.Japan--Social life and customs--1912–1945. I. Title. II. Series

NA 7451.S33 2003

306.85'0952'09045--dc21 2003047753

Index by the author

♾ Printed on acid-free paper

First paperback edition, 2005; ISBN 0-674-01966-0; *front cover illustration*: Culture Village at the Peace Memorial Exposition in Ueno, Tokyo, 1922. Postcard. Courtesy Edo-Tokyo Museum.

Last figure below indicates year of this printing

15 14 13 12 11 10 09 08 07 06 05

The real dwelling plight lies in this, that mortals ever search anew for the nature of dwelling, that they *must ever learn to dwell.*

—Martin Heidegger, "Building Dwelling Thinking," in idem, *Poetry, Language, Thought,* trans. Albert Hofstadter (Harper & Row, 1971)

When I think what might have been greatest among the causes for my tending toward pessimism, this is what I think: the time I realized that I could not do without what we call enlightenment was also the time I realized to my core that this enlightenment would not be enough to bring me satisfaction.

—Natsume Sōseki, *Bungaku hyōron* (Essays on Literature), 1909 (reprinted in *Sōseki zenshū,* vol. 10, Iwanami shoten, 1967)

# Acknowledgments

My sincere thanks to all of the people and institutions below.

Financial support from Columbia University, the Japan Foundation, the Yokohama Association for International Communications and Exchange, and the Edwin O. Reischauer Institute of Japanese Studies at Harvard University made the research for this book possible.

The staff at Columbia University's C. V. Starr East Asian Library, Tokyo University School of Architecture Library, Yokohama City University Library, and the Edo-Tokyo Museum went beyond their ordinary duties to assist me in locating materials.

Theodore Bestor, Elizabeth Blackmar, Fujimori Terunobu, Kano Masanao, Katō Yūzō, Koizumi Kazuko, Narita Ryūichi, Suzuki Hiroyuki, Tamai Tetsuo, and Uchida Seizō shared their wisdom with me on research strategies and sources.

I especially thank Uchida Seizō, who generously shared his library as well as his enormous funds of expertise on the history of Japanese houses.

Collaboration and conversations with the following people inspired or helped clarify particular ideas in this book: Gregory Clancey, Fukuhama Yoshihiro, Makita Tomoko, Matsuyama Iwao, Mori Mayumi, Muramatsu Shin, Muta Kazue, Niikawa Shihoko, Nishikawa Yūko, Ken Oshima, Satō Kenji, Satō Kōji, Takamatsu Mari, and members of the Kindai jūtakushi kenkyūkai.

The following people read and commented on portions of the manuscript at various stages: Kim Brandt, William Coaldrake, Laura Hein, Ken Ito, Tobie Meyer-Fong, Nakatani Norihito, Giles Richter, Julie Rousseau,

Ken Ruoff, Barbara Sand, Alan Tansman, Stephen Vlastos, Cherie Wendelken, Kären Wigen, and students in Henry Smith's seminar Material Culture in the History of Modern Japan.

Paul Anderer, Barbara Brooks, Carol Gluck, Henry Smith, and Gwendolyn Wright read and commented on my dissertation at Columbia. I carried their comments with me throughout the writing of this book and have done my best to respond to them.

Andrew Gordon, Harry Harootunian, and Louise Young painstakingly went through the entire manuscript at its penultimate stage. Their insightful readings helped me reframe it.

Carol Gluck and Henry Smith have been and continue to be my teachers. My debt to both of them is great beyond words.

Alice Gordenker provided me a temporary office in Tokyo.

An earlier version of Chapter 1 was published in *Mirror of Modernity: Invented Traditions of Modern Japan,* edited by Stephen Vlastos (Berkeley: University of California Press, 1998). An earlier version of Chapter 10 appeared in *Being Modern in Japan: Culture and Society from the 1910s to the 1930s,* edited by Elise K. Tipton and John Clark (Honolulu: University of Hawaii Press, 2000).

A complete acknowledgment of the influences shaping this book would include mention of all the houses I have inhabited in the United States, England, and Japan, and the people with whom I cohabited. I would particularly like to thank the friends and family in Japan who taught me how to dwell.

It happens that while this book was in its final editing stage, I became the owner of a bungalow built in a North American suburb in the 1920s, something very much like the object of desire I discuss in the final chapters of this book. Perhaps if I had known the rewards and frustrations of suburban homeownership firsthand when I started out I would have written a different book.

I.S.

# Contents

# Figures

# House and Home in Modern Japan

# Introduction

# Dwelling and the Space of Modern Japan

A house is a site, the shelter for a household, the bounds and the focus of a community. It is also an artifact, a product of human manufacture, a material extension of its occupants' lives. This book takes the Japanese house in both senses, as site and as artifact, and explores the spaces, commodities, and conceptions of community associated with it in the modern era.

Where property and family are relatively stable institutions, as they were for wealthy peasants, for samurai, and for the merchant elite of cities in Japan during the Tokugawa period, the dwelling gives concrete shape to the norms that maintain the household over time. For people without property, whose lives lack long-term stability, like the tenement-dwelling masses of the Tokugawa capital of Edo, the individual dwelling itself may have little significance, while the local community of surrounding households takes on a larger role in domestic life. In the modern era, however, these principles that relate house and family in widely recognized and accepted ways begin to break down. Modernity destabilizes, relocates, and reinvents community at every level of society. It dislodges material and practical forms from their local vernaculars and releases them into the market. Geographical and social mobility threaten the stability of multi-generational households, at the same time bringing into question distinctions within the house that had previously seemed natural. The authority of the state intrudes where local community or familial authority were once supreme. Thus, even where the traditional markers of social divisions surrounding and within the house persist, they become vessels for new meanings, since the institutions of dwelling are themselves resituated in a new nexus of relations.

The house as artifact and the artifacts it houses are affected in turn. In the fluid conditions of modern society, the construction and ornament of houses cease to provide stable indices of their occupants' social status. And just as people's lives begin to traverse multiple communities, the artifacts with which they are surrounded increasingly come to be goods circulating in national and global markets. By the same token, the creative acts of modern urbanites tend to revolve around the choice of things to acquire and consume.[1] Reflecting these conditions, sociological studies of the contemporary home, in contrast with ethnographies of peasant societies, most often root their analyses in conceptions of the home as a means of personal expression.[2] The home can only become this idiosyncratic creative project when the act of dwelling has been reconceived in terms of an ensemble of consumption activities.

From these twin transformations arises a seeming paradox, that amid the breakdown of inherited meanings in dwelling and the fluidity of modern society, where we might expect a radical diminishing of the dwelling's power to signify either internally or externally, the opposite has often occurred. Not only does the increased diversity of commodities lead to a material elaboration of the home, but home itself becomes an object of special attention, its importance emphasized in writing, invoked in politics, and articulated in architectural design. Where traditional continuity begins to dissolve, we are confronted with a sudden surfeit of discourse. In Japan, this turn in the history of dwelling occurred during the late Meiji and Taishō periods, the era that saw the institutions of the nation-state mature and Japan become a full participant in the global competition of the imperial powers. It was no accident that domestic space and the design of houses emerged as nodes of intellectual concern for the first time in these nation-building years. Although the ideological mask of private life was often used to conceal it, the modern imagining of domestic space was a highly political project.

This flourishing of discourse around the house and home was part of the production of a bourgeois culture, made possible by the abolition of ascriptive status distinctions, seeded by the state through a range of new institutions including the national school system, museums and expositions, and the imperial house itself, and nurtured in clubs, voluntary organizations, reform societies, and the mass press. The ideologies conveyed through this panoply of social channels engendered new notions of individual and social identity. The capitalist state promised and validated the free pursuit of wealth and social advancement (the famous goal of *risshin shusse*, establishing oneself and advancing in the world), and by the same token licensed the winners of wealth and social position not only to exploit others, but to claim the moral authority to provide a model for the way others should live.

The aim of this book is to show the features of this culture as it took shape within the milieu of the dwelling. For a number of reasons, dwellings bear particular weight in building class cultures. They are the primary locations for both inculcation and performance of class dispositions, particularly where women's occupations are largely domestic in locus. They also conspicuously manifest social position. Buying or building a house ties the owners to property, which has long been observed to promote conservative political and social behavior.[3] And regardless of how property ownership may affect the owners' habits, a house is often the largest investment of a lifetime, making it momentous both as a personal choice and as an embodiment of social values.

## Home as a Modern Space

Home was only one of many spaces being imagined or reimagined for political purposes at the end of the nineteenth century. Following the opening of ports to trade, the influx of goods and ideas from the West, and the establishment of the Meiji state, late nineteenth-century Japanese moved in a new space in both abstract and concrete terms. The first three decades of Meiji witnessed the creation of the political space of the nation-state, within whose boundaries governance was to extend identically to all national subjects; the ideological space of native landscape, in which writers and artists seeking to root blood in soil imagined a natural source of the nation; the technological space of a countrywide rail and telegraph network, which made the unified nation concrete by removing physical barriers; and the legal-economic space of private property in land, which capitalism made into an alienable commodity, removing it from the layers of local use rights and personal obligations in which it had been embedded. Although each of these spatial transformations had its own long past, they depended on specific acts of the Meiji state or conditions engendered by its development.[4]

For intellectuals, the political, ideological, technological, and economic components of modernity were entwined with efforts to conceive a national public, or society. Society was a space constructed through discourse, spoken and written into existence in mass-market print. A national newspaper-reading public took the span of the Meiji emperor's reign to develop, beginning with the first newspapers in the 1860s, and reaching a plateau of sorts with consolidation of the major dailies and the homogenization of their content, which occurred in the first decade of the twentieth century.[5] Accompanying the newspapers, national markets grew for a variety of magazines, which bound their readers into communities, enhancing individual awareness of the common space shared by an invisible public of companion readers (and letter writers). The modern term *shakai*, which had previously been used indifferently to designate any form of group enterprise, came into common written use as a translation of the English "society" in the first decade of Meiji. For long afterward, the term retained an ambiguity present in the nineteenth-century English word, sometimes indicating the total national collectivity, sometimes a subset defined by class norms. This ambiguity bespeaks the fact that nineteenth-century nation-building was a mutually constitutive project on the part of state and bourgeoisie, establishing new class cultures at the same time that it made national citizens.[6]

The same process of forming the homogeneous space of the nation-state generated distinct heterogeneous spaces, represented in new architectural typologies such as the schoolhouse, the military barracks, the train station, the office building, and the hospital, as well as new city landscapes, such as the boulevard, public park, and residential suburb.[7] As a consequence, while the nation-state was homogeneous in an abstract sense, the modern capital looked physically more heterogeneous than its precursor. Architecturally, most of Edo was a model of uniformity, and early Tokyo was much the same. Edward Morse, who visited Japan in the 1880s, described the cityscape of Tokyo as low and monotonous.[8] It is well-known that the Meiji regime broke with native building traditions by introducing Western architecture. In fact, the new government introduced something more fundamental, for which Western architecture was in a sense merely the tool: namely, the new system of functionally rooted building and spatial typologies that distinguish architectural space within the modern city.[9]

As the residuum rather than the direct product of this construction and differentiation of public space, the home possessed a double heterogeneity, not only distinct as one of many institutions within bourgeois society but also distinct as a space apart from the political space that was dubbed "society." The modern distribution of human activity among heterogeneous spaces supplemented the family's significance as a kinship-based institution by conscribing a sphere of domestic privacy, creating a site that was critical both as the place of retreat from larger collectivities and as the fundamental unit for governance. Privacy here became for the first time a space to be mapped in house and city plans, as graphic and material delineation of its boundaries acquired new significance. As Jurgen Habermas has pointed out in the European case, this new form of privacy was predicated on belief in the autonomy of the individual in free market exchange. In bourgeois society, the preservation of an intimate family refuge was a man's proof of his freedom and success in a competitive working world. By claiming to operate on different principles from public society, it also obscured the fact that families were themselves political structures, founded on patriarchal authority.[10] In the vision of bourgeois ideologues, the world within the home was to be what Habermas calls a "domain of pure humanity," and a voluntary "community of love." At the same time, the spatially bounded, family-centered household was made into an essential instrument of the modern state, which drew its strength from the productive and reproductive capacity of the entire population and saw in the intimate community of the family a mechanism for manufacturing citizens.

## The International Discourse of Domesticity

A generation of research has revealed domesticity as one of the peculiar ideological constructs of Western modernity. Since the publication of Philippe Ariès's *Centuries of Childhood*, social historians have steadily dismantled the notion that the intimate family is historically unchanging, universal and natural.[11] The Victorian "cult of domesticity," now a staple feature of nineteenth-century English and North American histories, has been described as manifested in a heightening of affection among family members or in a sentimentalization of home life and motherly duties and romanticization of childhood. The origins of the new family morality have been imputed to the growth of capitalism, to industrialization, to Protestant reform movements, and to the trend toward having fewer children.

This story of the emergence of the modern home is so familiar by now that it has taken on a naturalness of its own that may itself deserve "denaturalizing." The Japanese case offers a means to do this by providing an instance in which the ideology of modern domesticity was recognized from the beginning as foreign—its foreignness being an important part of its significance in fact—and posed against very different native domesticities. The moral importance imputed to the home was readily apprehended by modernizing ideologues in Japan, but even as they embraced it, a variety of basic questions emerged demanding answers: Who cohabits in the home? What do they do there? What kind of space should it be? How should it relate to its neighbors? "Home" in Japan thus struggled into existence, consciously cobbled together from a variety of native and foreign models. It bears reemphasizing that there was nothing inherently natural in the particular forms and practices of modern domesticity, nothing emerging inevitably from the social conditions of industrialization. These forms and practices had to be adopted and adapted or crafted anew. The history of domesticity in Japan between the 1880s and the 1920s allows us to see their conscious introduction, and the problems of their naturalization.[12]

Writers on Western domesticity have noted the new emphasis on the moral virtues of home in nineteenth-century writing. But what made nineteenth-century domestic discourse distinctively *modern* is not simply that it came with heavy doses of family morality (much of which had earlier roots, after all), but that it was carried on in mass-market texts. The textual sources on which most historians of nineteenth-century domesticity have relied reveal the central importance of female literacy and the growing market for inexpensive books and journals.[13] By the beginning of the twentieth century, writings on the home and its management were flowing across national borders as well, with at least as much ease as other commodities in the world market, impeded only by the costs of translation. International expositions and congresses further accelerated the global flow of goods and ideas. The new feminine discipline of home economics was promoted at the expositions, sparking the formation of bourgeois women's organizations in several countries and filtering from there into higher education.[14] American nutritional science, which had a transformative effect on food markets and kitchen work from the 1890s, drew its authority from German experts. Conversely, the modified Taylorism of American home economist Christine Frederick moved from the United States to Germany and Japan in the 1910s and 1920s.[15] At the turn of the twentieth century, Swedish author Ellen Key's writings on motherhood, translated into numerous languages after her first appearance at a Women's Exhibition in Copenhagen in 1895, sparked fierce debate in the feminist movement (itself highly international in character) and won her more devotees abroad than in her native Sweden. In Japan, a partial translation of Key's *Century of the Child* from the 1902 German edition was published soon afterward. Other works followed, and Key's ideas played a central role in the "Protection of Motherhood" debate (*Bosei hogo ronsō*) among Japanese feminists in the 1910s.[16]

Nor was Japan the only country outside Western Europe and North America where modernizing elites campaigned to sacralize, protect, rationalize, or beautify the institution of the home. Similar stories are told by historians of Finland,[17] of Turkey,[18] of Bengal,[19] and of British colonial Africa.[20] Although local meanings and concrete material manifestations varied widely, a common vocabulary and set of issues appeared in roughly the same period in disparate circumstances. Such a coincidence encourages us to view modern domesticity less as a response to new social conditions reiterated in multiple isolated regional and national contexts than as part of a discursive bundle of interpretations and reinterpretations, carried by imperialism and an accelerating global trade in texts and images.

Japan's contribution to the global exchange of domestic images and ideals was primarily in the realm of aesthetics. A "Japanese taste" became popular in American interiors following the Centennial Exhibition of 1876, where the Japanese exhibit and bazaar had attracted architects, aesthetes, carpenters, and housewives. It was propagated thereafter through travel writing and decorating advice articles in architecture journals and general audience magazines. Images of Japanese architecture and crafts played a crucial role in the aesthetic movements out of which architectural modernism emerged, movements that were both transnational in character and intensely concerned with reformulating domestic space. Such aesthetic influences might seem at first to belong to a distinct category of phenomena, but like housework, childrearing, hygiene, and other aspects of domestic discourse, architectural and interior aesthetics were regarded as bearing powerful moral valence, and specific objects and motifs were associated with enlightened family ideals.[21] Even where this connection was not explicit, the aesthetics of the modern home and the practicalities of its management were often propagated through the same popular media.

Some older textual traditions relating to dwelling enjoyed considerable longevity in Japan after the founding of the modern state and the propagation of new ideas from overseas. Tokugawa-period Confucian and Confucian-influenced moral tracts on the management of households and on women's education, including the *Greater Learning for Women* (*Onna daigaku*), made infamous by modern critics, were still popular reading in the Meiji period, and were sometimes used in the schools during the period before the national system of textbook review was put in place in 1903. Their influence continued long afterward. Manuals of geomancy, the Chinese divining method for siting and layout of houses, were regularly repackaged to keep up with popular tastes. They acquired a modern look and began featuring Western-style houses in the 1920s. The market for geomancy books (under the Chinese name, *feng shui*) became a global one in the late twentieth century. New guides continued to come out in Japan as well. Pattern books diagramming architectural details for carpenters continued to be printed, as they had been since the early Tokugawa period, and guides for tea aficionados to the design and decoration of tearooms and related *sukiya*-style interiors persisted into the twentieth century.

What these various textual genres lacked was a conception of the home as a space to be molded around an ideal model of family. The discourse on home and family that mobilized reformers in the late Meiji period was thus quite new, with little counterpart in the Japanese past. This is perhaps unsurprising, since so many of the institutions of its production and dissemination were new. New reform organizations, both state-led and private, were constantly being spawned after the Restoration. Architects, the most influential agents in the remolding of physical space, were the product of an education unlike anything that had preceded it, organized initially under Western instructors at the Imperial College of Engineering. The first generation of architects graduated in 1879. No less a product of modern institutions was the professional architect's counterpart in the project of reforming domestic space, the professional housewife, whose role was similarly a creation of the modern education system. The number of women receiving secondary education remained small for the first three decades of Meiji but grew exponentially after the turn of the twentieth century. Women's magazines, which until World War I drew their readers from the girls' higher schools, developed along a parallel trajectory. Their contents complemented and extended the girls' school curriculum. Although the bulk of the writing on home was by men, as were all of the architectural designs recognized in the profession and the market, these two sanctioned sites—women's education and journalism—made possible broad female participation in the public construction of home and daily life.

Domestic discourse molded a modern family that was both bounded and unbounded. It was founded on cohabitation in the morally charged space of the home, yet at the same time, the modern home's functions were exported to outside institutions such as the schools, and domestic life was ordered according to ideas and information from outside. This dual character is most evident in the efforts of women's educators to shape housewifery as a professional specialization in alliance with public health authorities and to reorient child-rearing toward state educational goals. But analogous processes of moral grounding and social disembedding affected men's roles, the division of labor and leisure, and the aesthetics of house design. Domesticity in nineteenth- and twentieth-century Japan must thus be conceived not only as a textually mediated process but also, more broadly, as the public construction of a private sphere.

## Middle-Class Rhetoric and Bourgeois Culture

Underlying all nineteenth-century domestic discourse was the production and reproduction of social positions, particularly the position that in Japan from that time came to be called, through various locutions, something like "middle class." Like "home," the term "middle class" too needs to be understood not as a simple social reality but as a discursive construct, and a highly contingent one. In the words of Pierre Bourdieu, "Social class does not exist. . . . What exists is a social space, a space of differences, in which classes exist in some sense in a state of virtuality, not as something given but as something to be done."[22] This is not to say that all talk of class stands on air: in the social space Bourdieu describes, individuals and groups make their competing claims to political and cultural legitimacy on the basis of real forms of capital, whether economic (capital in the classic sense), social (family ties, for example), or cultural (all the forms of competence acquired through formal and informal education); and capitalist society, by definition, distributes these things unequally.

Marx's two-class system of capitalists and proletariat derives its clarity from the fact that each social position is fixed vis-à-vis the means of production. A tripartite system of upper, middle, and lower, on the other hand, makes the definition of class a relative matter, so that every determination of an individual's class implies the presence of another individual as referent. A potentially infinite number of subdivisions of upper-middle, lower-middle, upper-upper-middle, and so forth, seem quickly and inevitably to follow.[23] Allowing in a "middle" thus causes designations of class to lose their solidity and become rhetorical devices of the historian, or of the historical actors themselves. This is why there are always disagreements among historians (and not only historians) about who was in the middle class and who was not.

The rhetoric of class and the normative value of middle-classness nevertheless deserve historians' attention because they are themselves fundamental to capitalist society. The modalities of class rhetoric also extend far beyond explicit verbal declarations, encompassing nuances of expression, physical comportment, dress, personal belongings, and every expression of taste. Even if class categories evade a single social scientific formulation, there can be no question that the language of class emerged from a systemic transformation of tremendous weight, that is, the abandonment of a social structure in which status was largely hereditary, unambiguous, and unquestioned.[24]

I will refer to the people who embraced and were served by the idea of middle-classness as bourgeois, not in the strict Marxist sense as the owners of capital, but following the broader usage common in writing on the history of continental Europe, where the word means first, urban, and second, belonging to the management side of capital, including both property-owners and professionals.[25] Admittedly, this category too threatens to unravel at the edges, with economically marginal professionals at one end—the precariously situated petit bourgeois quintessentially represented in Meiji-Taishō Japan by the primary-school teacher—and an artificial aristocracy at the other end, the majority of whom acquired rank on the basis of wealth, military achievement, and political ties to the state rather than traditional claims of land and lineage. Despite its empirical indeterminacy and the baggage of historiographic debate it drags behind it, the term "bourgeoisie" has the advantage of making explicit the grounding of class traits in the capitalist system, and of avoiding the ambiguous mix of socioeconomic and ethical dimensions latent in "middle class." Still, I will not be dogmatic in its use, since it is an imported term, and I am equally concerned with the way people on the managerial side of capital perceived themselves.

From the 1880s, bourgeois intellectuals designated themselves the "middle" (*chūryū*) within native society. This move asserted their centrality in the political structure of the nascent capitalist state at the same time that it announced a moral position in relation to the rest of the nation. Since the domestic reformers and propagandists came from among this group, the site of concern was always the "middle-class" or "middling" home (*chūryū katei*) in the rhetoric of domesticity. This was a class-affirming statement, but it was also a rhetorical dodge. As Anthony Giddens observes, it is part of the bourgeois disposition to view society as made up of autonomous individuals and deny the influence or reality of the class system.[26] Thus, although new Japanese bourgeois ideologues spoke of their own kind as "chūryū," the word "class" (*kaikyū*) was often avoided in favor of terms such as "the middle ranks" or "middle level of society" (*chūryū, chūtō shakai*).

It is impossible to completely separate the aristocracy from this class, although its spokesmen would urge us to do so. From the first elections for the House of Peers in 1890, writers in the political journals frequently criticized the privileges and condemned the extravagant lifestyles of the country's newly created aristocracy. The same writers called on aristocrats to contribute more to national welfare financially and by moral example. Yet the critics were no republicans: as sharply worded as their condemnations could be, they nevertheless maintained the expectation that aristocrats should indeed provide a standard of behavior for their countrymen. Although aristocratic wealth dissipated on gambling, mistresses, or "high mansions and gaudy finery" was held up to readers as an object lesson, wealth itself was hardly taboo.[27] Aristocrats had simply to display it the right way, which is to say, in keeping with a bourgeois morality that emphasized work, concern for family, refinement of taste, and devotion to the progress of the nation. Provided these rules were followed, their families and homes could appear in the women's magazines,[28] their calligraphy or cameo photographs could grace the front pages of books published by this or that reform society, and they could even be quoted as authorities on domestic matters, like Count Tokugawa Satotaka, descendant of the former dynasty who contributed regularly to the home journals of the late Meiji period.[29] Particularly after service as officers in the Russo-Japanese War brought distinction to several scions of the old daimyo families, a number of aristocrats became popular exemplars of bourgeois behavior.[30] Although their frequent appearance in the magazines and newspapers implied that they possessed some virtue deserving of emulation, in reality, publishers were playing off of their celebrity status, which in the case of old aristocrats derived from inherited wealth and privilege, and in the case of many new aristocrats, from wealth pure and simple. As Mark Jones has pointed out, the ideologues of Meiji domesticity had an ambivalent relationship to money, as they sought to stress the primacy of moral character over material possessions, yet were unable to escape the fact that "money was an enabler of class."[31]

Minami Hiroshi and other historians of early twentieth-century culture have referred to the large white-collar professional population that emerged in Japanese cities during World War I as the "new middle classes" (*shin chūkansō*).[32] A range of other terms was used at the time, including *hōkyū seikatsusha* ("people living on salary"), *seishinteki rōdōsha* ("mental workers"), *puchiburu* (a contracted transliteration of "petit bourgeois"), and the name that would stick, *sarariiman* ("salarymen," male salaried workers).[33] I will occasionally follow Minami's usage, to distinguish this group from the narrower bourgeois elite of the previous generation, as well as from the shopkeeping "old middle class." Although all empirical criteria to distinguish classes are in some measure arbitrary, it remains useful to allow some ad hoc application of widely recognized social distinctions within the capitalist system at the same time that we attend to the migrations of class language. Few of the "new middle-class" heirs of the Meiji invention could be called bourgeois in the strict sense of the owners and managers of capital. Yet I hope it will become evident in the chapters to follow that despite internal conflict, a single evolving cultural project extending across these two generations warrants the general rubric of bourgeois culture.

Secondary education and a white-collar profession for the household head were the first two indispensable factors in a family's recognition as part of this "middle level" of society. Two further characteristics of the modern bourgeoisie in Japan were connected with these: first, that since class identity was built primarily on bureaucratic or professional position, its legitimacy was not founded on property in land, and second, that the majority of its members had come to the city recently. This was particularly the case in Tokyo. The Meiji government had recruited new men from the provinces, and the middle and higher schools formed a magnet that continued to draw youth to the city, making old Edo residents and their descendants an increasingly small minority in the population.

After education and profession, the most conspicuous markers of bourgeois status related to the home. The basic elements were carried over from the past. A detached house with a garden and gate had been the prerogative of samurai households and became a common bourgeois marker after the Restoration. A British observer describing Japanese houses in 1915 noted that regardless of their wealth, merchants and farmers "appear to be regarded as a class apart."[34] Their houses distinguished them. On the other hand, households of property or status in all parts of Tokugawa society had kept servants, and the modern bourgeoisie was a servant-keeping class, although, in contrast to the situation in the past, the servant population became an overwhelmingly female one. As Eric Hobsbawm has written of nineteenth-century Europe, "to this extent, the middle class was still a class of masters . . . , or rather mistresses over some labouring girl."[35] The change here was significant, but the agents of middle-class discourse tended to see rather the continuity.

The first half of this book deals with four elements in the composition of Japanese bourgeois culture that emerged anew after the second decade of Meiji, all of them connected to the issue of dwelling: the idea of "home" itself, the formation of a profession of housewifery, the notions of taste and style in domestic architecture and interiors, and the ideal of suburban homeownership. In contrast to the open and communal world of the urban working class and to the peasantry's undifferentiated spheres of productive labor and consumption, the bourgeois family was sequestered from the public sphere and the market. It was treated as a sentimental investment in need of nurturing. The bourgeois woman managed this investment as a professional in her sphere, whose expertise derived from books rather than instruction within the household. Formal education distinguished her from working-class women and from women of the past. The bourgeois cultivation of personal taste in house design and interior decor was premised on the ability to choose and to regard the dwelling as an aesthetic project. The owner-occupied suburban house was the commodity form of all these domestic values, a materialization of the bourgeois investment in family privacy. The male homeowner not only sequestered his family but, in acquiring a suburban house, invested in a refuge away from the city, where home could be part of a romantic landscape, posed against the dangers and seductions of the city.

All of these things required some combination of money, higher education, and the kind of self-cultivation that only a limited part of the population could afford. All were unattainable by the working classes and rarely sought by them. Together, they constituted the domestic half of a culture that had little meaning without external counterparts in the space of bourgeois society: the public sphere corresponding to the home, male professions corresponding to the housewife's profession, the marketplace, and particularly the department stores, corresponding to the domestic interior, and the city of work and male play corresponding to the residential suburb.

The writing, speaking, and designing that gave expression to these values relied ineluctably on a cadre of intellectuals. In journalism, in clubs and reading groups and political parties, in lecture tours and other forms of expression and association, a well-known group of intellectuals can be seen in the Meiji period struggling to form and broaden a bourgeois public sphere.[36] As political critics, these are the figures Carol Gluck has referred to as "*minkan* [popular] ideologues," the writers and journalists who claimed to speak for "public opinion" (*yoron*).[37] Many of the same men prove to have been busy reinventing the private as well, publishing "family journals" and penning women's columns in the newspapers, speaking and writing on the need for reform of conjugal relations, childcare, employment of servants, hygiene, eating habits, music and art for the home, house design itself, and other issues that at first glance appear distant from public politics. Proselytizing a bourgeois conception of private life was integral to the realization of their ideals for society as a whole.[38] After World War I, they were joined by less privileged intellectuals, creating an expanded and fragmented field of discourse. Borrowing a term from Pierre Bourdieu, but applying it more broadly, I will refer to these intellectuals collectively as "cultural intermediaries."[39] Whether from elite or non-elite background, they positioned themselves between the sources of dominant class legitimacy and the literate public, seeking audiences for their opinions and cultural expertise.

## Translated Modernity and the Mass Market

Basing their theories on nineteenth-century Western European and North American experience, sociologists since Georg Simmel have regarded the abundance of goods made available by mass production as fundamental to the experience of modernity.[40] Yet, since information often flows more easily than material goods, in many parts of the world modernity is first apprehended as a set of conditions found elsewhere, before the results of industrialization are fully manifest at home.[41] This was vividly the case in Meiji Japan.

With regard to houses and the things kept and consumed in them, the first trait of the modern transformation in Japan was that the mass market in print and images of modern commodities came in advance of a mass market in the commodities themselves. Japan thus experienced a revolution in representations well before anything approaching a consumer revolution based on mechanical mass production.[42] Even this form of mass consumerism did not engage the majority of the country; the media purveying images of the bourgeois home targeted urban audiences, and their cultural vocabulary was Tokyo-centric. If we take Minami's new middle class (defined by secondary education and white-collar profession) as the likely audience for these media, only 5–8 percent of the adult population of the nation in 1920 were likely readers or potential buyers of the goods they advertised.[43] Mass marketing should not be measured simply in numbers, however. After the turn of the century, first the department stores and then the publishers of women's magazines constructed an image of the mass consumer of home-related goods and publications, conceived generally as female in gender, and developed strategies to reach her. Merchandise display techniques, graphic advertising, and the language and appearance of publications abandoned the conventions of a closed world of status-specific consumption, seeking by every means to attract new buyers, even as they displayed houses and household goods that were beyond the reach of most. For urban Japanese in the 1920s, these devices of marketing, together with the new technologies of film and sound recording, shaped an experience of mass-mediated modernity that greatly heightened the sense of living in a world of commodities and invitations to consume.[44]

Under the domination of the educated bourgeoisie, the most valuable commodity in social terms was translated knowledge from the West. This fact has encouraged many people discussing Japanese modernity simply to equate modernization with Westernization. The pages of late Meiji and Taishō publications presented their readers with countless images of European places and people, as well as sometimes improbable-seeming quotations from Western experts or anecdotes about figures drawn from pantheons of Western heroes. The use of Western images, stories, and opinions in Japanese print reflected an intellectual fixation produced by Japan's tenuous position as the only non-white country among the powers, and a latecomer—and the internalization of that position by many Japanese intellectuals. Yet Japanese print incorporated Western knowledge and representations in a dialectic of foreign and native too complex to be compassed by the notion of Westernization. Because modernity came from overseas, Japanese had continually to make accommodations in both directions, to fit the native into Western-based modern milieus, and to fit the Western into native cultural strategies.

For the first generation of intellectuals engaged in it, crafting bourgeois domesticity was a national project. It was impossible for the national project to hold a single course in the mass society taking shape after World War I. As more people claimed a stake in its definition, the terms of domesticity became material for manipulation in a competition of taste. The ideal of the intimate family itself, once it broke the confines of a narrow world of propagandists and moral exemplars, revealed new implications that could be disturbing to established bourgeois intellectuals. Conflict within the bourgeois project in the 1920s formed around what was called the "culture life," which is the subject of the latter half of this book. Postwar cultural intermediaries developed a new cosmopolitan language, envisioning a utopia in which Japanese would be neither bound by native tradition nor civilizing themselves under pressure from the West (an "externally motivated civilization" as Natsume Soseki had put it in 1911).[45] My focus is on material manifestations of these ideals in the new planned suburbs called "culture villages" and in the "culture house." These 1920s extensions of the project begun by Meiji ideologues reconfigured it as a cosmopolitan utopia. In the process, they displaced vernacular modes of building, making house forms into ephemeral commodities, and invented a new role for the architect as a purveyor of images in the mass market.

## Reforming Everyday Life

If the history of domesticity, middle-class rhetoric, and mass marketing reveals broad commonality between modern Japan and the bourgeois nation-states of the West, the powerful strain of national cultural reform that linked these things may be a particularly striking feature of Japanese modernity.[46] The Meiji government's efforts to reform manners in the name of Civilization and Enlightenment are well known. To shape a public acceptable to Westerners, officials prohibited a range of behaviors, including mixed bathing, exposure of bare limbs, cross-dressing, and inappropriate haircuts for women. The proposals of enlightenment intellectuals in the Meirokusha group were more far-reaching, extending to such extremes as the abandonment of the Japanese language. A proposal for the "reform of the Japanese race" through miscegenation (specifically between Japanese men and Western women) was published in 1883.[47] Privately initiated campaigns focusing on specific objects for reform were numerous enough to inspire parody. In 1888, the satiric magazine *Marumaru chinbun* listed thirty-two such campaigns under the title "The Recent Competition Among Fashionable Reforms" ("Tōsei ryūkō kairyō arasoi").[48]

Many contemporaries were skeptical of cultural reformism, particularly when it touched on the habits of their own daily lives. As the parody suggests, often the passion for reform of this or that native trait or custom had the ephemeral character of fashion. But in the eyes of skeptics, the issue was not simply this, it was what they perceived as the "Western infection" (*seiyō kabure*), which threatened Japan's national culture. The reformers themselves were at pains to emphasize that they were not advocating mere imitation of the West. In the process, they amplified the discourse of national culture by affirming reified conceptions of native and foreign, together with state-propagated nationalist ideologies. There was in fact no difficulty in combining concrete cultural reforms with promotion of the ethereal national essence and imperial mythology. The hegemonic discourses of progress and of nation had critical mass sufficient for fusion to occur.[49]

As the work of Sheldon Garon has demonstrated, this fusion of national rhetoric and progressive interventions into everyday life continued as a persistent feature of Japanese public life through much of the twentieth century, prosecuted by self-styled "middle-class" advocates in collaboration with bureaucrats in the Home, Education, Agriculture, and other ministries.[50] After the watershed events of the World War I years, these collaborative campaigns sought to engage Japanese women as consumers and domestic managers, opening a new front in the state's intervention. A symbolic juncture in this new stage of relations between households and the state came in 1919, when social bureaucrats brought architects, medical professionals, and women's educators together in a league with the comprehensive—not to say grandiose—goal of "reforming everyday life" (*seikatsu kaizen*). The experts called on to participate saw their work as quite practical, however. Most had been promoting their visions for the bourgeois home in print and in the classroom for years, making the official movement a welcome confirmation that their independent efforts coincided with state goals.

Through his analysis of everyday life reform and other forms of what he terms "social management," Garon provides a new perspective on the nature of the modern Japanese state. By revealing the larger role of civic groups in these campaigns, he refutes the long-held view of the prewar state as distant and authoritarian and of the people as either passive victims or bold resisters.[51] Historians in Japan since the 1990s have revised the standard narrative of prewar Japan in analogous ways, rejecting the view of Japanese modernity as "deformed" or "incomplete" and turning critical attention instead to the ways that the modern state created national subjects and to the myriad channels through which power operated, often invisibly, in everyday life. These reinterpretations have opened the way for a new history of modern institutions, including the family, that recognizes the political nature of private life.[52]

I believe the revision can be pushed a step further by excavating the strategies beneath the class rhetoric in social management and cultural reform. Why were certain "middle-class" men and women so enthusiastic about joining forces with the state to reform national habits? As Garon notes, reformers tended to see the modernizing stance of the state, enshrined in the Charter Oath of 1868, as agreeing with their own interests, which encouraged them to use the power of the state to make national lifestyles conform to their own bourgeois conceptions.[53] Until at least the 1930s, however, bourgeois reform was a minority struggle. The very claim of reformers to represent the "middle class" must therefore be seen as a political strategy, a way of claiming to represent the core interests of the nation. Moreover, the claimants to middle-classness themselves were internally divided. Although there was often strong unity of interests among educated professionals on a general level, the concrete standards and methods for reforming everyday life varied among the people using the language of reform.

Certain reform strategies won broader consensus than others, inside and outside government. For reasons that may reach beyond the direct effects of modern government campaigns, the constant pressure for frugality has been felt widely by Japanese throughout the century.[54] When everyday life reform delved more deeply into specific consumption practices and material choices, however, consensus was not as easily won. Propaganda for new models of family life, domestic management or house form exposed the gaps between city and country, between generations, between genders, and between bourgeois participants and aspirants with different backgrounds or different forms of capital.

Even when the message came from the state, in the form of textbooks, exhibitions, posters, and propaganda writings, reformers were neither in a position to impose their vision by force nor in a position of unchallenged cultural hegemony with relation to society at large. The lines of causality between reform discourse and actual practice were therefore never simple or unidirectional. The economic and cultural resources that bourgeois cultural intermediaries and their audiences brought to the field determined the ideals reformers were capable of envisioning, the reforms that managed to "sell," and the ways in which consumers made use of them. The historian's task thus becomes one of determining the contours of the field in which reform models were produced and the positions of particular agents within it.

This book presents two stages of Japanese modernity, a stage of nation-building in which intellectuals constituted a modern bourgeois culture as part of their struggle to find Japan's place in the imperial order, and a stage of global mass-mediated consumerism, in which intellectuals reconfigured that culture for a wider public as they sought to define a cosmopolitan identity and lifestyle. The two are roughly divided by World War I. They might even be called two modernities: bourgeois modern and mass-society modern. Yet a continuous search for new forms for everyday life bridges them. The ways that members of Japan's dominant class between the 1880s and the 1920s talked about, designed, and occupied houses articulated the positions they negotiated in the modern world. In the years since, the bourgeois model they shaped has been stretched and strained, but never replaced.

# 1

# Domesticating Domesticity

## An Abstract Space

As in many other countries in the nineteenth century, family in Meiji-period Japan was a new node of social concern both inside and outside government. The Meiji state's establishment of national institutions to replace the disparate systems of the shogunal and daimyo domains and the concurrent project of fostering national sentiment depended on defining the family's bounds and function as a unit of society. The national family register system introduced in 1871 began the process of codifying the family legally, and the marriage and inheritance laws promulgated under the 1898 Civil Code set in place a single national model, subsequently known as the "Japanese family system," defined by lineage and strongly patriarchal. During the preparation of the Civil Code in the 1870s and 1880s, legal scholars gave ideological weight to this construct by claiming it to be a unique and timeless native institution based on the ancestral cult, while linking it anew to the state myth of the emperor as national patriarch.[1]

While political leaders and legal scholars formulated modern state structures around the family, men and women writing in the emerging mass-market press constructed a framework of meaning for family that was grounded in everyday practices and the bonds of cohabitation. Although the basic forms of domestic life were not themselves new, the notion of "home" as an intimate space sequestered from society and centered on parents and children was alien. Nineteenth-century Japanese households were varied and fluid in composition, and among the wealthy they often included numerous servants, apprentices, and lodgers, in addition to extended family. Parents of all classes commonly sent their children away at a young age: to wet nurses or foster parents in infancy, to boarding schools and apprenticeships thereafter. The social and physical boundaries of the house were porous and often submerged in a network of intersecting relations of obligation with the village community, occupational association, or vassal group. Most of all, before the 1880s, no one in government, religious office, or the world of letters identified the physical site of family life as a special locus of moral meaning.

In Anglo-American texts and in the exhortations of missionaries, Meiji-period social reformers encountered the rich Victorian language of domesticity, something without parallel in Japan. Persuaded of the importance of the institutions of home to the bourgeois nations of the West, these reformers responded by inventing domestic discourses and norms of practice suited to their own circumstances. Initially called *hōmu* and, as the loan-word suggests, plainly Anglo-American in origin, home was thus among the new ideas fertilized by contact with the West after the Meiji Restoration. The West provided ideas and images to be adopted, interpreted, and recontextualized. Yet at the same time, Japanese reformers were compelled to invent a great deal, as there was little available in Japan corresponding to either the physical forms or the moral norms of the Victorian middle-class home.

The native family system and the modern ideal of home were products of the same historical moment, since they both emerged in the 1880s, during the debates around the drafting of the Meiji Civil Code. The family system, called *ie sei*, was championed by legal scholar Hozumi Yatsuka in his defense of the customs of patriarchal authority common among samurai.[2] The word *hōmu* was introduced by Protestant social reformers and began its career as a weapon against *ie sei*, or against conservative mores generally. In the first period of their formulation, the two concepts, *ie* and *hōmu*, thus appeared to be antitheses—indigenous and foreign, feudal and modern. But they were not, in fact, mutually exclusive. Whereas the central axis of the legal *ie* was heredity, a temporal concept, "home" posited a space, with definite boundaries. In the subsequent decades, both terms proved malleable enough to coexist without conflict. "Home," in particular, shed its polemical connotations as it was manipulated and transformed to become part of a Japanese discourse on women, family, and dwelling.[3]

Members of the small progressive vanguard instrumental in promoting domesticity at the turn of the century were anxious first to assert their own social place before turning to the reform of others' homes. In its Meiji construction, the Japanese domestic ideal was vehemently "middle class," representing the segment of society in which the journalists, educators, and architects doing the writing, speaking, and designing located themselves and their audience. New gender roles were invented and new moral meanings invested in material life and daily practice to provide substance to the middle-class image. New house designs and interiors followed, providing a means to shape bourgeois identity through material possessions and taste. Thus, in defining home, the framers of Japanese domesticity were also defining themselves.

The first reformers to address domestic forms and customs were Protestants, whose points of reference, dictated by the source of their conversion, were invariably Anglo-American. Their criticism began with the social strictures imposed upon their generation by traditional family obligations, which they perceived to embody a general principle, what popular-rights activist Ueki Emori called a "certain special family philosophy" (*isshu tokubetsu naru ie no shisō*), penetrating the whole outmoded "feudal system."[4] But in describing the Anglo-American alternative, even Protestant reformers looked often to practical and tangible aspects rather than religious philosophy—the kind of households and the activities and behavior of family members that they had seen in the West, encountered among missionary acquaintances, or read about in moral literature. Iwamoto Yoshiharu, principal of the Meiji School for Women and editor of *Jogaku zasshi* (Women's Education), Japan's first major women's magazine, was the premier spokesman of the Protestant home ideal and proudly claimed responsibility for discovering and popularizing the English word. Iwamoto attributed a lack of harmony and joy in Japanese families to the practice of adoption and to the presence in the house of parents, other in-laws, concubines, and lodgers, all of whom inhibited conjugal happiness and provided a poor environment for children. Japan would have no "*hōmu*," he professed, until adoption was ended and these interlopers were removed.[5] Echoing Iwamoto, Ueki called for physical separation of the older and younger generations. The fundamental problem for both of these men was one of composing households of the proper members.[6]

Addressing a women's temperance union meeting in Tokyo, Uchimura Kanzō described the Christian home as characterized most of all by efficient management. Seeking Japanese words to capture the essence of "home," Uchimura spoke of it as the "native place" (*furusato*) where one's parents and siblings were; the source of food, clothing, and shelter; the place in the world a person most wanted to be. Yet "this home (*hōmu*)," he concluded, was not something that could be described in words—one had to enter it and "breathe its air." Drawing from the experience of a recent visit to the United States, Uchimura told his audience that in the American home, there was a fixed order to each day, marked by bells the servants rang. The housewife led her daughters in a strict cleaning routine. Meals were taken with all the family together and followed by music or conversation. The interior was always dust-free and frugally appointed. Childrearing was the family's highest priority. For the education of small children, there were generally "ten or fifteen of the implements used in nursery school." In contrast, houses in Japan were unconducive to accomplishing things efficiently, and people kept too many servants.[7] Uchimura's readers would have found ample ideological ground in native tradition for his emphases on maintaining the household through daily routines and on cleanliness and frugality. More than this, however, Uchimura was urging that the round of domestic routines—not only chores but shared meals, pastimes, children's lessons—work to reinforce family togetherness.

The conjugal relationship had an ambiguous place in the first generation of Japanese writing on domesticity. Iwamoto and his Christian peers recognized that romantic love between husband and wife formed the core of the Anglo-American domestic ideal, and initially advocated reducing the household to conjugal couple and offspring in order to foster intimacy among Japanese couples. Yet their position was a radical one, since the multigenerational household was normative (if not numerically dominant), and little of the previous moral literature had placed such value on affection between husband and wife. *Jogaku zasshi* continued to promote the mutual duties of husbands and wives, but Iwamoto later turned away from advocating nuclear households.[8] Domestic texts reinterpreted native tradition to accord couples a new centrality (the frontispiece of one, for example, presented the mythic creators of the Japanese archipelago, Izanagi and Izanami, as the ancestral gods of marriage).[9] The private pleasures of conjugal love were infertile ground for public morality in Meiji Japan, however. It proved easier, instead, to stress the importance of the home as an educational environment for children, which accorded with the widespread hopes for advancement (the pervasive Meiji ideology of *shusse*), or to write of the modern housewife's responsibilities as domestic manager and moral instructor, which offered a fitting new role for women without threatening the foundations of patriarchy.

In addition, the first reformers to write of "home" rarely used the term to speak of the physical house. They understood home as an environment, a family group, and a set of practices rather than a building. At least among urbanites, suitable precedents were not available to foster an association of the dwelling itself with the affectively bonded family. Indeed, few owned their own homes. Early reformers thus had little to say about the architectural specifics of the new domesticity. Yet a lack had been identified, and a problem posed. Domestic space provided an arena for social reform, and domestic practices the specific objects upon which reformers could exercise their influence. Home was an abstract space waiting to be molded in concrete form.

## An Audience for the Home

The first step toward diffusion of the new domesticity outside the circle of Christian social reformers was linguistic naturalization. Although proponents uttered the caveat that the English "home" was untranslatable in any language (Uchimura attributed this observation to Bismarck), the Japanese neologism *katei* came increasingly to stand in for the English term. Unlike *hōmu*, it served also as a modifier, in expressions such as *katei kyōiku* (home education) and *katei eisei* (home hygiene), each of which gave a special valence to the second term beyond simply locating it in the domicile. "*Katei*" as a modifier feminized. It also implied half of an equation, in which new public institutions and the nascent public space of society formed the other half. With the assistance of such expressions, the word entered common usage.[10]

If the nuance of the term *katei* was feminine, conversely, its popularity in print represented the discovery of a growing market of literate women. Tokutomi Sohō was the first publisher to exploit the term as a device to open this market, beginning the journal *Katei zasshi* in 1892 as a companion to his monthly *The Nation's Friend* (*Kokumin no tomo*). The first issue contained columns on household management, cooking, and prices of daily necessities, as well as an article on trends in women's education and a biography of Garibaldi's wife.[11] The general-interest magazine *Taiyō* began a column entitled *Katei* in 1896, expanding it under the editorship of Iwamoto Yoshiharu the following year. In 1898, the *Ōsaka Mainichi shinbun* was the first major newspaper to introduce a *katei* column, followed by the *Yomiuri* in 1900. By the first years of the twentieth century, there were at least five magazines on the market with *katei* in their titles. The first issue of *Nihon no katei*, published in 1905, sought to explain this development:

The word *katei* has recently been circulated in this country in both high society and low as if it bore a peculiar new gospel. Needless to say, this *katei* existed here in Japan long ago. Then why is it that it has drawn everyone's attention and produced such great response in society, as if it were something new? It is probably due to the rise of civilized education for women, along with women's awareness that their mission (*tenshoku*) is not an easy one, on the one hand, and the expansion of national fortunes, on the other. Various conditions, both domestic and foreign, have called for great activity on the part of women. As a result, people have recognized the necessity for attention to the home (*katei*), which is primarily a woman's domain.[12]

The author captures two key causes for the sudden blossoming of interest in the moral importance of the home: the expansion of women's education and the extending reach of the Japanese state. In the period of Japan's imperial wars, a nationalist press eager to engage every literate Japanese subject, male and female, helped elevate the *katei* to the level of a national cause.

Shifts of connotation accompanying the word's propagation in journalism during the years prior to the Sino-Japanese War had eased the way to mass acceptance. First, *katei* lost its Christian tone. Iwamoto's preaching had considerable influence on the content of Tokutomi's *Katei zasshi*, but religion was not an explicit subject in the journal. In place of Christianity, Tokutomi offered the "common man's faith" of *heiminshugi*. Also largely absent from Tokutomi's journal, and from the *katei* landscape generally as it developed in the magazines that followed *Jogaku zasshi*, was Iwamoto's emphasis on the romantic bond between husband and wife and the need to purify the domestic environment of anything that might vitiate it. Frequently, this was supplanted by a solitary focus on the wife/mother. At the same time, parents-in-law crept back into many of the magazines' depictions of home life—although significantly, concubines and adopted children did not.

In *Taiyō*, a more aristocratic focus than *Katei zasshi* offered photographs of Count Ōkuma and his mother, lessons in traditional etiquette, or rules of interior decoration taught by Shimoda Utako of the Peers' School for Girls (Kazoku jogakkō). But whatever the social position of the writer, *katei* journalism from Tokutomi onward overwhelmingly proclaimed itself to be addressing the "middle level of society" (*chūtō shakai*). Tokutomi's common man's home was ideally that of a "country gentleman," reflecting the publisher's own rural samurai origins, and the important distinction between the social middle as conceived by Tokutomi's Minyūsha and the traditional urban bourgeoisie. Rural or urban, the model families of late Meiji-period *katei* literature were with few exceptions headed by the company directors, elite bureaucrats, university professors, and military officers who constituted the new class of professionals. Although Minyūsha writers had criticized the government for its favoritism toward the newly established aristocracy in the 1880s, they were more deferent toward the aristocrats themselves, some of whom also provided *katei* models. The magazines frequently included portraits of particular households, detailing everything from the appointments of their interiors and daily life within them to the particulars of the family budget. For readers, these portraits provided checklists of the goods and behavior that marked class membership.

A special issue of the magazine *Jogaku sekai* in 1904, titled "One Hundred Walks of Life" ("Shakai hyaku seikatsu"), situated the "middle-class" home model within a spectrum of social types. The issue contained descriptions of twenty-two households. A diagram of class structure was included, showing Japan to be among the healthy societies (along with England and Germany) with 65 percent of its population in the middle class. An accompanying list of the attributes of upper, middle, and lower classes showed all virtues adhering to the middle, which was described as the "producing class," in contrast to the "unproductive" upper class and the lower class "low in productivity" (see Fig. 1.1).[13]

Individual portraits in the issue elaborated this claim, and added a moral dimension to the distinction between the new professional and old merchant bourgeois. "The Home of an Osaka Merchant" presented a largely denigrating stereotype that stressed the divergence of Osaka families generally from recognized norms. Education was not valued, boys in the house were taught feminine manners, family members shared little affection—and in any case had little to talk to one another about.[14] In contrast, articles describing Tokyo professional households introduced particular families through interviews with the housewife or records of a visit to the house. A portrait titled "Life of a Naval Officer," for example, opened with an enumeration of each piece of furnishing in the reception room, from the arabesque-patterned carpet and leather-covered chairs to the pair of Kanō-school scrolls, the Kutani vase, lion-shaped incense burner, and miniature jade cannons in the *tokonoma* alcove. The other six rooms in the house were also described, and a dinnertime conversation recorded, along with a month's menus and the husband's salary.[15]

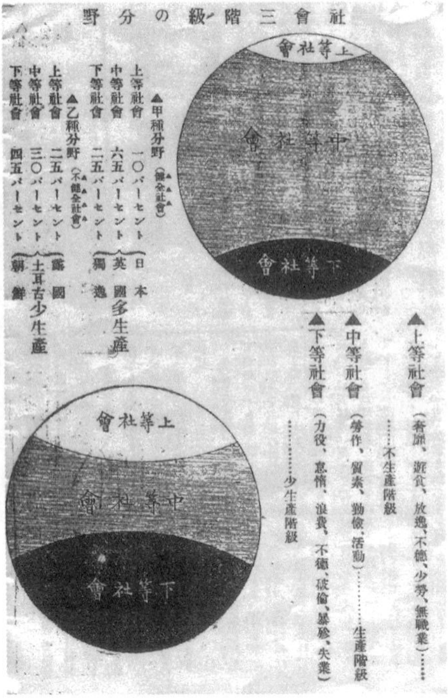


Fig. 1.1 Societies distinguished by the size of the three classes: healthy societies (*top right*), with 65 percent of the population in the middle, and unhealthy societies (*bottom left*), with only 30 percent ("Shakai hyaku seikatsu" [One Hundred Walks of Life], *Jogaku sekai*, 1904).

These minutiae of family possessions and practices advertised a lifestyle that was at least in some measure a product of choice. The naval officer's house was rented, not inherited from his father. The furniture in the reception room would probably have been purchased after marriage. Other stories of model households in "One Hundred Walks of Life" and elsewhere in turn-of-the-century women's magazines described second or third sons and their wives starting married life without house or belongings and having to shop for them. These households belonged to a sector of the professional class that enjoyed special privilege in determining the norms of taste as well as enlightened behavior in progressive society. The bureaucrats, company elites, and officer corps of this period were a new generation, largely urban, and many of them literally without the baggage of the old house. Ueki Emori had perceived in 1888 that a greater number of "convenient and complete" rental houses would have to be made available in order for progressive young couples to live apart from their conservative parents.[16] In fact, a new housing market was beginning to develop around the desires of Tokyo youth free of the obligations of heredity. *Kashiya fuda*, Tokyo's first specialty publication advertising houses for rent, began in September 1890.[17]

## Family Performance

*Ikka danran*, or *kazoku danran*, was another phrase that, like *katei*, became ubiquitous after the 1880s through propagation in the language of domestic reform. *Danran* implies a circle or gathering; together with "household" or "family," it meant something like "the family circle." A chorus of texts incanting the same phrases called the *katei* life's "sanctuary" (*rakuen*), and the family circle "life's greatest pleasure" (*jinsei no saidai kōfuku*). They also stressed the moral influence (*kankaryoku*) of the gathering, placing it at the center of "home education." Iwamoto wrote paeans to the virtues of conversation among family members, finding transcendent moral value even in inconsequential small talk around the brazier.[18] But since the moral discourse of domesticity was alien, others were not content to leave the form the family gathering should take to chance. To make its moral value self-evident, champions of the *katei* gave the family circle a ceremonial character, providing specific protocols for its enactment and investing it with symbolic significance (see Fig. 1.2).

*Harmony of the Home* (*Katei no waraku*), the first volume in a series of home manuals published by Minyūsha concurrent with *Katei zasshi*, devoted a chapter to pastimes suited to the family circle, encouraging music in particular. But the lack of morally appropriate music for Japanese homes was a problem that aroused the concern of social reformers. Elsewhere, liberal politician Itagaki Taisuke lamented the lack of "domestic music" (*katei ongaku*) in Japan, observing that all Japanese music with the exception of that of the Nō theater had degenerated into brothel entertainment, and calling for the establishment of schools to develop a musical form that could be enjoyed in the home.[19] The Minyūsha writer specified which new instruments were suited to the home. "But since the true essence of domestic entertainment," the author concluded,

> is for everyone in the house, old and young, man and wife, master and servant, to come together and enjoy themselves, one should choose common, simple, and inexpensive pastimes that anyone can appreciate. This is not so difficult to do. Institute a conversation or [tea] gathering at home every evening for an hour or two after

Fig. 1.2 The family circle in four social classes: upper class (*top right*), middle class (*top left*), lower class (*bottom right*), and lowest class (*bottom left*) ("Shakai hyaku seikatsu" [One Hundred Walks of Life], *Jogaku sekai,* 1904). The artist distinguishes each class by the manner in which the family members sit and their orientation to one another. The upper-class family sits on chairs, and their nursemaid sits on the floor. The middle-class family are shown as the most orderly and egalitarian group. Both the circular configuration of the group and the bodily comportment of individuals breaks down in the lower classes. Only in the middle-class family is a mother shown holding her child, thus subtly marking the mother's direct role in childcare as a class trait.

supper, bring the family together, and console one another with mutual love and kindness after the day's labors. Tell one another amusing anecdotes of things you have seen and heard during the day, tell old tales of educational value or read light and interesting passages from a newspaper or magazine, gaze at the baby's endearing face and smile together, or listen to the innocent voices of the children recounting the subjects they studied or the moral lessons they learned at school.[20]

The text was accompanied by an illustration labeled "The Family Tea Gathering" ("ikka danran no sawakai"). Its emphasis on the instructive value of the event appears to have found sympathetic ears at the Ministry of Education, since the entire passage reappeared almost to the word (including even the neologism *sawakai*) in state-compiled morals texts for the upper primary school nine years later.[21]

Elsewhere, the prescription was for a weekly rather than nightly household meeting. The family of Viscount Kano Hisanobu held a "home conversation group" (*katei konwakai*) each Saturday evening, in which speeches were reportedly given.[22] Matsuura Masayasu, an instructor at the Japan Women's Higher School, described a family gathering in his own house called the Saturday Club (Doyōkai) as a model for the readers of a home encyclopedia. His list of activities resembled that for the Minyūsha tea gathering, with the addition of music and comic impressions, and the significant feature that each member of the household performed, read, or told something to the group in turn.[23]

Still greater choreographic care was evident in the portrait of a household of twelve, including in-laws and servants, that appeared in *Katei no kairaku*, a book published in Osaka in 1901. The book's author announced that the home he was describing actually existed; it belonged to a "middling family" (*chūtō no katei*), formerly samurai with a one hundred *koku* stipend. The family meeting commenced at three o'clock each Saturday afternoon. Tea was prepared in the room of the master of the house, and the master had his wife escort his parents into the room, followed by the rest of the household. Each member took an assigned seat after first greeting his or her superiors. The master then proceeded around the room, telling "unusual stories from the newspaper and such," first for the benefit of his parents, then his younger siblings, followed by his own children. Following this, he had his wife pour the tea for his parents, while the children received confections. After tea, the grandmother instructed her daughter to play the *koto*, the nursery-school age boy began to sing the national anthem, and the other children played with their grandparents.[24] In this model household, a drama whose not-so-distant origins lay in an idealization of the exclusive conjugal family became a ritual embodiment of the very patriarchal ideal being promoted by conservative legal thinkers at the time (see Fig. 1.3).

Japanese families had gathered before—and doubtless shared affection—without the aid of these heavily formalized models of the family circle. In farmhouses where a single open hearth provided the only source of heat, all indoor activity during the winter would have taken place in one room. In fact, it was the passing of this picture of domestic community that worried folklorist Yanagita Kunio, who wrote in 1930 that improvements in farmhouses were permitting a "division of the fire" that encouraged individualism

Fig. 1.3 The family circle in a household of twelve, including servants and nurse. The patriarch and his wife sit on cushions in front of the *tokonoma* alcove with a brazier between them. The eldest son, who sits with his wife on the right, conducts the meeting (Chokei Dōjin, *Katei no kairaku* [The Pleasures of the Home], 1902).

and estranged family members from one another. Away from the presence of the patriarch, young people had become free to read and think what they wished, occupying a private world Yanagita called a "small sitting room of the heart" (*kokoro no shō zashiki*).[25]

Meiji reform ideologues had set the stage for Yanagita's nostalgia by identifying the gathering of family members as something morally significant. Unlike Yanagita, however, they tended to emphasize the morally unimproving character of homes of the past. Ritual enactments were designed to reinforce the cohabitant family with a substantial embodiment and to assure that private thoughts and private talk had public, communal value, particularly edifying value for children. The artificial quality of the event promoted in these texts reveals that as much as the public lecture (*enzetsu*), which was first promoted by Fukuzawa Yukichi and propagated through the popular rights movement in the 1870s, the private family conversation (*danran*) was a consciously shaped Meiji institution, and as much as the public lecture, it had political ends.[26]

## Family Meals

Judging from the domestic settings depicted in these scripts it seems likely that such enactments of the "family circle," although not requiring particular expense, occurred chiefly in larger, propertied households. Less grandiose prescriptions, better suited to the occupants of modest households but equally addressed to readers of all classes, applied to the most basic of human rituals: the taking of a common meal. This was no less a matter of orchestration, however, since establishing a fixed practice of family dining meant synchronizing mealtimes and sharing an eating place, a fundamental change of habit for many families. Barriers of status in samurai and elite commoner households had commonly been maintained by segregating members' meals, and these customs persisted after the Restoration. In some households, children, apprentices, and servants were grouped apart from the patriarch and his wife and allowed to eat only after they had finished their meal; elsewhere, the room in which the husband dined was off limits to his wife. Even for modern professionals whose lives were less bound by these status taboos, there was no general expectation that dinner would be taken together with the father present.[27]

Many reformers felt, however, that it was not enough simply to assemble in one place for meals. To make the gathering "life's greatest pleasure" required introducing one central prop: families did not enjoy dining together, they argued, because they had no dining tables. Sakai Toshihiko, who would later become a founding member of the Japan Socialist Party, began his social activism as a vigorous proponent of reform in the middle-class home, founding a *Katei zasshi* of his own in 1903. In *Katei no shin fūmi* (A new taste for the home), a serial written in 1901–2, Sakai couched his faith in simple terms: "A family meeting is held at mealtime. Scenes of the so-called family circle occur most often at mealtime. In light of this, meals absolutely must be taken at the same time and the same dining table. When I say dining table, I mean one large surface, whether round or square—you can call it a *teeburu* or a *shippokudai*. In any event, I believe we should abandon the old trays (*zen*)."[28] Meals in most Japanese houses at this time were taken on individual trays, with one tray and set of utensils for each member of the household. This practice appears to have been general among all classes in dwellings of the Tokugawa period. The *shippokudai*, a Chinese-based novelty popular for banquets in Nagasaki, was exotic because it offered a single surface from which several people could eat at once. Sakai believed that sharing one table would also entail that everyone in the house eat the same food, thus putting an end to the feudal habits of husbands who behaved like "little lords" and impeded the development of a "beautiful common-man's home" (*heiminshugi no utsukushii katei*).[29] Historians have regarded the use of separate trays in a similar light, as a manifestation of feudalism: in Japan's status society, each individual stood in a position of either inferiority or superiority to others, making it an impropriety for two people to eat from the same surface.[30]

Many professional men in the cities at the time Sakai was writing—the men he censured as "little lords"—were in the habit of having a separate meal delivered from the local restaurant in the evening for private consumption in the master's room, one of the finest rooms in the house. The women of the house, often both mistress and servants, would take supper together in a room near the kitchen. The maid in Sakai's unusually progressive household reportedly joined master, wife, and children at the dinner table—a practice that was certainly the exception among bourgeois families.

The common dining table was not promoted only by social liberals like Sakai. A compilation of moral instruction and household management advice published in 1907 under the title *Ie* began with a discussion of the house as foundation of the state and chapters on ancestor worship and the role of the patriarch but also instructed that "houses of the middle level of society (*chūtō shakai*) should make a custom whenever possible of gathering the whole family for meals." Meals should be taken in the most pleasant place in the house, conversation should be encouraged, and "to the degree possible, trays should be abandoned for a table structure (*shokutaku soshiki*)." Assembling for meals provided a time for the household head to hear the progress of the day's work and to give instructions.[31] The word *katei* was conspicuously absent from *Ie*, as was the romantic vocabulary of domestic happiness. But both Sakai's proto-socialist *katei* and this author's vision of the ideal house made the common table a device for imposing a regime on the household's time and bringing about, at least in appearance, a convivial domestic group.

New practices associated with the communal family meal were encouraged for reasons of hygiene and moral improvement as well as better family ties. Eating quickly and silently, which had been widely considered a virtue, was criticized as bad for the health.[32] Proponents of conversation during meals asserted that talking was also beneficial to digestion. Many people, however, continued to regard talk during meals as vulgar. In a survey of eating customs conducted by ethnographers in the 1980s among women born in the late Meiji period, the majority of respondents recalled that they had been forbidden to speak at dinner when they were children. Where silence was not the rule, most recalled parental lectures. Although women who had taken meals at a common table were twice as likely to say that they had been permitted to speak compared to those who had grown up eating from individual trays, it is clear that ambivalence about mealtime conversation was widespread and not quickly overcome.[33] The persistence of such stern norms presumably explains why some reformers counseled staging the family circle apart from mealtime, like the authors of the Minyūsha volume *Katei no waraku*, who recommended conducting it after dinner. Still, none of the new mealtime moralists made a virtue of dispatching one's meal quickly, since all accepted the intrinsic moral importance of the gathering.

Written and illustrated depictions of the "family circle" in most domestic management texts represented an assembly of children, parents, and sometimes grandparents, omitting other household members, with the occasional exception of a maid, who waited on the family but did not join them at the table. The prop-less weekly ceremony of *ikka danran* practiced in some households manifested a strict hierarchy of authority, but it was an open structure, since the ring could be expanded to accommodate any number of participants. A common table, on the other hand, created a focus of limited size for a closed and intimate family circle, delineating inside from out at the same time that it implied greater equality within (see Fig. 1.4). Peripheral household members, particularly servants, were placed on the outside.[34]

The houses of the wealthy bourgeois exemplars who provided endorsements for Meiji domestic manuals usually had Western dining rooms with tables and chairs. But most families who abandoned their trays instead took meals sitting on the floor around a low table. The beginning of this practice is commonly associated with an innovation known as the *chabudai*, a simple wooden table usually under one meter wide, with folding legs.[35] Manufactur-

Fig. 1.4 Three generations of a family eating at a common table. Here the gathering takes place in a sitting room without *tokonoma* alcove or other markers of status. The wife serves from the rice bucket to her left, and there are no servants in the room (Miwada Masako, *Shin katei kun* [New Lessons for the Home], 1907).

ing data indicate that the folding-leg *chabudai* became popular from around 1910, although the majority of households nationwide probably did not abandon individual trays until the late 1920s.[36] Some domestic management texts, however, were already exhorting readers to use a low table in place of trays for family meals as early as 1889.[37] Illustrations of such a scene, accompanied by homilies to the housewife and instructions on proper comportment at the table, appear in many texts after the turn of the century (see Fig. 1.5).

Because of its convenience, working-class families probably adopted the *chabudai* earlier than their bourgeois neighbors. A survey conducted by the Ministry of the Interior in 1921 found that 89 percent of the houses in four Tokyo slums had some form of dining surface (*shokutaku*). The term is ambiguous, but in light of the fact that this statistic was grouped alongside figures for large items such as bedding, it probably referred to folding tables rather than trays in most cases.[38] National diffusion in the 1910s and 1920s

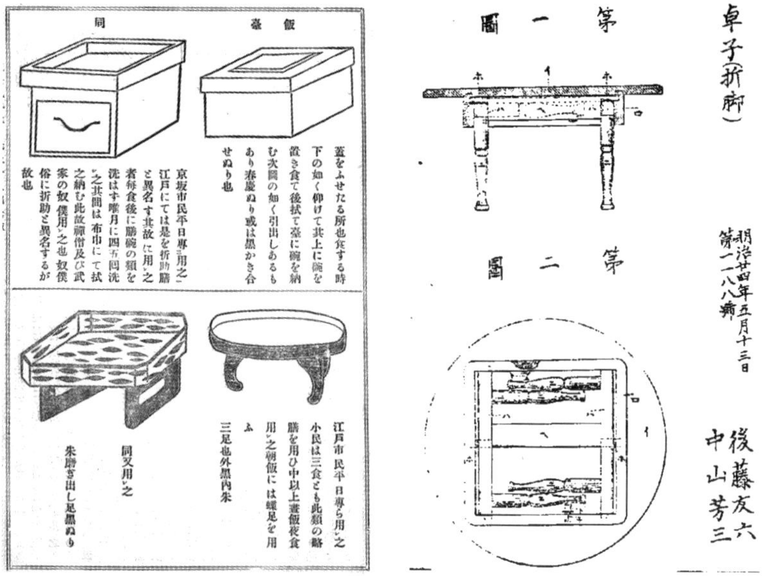


Fig. 1.5 Trays (*ozen*) and small tables (*chabudai*) for meals.

(*a, above left*) Common types of *ozen* used by residents of Edo, Osaka, and Kyoto in the early nineteenth century (Kitagawa Morisada, *Kinsei fūzokushi: Morisada mankō* [Modern Customs], ed. Muromatsu Iwao, 1908, 2: 412–13). According to this text, the box type, which provides storage for eating utensils, was used by commoners in Osaka and Kyoto as well as by Zen monks and servants in samurai households. The legged trays depicted below were used for daily meals in Edo.

(*b, above right*) Patent application no. 1188, a table with folding legs. Two men residing in Nihonbashi-ku, a commercial district in central Tokyo, applied for this patent in 1891. The legs in the illustration appear to be of ambiguous length, short for a table with chairs but longer than would become standard in *chabudai*.

(*c, overleaf top*) Photographer Kageyama Mitsuhiro and his wife having breakfast at a *chabudai* in their Tokyo apartment, late 1920s. By this time, the *chabudai* had become standard in most Tokyo sitting rooms, having spread with the proliferation of small nuclear households. Here it contributes to the intimacy of the scene while announcing the couple's modernity: they drink English tea from Western cups and eat toast (on the small brazier in the foreground). (Photograph by Kageyama Mitsuhiro. Courtesy of Kageyama Tomohiro.)

(*d, overleaf bottom*) *Ozen* in use in a farm household in Niigata Prefecture, 1951. Some rural families continued to take daily meals from individual trays until houses were modified and central hearths abandoned in the early 1970s. (Photograph by Nakamata Masayoshi. Courtesy of Nakamata Toshiyo.)

(Fig. 1.5c)

(Fig. 1.5d)

correlates with rapid growth in the population of independent households occupying small urban dwellings, and particularly of white-collar households. A complex web of social factors were involved in the switch of the mass of Japanese from meals on individual trays to common tables, including increases in the housewife's kitchen labor and service responsibilities, the spread of ideas of hygiene, and changes in diet.[39] From the 1890s, the "family circle," the central embodiment of the *katei* in practice, was woven through all of these strands of social change.

## A Land of Duties and a Land of Beauty

Despite the growing movement for domestic reform at the turn of the century, in the male world of architecture, the home had yet to receive clear articulation. Certainly, change had taken place in elite residential architecture, but there was little discussion in the academy of redesigning houses to meet the values of the age. The first men to raise the issue of proper architectural forms for the *katei* were men of letters. In an essay entitled "Kaoku" (House) in October 1897, novelist Kōda Rohan called for a reform of "the relationship between people and houses," to bring houses into step with the progress of the nation. After tracing an outline of the history of Japanese houses, Rohan concluded that the houses developed under the pacific rule of the Tokugawa shogunate were "comfortable like armchairs, but prone to encourage indolence." They may have been adequate for people of the Tokugawa era, but in a fiercely competitive world, the people of Meiji needed separate "specialized houses" (*senmonteki kaoku*) for work and for rest. Not only could one not expect Japanese to work efficiently in houses that did not distinguish the two, but also one could not teach them the pleasures of the home. There were some men of property, Rohan noted, who had already built themselves two houses and accomplished the separation. The rest of society would have to follow suit. The house for work would be a "land of duties" (*gi no kuni*) and the second, for rest, a "land of beauty" (*bi no kuni*).[40]

A series of articles in *Jiji shinpō* in 1898 enumerated the shortcomings of Japanese houses in greater detail. The author pronounced Japanese houses primitive and unsanitary, no better than the "natives' huts of Java." *Tatami* mats were among the chief culprits: they were unclean, damaged the body, and promoted lazy habits. Such houses were therefore ill suited to work. But advocating such an appalling extravagance as the maintenance of two separate houses was of no utility to the middle class. The solution would have to be in one structure. The next problem calling for broad reform was the house's interior layout: rooms were not designated for specific functions and lacked proper partitions. Family members should have their own bedrooms, the author urged, and one room should be set aside for dining.[41]

This polemic was probably the first public utterance to be quoted and discussed in the pages of both *Jogaku zasshi*, still the premier organ of women's education at the time, and *Kenchiku zasshi*, official journal of the Society of Architects (Kenchiku gakkai). Both praised the author, but *Kenchiku zasshi* noted that the articles had offered more criticism than solutions. This put the ball in the architects' court. Everyone had long been aware that Japanese houses were "imperfect" (*fukanzen*), the journal observed, but the solutions, after all, were the responsibility of "our nation's only Society of Architects."[42]

Architects in the society had in fact designed many of the "specialized houses" for men of property to which Rohan alluded. From early in the Meiji period, a few of the nation's leaders had constructed separate "Western buildings" (*yōkan*) adjacent to their dwellings (see Fig. 1.6). The earliest such buildings were constructed by statesmen and aristocrats for the purpose of receiving the Meiji emperor.[43] In this respect, they were a variety of ritual architecture akin to the elaborate gates (*onarimon*) and pavilions once built by daimyo for reception of the shogunal entourage. Subsequently, other high government officials and wealthy businessmen constructed their own, using the buildings for formal reception, particularly of non-Japanese visitors. These buildings represented Rohan's land of duties. They were distinguished by proportions and ornament derived from European texts (and the instruction of Englishman Josiah Conder, who taught architecture at the state-managed Imperial College of Engineering) and by the absence of *tatami* mats on the floor. The most prominent of them were also distinct from native houses in being the work of architects—since "architect" itself was a new professional status claimed only by graduates of the Imperial College. Clients usually maintained their families in dwellings designed by traditionally trained carpenters.

Prior to 1898, *Kenchiku zasshi* had not published plans for a dwelling of traditional wood construction. On the heels of the *Jiji shinpō* series, however, two articles appeared proposing reforms to the dwelling that incorporated both Western and Japanese features. Plans for a house submitted by archi-

Fig. 1.6 *Yōkan*: a Western house built for formal reception. The house of former daimyo Kuroda Nagahiro, built in Akasaka-ku, Tokyo, 1874. This was reportedly the first *yōkan* built as part of a Japanese private residence. The emperor was received here in January 1875. The two-story *yōkan*, to the right, with double-hung glass windows and white-painted clapboards, was linked to an existing Japanese dwelling by a corridor (*Kenchiku zasshi*, no. 150 [1899]).

tect Kitada Kyūichi represented in essential form the perspective of the profession at the time (see Fig. 1.7). The design placed on either side of a common entry vestibule a *tatami*-floored traditional dwelling and a suite of Western-style rooms consisting of a reception room and study. This plan was no radical innovation—in fact, many occupants of vernacular urban houses had already improvised some simplified form of what Kitada called "combined Japanese-Western house" (*wayō setchū jūka*). Kitada's aim was to demonstrate that such a house, indispensable "to the middle class of the twentieth century," could be built affordably, and that the task of its design was one worthy of professional architects. Revealingly, he focused attention on the Western rooms.[44]

Other architects soon added theoretical flesh to this framework for reform. In 1903 and 1904, three of the society's leading architects discussed the problem of domestic reform in the pages of *Kenchiku zasshi*, reiterating many of the arguments made earlier in *Jiji shinpō*, particularly about the ill-suitedness of *tatami* mats to work and the lack of proper interior partitions.

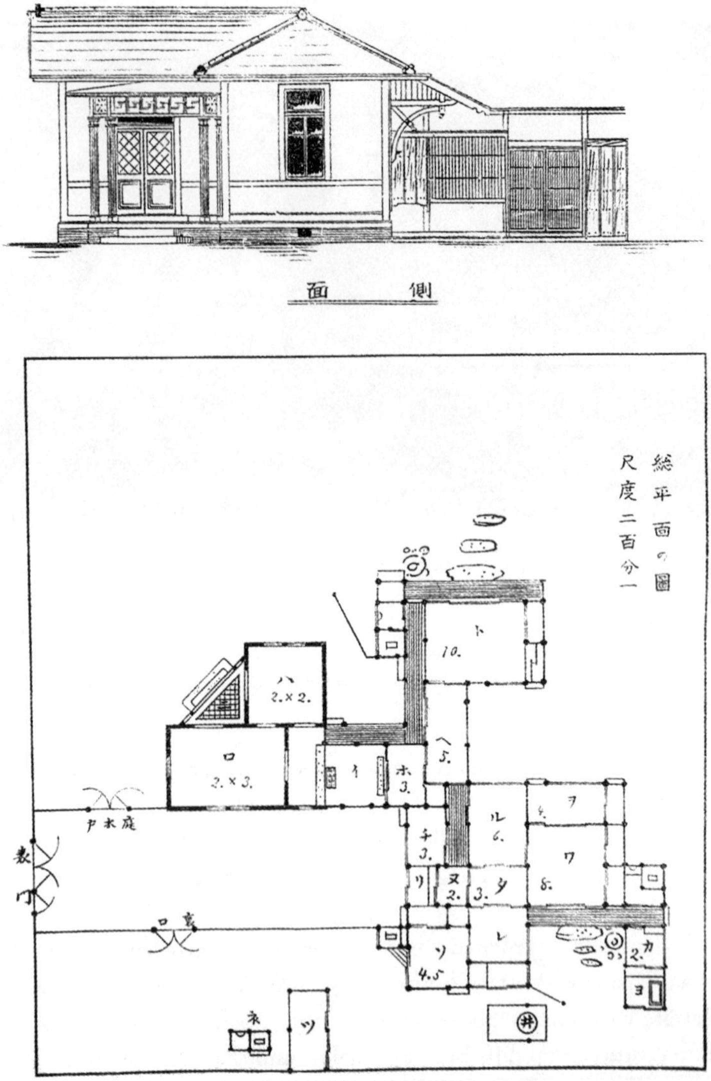


Fig. 1.7 Architect Kitada Kyūichi's plan for a mixed Japanese-Western house, featuring study (labeled ハ) and reception room (ロ) next to the earth-floored entry vestibule (イ). Measurements on the plan are in *ken* (units of approximately six feet) for the Western rooms and numbers of *tatami* mats for the Japanese rooms. Kitada provides a small entry hall between the Western rooms and the earth-floored vestibule, mirroring the *genkan no ma* on the other side, which was standard in urban houses of this time. He expected that visitors would remove their footwear before stepping up into this entry hall, just as they did on the Japanese side of the house (*Kenchiku zasshi*, no. 144 [1898]: 379).

The latter problem was described with the English words "privacy," and "secrecy," neither of which was in common parlance, as the writers' use of the English terms and proposals for possible Japanese translations (*inmitsu, himitsu*) indicate.[45] The use of rooms opening directly to one another, it was observed, put Japan 450 years behind the West, where they had had corridors since the Renaissance. Voices carried easily through paper sliding doors, often causing unpleasantness to visitors and embarrassment to the household. Private space for individual family members, however, was not discussed. Privacy as presented by these architects was a matter of the contact among three groups: the family, servants, and outsiders. The household was posed against its neighbors and guests, and the family against its servants.[46]

In 1908, in one of the rare cases in which the Meiji government involved itself in matters relating to housing, the Ministry of Education provided grants to build new dwellings for primary-school teachers throughout the country.[47] Anxious that teachers in the provinces properly represent the state not only by their conduct in the classroom but by the maintenance of proper homes, the ministry sent prefectural offices a set of sample plans and had them published in pamphlet form with commentary. The houses were simple, with three and four *tatami* rooms and large kitchens—"countrified" (*inakateki*), in the ministry's own words. Still, provision was made in each for at least two main rooms with separate access. Comments from the vice minister included the admission that "although houses for primary-school teachers have been built in the past, there has often been doubt whether one could maintain the respectability (*taimen*) of a teacher in them. We must take care that this does not happen in construction and additions in the future. It is necessary at least to separate the family living quarters and the guest room enough that when there is a guest, the family can still maintain its family circle."[48] From the ministry's point of view, the respectability of a primary-school teacher (in this document presumed to be male) thus depended not only on his personal manner or appearance but also on the proper enactment of family life and the ability to properly conceal it.

Although dwelling reform was thus beginning to produce concrete architectural changes outside the domain of the academy, academy architects themselves were still far from taking the lead in devising a new national model. The architects who wrote in *Kenchiku zasshi* during 1903 and 1904 lamenting the state of the native dwelling did not accompany their critiques with plans for new houses. One half of the profession's solution had already been laid out in Kitada Kyūichi's earlier proposal, which sequestered reception and the male household head's study at a position to one side of the entry vestibule, creating a *tatami*-less zone and ensuring the separation of household and guests. As a reduced version of the formal reception pavilion of the upper class, this space was viewed to be necessary for maintenance of a gentleman's proper relation with society. For Kitada and his bourgeois peers, such a space had to be in Western style, since "society"—the world of duties and work—wore Western trousers and shoes and sat on chairs. Architects commonly noted that no one sat on the floor in government and company offices.

This reception room was a male space, and its interior was given more than chairs and tables to articulate its status as such. The naval officer and his family described in "One Hundred Walks of Life" had created a makeshift reception room in their rented house by putting a carpet and chairs in a room with *tatami* mats and *tokonoma* alcove. They completed the conversion by filling the room with objects associated with the officer's career. In addition to lining the walls with photographs of battleships, books on naval science, and a mounted piece of Chinese calligraphy reading "Courage touches the sky," they had selected items for the alcove that bore connotations of masculine taste. No comparable decoration was given to other rooms in the house.

Since the remaining problem for architectural reform after this masculine cloister had been defined was an undivided interior, the other half of the solution was naturally to put corridors between rooms. This was achieved by the "interior corridor type" (*nakarōka gata*) plan, which appeared with increasing frequency in pattern books and magazines after 1910. The exterior corridors or verandas (*engawa*) that were usual in houses prior to this time allowed passage through the house without traversing each *tatami* room, but since rooms were typically opened toward the *engawa* in summer, they afforded little privacy. *Engawa* also provided no aid in segregating family from servants. Houses built on the new plan had a wood-floored corridor, typically three feet wide, running the length of the house. The kitchen and servants' room were grouped on one side of the corridor, with family living quarters on the other. In full realizations of the type, a Western-style reception room was placed beside the entry.[49]

The term "interior corridor plan" is of later coinage. Although not all houses labeled as such have all the defining attributes, there is little question that a new type of interior plan did emerge around 1910, and that it was widely popular thereafter in detached houses of more than three rooms, particularly in the Tokyo area. The type was abandoned after World War II, but many survived until the 1980s. Architecture historians have debated the precise origin of the interior corridor plan, disagreeing over whether to regard it as a product of vernacular ingenuity, the response of carpenters to new family needs; or as an elite design, product of the growing reform impulse within the architectural academy. On the one hand, the combination of its wide diffusion and comparative conservatism (since it involves little more than the addition of a corridor and one new room) suggests vernacular evolution.[50] On the other, the segregation of family from non-family in the interior-corridor plan clearly embodies the concerns voiced by reform-minded architects at the turn of the century prior to its wide diffusion. Architecture historian Kimura Norikuni, who coined the term, regarded the interior corridor as an architect's adaptation of non-Japanese plans, which subsequently filtered down into the general market.[51]

The assumption on both sides of this debate, that a unique genealogy must be traceable to either the elite architect or the anonymous carpenter, reifies a typology created ex post facto and misreads the relationship between vernacular and elite production in the modern era. Modern discourses of domesticity and attitudes about domestic space were entering house design through multiple channels. In the 1910s, collections of house plans were published in increasing numbers. Competitions judged by academy architects appeared in the newspapers and elsewhere, and interior corridor plans tended to win. Clients and literate carpenters both had access to these media; at the same time, the needs of families were changing, as bourgeois families were reconceiving their own domestic lives and turning new attention to shaping the space around them.[52]

## Architecture and Manners

This process of fashioning a space primarily for the household head's contact with the outside world and creating functional zones within the house purified the main *tatami* portion of the house as a place to cloister the family from society. The interior could not be secured entirely as a refuge for the conjugal family, however, because dwellings were still requisitioned as the stages for more public uses, chief among which were weddings, funerals, and memorial services for the dead. On these occasions, the interior of the house was opened to gatherings of extended family, local community, or professional associates. To accommodate a large occasional group, the interior-corridor house retained at least two contiguous *tatami* rooms that could be used in combination. These rooms were typically designated *ima* (day or living room) and *kyakuma* (guest room; distinct from *yōma*, or *yōshiki ōsetsuma*, the Western-style reception room). In ordinary use, both rooms could be part of family living space, but on the occasion of large gatherings, sliding panels between them were removed to create a single *zashiki* (*tatami*-floored gathering space).[53]

As long as weddings and funerals continued to be held in the home and to involve broader communities that overlaid the household, *tatami* rooms would retain the occasional function of formal reception.[54] The *zashiki* combination was retained in model house plans until the 1920s (and usually in interior-corridor houses constructed afterward), but reform writers and architects rarely voiced the practical necessity of linked rooms explicitly.

Reform advocates were less forgiving of casual reception, however, which they viewed as wasteful and an unnecessary burden on the household. Girls' school texts and women's magazines discouraged unscheduled visits and service of anything more than tea and confections to unscheduled visitors. Conversation at these times, they urged, should be limited to business as much as possible. A chapter titled "The Housewife and Social Exchange" in the Greater Japan Domestic Science Association's manual *A Lady's Home Library* began by observing how "very unfortunate" it was that unlike the West, Japan had no custom of fixed visiting times. Things may have been different in "the extreme leisure" of the feudal era, but in the twentieth century every minute was money.[55] "Fifteen to thirty minutes" were the polite limits, according to another text.[56] Anterooms linked to the guest room, associated with elaborate feudal practices of reception, were counted unnecessary and omitted from reformed house plans.

Despite calls for rationalization, traditions of reciprocal visiting and the extensive gift economy were not easily disrupted. Apart from the major events in the family life cycle and holidays such as the New Year, there were numerous minor occasions to pay visits. In an era before telephones, even trifling matters had to be communicated by letter or in person. Since a scheduled visit compelled the host to make special preparations, it was considered better etiquette to arrive unannounced than to fix a precise day and time. Except in the case of tradesmen and complete strangers, it was usual to invite the visitor in and serve tea and food or even *sake* and a meal.[57]

The layout of late Tokugawa-period middle and lower samurai households was in large measure determined by the needs of formal and informal reception. The master's region of these houses typically comprised a progression of two or three rooms leading from the entry to the *zashiki* guest room (which might also be the master's living quarters). This sequence of spaces formed the stage for rigorous performances of status in receiving official visitors, as well as for family-related ceremonial occasions. As the portion of the house associated primarily with occasional rather than everyday use, these rooms tended to be more ornamented and brighter, enjoying better prospects of the garden. In contrast, unannounced daily visitors were received in the region of the house governed by the mistress. In surviving plans from Iida han, for example, a large room or pair of rooms linked with the kitchen and labeled *daidoko* (a common designation for a room with a hearth) and *ōtai* ("receiving," but implying more casual reception than *zashiki*) forms a second zone parallel or perpendicular to the rooms for formal reception (see Fig. 1.8).[58] Meiji reformers seldom acknowledged such distinctions, as a redefinition of guests mirrored their redefinition of the family. Late Meiji plans reflected the continued practical necessity of an extendable *zashiki* space, but the vernacular gradations that included a middle area for casual visitors, not quite front and not quite back region, were no longer recognized. When family ideologues spoke of guests, they meant outsiders, whose reception was now construed fundamentally as part of the master's business world, to be kept as much as possible in the Western reception room.

Yanagita Kunio observed an analogous change in farmhouses with the waning of the *dei*, the room best suited to casual reception of visitors. His description is characteristically vague with regard to time period but pointed with regard to the social implications of the change:

> People from outside came to fall either into the category of those one compelled to come up into the *zashiki* and entertained as guests, and those one tried, if possible, to have sent away at the door. I think perhaps the reason that the Japanese manner with guests is judged too heavy by some and interpreted as rather cold (*reien*) by other observers comes mainly from the etiolation of the *dei*.[59]

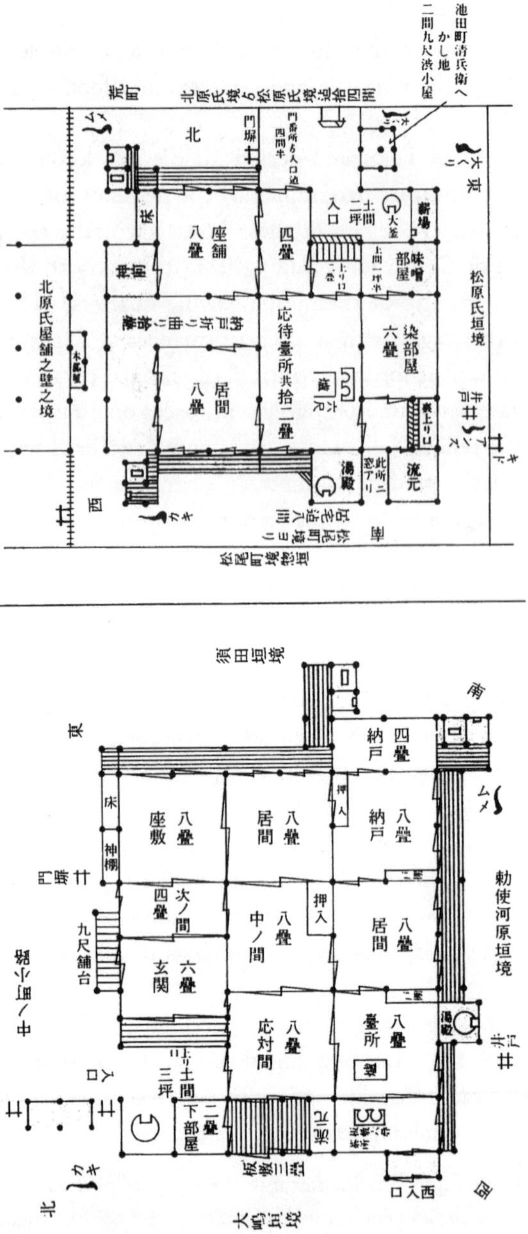

Fig. 1.8 Plans of two houses built prior to 1858 for middle-ranking samurai of the Iida *han*. Three linked rooms, the master's *zashiki*, with *tokonoma* alcove, an antechamber, and the entry chamber (*genkan no ma*), define a zone for formal reception; household functions and the reception of more casual visitors take place elsewhere (Ōkawa Naomi, *Sumai no jinruigaku*). Entry to the house above is from the top right. The master's *zashiki* is at top left. Entry to the house below is from the bottom left, and the master's *zashiki* is at the top left.

This was a subtle but profound change. The room itself did not disappear from standard four-room farmhouse plans, but according to Yanagita, people no longer understood what its original purpose had been. Yanagita noted that in its place, modern houses had the reception room (*ōsetsuma*), which "retained many guest-room elements" and lacked the cozy informality of the old *dei*.[60]

Domestic reformers more interested in the woman's side of the home ideal than in questions of men's formal reception sought to further articulate the dwelling as a family space by calling for a layout in which guest rooms were placed to the north and family rooms given the healthy southern exposure. Reform texts came to refer to this in shorthand as the "family-center idea" (*kazoku chūshin setsu*) or the "family-based house" (*kazoku hon'i no jūtaku*). Since most middle-class houses still had a *tatami* "best room" (*kyakuma* or *zashiki*) for formal meals and overnight guests, this became the reformers' target. It was a fine thing to honor guests, they argued, but the best room in the house ought not to be set aside for non-family use. Opinions on the proper solution differed, and not all floor plans, either in reality or in the prescriptive literature, demoted the "guest room" to an inferior position.[61] Since *tatami* floors made a range of living arrangements possible within any layout, the particular solution offered by each text is less significant than the fact that most addressed the issue in the same terms, using a vocabulary that reflected the normative role of the family in dwelling design.

It is easy to interpret these admonitions as part of a general effort to reduce formal etiquette. Viewed broadly, however, the reverse is probably true. The rules of etiquette taught to samurai by the Ogasawara school since the medieval period filled textbooks for girls' instruction in the modern period. The choreographic protocols of reception for guests of higher rank, equal rank, and lower rank, each with graded distinctions regarding where one was to kneel and bow, and where to place the hands while bowing, were taught in girls' school classes from texts illustrated with drawings of young women performing them (see Fig. 1.9).[62] The cult of tea, which had been a primarily male literati pastime, was appropriated by the girls' schools as a device to inculcate elaborate rules of comportment and behavior for reception of guests.[63]

The portion of the female population able to have etiquette lessons at girls' higher school in this era was small, but magazines and other media

Fig. 1.9 Proper forms of greeting for a visitor of inferior station (*left*), equal station (*middle*), and superior station (*right*), from an etiquette text for use in girls' schools (Takahashi Bunjirō, *Shōgakkō onna reishiki kunkai* [Etiquette Lessons for Primary-School Girls], 1882).

transmitted the same ideas to a larger audience. Even some progressive writers and educators treated the dictates of the Ogasawara school as the essential canon of manners. The traditional etiquette masters themselves published texts and manuals for popular consumption, aimed particularly at the female reader. Articles on the etiquette of guest reception and visiting in women's magazines assumed a common sequence of spaces and interactions, beginning with an encounter in the entry vestibule (*genkan* or *genkan no ma*) between the visitor and a servant or other representative of the household whose task it was to answer the door and greet visitors (*toritsugi*), and progressing to the *zashiki*, where bows were exchanged again, and the visitor was asked to wait. The master or mistress of the house was expected to time his or her entrance to the *zashiki* according to the nature of the visit and the status of the visitor.[64] Servants and other go-betweens sometimes played a larger role than they had in the past. Manners now were looser, one Ogasawara master explained to Hani Motoko, the editor of *Katei jogaku kōgi* (precursor of the magazine *Fujin no tomo*); hence it was acceptable in "ordinary homes today" to have a servant go to the door in place of the host "unless receiving someone of much higher station."[65]

Since the modern bourgeois class for whom these social rules were most significant was still taking shape, the codes, too, were being molded to modern requirements. Samurai etiquette was modified to incorporate calling cards, and separate forms were developed for reception in Western dress. In either case, gesture and comportment were formulated in a strict hierarchy to match social position. It is important to bear in mind that not all the people learning and practicing this etiquette were children of samurai who had grown up in such habits. Lessons provided in girls' schools, women's magazines, and domestic manuals were needed because both the codes themselves and the class practicing them were in flux. The two constituted each other.

If the expulsion of casual visitors gave the family more of the house to themselves, it was not given unconditionally. As the universal application of an elite canon of etiquette and the prescriptions for performance of the "family circle" suggest, women's education and journalism sought to remodel the family for the parlor as much as the parlor for the family. This was true of everyday mealtime gatherings no less than formal occasions involving guests. Reformers stressed proper attire and morally beneficial conversation topics, holding up "the West" in contrast to native habits. The family meal would ordinarily be taken in a sitting room (*chanoma* or *shokudō*), which was treated as part of the woman's sphere. While the patriarch presided at non-mealtime family meetings, mealtime was orchestrated by the housewife, who was the one expected to see that these standards were maintained (for a different vision, see Fig. 1.10).

The reformers who sought to redesign domestic architecture for a more intimate family had much in common with the authors of an earlier literature of domestic reform in the United States. American architect Calvert Vaux, for example, had criticized the custom of setting aside rooms for company, asserting that the most pleasant rooms should go to daily use.[66] Also comparable was the effort paralleling architectural reform to modify occupants' behavior. Indeed, Japanese reformers were prone to regard as evidence of Western standards material from the prescriptive writings of Anglo-American reformers who, like themselves, were devising ideal models out of dissatisfaction with native conditions.

Unlike the ideal of the domestic haven that developed in England and the United States, however, the vessel for domesticity proffered to Japanese retained a small piece of the household head's working world, albeit enclosed in solid walls and kept near the entry in the name of "privacy." Rohan's two types of house were not the suburban residence and office in town that bourgeois men in England and the United States were coming to possess. The residential suburb in Japan had hardly begun to develop in 1898, when Rohan wrote his essay on the dwelling. Tokyo's physical landscape would only begin to catch up with the discursive one in the years after World War I. But the fact that the Japanese middle-class model placed the "land of

Fig. 1.10 Kosugi Misei, "Home" ("Katei"). Simply by labeling this chaotic domestic scene with the neologism *katei*, the artist pokes fun at the florid idealizations that more often surrounded it in the popular press of the time. As if in an ironic inversion of the "family circle," everyone in the household, including the cat, faces away from the others. The scroll in the *tokonoma* reads "flourishing, boisterous, and noisy" (From *Hōsun*, Feb. 1909).

duties" and the "land of beauty" not only on the same lot but under one roof reflected distinctive characteristics of both domestic management authors and the architectural profession in Japan. The image of home as a sacred haven and the housewife as its spiritual center persisted in *katei* rhetoric even after overt Christianity had been purged from the literature, but the sacred nature of the conjugal relationship ceased to play a large role in Japanese domesticity. A new perception of childhood whose seeds were evident in textbooks of the Meiji period would later swell into a cult of motherhood comparable to that in the West.[67] Nevertheless, the ideologues of the *katei* did not demand conjugal hegemony over the entire house. A gender-specific cloister could be retained under one roof together with the family haven without fundamental contradiction.

Part of the architects' reform agenda echoed the concerns of women's educators. Awakened to the native dwelling as both an architectural type and a social problem, they responded with designs to establish an internal zoning of functions and social groups. Whether their zoned plans gave preference to the guest or to the family, they served to enhance the stage for domesticity by separation of the two. Meanwhile, the larger context of architectural reform was dominated by the enormous difference between structures of the native building tradition and the European architecture that housed the institutions of modern society and stood as a gauge of national progress. To some, as public life was transformed for hygiene, efficiency, and the aesthetics of civilization, Japanese buildings came to seem increasingly barbaric. It was in this context that *tatami* mats were particularly vilified. But most architects stated that, despite their being unhygienic, mats could not be removed from the dwelling at once. Their reasons ranged from personal fondness for the comforts of floor living to nationalist defense of native cultural traditions to a kind of colonial rhetoric in which the light of civilization would eventually reach the home, but the women who were its chief occupants could not quickly be brought into the modern age. This ambiguous stance toward native forms added a second filter over dwelling reform, making the problem one not only of morality and family well-being but also of the level of civilization of the nation itself. It led Meiji-period architects inevitably to the "combined Japanese-Western style" solution, in which the conditions of being civilized were met without disrupting more than necessary the individual architect's sense of cultural identity or of gender hierarchy and proper domestic roles.

## The Common Ground of Domesticity

After the 1898 Civil Code, the *ie* trod its own course. The *katei*, meanwhile, having made its peace with the older generation (still cohabitant with their children in many cases) and identified itself with the bourgeois vanguard who claimed the social "middle" (*chūryū*), was becoming a nexus between reformism and a nascent consumer culture. The "home" Meiji reformers constructed under the name *katei* was a human community circumscribed in space. It assumed conjugality at its center, but was not antagonistic to lineage. This new spatial configuration of people, along with the practices designed to nurture and sustain it, served the interests of the state. This was the reason that nation-building ideologues like Tokutomi Sohō, whose primary preoccupations were in the public sphere, saw it as a cause equally to be championed. But the *katei* was not invented by the state—its material and ritual contents were cobbled together by men and women purveying their moral wisdom on family matters and their expertise on Western domestic practice through popular magazines and other commercial vehicles that must be considered only partial in their normative power. Their readers, to the degree that they accepted the advice being offered, presumably believed they were buying useful components of class membership.

The material elements were in some cases quite distinct from those in other countries where the discourse of domesticity had currency (*tatami* mats, for example, were a problem peculiar to Japan), in others ostensibly the same but very different in their local meaning (dining tables in Japan possessed a significance without counterpart in the West), but in Japan as elsewhere, modern domesticity proved fertile ground for the growth of bourgeois culture. By World War I, a new ensemble of bourgeois family norms and accompanying spatial practices had taken shape. *Katei* signified the space of these norms and practices. The architecture of the dwelling was belatedly incorporated into the process of ideological construction, setting the stage for a broader reshaping of domestic space and everyday life.

# 2

# The Housewife's Laboratory

## Domestic Knowledge in the Schools

For women, the site of family harmony was also a place of work. As bourgeois ideologues reconceived the dwelling around a new configuration of family, they redefined the nature of women's work as well. Feminist historians and theorists have made clear that words like "housewife" and "housework"—in modern Japanese, *shufu* and *kaji*—are ideological constructs that function by making specific relations of power appear natural and timeless, thereby concealing their historical origins.[1] A moment when the use of these words changes thus provides the opportunity to scrutinize the workings of gender ideology. In Japan, one such critical moment came at the end of the nineteenth century.

The same Meiji-period institutions and media in which domesticity acquired shape provided the social and discursive instruments for a new gendering of housework and, in the process, defined the new profession of housewife. As participants in the constitution of new fields of expertise surrounding the dwelling and as the target consumers of much of that expertise, housewives were not simply left at home while their men became commuting workers; rather, they were integrated into new roles in a redefined social space. Modern housewifery, that is, took shape as the counterpart not to the work of husbands (men : work :: women : home) but to other specific professional disciplines: child psychology, medicine, hygiene, nutrition science, industrial management, and architecture. Although women's lives appeared on the surface less radically transformed, their imbrication in modern professional formations restructured labor roles and practices in ways that would ultimately prove as fundamental as the regulation of male labor and leisure under modern capitalism.

Schools provided the first channel for conveying a modern discipline of household management. A new curriculum developed during the Meiji period, referred to as *kaji* (household matters) or *kasei* (household management), isolated a set of tasks and responsibilities from the activities that sustained Japanese households and assembled them into the new profession of housewife. Cooking, cleaning, and childcare, the duties commonly delegated to modern housewives, had long been parts of a system in which production and consumption, and male and female responsibilities, were interwoven. Universal education under the modern state, which removed boys and girls alike from household labor regimes, trained girls to return to the household, but with new values that would serve the state and a modern bourgeois conception of family.

Girls received lessons in domestic management in both primary and secondary schools, but the secondary schools for girls known as *jogakkō*, or girls' higher schools, became the true hatcheries for professional housewives. At these schools, teenage girls whose families could afford to do without their labor studied the arts and etiquette that provided the finishing for a good marriage. They also learned habits of domestic work that would distinguish them from their mothers and grandmothers, as well as from less-educated women of their own generation. The institution of the girls' higher school itself contributed powerfully to a cohesive class consciousness by bringing privileged young women to live together in cities away from their families. For the women who went, the experience created strong bonds, forming transregional communities of classmates and graduates. These communities were subsequently fostered and extended in women's magazines. And just as these new institutions of bourgeois culture shaped women, the family ideals and specialized knowledge of modern housewifery shared among this educated sisterhood contributed significantly to shaping bourgeois identity.[2] Prewar Japanese women's education has often been described as conservative, but the institution itself was profoundly antitraditional, and domestic management as a modern discipline was driven by perpetually evolving reformist ideals. Women's secondary education engaged in new discourses of science and economy in response to the changing forces and demands of the state and capital.

Admittedly, much of housewifery in the late nineteenth and early twentieth centuries consisted of tasks that had been performed by women in earlier generations as well. The association of women with domestic labor was not a modern contrivance; Confucian texts had repeated homilies about "women governing within and men without" for centuries. Although Victorian writing provided a new rhetoric about woman's natural disposition to things domestic, the primary tasks for Meiji women appear at first glance to have changed little. The kitchen was a predominantly female space in most households before cooking became part of the girls' school curriculum. The manufacture and repair of clothing had long been the most time-consuming task of married women and continued to be so in the modern period. Reflecting this, girls' education in the modern period devoted more hours to sewing than to any other instruction.

Nevertheless, Meiji pedagogues presumed, as none had before, that girls' education, like that for boys, should serve the needs of the state. This meant not only that the girls would now sew sacks and uniforms for the military but also that the rest of the curriculum as it developed would have to be justified on the basis of more than feminine cultivation—it had to claim universal principles of utility. In the 1870s, during the first years under the new system, practical instruction specifically for girls was given in classes called "hand crafts" (*shugei*) and "economics" (*keizai*). Some of the texts later to be used in *kaji* classes served first here. Regulations for the primary school curriculum issued in 1881 specified "household economy" (*kaji keizai*) for the girls' higher primary school, with "clothing, laundry, dwelling, furniture, food, cooking, hairdressing, budgeting, and other matters concerning the economy of a house" as appropriate contents. "Household management" (*kasei*) appeared in the curriculum of state-sponsored girls' higher schools from the time of their establishment in 1882.[3] Subsequently, it was taught consistently in the higher schools but existed only as an independent course in the primary schools intermittently until 1914, when it became a permanent part of the compulsory curriculum for girls. In 1947, it was combined with sewing, which had been taught in separate classes since the 1870s, to form "home class" (*kateika*).[4]

From the creation of the first state-mandated girls' schools in the 1870s, the Ministry of Education and private publishers following ministry guidelines produced a diversity of textbooks relating to management of the home. These texts began by codifying knowledge previously conveyed orally or through practice within households and became increasingly technical with time. They represent the effort of educators to impose a set of national standards in place of the range of local practices without appearing to reject native traditions. *Kaji*, or "domestic matters," as the subject was known generically, was thus an eclectic discipline. Early instruction drew material from moral texts by Tokugawa Confucianists and merchant house codes, as well as a number of translations or adaptations of Anglo-American works. The curriculum was in flux until the end of the century, as was the education system as a whole. Yet, by the 1890s, when "home" developed a discourse outside the field of education, girls' school teachers were contributing a consistent message to the swelling ideological current that would come to engulf domestic life. The divide between domestic reform journalism and women's classroom education was not always a clear one, since educators often wrote columns in the women's magazines and the popular press at the same time that they taught and wrote textbooks.

Hygiene and efficiency, two quintessentially modern obsessions, came increasingly to separate the new domestic knowledge from the old. Both had native precedents: modern hygiene (*eisei*) in Japan could look to the older science of fostering health called *yōjō*, and "efficiency" (*nōritsu*) was in part a metamorphosis of older notions of "economy" (*keizai*). Their modern forms, however, came to the household from outside, as manifestations of state and municipal authority and of industry. The print market brought female readers the counsel of experts, images of wealthy bourgeois exemplars' lifestyles, and the experience of other literate women. These ideas thus penetrated daily life through many channels besides the schools.

The first textbooks authorized by the Ministry of Education were translations or adaptations from works in English, but most girls' school students in the first decade of the new curriculum read from native texts. In some instances, texts not written specifically for a female readership came to be treated as such. Schools assigned Tokugawa-period manuals for merchant households, which combined moral prescriptions with specific advice on matters such as finance, housekeeping, and relations between master and servant. Kaibara Ekken's *Kadōkun* (Instructions in the way of the house), first published in the late seventeenth century, was still read in some schools during the Meiji period. Other schools used newly published texts based on these earlier genres.

Enterprising authors and publishers modified their strategies to respond to demand for a gendered product that was still in the process of being defined. *Danjo futsū kasei shōgaku* (Boys' and girls' ordinary domestic management primer; 1880), a textbook written in simple language for primary school pupils, for example, was reissued in 1882 as "Revised Domestic Management Primer," with the words "boys' and girls' ordinary" omitted from the title. New chapters covered cooking, laundry, and hairdressing, to conform to 1881 Ministry of Education guidelines for the girls' curriculum.[5] The author of one inexpensively produced domestic manual published in the 1880s felt obliged to justify the change to readers, noting that "as trends have changed in recent years, study has been divided into numerous different subjects, so that men's education and women's education now differ in their purposes and methods, and study relating to household economics has become a field to be pursued only by women."[6]

Popular domestic manuals, identifiable by the extensive use of Japanese readings to paraphrase Chinese characters in the text, and often also by the word *tsūzoku* (popular) prefixing the title, continued to be published by non-specialists into the first decade of the twentieth century, conveying a blend of old and new notions and images in inexpensive, small volumes suited to a non-elite public. By 1910, however, primary-school attendance of both boys and girls neared 100 percent, the numbers attending girls' higher schools were rising rapidly, and a diversity of magazines and other publications explicitly targeted female audiences with new knowledge for the home. In this context, the eclectic older texts gradually faded from the market.

Despite the retailoring of domestic training for young women, few of the early textbooks written by Japanese authors discussed the nature of womanhood itself or the suitedness of women to domestic roles. Absent also was any idealization of the family. This contrasted them with the works of Anglo-American authors of domestic management texts like the Beecher sisters, for whom the moral influence on the family of woman's innately charitable disposition was a theme of central importance. Instead, Japanese writers emphasized a wife's responsibility to the institutions of the house. Kasukabe Sannosuke's *Shōgaku kaji keizai kunmō*, published in 1883, opened with a list of the topics specified for domestic economy classes in the Ministry of Education guidelines and then explained to readers "why domestic economy is a subject exclusively for girls." When they grow up, the introduction stated, girls would be required "to manage the house and preserve its property (*kasan o tamotsu*)," while helping their husbands to ensure the "prosperity of the house" (*ikka no hanjō*). Later passages spoke of pursuing the "occupation of the house" (*kagyō*) and building the foundation for its independence (*ikka dokuritsu*). The term *katei*, yet to gain wide circulation at this stage, was absent. Translations of Anglo-American texts often spoke of "household management" in the economic sense (usually translated with the Confucian term *saika*) but not of the house as a business concern. Early Meiji-period textbooks like Kasukabe's still evoked a domestic world congruous with that of Kaibara Ekken's *Kadōkun*, written two centuries earlier. The difference was that where Tokugawa texts had included a corresponding set of rules for men, these rules were no longer taught.[7]

By the turn of the twentieth century, a new girls' higher school curriculum had developed, along with a new generation of educators, many of whom were women, to write the textbooks and use them in the classroom. *Kaji* (domestic matters) was becoming *kaseigaku* (domestic management studies), the discipline of a corps of specialists. New textbook guidelines were issued in 1895 and 1901, and finally in detailed form in 1903. Under these guidelines, the scope of domestic training was expanded to encompass childcare, nursing of the sick, and prevention of contagious disease. Cooking instruction, present in the earlier guidelines for primary school but not universally taught in the higher schools, was given new prominence, with thirteen topics and over twenty foods specified.[8]

In 1899, the Ministry of Education ordered that a minimum of one girls' higher school be established in each prefecture. Attendance climbed severalfold in the following decade. It was 75,128 in 1912, still only 2 or 3 percent of the figure for girls in primary school at the same time, but it continued to climb exponentially afterward, multiplying by sixfold again between 1910 and 1926. By 1926 the number of students in the girls' higher school had approached 10 percent of the primary-school girls' population and was only slightly lower than the number in the boys' middle schools, which represented the equivalent level in the boys' system. Thus, among couples married after the 1910s, it was increasingly common for both members to have had some experience of secondary education, a critical element of bourgeois class consciousness.[9]

In contrast with the texts of the 1880s, both *Kaji kyōkasho* (Textbook in domestic matters; 1898) and *Kaji kyōhon* (Domestic primer; 1900), two standard texts of the second generation of girls' higher school education, opened with declarations that woman's innately gentle and sensitive character made her peculiarly suited to the duties of housekeeping. *Kaji kyōkasho* described the house as a "place where husband, wife, and children, the most intimate relations, wake and sleep together, sharing love and helping one another," a place to which the household head, "away all day pursuing his affairs," returned fatigued from work, to be nurtured by his family. Removal of the male household head's work from the home thus made explicit, these textbooks spoke little of women working for the "occupation" or "prosperity of the house."[10]

*Kaji* textbooks aggrandized the importance of work in the home with metaphors borrowed from the Anglo-American domesticity literature, which compared housewives to figures of power in a male world outside. The housewife was the "prime minister" of the household or a soldier whose "battlefield" was the home.[11] At the same time, the modern terms describing housework and housewives reflected the delimiting of the field of domestic work and female roles that was taking place. *Kaji*, which became the standard modern word for housework, had had a broader meaning in Tokugawa texts such as Kaibara Ekken's *Kadōkun*, where it was used to encompass literally all "things of the house," including commercial activities and farming. *Kadōkun*, in fact, addressed primarily the master of the house, assumed to be male.[12] Commerce and farming were excised from the modern field of *kaji*, which was reduced to the set of tasks comparable to what is called "housework" in modern English.

Similarly, words referring to the woman of the house underwent a subtle shift in nuance in the late nineteenth century. *Shufu*, the equivalent to "housewife," combines the characters "master" or "chief" and "woman." It appears in Chinese classics as a term distinguishing a primary wife from concubines. In Meiji Japan, it bore the sense of "mistress [of the house]" but was not commonly used in popular texts, where *fujo* (women) and the colloquial *nyōbo* (wife) were preferred. Gradually from the 1880s, *shufu* became an independent label, reflecting its transformation from a status designation within a household to a universal occupational category. Letters published in the housekeeping advice column of *Katei no tomo* magazine, which began publication in 1903, were often signed *ichi shufu* (a mistress), a locution (whether chosen by the writer or the editors) that could imply only "housewife," as a general description of the writer's social position, particularly when juxtaposed with letters signed "a laborer" (*ichi rōdōsha*) and "a young father" (*wakaki chichi*).[13] Whereas "*shufu*" had formerly been equally applicable to a female household head or the proprietress of a business such as a restaurant, in the early twentieth century it shed these meanings and became the universal term for a married woman without work obligations outside the house.[14]

As Kano Masanao has observed, this occupation was one to which many women aspired, since it connoted freedom from the toils of farm or shop labor and usually the presence of a maid to do the housewife's least pleasant chores and call her *okusama* (madam).[15] Even without a maid to confirm her social superiority, the professional housewife who answered only to her husband enjoyed a status far preferable to that of the young bride (*yome*) in a multigeneration peasant household, who was commonly treated like a farmhand.[16] Compared to the lot of the young bride under the harsh rule of her parents-in-law, being a *shufu* placed a woman in a position of authority, however small her actual dominion.

The inauguration in 1917 of *The Housewife's Companion* (*Shufu no tomo*), a magazine that soon had a wider readership than any of its predecessors, represented the term's arrival in its modern lexical position as "housewife": no longer the mistress in any institution other than the home, often the director of only a small kitchen and sitting room, but a recognized professional identity nonetheless. Desirable as it was to the laboring majority, once *shufu* came to be a generally recognized social position, the connotations of this identity were not lofty by all standards. According to the publisher's later recollection, when the magazine began publication, *shufu* had already come to imply a baser status alongside the more elegant *fujin*, a general term for woman or lady.[17]

## Reforming Kitchens

No part of the house was more heavily invested with importance in the texts of the new profession than the kitchen, for it was here that the modern *shufu* was to establish herself as an expert. At the same time, domestic ideologues anxious that education should not lead young women to harbor ambitions for careers outside the home found in the elaboration of knowledge around the kitchen the means to claim that housework was a calling as intellectually rewarding as any technical profession. The kitchen was, in fact, a "laboratory" for the housewife, *Jogaku zasshi* declared, and women should think of their work there as "research." Girls' school graduates who became dissatisfied with the monotony of a life spent in the kitchen should recall, the journal urged, that scientists too spent years doing the same tasks in tiny rooms without complaint, never knowing when or whether their work would lead to "the discovery of a microbe or invention of a vaccine" that could save the lives of thousands of people.[18] The girls' higher schools set the research agenda for professional housewives and sought to instill the habits of perseverance and meticulousness proper to solitary study.

At the same time, the educated woman's commitment to the kitchen was an expression of class identity as much as a response to state indoctrination. The vision in school texts of the housewife laboring to ensure the welfare of her family served the interests of bourgeois progressives eager to distinguish their own lifestyles from the "feudal" or "aristocratic" customs of past elites. Meanwhile, the popular media for women echoed the higher school texts in insisting that the mistress of the house handle food preparation for the sake of the family's health. Hygiene discourse inflected the problem of class in a new way, making it a housewife's duty not only to care for her family but to protect them from the invisible threat of disease. For this, she was to forge an alliance with medical experts against the ignorance and negligence of the working class, embodied in the servants and tradesmen through whose hands household provisions passed.

As part of its distinctly modern, urban character, the bourgeois conception of food preparation that emerged at the end of the nineteenth century put new primacy on novel recipes and ingredients. The need for novelty was inherent in the logic of the periodical mass media, which introduced culinary features in order to attract and keep female subscribers. Newspaper and magazine columns thus aided the schools in naturalizing the idea that the kitchen was a housewife's special domain while adding a new emphasis on daily invention and variety.

These new perceptions of food preparation, and hygiene consciousness in particular, created a profound rift between housewives who had attended the girls' higher schools and their maids, who rarely had more than the mandatory four to six years of primary school. Hygiene received far greater elaboration in the second generation of texts printed from around the turn of the twentieth century. Higher school graduates and women's magazine readers absorbed heavy doses of hygiene discourse and lived in a world where "reform of the kitchen" was viewed as a matter of urgency. Ignorant servants were often treated as the primary impediment.

Changes in the structure of urban households reconfigured the mistress-servant relationship, enhancing the tensions created by education. The small, newly formed professional households whose numbers were growing in the cities were likely to have one or two live-in maids together with the family, in contrast to the long-established houses of propertied families, where work was commonly shared by several female and male servants, along with farm tenants, apprentices, or other subordinates in the household enterprise. Jukichi Inouye's 1910 account of Tokyo life, which portrayed primarily households of the upper bourgeoisie, spoke of three maids—a cook, a housemaid, and a "lady's maid," who served as personal attendant to the mistress—in addition to a wetnurse and sometimes a head housekeeper. When present, Inouye noted, the housekeeper enjoyed great authority over other servants, who held her in "hardly less reverence than her mistress."[19] But as frequent letters and articles on the "servant problem" in the women's magazines reveal, many educated women oversaw only one maid and worried over what to entrust to her and how to treat her. *Fujin sekai* began a series on maids in 1909, soliciting letters from both employers and employees. The editors and letter writers mentioned no division of roles in the household other than that between the mistress and her maid, who was referred to with the more neutral-sounding new term *jochū* rather than traditional appellations such as *kahi*, *hiboku*, and *gejo*, all of which connoted lowliness. The letters chosen presented instances of loyal "model maids" and employers' descriptions of successful methods for assigning work responsibilities.[20] In addition to the increased competition in the employment market engendered by opportunities in factories and elsewhere, this new concern reflected status uncertainty accompanying the changed composition and dynamics of the household. In small bourgeois households, the new role constructed for the mistress of the house meant, in effect, that there were now two women in the kitchen, with the same basic duties, one of whom was paid and one of whom was not.

Before reform of the kitchen could become an issue of wide concern among educated women, however, educated women had first to take an interest in cooking. Women in most nineteenth-century households had doubtless had more involvement in domestic food preparation than men, but as with other tasks, the distribution of kitchen labor was determined by status as well as gender. The rice scoop is a well-known symbol of the privileges of the mistress of the house (*shufuken*) in rural Japan. It represented the authority of the *shufu* over the distribution of food, but it did not signify that she herself prepared it.[21] *Kaji* textbooks from the 1880s often urged women to obey their "calling" (*shokubun*), to manage the kitchen, and not leave everything to servants. Yet the frequent repetition of such exhortations also intimates that among households that had servants, there were indeed many where food preparation was left to them. The model mistress of the house was an overseer in the kitchen, not a cook. Stereotypical nicknames given to maids, such as "Osan," "Osandon" and "Onabe," had meanings referring to meals, since preparing them was often their primary duty.[22] Nor were kitchen tasks exclusively the work of female servants. Illustrated books of the Tokugawa period often showed men involved in kitchen work, particularly heavier work. The readers of an almanac of practical knowledge published in 1886 presumably found nothing peculiar in seeing explanations of pickling methods illustrated by pictures of both men and women[23] (see Figs. 2.1–2.2). In the upper class it was sufficiently unusual for the mistress of the house to cook that when Naka Michiyo, principal of the Tokyo Women's Normal School (Tōkyō joshi shihan gakkō) from 1881 to 1885, introduced cooking instruction to the curriculum there, he met with protest from the wealthy men whose daughters attended the college.[24]

From the mid-1880s, the newly emerging women's press began to call for more cooking instruction in the girls' schools. Yet even in 1899, four years after the Ministry of Education had ordered that time be allotted for actual practice in *kaji*, a magazine survey found that no cooking practice took place at the majority of schools. The magazines themselves sought to compensate, printing recipes provided by professional chefs. The first newspaper to join the effort was *Jiji shinpō*, which began running the cooking column "Nani ni shiyō ne" (What shall I prepare?) in 1893. Introducing the column, the editors wrote, "Since wives in every house are troubled by the same question—'What shall I make today?'—we have decided to present daily dishes in a corner of the *Jiji shinpō* for their convenience. . . . Of course, since these recipes have the strength of advice from experts like the master of Kagetsurō in Shinbashi, we can recommend them with confidence for method and accuracy."[25] Cooking classes and professional demonstrations for female

Fig. 2.1 Kitchen labor in the eighteenth and nineteenth centuries.
(*top*) A fishmonger squats in the earth-floor section of the kitchen to gut a fish (*Onna juhō saidai* [The Woman's Eternal Mugwort Board], 1819). (*bottom*) The manservant on the wooden floor in the foreground uses a large mortar and pestle. Maids kneel on a *tatami*-mat floor to scoop rice and ladle water (*Onna yō chihiro hama* [The Woman's Thousand-Fathom Shore], 1780).

audiences also began at this time. Formal instruction in food preparation had previously been restricted to men and women seeking to practice professionally.[26] For consumers in urban areas, restaurants and fish merchants delivered prepared foods for special occasions or everyday ones. Simpler preparations were learned at home, primarily in a transmission between

Fig. 2.2 Two pages from *Shobutsu seihō myōjutsu kihō: banmin no jitsueki* (Curious Techniques, Ingenious Methods of Manufacture: Real Profit for the Multitudes; 1886), a miscellany of popular knowledge. A man prepares a chicken for preserving, and a man and woman pickle melons and eggplants.

older women and younger.[27] The recipes in *Jiji shinpō* were not exotic; the vast majority used familiar Japanese ingredients. Their significance lay in the fact that they were collected from professionals for the edification of "the wife in every house," and the underlying assumption that the reader would be preparing something new each day. In large urban households as in the countryside, the kitchen had been a factory where production and preservation followed seasonal and annual cycles rather than a daily one. Newspaper recipes entering this system not only diversified cuisine but created implicit pressure for daily variety.

Despite the long period during which actual cooking practice had only a marginal role in the classroom, the first two generations of girls' school *kaji* textbooks reflect the change in perceptions of the kitchen's function and the rhythms of kitchen work. *Kaji keizaikun*, a text from the 1880s that treated food preparation with comparative thoroughness, included charts dividing foods by type, and listed different preparations for each season.[28] In contrast, higher school textbooks after 1903 charted foods according to their nutritional content and then offered sample menus for single meals.[29] Nutrition took a place of increasing importance in the 1910s and 1920s, with the establishment of Japan's first institute for nutrition research in 1911 and a national institute in 1920.[30] Textbooks from this period include recipes provided by doctors from the National Nutrition Institute as well as by chefs.[31] Kitchens themselves gained new prominence in texts beginning in the 1910s, with frequent illustrations of model kitchen interiors and new appliances. A generation after cooking had first been introduced in the normal school amid parental protest, the qualifying examinations for *kaji* instructors were dominated by questions about food preparation and nutrition.[32]

## Hygiene and the Bounded Space of the Home

Spatialization of the idea of the family in the *katei* heightened the sense that there were invisible boundaries to be protected. The hygienic regime made explicit the house's function as a bulwark against violation from the outside. Rats, flies, street dust, and wellwater bore with them invading armies of germs, threatening the family.[33] The threat was greatest in the kitchen, which was an orifice exposing the bounded family space to the world outside.

Amano Seisai's *Home Treasury: Kitchen Reform* (*Katei hōten: daidokoro kairyō*), published in 1907, encapsulates the characteristics of this rhetoric of kitchen reform in the late Meiji period. The kitchen is the source of health or illness in the family, the introduction informed readers. The "dark and unclean kitchens of the Tenpō period" could not possibly provide food conforming to standards of health and hygiene, Amano continued. Yet when people build or rent a house, "all too often the wife consents to put up with a dark, unclean kitchen for the sake of having well-appointed guest rooms, disregarding the fact that horrible germs attach to food prepared in the unhygienic kitchen, attacking the body."[34] How the mistress of the house should equip herself to protect the kitchen from this threat (reintroduced shortly afterward as "a bug called the germ that causes all kinds of bad diseases")[35] was the chief theme of *Kitchen Reform*. The battle, however, was complicated by the presence of servants. Reference was made to Western housewives who had dispensed with servants, and the mistress of the house was urged to involve herself in each aspect of kitchen work. Still, throughout the text the author assumed the presence of one or more maids in the kitchen. A maid appeared in every illustration, and the frontispiece depicted three kitchen maids and a parlormaid preparing to serve a meal, with the mistress of the house absent from the scene.

In the bounded *katei*, the maid was an outsider. The kitchen door, necessary for the daily traffic of the tradespeople who supplied the household provisions as well as for the carriage of water from the well and firewood from the woodpile, was a passage not only for invisible germs but for the maid herself, who occupied both her master's house and a community beyond the house over which the enlightened mistress could not exercise direct control. From the point of view of the maid herself, the kitchen door was also the door to her social world; not only the door she would use to come and go, but the place where tradesmen, servants from neighboring houses, friends, and kin might come to visit.[36]

In the course of describing the requisites for a safe and sanitary kitchen, *Kitchen Reform* enumerated the sinister attributes of the maid, treating her as an interloper whose communicability with both inside and out made her a menace: she was uneducated and her manners were rustic, she neglected her own bodily hygiene and did not distinguish clean from unclean in the kitchen, she was possibly diseased and possibly a thief, she spoke ill of her masters to others at the local well, and she wasted time consorting with tradesmen, who themselves posed a threat to the family because of their ignorance of proper hygiene.[37] Irresponsible and unclean, the villainized maid in *Kitchen Reform* was shown endangering family health by letting dust gather on the soy sauce, throwing rubbish under the floorboards, and putting the dishtowel together with the floor rag. Unaware that she has developed typhoid, she washes her kimono and allows the water to drip into the well, infecting the family and threatening the whole region (see Fig. 2.3).[38]

Accusations of servants' careless habits had certainly been made in earlier eras, but the context of hygiene reform at this time, with the discovery of bacteria still recent knowledge in Japan, gave the condemnation an import

Fig. 2.3 Mistress and maid in *Kitchen Reform* (Amano Seisai, *Daidokoro kairyō*, 1907). (*upper left*) The kitchen maid allows dust from the soy sauce jar to get into the food. (*upper right*) She disposes of rubbish under the floorboards. (*lower left*) She unknowingly allows wash water from her typhoid-infected kimono to drip into the well. (*lower right*) She receives a white "cooking garment" from her employer.

that it could not have earlier possessed. The communicability of disease between bodies, and of servants between the house and the street, meant that the ignorant maid was not merely an annoyance but a potential agent, carrying the invisible pollution of bacteria within her. As such, even if her habits were better than most, the maid's ignorance demanded that the mistress guard her family, and provided a compelling reason for her close surveillance in the kitchen.

The need to disinfect also followed from such concerns, and *Kitchen Reform* devoted considerable space to explaining in lay terms what disinfecting was about, and how women should practice it. The author recommended a copper-lined boiler for disinfecting dishtowels. Interviews introduced four "model kitchens" and described the reforms their owners had made. At the house of Dr. Kitazato, the renowned plague specialist, the doctor himself guided the tour, exhibiting the copper boiler in which they had trained the maids to disinfect the dishtowels once daily.[39] Dishtowels must always be "pure white" (*junpaku*), explained the author, but in contrast to the West, few Japanese towels were pure white, and people thought nothing of using dirty gray or brown dishtowels. Dishtowels were to be washed daily in soap.[40]

With the gradual shift to greater practical instruction and the transformation of the curriculum by ideas of science, making things white—the color not only of purity but of public hygiene and laboratory coats—came to figure prominently in *kaji* instruction as well. The qualifying examinations for *kaji* instructors given between 1912 and 1924 included questions about the proper way to bleach a child's bib, the mixing of a solution for the economic and effective laundering of white cotton, the characteristics of soap and the proper use of bleach powder, as well as questions on reforming Japanese bedding (the correct answer to which involved adopting the use of white sheets), and the application of the national contagion disinfectant law in the home.[41] Soap itself was a new product in late nineteenth-century Japan, the spread of which paralleled the growth of hygiene education. Hōmu was among the first brand-named laundry soaps. During the World War I boom, the industry expanded vastly, and domestic consumption increased along with exports. Japanese soap production quintupled between 1912 and 1919.[42]

In their capacity as health workers within the home, housewives would eventually don a white uniform. Aprons in the nineteenth century, like almost all daily wear, were made of blue-dyed cotton. They were cut to hang from the waist and worn chiefly by shopclerks. There was no special attire for kitchen work, apart from a cord to tie back hanging kimono sleeves. An apron appears among the items advertised in the back of Hani Motoko's *Home Companion* (*Katei no tomo*—retitled *Fujin no tomo* in 1908) for purchase by mail order direct from the magazine's sales department, which was established in 1906. Identified as a "work garment for home use" (*kateiyō shigotogi*) designed by Sasaki Sachiko, one of the magazine's contributors, it was avail-

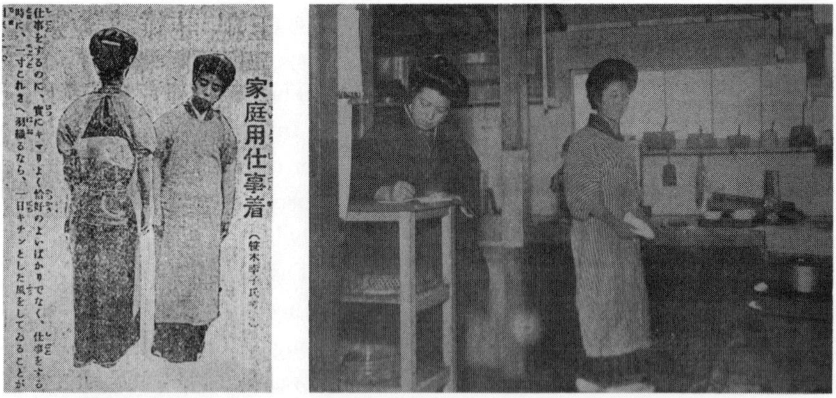


Fig. 2.4 (*left*) *Ladies' Companion* advertisement for a "work garment for home use" (Sept. 1913). (*right*) "Mrs. Sakurada's Household Management" (*Fujin gahō*, no. 145 [Apr. 1918]). Mrs. Sakurada stands to the left, making notes in her account book. Her maid wears the *Ladies' Companion* "work garment."

able in adults' and children's sizes. It covered the front of the kimono with a light patterned cotton. Half sleeves gathered below the elbow to keep kimono sleeves out of the way. The model kitchen maids shown in the illustrations of *Kitchen Reform* (in contrast to the unhygienic and dangerous ones) wore aprons. One of the housewives interviewed, when asked what sort of innovations she had introduced regarding kitchen utensils, told the interviewer, "Everyone seems to be doing it recently, but I have my maids wear cooking garments (*ryōrigi*) when they work in the kitchen."[43] The author urged readers to have their maids always wear aprons of "pure white."[44]

As bourgeois women took on more kitchen labor themselves, the aprons gravitated from maid to mistress. A photograph of mistress and maid in the kitchen, published in upper-class-oriented *Fujin gahō* (The ladies' graphic) in 1918 shows that the *Home Companion* "work garment" was still being worn (see Fig. 2.4). The "work garment" in this instance was on the maid; the mistress wore a dark jacket (*haori*).[45] Photographs of classes at two cooking schools published in the same issue showed female pupils (future *shufu*) wearing the same type of garment. With the exception of one figure, all of their aprons were white.[46] By this time, the new sleeved aprons were coming to be worn far more widely among housewives, and not only in the kitchen. They are ubiquitous on the model housewives gracing advertisements and textbook pages in the 1920s, showing that they had become a standard marker for the *shufu* rather than the maid by this time. They remained the Japanese housewife's uniform until the late 1960s, when kimono ceased to be daily wear for most women. The more attractive-sounding name *kappōgi* (cuisine garment) replaced "work garment" and "cooking garment" some time in the process of normalization. Solid white was the standard.

Donning a white apron might not seem of itself a revolutionary change in behavior, but Yanagita Kunio noted its cultural profundity in 1931, when the shift was still in recent memory: "Today white has come to be used even for kitchen aprons, but originally it was a taboo color. Formerly it was never worn in Japan, except in the robes for sacred festivals and mourning." He attributed the change to confusion in the modern era between the special and the everyday and a tendency to treat lightly "the excitement of things that only occur rarely."[47] But the housewives who dressed in white also unconsciously marked the opposite tendency: that the everyday world of kitchen work had been transformed by the modern hygienic regime into a realm of special danger and taboos.

## Home Cooking and the Market

One remarkable, and remarkably popular, contribution to the discourse on kitchen work was a serial novel titled *Shokudōraku* (The Gourmet's Delight), published in the newspaper *Hōchi shinbun* in 360 installments between 1903 and 1904. The author, Murai Gensai, was a writer for the newspaper who had earlier serialized a number of novels. *Shokudōraku* was a novel in form, but in keeping with the author's didactic intent, it conveyed a wealth of information on many topics, particularly the preparation and consumption of food. The serial met with unprecedented success. It appeared in four paperback volumes sequentially during serialization, and the first of these volumes went through thirty printings in six months. A stage version appeared in 1905, and the *Ladies' Graphic* issued an accompanying book of photographs in 1906. The original paperbacks were still in print in the late 1920s.[48]

The main lesson of Murai's novel was the moral and physiological importance, as well as the pleasure, of what he called *katei ryōri* (home cooking). The prefix "home" gave *katei ryōri* prescriptive significance, especially for women. As he expatiated on "home cooking," Murai also censured wives who depended on bought meals (*kaikui*) or tried to take shortcuts in meal preparation, as well as husbands who ate outside the house or had meals delivered to be eaten apart from their families. *Katei ryōri* in Murai's formulation did not merely connote food prepared at home, however; it was a distinct style of cuisine, with its own principles and techniques. The pleasure of this cuisine, if properly prepared, would be sufficient to turn family members away from its rivals. "If you have *katei ryōri* every day," Murai wrote, "you can hardly eat food from the restaurant."[49] This ideal placed the burden of family happiness squarely on the shoulders of the woman doing the cooking, who was supposed to master the art of home cooking in order to defeat her professional rivals.

*Katei ryōri* was a summation of the two new perspectives that had made kitchen work a housewife's special responsibility, treating cooking as an art involving constant innovation and the kitchen as the source of family health. The main narrative was a romance about finding the perfect wife.[50] The daily ingenuity of the enlightened housewife was manifested in every act and utterance of the novel's heroine, O-Towa, and imparted to the reader as directly as possible by a supplement printed along the top margin containing over six hundred recipes for preparations referred to in the main text. Many of the recipes included new ingredients associated with the West, and it was repeatedly stressed that Western food was not something only for special occasions. It provided necessary nutrition and should be combined with food from the Japanese diet. Diversity was essential; the family should have different foods every day and the differing nutritional needs of father and children should be separately accommodated.[51]

O-Towa's brother Nakagawa, the author's mouthpiece and a social critic prone to long monologues, established the second theme, which was woven through the romantic plot and descriptions of countless meals. Nakagawa instructed readers that nutrition, hygiene, and dwelling design were all intertwined, and that true home cooking was inseparable from the reform of all of them. Explaining his "cooking principle" (*ryōrihō*) to justify time-consuming recipes, he asserted that the level of a civilization was revealed by the amount of effort expended in food preparation, which saved a proportional effort on the part of the internal organs of the eater.[52] The kitchen where this crucial civilizing process took place was the "center point of the home." But too many people, Nakagawa declared, spent their money ornamenting the parlor and left the kitchen dark and unsanitary.[53]

The class characteristics of Murai's *katei* emerge in the course of Nakagawa's diatribes, which set the educated bourgeois ideal in opposition to stereotypes of other classes. The dearth of dishtowels in the kitchen, which revealed Japan's unhygienic habits, for example, also revealed what Nakagawa regarded as a troubling absence of class distinctions: "Someone living in a nine-by-twelve foot tenement on ten yen a month has two or three plain white cotton dishcloths. It is quite incongruous that a house like yours, living on two or three hundred yen, should have only five or ten plain cotton dishcloths. The tenement's dishcloth is gray, and yours is gray too—something seems out of balance here."[54] The focus here was not on reform of hygienic conditions among the poor but on the educated bourgeois, who was obliged to know better. Among the educated, however, the aristocrats were characterized by an inexcusable preference for private luxuries over family well-being. The man reproached in this passage for not having recognized the importance of his kitchen was a viscount, who had invited Nakagawa to see his expensive new house, tearoom, and ornamental garden. Propounding a theory he calls "ruin of the country through refinement" (*fūryu bōkokuron*), the author's spokesman rebukes his host.

Countryfolk depicted in the novel were even further beyond redemption than careless aristocrats or benighted tenement-dwellers, since they were not only oblivious to good hygiene and nutrition but endangering the Japanese race itself. A wealthy family from the country trying to force the eldest son to marry a cousin provides the opportunity for a lesson about the dangers of marriage between relatives and the virtue of "free marriage" (by which Murai meant a young man's free choice of a bride not forced on him by his family).[55] What's more, the rural family's servant, brought into an urban kitchen, is found to be incapable of cooking, since she has spent her life managing a crew of subordinates and has never herself had to cook. The novel's caricature of the rural propertied class thus manages also to ridicule the distribution of domestic authority by status that characterized large traditional households.[56]

Although *Shokudōraku* used a fictional viscount to introduce the author's critique of luxury, for Murai as for other Meiji journalists, titled aristocrats still served as bourgeois exemplars, helping the author to promote a domestic regime reformed by new commodities. The kitchens of two forward-looking members of the aristocracy were depicted in color frontispiece illustrations of the novel's first two volumes. Murai promoted the kitchen of Count Ōkuma Shigenobu, a perennial favorite in mass-market journals. The

Fig. 2.5 (*top*) The kitchen of Count Ōkuma Shigenobu, as depicted in the frontispiece of *Shokudōraku*. The gas stove imported from England for 250 yen can be seen in the earth-floor area to the rear (Murai Gensai, *Shokudōraku, Haru no maki* [The Gourmet's Delight: Spring], 1903). (*bottom*) The kitchen at author Murai Gensai's residence in Hiratsuka. A worktable stands to the left on the raised floor, but cooking devices and sink are at floor level or in the lower earth-floored area, reflecting the fact that Murai did not extend his campaign for hygiene and dietary reform in the kitchen to include the rationalization of kitchen labor (*Ladies' Graphic*, Sept. 1906).

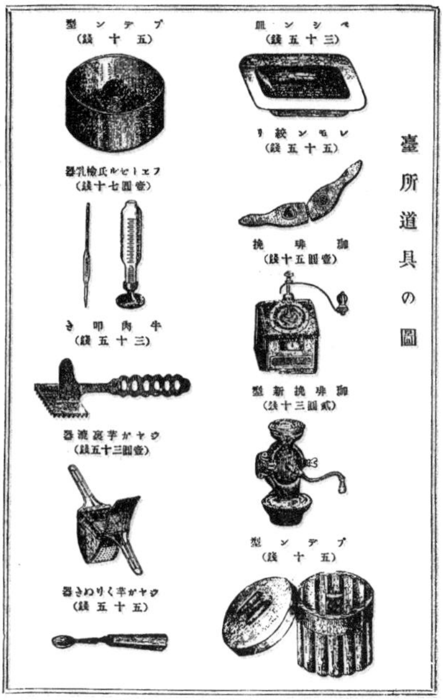


Fig. 2.6 Kitchen utensils advertised in *Shokudōraku* (from top left to bottom right): bundt pan, basin, Fessel milk-testing instrument, lemon press, meat pounder, coffee grinder, potato strainer, new type coffee grinder, potato scoop, lidded bundt pan (Murai Gensai, *Shokudōraku, Natsu no maki* [The Gourmet's Delight: Summer], 1903, appendix).

Ōkuma kitchen later appeared in other publications.[57] *Shokudōraku* made special note of the large iron stove imported from England and its price tag of 250 yen. For a single kitchen device this was an extravagant sum that would have impressed readers at the time. Piped gas itself was still a rarity, available only in Tokyo at the time that *Shokudōraku* was being serialized. The count in Murai's story was counseled to remodel his kitchen after Ōkuma's and use gas.[58] For readers of more modest means, there were other conveniences to be purchased. Indeed, Murai's *katei ryōri* and hygienic kitchen were dependent on such purchases, since they required particular foodstuffs, cooking devices, and cleaning products, some of which were illustrated in the margin along with their prices and the addresses of shops that sold them (see Figs. 2.5–2.6).

## Gas Cooking and Civilization

Infrastructural improvements such as electricity, piped water, and gas intrinsically altered domestic labor as well as the shape of houses. At the same time, they did not simply arrive in the house—they had to be bought by its occupants. Marketing conjoined with the interests of domestic reform to give these commodities a significance that made them more than simple conveniences. Bourgeois reformism served the interests of the gas companies particularly well, since it provided the language to sell gas cooking to educated housewives.

At the turn of the twentieth century, the Tokyo Gas Company began developing new cooking devices suited to the Japanese kitchen in order to hedge its investment in lighting. The first gas-burning rice cooker was introduced in 1904.[59] A single-burner gas stove for open cooking came out the same year as a substitute for the portable coal-burning *shichirin* on which most light cooking was typically done. These items were intended to be used in the same manner as existing cooking devices. Large Western-style ovens were also sold but had only a limited market.[60]

Advertising for household goods that directly targeted female consumers was new in the first decade of the twentieth century. The women's magazines primarily advertised cosmetics and medical products. But as bourgeois women took to cuisine, the gas company recognized the new potential market. Advertisements run in the newspapers in 1904 depicted a well-dressed woman surrounded by kitchen devices, a gas boiler, and a gas heater, under the slogan "With Just One Match" (see Fig. 2.7). The appeal of gas lay not only in its convenience but in its tidiness. The company's 1910 product catalogue touted the merits of gas cooking in terms more expressly intended for affluent housewives. Gas, the catalogue explained, made it possible to cope with one less maid. Since gas produced no ash or soot, the kitchen could be kept very clean. So could the woman in charge: "Since it won't soil ladies' hair, skin, or clothing," the advertisement emphasized, "you can manage the kitchen without fear." The domestic ideal was served as well: "A Western cooking device . . . installed in a middling or better home (*chūtō ijō no katei*)," would "assist the enjoyment of the family circle."[61]

An advertisement appeared in the *Ladies' Companion* the same year, appealing to the reform-minded audience of that magazine with the slogans "Reform

Fig. 2.7 "With Just One Match." Advertisement for gas cooking and heating devices, 1904 (courtesy Gas Museum).

of the Home Begins with Reform of the Kitchen," and "Reform of the Kitchen Is Achieved Through the Use of Gas." The advertisement repeated the claim that gas equipment could replace one maid, announcing that "everyone calls the gas cooker the 'no-need-for-a-maid (*gejo irazu*).'" The slogan "no need for a maid" had earlier advertised new oil-burning stoves as well.[62]

In 1907, there was only one gas connection for every nine households in Tokyo, and the majority of these were for lighting only, but by 1922, one-third of the households in the city had gas.[63] The market was thus changing quickly during the 1910s. In 1911, the Chiyoda Gas Company entered the Tokyo market, claiming to provide the service more cheaply. The same year, prices for firewood and coal rose dramatically.[64] As the gas companies began advertising lower prices and equipment rental, consumers were presented with a changing array of fuel choices. Girls' higher school texts and women's magazines responded by devoting considerable space to the new technology. The 1912 qualifying examination, for example, asked prospective *kaji* instructors to compare the economic merits of different cooking fuels.[65] Textbooks by the late 1910s were full of illustrations of various cooking devices, gas-burning and otherwise.

In January 1912, Hani Motoko's *Ladies' Companion* printed the results of an "economic study of fuels." The article was at once a thinly veiled adver-

Fig. 2.8 (*left*) Cooking on the floor with a coal-burning *shichirin* (*Fujin no tomo*, June 1913, 139). (*right*) Cooking on the floor with a single-burner gas *shichirin* (*Jiji shinpō*, Dec. 20, 1910).

tisement for piped gas and an outline of the social order that new sources of knowledge had built around educated housewives and their kitchens by this time. The world in which these women found themselves differed markedly from that of their mothers and of the nineteenth-century *kaji* texts.

Gas called for particular study, the article contended, because it was "the fuel of civilization." Advice was solicited from a gas-company spokesman, recently returned from a study of the industry in the West. Home use of gas there had progressed remarkably, the expert explained, noting that second year students at the girls' schools in France took classes in the use of gas. The article continued with an anecdote illustrating the dilemma in Japan, where ignorance reportedly prevailed regarding the proper use of gas. A certain widower had left his house in the hands of the maid for a week while he was away and returned to discover that she had kept the kitchen stove lit uninterrupted for the entire week. Maids will waste gas and must be educated, the magazine warned. Left on their own, they will use the gas to boil water for every little task. In the West, the passage concluded, they say that if you waste gas, you'll "get a disease of the private parts" (*sic*).[66]

Technology, even technology promoted for its simplicity, brought with it a burden of knowledge that integrated its audience in social and cultural hierarchies. All the players were present in this article, in proper configuration for the modernization of housework: civilization embodied in the new commodity; Europe and the United States as the sources of authority; the girls' schools as the places of transmission for authorized knowledge; and—a new player—the company representative as a messenger bearing news of the latest products and lessons of civilization. In the home, the article hinted at the tense hierarchy of mistress and maid (here with the twist that the mistress herself was dead, leaving the problem to a master prone to absence). Finally, there was the threat of disease, appended in a curiously improbable-sounding piece of lore that nevertheless bore the authority of a Western source, suggesting the association of disease with poor adaptation to civilization. The housewife drawn into the market for modern conveniences bought more than mere convenience.

## Economy, Efficiency, and the Body

Hygiene was the first gospel of kitchen reform. Economy was the second. But economy could be understood in different ways, and one person's economy was not always another's. Whereas the *Ladies' Companion* counted fuel economy in terms of the cost in yen of the fuel expended to cook family meals, the vexing maids whom the magazine warned readers to monitor chose an economy of effort.[67] Murai Gensai's economy followed yet another logic: nothing was more "uneconomical" than for the cook to reduce the time invested in food preparation and thereby increase the labor expenditure of several people's digestive systems.[68]

An older "economy" rooted in conceptions of household governance distinct from the modern discipline of political economy still informed the textbooks used by girls and women in the early period of the Meiji education system.[69] *Kaji keizaikun* (1881) and *Kaji keizairon* (1882), two textbooks written under the Ministry of Education's 1881 guidelines, addressed themselves to female readers but, befitting the conception of the house as a corporate enterprise, described household economy as a matter of concern to both sexes. "Economy" in these texts encompassed the maintenance of a self-contained system, the "managing of the interior," which was primarily the mistress's domain of authority. Her management was conceived in broad terms, consistent with the long cycles of the premodern household economy. The unifying component in these texts was an injunction to frugality. Domestic practices that would later be understood within different categories were enjoined or admonished in terms of economy. *Kaji keizairon* warned that if the mistress were careless in housekeeping, there would always be a foul smell and insects in the kitchen, household members' clothes would be dirty, and food would be damaged by mice and cats. This was termed not dangerous to family health but "in every respect uneconomical."[70] *Kaji keizaikun* introduced the topic of cooking as "the economy of food" but described it in terms distinct from the economical procurement of foodstuffs, and from the digestive economy of *Shokudōraku,* in which the success of food preparation correlated directly with how troublesome the food was to prepare. The problem was one of effective use of what was at hand, rather than of either market calculation or clinical attention to family health.

In this earlier understanding, there was an economy of cooking and an economy of cleaning, just as there was an economy of managing money. Each could have its own autonomous logic. Later, these alternative economies would be overcome by discourses of home cooking, nutrition, and hygiene, leaving only the management of money and scarce commodities in the field of economy. Yet as the mix of moral instruction with advertisements for dozens of unusual new commodities in *Shokudōraku* suggests, new domestic discourses altered the mechanics of household economy in the strictly monetary sense as well. In reference to kitchen tools and other household goods, the *kaji keizai* text of the 1880s counseled readers that it was best "to use the ordinary products available (*seken tsūjō no shina*)" and avoid the unusual.[71]

Extravagant dreams of 250-yen ovens found no place in Hani Motoko's domestic economy either. With copious concrete advice and point-by-point critiques of household budgets submitted by readers, Hani's *Home Companion* and *Ladies' Companion* shared the tradition of preaching frugality. Yet Hani's efforts to rationalize the housewife's managerial work resituated educated women and their households as significantly as Murai's discourse of home cooking. The crystallization of Hani's method of domestic economy, and its most enduring legacy, was the *Home Companion Household Account Book* (*Katei no tomo kakeibo*), a hardbound annual volume first published in 1904, containing daily and monthly charts for recording income and expenditures. These account books differed in two respects from the simple cashbooks (*kozukaichō*) Hani's volume was intended to replace. First, instead of recording only expenditures as they occurred, Hani's account-keeper drew up a monthly budget and compared expenditures to the allotted amounts as she recorded them. Second, the charts divided expenditures into categories, distinguishing, for example, entertainment expenses from family meals and staple foods from side dishes.[72] Transactions in Hani's model household were thus carefully planned in advance and classified according to purpose. The charts provided no way to record gifts, except those of known monetary value. This level of elaboration in detailing the household's cash exchanges announced that the efficiency of the housewife's work rested to a large extent

Fig. 2.9 Cooking by the book. With a growing market of young women experimenting in the kitchen without the supervision or help of another woman, new cookbooks taught basic techniques in precise detail. The cartoonist affectionately presents the young housewife in her laboratory with a cooking manual in hand (*Ōsaka pakku*, Oct. 1917). Together with the household account book, the cookbook made numerical measurement and the written word central to modern kitchen work. The chart on the wall appears to list the nutritional values of various foods.

on her skill as a purchaser of commodities. The recipe book and the account book proved to be the two enduring genres of writing for the modern kitchen, the former representing the demand for novelty and constant variety, the latter codifying the management of consumer goods into a feminine discipline (see Fig. 2.9).

The conceptual refinement in the scope of "household economy" evident in Hani's bookkeeping reflected a subordination of transmissions and transactions within households to the logic of a larger, external economy. From the 1910s, other terms came to supplement *keizai* in the language of domestic reform conveyed by Hani's magazine and the girls' school textbooks. "Efficiency" (*nōritsu*) was the new goal for reformers in the mid-1910s. The *Ladies' Companion* published a special issue, "Increasing Domestic Efficiency," in 1917. Taylor's *Principles of Scientific Management* had been translated into Japanese four years earlier, and a native efficiency movement was bringing the language of Taylorism into common parlance.[73] The industrial world was a source for more than nomenclature, however; "efficiency" in the home entailed physical modifications of domestic space and the working habits of its occupants corresponding to those taking place in industry. As with hygiene, when domestic reformers adopted the public rhetoric of efficiency, they targeted the kitchen as the critical site for its application.

The first effort to reshape Japanese kitchens physically for greater efficiency, discussed even before the arrival of Taylorism, was the move to redesign them for work standing up. In kitchens in the Kantō region, most tasks had been performed on the floor, in a sitting, kneeling, or squatting position. Low cooking stoves were placed freestanding on a wood floor, and the sink at floor level. An earth-floor area one or two feet lower than the wood floor made up part of the workspace and provided entrance and egress. In Kyoto and Osaka, by contrast, sink and stoves were used in a standing position in the earth-floored corridor space (*tōri niwa*) that ran along one side of the raised-floor portion of the house. Cooking was done traveling between the two spaces. Both Kantō and Kansai kitchens had the earth-floor space, used for water storage and wet jobs as well as for delivery traffic, and both used the wood (or sometimes *tatami*-mat) raised floor to prepare trays for service, but the Kantō kitchen was designed so that chopping, washing, and watching the stove were more easily done in a position low to the floor.

Reformers in the 1910s viewed the table-less kitchen as a hallmark of the unhygienic and inefficient house. Their view seems to have won broad acceptance, since, aided by the introduction of piped gas and water, Tokyo kitchens built in the following decade generally incorporated standing sinks and work counters.[74] To someone accustomed to chairs and tables, the inefficiency of the old kitchen may appear obvious, but it was a flexible workspace for bodies correspondingly flexible and comfortable sitting on the floor. The floor was well-suited to heavier tasks, such as grinding large quantities with a mortar and pestle or carving a fish. Aware that such heavy tasks were becoming less common in the houses of many of her urban readers, Hani Motoko published plans of improved kitchens with standing sinks beginning in 1904. As with the household account books, Hani promoted her kitchen designs as products of experimentation aimed at improving the results of a housewife's labor. It was not generally assumed, however, that working standing up would be easier. The magazine's attention was focused more on hygiene and a general notion of rationalizing routines that would later come under the rubric of *nōritsu*. Katayama Teruko, the wife of a Tokyo architect, told Hani's *Home Companion* in 1903 that she had heard from an acquaintance who had grown accustomed to the Kansai-style kitchen that "doing all the cooking standing up . . . was probably a bit more tiring than working sitting down, but your clothes didn't get soiled and the area around you had a nice tidy feeling." As a Tokyo resident, she herself had not had first-hand experience.[75] By 1913, the mail-order division of the *Ladies' Companion* was offering a high kitchen worktable featuring a variety of special drawers and slots for tools, whose advertised merits were that one could work in a "clean and orderly" way (see Fig. 2.10).[76]

These practical questions of kitchen labor appear not to have caught the notice of male reformers until later. The position of the body when doing

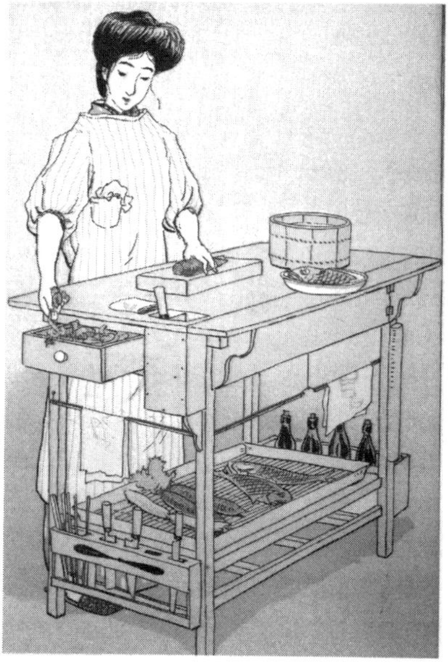

Fig. 2.10 The *Ladies' Companion* kitchen worktable for the home ("Katei yō ryōridai," advertisement in *Fujin no tomo* 8, no. 7, July 1914).

kitchen work was not discussed in *Kitchen Reform* or *Shokudōraku,* although both books bore frontispiece illustrations showing reformed kitchens with servants standing at work tables. Murai Gensai's own kitchen, a photograph of which appeared in the *Ladies' Graphic* in 1904, had a standing-level worktable on the raised floor, but cooking stoves and sink in the earth-floor area below, requiring the cook to move between two levels, and encouraging use of the sink in a kneeling or squatting position.[77] Focused as he was on the welfare of those doing the eating, Gensai did not reach beyond matters of hygiene and digestive efficiency to consider labor efficiency.

In the Taylorist regime, standing in the kitchen took new priority as part of a streamlining of the motions involved in food preparation. Two kitchens were featured in the *Ladies' Companion* "Efficiency" issue of 1917, one in which the floor was entirely concrete and one with a raised wood floor and no ground-level floor space, so that "everything could be carried out smoothly in a standing position." For the sake of "motion economy," the designer also put all work surfaces at the same level, explaining:

> If there are differences of height among these tools, or if there are obstacles to motion, things may be carried out well enough once one is accustomed to them, but actually, without being conscious of it, one is using a tremendous amount of concentration. This unconsciously operating concentration is not without a price—it accumulates to induce fatigue, and naturally mistakes will occur somewhere.[78]

The other thing that distinguished this kitchen, and would distinguish model kitchens from this period generally, was its size. Misumi Suzuko, principal of Tokiwamatsu Girls' Higher School, who was to become the champion of "scientific management" among Japanese women educators, promoted the compact kitchen as a way to dispense with maids.[79] Her own house, newly built with a six-by-nine-foot kitchen, was featured in the *Housewife's Companion* in the same month as the *Ladies' Companion* "Efficiency" issue.[80] Kitchens in the house plans found in textbooks and in builders' pattern books were becoming tight, highly determined spaces. The 1912 edition of Sakata Shizuko and Gokan Kikuno's *Domestic Textbook for Girls' Higher School* (*Kōtō jogakkō yō kaji kyōkasho*) had included plans from a contemporary architectural pattern book depicting three houses, the kitchens of which were the equivalents of nine, twelve, and sixteen mats in size (162, 216, and 288 square feet). Two of these included large earth-floor areas, making the kitchen larger than any other room in the house.[81] In contrast, textbooks

Fig. 2.11 This illustration of a kitchen with standing sink, worktable, gas, and a prominently displayed clock appeared in several girls' school textbooks (Yoshimura Chizu, *Jitchi ōyō kaji kyōkasho*, 1919).

after the late 1910s seldom showed a floor plan with a kitchen larger than three *tsubo*, or six mats in size (108 square feet). The cooking chapters of the same texts featured illustrations promoting the worktable, and often showed the interior of a kitchen with worktable, standing sink, and a prominently displayed wall clock (see Fig. 2.11). The accompanying texts stressed the importance of working standing up.[82] A similar shift may be traced in books of house plans. By 1930, it was assumed that work would be done standing, and some *kaji* textbooks were also emphasizing the importance of having the sink, cooking stove, and worktable (the "three centers of kitchen activity") located as close to one another as possible to minimize vertical and horizontal movement.[83]

Even if the actual apparatus of the Japanese kitchen remained relatively primitive, the compact laboratory model was convenient to the companies marketing new equipment, since scientific management reduced the kitchen to a countertop row of efficiently placed devices. Hisanoki honten, a manufac-

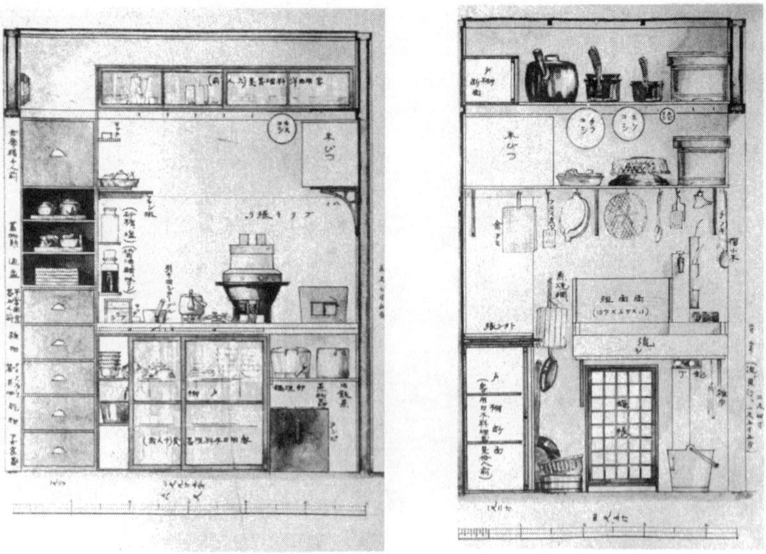

Fig. 2.12 Mrs. Irizawa's 1.5-mat model kitchen, at the home exhibition sponsored by the newspaper *Kokumin shinbun* in 1915.

turer of oil-burning stoves, presented a model "one-tsubo [36 sq. ft.] kitchen" at an exposition in 1928 and used Taylorist language to promote its "extremely efficient" layout: "With the body in the center, everything is situated appropriately on three sides, such that, without moving the feet, one can operate (*sōsa*) the shelf, stove, and sink on roughly the same horizontal level."[84]

Work in a nineteenth-century Japanese kitchen had involved use of the body in a range of postures and motions between two floor levels, and between indoor and outdoor space. In addition to use of coal and wood fire in a *kamado* or *hettsui* (a large fixed-position clay stove with two or more burners) and one or more *shichirin* portable burners, kitchen operations included tasks such as pounding rice cakes, grinding bean paste, drying fish and vegetables, and pickling—tasks that required space, use of the whole body, and sometimes several sets of hands. Kitchens had been not only large and unconstrained spaces but also social ones. This remained the case in farmhouses through the modern period. To the hygienist, this openness could signify menace. The hygienic kitchen was a brightly lit and closely monitored space, and not to be entrusted to an outsider. Following the inducement of the housewife into a tidier kitchen, the discipline of efficiency

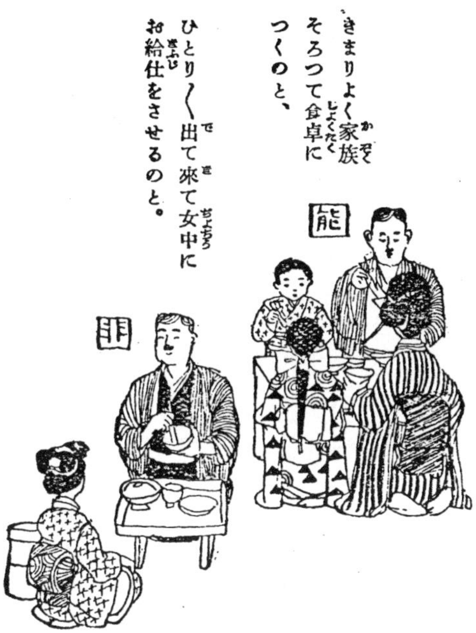


Fig. 2.13 "Efficient and Inefficient Ways of Working: Meals." Taylorism provided both a new way of conceptualizing domestic labor and a new rhetoric for addressing older problems. This illustration from *The Ladies' Companion* advocates the family meal at a common table not to promote morality but to save time and labor (*Fujin no tomo*, Mar. 1917).

dictated a new program in which kitchen activity was contracted to a set of manipulations in a cockpit-like enclosure.

Technological change played a role in the reduction of kitchen space too. Gas and piped water made kitchen work in a closed space possible, eliminating the need to cart firewood, coal, or water and reducing the need for storage. This also allowed the reduction in size. For two reasons, however, technology cannot be viewed as the decisive agent of change. On the one hand, the early technology accommodated old practices. The first gas equipment marketed for the kitchen was designed simply to be set on the floor in place of the old *kamado* and *shichirin* and used in a squatting or kneeling position (see Fig. 2.8 right). Thus, there is no reason to suppose that rebuilding the kitchen with piped gas burners necessitated or naturally engendered the shift to work done in a standing position. Second, despite propaganda in a number of media (including classroom instruction), until the high economic growth of the 1960s,

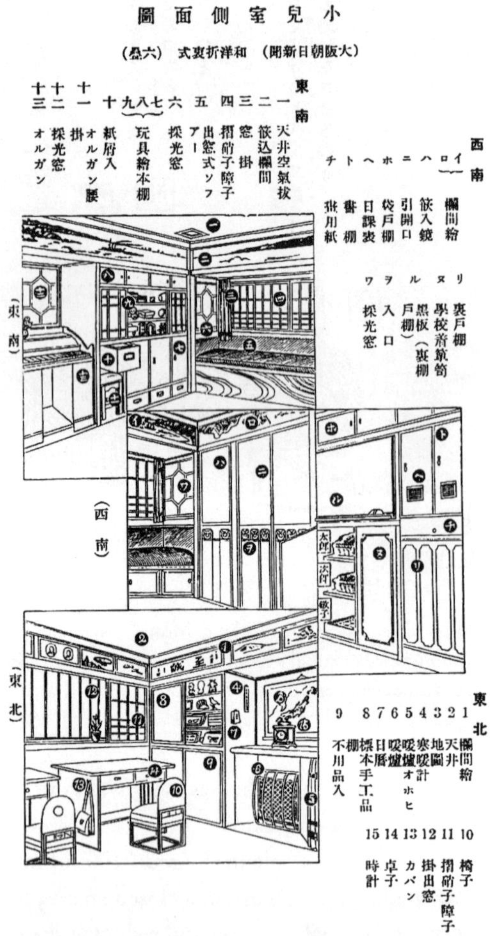


Fig. 2.14 Children's rooms. Household management texts began promoting the notion of a room designed specially for children's play or study in the first decade of the twentieth century. Images of children's rooms received increasing elaboration as child psychology emerged as a significant new node of discourse in the women's press and girls' higher school curriculum and as the competition to enter secondary schools intensified. The "home education" chapters of several girls' school textbooks after 1918 carried these diagrams of an ordered and minutely programmed children's room, originally the winning entry in a competition sponsored by the *Ōsaka Asahi shinbun*. The extreme degree of compartmentalization in this gratuitously detailed design symbolically mirrors the contemporary elaboration of systems of expertise around child-rearing (Uramori Fumi, *Shintei kaji kyōkasho*, 1918, 2: 80–81).

the market for electrical appliances was small. The pristine white kitchens filled with conveniences that were common in magazines and textbooks in the 1920s and 1930s remained a dream for most Japanese women, who were still dazzled by similar images in the propaganda films depicting American home life that the Occupation authorities distributed in the late 1940s.[85] Decades before toasters and shiny electric refrigerators actually became part of many Japanese households, therefore, the discourse of reform had changed the meaning of the kitchen, its spatial configuration, and the work practices within it.

In the modern classification of human activity into leisure and labor, the axis for labor was vertical. For Japanese architects in the 1890s, this geometry had shaped the problem of what they perceived to be an undifferentiated domestic space; how could Japanese dwellings be brought into the civilized world, when eating, sleeping, working, and playing all took place on the same plane? The replacement of *tatami* mats with chairs and tables in the master's portion of the house, making it a more worklike space, was the first spatial solution. The re-encoding and reshaping of the female workspace of the kitchen in the subsequent two decades grew inevitably from the same premises.

Kitchen work in the nineteenth century was unquestionably more strenuous than in a modern kitchen. Images of the modern kitchen could have a powerful attraction to women burdened with the heavy responsibilities of food preparation in large country houses. But sacrifices were made in the name of efficiency as well. Like many of the losses that occur in the course of broad cultural change, they were sacrifices made largely unconsciously. A freer use of the body, a sense of time less bound by the clock, along with practical knowledge derived from local transmissions primarily between generations of women, constituted work in the environments where food preparation had previously taken place. Some would consider the loss of these things a small price to pay for greater convenience and more time available to be spent outside the kitchen. Kitchen reformer Misumi Suzuko, busy with a career that itself would have been unthinkable to a woman of her grandmother's generation, certainly never looked back to ask whether the loss of tradition had been worth it. Yet it was in the nature of the media through which new forms and behaviors were conveyed and appropriated that it was difficult, if not impossible, to put the new and the old in the scales and judge their respective merits. The care of a family, including

Fig. 2.15 With housecleaning as with cooking, as girl's higher-school texts increasingly presumed the reader to be a young woman destined for the management of a small household, they treated tasks that might once have been performed by multiple hands as solely her responsibility. By the 1920s, texts frequently portrayed lone housewives in the regulation *kappōgi* holding cleaning implements. The text accompanying this illustration reads: "The housewife should clean inside the house and out every day and, in addition, fix a special day for cleaning each week or month, as well as conducting periodic general cleaning in spring and autumn" (Inoue Hideko, *Gendai kaji kyōkasho*, 1928).

provision of their daily meals from a compact urban kitchen equipped with gas, standing sink, and perhaps an inexpensive imitation of Hani Motoko's kitchen worktable, awaited the majority of Misumi's students and others graduating from the girls' higher school, not a professional career outside the house. Those who enjoyed the luxury of having a live-in maid to assist them had learned things that introduced an unresolvable tension into the employer-servant relationship. Lessons in hygiene had taught them the many hazards that lurked in the kitchen and had given them the duty of on-site surrogates for the public health authorities. Kitchen work had been inculcated in them as both a daily duty and the primary outlet for their creativity. Taylorism had narrowed the physical scope of performance of this duty to conform to principles of time-motion optimization formulated for the factory assembly line.

More generally, by defining the *shufu*, or housewife, as a universal category, the discipline of domestic management had inculcated the idea that all the tasks of maintenance and reproduction in the dwelling were directly incumbent on one woman. This applied to housecleaning, laundry, and childcare, as well as food preparation. To understand how radical a relocation this signified, even for women in small households, we need only revisit briefly the world of a woman who might be considered a premodern counterpart to the "middle-class housewife" of the twentieth century. A diary maintained between 1785 and 1843 by Rai Baishi, the wife of a Confucian scholar and low-ranking samurai of Hiroshima domain, offers such a comparison. Baishi's household was small, without extended family. Baishi herself worked hard, but what she recorded daily in her diary simply as "work" (*shigoto*) was weaving, which was the prime responsibility of the mistress of the house. Under the mistress's direction, there was a division of labor in the manufacture of cloth that involved the two maidservants, the nurse, and Baishi's daughter, as well as the assistance of women from outside the house. Cleaning, at least periodic general cleaning, was dominated by male household members. A manservant tended the vegetable patch and prepared pickles. In addition, a number of tasks were hired out to people who came periodically, including the wife of a local merchant who did laundry and taught weaving. A wetnurse shared in the care of the children from their infancy. Food preparation is seldom mentioned in Baishi's diary, and only on occasions when guests were received. Nothing suggests that the mistress herself worked in the kitchen at other times. Thus, all the "chores" typically associated with a housewife's work—cooking, cleaning, and laundry—were distributed among members of Baishi's household and people from the outside.[86]

Teaching a new regime in school did not bring about the change alone, of course. Nor could any amount of hortatory writing in the popular press. Until their families had the buying power to become consumers of the new goods that embodied modern living—new foods, kitchen equipment, services such as gas, electricity, and piped water, and new houses themselves—women were not likely to experience the full dislocation from traditional work patterns that was being promoted. It took decades for the national economy to catch up with the rhetoric of reform. Indeed, in rural areas right up through the 1970s, reformers sponsored by government and private groups were still promoting the same agenda—standing sinks, disinfecting, variation of diet for nutritional balance—that had first appeared in girls' school textbooks at the turn of the century.[87] But as the markets did develop, first in the cities from the 1910s, new commodities were fit into the developing regime. Education made women's roles, bourgeois domestic reform, and the market for consumer durables inseparable from one another.

The trained professional housewife acquired a bourgeois cultural identity grounded in universal forms of knowledge and a rational, scientific disposition toward domestic work. Rationalization meant not only frugal habits, for which absolute scarcity had long provided sufficient incentive among peasants, but a modern awareness of the power of a woman's economic and managerial expertise when allied with institutions beyond the home. Universal knowledge promised to elevate the bourgeois household above tired conventions, to align the management of the household with the advancement of the state, and to wisely organize a woman's time, which was a precious commodity in bourgeois society. Seeking a place in this society and given little other social space in which to operate, educated women made themselves scientists of the home and turned the kitchen into their laboratory.

# 3

# Domestic Interiors and National Style

## Mass Marketing and the Idea of Taste

The Meiji discourse of home and the disciplines of housewifery that accompanied it had little to say on matters of aesthetics. More than clothing or individual decorative objects, more than architectural forms themselves, interiors, which involved manifold choices and combinations of goods, traveled poorly. Reformers reshaped family practices and began to replan the layout of dwellings, but with the exception of the one room given over to the eclectic East-West hodgepodge of the new male preserve, domestic interiors remained little affected. The majority of household objects continued to come from the same systems of local production and continued to function in domestic life as they had before the reformers' intervention. The "new taste" (*shin fūmi*) for the home, as Sakai Toshihiko had called it in his manifesto for a better family life, brought with it no distinctive change in design. After the Russo-Japanese War, however, architects and intellectuals turned new attention to the aesthetics of the dwelling. By no coincidence, the same years saw the advent of Japan's first department store, which in the long run would have a massive effect on domestic interiors.

Like *hōmu/katei*, *shumi*, the modern Japanese word corresponding to "taste," was new in common parlance at the turn of the twentieth century. One source of its diffusion was the journal *Shumi*, which began publication in June 1906, with contributions from well-known figures beginning with the doyen of Japanese literature, Tsubouchi Shōyō.[1] Although not the first publication to use the word, *Shumi* gathered expert opinion on everything from contemporary European painting to the popular native storytelling art of *naniwabushi* to conjure into existence an autonomous world of taste (which writers called *shumikai*). The journal, its editors promised, would not only entertain the public but contribute to improvement of the arts and—inevitably—promote the "cultivation of the home." Tsubouchi opened the first issue with an article that at once acknowledged his subject as a matter of personal preference, for which there was no accounting, and, quoting Carlyle's definition, declared taste (*teesuto*) to be the "discernment of the true and great."[2] Other writers repeated the theme that *shumi* applied in all spheres of life, and that a man's character could be judged by his *shumi*.

The ability to discern the "true and great" presumed a selection of things. Beyond literary circles, the pressure of things—commodities seeking selection and placement—was encouraging a broad reordering of matters of taste. For in the same historical moment that the neologism *shumi* emerged in literary and popular discourse as a device for distinguishing value in things (and by extension, people), new encounters with commodities and opportunities for acquisition were awaiting the populace in the emporia of Japan's major cities. Although most journals of the time advertised books, cosmetics, and patent medicines, advertisements in *Shumi* introduced readers to gramophone shops, dealers in art and antiques, a maker of gold and silver dishes bearing the title of imperial arts commissioner (*teishitsu gigei iin*), and a specialist in frames for windows and Western paintings, as well as purveyors of personal adornments such as diamonds and panama hats. Reigning over this pageant of decorative goods was the department store, particularly the Mitsukoshi department store, which became the premier trendsetter in early twentieth-century Japan. Elite intellectuals like Tsubouchi were central players in Mitsukoshi's effort to recast Japanese tastes.

The Mitsui dry goods store in Nihonbashi changed its name to Mitsukoshi in December 1904 and advertised in the new year that it would expand its range of merchandise to become a "department store of the kind operating in America." This was the culmination of a process of several years. At the turn of the century five years earlier, the store had taken the first crucial step in converting sales practices for a mass market by introducing display cases and eliminating the traditional mode of transaction through orders placed individually with seated clerks. Display windows were added to the streetside facade of the building in 1904. By 1908, the four other large dry goods stores in Tokyo had followed suit.[3]

This conversion altered the space where urbanites shopped from a void, bespeaking an economy of scarcity, to a visible embodiment of abundance and transformed the act of acquiring goods from a matter of personal negotiation to one of anonymous liberation. As Edward Seidensticker notes of the commercial city before the department store, "Edo was a closed world. . . . People knew their stores, and stores knew their people."[4] Transactions between clerk and customer in the traditional dry goods store took place on the broad and empty *tatami*-mat floor of the shop. The merchandise was kept out of sight in rows of storehouses behind the shop, and items the clerk judged appropriate to his client (the clerks being male) were brought out in the course of negotiation. An early woodblock print of the new store in the first stage of its conversion shows women climbing the staircase to the upper story, presumably for the first time, to find rows of cabinets displaying the shop's wares in the same manner as the government-sponsored expositions of the era (see Fig. 3.1). Mitsukoshi immediately became a tourist site. With the subsequent reconstruction in Renaissance style and additions of richly ornamented dining rooms, lounges, playgrounds, and exhibition spaces, it also became a place for properly attired urbanites to bring their children and spend the whole day. Mitsukoshi managers put particular emphasis on special exhibitions, since the Japanese department store's role was not only to multiply the opportunities for consumption and stimuli to consume but to provide potential consumers with object lessons in the meanings and uses of new commodities.[5]

Taste is the distinguishing trait par excellence of class. Yet the explicit content of the Meiji discourse of taste revolved more around the definition of nation. Tsubouchi treated the nurturing of taste in Japan as a problem of nationhood, announcing that the journal would seek to "contribute to the nation" by responding to the urgent need to promote "both the progress and the preservation" of Japanese taste.[6] Mitsukoshi's managers spoke of the department store's role in a similar manner, claiming that the progress of their business was inseparable from the progress of the nation. Toward this lofty purpose, the store sponsored several "research groups," inviting prominent intellectuals, who gave talks on contemporary trends, evaluated new patterns

Fig. 3.1 Interior of Mitsui dry goods store during its conversion to a department store. While the traditional transactions between individual customers and their designated clerks continue on the *tatami* floor below, shoppers upstairs browse the display (courtesy Mitsukoshi Archives).

of fabric the store had designed, shared personal collections, and planned exhibitions. The "trends research group" (*ryūkō kenkyūkai*), the longest-lasting of these, began meeting monthly in 1905 under the direction of Iwaya Sazanami, a popular writer hired by the store. Mitsukoshi thus became an occasional salon at which such prominent men as Nitobe Inazō, Mori Ōgai, Yanagita Kunio, and Tsubouchi himself met with store executives, in-house designers, and intermediaries like Iwaya. The store derived propaganda value from the presence and support of these luminaries, who were referred to in Mitsukoshi publications either by name or with grand-sounding collectives that evoked the pantheon of bourgeois cultural legitimizers—terms such as "eminent authorities" (*sho taika*), "renowned specialists" (*senmonka meishi*), and "the first rank of celebrated men in this generation" (*tōdai ichiryū no meika*). *Mitsukoshi* magazine, one of three publications the department store produced, was an amalgam of literary journal, fashion-watcher, and merchandise catalogue.[7] Here the speeches given at study-group gatherings were reprinted alongside reports on new sales displays and photographs of the latest merchandise, often sponsored by or promoted as the invention of one of these specialists or men of renown.

For Tsubouchi Shōyō, translator of Shakespeare and author of the first Japanese treatise on the novel, it was natural to see the problem of taste first in terms of national culture. The same can be said of most of the luminaries invited to Mitsukoshi. Men who by the nature of their social position were national intellectuals tended to find national rationales for their class concerns. The department store's motives were of a different character. However high-minded—or nationalistic—the management's rhetoric, from a business perspective, the nation provided a legitimating device, a means whose end was to generate consumer desire. These distinct interests, of the bourgeois intellectual seeking audiences for a class-based vision of nation and of the commercial enterprise seeking customers, were brought together by the Mitsukoshi research groups.

With the collapse of an ascriptive order governed by convention and sumptuary regulation, bourgeois society places aesthetic choices in an autonomous sphere, just as the bourgeois individual is conceived as isolated and self-governing.[8] By extension, the bourgeois interior is composed as the personal expression of its occupants. Bourgeois taste may still be hemmed in by social convention—indeed, when fixed rules no longer define what is permissible, the pressure to keep up appearances is greater than ever—but it is as consumers making choices that families and individuals in bourgeois society express themselves. The ideology of the autonomous individual is tied to the ideology of a personal taste that transcends status or practical necessity. At the same time, bourgeois society treats aesthetic discernment as indispensable cultural capital. Thus it cloaks what is in fact a class strategy—and in this sense eminently "practical"—with an appearance of disinterestedness and purity.

Sparked by the encounter with Western bourgeois culture, the Meiji discourse of taste gave primacy to national definition. It contributed no less, however, to a specifically bourgeois sensibility regarding the home. Like the propagandists of the *katei*, promoters of *shumi* targeted an audience for whom higher education, sentimental and practical investment in domesticity, and knowledge of how things were done in the West underwrote class identity. Selecting new goods for the home was now becoming an important element of this identity. Yet the vast differences between the design and decorating methods of nineteenth-century Japanese houses and their contemporary Western counterparts set the problem of negotiating commodities in sharp relief. Compared with densely populated Victorian interiors, Japanese rooms appeared empty. To cope with this difference, one either had to claim that minimalist "simplicity" was the essence of Japanese taste or to view the Japanese interior as a blank canvas awaiting the expression of individual artistic impulses liberated from feudal convention. Since no bourgeois ideologue advocated indiscriminate Westernization, and none believed that things could remain as they had been, finding a way to redesign the domestic interior to express both of these positions became a vital part of the bourgeois project.

## Recoding Interiors

The dialectic between native and Western that constituted Meiji bourgeois taste reinterpreted native aesthetic traditions as much as it accommodated imported ones. Even at the height of the high-society boom for Western fashions in the 1880s, nativist impulses, often expressed by the leaders of Western fashion themselves, brought to the fore some native style or art form to show that Japan was at least a match in aesthetic terms for the enlightened West. The imperial house itself was the master synthesist—or, more precisely, the device with which national leaders legitimated their synthesis. So, for example, in summer 1887, a week after the Rokumeikan masquerade ball for whose Westernizing excess he would subsequently become infamous, Foreign Minister Inoue Kaoru received the emperor and empress at his estate for a celebration that included a viewing of his teahouse and performances of kabuki. The event not only balanced the flamboyant Westernness of the previous week's ball but put the imperial imprimatur on kabuki, transforming it from a vulgar urban entertainment to a legitimate national theater. Dealers in teawares also profited from official recognition and the patronage of Japan's power elite, and the practice of tea was similarly transformed by its incorporation into Meiji bourgeois culture.[9]

Prior to the importation of Western goods and texts illustrating their use, the predominantly male literati maintained highly evolved aesthetic traditions associated with tea and other codified practices of social exchange, art collecting, and art appreciation. Traditional decorative techniques in the elite domestic architecture of the *shoin* focused mostly on the proper place-

Fig. 3.2 *Zashiki* decorated for the annual first Day of the Rabbit in the Chinese zodiac, from Sugimoto Buntarō, *Zukai Nihon zashiki no kazarikata* (Illustrated Guide to Decorating Japanese Guest Rooms), 1912. The accompanying text explains that "solemnity is to be observed in all cases of decoration for annual holidays and celebrations, which must rely on decorum of the highest level of formality (*shingyō no sahō*)" (129–130). The fern-like ornament hanging in the alcove is *hikage no kazura*, an archaic Shinto ritual element that the author reports was enjoying a revival at the time. Architectural features of the room such as the unplaned alcove post, the semicircular cut in the sleeve-wall, and the lack of a continuous molding (*nageshi*) reflect the *sukiya* style.

ment of objects and painted scrolls in the *tokonoma* alcove of a guest room. This approach to interiors, generically known as *zashiki kazari*, persisted in some Meiji texts on interiors. Sugimoto Buntarō, for example, author of several popular books teaching readers how to decorate Japanese rooms, redacted principles from these traditions and synthesized them into a unified system. His books won the endorsements of a list of titled aristocrats beginning with the Imperial Household minister. Although Sugimoto positioned himself as an aesthetic conservative, his advice was distinctly modern, for it reconstituted diverse past practices in the name of a single national tradition. He regarded the composite he created as representative of the "Japanese" taste and temperament, and contrasted it in every aspect with the West (see Fig. 3.2).

Sugimoto and other writers constituting the native style in interiors taught minutely detailed codes for decorating guest rooms. His books first adduced examples from Western and native texts to show the contrast of taste, claiming that the unique Japanese preference for "elegance" (*fuzei*) and "variety of form" had been transmitted since ancient times together with the essence of the national polity, and then compiled permutations of objects to ornament particular alcove, shelf, and *shoin* desk combinations, thereby constituting a comprehensive code.[10] *Rules of Japanese Domestic Interior Decoration* (*Nihon jūtaku shitsunai sōshoku hō*) classified alcove treatments by decorative element, indicating principles for the handling of each type of object, flower, or painting theme. These were assembled according to an overarching principle of creating harmonious compositions suited to the season and the circumstances of display. Arrangements of flowers and objects on a decorative stand to be placed in the alcove were ordered according to three basic grades of formality with six intermediate grades.[11] Interior decorating was treated as the application of predetermined rules derived from literate tradition. Sugimoto encouraged placement of folding screens in the entry and other parts of the house as well as in the guest room, for example, but told readers that putting decorative objects in front of a screen in the entry was "not in the rules" (*hō ni nai*).[12] At the same time, this system of rules constituted a ritual aesthetic, which functioned only in the service of the social interaction that took place between host and guest. There existed no "rule" for decorating rooms intended for private use.[13]

While domestic management and etiquette texts for women repeated elements of Sugimoto's rules of alcove decoration, they also revealed the pervasiveness among late Meiji educators of Victorian ideas about the moral influence of environment. These ideas constituted a second strain in Meiji writing on interiors, distinct from the tradition of treating the interior as a setting for formalized social exchange. Claims that the decoration of a room had the power to influence the morals of its occupants were common in nineteenth-century Anglo-American writings on the home. As revealed in the domestic manual *Katei no shiori* (1909), this notion arrived in Japan with its own lore. The authors provided a story, reportedly from the United States, of a woman who had lost two of three sons in shipwrecks because a painting of a ship that hung in the house had instilled in them the longing to become sailors. The story was described as illustrating the hazards of decorating without due care for the effect of the domestic environment on impressionable children's minds.[14] Since domestic management writers had recast the home as a moral sphere under female dominion, such tales had natural relevance for women.

No conflict existed between the prescriptions of *zashiki kazari* writers and those of women's educators. Yet treating interior decorating as a subject for the study of elite women was itself a departure from past practice. Sugimoto Buntarō could only note wistfully in 1912 that before the Restoration "men had considered interior decoration their indispensable obligation, just as women consider the adornment of their persons first among their accomplishments."[15] *Joshi sahōsho*, an etiquette text for the girls' higher school, fused the two systems of norms by applying the ritual-aesthetic rigor of Sugimoto to modern ceremonies of morally didactic intent. Readers learned the proper appointment of rooms for celebration of such events as the Emperor's Birthday and National Founding Day, the two major state holidays invented in the Meiji period. For the Emperor's Birthday, they were instructed to prepare a front room with photographs of the Emperor and Empress to which the family would pay reverence and then to invite relatives and friends for a celebration in a separate guest room. Instructions included the appropriate alcove decorations and menu. A separate exegesis was then provided for performance of the ceremony in a set of Western-style rooms, beginning, in the reception room, with a large rosewood shelf on which were to be placed an ivory sculpture of a shepherd, a Nō mask with a half-fan beside a "sufficiently ornamented" table clock, and seven other objects, progressively more arcane. Further specifications were provided for the dining room, entry vestibule, and corridors.[16] Even for students in the rarified air of the most elite women's institutions, all the elaborate appurtenances called for in this text could not have been waiting at home. The instructions served less as a literal blueprint than as a means to impart to elite women principles for setting the domestic stage in a manner suited both to their social position and to the new national culture.[17]

Texts not explicitly concerned with ceremony still approached interior decorating through the application of distinct principles for things Western and native. They typically treated the Western interior separately from the Japanese interior and outlined distinct parallel formulas for the appointment of each. Decoration of the Western room was always to be "rich and gorgeous" (*nōkō kabi*), and the Japanese room "refined and light" (*seiga tanpaku*).[18] But a simple division of imported objects for Western rooms and

Fig. 3.3 Decoration for a *tokonoma* alcove in a Japanese room and a mantelpiece in a Western room (Kondō Masakazu, *Kasei hōten* [Household Management Treasury], 1906).

native objects for Japanese rooms did not follow inexorably from this principle. Some writers even encouraged mixing of native and foreign goods. Shimoda Utako's instructions for decorating a Western room recommended the use of "items unique to our country."[19] Rather, within these antithetical settings, the texts followed the same logic of aesthetic prescription found in Sugimoto Buntarō's writing, treating decoration as a problem of creating harmonies within the bounds of socially determined protocols. The hearth in the Western room was often described as like the *tokonoma* alcove of the Japanese room, and decoration of the mantel was treated with similar formal rigor (see Fig. 3.3).[20] Like the *zashiki* and the tea house, Western rooms were performance spaces. To the reader placed in the role of guest, texts indicated protocols for sitting in a chair that were as exact and exacting as the rules for receiving tea or viewing objects displayed in an alcove.[21]

Nowhere did these texts speak of expressing individual taste. They nevertheless expected their readers to possess not only a capacity to discern objects of generally regarded worth but the means to own a stock of such objects sufficient to select and match in accordance with the aesthetic principles prescribed for different settings or times. Despite the rule of lightness in Japanese guest rooms and repeated asseverations that the art of decorating a Japanese room lay in combining the humble objects at hand to harmonious effect,[22] the appearance of simplicity was deceptive. The artfully spare interior was predicated at the very minimum on having enough space to keep a room free of aesthetically undesirable objects of daily use, that is, on possession of a *zashiki* that could be dedicated to display and reception. Appropriate decoration also presumed the accumulation of goods (and the access to seasonal flowers) necessary to change a room's appearance seasonally and according to the formality of the occasion. Even a very partial array of the scroll paintings, flower vases, pieces of sculpture, decorative shelves, and folding screens discussed in Sugimoto's books would have required a storehouse (the essential architectural embodiment of wealth in the premodern city) for safekeeping of items not in use. Texts like Shimoda's also explicitly assumed the presence of several servants for maintenance of these goods and the *zashiki* in which they were to be displayed.

Much more costly still would be the maintenance of a proper Western room following protocols demanding that it be "rich and gorgeous." Shimoda Utako even specified that this was a matter of quantity, instructing her readers that "in a Western building, one should array lots of objects and furniture, not allowing too much empty space even in a large room."[23] An article describing the typical high-ranking bureaucrat's household in "One Hundred Walks of Life" (1904) considered ownership of one room in proper Western construction beyond the reach of a bureaucrat with an annual salary of 1,000 yen, unless he had an auxiliary source of income.[24]

The aristocracy and haute bourgeoisie therefore held a near-monopoly on Western domestic architecture and its proper appointments at the turn of the twentieth century. From time to time, their decorated interiors were photographed for the edification of readers of the *Ladies' Graphic*. A special issue on interior decorating published in 1906 showed the guest rooms, dining rooms, and reception rooms of fifteen such illustrious households, along with interiors at the Mitsukoshi department store and an unidentified building belonging to the Imperial House. These photos reveal that members of the upper class were mixing pieces of Western furniture and ornament with Japanese in a surprising range of combinations in both *tatami* rooms and Western rooms. Befitting the high elite of an era of cultural redefinition, the

Fig. 3.4 Eclectic interiors of "Western rooms" (*yōma*) in the houses of late Meiji aristocrats. In the Kuroda house (*top*), Japanese paintings have been mounted in roundels and fan-shapes as part of the wallpaper. Similarly, in the house of Kaneko Kentarō (*bottom*), the heavy Victorian furniture makes the rooms functionally "Western," but the exposed posts, *nageshi* moldings, and sliding panel doors reveal that they nevertheless adhere to the standard methods of vernacular house construction (*Ladies' Graphic*, 1906).

decorators of these houses appropriated objects from West and East (including Orientalia of non-Japanese origin) to display both wealth and cosmopolitanism. Rugs and animal hides appeared in several of the *tatami* rooms photographed—a recent fashion that Sugimoto Buntarō considered particularly repugnant.[25] Carpeting, another decorative feature that was anathema to indigenous traditionalists, was found in Japanese and Western rooms alike. All rooms with chairs had carpeting—the minimum two elements needed to make a room "Western." Most of the rooms with chairs had pieces of Japanese sculpture and porcelains displayed as objets d'art, often on delicately made ornamental shelves. Nevertheless, the dualist principle of "light and refined" for "Japanese rooms" in which floor sitting prevailed and "rich and gaudy" for "Western rooms" with chairs was maintained in some form throughout. Revealing the transposition of a rigidly codified native decorating approach to Western rooms, mantels were decorated with a symmetrical combination of the prescribed flower vases, candelabra, and clock or statuette, an equivalent to the *shin* or formal protocol for decorating a *tokonoma* (see Fig. 3.4).[26]

A larger population whose guest rooms were less likely to grace the pages of the *Ladies' Graphic* than the *Ladies' Graphic* was to grace their guest rooms pursued an eclecticism predicated on making do, the operative principle in the house of the naval officer and his family in "One Hundred Walks of Life." The assembly of goods that served to convert one room of this rented house into the "Western room" articulated the master's occupation and career more than any unified aesthetic effect. Novelist Nagai Kafū, returning from Paris with an eye accustomed to French interiors and an aesthete's disposition, reviled the hodgepodge of such rooms, calling them "degenerate and chaotic."[27] Kafū's European purism matched the Japanese purism of Sugimoto Buntarō. However, aesthetic codes more expressive of the bourgeois society developing in Japan at the beginning of the century and of Japan as a modern nation were to be formulated less by these aesthetic purists than by designers and marketing experts courting the mass public.

## A National Style in Interiors

The history of the modern interior design profession in Japan begins properly at the Mitsukoshi department store. At least it is safe to say that Mitsukoshi was the first institution with the possible exception of the Imperial Household Ministry to establish a position with the professional title of "interior decorator" (*shitsunai sōshokushi*). Hayashi Kōhei, Mitsukoshi's first chief interior decorator, began his career as a child apprentice in the Mitsui dry goods store preceding its rebirth into a department store. The store's manager discovered his talent for drawing and in 1904 sent him overseas to study window display. In 1906, he returned from studying in New York and a period at an interior decorating firm in London to begin work on Mitsukoshi's first interior design commission, the Japanese Embassy in Paris.[28]

Hayashi created distinct motifs for the surfaces and upholstery of each room of the embassy, including "autumn colors," "cherry blossoms," "chrysanthemums," "bamboo," and "weaponry."[29] Upon its completion in 1908, the embassy design was well-received in Paris, where it served to represent traditional Japanese taste. In Japan, Mitsukoshi promoted the design by publishing a book by Iwaya describing a fictional visit. Here the novelty of the design and its distinction from traditional architecture were emphasized. One of Iwaya's fictional visitors opined:

> I think the most praiseworthy thing is that it adds pure Japanese-type decoration to a purely European type of structure and ingeniously blends them, without falling into the slightest disharmony. If you were to demand that everything be Japanese, there would be no need for plans and designs. One merely needs money to do that . . . there's neither artistic design nor planning effort in it.[30]

From Mitsukoshi's perspective, Hayashi's innovation was to create a Japanese style distinct from the work of vernacular carpenters. In the context of European Japonisme, its only true distinction may have been that it was the authentic work of a Japanese designer. But within Japan, Hayashi's work could claim to bear Japanese interior aesthetics across the threshold from an unconscious and artless vernacular past into enlightened modernity.

Thanks to Hayashi's synthesis, it was now possible for Mitsukoshi to promote "Japanese style" in a Western room (*yōma*) as a positive virtue rather than as the inevitable product of compromise with native materials, craft techniques, and living habits. Back at the Tokyo store, a lounge was installed in the style of the Paris Embassy's "Bamboo Room."[31] Meanwhile, Mitsukoshi had begun display of other national styles for the consumption of the Japanese public. A lounge in Louis XV style was installed in 1908, and two model rooms in the style of an "English cottage" were put on display in 1912. These were followed by a study in "Adam Style," a guest room in "Louis XVI," a dining room in "Jacobean," and a "modern English" bedroom installed in the department store's new building in 1914.[32]

In the January 1912 issue of *Mitsukoshi* magazine, Hayashi described the interior of a house he had recently "decorated in eclectic style at the request of a certain gentleman." Accompanying photographs showed a ladies' lounge, guest room, smoking room, dining room, and study. As in Paris, Hayashi applied a palette of motifs and materials to the furniture, walls, and other available surfaces of the room to evoke a Japanese style. In this case, however, the rooms were in a dwelling of native construction rather than a European public building; meaning, in effect, that Hayashi was appointing a Japanese interior to make it look Japanese. Still, the task was the same in Hayashi's eyes: to create something that would evoke a "twentieth-century Japanese style (*sutairu*) of decoration." Hayashi wrote that the growing demand for eclectic interiors was a welcome sign and reflected the fact that the Japanese people were "becoming conscious of their status." For Hayashi, the object of decorating was to incorporate pieces of Western furniture but apply ornament that reduced their Westernness. At the same time, Hayashi's decorating transformed the vernacular interior of the original rooms into a consciously contrived Japanese style (see Fig. 3.5).

Although Hayashi spoke of the need to attain "the most harmonious, pleasant style for the least expense," he applied liberal quantities of gold and silver dust, plate, and leaf. Tables and chairs in the guest room were given "Japanese taste" by the attachment to legs and corners of openwork metal fittings in the design of cherry blossoms and butterflies. Elsewhere, Hayashi drew from various periods, using coffered ceilings characteristic of sixteenth- and seventeenth-century architecture and "patterns from the ancient period" (*kodai moyō*) on the frame of a mirror. Light fixtures were modeled after lanterns ordinarily used outdoors.

It is perhaps not surprising that Hayashi, having been trained in Europe, should arrive at a decorative style reminiscent of the European "Japanese taste." Certainly in Paris he was under pressure to produce something that, as Mitsukoshi manager Hibi would later describe it, "demonstrated the true value of the Japanese arts"; something that would not simply "be laughed at for trying European decoration without the money to do it."[33] But to establish a position of expertise at home, Hayashi needed most of all to distinguish his work from vernacular precedents. Rather than leave the native element of the new eclecticism to carpenters, he treated the carpenter-built *shoin* room—ostensibly already "Japanese"—as a volume composed of blank

Fig. 3.5 Mitsukoshi interior designer Hayashi Kōhei's decoration for a gentleman's house (*Mitsukoshi* magazine, 1912).

surfaces to be papered over with motifs that would evoke Japaneseness. And although the result was unquestionably ornate, Hayashi criticized earlier eclectic interiors, the work of wealthy amateurs who, in his view, had failed to be selective in their use of native elements. "Many of the Western rooms in Japanese taste to date," he wrote, "have been fitted with copious sculpture, and gold and blue (*kinpeki*) everywhere, giving one the feeling of being in Nikkō or Hongan-ji Temple." It was a style "inappropriate to a private dwelling." Perhaps the guilty parties here had turned to contemporary domestic manuals for advice. Their choice of heavily decorated vases, gold-leaf screens, and other Orientalia for Western rooms would have been extrapolated naturally enough from the decorating instructions of Shimoda Utako, for example, who urged readers to use Japanese goods in their *yōma* while prescribing "rich and gorgeous" as the governing aesthetic for these rooms.[34]

Hayashi positioned himself as an artist. In contrast to the conventions of Shimoda's dualistic code of East and West, his aesthetic fusion claimed to be at once as Japanese as possible and the expression of a transcendent prerogative of individual taste. Viewed from a point of greater remove, interior decorating as a commercial profession, which began in Japan with Hayashi Kōhei, stood in basic opposition to the traditional syntheses that made up the rules of *zashiki* decoration. The interior done in Japanese style dispensed with the permutations of existing architecture and decorative objects in favor of adapting motifs from the decorative arts to dress any sort of space. The textual tradition preceding him was a long chain of redactions and codifications of practice, in which aesthetic choices were inseparable from proper conduct. Hayashi's notion of tasteful decoration severed aesthetics from the practical contents of interior space; treatment of the interior was no longer constrained by the seasonal, occasional, and status-determined dictates of ritual.

## Architects and Style

The need to formulate a national style was felt as urgently in the architectural academy as in the field of interior decorating. This urgency was impressed upon many Meiji architects for the first time by the experience of study in Europe. Tatsuno Kingo, who went to England in 1879 as Japan's first architecture student to be sent overseas for training, found himself at a loss when called upon by his hosts to explain the historical styles of architecture in his country.[35] Europeans' queries doubtless posed the same challenge to those who followed him. Yet the issue of national style that Japanese architects confronted in late nineteenth-century Europe was both deeper and messier than the naïve and perfectly natural "tell us about your country" would imply—deeper because behind it lay the claims to unique ethnic traditions, the theories of architectural evolution, and the stylistic appropriations from colonized cultures that gave architectural expression to the furious competition of the powers; and messier because individual European architects' choices of expression in this grand potlatch of style and theory were eclectic and protean. Every historical form that appeared serviceable could be fit to the logic of some interpretation of national style. As architecture historian Fujimori Terunobu has put it, it was as if someone had "turned out all the drawers from the cabinet of styles at once."[36] Yet despite the appearance of a stylistic free-for-all, there was an implicit hierarchy. The Japanese architect faced the dilemma that if he adopted the eclectic styles of his European counterparts, he was seen by them (and sometimes by his Japanese peers) as betraying his native tradition, whereas if he championed a native style, he risked falling back into the drawer prepared for him by European Orientalism.[37]

The historical eclecticism that was at its zenith in Europe, particularly in England, during the 1870s and 1880s thus differed in logic and conception from the eclecticism of Meiji *wayō setchū*, which was born of practical necessity—that is, literally as a solution to problems of practice. The Japanese architectural academy might have gone down a different path had it not been baptized in European modernity at this moment of profuse historical revivals and exotic appropriations. In the event, Japanese architects brought home two seemingly contradictory messages. These were, first, that every nation must possess its own unique style, sustained by an orthodox lineage of orders and motifs, and second, that, within the bounds defined by these lineages, appropriation of other national styles was in fact the order of the day. As political subalterns, they sought to negotiate their way through this international arena with a national style of public architecture in which the Western was equated with function and the native with aesthetics.[38]

The profession of architecture in Japan at the end of the century was itself only beginning to develop self-consciousness as something other than the application of imported technology. The European category of "fine arts," with its emphasis on form, was alien when instruction in sculpture began at the nationally sponsored Technical Art School (Kōbu bijutsu gakkō) in 1876.[39] It took yet longer for students of the applied art of architecture to conceive of the formal component of their practice abstracted from construction. The name of the Society of Japanese Architects was Zōka gakkai, literally "Society for the Study of Building," for its first ten years of existence, from 1887 to 1897; during this time the term *zōka* (building) was used interchangeably with *kenchiku*, the term that subsequently became the standard translation of "architecture." The society finally changed its title at the instigation of Itō Chūta of Tokyo Imperial University, the country's first architecture historian. In an aggressive polemic calling for a unification of terminology, Itō observed that the real nature of "architecture" (*aakitekuchūru*) was the "manifestation of true beauty in an appeal to line and form," and that the word *zōka* failed to encompass the tombs, memorials, and triumphal gates that "architects" (*aakitekuto*) planned and the pagodas and temple halls whose construction they managed.[40] The new name thus made clear that the society's business was the art of design rather than the mere construction of shelter.

The society debated the problem of national style first in 1910, when a conference was held on the theme "What Should Be the Future Architecture of Our Country?" Here Itō reiterated an "evolutionary theory" of architecture he had earlier developed to assert that the formal elements of ancient Japanese Buddhist architecture could become "the orders" of a Japanese style if they were constructed in stone. Other architects called for construction of a new national style that incorporated elements of foreign styles on the basis of "the taste and spirit" (*shumi seishin*) of Japanese architecture.[41] Talk of a "Japanese taste," "Oriental taste," or "new eclectic taste" in architecture appeared in numerous other articles in the society's journal in the same year. It also became commonplace to make Japanese or "Oriental" *shumi* a condition for entries to design competitions from this time.

For the most part, the architects who participated in the 1910 conference had no program for residential architecture. Those who mentioned it did so chiefly to allude to the persistence of habit in private life and the necessity therefore to treat dwellings as distinct from "architecture" proper.[42] A Japanese style in residential architecture therefore remained relatively unexplored territory. The proposals for dwelling reform that had appeared earlier in the pages of *Kenchiku zasshi* had made no mention of aesthetics or taste. Although Josiah Conder conceived the architect's education in broad liberal-arts terms, his students at the Imperial College of Engineering knew that they were being trained to build monuments and public structures for the state, not to enter private practice designing houses.[43]

The first Japanese architects to explore new aesthetic expression in house design were men rediscovering native traditions through contact with the modern design rebellion against historicism in Europe. It is a well-known irony that Art Nouveau and the parallel movements Japanese encountered in Europe at the turn of the twentieth century were heavily influenced by late nineteenth-century Japonisme, which had absorbed motifs from Japanese vernacular architecture and decorative arts through illustrated books, expositions, and goods in the curio trade.[44] Contemporary Japanese were quite aware of this irony, although in Europe's rich variety of Japanesque interpretations, it was not always certain what the original stylistic sources or modes of transmission had been. Mitsuhashi Shirō, one of the proponents of a national style at the 1910 conference, guessed at a variety of possible lines of influence:

> I don't know whether it is from Westerners who came and saw Japan as tourists, or whether they have relied on Japanese drawings, but [Art Nouveau styles] contain a great deal of Japanese taste. . . . For example, things like the checkerboard (*ichimatsu*) pattern, the fish-scale pattern, the scroll pattern, or things like square brackets (*masu*) are all Japanese style. Also the exposing of second-floor joists as a decoration of the ceiling is something I think they may have learned from looking at Japanese shops.[45]

Japonisme thus helped Japanese architects envision a native Japanese style composed of disparate elements formerly outside their own area of concern. Whatever their precise relation to Japan, however, the decorative motifs of Arts and Crafts, Art Nouveau, and the Viennese Secession movement attracted the attention only of Japanese architects with an eye for things other than large public buildings.

Takeda Goichi, who belonged to the second generation trained at Tokyo Imperial University, was one such architect. Takeda would later become the leading figure in a circle of architects devoted to developing a new style in residential architecture. Arriving in London in 1901, Takeda visited Rennie Mackintosh's Glasgow School of Art and then followed the trail of Art Nouveau to Brussels, Paris, and Vienna before returning to Japan in 1903 to take up the country's first professorship in design (*zuanka*) at the Kyoto Higher School of Arts and Technology (Kyōto kōtō kōgei gakkō). Takeda's first commission on returning to Japan was the house of Fukushima Yuki-

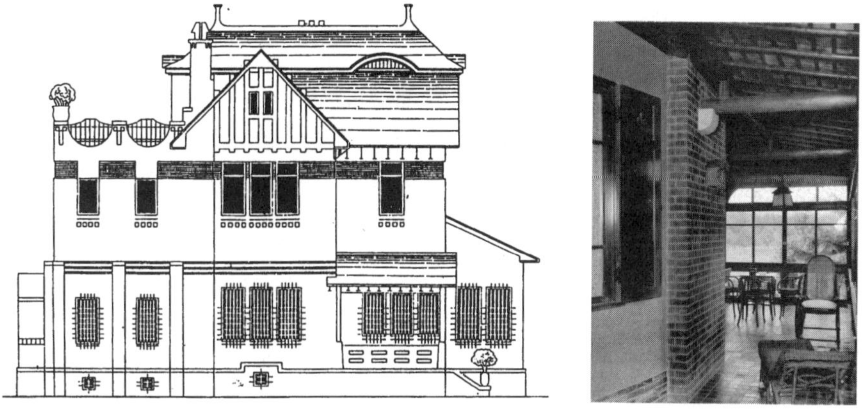

Fig. 3.6 Houses by architect Takeda Goichi. (*left*) Fukushima house, 1907 (*Takeda hakase sakuhinshū*, 1933). (*right*) Shibakawa house, 1912. This interior shows Takeda's fusion of *sukiya* elements such as decorative exposed rafters and woven bamboo in the walls and ceiling with Western construction, including glass, brick, and stone. (*Takeda hakase sakuhinshū*, 1933).

nobu, president of the Shirokiya department store. Completed in 1907, the house was done in what was called *Sesesshon shiki* (Secession style), with white furniture and fine-lined rectilinear detailing reminiscent of the work of Austrian architect Josef Hoffman and of Mackintosh.[46] On the exterior, the roofline and an exposed half-timber gable evoked German folkhouses (see Fig. 3.6).

Takeda emulated his European sources faithfully in all rooms but one, which he floored with *tatami* mats and built with elements of indigenous residential architecture including exposed posts, *nageshi* molding and decorated transoms (*ranma*). Unlike the typical *zashiki*, however, the room had double-hung windows facing the garden instead of sliding doors and an exterior corridor.[47] Also unlike the vernacular *zashiki*, it stood alone, without an adjacent *tatami* room that could be used as an anteroom for guest reception or combined with it for large gatherings. In fact, Takeda's building appears to have been linked to a carpenter-built native house in the manner of the standard *yōkan*, so the single *tatami*-floored room in Takeda's building may have been more a design experiment than a response to the practical needs of the client.

Takeda's interest in non-monumental traditions in Japanese architecture predated his study in Europe. In 1898, he had been the first modern architect to write a treatise on the tearoom.[48] The delicate, stylized rusticity of *sukiya* architecture, derived from the aesthetics of tea, provided Takeda with a native vocabulary that could be used in residential designs, and that seemed a comfortable marriage with the vanguard of European design. Europeans looking east in this period recognized little distinction of style among Japanese houses, but from Takeda's vantage point, *sukiya* represented the most aesthetically evolved in a range of indigenous building traditions.[49] Unlike the vernacular idioms of most domestic architecture, *sukiya* was a conscious style; its rules were shared by practitioners everywhere that it was practiced. There were pattern books an architect could turn to for particular motifs and famous, much-coveted paper models of tearooms. In subsequent residential designs, Takeda tried combining *sukiya* motifs, such as the use of woven bamboo or wood strips on walls and ceilings, with architectural features from Art Nouveau, the American bungalow, and later the Spanish Mission style.[50]

*Sukiya* style offered an alternative that contrasted markedly with the mix of lacquer, gold leaf, inlay, and openwork silver that Hayashi Kōhei was installing at the Japanese Embassy in Paris and in the homes of wealthy Tokyo clients. Whereas Hayashi's interior aesthetics drew more from decorative arts associated with the daimyo lords, *sukiya* belonged to the pre-Meiji merchant bourgeoisie. As an architect with Western training rehabilitating this non-aristocratic native style, Takeda was beginning the process of shaping a modern bourgeois style in Japanese architecture and expanding the role of the architect beyond state builder to bourgeois tastemaker. Takeda's clients were wealthy too, and his designs remained far removed from what most professionals could afford. Most of his clientele were in the Kyoto-Osaka area, where he taught, and where *sukiya* style enjoyed particular favor. Many had attended university, which was a rarity until the 1920s, several were company presidents, and several more had been granted court rank on the basis of their wealth or contributions to the state. Still, they were not statesmen or members of the imperial family, and they had commissioned the architect to design a house for their personal tastes rather than their public duties.[51]

Other architects who visited Europe absorbed different fashions in design. Half-timber construction, revived in the English picturesque style, struck Japanese designers as congruent with native tradition, in which exposed wooden posts and beams were common (although exposed timbers were a trait of the interiors of Japanese houses rather than their exteriors). French Art Nouveau was less influential but not ignored. Tsukamoto Yasushi, an advocate of dwelling reform as well as an active participant in numerous cultural activities sponsored by Mitsukoshi, was in Paris to witness the French Art Nouveau at the same time that Takeda was in London. In 1911, Tatsuno Kingo, the reigning master of public architecture in this period, collaborated with younger architect Kataoka Yasushi on a mansion in half-timber style with interior details in the manner of the French Art Nouveau.[52]

These aesthetic adventures were free of many of the social meanings that vanguard styles bore in their places of origin. Movements espousing strong anticlassical rhetoric and charged with political import surfaced and sank with increasing rapidity in the European design world beginning in the 1890s.[53] Since Japanese architects in these years visited only occasionally, in small numbers, and seldom stayed long enough to become closely acquainted with their European counterparts or the context in which they worked, it was inevitable that the social and political contours of the field would be flattened to some extent in the process of importation to Japan. Revolutionary styles brought from Europe tended to lose their revolutionary significance also because the weight of classicism bore down on Japanese far less than the weight of European culture itself. The pilgrimage to the monuments of Italy that was the culmination of every European architectural education (and an object of Secessionists' condemnation) had its counterpart for Japanese architects in study tours of England, Germany, and the United States.[54]

The encounter with Art Nouveau and related movements was nevertheless important for the mediating role it played in a turn among Japanese architects toward the aesthetics of the dwelling. This was more than a problem of ornament, since Takeda and some of his contemporaries were blending indigenous and European forms with the ultimate aim of creating a more intimate domestic space. For these architects, aesthetic concerns were inseparable from conceptions of comfort and, at root, of the true function of the dwelling. This problematic, too, resonated with trends in Europe. The vanguard of Japanese architects in the 1910s thus participated in an international search for a new architecture of domesticity, in which sources from distant times and places were drawn upon to answer genuinely felt human needs.

## Furniture as a New System of Goods

The developments discussed thus far, of a discourse of "taste" to supplant earlier aesthetic conventions and of an aesthetic reconception of the dwelling, in practice touched only the wealthiest fraction of Japanese society at the turn of the twentieth century. They might have been of little consequence to the rest of society if it were not for the fact that in the same years the old conventions of domestic architecture and interiors were being attacked on other, more popular fronts.

Model rooms and special exhibits at Mitsukoshi department store provided a general education in interior style classified by nation and period. The simulation of a global catalogue of historic styles, each with its own forms, motifs, and internal rules, added nuance to the existing dyadic view of things Japanese and Western and provided a setting for imagining Japan's national style. Teaching department store visitors the vocabulary of national styles did not make the furniture pieces themselves any more accessible, however. The chairs and tables labeled "Louis XVI" or "Jacobean" belonged in the category of exotic luxuries. Mitsukoshi's early model rooms were literally museum displays, whose objects were not intended for sale. It was in less extravagant forms that the department store assisted the entry of "taste" into the popular lexicon and the penetration of design fashions into the homes of its customers.

Mitsukoshi began selling furniture in 1909. The following year a furniture assembly division was set up, and the department store began manufacturing its own brand.[55] Other manufacturers of Western furniture were already in business in Tokyo; a group of specialists were clustered in the Shiba district, and Maruzen, a store better known for its books, also sold chairs and tables.[56] The Shiba district dealt primarily in furniture handcrafted to customers' specifications. In contrast, Mitsukoshi offered ready-mades, as well as Hayashi's design services. Yet by making and selling its own furniture, Mitsukoshi was not simply supplanting a craft tradition with mass production and marketing. For unlike the Americans to whom the Montgomery Ward catalogue offered cheap furniture in imitation of expensive handcrafted styles, many of the Japanese who would buy the merchandise listed in Mitsukoshi magazine had never owned tables and chairs at all.[57]

Ready-made Western furniture called not only for new uses but for a new system of acquisition of household goods. Here again, nomenclature is revealing, as the Japanese word *kagu,* used today as an equivalent to the English "furniture," acquired this meaning only in the 1910s and 1920s, that is, in the period that department stores began to sell goods under that name. Prior to this time, *kagu*, the Chinese characters for which literally denote "household articles" generally, referred to all movable property in a house, from artworks to bedding to cooking utensils. Books describing *zashiki* or reception-room decoration therefore had not spoken of *kagu* but instead used locutions such as *dōgu* (tools), *kizai* (receptacles), and *buppin* (articles).[58] The word *kagu* came to refer specifically to the appointments of a room rather than to all material possessions of the household as, through the diffusion of Western furniture, more people learned the experience of *furnishing*, acquiring things to fill domestic interiors.

It has long been a commonplace that the traditional Japanese house has no furniture. This is not to say that Japanese households lacked possessions. Apart from the screens, scroll paintings, and other decorative objects desired for the properly appointed *zashiki*, every household had some quantity of objects for daily use, along with chests for storage. The most important items of such movable property were usually acquired in the form of dowry. Decorative objects and writing tools of the *zashiki* constituted a system of goods belonging primarily to the master of the house, whereas dowry articles made up the core of a female domain outside the *zashiki*.[59] The size and content of dowries varied widely with class and region, but there were some basic common elements. These included a toilet-table and mirror, a sewing box, lightweight wooden chests of drawers (*tansu*), and lidded oblong chests (*nagamochi*) containing kimono and bedding. Kimono and bedding were often among the most valuable assets a family possessed.[60]

The two gender-specific systems of goods circulated differently in society and occupied space differently in the home. Before modern mass production and marketing, men acquired decorative objects through inheritance, orders to craftsmen, or purchase and exchange among connoisseurs and dealers in antiquities. In the canons of *zashiki* decoration, pieces of artistic value were stored out of sight, to be displayed seasonally and selectively. Selective display also sustained the functioning of connoisseurs' circles, in which the value of objects was determined according to rarity and lineage. Where the custom of dowry prevailed, the most valuable items in the female system of goods for the house were made at home or ordered from craftsmen to be assembled for the wedding, an event that occurred once in a lifetime. These goods then entered the storehouse or private rooms of the dwelling, where they would reside until transported as dowry in a later generation.[61] Indeed, for urban dwellers, dowries could be permanent in a way that houses were not, since they were carried (and designed to be carryable) wherever the household went, and it was common to move house (or rebuild after fires) many times.

To introduce ready-made goods, the department store needed strategies to penetrate and alter the world configured by these two systems of goods. Mitsukoshi engaged each in a different manner. It began by expanding its commercial role as a traditional dry goods shop to include all the elements of the standard dowry. Although the infrequency with which people invested in dowries was a demerit from the point of view of mass marketing, the custom assured steady demand. Using advertising and mail ordering, the store made every effort to aid the diffusion of more elaborate dowries throughout the country, including places where the transfer of dowry was little practiced.[62] Early issues of Mitsukoshi's publication *Jikō* included advertisements for complete sets of dowry chests made to order by cabinetmakers in Tokyo. By 1912, *Mitsukoshi* magazine was displaying a complete dowry, replete with garments and bedding, chests, and other articles that the store had marshaled for the marriage of a wealthy publishing magnate's daughter.[63] In the same years, the store moved to extend its geographical range. A form for readers in the provinces to place orders directly to Tokyo replaced the advertisements for Tokyo cabinet shops in the back of the store's general-circulation magazine. Women's magazines advertised Mitsukoshi's nationwide rail delivery service.

Mitsukoshi's incursion into cabinetmaking affected the trade more indirectly than directly, as department store advertising spurred a general cultural urbanization of dowries. More people came to assemble their dowries according to Tokyo or Osaka practices, opening new markets for fancy kimono, which in turn required more storage chests. By the late 1920s, the national diffusion of metropolitan dowry customs had resulted in standardization of storage chest manufacture, as regional craft designs were replaced by a plainer, more uniform "Tokyo style."[64]

## Art and Decor

Carving a niche in the predominantly male world of art was somewhat more complicated. To make paintings into commodities as available and casually acquired as any household article, it was necessary to dislodge them from practices of production, exchange, and appreciation that had kept them in a closed world inhospitable to mass marketing. Defenders of this world regarded the proper expression of national taste to be manifested in the custom of keeping precious goods concealed. From a Japanese point of view, one collector writing in *Shumi* magazine in 1907 noted, European interior decoration appeared "childlike," because Europeans put everything they owned on display, whereas Japanese displayed only one thing at a time. "You may have lots of gold screens," he observed, "but only one will be standing [in the house], and the rest are shut up in the storehouse." Westerners also differed from Japanese in their attitude toward individual works of art. In an ordinary house in the West it was usual to have two or three original oil paintings and a number of copies and photographic reproductions (*shashinban*) of famous works. The idea of displaying copies or prints was anathema in Japan, where people would accuse you of being "vulgar" or "lacking taste" if you hung such things in the house.[65] He explained this by presenting the elite connoisseur's mode of appropriation as a national trait: "Japanese have a tendency to appreciate in paintings or works of calligraphy not the thing itself but the work together with the personality of the artist or calligrapher. Therefore, no matter how great the original painting may be, if the work is a copy and not the original artist's hand, it is dismissed as tasteless and unrefined."[66] "Japanese" in this case meant Japanese with the means to acquire scrolls and screens by known artists and the storehouses to keep them. This naturally limited the market. The department store's interest, in contrast, was in the growing number of Japanese who had been familiarized with high art, both Eastern and Western, through expositions, museums, formal education, and popular media but who lacked the trappings of established wealth.

In the same year, Mitsukoshi's Osaka branch opened a painting department. Eager to reach as large an audience as possible, promoters of the business took a more populist view of Japanese taste. "Pictures are indispensable as interior decoration," observed the store organ *Jikō*. "The Japanese are a nation who love art":

> even in a nine-by-twelve foot backstreet tenement, one often sees picture supplements from the newspaper or prints from magazines in frames. How much more so the house with an entry vestibule and a *tokonoma* alcove. Picture frames are put up over the lintels everywhere, and there isn't a wall without a painting hanging on it. Setting aside the question of how shallow or profound the love of art may be, among Japanese, the desire for pictures is a social custom that comes from a definite need.[67]

Here national taste was invoked again, to precisely opposite effect, since the highly personalized mode of elite appreciation was inimical to the store's aims. Regretfully, the writer explained, impediments stood between the art-desiring consumer and suitable works of art. There were lots of forgeries among old paintings. When one tried to order a painting from one of the contemporary masters, on the other hand, there was no telling when it would be ready, if the artist agreed to do it at all. One could have a mounting shop act as broker, but the fees they charged were extremely high. The newly created Mitsukoshi gallery offered a means around these inconveniences, the article promised. The paintings could be purchased immediately, and the store guaranteed their authenticity with its own reputation. In addition, since the works were there for view, customers could choose what appealed to them. Several painters were listed whose works had recently been sold at Mitsukoshi. "Among the many paintings handled since opening last September, there were quite a number of works that were the masterpieces of a generation," the writer noted, hinting at future value.

A further effort at solicitation was made in the description of a few works recently arrived, each title dressed with the enticing adjectives of fine art appreciation: "possessing a delicate touch" (*shōsha taru shuchi o obi*), "a light stroke with deep overtones" (*hitsuro keikai ni shite yojō fukaku*), "true to life yet departing from realism, a use of so-called idealist representation that brims with subtle elegance" (*shasei o mamotte shasei o dasshi, iwayuru risōteki byōsha o motte shitaru tokoro, gami shinshin*). Photographs that commonly appeared in *Jikō* and *Mitsukoshi* magazines showed Japanese ink paintings as well as Western oils, each listed with artist, title, some more advertising copy, dimensions, and price. The lowest prices were 18 yen for an ink painting and 50 yen for an oil painting.[68]

These were, in effect, the prices of admission to an imagined world of connoisseurship, proffering its own "masters" and marks of value, without the requirement of personal intimacy with the producers and purveyors in the art business or the need to fear embarrassment in the game of authentication. Thanks to Mitsukoshi's prominence as a cultural institution and its close ties to a coterie of well-known intellectuals (the frequently summoned *meishi* and *taika*), some of what was sold actually did come from recognized figures in the academy and their students. But the primary selling point was ready availability. Mounted and *prêt-à-porter*, the art department's merchandise offered a convenience, which promotional materials described as valuable for "foreigners visiting for a short time or people building a new house and requiring [art works] immediately."[69] Homeownership was still uncommon in the city before World War I, and the buyers of these instant emblems of taste were more likely to be renting a new house than building one. Yet if one had neither the inherited collection nor the experience with the art trade, the "need" for art was the same. *Tokonoma* alcoves had proliferated in rented houses since the Meiji restoration, when the Tokugawa sumptuary codes that restricted their use according to rank were abolished. All but one of the one hundred plans for detached houses in a builder's guide published in 1913 possessed alcoves.[70] To maintain appearances—in other words, to maintain a *zashiki*—in such houses, the occupants needed at least one piece of art for the alcove, and preferably several to change with the seasons.

The buyers of these paintings, it was anticipated, were not going to keep them rolled or folded away in the storehouse. The emphasis was on use, for which new works were actually preferred, as both affordable and free of the complexities of pedigree. Let the antique dealers handle old paintings, one journalist said at the opening ceremony of one of the store's exhibitions; "the works by the masters of this generation are decorations that Japanese homes should not do without. In truth, they are practical necessities (*jitsuyōhin*). Works of this sort should be in the hands of practical merchants."[71] Although the Mitsukoshi art department borrowed the legitimating devices of high art criticism, it clearly shifted the art object into the more visible, less rarified, role of decor.

Oil paintings fit easily into this role since they were not part of the traditional system of connoisseurship in Japan. However, they fit less easily into Japanese houses. A petit-bourgeois house without the stored collection of scrolls and screens was also unlikely to have a Western room with the expanse of wall space necessary to hang a framed painting. Behind the claim in *Mitsukoshi* magazine that every wall in the typical house was adorned with a painting lurked the reality that vernacular dwellings often had no interior walls whatsoever apart from the back wall of the *tokonoma* alcove and the narrow space between lintels and ceiling. Since *tokonoma* usually housed scrolls, the only place left to display a framed piece of art was between the lintel and ceiling, a space between one-and-a-half and two feet in height. The newfound need, then, was for small paintings (see Fig. 3.7).[72]

Fig. 3.7 Takahashi Yuichi, *Enoshima*, 1873–76 (courtesy Konpira Shrine). Takahashi created narrow-format oil paintings designed to fit above a standard *nageshi* molding or hang from posts. As art historian Kinoshita Naoyuki has shown, Takahashi took up the problem of placing Western-style paintings in Japanese interiors early in the Meiji period. Decades would pass, however, before a substantial market emerged for oil paintings suited to Japanese rooms and small *yōma*.

The institutional framework of art schools, exhibitions, and critics for the new field of oil painting had recently taken shape when, in May 1912, Tokyo Mitsukoshi held its first "exhibition of small Western paintings" (*yōga shōhin tenrankai*). Paintings by twenty-nine living artists lined the walls of the small space, with prices that ranged from 60 yen for a modest canvas by Kuroda Kiyoteru, the leading artist of the day, down to 3 yen for a postcard-size miniature. Specializing in small pieces allowed the store to promote the affordability of an exotic commodity, and at the same time to domesticate it by offering it in a size that would fit anywhere in the house, even a Japanese house with limited wall surface. Newspapers reported on the exhibit in the manner of reviews of the annual exhibits sponsored by the Ministry of Education (the so-called *bunten*, begun in 1907), describing the works of the best-known artists and listing the schools they represented. Mitsukoshi could readily be accepted as an institution of high culture. Yet, press responses also show some ambivalence toward the mass marketing of art. One newspaper praised the timeliness of the show, suggesting that the department store was performing a public service by introducing a wider public to Western art; another paper noted that the prices were low, "perhaps because the paintings are primarily intended for practical use." Yet another registered discomfort at the juxtaposition of an exhibit of oil paintings with the other commodities ordinarily on display at the store, commenting that the first impression one got was inevitably "They're up for sale!" which, the reviewer commented, "is not a very

Fig. 3.8 Exhibit of "small Western paintings" at Mitsukoshi, May 1912. By offering small-format oil paintings framed and *prêt-à-porter*, the department store promoted an affordable cosmopolitanism and sought to attract new bourgeois and petit-bourgeois customers who lacked the knowledge or capital to buy with confidence through established art-world channels (*Mitsukoshi*, 2, no. 6 [June, 1912]).

pleasant sensation." But after all, a trade newspaper noted with a hint of cynicism, it was an exhibit of paintings to "look at lightly and purchase lightly."[73] The exhibition was enough of a commercial success for the store to repeat the event before the end of the year, this time with nearly twice as many entries (see Fig. 3.8).[74]

On the basis of the titles of works mentioned, it can be surmised that none of the art in these exhibitions came from the avant-garde. Mitsukoshi was both a key site and an agent in the formation of a middle-brow cultural field.[75] Minami Hiroshi has written that Tsubouchi Shōyō, the founder of *Shumi* magazine, sought to create a culture between pure art and entertainment, and promote it in the name of "taste."[76] The contents of the magazine *Shumi* were less consistently popularizing than this statement would suggest, but it is unquestionably true of the new idea of "taste" as it was promoted at the department store.

## Style in the Creation of a Furniture Market

Whereas Mitsukoshi's Art Department could rely on references to existing collecting traditions (even as it challenged them), the Western-style Interiors Department, created to sell a category of goods that slotted into neither of the gendered systems of movable property, had to enter into the interstices between the two and establish a social space that was governed by neither.[77] Modern trends in European design came to the aid of Japanese marketing here, providing models for more affordable furniture that was not strongly stamped with the style of a particular nation or period. *Mitsukoshi* magazine began by advertising expensive sets of chairs and sofas upholstered in silk and leather but quickly followed with cheap and lightweight rattan and bentwood chairs. Rattan was particularly successful, since, as a tropical fiber like the *igusa* reeds used to cover *tatami* mats, it agreed aesthetically with Japanese rooms. The lightweight, informal rattan chair had traveled with Europeans from colonies and treaty ports in Asia back to resort houses in the metropole. Japanese now reappropriated it as up-to-date, Western, and suited to native dwellings. The "Mitsukoshi-type rattan chair," introduced in 1911, was ubiquitous by the mid-1920s, having colonized the verandas and, in some cases, *tatami* interiors of many houses without Western rooms (see Fig. 3.9).[78]

The magazine soon advertised a wide range of Western furniture that expanded on this trend toward light and inexpensive pieces. Glass-doored cabinets with carved scrolling in Louis XVI style, recommended for guest rooms, were joined by flat board-cut bookshelves, stackable sidetables, and smoking cabinets with simple openwork decoration, recommended for "either a Western or a Japanese study," and costing less than one-third as much.[79] The shapes and motifs of these pieces of affordable cabinetry clearly reflected the influence of Art Nouveau. The term was not used in their descriptions, but it had already gained currency outside architectural circles through graphic design and other media. Things described as *nūbō* ("nouveau") appeared several times in the novels and stories written by Natsume Sōseki in this period, for example. One character in a story written in 1907 had a table "put together in a way that combined Chippendale and nouveau," and a reception room elsewhere had "nouveau style bookshelves." Learning that the architecture of a particular shop was "nouveau," the young protago-

Fig. 3.9 The Mitsukoshi-style rattan chair (*Mitsukoshi* 1, no. 3 [Apr./May 1911]). These inexpensive and popular chairs appear in numerous photographs of domestic interiors from the 1910s and 1920s. For many they were the first chairs to enter the home.

nist of the novel *Sanshiro* "became aware for the first time that there was nouveau style in architecture as well."[80]

The closely related Secession style was the fashion among young designers beginning in the 1910s. When Mitsukoshi sponsored a furniture design competition in 1913, the majority of the designs submitted were in Secession style (Fig. 3.10). However, these students and graduates of the engineering and art colleges lacked the store's concern with mass production. Commenting on the pool of entries, one of the judges observed that while Secession appeared to be popular because it "felt the newest," the essence of its "simple taste" could already be found in Japanese tearoom decoration. Unfortunately, he continued, all these entries had pursued unusual designs at the cost of practicality, and none had arrived at something that the judges believed could be inexpensively manufactured and sold.[81] The new field of design (comprising both *zuan* and *kenchiku*), divorced from craft, was beginning to generate a cadre of young specialists who saw their work in purely aesthetic terms, transcending obligations to either the state or the market.

Academy architects traveling in Europe had discovered the style of the Viennese Secession, but it soon left their hands at home, picked up by young designers and the mass market to provide the aesthetic vocabulary and the name for the first design vogue in Japan to unite architecture, inte-

Fig. 3.10 (*top row*) Secession-style furniture designs submitted in a competition at the Mitsukoshi department store in 1913 and (*bottom row*) simpler pieces with Art Nouveau features advertised in the catalogue pages of the store magazine (*Mitsukoshi*, 3, no. 6 [June 1913]; 1, no. 9 [Sept. 1911]).

rior design, graphic arts, and fashion. In 1914, the year that pavilions of the Taishō Exposition displayed Secession style architecture in Tokyo, "furniture dealers, shophands at the notions shop, and clerks at the clothiers" were all pushing *sesesshon*, or *se shiki*, as it was known for short. Even dolls for the girls' festival reportedly came in *sesesshon* designs.[82] As others played with its aesthetic possibilities, academy architects debated questions of authenticity, and the true meaning of the original movement. Most regarded it as popular in Japan because it accorded somehow with "national" or "Oriental taste" but were disturbed that it was not in fact native and decried the sudden vogue as evidence that young designers were blindly following the latest fashion from

Fig. 3.11 Re-styled rattan chairs, "the chairs best suited for placing in a Japanese room" (*Mitsukoshi* 10, no. 3 [Mar. 1920]).

Europe without having absorbed the lessons of the historical styles. These debates mark the first moments of a competition between established and parvenu architects and tastemakers that would expand in the 1920s.[83]

The simple, rectilinear forms associated with new European design as it came to Japan, particularly with Secession style, were unquestionably easier to mass-produce, however, even if idealistic art and architecture students overlooked this crucial characteristic. The new style also encouraged clear-varnished wood. With the aesthetics of the tearoom recovered as evidence of an inherent sympathy between native tradition and modern styles from Europe, these design features were easily promoted as suiting Japanese taste. The furniture department went on to produce inexpensive lamps, tables, desks, tea shelves, and stands for hibachi braziers and potted plants in simple designs dominated by square-cut clear-varnished wood, fine linear etching, and sometimes small amounts of "nouveau" openwork. These things exhibited an aesthetic that was a far cry from the national taste of Mitsukoshi designer Hayashi Kōhei's richly ornamented eclectic interiors.[84] The difference was less a matter of changing design fashions than of different clientele, however. Mitsukoshi had identified a market of people without the requisite formal Western room, but with an interest in the latest fashions in native and European design. The idea that simplicity was the essential characteristic of Japanese taste permitted these customers to make a virtue of necessity. By 1922, *Mitsukoshi* magazine had dubbed the lightweight chairs and the line of inexpensive wooden cabinetry it sold "the new Japanese furniture" (*shin wakagu*). The line offered in October of that year was intended to capture this aesthetic developed for the Japanese house: "In style, the delicate craftsmanship and heavy ornament of Western furniture are banished. The furniture must appear as simple as possible, so we have emphasized straight lines, valued light colors, and given just a hint of roundness. For ornament, the pieces are accented with openwork, etching (*kiwamebori*), and latticework at key points to bring the whole together."[85] A taste for the affordable thus reigned in the world of new goods for Japanese houses, goods that belonged to neither the category of the everyday and permanent, which was primarily gendered female, nor the category of the decorative and occasional, primarily gendered male.

## Liberated Taste

The emergence of an intellectual discourse of national taste, the commercial promotion of hybrid interior decoration, and the experiments in search of a modern national style in residential architecture were all processes working ultimately in the same direction—to divorce aesthetics from practice and, more particularly, to extricate the formal aesthetics of architecture and interior design from the intimate social space of the *zashiki* and the tearoom, where they had been monopolized by connoisseurs. "Taste" conceived as a transcendental value made it theoretically possible to abstract a pure aesthetic from its context. To Tsubouchi Shōyō and the intellectual group writing in *Shumi*, however, the refinement of national taste was as important as more universal romantic conceptions of beauty. This meant educating more people in a common aesthetic sensibility, to make *shumi* a property of the nation. Hayashi Kōhei extracted aesthetics from its practical setting in a concrete sense by selecting motifs from the decorative arts for a national style that could be applied in any interior. The second generation of European-trained architects, men like Takeda Goichi, in dialogue with trends in high design overseas, also went foraging in indigenous traditions and appropriating from abroad for elements that would compose a national style. Their reinterpretation of *sukiya* and of vernacular domestic architecture elevated the dwelling into a national and international arena of academic architectural discourse and design practice. For these architects the native became one of any number of stylistic techniques to be applied for what Itō Chūta had called the object of the architect's work: the "manifestation of true beauty."

Selecting from multiple possible "national tastes," mass-marketers chose a "national" taste for simplicity that happened to be affordable. The simplicity of *sukiya* was not, however, ordinarily cheap—on the contrary, connoisseurs paid extravagantly for rare materials and delicate craftsmanship that would distinguish their houses from the genuinely rustic architecture that *sukiya* style artfully quoted. In view of the bourgeois market then emerging, Hayashi's proposal for a national style proved a less accurate prognostication than Takeda's mix of *sukiya* and "Secession style," since the aristocratic traditions in decorative arts on which he drew were less suited to the production techniques of the modern era and less in keeping with the international trends in design that modern mass production had catalyzed.

Although both these men served an elite clientele distant from the mass market, their work contributed to the redefinition of taste and style occurring simultaneously at the department store. With the aesthetics of dwelling space liberated from past conventions of practice, and art and decorative goods disembedded from older institutions of production and exchange, the department store's promise of liberated consumption extended to furniture and decoration for the home. As a critical step in the forming of modern bourgeois identity, Japanese city dwellers in the early twentieth century learned the experience of choosing things for the home and became conscious that their choices were expressions of personal taste. Since defining and defending national culture in the face of the onslaught of Western modernity was the abiding mission of intellectuals, they treated the problem of taste in furniture and interiors as one of establishing a national style. Mass-marketers recognized the universality of the issue for the bourgeois public and used the idea of national style to habituate bourgeois men and women to displaying their own cultivation through new goods and ornament.

# 4

# Landscapes of Domesticity

## The Railroad Company as Cultural Entrepreneur

As new ensembles of goods occupied and redefined the space of the home, bourgeois practices began to redefine space in the city. The residential suburb, like the intimate family-centered home, was consciously promoted by late Meiji period cultural intermediaries looking to Western models. And like the ideologues of Japanese domesticity, the men promoting suburban living molded the new ideal from a mixture of cultural material that reflected native conditions as well as foreign models.

Regional differences in the growth of rail capital within Japan also played a role in determining the shape of suburban development. Although railroad construction began in the capital, the first planned suburbs were built by railroad companies in the Osaka-Kobe region. From the opening of the first line between Shinbashi Station in Tokyo and Yokohama in 1872 until the 1910s, the state dominated the construction and management of railroads, pursuing the military and economic goal of linking the entire country by rail. Several private railroad companies were formed with support from the state, but in 1906, under pressure from the Army, the government unified all the lines under a single state authority. By this time, the national network was essentially complete. With few exceptions, private rail companies were required to sell their assets to the government. Around Osaka, however, the situation was different. Private rail here had developed earlier. Taking advantage of a legal loophole, several companies had received licenses treating their lines as tramlines rather than railroads, thereby exempting them from nationalization. The result was that although 91 percent of the national network, including the Yamanote loop line which would become the core of Tokyo transit, fell under state management, Kansai became what historian Hara Takeshi has called a "kingdom of private rail," dominated by five local companies. Several of the lines ran roughly parallel to sections of the national lines, but had separate terminals, used wide-gauge instead of narrow-gauge track, and converted to electric power earlier.[1]

Rail construction in western Japan thus occurred in an environment of direct competition among multiple private authorities limited geographically by the nationalization law to the immediate environs of the Osaka-Kobe conurbation. With the opportunities to profit from long-distance transport closed to them, the directors of private rail companies recognized that they would have to generate steady demand for regional passenger transit. They did this by advertising famous sites, building amusement parks and resorts, attracting schools and other institutions, and, most of all, developing residential suburbs. The railroad companies thus became cultural entrepreneurs.[2]

No individual contributed more in terms of both actual construction and imaginative labor to the bourgeois redefinition of urban space than Osaka entrepreneur Kobayashi Ichizō, director of the Hankyū (Osaka Express) Railroad.[3] Like Iwaya Sazanami, Murai Gensai, and other cultural intermediaries of his generation, Kobayashi participated vocally in the public discourse on private life in which the terms of bourgeois culture were forged, while at the same time probing the growing bourgeois public for points to insert new opportunities to consume and to awaken new desires. Also like other successful Meiji propagandists, he adopted the rhetoric of social and domestic reform, presenting his own business goals as closely tied to the progress of the nation. Toward the end of his career, he himself occupied high government positions.

When the two branches of Hankyū's Minō-Arima Line opened in March 1910, the terminus at Minō was a minor local tourist spot and the Takarazuka terminus little more than a farming village. The line had originally been intended to continue past Takarazuka to the established hot spring resort of Arima, but this plan failed for lack of funding. What resulted was a rail line that led out from its urban hub into the nearby countryside without a socially or economically significant destination—a train to

Fig. 4.1 The exotic Takarazuka Paradise, called a "Western building" in company literature but redolent of what English architects of the time called "Saracenic" style, opened in July 1912. The building originally housed Japan's first indoor swimming pool, but this failed, in part because the authorities forbade mixed bathing. The pool was then converted into an exhibition space and theater for the revue (courtesy Ikeda bunko).

nowhere.[4] In the early years, making a somewhere out of this nowhere tested Kobayashi's ingenuity. He built a zoo in Minō and a modern hot spring resort called "Paradise" in Takarazuka, with one of the country's first indoor swimming pools (see Fig. 4.1). When the zoo failed, the company promoted the natural landscape of Minō for picnicking and hiking. When the pool in Takarazuka proved unpopular, it was converted to a theater for a "girls' chorus," which would subsequently grow into the most famous product of Kobayashi's cultural empire, the Takarazuka Revue.[5]

Eventually, Kobayashi would arrive at his empire-building formula, which linked three consumption sites on one private rail line: the urban terminal with a department store and shopping center at one end, leisure and tourist sites at the other, and residential subdivisions of single-family detached houses in between, all managed by the railroad company. It would be no hyperbole to say that with this formula Kobayashi invented the most influential commercial structure to shape the twentieth-century Japanese metropolis, since it was subsequently copied by all the major private lines that developed in Tokyo in the 1920s.[6] Suburban housing provided this structure its backbone, ensuring daily riders as the company accumulated capital for further expansion.

Kobayashi's marketing strategies for suburban real estate included other elements unprecedented in Japan, several of which were subsequently imitated in Tokyo. First among these was the subdivision itself, with ready-built houses for sale, promoted in print advertisements that included house plans, maps, and blurbs itemizing the merits of the site. Equally innovative was Kobayashi's offer to sell the houses on an installment plan. The least expensive could be purchased for a down payment of 200 yen followed by ten years of monthly payments of 12 yen.[7] Since the starting salary for a bank employee with higher education was about 40 yen per month at the time, the installment plan put Hankyū houses within reach of many professionals.[8]

Yet buying property was unusual at the time, particularly in Osaka. Although possession of a house was the usual basis of citizenship rights in the commoner quarters of Tokugawa-era cities, and the franchise was limited under the modern state to taxpayers, almost all of whom were landlords, homeownership was not a goal widely pursued before the twentieth century. The article in "One Hundred Walks of Life" describing a typical upper-level bureaucrat in Tokyo in 1904 assumed the man's family would be living in a rented house.[9] In Osaka during the Tokugawa period, even some well-off merchants with large households of clerks and apprentices lived in rented houses, presumably to avoid the public duties imposed by the government on householders. City authorities issued edicts urging those who could afford property to buy.[10] That the authorities felt compelled to do so is a fair indicator of the preference for renting. The housing rental system was so well developed that specialist businesses leased *tatami* mats and interior sliding doors, since houses were typically rented without flooring or partitions to allow tenants greater flexibility.[11]

The suburban spec-built house put its occupants in a new relation to the dwelling site, different from either the transiency of the urban tenant or the multigenerational stability of the landed peasant household. "Modern house sites are chosen according to an 'abstract function,'" as Suzuki Hiroyuki

Fig. 4.2 Advertising pamphlets for real estate sold by the Hankyū Railroad: (*left*) "This House Is Yours!" (*right*) "House and Lot for Two Yen per Month" (courtesy Ikeda bunko).

notes; consumers consider a list of factors, from sanitation to social status, often without having any personal connection to the place.[12] At the same time, the buyer in a new district gambles on the prospect that a place lacking history as a town will develop into a town worth staying in or worth the investment. Propaganda issued by the rail lines sought to allay anxieties that an unknown area would prove inhospitable or ultimately fail to develop as promised.[13] These traits in speculative housing—its removal from any traditional community context and its lack of history—also made a space for advertising to fill with fantasy images. As compensation for the risks of buying property and moving away from the convenience and familiarity of the city, Kobayashi and the developers who followed him conjured an entire lifestyle associated with the suburbs. Central to this lifestyle were images of leisure, to be enjoyed in new tourist sites and occasional activities and made habitual in the home. A sense of place was thus created anew on the *tabula rasa* of suburban tracts.

Whereas the other railroad companies sold land or built rental houses, Kobayashi chose to go a step further and offer the suburban house and lot as a finished product. In a culture of tenancy, this meant persuading consumers of the value of homeownership. Certainly, property had some intrinsic appeal, which was addressed directly in Hankyū advertisements with banners declaring "Fine Estates You Can Afford to Buy" or "This House Is Yours!" (see Fig. 4.2).[14] The company's publicity magazine *Sanyō suitai* (Mountain and Water Vistas) went well beyond this direct approach, however, bringing together several elements from contemporary bourgeois discourse and embellishing them to make the suburban house and garden an essential part of the new cultural identity. *Sanyō suitai* played to class desires by hinting that suburbanites would be guaranteed the exclusive company of others like themselves. The magazine also exploited emerging bourgeois fears of the city by promising a healthy environment and promoting the bucolic suburban landscape. It also drew upon the ideology of domesticity, which had by this time saturated the women's popular press. It was here that Kobayashi exercised the greatest imagination, repackaging the domestic reformers' *katei* in a form that would give it allure, and ultimately planting in Japanese soil a cultural model of remarkable power and longevity.

## A Class-Based "Tokyo Style"

Ikeda Muromachi, the first of more than ten planned developments of ready-built houses, went on the market the day the line opened in March 1910. Construction began on four other districts soon afterward. Ikeda consisted of 200 detached houses of four to seven rooms, on rectangular lots of 100 *tsubo* each, laid out on a ten-block grid. The houses were offered at prices between 3,000 and 4,500 yen on a ten-year installment plan. Advertisements in each issue of *Sanyō suitai* stressed that the best properties would go first, further feeding the speculative sensibility that new suburban property invoked. Maps were printed showing the dwindling number of houses still available on the site. Together with the planned subdivision, this bargain-table display of property was something novel, since real estate trading had only recently emerged as an independent profession, and sales of residential property were often conducted secretly to avoid embarrassment to the seller (see Fig. 4.3).[15]

Although *Sanyō suitai* made frequent mention of Europe and the United States, Hankyū's immediate points of reference for architecture and town planning were the streets lined with modest two-story houses on regular

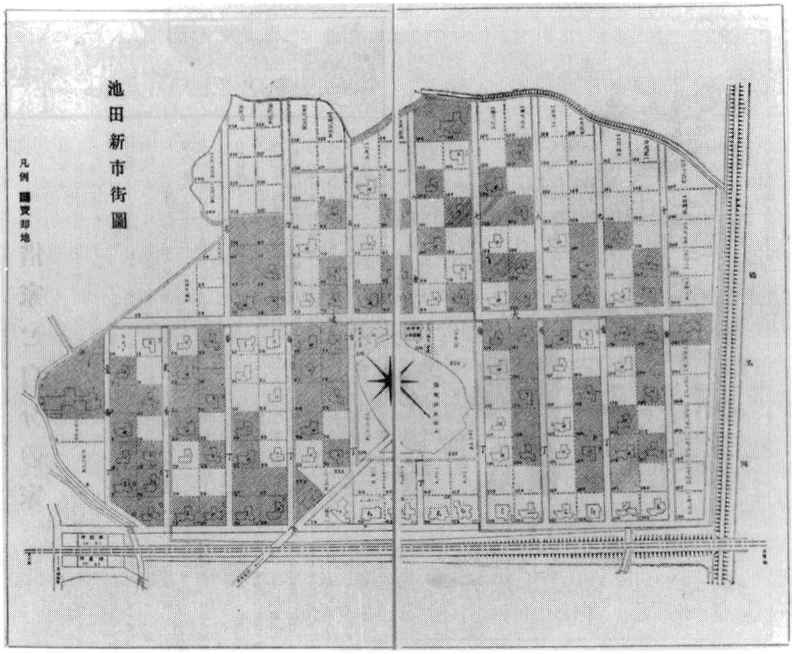

Fig. 4.3 (*top*) The first map of lots in Ikeda Muromachi to appear in the Hankyū line promotional magazine *Sanyō suitai* (1914 *rinjigō*). Lots already sold are blacked out. (*bottom*) Ikeda Muromachi in the early 1910s, shortly after its completion (courtesy of Ikeda bunko).

fenced lots in Tokyo's Yamanote district. *Sanyō suitai* referred to the Hankyū houses as "Tokyo gentleman's style" (*Tōkyōfū shinshi muki*) or "in the stylish Tokyo construction" (*Tōkyō no sukina kamae*). From the perspective of Osakans, who were accustomed to living in a commercial city of densely built rowhouses, the small detached houses occupied by Tokyo's bureaucrats, company professionals, and intellectuals, neither urban shophouses nor farmhouses, belonged to an alien culture.[16] Since the Meiji government's abolition of ascriptive status groups, occupying a house with a gate had become the common aspiration of young men seeking success in Tokyo. Hankyū packaged and promoted this ideal, seeking to persuade Osaka men that a more cosmopolitan bourgeois lifestyle was only a short train ride away. At the same time, as the use of the word *suki* (here translated "stylish") hints, having a house and garden outside the city's commercial districts, far from one's place of business, evoked older images of male retreat and devotion to elegant leisure pursuits.

Suburban development itself did not dictate either owner-occupied housing or the "Tokyo gentleman's" model. The first suburban houses built by the rival Hanshin railway, for example, one year before Ikeda Muromachi, were rented rowhouses.[17] Hanshin and Kobayashi's other rivals tended to sell or rent land to developers rather than build whole districts themselves. Unlike Hankyū's planned neighborhoods of ready-built houses, piecemeal development brought a mixture of housing types and consequently of classes. As one resident of the Kobe suburb Tengachaya lamented to the letters column of Hanshin's *Suburban Life* (*Kōgai seikatsu*) magazine, indiscriminately built houses of *nagaya* construction—"the chaff of Osaka style" housing—invited an influx of "porters and rickshaw drivers."[18] Hankyū advertising promised that their houses would "appeal to the taste of Osaka citizens" but stressed the contrast with the city and with other new suburbs:

> Just have a look at the houses for the so-called suburban life being offered to you along all the rail lines. If they are not the same type of designs as the houses built in downtown Osaka, where the houses are crowded together, they're unpleasant things of the back-to-back tenement type, and moreover with tasteless high fences and thick hedges—you will be surprised how woefully ill-suited to your desires they are.[19]

Bourgeois readers would have had no difficulty grasping the implicit message: where back-to-back tenements went, porters and rickshaw drivers were not far behind. Explicitly and implicitly, other Hankyū publications suggested the advantages of social homogeneity. An article in the first issue of *Sanyō suitai* stated that "all the residents are middle-class (*chūryū*) or above, and the harmony [between neighbors] overflows outdoors."[20] Elsewhere, a woman described having moved to the "gentleman's village" of Okamachi on the Hankyū line for the sake of her children, to get away from the prostitution quarters, moving-picture houses, and sideshows of the city. Since the residents of Okamachi were all "wealthy merchants, company, or bank employees," the children were "neat and tidy" (*kogirei ni kichinto shite iru*), and she had no worries about their playing with her own children.[21] Less-expensive developments such as Ikeda and Sakurai were equally certain to be homogeneous, since the prices of houses and lots within each varied little, and all would be occupied by the families of commuters.

Several recent Japanese authors have spoken of Hankyū as marketing a *yūtopia* (utopia). The term is attractively vague, and Kobayashi himself might well have used it had it been common at the time, but these first planned residential suburbs were neither social-reformist utopias like Ebenezer Howard's garden cities nor private arcadias for the rich like Norman Shaw's Hampstead Garden Suburb in London or Frederick Law Olmsted's Riverside, Illinois.[22] *Sanyō suitai* occasionally referred to "garden cities," but Ikeda Muromachi and the Hankyū developments that followed it were more commonly called simply *shin shigai*, "new towns." Their design was firmly rooted in mass marketing, based on repeated tests of what the Osaka market would bear. Western houses the company built failed to sell, prompting Kobayashi to abandon them quickly, although the few that were completed provided conspicuous landmarks for the developments.[23] The first promotional pamphlet promised tree-lined streets, a park and flower garden, a club with billiards, a buying co-op, electricity, and sanitary facilities,[24] yet the Ikeda streets ultimately had no trees or sidewalks, and the park was dominated by the precincts of a Shinto shrine that had been on the site before Hankyū purchased it. Subsequently both the club and buying cooperative failed, two signs that the new suburbs would not develop easily into autonomous communities. Thus Hankyū experimented in only a limited way with providing more than private houses and uniform lots, abandoning whatever proved to be an ineffective investment. Limiting its investment in facilities and landscaped open space, Hankyū offered instead an affordable "Tokyo style." Yet Kobayashi's strategies were no less innovative for this.

Hankyū's new towns were the first real estate enterprise in Japan to target a wide audience of urban professionals and appeal to them with the rhetoric of the emerging bourgeois ideal.

## Healthy Areas

Late Meiji urbanites contended with frequent alarms about dangers to their health. More often than not, the source of danger was in the cities, and those threatened as well as the already ill were advised to expose themselves to country air. With characteristic cynicism, the narrator of Soseki's *I Am a Cat* (1906) noted the proliferation of outdoor cures:

> Only recently have we heard that we should take exercise, drink milk, dash cold water over ourselves, dive into the sea, seclude ourselves in the mountains, and eat mist for the good of our health. These are all recent maladies which have infected this divine land from Western countries, and these suggestions should be classified as being as dangerous as the pest, tuberculosis, and neurasthenia.[25]

Both the ailments and their cures were new and strongly associated with the environment. One could almost say that hygienic discourse *invented* the notion of "environment," something invisible and enveloping that could nurture or endanger human health. Environmental thinking, frequently fusing notions of physical and moral health, endowed the suburbs with an intrinsic value they had not possessed before.[26]

There can be no question that the epidemics that afflicted late nineteenth-century cities provided good incentives to leave for those who could afford it. Measles, cholera, dysentery, typhoid, and tuberculosis spread through urban populations throughout the country after the opening of ports to international trade.[27] Particularly in the summer, when food spoiled and water-borne disease spread easily, hot springs and seaside resorts offered havens from infection. The skeptical view of Soseki's cat—and his telling inclusion of the Victorian malady of neurasthenia—should remind us, however, of the various ideological and physical mediators between the diseases pushing urban residents to leave and the salubrious mountain and seaside locations attracting them.

The discourse of public health that sustained bourgeois anxiety about the city evolved constantly as the diseases themselves changed. By the turn of the twentieth century, the threat of cholera had largely passed, but its place was taken by other contagions. Plague created a panic when the first Japanese deaths in the port of Kobe announced its arrival in 1899. Tuberculosis had been known for some years, but with the passing of the big cholera epidemics, it became the next major focus of hygiene efforts.[28] Just as each contagion had its own life cycle and mode of transmission, the public responses to each mapped urban space differently. Cholera, renowned for its rapid spread, prompted cordoning, disinfecting, and immediate quarantining of victims. Plague was strongly associated with the ports, as well as with the cotton mills, since a large proportion of the deaths in 1899–1900 were linked to raw cotton imported from China to Osaka's booming textile industry. Authorities responded to plague by cordoning larger areas, enclosing whole neighborhoods with metal fencing, and placing them under daily surveillance. The Home Ministry had police draw detailed maps of Kobe and Osaka, numbering and marking the residence of each victim. Finally in April 1900, amid increasing panic, authorities razed a block of forty-four slum dwellings believed to be a source of the disease.[29] Like the hygienists' home, the plague-afflicted city was envisioned as a bounded space, threatened at its borders. In contrast, tuberculosis was airborne and chronic. It could not be entirely expunged and called for public education and vigilance. Personal hygiene took precedence over broad urban sanitation projects. Together with the schools, newspapers and popular magazines conveyed word of the threat and the precautions to be taken. Instead of an embattled fortress, the city became something organic and threatening itself, its contours determined by carbon levels and mortality statistics. The meaning of the urban environment thus took on a new aspect with each shift in epidemiology and hygiene policy (see Fig. 4.4).[30]

Physically, the growing rail network brought country resorts closer to the cities, making possible short stays that fit within the new time regime of the working week, the weekend, and the summer vacation (all instituted for state employees in 1876). By the end of the century, many of the major spas around Tokyo and Osaka were reachable by train, and new seaside and mountain resorts had been opened with the arrival of rail lines. Hirade Kōjirō's compendium of manners and customs in the capital, *Tōkyō fūzokushi*, published in 1898, reported that the tradition of escaping the summer heat by hiring boats on the Sumida River in town was on the wane, since those who could afford it boarded the trains for leisure places elsewhere: "People

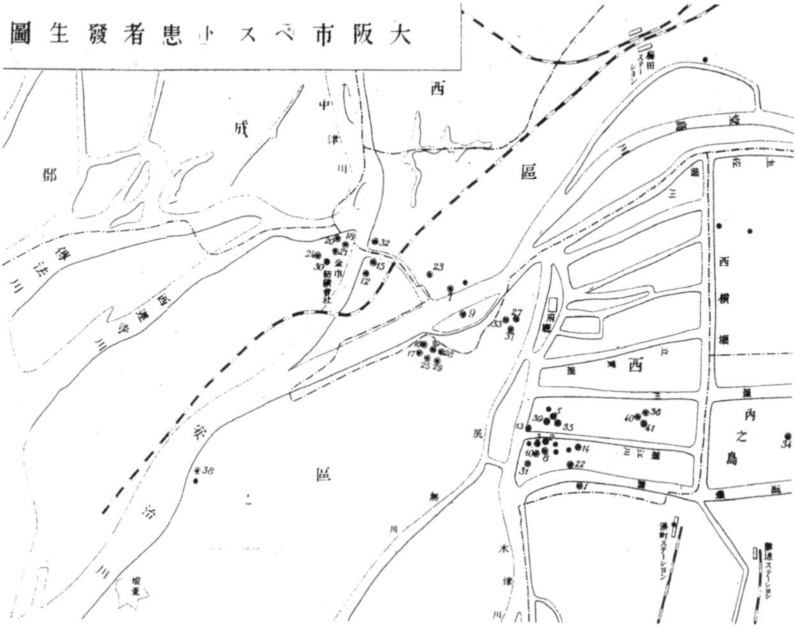


Fig. 4.4 The city as a dangerous environment: Home Ministry map of plague victims (solid dots) in Osaka, 1900.

today go to Kamakura, Zushi, Oiso, and Hakone, head into the mountains far from the city at Nikkō and Chūzenji, or pass their time at the shore, visiting hot springs and sea-bathing." Hirade added that as a result the recreation boats and restaurants along the riverbanks were enjoying only a fraction of the summer trade of former days.[31]

The model provided by resident Westerners, together with native exemplars such as doctors and military officers, inspired general interest in outdoor recreation activities and put new resorts on the map. When cholera caused many families to flee Tokyo in the summer of 1886, resulting in a rush on lodging in Kantō-region hot spring towns, German doctor Erwin Baelz, physician to the imperial family, boosted the popularity of the mountain spa at Kusatsu by endorsing the medical value of its waters. Army Surgeon-General Matsumoto Jun is said to have popularized the custom of sea-bathing when he went to Ōiso to cure his rheumatism in the same year. Tokutomi Roka's best-selling novel *Hototogisu* (1898) sparked a hot-spring boom with its idyllic depiction of the landscape around the spa town of Ikaho, where the hero and heroine were portrayed enjoying a fleeting

Fig. 4.5 The family of agronomist Yokoi Tokiyoshi "spending a pure and beautiful day enjoying the pleasures of the family circle out of doors," on the banks of the Tama River, captured by a photographer for the *Ladies' Graphic* (*Fujin gahō*, no. 102 [Nov. 1914]). Photographs like this of prominent figures with their families in rustic suburban locations, at the shore, or at the mountain resort of Karuizawa became common in the *Ladies' Graphic* of the 1910s, displaying the bourgeois fashion for outdoor recreation and registering a new informality in the presentation of the bourgeoisie.

moment of domestic happiness before he departed with the Navy to fight in the Sino-Japanese War and she contracted tuberculosis.[32] Ikaho was already known for its hot springs—the opening line of Roka's novel referred to its fame—but in *Hototogisu* it became a setting for conjugal romance and the great romantic affliction rather than simply a spa; and the premise for the scene was itself modern, since the couple had come to Ikaho for a honeymoon, an imported new travel experience (see Fig. 4.5).

In addition to disease, pollution gave health-conscious residents cause to leave the cities, particularly Osaka, at the turn of the century. As the heart of the country's textile industry, Osaka had become a city of smokestacks, known in Japan as the "Manchester of the Orient."[33] Unlike Tokyo, where the Yamanote district in the west still retained the generous lot divisions and much of the rich vegetation it had possessed when it was made up of samurai estates, residential Osaka was confined within the grid of the commercial and industrial city, whose streets were lined with rowhouses. By the 1910s, the air in Osaka was reported to be worse than London.[34] Already in mid-Meiji, some of the upper tier of the city's commercial bourgeoisie had begun moving their primary residences outside the city, in the pattern seen earlier in English industrial cities like Manchester and Birmingham.[35] The incidence of tuberculosis was high in the mills, which were also the source of Osaka's smog. The emphasis on fresh air as both precaution and cure served as excellent propaganda for the suburbs.

Yet with pollution as with epidemic disease, the relationship between industrialization and bourgeois flight was not a simple one. The bourgeois exodus from industrial Osaka was precipitated as much by changed consciousness of the city as by actual bodily discomfort caused by pollution. Through the activities and public pronouncements of police, municipal officials, and Home Ministry bureaucrats and through the writings of journalists and social reformers, residents of Japan's major cities came to perceive the city as an organic body whose overall health affected the health of individual residents. Apprehended through maps and statistics, the environmentalist city was a place that no one had actually seen. The authority of official sources and of Western scientific expertise gave it substance. Already dominant in Western urban discourse, environmentalism filtered gradually downward from state institutions to popular consciousness during the last two decades of the Meiji period.

Environmentalism was written into the country's first city-planning law (known as *shiku kaisei*), passed in Tokyo in 1888, as well as police regulations on housing in slum districts and similar initiatives in Osaka. Advocates of slum clearance stressed that contagious disease tended to begin among the lower classes and, "when most virulent, attack people of the middle ranks and above."[36] Already in 1881, members of Tokyo's Prefectural Assembly arguing for the demolition of slums in Kanda Hashimoto-chō had spoken of the policy's benefits to "general hygiene" (*ippan eisei*), expressing an idea certainly learned from European urban planners, since it had no native precedent.[37] Accounts of conditions in the poorest pockets of Tokyo and Osaka appeared in newspapers from the 1880s. Following the model of the London studies by Booth, Mayhew, and others, reports such as Matsubara Iwagorō's *Saiankoku no Tōkyō* (In Darkest Tokyo, 1893) and Yokoyama Gennosuke's *Nihon no kasō shakai* (Lower-Class Society in Japan, 1898) exposed the living conditions of the poor in vivid and intimate detail, awakening bourgeois alarm.[38]

As the study of cities developed, urban discourse evolved from reportage on specific places, the "dark continent" of the slums in Tokyo's Samegahashi and Osaka's Nago-chō, to greater scientific abstraction, describing the city in aggregates, human and nonhuman, tangible and intangible. Newspapers in eastern and western Japan published and analyzed statistics on the poor, divided by sex and age cohort, on mortality from respiratory disease, on numbers of factories and chimneys, and on the area of farmland versus residential land within city limits.[39] In a series of articles in the *Yomiuri shinbun* in 1906, agronomist Yokoi Tokiyoshi demonstrated the detrimental effect of urban overcrowding by calculating the total volume of carbon dioxide produced by Tokyo's two million residents.[40]

Where the numbers were unavailable for Japanese cities, writers relied on examples from elsewhere. Indeed, comparisons to Western cities, usually unfavorable to Japan, were an equally essential feature of environmentalist discourse. Police in Japan monitored hygiene and social statistics after 1877, but comprehensive urban surveys were not conducted until Tokyo's first modern census in 1908.[41] In their place, writers introduced figures for Berlin, London, and New York. By inference, conditions in Japanese cities were as bad or worse. The irrefutable logic of social statistics erased other differences. Waseda professor and social reformer Abe Isoo, the country's first scholar to speak explicitly of "urban problems" (*toshi mondai*),[42] based his seminal treatise on the subject, *Ōyō shiseiron* (Applied urban administration; 1908), entirely on cases from the West. Abe asserted that all social problems were urban problems and stressed hygiene as the first priority of urban reform, noting that Japan lagged far behind Western cities in this measure of civilization.[43] When Dr. Kitazato published the first statistics on tuberculosis in Tokyo in 1902, he reported that Tokyo compared poorly with every major Western city except St. Petersburg.[44] Readers of the *Ōsaka Asahi* newspaper in November 1911 learned that the English slum reformer Sydney Webb, touring Japanese cities in the company of Abe Isoo, judged the living conditions of Osaka's citizens to be "fifty years behind London."[45]

Beginning around the turn of the twentieth century, then, Japanese newspaper readers were encouraged to visualize their cities as organic totalities and barometers of national progress and well-being. In place of the local specificities of urban culture, environmentalism defined Tokyo and Osaka's identities in terms of enumerated quantities, and the data of these aggregates were then translated back to the personal level in warnings to the individual resident. In this new urban consciousness, the suburbs offered not only tangible pleasures or a temporary refuge, but long-term invisible benefits to the body. As Satō Kenji has observed, "The element of uncertainty in contagious disease always generates an excess of meaning," creating a space to be filled by the imagination.[46] This ominous uncertainty characterized not only contagions but also the city generally in environmental discourse. At the same time, the new territory opened by the railroads generated another excess of meaning, a fantasy surplus attached to unoccupied land, rural vistas, new towns, and private homes. Images of the corrupt city and the pure suburb promoted by intermediaries like Kobayashi insinuated themselves into these spaces of fear and anticipation.

The Hanshin railroad company was the first of the private developers to exploit environmentalist perceptions, in a booklet containing fourteen doctors' endorsements of suburban living.[47] The doctors offered predictable if sometimes hyperbolic statements, reminding readers that the air and water were cleaner in the suburbs, providing examples of patients cured by leaving the city, and claiming that suburban living assured longevity. The booklet labeled the Hanshin suburbs "healthy areas" (*kenkōchi*), a term that would be used frequently thereafter.[48] *Suburban Life* (*Kōgai seikatsu*), a biweekly newspaper published in the offices of a local developer on the Nankai line, took a similar approach, printing a doctor's report on the healthful effects of country air, along with statistics from London and Tokyo (in lieu of data for Osaka) and a series introducing the Garden City movement.[49]

Kobayashi followed suit in Hankyū promotional publications, borrowing the authority of other medics to support the claim that the hills north of Osaka, reached by the Hankyū line, were healthier than the shore, where the Hanshin and Nankai trains ran. At the same time, he assembled statistics and medical opinions to show how dangerous it was to live in the city. Announcing that "Osaka is the Number One Place for Tuberculosis in the World," *Sanyō suitai* reprinted the findings of a report on the health of paupers in the city, among whom it was found that 11.67 percent were infected with the disease. Estimates by two doctors of the percentage of the national population with various diseases followed, along with the experts' conclusion that in sum, roughly half the nation was sick. These sources provided the grounds for the article to claim that Osaka must have the highest tuberculosis rate in the world, and that one could safely say that half the city was ill. Noting that the consequences for the welfare of the nation were grave, and for individual homes tragic, the article called for comprehensive hygiene reform before reaching its goal of counseling, "without any intention of self-promotion," that the reader's safest choice was to retreat to the pure water, pure air, and beautiful vistas along the Minō-Arima line. A photograph of the company's houses set against a backdrop of verdant hills accompanied the article.[50]

## A Taste for the Country

Even as suburban entrepreneurs appealed to hygienic concerns, they could draw upon a strong contemporary interest in rural landscapes and country living that was both aesthetic and moral. Hankyū real estate's first promotional pamphlet began by evoking the environmental dangers of the city, but shifted gears to make a positive appeal to what it called "country taste":

> Citizens of Osaka! The beautiful city on the water is a fading distant dream, and it is your misfortune to live under dark skies in a capital of smoke.
>
> How you must feel the cheerlessness of urban life with a shudder of terror when you contemplate the sanitary conditions of Osaka's citizenry, among whom the mortality rate is eleven people for every ten born. And at the same time how desperate must be your desire for an enjoyable suburban life rich in country taste (*den'en shumi*)!

The phrase *den'en shumi* had special resonance in 1909. The previous year, drawing upon Ebenezer Howard's famous utopian tract, the Home Ministry had published a book called *Den'en toshi* (Garden Cities), using the same word *den'en* (made up of characters that literally mean "rice-paddy garden"), and journalists were writing about application of the Garden City idea to Japan. The Home Ministry's book was not a translation of Howard; after introducing Howard's plans and summarizing portions of a different English work, it concluded with a conservative response that sought to establish that Japan had always been a nation of ideal "garden villages," populated by diligent rice-farming peasants.[51] Nevertheless, it contributed to an emerging idealization of space outside the city as the countryside, an abstract landscape; as *den'en*, that is, rather than as the collective provinces (*chihō*) or individual native places (*furusato*). Since the turn of the century, new movements in prose, poetry, and painting had reconceived nature for the first time in Japan as the antithesis of civilization and prompted the excursions of young intellectuals (and legions of schoolchildren) into the hinterlands of major cities in order to apprehend the beauty of the rural landscape through direct experience (*jikken*). The popular suburban excursion and the representations of suburban places that writers and painters produced from it shaped a new consciousness of landscape that coupled aesthetic appreciation to individual discovery, exploration, and occupation. The Home Ministry's paean to the beauty of rural Japan adopted the same romantic perspective for its conservative social aims.[52]

The expansive and expansionist aesthetic of landscape was counterbalanced by a bourgeois ethos of self-improvement through simple living and physical labor in a rural setting. Another rhetorical commodity circulating internationally at the turn of the century, the "simple life" was introduced to Japan in 1905 through translation of a popular work by French minister Charles Wagner titled *La vie simple*, which came with the endorsement of U.S. President Theodore Roosevelt. The following year, the book inspired a Japanese magazine called *Kan'i seikatsu* (The Simple Life). The editors quoted Wagner and Thoreau, as well as socialist writers, sometimes advocating radical social reforms but more often simply promoting domestic intimacy, the abandonment of social formalities, and the pleasure of suburban activities such as vegetable gardening. Simple-life advocates came from a broad political spectrum. Popular writer Tokutomi Roka, who had adopted pacifism after visiting Tolstoy in 1906 and had strong socialist ties, moved to the suburbs of Tokyo to farm in 1907 and addressed his large public with introspective novels and essays about the experience.[53] Meanwhile, harking back to the ancient Chinese ideal of the gentleman recluse, several prominent military men built themselves suburban retreats where they donned work clothes and farmed on weekends.[54]

*Sanyō suitai* and rival magazines elaborated their own versions of the suburban gentleman farmer. The front page of the Nankai Line's *Suburban Life*, which described itself as the newspaper for the "country taste," bore a sketch of a man in boots, small-brimmed hat, and moustache, carrying a hoe. A bucolic landscape with thatched farmhouses spread across the masthead above him. This gentleman farmer—neither peasant in straw sandals nor businessman in a Western suit—was an eclectic invention much like the new suburbs themselves. *Sanyō suitai* featured its own suburban farmer in a sketch at the front of some issues. He was dressed in a style closer to that of the typical peasant but depicted gazing with satisfaction on a crop of two sun-

Fig. 4.6 Suburban gentleman farmers. (*left*) Sketch of a gentleman-farmer on the masthead of *Suburban Life*, the Nankai Railroad's promotional newspaper (*Kōgai seikatsu*, no. 14 [Sept. 1908]). (*right*) "Country Life in the Autumn" ("Aki no den'en seikatsu," *Sanyō suitai* no. 4 [Oct. 1913]). The Hankyū Railroad's homelier gentleman-farmer admires a crop of two sunflowers beside his "common-man's house."

flowers beside a small tile-roofed house (see Fig. 4.6). This must have reasonably represented the actual scale of operations most weekend farmers on the Hankyū line would engage in, but the magazine also implied that suburban living might develop into a true return to the land. The "ideal common man's house," according to Kobayashi, occupied 100 *tsubo* with a garden of fruit trees separated by a low hedge from a vegetable garden, grape vines on a trellis over the path, and goats, chickens, and rabbits on the other side, "as facilities developed with each year."[55] Gesturing toward an international icon of the rural simple-life ethic, the magazine enjoined readers to try the "country life of Tolstoy," a "life of taste."[56]

## Selling Domesticity

Invoking classic metaphors in the Anglo-American lexicon of domesticity, Hankyū's promotional pamphlet told readers, "Gentlemen, your house is your castle and refuge," and stressed how important it was to the working man to retreat at the end of each day to a house in healthy surroundings where his family waited.[57] Familiar as this image was to Japanese who had contact with Westerners or literature from the West, however, the ideal of the suburban house as family refuge suffered from a lack of native Japanese models. Both Edo and Osaka had seen large suburban expansions under Tokugawa rule, but the new suburbs were not associated with family life. Already in the late seventeenth century, shogunal officials and wealthy merchants in Edo had built villas in former farmland and reclaimed land east of the Sumida River.[58] The merchant elite of Osaka retreated to unlicensed pleasure quarters known as "the islands" (*shima*), also built in districts of reclaimed land at the periphery of the city. In these places, an antinomian culture of play (*asobi*) developed, beyond the bounds of Tokugawa society as the districts themselves were beyond the bounds of the established city.[59] Although prostitutes were frequent participants in this culture, and stories abounded of fortunes lost in it, many intellectuals, far from condemning it as decadent, regarded it as the flower of urban civilization, since it was founded on elegant leisure pursuits such as music, poetry, and tea, which required long cultivation. For the merchants of Osaka, banquets at the teahouses often sealed a deal in lieu of a written contract, making these districts integral to business relations as well.[60] This world of leisure in the suburbs of the major cities still flourished in cities of the Meiji period, although aficionados lamented the loss of past cultural standards. Since men's leisure here was taken in the company of other men and of professional women, not family, and the favored pastimes were considered unproductive, moral reformers decried it.[61]

Historically, places of private retreat from the mundane affairs of the world had also been divorced from the family. The typical forms of nonreligious seclusion included the retirement cottage, the scholarly hermitage, and the mistress's house.[62] All these were places for men to isolate themselves from their families. The history of the word *ryō*, which was often used to describe suburban houses near Edo, suggests the association with places and activities anathema to domestic reform advocates. Originally used to refer to a monk's dormitory, it came also to mean a tea connoisseur's hut, a private villa, the house of a kept woman, and an illicit house of assignation.[63] In contrast to nineteenth-century England and the United States, where the bourgeois suburb was built as a refuge to protect the family from the evils of the city, the nineteenth-century suburb in Japan was primarily a male pleasure ground.

Despite their tension with domestic ideals, the traditional connotations of suburban retreat could not readily be suppressed. Equally important, men still enjoyed diverse opportunities for play in the city, including legal prostitution. The rail line's single-family cottages presented an entirely different model of the suburb and of uses for a man's leisure time. In the articles and stories in *Sanyō suitai*, many of them penned by Kobayashi himself, one can see the special effort that was made to attract men to this model. A novelist manqué as well as a canny salesman, Kobayashi used his literary talents to invest the ideology of bourgeois domesticity with subtle promises of male pleasure. If claims for the healthfulness of the suburbs and the promise of homeownership were Hankyū's overt sales devices, the magazine also reveals other, subtler devices, calculated to sublimate the libidinal forces in the traditional modes of male leisure and redirect them toward an erotically charged yet safely domesticated commodity.

By 1910, the word *katei* was in common parlance, and the bourgeois family image it conveyed (albeit unspecific with regard to actual economic status and household composition) required no new advocates. The same talk of domesticity, or "*katei*-orientation," as the magazine called it, suffused the pages of *Sanyō suitai* and the advertising for events at the Takarazuka resort. *Katei* rhetoric to this time had been evangelical in tone and overwhelmingly directed toward women. By contrast, Kobayashi's interests were commercial, and his primary customers were male. In its commercial appropriation, *katei* became more than the reformers' code-word for a new social regime within the household; an object for a man to imagine and then possess.[64]

The "domesticization" of Hankyū culture marked a decisive shift early in the company's career, succinctly recorded in the calendar of events at the Takarazuka spa. During its first two years of operation, 1911 and 1912, the spa sought to entertain men in the pattern of many other hot spring spas. Geisha from Osaka danced and staged a "theater of beauties." An exhibit of art and curios associated with prostitutes, called the *yūjokai*, was held at the end of each year. Then, in the spa's third year, the geisha were supplanted by the Girls' Opera Troupe, and in place of the *yūjokai*, Kobayashi sponsored a "Women's Exposition" (Fujin hakurankai). This was followed in 1914 by a "Wedding Exposition" (Konrei hakurankai), and in 1915 by a "Home Exposition" (Katei hakurankai), as if tracing an imaginary female life cycle (see Fig. 4.7).[65]

Fig. 4.7 Promotional pamphlet for the Women's Exposition, held at Takarazuka in spring 1913 (courtesy Edo-Tokyo Museum).

In the suburban developments, domesticity found architectural expression in the "family-centered house" championed by reformers since the turn of the century. The 1913 women's exposition included a competition to design floor plans for future Ikeda houses, with prize winners published in *Sanyō suitai*. The first prize winner followed the basic layout of the interior-corridor house type and was praised for it by the judge, who noted that "the plan abandons the traditional guest-orientation and approaches a family-orientation," and that by "arranging communication of the maid's room with the living and dining rooms in a convenient manner, it harmonizes the Western-style distribution of rooms with Japanese style." Similar virtues were cited for other Ikeda houses published in the magazine.[66]

Much of the domestic culture promoted by Hankyū was the imaginative creation of Kobayashi himself. His idea of a musical theater performed entirely by innocent teenage girls made a decisive break with existing entertainment forms, and he defended it on both moral and financial grounds against a musical director who wished to include male performers.[67] *Sanyō suitai* can be read as the script of Kobayashi's project of *katei*-imagining, a theatrical production of a kind itself, with roles for the doctors and other sources of scientific expertise, the writers, architects, and other cultural intermediaries, and, most important, for the new commuters, housewives, and children living on the Hankyū line. The magazine distributed these roles according to a gendered division of literary labor. Female contributors appeared as mouthpieces for reform, describing the suburbs' advantages for health, childrearing, and family harmony. A familiar cast of female educators offered expertise at the expositions and in the magazine on matters such as household budgeting, children's clothes and furniture, and kitchen reform. Male contributors, on the other hand, if not introduced as housing managers or health experts, wrote of personal pleasures: the pleasures of home, of gardening, even the pleasure of riding the train.

The magazine also included advertisements in the guise of news, reportage, and occasional fictional monologues and dialogues, most printed anonymously. In the last, the purest products of the editor's imagination, the *katei* as a man's object of desire emerged most vividly—not in isolation, however, but as part of a picture of the suburban lifestyle that was sketched with subtle erotic overtones. The speaker in a monologue called "Luncheon Time" ("Ranchon taimu"), for example, confessed to an invisible audience of officemates that since buying his own house, he had developed a "taste for home" (*katei no shumi*), and told them in detail what "home" signified to him:

> Boys, I bought a house and lot. You think I'm lying? If you think it's a lie, then come have a look at my estate some time; [I walk] through the elegant gate and down the concrete path, with oaks neatly planted on both sides, and as my shoes strike the pavement sharply I put my hand to the lattice door, the bell tinkles, and my wife comes out. I just pass from the entry through the hall to the room in the back, get out of my Western clothes and that's it—my house and my land are my castle, as they say. This is a feeling renters like you boys couldn't possibly understand.[68]

Reformist *katei* advocates had choreographed rituals that reinforced family togetherness. The *katei* promoted here was constituted instead through a daily ritual that confirmed the male householder's possession. Some form of this scene of the white-collar commuter returning to house and garden and waiting wife would be repeated by millions afterward (with the shedding of Western clothes marking the transition from public to private a distinctively Japanese feature). Homeownership was not in fact a prerequisite; other Osaka professionals commuted daily from rented houses and returned to waiting housewives. But this articulation, with its stagy details, was new.

This was Kobayashi the ad-man, inventing roles, or sketching roles just emerging, so that his gentlemen readers might imagine themselves on center stage. Only by buying a house, Kobayashi's script implied, could one transcend the prosaic experience of commuting and become master in this dramatic enactment of home.

Although he borrowed the elements of *katei* ideology, Kobayashi omitted the original stress on intimacy among family members. The remainder of the homecoming ritual for the man in the monologue above was a little gardening, then dinner taken on the veranda from an individual tray, and a private drink. Not a word of his lecture to the boys at the office was about the harmony of the family circle. Other family members beside his wife were not mentioned.

An anonymous article titled "My House" presented one man's experience buying a house in Ikeda Muromachi and showed the rites of possession in another form: the allocation of space within the house. The "family-centered" layout that *Sanyō suitai* had elsewhere endorsed did not dictate a program for actual occupants' use, particularly because of the flexibility of *tatami* rooms. The arrangement described by this Ikeda resident suggests that the Hankyū rendition of the *katei* ideal in no way impinged on the patriarch's domestic hegemony:

> On moving day, I determined the division of rooms and made strict orders to the members of the household—true, it's just four of us including me—not to interfere with one another. First of all, the eight-mat room next to the two-mat entry is my living quarters and study, the four-and-a-half-mat room to the right is the kitchen and maid's room, the six-mat room next to that is my wife and children's room and the dining room, and the eight-mat room on the second floor I've made a study and guest room.[69]

To prevent family members "interfer[ing] with one another," the master of the house here allocated himself the only private room, and the largest. It is likely that he conceived the second-floor study and guest room as his own space as well. This portrait of a *katei* also omits mention of the "pleasures of the family circle" or the "family-centered" house.

Since men in *Sanyō suitai* stories typically play the role of satisfied customers, proselytizing to other men, it is perhaps not surprising that women enter chiefly as part of the package. Issue number one, published in July 1913, follows articles advertising the natural beauty of Minō and new houses in Sakurai with "A Half-Hour in Sakurai," an anonymous piece of first-person reportage describing a visit to the newly built suburb at four o'clock one afternoon. The reporter opens his sketch by depicting a young woman alighting from the train, described as "a housemaid of seventeen or eighteen." The sketch proceeds to note her hairstyle and kimono sash, the bundle she is carrying, and her delicate steps, following her until she disappears through the gate of a house along the main street. Details of the townscape follow: workmen digging a well, the regular rows of houses, the variety of gates, the hills in the distance.

Repeatedly in this sketch, the narrator's eye stops to linger on a human element in the scene. A woman is espied through a bamboo screen and, beyond the boughs of a willow in the back garden, emerging onto the veranda of a house "as if in a picture." At a nearby house, a boy of twelve or thirteen is seen straddling the bough of a peach tree, lapping with relish at a peach. "The beautiful color of his cheeks could be mistaken for the peach itself. This must be the precious young master (*hizō no botchan*) of the house." Back at the station, again the reporter is among women: "a lady of 22 or 23" is described being sent off by her maid and little girl. The reporter records her appearance and words to her daughter and then speculates that she is going to bathe at the new Takarazuka spa.

In themselves, these vignettes from everyday life seem unremarkable, but as the observations of an anonymous male visitor, they acquire a voyeuristic character, evoking the pleasure of the male outsider as an invisible witness to others' (particularly women's) intimacy. The suburban bedroom town was a newly constructed world of women and children, which male householders rarely saw during the day. In the eyes of the visitor, the town during the day had an air of domestic privacy about it. The absence of other men added an erotic appeal to the sketch.[70]

In place of evocations of the "family circle," the domesticity of *Sanyō suitai* centers on conjugal romance. The fact that men departed from the bedroom suburb each day, leaving their wives behind, presented another opportunity for erotic innuendo, this time in a dialogue titled "Waiting Evening" ("Machi yoi"), in which two unnamed characters enact the familiar scenario of the husband returning home late to find his wife alone waiting. She has bolted the gate, and he must knock to be let in. When she admits to worrying about an intruder, he asks, "But what do we have to steal?" then catches her blushing and laughs, "Ah-hah, I see. If I'm not careful, you might be abducted." She replies, "It's no joke, dear. I truly am lonely." A lovers' spat ensues, as the wife becomes jealous at her husband's mention of the geisha in Takarazuka (this was before they had been replaced by the girls' opera). The dialogue closes in a literary equivalent of the cinematic fade-out: "The waiting evening moon secretly casts their shadows, jealously lighting the two whispering figures."[71]

Although the actual women writing about suburban life in *Sanyō suitai* speak of virtues rather than pleasures, women in the magazine's fiction are to be found enjoying themselves and advertising the attractions of the Hankyū new towns to one another. Here, too, the image of isolated women in the suburban landscape could be used to add allure. "Story of a New House," a dialogue between a young woman from town and a suburban acquaintance, sets the stage in the manner of a pocket romance: "'What a lovely house! How I envy you,' said the artless, round-faced housewife of eighteen or nineteen as she leaned on the second floor railing, heedless of the cool breeze that came across the verdant hills of Minō and disordered her hair." The ensuing dialogue served as an advertisement for the new Hankyū houses in Sakurai. "Why don't you ask your husband and move out here?" the suburban woman finally suggests. "But it must be lonely." "Not at all. A hundred new houses have been built here in Sakurai. They even have billiards at the club, and there's not the slightest inconvenience in getting daily necessities."[72] The slightly jarring reference to the masculine pastime of billiards in this conversation between two women is just another sign that these vignettes were written by and for men. Waiting wives, whether pining alone or entertaining one another with polite conversation, were part of the fantasy landscape.

A dialogue titled "Sisters" combines the themes of health and suburban isolation. The pale, hysteria-prone wife of an urban merchant visits her healthy and energetic younger sister, married to a scholar and living in the suburbs. The urban woman's husband, as she tells her sister in frustration, is frequently out on the town (*yoku asobu*). The suburban husband, by contrast, has become a faithful homebody, since he finds it too much trouble to go back to Osaka once he has returned from the office. "Bring your husband out on Sunday," the younger sister offers. "He can hear my husband's ideas on suburban living, and we'll take you to see an available house."[73]

Despite the common ground of the *katei* ideal and of new house designs that Kobayashi shared with the moral reformers of a decade earlier, these narrative vignettes set the home in a different discursive frame. Men extolling the return to a private house and waiting wife as a daily re-enactment of the pleasure of acquisition, men describing the titillation of visiting the Hankyū neighborhood when no other men are present, couples shown deriving erotic sustenance from the privacy of the suburban home, and women portrayed as part of an alluring landscape: each seems subtly calculated to arouse the desire of the male reader, while adroitly sublimating it toward the central proposition—which could be stated overtly but was made immeasurably more appealing by the libidinal surplus—namely to embrace domesticity by buying one of Hankyū's houses.

## The Economy of Domesticity and Desire

Utopian neither as a manmade natural landscape nor as a social reform experiment, the new towns on the Hankyū line did nevertheless represent a highly innovative vision with broad subsequent impact. It was most of all a commercial vision. Like Mitsukoshi and other contemporary commercial enterprises, Hankyū was selling the trappings of a lifestyle, and also like them, the company exploited the rhetoric of domestic reform. The pages of *Sanyō suitai* and other Hankyū publications reveal Kobayashi's sensitive ear for the language of bourgeois reformism and his ability to draw from the intellectual trends of the time for marketing purposes (see Fig. 4.8).

Kobayashi contributed to Japanese bourgeois culture the ideals of homeownership and of the suburb as family refuge. To promote these values, already well established in the Anglo-American context, he and other suburban entrepreneurs drew on environmentalist ideas from Europe and the United States as well as on images of the conjugal family. Each received a native inflection, however. In particular, since his audience could not be assumed to recognize the supreme virtue of either homeownership or monogamy, he sought to appeal with the added component of erotic pleasure as something the commuting homeowner could keep stored in his suburban home.

Yet this eroticized commodity was never so distant from the social reformers' model of the ideal *katei*, which provided a necessary cloak of sanctity to the enterprise. Just as the urban environmentalism of Abe Isoo served early efforts to sell the suburbs, Kobayashi's commercial successes later enjoyed the endorsement of Abe himself, who surveyed the Hankyū plans with care, and even lectured on them at Waseda. In these lectures, the Hankyū subdivisions became "garden cities," farsighted solutions to the housing problem. Abe explained that the railroad company owned the land and not only sold houses

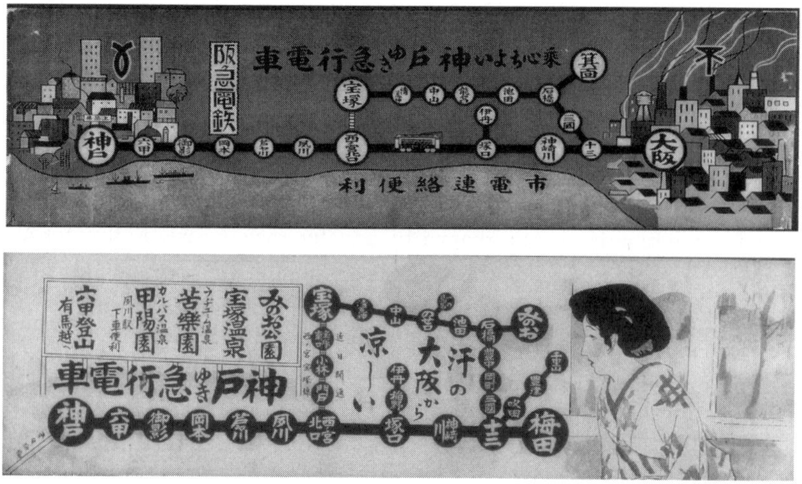


Fig. 4.8 Taishō-period posters advertising the Hankyū suburban line to Osaka tram riders. (*top*) This poster announces the line simply as a pleasant express route to Kobe, but the rendering highlights Osaka's reputation as a city of smokestacks, the "Manchester of the East," in keeping with the company's propaganda for suburban living. (*bottom*) The attractions listed here are a park, three hot springs, and hiking trails. The inclusion of a lone female train passenger shows the kind of subtle eroticism that Kobayashi Ichizō exploited in many of the company's promotional activities. (Courtesy Ikeda bunko.)

but could build them to order, and that buyers paid on a ten-year plan. "It is clear that if a method like this is gradually put into effect throughout the country, it could solve part of the urban social problem," he asserted. Although Hankyū had made not the slightest pretense of philanthropy and no direct reference to the Garden City movement, from Abe's vantage point, the contractual arrangement resulting in homeownership, and perhaps more importantly the planned suburban development itself as a physical form on the landscape, were sufficient grounds to treat the venture as a contribution to public welfare. These Japanese "garden cities," Abe acknowledged, were so far only for the middle classes, but if the same system could be extended to the working class in the future, with low-interest loans provided by the government, then Japan might achieve the fine results seen in Belgium.[74] Abe was a social reformer, whose political career included participation in the founding of the Socialist Party, chairmanship of the Fabian Society, and later election to Diet as a representative of the Social Democratic Party.[75] Yet his notions of social good and national progress allowed him to regard Kobayashi's suburban developments as a step toward the ideal society rather than merely another form of commercial capitalism. For the Meiji generation of reform ideologues and cultural intermediaries, the priority of establishing a common bourgeois culture permitted unlikely bedfellows.

As in the "paradise" of innocent teenage dancing girls at the end of the line, the eroticism that Kobayashi's housing advertisements imbued in Hankyū suburbs was ambiguous, fusing the purity of the place and the purity of its women into a landscape shaped by and for male desire. Reflecting its modern romantic sensibility, this landscape of desire, built around a domesticated female object, posed an antithesis to the shape of desire in the urban prostitution quarters that were the traditional locus of eroticism. Where the prostitution quarter offered the objects of desire sequestered but explicitly displayed and commodified, here a landscape without limits was suffused with desire, ever-present and inviting, but latent. The male consumer was asked to learn to savor the wait. Even the method of payment functioned as part of this psychic economy. The installment system, which promised complete possession in exchange for a long-term commitment, proposed to delay gratification in a manner that made it analogous not only to the reward of fidelity in companionate marriage but to the reward of leisure (in a suburban home occupied by a waiting wife) won in exchange for the male office-worker's daily commitment of his labor to his employers in the city. The normative valuation of this combination of investments has become so obvious today in Japan as in the West that it seems barely worthy of comment. Yet where erotic alternatives were very openly available in the city, and the housing market (plus the state of lending institutions) still made renting not only easier but often the more rational choice, Kobayashi had to do a lot to make his product appeal.

Kobayashi's stories teaching the pleasure of delayed gratification spoke to a bourgeois sensibility essential to modern consumerism, what Colin Campbell has called the "romantic ethic." In Campbell's words, "individuals do not so much seek satisfaction from products, as pleasure from the self-illusory experiences which they construct from their associated meanings."[76] Once the moral imagination had been seeded with ideas of the intimate home and the healthy, bucolic suburb, cultural entrepreneurs like Kobayashi latched onto Japanese consumers' capacities to imagine that homeownership or acquisition of other goods might make real the chimerical realm of these ideals. The investment in a suburban house, and the fantasies associated with it, were neither purely hedonistic nor strongly tied to notions of status and propriety—in this sense, this new ethic looked forward to an era when neither working-class fatalism nor the stern ascetic morality carried over from the culture of the old *samurai* gentry would hold sway, and when the acquisition of *mai hōmu* (the 1960s term for a private home) would be the desire and the burden of the typical white-collar Japanese male. Implicitly at least, this ideal home was free of extended family and in-laws, who were never mentioned in *Sanyō suitai*. Homeownership in Kobayashi's eroticized vision of it implied a man's command over a woman's sexuality and her affections, and some gesture of faithfulness from the man—in short, a romance. Private conjugality (achieving your own *katei*) would be the continuing attraction of the single-family suburban house afterward.

# 5

# Middle-Classness and the Reform of Everyday Life

## Emergence of a Mass Society

By the 1910s, there were signs of a fundamental shift in urban Japan beyond the halls of the girls' higher schools and the gatherings of the Society of Japanese Architects. The Portsmouth Treaty that concluded the Russo-Japanese War in September 1905 had inaugurated a new era of what Andrew Gordon has called "imperial democracy." Angry crowds, loyal to the emperor and enthusiastic for imperialism but demanding a voice in domestic politics, took to the streets to challenge the legitimacy of the oligarchs who claimed to represent the imperial will. The Hibiya riot of 1905 marked the emergence of the urban masses in Tokyo. Public rallies supporting constitutional government in 1912 and 1913 and labor rallies in subsequent years also gathered antigovernment crowds in Hibiya. In the culminating moment of prewar popular unrest, rice riots in cities throughout the country in 1918 demonstrated that the urban masses were now a national force.[1]

In precisely the same years that a mass politics borne by the working class was emerging, a second kind of massification had begun. Mass consumer culture was taking shape around the department store and other new urban institutions. Amid increasingly diverse commodity choices, reformers resituated their programs for house and home within a new problematic of everyday life founded on consumption. Yet the issue for what came to be called "everyday life reform" was not the problem of mass consumerism as such but the problem of how to consume. Reformers sought to channel and rationalize consumption behavior by rendering concrete the ideals for the home that they had developed in the earlier encounter with Western domestic practices and ideology. They continued to promote family intimacy, efficient and hygienic habits of domestic work, and the nativized hybrid forms of the modern interior with chairs and *tatami* mats. Now, however, they reached out to a mass audience through advertising, public display, and even through direct appeals to passersby on the streets of Tokyo.

The growth of the urban white-collar population during the economic boom and bust precipitated by World War I led the government to recognize for the first time a "middle class" whose housing and living conditions could be matters of national policy, engendering a new confluence of interests between the state and the progressive bourgeoisie. Perception of the "living issues" (*seikatsu mondai*) of this class as a national concern led in 1919 to a state-sponsored movement for comprehensive reform of the material conditions of middle-class life, including dwellings. However, problems of class definition lay thinly concealed under the surface of a reform discourse dominated by talk of nation. Reformers' efforts to encompass the growing numbers of educated urbanites beyond their own immediate social circles exposed fissures within the structure of bourgeois dominance.

The popular press expanded in the first two decades of the twentieth century to take on more of the characteristics of a mass-market industry, with both larger circulation for general-interest magazines and the development of specialized journals for particular audiences. Women's magazines grew most remarkably. Nineteenth-century pioneers such as *Jogaku zasshi* had found their audience among the first generation of students at the girl's higher schools. As the number of graduates grew, so did the potential market. Journalist Ōya Sōichi wrote in 1926 that the growth of a female readership in recent years had influenced journalism "like the discovery of a vast new colonial territory."[2] The boom had begun at the turn of the century. A total of sixty-four women's magazines are known to have been founded in the years 1901 through 1906 alone.[3] By January 1925, the most popular, *The Housewife's Companion* (*Shufu no tomo*, first published in 1917), was publishing between 230,000 and 240,000 copies twice monthly, and the cumulative monthly volume of the major women's magazines exceeded 1,200,000 copies.[4]

Increased readership was not immediately accompanied by any changing of the guard among home ideologues. Several of the same journalists and women's pedagogues who had been writing magazine articles and textbooks on domestic management in the 1890s were still writing in the same manner more than two decades later.[5] Expansion of the audience that reformers addressed, however, made it increasingly difficult to assume general agreement on the standards of the "middle-class home" that was the object of concern. The combination of rapidly expanding secondary education and economic instability after World War I produced a large reading public in new white-collar households with pretensions to bourgeois status but without the social privilege or financial security of the generation educated earlier. The widening audience for household advice and reform journalism is most evident in *The Housewife's Companion*, whose discussions of readers' low household budgets and strategies for ladylike side-jobs reveal a readership barely maintaining its social position.

Awareness of this new middle class had a marked impact on the relation of the architectural profession to dwelling reform issues. The few architects making proposals for reform of the dwelling at the turn of the century had published their ideas for a limited audience in the single journal of their profession. When they spoke of the middle-class gentleman's home, they envisioned a "class" that did not extend much beyond the immediate circle of reformers and their colleagues. By the end of World War I, however, the boundaries of the middle class were in dispute, and new designs for houses were appearing in a variety of places outside the academy. As specialty publications multiplied and interest in dwelling reform grew, architects came to share reform venues with a range of non-architects. After the war, the narrow class politics of reforming the home intersected with the politics of a newly formed mass society.

## The Nation, the State, and the Middle-Class Home

The efforts of architects, domestic science experts, and other cultural intermediaries to make reform of the home a national issue began to converge during the war, beginning with two events in 1915: a home exhibition sponsored by Tokutomi Sohō's newspaper *Kokumin shinbun*, and the founding of the Dwelling Reform Society (Jūtaku kairyōkai), organized by builder Hashiguchi Shinsuke and girls' school principal Misumi Suzuko. Participants in both considered only single-family detached houses and treated them exclusively as places of consumption and female labor. Adopting the methods of the public exposition and the voluntary society, they addressed themselves to a national public, not only endeavoring to attract wide audiences but, more than previous reformers, claiming to offer concrete national models. Yet what they sought to define was also centrally a "middle-class" lifestyle. Their picture of an everyday life centered on consumption had no space for the producers of commodities, and their conception of dwelling needs ignored the urban masses who lived in shophouses and multifamily tenements, as well as the peasantry, whose dwellings had to accommodate a wide range of community social and work functions in addition to housing humans and animals. If reform of the dwelling was now to be a national cause, it was for a bourgeois nation.

In early 1915, the *Kokumin shinbun* trumpeted its Home Exhibition (*Katei hakurankai*) as a major news event, announcing the formation of a managing committee consisting of such public figures as Gotō Shinpei, the renowned former colonial administrator who was soon to become home minister, and 190 other prominent patrons.[6] An article advertising the exhibition posed as its unifying theme the problem of what to consume:

> With the changes in society that have accompanied the progress of civilization, the problems of actual home life (*katei no jisseikatsu*) have become increasingly complex. What sort of house to live in? What sort of food to have? And what sort of clothes to wear? The problems of the home are matters of food, clothing, and shelter, as they have always been, but the food, clothing, and shelter of the new era must naturally be something different from those of the old. Our home exposition was planned to present a home and home life suited to the age, in actuality (*ari no mama no jissai*), not described in theory.[7]

In the introduction to *Risō no katei* (The Ideal Home), a volume of essays that accompanied the exhibition, editor Tokutomi expressed the issue of reform as a matter of finding an ideal suited to the Japanese nation, using language that reflected his shift toward conservative nationalism since the founding of *Katei zasshi* before the Sino-Japanese War. Comparing the unique self-sacrificing spirit of Japanese womanhood to the women of other nations, he observed that because of the "ancient family system of the Yamato people," Japan, unlike the countries of the West, was a "home-based (*katei hon'i*) society."[8] The imported idea of "home" was now so completely naturalized that it could be claimed as more essentially Japanese than it was anyone else's. Tokutomi assembled authorities (*taika*) from disparate fields to flesh out this domestic national ideal.

Just as the exhibition was one of actual goods rather than abstract ideals, however, the common ground on which participating experts met was that of material goods. The tradition of moral discourse on the virtues of the home was becoming increasingly marginal in the women's popular press as the market expanded. Tokutomi peppered *Risō no katei* with homilies in the same moralizing vein that had dominated his *Katei zasshi* in the 1890s, but none of the other contributors devoted page space to proselytizing family morality. All were concerned more with concrete aspects of bourgeois domestic life. Several women in the field of domestic management, including journalist Hani Motoko and a group of students from the Japan Women's Higher School, presented model room interiors at the exhibit, and articles discussed kitchens, storage and sewing rooms, gardening, and interior decorating. The house exhibit included plans for a model middle-class house designed by Itō Chūta and the young architect Endō Arata that neatly encapsulated the late Meiji-period dwelling reform solution: "family-centered," with a good garden exposure for the *tatami*-floored dining room, a Western-style reception room and study set off to the right of the entry, and a corridor separating family from servants. Revealing where the designer's primary aesthetic interests lay, the Western-style rooms were the only rooms with innovative details represented in interior perspectives (see Fig. 5.1).[9]

Itō's article describing the house began with the problem of what was meant by "middle class" (*chūryū*), noting that despite the term's vagueness, he had designed a house that aimed at "about what everyone conventionally has in mind." His prescription was specific: this meant a family of four with one maid, the father a professional and the two children in primary school. Their home would be a single-story house in the suburbs. The husband would read and receive intimate guests in the study, receiving others in the guest room; the wife would work in the day room next to the dining room; the family would dine and enjoy after-dinner conversation in the dining room and play music in the guest room.[10] Using the national staple as a metaphor, Itō concluded that the ideal house should be "like boiled rice rather than beef or eel." Unlike these delicious but rich foods, rice was something one could consume three times a day without ever tiring of it. His house design, whose features embodied what had been the progressive vanguard of dwelling reform a few years earlier, was now presentable as conventional and conservative, a model for the middle-class nation.[11]

Fig. 5.1 Model house plan for the Home Exhibition of 1915, by architect Endō Arata under the supervision of Itō Chūta. Guidelines for the design specified that the house should be "family-centered" and accommodate tables and chairs (Kokumin shinbunsha, *Risō no katei* [The Ideal Home], 1915).

The activities of Hashiguchi Shinsuke and Misumi Suzuko's Dwelling Reform Society, which began concurrently with the Home Exhibition, reveal how closely tied the national agenda of reform was to both the definition of a "middle" and the marketing of Western goods and lifestyles. Hashiguchi, who had little background in architecture, had entered business in Japan in 1909 by attempting to sell imported ready-to-build American bungalows in Tokyo, determined to bring a Western domestic lifestyle to a broad Japanese public beyond the bourgeois elite to whom it had been restricted until that time. Inspired by personal experience in Seattle, he named his business Amerika-ya (the suffix *-ya* meaning "shop").[12] The venture foundered. It did so in part because buying one of Hashiguchi's imported houses was still no cheaper than hiring a carpenter to bring lumber and cut and finish it all on site in the usual manner.[13] But the larger problem was that of finding a market for the unusual product. Unpretentious structures designed for middle-class Seattle families fit poorly with either the aesthetic preconceptions or the practical needs of the upper-class urbanites who were the chief—practically the only—clientele for Western-style houses in Japan before World War I. Few others were seeking to own a house without *tatami* mats. Eventually, five of the six bungalows were purchased by a man who wanted them to rent to foreigners. Amerika-ya shifted to custom-building Western-style houses and resort cottages for a largely elite clientele (see Fig. 5.2).

During the same years, Misumi Suzuko, who had graduated from the Women's Normal College in 1892, was making innovations in women's education and introducing Taylorism into the design of kitchens. The two met in 1915 when she commissioned Hashiguchi to design her house. Hashiguchi was impressed by her ideas, and they decided to collaborate, founding the Reform Society and beginning publication of a graphic magazine called *Jūtaku* (The House).[14]

Like Tokutomi, they followed the well-established Meiji formula of bourgeois voluntary societies promoting state modernization goals. Together they drafted a prospectus that began with a loftily worded reform manifesto and, armed with this document, succeeded in gathering the sponsorship of 134 political figures, academics, and members of the peerage, beginning with Ōkuma Shigenobu, who was then prime minister.[15] Their manifesto further dressed the campaign in the borrowed robes of the state

Fig. 5.2 Advertisement for the design firm Amerika-ya, published in *Jūtaku* magazine, May 1918 (reprinted in Uchida Seizō, *Amerika-ya shōhin jūtaku*). By this time, the company had opened branch offices in Osaka, Nagoya, and Karuizawa and was advertising design and construction services for a range of buildings beside private residences.

by using the sinified Confucian language of classical essays and official documents, appealing to "men of virtue" (*kunshi*) concerned with "affairs of governance" (*keisei*) and proclaiming that dwelling reform was the "very foundation" on which to "construct the healthy state."

In fact, the work of this voluntary organization was firmly based in Hashiguchi's commercial enterprise. The society listed Amerika-ya's address as its own, and activities described in the prospectus included the introduction to members of specialists in residential architecture and reliable workmen, as well as manufacturers and traders in building parts, furniture, and ornament. At least initially, these products and services were to come from Amerika-ya. In accord with Hashiguchi's original vision for the business, the society promoted Westernization and targeted what were described as "middle-class" dwellings. The magazine's inaugural issue solicited readers' submissions to three competitions, one for design of a "middle-class gentleman's house," another for proposals on reforming the height of doors in Japanese houses to accommodate increases in the average height of Japanese and the fact that increasing numbers of people were receiving foreign visitors at home, and a third for reforming toilets both for hygiene and in order to better accommodate people wearing Western clothes.[16]

*Jūtaku* attracted a favorable response, becoming a stable presence in the print market for over two decades. In the 1910s it was the only popular publication of any kind to deal regularly with architecture.[17] It carried articles on dwelling reform by the leading members of the architectural profession, as well as a number of well-known social reformers and men and women of letters. Early in the magazine's second year, educator Nitobe Inazō called for the construction of houses adapted for sitting in chairs,[18] social reformer Abe Isoo described the enhancement of privacy and convenience his family enjoyed after moving to a Western house,[19] and politician Ozaki Yukio commended the virtues of summer life in a mountain resort for achieving a "peaceful and harmonious home life."[20] These bourgeois exemplars enhanced the legitimacy of Hashiguchi's enterprise, rooting it securely in the tradition of domestic reform discourse that went back to the 1880s.

As the first consumer-oriented magazine in the market for houses and house decorating, *Jūtaku* took American publications like *House and Garden* as its models. However, the reform focus of articles and the constant presence of Western referents in all the writing that appeared in *Jūtaku* demonstrate the fundamental difference of character between this magazine and contemporary popular-market counterparts in the United States. *Jūtaku*'s editors were not so much responding to a broad change in the housing market as seeking to instigate such a change themselves. Although consumption and the home came to occupy larger regions of public discourse, the "middle class" remained elusive. Hashiguchi, Misumi, and their associates thus groped for a mass market amid the changing configuration of people claiming the "middle," which, in practice, meant claiming the nation.

## The Housing Problem and the Definition of Middle-Classness

Expansion of the white-collar population and the diminished prospects for social advancement it meant for many of them caused intellectuals to worry over what was perceived as the progressive impoverishment of the "middle ranks." Even prior to World War I, there was ample evidence of a growing disparity in career chances and wealth among professionals. Despite large increases in the total number of corporate and bureaucratic jobs, the probability of rising to elite positions dwindled markedly after the Russo-Japanese War. In the course of World War I, commodity prices would double while wages remained constant, and the problem of a poorly compensated "white-collar proletariat" (often called *yōfuku saimin*, or "paupers in Western clothes") would continue in the following years.[21]

Thus, the material conditions of bourgeois identity—a house with a reception room, an improved kitchen for the professional housewife, and a separate room for the children, for example—were becoming a focus of attention not only because of the new commodities for the home that the department stores had made available and mass-market magazines had encouraged, but also because of a growing population that was struggling to achieve such standards in any form at all. Reformers who wished to address a bourgeois nation that included these new members of the "middle ranks" were compelled to recognize that before defining what the organizers of the 1915 Home Exhibition had called "a home life suited to the new age," they would have to offer solutions to the difficulties of getting by.[22] The disjunction between reformers and their mass audience created insoluble tensions in the reform campaigns of the 1910s and early 1920s and raised questions about the definition of middle-classness itself (see Fig. 5.3).

The war boom also brought about Japan's first urban housing crisis. The expansion of heavy industry to meet the almost unlimited demand created by war in Europe attracted workers to the major cities in unprecedented numbers. Construction of new housing failed to keep pace. Following steady annual increases of 1 percent to 4 percent from 1900, the Tokyo region's population leapt 14.5 percent (an estimated 421,900) in 1917.[23] The population of Osaka was increasing at a rate of roughly 100,000 per year during the war, but a bare 5,000 new dwellings were built annually. A 5.5 percent availability rate in 1915 dropped the following year to 0.8 percent.[24] The wartime shortage combined with inflation to cause rampant rent increases, which were not followed by reductions in the subsequent slump. Tokyo rents rose two and a half times between 1914 and 1922. Population pressure and the inflationary war economy thus affected the entire rental market until the year of the Kantō Earthquake.

The impact of this crisis was felt by the tenement-dwelling working class and white-collar households alike. In 1922, Tokyo's Social Bureau conducted a survey of "middle-class" (*chūtō kaikyū*) housing conditions in the Tokyo area

Fig. 5.3 Comparison of the proportion of food required by a manual laborer and a non-laborer. The non-laborer needs only 25 to the laborer's 30 (units unspecified) (Nukada Yutaka, *Anka seikatsu hō* [How to Live Inexpensively], 1915). Although manual laborers earned less than members of the middle class, they suffered less from living difficulties, Nukada claimed, because they received clothing from their bosses or patrons and needed only the simplest dwellings. In contrast, middling "mental workers," i.e., "salaried workers, those with comparatively more education, knowledge, and a sense of shame," were compelled to spend far more in order to maintain their social standing. Budgeting food intake based on nutritional science, Nukada maintained, would rescue the middle class from living difficulties.

and found that over 85 percent of bank employees (with an average monthly wage of 174 yen) and over 90 percent of company office workers (with an average monthly wage of 156 yen) lived in rented dwellings. Disputes over rent became the most common cause for suits in Tokyo in this year, and tenant unions formed in both working-class and white-collar districts.[25]

Prior to 1919, neither national nor municipal government had had any involvement in housing provision. The crisis brought the first tentative steps toward a public housing policy. A Relief Projects Research Committee (Kyūsai jigyō chōsakai) was established within the Home Ministry in 1917. The following year, the committee submitted a report proposing government loans to promote the construction of public housing and the formation of private housing associations that would encourage homeownership. This report provided the catalyst for the first government response to the housing problem, albeit on a limited scale. Using low-interest loans provided by the Ministry of Finance, the Tokyo municipal government took immediate advantage of the financing to build 344 row-house units in the factory district of Tsukishima and 52 detached and semi-detached houses in Hongō Masago-chō.

The Housing Association Law (Jūtaku kumiai hō) of 1921, which provided further low-interest loans for associations of seven or more private individuals to buy or rent land and build houses for their members, also resulted from the recommendations of the Relief Committee's 1918 report. Between July 1921, when the law was enacted, and November of the following year, 298 associations were formed nationwide, with a total of 5,739 members. Compared with the housing construction and aid programs in countries such as England in the same period, the numbers involved were small.[26] Roughly 35,000 houses were built nationwide under the Housing Association Law between 1921 and 1938. Even after the expansion of housing provision under the Dōjunkai, a semi-public body created in 1924 to build temporary and permanent housing as part of the earthquake recovery effort in Tokyo and Yokohama, neither national nor municipal government showed signs of meeting more than a small fraction of market demand in the 1920s and 1930s. In eighteen years, the Dōjunkai built a total of less than 11,000 units.[27] Housing policy was directed more at presenting suitable models for builders to follow than at providing a direct solution to the housing shortage or significantly altering market conditions as a whole.

There were precedents of housing legislation for the purposes of slum reform prior to the Relief Committee's housing report, in particular the tenement regulations (*nagaya kinshi rei*) issued by the Tokyo police in 1909. Previous intervention, however, had been restrictive in nature and had apprehended the problem at the level of the district or the tenement building, not the individual dwelling. The social bureaucrats of 1918, while reaffirming the traditional goals of slum reform, turned their gaze away from the aggregate problems of the slum environment and its denizens toward the dwelling itself. Their new interest grew in part from the perception of a "middle class" whose members had special housing needs.

The first indication of this new awareness can be found in the title of the Relief Committee's *Report on the Improvement of Small Houses* (*Shō jūtaku kairyō yōkō*). Choosing the term "small houses," rather than terms that had been used previously such as "tenements" (*nagaya*) and "houses of the poor" (*saimin jūtaku*), removed the housing problem from the limits of environmental or class-specific legislation. In discussions during the drafting of the report, two of six committee members proposed removing the word "paupers" (*saimin*) from the legislation, and a third called for "consideration of the improvement of houses for the middle [classes] and above (*chūryū ijō no jūtaku kairyō*) as well." All references to "houses of the poor" appearing in the original request from the Home Ministry were excised in the final report.[28]

The types of houses built under the new legislation further confirm that the purview of public welfare was being extended to include professionals and, at the same time, that the bureaucrats' aim was to provide a middle-class model rather than a solution to the housing shortage. Of the first two housing estates built by the city of Tokyo with the financing provided in 1919, the Hongō houses were clearly intended for tenants with means well beyond those of the typical factory worker. Rents ranged from 30 yen per month for a semi-detached unit with four rooms to 65 yen for a six-room detached house.[29] In light of the fact that the 1922 survey of what the Social Bureau considered "middle-class" living conditions found the average monthly rent of a Tokyo bank employee to be roughly 32 yen and that of members of other occupational categories even lower, the rent of 65 yen for these first detached houses appears well out of the range of what even white-collar workers could afford at the time.

The Housing Association Law set its sights similarly high. It was intended to encourage mutual aid among small investors, but formation of associations was restricted by minimum figures for start-up capital and other encumbering membership conditions. Statements made in Diet debate on the topic make clear that the politicians who promoted it regarded this law as explicitly for the benefit of white-collar professionals, in contrast to the English Housing Act on which it was loosely modeled. A separate bill was proposed to offer financial assistance for the formation of housing companies that would rent improved dwellings to people without the capital to build their own houses, and the two were described by an advocate in the House of Peers as intended for "salary-earning workers" and "the poor," respectively. The housing bill to provide for the poor ultimately failed due to lack of support from the Ministry of Finance.[30]

## The Social Turn in Architecture

In the same years that relief of the middle class became an issue for public policy, housing and urban policy became topics of discussion among architects, few of whom had previously shown professional interest in the problems of any social group beyond that of their elite clients. As architects of the late 1890s had departed from their classical training in the design of

Fig. 5.4 Masthead of the *Kansai Architecture Association Journal*, 1917.

public buildings and monuments to take up the issue of dwelling form, architects of the 1910s took a further step and identified urban housing generally as a matter to be treated within the discipline of architecture.

The journal of the Kansai Architecture Association, *Kansai kenchiku kyōkai zasshi*, founded in 1917, was more active in extending the sphere of architectural discourse than the older *Kenchiku zasshi*, based in Tokyo. A heady statement of purpose in the first issue spoke of the editors' "great aspirations to lead society in this era of progress" and to be the "clapper that rings the first bell of dawn" for an age of "scientifically organized" city-building (see Fig. 5.4).[31] Contributions on urban reform by figures such as Kataoka Yasushi, the Kansai Association's director, and Seki Hajime, who was deputy mayor of the city of Osaka from 1914 and became mayor in 1924, revealed the internationalism and sense of social mission that distinguished the new architectural journalism.[32] To these men, the "housing problem" (*jūtaku mondai*) was a universal product of modern civilization. Their writings analyzed statistics on overcrowding and mortality, introducing slum reform ordinances from Germany and England along with the plans of public apartment complexes and the ideas of the garden city movement. Translations of housing and planning laws from overseas were appended to the back of several issues.

The Kansai Association's journal was only one of several places where one could find similar discussion of urban planning and policy in the late 1910s and early 1920s. A new Town Planning Law (Toshi keikaku hō) for the six major cities in Japan, an Urban Building Law (Shigaichi kenchikubutsu hō), and a Tuberculosis Prevention Law (Kekkaku yobō hō) were all promulgated in 1918. The following year, the *Ōsaka Mainichi* newspaper ran a series of articles entitled "Jūtaku mondai" (The Housing Problem) that included statistics and examples describing conditions in the United States, Britain, and Germany, now for the first time alongside comprehensive data for Tokyo and Osaka.[33]

In the years after the war, the national Home Ministry and municipal social bureaus surveyed numerous aspects of urban living. These scientific studies placed Japanese dwellings for the first time in the homogeneous category of housing, irrespective of location or social class, and treated their characteristics as numerically representable.[34] As the hygiene movement had earlier revealed the city as an organism whose health was measured in mortality statistics, housing studies now showed the dwelling to be not only the site of family unity, of domestic labor, or of the exercise of taste, but a cell within the urban body, whose condition could be analyzed to determine its effect on the well-being of the whole. This provided a new tool for architects and dwelling reformers, enabling them to situate their expertise within a larger framework of scientific endeavor.

Yet architects writing in the 1910s still bore the burden from earlier years of unresolved cultural questions that defied conventional statistical analysis. In the pages of the *Kansai Architecture Association Journal*, alongside translations of European planning laws and analyses of the environmental causes of disease in Osaka's slums, they discussed the maleficent effects of *tatami* mats and the overattention to guest reception in Japanese dwellings. Nothing makes plainer the ambiguity with regard to the object of reform that was endemic to discourse in this period than the fact that the social problems of housing and the cultural dilemma of the dwelling were described with the same terms: *jūtaku mondai* and *jūtaku kairyō*. The word *jūtaku* could signify both the aggregate, housing, and the individual dwelling. It was not out of ignorance that architects allowed the two to be conflated, however. Some indeed were careful to specify which problem they wished to emphasize by speaking of housing with the English word in transliteration or by distinguishing the term *jūkyo*, which bore the more general sense of "shelter," from *jūtaku*, which they used when referring to individual residences. Rather, they perceived the reform of domestic life, which had been framed as a middle-class problem—and had provided the material indices with which to frame the middle class—in continuity with the problems of reforming the urban environment, which had originally been defined in relation to—and used to define the physical boundaries of—the urban poor.

Architects of the Kansai Association decried the inefficiencies of the Japanese style of living. In an article entitled "The Reconstruction of Dwelling Architecture from the Perspective of the Nation's Economy," published in the second issue of the *Kansai Journal*, association member Motono Seigo stated that the dwelling could be observed from two points of view: that of the "pure materialist" and that of the "pure spiritualist." The materialist regarded dwellings as no more than "boxes" and humans as "machines," whereas the spiritualist saw dwellings as "extremely subtle vessels for harboring the spirit." Motono advocated taking a position between these two extremes, since the "dwelling problem" (*jūtaku mondai*) lay precisely in the fact that humans were indeed machines, but very subtly crafted ones. In Motono's view, the pressing question in Japanese life was how to conserve space and the energy of the people. From the aristocracy down to the poor, Japanese squandered time, labor, and money, Motono wrote, and the present manner of living was one of the chief reasons for this waste. The solution, he declared, lay in abandoning sitting on the floor.[35] One year later, architect Katsuno Sōichirō echoed Motono's call for the abandonment of *tatami*, asserting that only a fundamental reconstruction of the dwelling would lead to a complete solution of the housing difficulties (*jūtakunan*). Housing difficulties, Katsuno continued, beset not only those who were seeking housing but the majority who already had houses, and not only the poor but all classes.[36]

Tokyo's Japanese Society of Architects, although still less socially concerned on the whole than the newer Kansai Association, joined the wave of reform after the end of the war. Urban planning was the theme of the society's annual conference in 1918, and "cities and dwellings" (*toshi to jūtaku*) the theme in 1919. On the first day of the 1919 conference, architect Yasuoka Katsuya addressed the society on the future of urban dwellings, noting that discussion to date had focused on the individual dwelling, but with the new Town Planning Law, the time had come to examine housing at the district level. The aristocracy, Yasuoka asserted, occupied too much valuable urban land and should be required to resituate in the suburbs. Houses of the middle classes (*chūryū no jūkyo*) in Japan were too large—"puffed up like baked bread"—and architects ought to learn from the example of England, where the middle classes lived in compact rowhouses and semi-detached houses. Citing figures on the rapid growth of Tokyo's population, Yasuoka estimated that if each middle-class

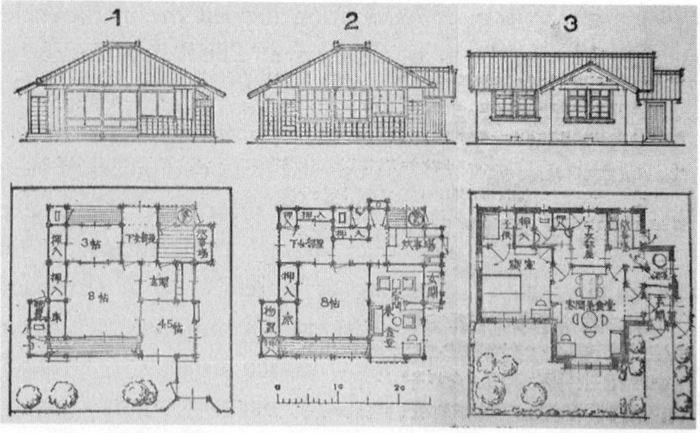


Fig 5.5 Plans for converting a rented house in Tokyo presented by architect Tanabe Junkichi to an audience at the Everyday Life Reform Exhibition in 1920. The problem with the original house, Tanabe explained, was that room functions were poorly defined. In the final stage of the conversion, rooms gain distinct functions (significantly including a separate bedroom for the couple), floor-living is abandoned, and the "empty ceremony" of traditional guest reception gives way to family leisure. As was almost always the case in reformed middle-class houses, the maid's room remains unchanged: three *tatami* mats located next to the kitchen. The entrance to each house is from the right side of the drawings (Seikatsu kaizen dōmeikai, ed., *Monbushō kōshūkai*, 1922).

house covered 60 to 70 *tsubo* (2,160 to 2,520 square feet), newly established residential districts would be filled in a short time.[37]

At the same conference, Tanabe Junkichi addressed the issue of dwelling reform for each social class, noting that urban reform in Japan was complicated in part by the many classes of dwelling in the city. The houses of the poor were easier to reform than "ordinary houses," Tanabe believed, since the poor could not afford to manage buildings themselves, making it possible for government or large organizations to alter them freely. Of all the classes, the educated class most keenly desired dwelling reform, yet sadly, the people of this class, "ourselves included," were "so-called paupers in Western clothes" (*iwayuru yōfuku saimin*), without the financial means to realize the dream of reform. Tanabe offered no specific program for reforming the dwelling, but concluded with a call for more architects specializing in house design to cure the "diseased architecture of the present," just as the numerous specialists in different fields of medicine assisted ordinary physicians in protecting and advancing the health of the nation (see Fig. 5.5).[38]

Through the experience of the housing crisis and the opening of a discussion of comprehensive housing policy, the universalizing rhetoric of public health and urban administration were thus added to the vocabulary of architecture, but without altering the essential problematic of reform architects with regard to dwelling. These architects treated the "housing problem" as simultaneously a problem of their own lifestyle and a problem of the city and the nation as a whole. The concrete solutions they proposed began with the needs of the people they defined as "middle class" (or some circumlocution such as the "middle ranks of society"), but the economic and social criteria of that class were no longer clear. An anonymous, vaguely bounded "middle class" arrived on the stage of journalistic and architectural discourse, and in the same moment bourgeois architects redefined the problem of the middle-class home in universal terms as a social question.

## "Reconstruction" and Postwar Social Policy

While ambiguities about class continued to pervade the architectural discourse, for some, solutions to the dwelling problem required transcending the nation itself. Katsuno Sōichirō's articles on "reconstructing the dwelling," written just as World War I was coming to an end in late 1918, went a step beyond calling for improvement of Japanese houses for the sake of the nation and demanded the "globalization" (*sekaika*) of Japanese habits of life. The "civilizing projects" pursued in the half-century of Meiji always started from a strict distinction between Japanese and Western styles and therefore "lacked digestibility," Katsuno wrote. "But now the time has come; we will no longer be able to persist in standing on such petty discriminating notions (*sabetsuteki kannen*)."[39] Comparison with the West had long been the foundation of criticism of native practices, but this idea of abandoning all national distinctions in everyday life was something new.

"World trends" were being cited in all quarters in 1918, born of a sense that a great wave of change, either threatening or promising, was lapping at the nation's shores. In addition to the end of the war and evidence of democratic transformation in Europe, the Russian Revolution and the growth of labor unrest in Japan were potent threats to some and inspiration to others. More than anything else, the rice riots that swept through Japan in the summer of 1918 revealed the sharp divisions within Japanese society, contributing to the radicalization of political language at every level of discourse. Countless books and articles called for reconstruction (*kaizō*). The left-wing political journal *Kaizō*, whose first issue appeared in April 1919, became the most famous emblem of the change in the postwar intellectual environment, but the belief that Japan was on the verge of a new era was in no way restricted either to the left or to political thinkers.[40]

Within the bureaucracy, a trend toward greater interest in social welfare that had already begun during the war was spurred by the shock of the rice riots. The Relief Section in the Home Ministry (created concurrently with the committee responsible for the Housing Report of 1917), was expanded and renamed the Bureau of Social Affairs in 1920. The city of Tokyo had set up its own Bureau of Social Affairs in 1919. Young men returning from study tours in wartime and postwar Europe with strong influence from the contemporary social thought of the countries they had visited staffed the Home Ministry's new bureau.[41]

A similar new guard entered the Ministry of Education during the war years, and sought to alter the role of government in the changed social climate after 1918. These new education bureaucrats urged replacement of the condescending tradition of "popular education" (*tsūzoku kyōiku*) with what they called "social education" (*shakai kyōiku*), just as their peers in the Home Ministry had replaced "relief" with "social affairs." "Popular education" programs attempted to inculcate patriotic sentiment and Confucian values through moral stories conveyed in the guise of entertainment, using storytellers, films, and illustrated books written in simple language. Norisugi Kaju, one of the leading ideologues of the new social education, envisioned a broader relationship between the state and the masses, and a style of education that would foster a nation of individuals with "little governments in their hearts," as he put it, rather than merely dictating the law. Norisugi entered the ministry in 1913, and became section chief in charge of popular education (soon changed to social education) in 1919. The ministry began publication of a periodical dealing with morality and social welfare titled *Society and Moral Suasion* (*Shakai to kyōka*) in 1920 and issued a directive to regional offices in the same year ordering the establishment of one post in each region for a "secretary of social education."[42]

The social policy promoted by this new generation of bureaucrats was both more liberal in its conception of the nation and more interventionist in its vision of the role of government in the life of its citizens. The government response to the social upheaval of the war years began in the tradition of earlier "local improvement" campaigns, exhorting hard work and frugality. These campaigns were in turn rooted in late Tokugawa moral philosophy. To promote state aims, the ministries took advantage of the many town- and village-level organizations, such as youth and women's groups, that the government had been nationalizing since the Russo-Japanese War.[43] The chief targets of these programs were peasants and the urban working class. In the climate of experimentation after 1918, however, younger bureaucrats invited the collaboration of bourgeois reformers outside government, who used the bureaucracy's campaign and the new conception of state-society relations to pursue their own aim of establishing a modern "middle-class" identity.

## The Everyday Life Reform Movement

Social policy encountered the material concerns of bourgeois architects and domestic ideologues in 1919 in the formation of an organization called the Everyday Life Reform League (Seikatsu kaizen dōmeikai), which emerged from one of these thrift and diligence campaigns, the Movement to Foster the Nation's Strength (Minryoku kanyō) initiated by the Home Ministry in 1917. After the end of the war, a set of five guidelines were issued, the last of which referred to "stabilizing life" through increased hard work and production, specifying further the "reform of clothing, food, and dwellings, and [the practice of] simple living."[44] By this one allusion to material conditions, the directive hinted at a departure from strict "moral suasion" and the beginning of state participation in the search begun by bourgeois home ideologues a generation earlier to find solutions to the problems of everyday life. It remained to movement participants to determine the concrete substance of the reforms. Although initiated by high officials, the movement would be carried on by lower bureaucrats, pedagogues from the elite women's schools, architects, and other bourgeois proselytizers.

Tanahashi Gentarō, director of the Ministry of Education's Tokyo Museum of Education, joined Home Ministry bureaucrats to formulate the campaign in greater detail and present its aims to the public. The Everyday Life Reform Exhibition opened on December 1, 1919 (see Fig. 5.6). On December 2, Tanahashi and Norisugi Kaju sent a letter to over thirty Tokyo intellectuals, most of them outside government, calling for participation in the formation of the league. Later in the month, the first planning and promotional meetings were held at the museum, and the league was made official.

主人本位の住宅
骨董弄りよりは家庭の團欒
家庭の改良は先づ臺所設備から


Fig. 5.6 Posters from the Everyday Life Reform Exhibition of 1919–20 (courtesy National Science Museum). "The Master-Centered House" (*top*) and "Family Gathering Rather Than Tinkering with Antiques" (*middle*) criticize Japanese men for indulging themselves and their guests at home while letting their wives and children suffer. The native *zashiki* is blamed, and a Western room with chairs, glass windows, and steam heating is contrasted as the appropriate setting for health and family togetherness. In "Reform of the Home Begins with the Kitchen Equipment" (*bottom*), an enclosed modern kitchen designed for work in a standing position, with piped gas and water, electricity, and a clock, is juxtaposed with a dark and smoky kitchen, lacking amenities and open to the outdoors.

In keeping with the initial aims of the campaigns to educate or "foster the strength" of the nation, the state officials who participated in the league regarded its reform program fundamentally as a means to ideological ends. "We started this movement," Norisugi told an audience in 1921, "with the thought to touch upon the practical problems of our so-called 'everyday life,' and from there proceed naturally to our spiritual problems."[45] Similarly, Home Ministry official Tago Ichimin declared: "I believe that the foundation of this everyday life reform is thought.... Everyday life is the expression of the nation's thought, and national thought appears and takes the form of everyday life."[46] Talk of "thought" (*shisō*) in this context evoked unmistakably the battle with socialism, which was the ministry's foremost preoccupation.

The specialists they invited from outside government, however, tended to see the immediate practical or material object of their reform as the essential problem, rather than transcendent questions of the nation's spiritual or political life. Materials for the exhibit were prepared by architects, utility companies, technical schools, and several girls' higher schools. Treating daily life reform as primarily a women's issue, the movement's male organizers gave women from the girls' higher schools in particular a large role. Six of the eighteen people present at the founding meeting were women. This substantial female participation in the movement's directorate distinguished Everyday Life Reform from earlier Home Ministry campaigns. In composition and style, the league had more in common with the groups behind privately sponsored events such as the *Kokumin shinbun*'s home exhibition and similar events held by Mitsukoshi.

The girls' school pedagogues, who had formed a discipline out of domestic practices, found the movement a natural way to extend their pedagogical work beyond the walls of the classroom. Substantially, this is what it was. Four committees were created to promote the reform of clothing, food, dwellings, and etiquette, dividing "everyday life" into categories that corresponded to the contents of the girls' higher school curriculum. The problem in each of the three areas of material life to be reformed was explicitly posed as one of consumption behavior, as both the exhibits at the Education Museum and the league's first publications focused on end-uses in the home rather than on production. Even etiquette reform began with consumption habits, putting first priority on the problems of extravagant weddings and gift-giving customs.[47]

With the reformist tradition of girls' school education and precedents like the Home Exposition, the main ideas of the movement's agenda were not new in 1919. What gave everyday life reform a new appearance and made it newsworthy were the facts that the Ministry of Education's sponsorship made it a national movement with the active endorsement of the state and, equally significantly, that members of the league sought through a variety of means to appeal directly to the general public. The league's propaganda campaign began on January 25, 1920. Female students and members of the Japan Domestic Professions Research Association (Nihon katei shokugyō kenkyūkai), under the direction of Kaetsu Kōko, principal of the Japan Girls' Commercial School, canvassed the central districts of Tokyo with 20,000 flyers and solicited members for the league. For a fee of 50 *sen*, new members were given a silver badge bearing the roman letters "BL," for "Better Life." Forty members of the Buddhist Girl's Youth Association (Bukkyō joshi seinenkai) joined the canvassers the following day and continued the campaign at major rail stations.[48]

With the additional sponsorship of women's organizations and regional newspapers, the exhibition traveled to Osaka and roughly a dozen other cities in the year after its run in Tokyo.[49] The Ministry of Education sponsored an exhibition around the theme of "time" the following year, in keeping with the Everyday Life Reform League's punctuality campaign. Subsequent exhibitions featuring league exhibits included a Consumption Economy Exhibition in 1922 and a Hygiene Industry Exhibition in 1924.[50]

## Critics of the League

Viewed in the records left by the Ministry of Education and the league itself, the movement of 1919 appears to have grown nationwide. Yet newspaper reports reveal that the league's campaign failed to gather the momentum that its organizers had anticipated. On December 26, 1920, precisely one year after the league's founding, the *Asahi shinbun* reported that despite the league's aim to "unite their seventy million compatriots," the national campaign had brought in barely over 2,000 new members, "no more than one person in 35,000." The article further noted the "interesting phenomenon" that the rural prefecture of Okayama had more members than Tokyo, which had fewer than 700. "In this light," the article continued, "it seems uncertain not only whether the average home has yet been reached by the benefits of reform, but whether or not in their hearts people even desire them."[51]

In the cities, the league was more successful at consolidating women of common background and interests in a cause that confirmed their own social position than it was at winning recruits. After the first day of promotion in January 1920, Kaetsu Kōko, the director of the membership campaign, admitted to the *Asahi* that people in the commercial district of Kanda had been "too busy even to have a look (*mimuki mo shinai*)."[52] In its attempt to appeal directly to the Tokyo public, the league had encountered the wall of urban anomie. Moreover, although between 100,000 and 200,000 people attended each of the exhibitions at the Museum of Education, the league's total national membership at the end of a year barely exceeded the average attendance in one day at the first exhibition in Tokyo. Passive attendance at the exhibition did not lead large numbers to active involvement in the movement. Campaigns of "moral suasion" could attract popular interest, but it was more difficult to induce people to sign up and pay to participate.

In rural areas, state-sponsored campaigns were able to assemble people by exploiting local organizations embedded in the semi-obligatory relations of village society. Concurrent with the league campaign in the cities, schoolteachers and the village leaders of women's associations were encouraged by national and prefectural authorities to begin their own everyday life reform campaigns. A 1921 Home Ministry report on women's groups could observe with satisfaction that "these groups appear recently to be transforming themselves into organizations for self-improvement and study or for everyday life reform and regional reform." In fact, the ministry gave awards to women's groups sponsoring activities of this kind.[53] In its first years, the Everyday Life Reform League focused all its efforts in major cities, but a committee for farm villages was added in 1924, which then created subcommittees for each of the established categories of everyday life. Everyday life reform campaigns continued in the countryside in many institutional forms, promoting similar goals decades later.[54]

Difficulties in Tokyo were not limited to the cold response on the streets; friction surfaced within the ranks of the organization as well. At a general board meeting in 1921, new members raised a cry of elitism. One of the critics told the *Asahi shinbun* that no progress was being made because wealthy members had taken control, leaving others no room. Naming several well-known figures of high society by name, and invoking "feudalism," the perennial charge against the old elites, the newspaper reported in bombastic prose: "The inflammation of reverence for wealth brought about by these members' unrestrained demonstration of feudal spirit [has] swollen to the point of bursting."[55]

Despite a change of personnel reported later in the year, the *Asahi* had adopted such a critical stance toward the league's bourgeois core that when members gathered for a dinner party in December, coverage treated the group unambiguously as an object of ridicule. A photograph of the assembled members in formal Western attire at a Western banquet table was juxtaposed with another of day-laborers in a crowded bar. Printed below an interview revealing the laborers' desperate working conditions, conversation at the league dinner was reported with the headline "End This, Abolish That—A Hundred Demands at Final Assembly." The article reported dinnertable conversation that revolved around manners, temperance, reforming calendars, and reducing the number of days spent in New Year's greetings. These topics were treated plainly as the idle chatter of the rich. For the *Asahi shinbun*'s projected readers, who were educated but not necessarily privileged, "everyday life reform" would have to better reflect what seemed urgent in their own lives.[56]

Criticism of the Westernizing excesses of high society dated at least to the 1880s, when lavish balls held at the Rokumeikan (Deer Cry Pavilion) had incited a nativist reaction. There had been inveighing against "feudal" customs in the nineteenth century, too, indeed from among the very same elite who now represented the old guard in the Everyday Life Reform League. Although the progressive Meiji press had excoriated anyone seen as either blindly adulating the West or idly rich, it had not challenged the cultural legitimacy of bourgeois ideologues who advocated reform for the good of the nation. Twenty years earlier, these members of the top ten thousand of Meiji society could claim on political grounds to speak for the "middle ranks." A new middle-class voice now rose to challenge their authority and the basis of their legitimacy.[57]

One of the most significant targets of criticism in the newspapers after the war was urban landowners. In 1912 the majority of the land in Tokyo was in the hands of barely one-fifth of 1 percent of the population.[58] A vocal public campaign developed in 1920 to pressure large landowners in Tokyo to sell their property in order to relieve the housing shortage. The press served as a mouthpiece in this campaign, openly expressing the antagonism of white-collar workers, referred to this time as the "educated propertiless class" (*yūshiki musan kaikyū*). Exposés and editorials in the Tokyo newspapers called for the "liberation" (*kaihō*) of estate land, and city council member Nonoyama Kōkichi announced the results of a survey revealing that 25 estates of over ten thousand *tsubo* in the city went completely unused.[59] The progressive bourgeois exemplars whose households had often been featured in journals since the 1890s, and most of whom owned enough property to live as they pleased, were no longer recognized as models for "middle-class" living.

## Varying Constructions of Everyday Life Reform

None of this, however, led to a general challenge against bourgeois reformism. The individual committees for housing, food, and clothing reform within the league were composed largely of academics and professionals. Coming from the imperial universities and the girls' higher schools, they shared a community of privilege with the wealthy core of the league, but they were not people known for their wealth or rank. The content of their programs for reform, in contrast to the behavior of the central committee's wealthy members, met with little direct criticism in the press. Indeed, the league's projects were widely reported, and regarded favorably as efforts on behalf of the middle class.

In July 1920, the League's Dwelling Reform Committee announced a program for the improvement of houses under six tenets:

1. Dwellings should gradually be modified for chairs.
2. The layout and appointments of dwellings should be modified from the past orientation toward guests to a family orientation.
3. The construction and equipment of dwellings should avoid empty ornament and place weight on practicalities such as hygiene and safety.
4. Gardens should place weight on practicalities such as health and safety and not have the decorative bias of traditional gardens.
5. Furniture should be designed for simplicity and sturdiness, in keeping with the reform of the dwelling.
6. In large cities, the construction of common dwellings (apartments) and garden cities should be encouraged, according to the conditions of the area.[60]

The following year it was reported in the *Tōkyō Asahi shinbun* that the committee would be establishing a consultation section to offer free advice for people building houses. The committee's chairman told the newspaper that member Tanabe Junkichi had already drawn plans for new "middle-class" houses costing 2,000 and 3,000 yen.[61] Journalists concurred with league architects that the task was to bring the reforms already achieved by a small elite vanguard to the broad middle class. The *Yomiuru shinbun* reported that members of the Dwelling Reform Committee had searched Tokyo suburbs to find suitable houses for a lecture-demonstration series offered to girls' higher school teachers and had found a handful of candidates only with difficulty. According to the newspaper, almost all the "reformed houses" in the city were "aristocratic ones," which were not "suited to the intentions of everyday life reform."[62] Despite its cynicism toward the central committee, the *Asahi* continued to report on the activities of the league. Establishment of the Shotai no kai (Household Association), a group with similar aims formed in September 1921 under the direction of the Ministry of Agriculture and Commerce, was announced in the pages where news of the Reform League's start had earlier been reported, and the new group's activities were earnestly chronicled.[63]

Reform or improvement (*kaizen* could mean either) of everyday life was in itself an unimpeachable aim.[64] In an era of idealism, appeals for reform resonated widely. Even before the official proclamation by the Ministry of Education, "everyday life reform" had had a life of its own in print, and once given the official stamp of a national cause, it became more popular, appearing in newspaper and magazine articles and advertisements and joining the arsenal of department-store publicity. After the league's campaign, "everyday life reform" also entered textbooks for the girls' schools and was sometimes used as a prefix to the titles of domestic manuals. Mitsukoshi advertised a new line of simpler furniture that claimed to be tailored to the tenets of everyday life reform,[65] and other department stores gained the cooperation of the league for their own everyday life reform exhibits.[66]

Women's magazines were the most visible print vehicle for the popularization of everyday life reform. In order to survive in what had become a highly competitive market, the major women's magazines followed contemporary trends closely, running special issues on the most current topics. Several magazines published descriptions or reviews of the reform exhibition in January 1920. *Fujinkai* magazine included two articles by museum director Tanahashi and a colleague of his in the Ministry of Education, and one article by Home Ministry bureaucrat and League member Tago Ichimin, along with a catalogue of the exhibits.[67] Most of the magazines also ran "everyday life reform" special features during or even slightly before the exhibition. These features included submissions from journalists, educators, and central figures in the movement, as well as reform proposals from readers. The resulting spectrum of interpretations of everyday life reflected the different social positions of the magazines and their readers.

Inoue Hideko, a professor at the Japan Women's College who had earlier contributed to the *Kokumin shinbun*'s home exhibition, described her newly built Western house to readers of the elite *Ladies' Graphic* in the magazine's special issue of September 1919, "New Life" ("Atarashiki seikatsu"). Inoue subsequently became a member of the Everyday Life Reform League's Dwelling Reform Committee. As she reported in the magazine, she and her family were beginning a new life, having established a home in Tokyo free of all connection with "ancestors and the past." Without need to worry about tradition, they had built the house entirely in Western style, as Western houses were superior with regard to "economy of time and movement." The house was three stories and originally had thirteen rooms, which they had recently enlarged to eighteen. Inoue was not one of the Meiji elite whose "feudal attitude" would soon rouse dissent in the league, but a lifestyle like hers was practically as unattainable for the salary-earning middle mass as the estates of the aristocracy.

*Fujin kōron* (The Ladies' Review) and *The Ladies' Companion*, both relatively high-brow progressive publications, contributed to the discourse by polling the opinions of prominent intellectuals on what sort of reform was most needed in contemporary life. The editors did not specify food, clothing, and dwellings in the manner of the reform exhibition. Some respondents called for radical political change (ending capitalism, for example), and others replied that all reform must begin with a reconstruction of the human spirit. Roughly half of the writers published in *The Ladies' Companion* and a third of those published in *Fujin kōron*, however, discussed some aspect of everyday life as the league would construe it and made proposals prefiguring the Reform League's agenda. Most numerous among these were references to redesigning houses and clothing in order to abandon sitting on the floor, ridding social relations of "empty ceremony," and increasing efficiency in the home.[68]

Ordinary readers' ideas of how to reform everyday life were dominated by humbler goals. Most of the winners of *Fujinkai* magazine's competition for everyday life reform ideas, published in the same issue with the exhibition report, described ways they had found to save money and cope with inflation. First prize went to the wife of a local official in the city of Kanazawa, who related how she and her husband had elected a "reduced living" and found that they could make do with a smaller house. Other winning entrants were farming their own land rather than renting to others, reducing the number of midsummer gifts (*o-chūgen*) they distributed, remaking old shirts into slippers, and cooking steamed bread from a recipe in the newspaper instead of buying rice.[69]

Although none of these writers presented a very bright picture of life, their economizing strategies were at least told in the form of success stories of the "helpful hints" genre. But the need to maintain appearances and the pressure of the norms of class and community lurked just behind these women's stories. When *Fujin kōron* defined the assignment in the opposite terms, soliciting letters on the theme "discontents with contemporary life," other housewives revealed with bitterness the daily struggle necessary to maintain their tenuous social position. "I would like to say," wrote the wife of a middle-school teacher under the pseudonym "White Orchid," "that I think the tax system is cruel to salaried workers and generous to everyone else." The dyers' business next door, whose profits were high and taxes low, was the primary source of her discontent. The discrepancy between the two households extended to every aspect of life. "They wear only work trousers and shirts, with no socks. If someone comes they stand and chat with them just like that; they haven't even got a brazier warm or tea on. Even the wife wears only a single narrow sash." Among her own class (which she called *kono shakai*, "this society"), the possibility of an unexpected guest demanded constant readiness:

> [We] live in houses of at least three or four rooms, and when there are guests we invite them into the guest room. If it is winter, I put lots of charcoal in the brazier (although I ordinarily try to conserve every piece), and offer tea and confections—in summer, sweet ice and cider, or some other cold confection appropriate to the season. Without necessarily offering great amounts, I try to give it a bit of elegance. If I don't, they'll say we're bad hosts, or tight-fisted, giving a bad reputation not only to the housewife, but even to the husband. It seems that people in this society notice quite a bit about the tidiness of the house and such, so one needs a room or so extra as a combined study and reception room.[70]

There was no place in any of the schemes of everyday life reform for the other petite bourgeoisie, whose daily lives were inseparable from the small manufactories and shops they owned. Whether composed by the Everyday Life Reform League or by the educated female writers whose letters appeared in women's magazines, programs for reform were confined within the social bounds of the professional bourgeoisie, which also determined professional standards for housewives. The key was thus to "dispense with empty ceremony" (in the popular phrase of everyday life reform) and achieve the more rational and efficient life while maintaining the niceties of decorum expected of the social position of the reform-conscious class. The closer one stood geographically and socially to one's perceived social inferiors, the more anxiety-ridden was the struggle to preserve these niceties.

*Shufu no tomo*, the best-seller among the postwar women's magazines, suggested the upper and lower boundaries of the "middle-class" community in its September 1919 issue, which carried a special feature on everyday life reform. The editors contributed an odd satire of the fashion for reform talk, brimming with reproach for the rich. Under the title "A Great Success in Fundamentally Reforming Our Everyday Life," the piece began:

> Since prices for everything keep rising today, we thought that we had better institute a great reform of matters concerning our living. To begin with, we had our house, which had been made of straight-grained cryptomeria wood, rebuilt entirely in straight-grained cypress. Then we bought a new automobile. We evicted the tenants in the rented houses adjacent to our estate and expanded our garden, increasing our fountains to three times their former size. We used tiles of the highest polish for the roof, so the poor people who pass by look round-eyed in wonder at such a palace. We recognized that the times also called for a major reform of the family's clothing, so we have decided not to employ any kitchen maid, let alone general house maid, who cannot wear ordinary silk or better. . . . We also send our shopclerks all over the country to buy up rice and cotton cloth at any price, and we don't let go of it until the market prices skyrocket, so our profits just get bigger. In this way, we pile reform upon reform, and our assets grow in a way that is quite amusing. Everyone in the family worries only about what luxury we can indulge in to shock the poor people of society. It is too funny for words to hear them speaking of whether or not the middle classes and the workers shall be able eat.[71]

The precise target of this satire is not clear, but its bitter caricature of people who were profiting from the economic crisis reflects the widely felt outrage that had fomented the rice riots of the previous year. Published in the month that the Everyday Life Reform Exhibition opened, but before the official establishment of the league, it could not have been directed at the League itself, as later charges of elitism would be. "Everyday life reform" was already very much in the air, however, and it was not difficult to find irony in the rhetoric of austerity and reform for the national good when it came from the mouths of aristocrats. The elite women's educators, although still recognized as authorities on etiquette and domestic management, emerged from the war years in a class position removed from the majority of educated housewives. Inoue Hideko, who could afford to expand a thirteen-room house of Western construction to eighteen rooms during these same years of crisis and offered her "new life" as a model for the readers of the *Ladies' Graphic*, found no place for her life reforms in the pages of the *Housewife's Companion*.

Readers of *The Housewife's Companion* still sought to define a class community around habits that accorded with the reforms of the dominant fraction of the bourgeoisie. But with pressure to secure their foothold in the "middle ranks" that the elite had never felt, they focused their life reform efforts more around the housewife's assertion of independence from social obligations. Provided that the ties reinforcing class community were not damaged, the ideal of "simple living" could be accomplished (and indeed was best accomplished) at the cost of other kinds of community—those of locality or extended family, for example. The readers who related their own life reform successes in the same issue of *The Housewife's Companion* followed the pattern of the housewives in other magazines, describing their strategies and innovations to make ends meet. Here, however, these strategies stressed reducing or limiting contact with outsiders, of both a commercial and a socializing nature. One woman wrote that she had begun her reform by dispensing with the maid and then parted from local custom by not serving *sake* to visitors. Another put an end to "empty ceremony and vanity" (*kyorei kyoei*) in similar fashion, omitting *sake* and fancy meal preparations for guests. Having moved away from the city, she had also developed the habit of going to market and paying in cash rather than relying on the tradesmen who used to come to the house. A woman in Tokyo had also "resolved to refuse the tradesmen" and was meeting her family's needs through a cooperative she had seen advertised in the pages of the magazine. Buying from the cooperative saved her not only money but time, since the delivery man came once every two days, unlike the tradesmen who were constantly coming around.

Doing without maids and tradesmen, however, often meant replacing the labor of these people with the housewife's own and therefore investing more time rather than less. These reform-conscious housewives economized on time by changing their socializing rather than their work habits, tightening their social circle to intimates who would share a simple meal at the family dinner table or consorting during the day only with women "of higher

Fig. 5.7 Kitazawa Rakuten, "The Japanese People's Double Life: When the architecture is pure Japanese in construction and only the master's clothing and the chair and table are Western style, no wonder there's confusion about whether to use Japanese or Western etiquette." The confusion illustrated here is on the part of the male guest; the woman receiving him is a component in the unity of native architecture, dress, and manners (*Jiji manga*, no. 20 [June 26, 1921]) (courtesy Saitama Municipal Cartoon Art Musuem).

station" (as one contributor put it) from whose conversation they could profit. In contrast to "White Orchid," the schoolteacher's wife whose lifestyle contrasted so greatly with that of her manufacturing neighbors, the writers in *The Housewife's Companion*'s everyday life reform issue had moved with their families to suburban or rural districts, which both facilitated the break with established ties of local society and increased the burden on the solitary housewife. But like her, they could modify their lives only within certain narrow confines, limited both by the norms of bourgeois social exchange and the small means they possessed with which to meet those norms.[72]

Everyday life reform could have almost as many interpretations as it found advocates. For most of the reformist elite who had dominated the home journals since the 1890s, the primary aim of everyday life reform was to bring native manners in closer line with those of polite society in Europe (see Fig. 5.7). The more cosmopolitan of their number, including Inoue Hideko and most of the men on the Dwelling Reform Committee, regarded the project at hand to be a complete alteration of the material forms of everyday life, particularly the house itself. For the women whose letters appeared in *The Housewife's Companion*, the forms of "middle-class" society as they had been established by an earlier generation were a difficult onus to bear, making calls for the abolition of "empty ceremony" welcome. But abandoning social norms was a risky enterprise for newcomers. Moreover, only a small minority had the means to build and furnish new houses according to the tenets of the Reform League or were prepared to make the radical adjustment of domestic practice that a reformed house would require. Among the housewives writing in the pages of *The Housewife's Companion* and most of the other women's magazines that had appeared since the war, the consensus view of everyday life reform was built around coping—economizing without making costly mistakes, simplifying without abandoning the marks of a hard-earned social position.

A step back from the particular contents of these women's reform proposals brings into clearer perspective the relationship between everyday life reform and class self-definition. Each magazine in this period had come to represent a specific community and social stratum. Readers' letters were prominent in all of them, and the exchange of hints, advice, and sympathy for which they created a forum in many ways perpetuated and strengthened the sorority established in the girls' higher schools, which were the strongest single contributor to bourgeois identity for women. In addition, reformism itself represented a form of cultural capital in the hands of the educated, even if the material content of individual reforms might differ. In speaking of the "abandonment of ceremony" or "time-motion efficiency," the professional housewife shared the symbolic commodity of everyday life reform rhetoric with others claiming or aspiring to enlightened "middle-class" status.

## The Culture Life

While accusations of elitism dogged the campaigns of the Reform League, a new slogan soon emerged to fill the magazine headlines and form a second node of discourse complementing everyday life reform. Talk of the "culture life" (*bunka seikatsu*) was popularized first through the writings of economist Morimoto Kōkichi, whose Culture Life Research Group (Bunka seikatsu kenkyūkai) published the first issue of its journal, *Bunka seikatsu kenkyū*, in May 1920. The Research Group followed this with publication of a general-market magazine, *Culture Life* (*Bunka seikatsu*), in 1921, along with several volumes on architecture, domestic management, and other topics. The term soon gained wider currency than the state-promoted slogan "everyday life reform" had succeeded in attaining, appearing in advertising for household products as much as in scholarly writing.[73]

As slogans, everyday life reform and the culture life were interchangeable, and interchanged in fact following the vogue of the moment. In 1920, the Society of Architects announced that the theme of its annual conference the following year would be "architecture and everyday life reform," but by the time of the conference in April 1921, the sponsors had changed the theme to "architecture and the culture life." In inaugural remarks, society chairman Nakamura Tatsutarō explained that "in substance they are almost the same; we changed the title simply on the basis of culturalism." Not surprisingly, each speaker had his own notion of what "culturalism" was.[74]

*The Ladies' Companion* published its "Culture Life Issue" in January 1921, a year and two months after the magazine's "Everyday Life Reform Issue." Journalist Miyake Setsurei penned the lead article for both. In 1919, Miyake assessed the reforms most needed in food, clothing, and housing, concluding that the essence of everyday life reform lay in a simplification of life to reduce the differences between classes. His exegesis of the culture life in 1921 followed the same theme, noting that habits of dress in Europe had become more democratic since the war and that the qualifications for becoming a "gentleman" (*zentoruman*) were now much broader. "The culture life can be interpreted many ways," the article began, "but in plain terms, we can call it the style of gentlemen and ladies minus the associations of wealth and nobility."[75]

Miyake's image of the democratic gentleman sans silk hat suited the liberal and cosmopolitan climate of the time. Although it was often linked to the same programs, the rhetoric of "culture" possessed a capacity for positive appeal that government prescriptions for everyday life reform lacked. However, the culture life—"living a life in keeping with the culture of the era," as Miyake defined it—still required a material model. By speaking of "culture" instead of everyday-life reform, proponents had simply turned the focus of attention from prescription and process to expectations and goals.

The Culture Life Research Group's chief enterprise at the time of its founding was a correspondence course for girls' higher school graduates. Morimoto recruited the support of writer Arishima Takeo and political thinker Yoshino Sakuzō, whose lectures on topics such as "life and literature" and "women and politics" appeared in the journal alongside Morimoto's discussions of the economics of consumption and the culture life, lectures on domestic management by Morimoto's wife Shizuko, and lectures by prominent male academics on a variety of topics, most including "home" or "family" in their titles.[76]

At the core of Morimoto Kōkichi's economic studies was his effort to determine an empirical standard for what he conceived the culture life to be. Having taken a doctorate in economics at Johns Hopkins University, Morimoto was influenced both by the work of contemporary Anglo-American economists and by the experience of life in the United States. In books such as *Living Problems: An Economic Study of Life* (*Seikatsu mondai: Seikatsu no keizaiteki kenkyū*; 1920) and *From Survival to Living* (*Seizon kara seikatsu e*; 1921), as well as in the two periodicals of the Culture Life Research Group, Morimoto compared data on income and living costs in American and European cities with Japanese government statistics and his own survey results to adduce the discouraging fact that Japanese were on average far poorer than the denizens of the dominant Western nations. His opening lecture in *Bunka seikatsu kenkyū* introduced the statistics of a French insurance specialist on the monetary value of an individual citizen in different nations at the time of the war, with the value of a Russian at the bottom of the list, recorded as 4,040 yen. Morimoto went on to report that calculation revealed the value of a Japanese to be the same as that of a Russian. This was less than half the value of a citizen of England or the United States. The statistical disparity represented "primarily the scale of productive capacity in a society," and the fundamental reason that Japan was unproductive was to be found in "living problems of the people themselves": bad consumption habits, in Morimoto's view, were the basis of Japan's low level of productivity. Japanese had not yet achieved what he called "an efficient standard of living" (*nōritsuteki seikatsu hyōjun*).[77]

This "efficient standard" played a central role in Morimoto's construction of the culture life. Morimoto posited three living standards, correlating them with three modes of consumption. The first was the "absolute living standard," signifying a bare subsistence level of consumption. This was followed by the "relative living standard," signifying the ability of individuals to satisfy desires for things recognized by custom as necessary (*mibunteki yokubō*, or "decency"), along with "desires for comfort" (*kairakuteki yokubō*), and "desires for luxury" (*shashiteki yokubō*). Above these two standards stood the "efficient standard of living," achieved when individuals excised all luxury and satisfied the other desires to the greatest degree possible within the conditions of a

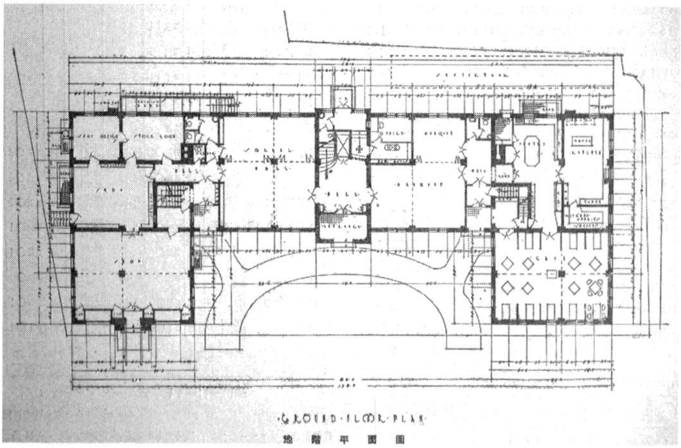


Fig. 5.8 The Culture Apartment Building built in central Tokyo by Morimoto Kōkichi's Culture Promotion Society, 1925. Design by William Merrill Vories. Morimoto believed that this entirely Western-style apartment building, with communal facilities on the ground floor and private units designed for chairs and tables, would provide a model for a more efficient lifestyle. Because of the prohibitive cost of units, however, Morimoto had few imitators. According to public housing historian Ōtsuki Toshio's count, only twenty-three other apartment buildings were built in Japan between 1925 and the war, of which only five were entirely private ventures (Uchida Seizō, *Nihon no kindai jūtaku*, 126–27).

given era, place, and society.[78] The culture life was one that took full advantage of the products of civilization to be "highly efficient" (see Fig. 5.8)

After 1920, Morimoto referred to the "efficient standard" alternately as the "new standard of living," the "new Japanese standard," and the "national standard."[79] He was explicit, however, that by "standard" he meant a level to be achieved and not one that the majority of the population had already attained. Morimoto developed a formula to calculate the necessary expenditure for a family of five to achieve this ideal standard and arrived at the figure of 2,076 yen for the year 1919. He explained that the standard applied specifically for the middle class, since his surveys of living expenses were limited to urban households that the author judged to be middle class. Yet in 1919, Morimoto found that only 2 percent of the total Japanese population was enjoying this middle-class standard.[80] By 1924, he had arrived at the pessimistic conclusion that the class itself was threatened with extinction. Two things were necessary to reverse the decay: class solidarity and the reform of everyday life.[81]

Reform aims took precedence over the analysis of economic conditions in Morimoto's work. Beginning with data from a sample population selected by what he judged to be criteria for middle-class status and arriving at a living standard that determined membership in that class, his calculations built only a model for the middle class as, in the researcher's own eyes, it ought to be. Lexical confusion between the existing economic bracket he called "middle" and the ideal middle class, defined as the class able to meet the "efficient" or "cultured" living standard, compounded the problems created by statistical samples selected according to preconceptions of class. In the end, Morimoto's economic writings were a loose manifesto for an imagined middle class. More ineluctable for Morimoto than economic principle was the material example of the Western nations, particularly the United States as he had experienced it. So, for example, if his sample population's average expenditure on housing was approximately equal to that found in American surveys, the point this illustrated was not parity in this area of consumption but that Japanese middle-class households were actually paying more for housing, "since our houses are extremely poor in comparison to theirs."[82]

Morimoto maintained that the middle class, led by the educated class (*chishiki kaikyū*) within it, had the obligation to provide a model for other classes to follow. Eventually, the whole nation should enjoy the same culture life. Yet the immediate crisis was that the vanguard was still hampered by backward customs. Locating the root of "living problems" in a Japanese home life that was "immature" (*yōchi*), Morimoto sought solutions in the same reforms of dwellings, clothing, and practice espoused by the Everyday Life Reform League, to be promoted first through the education of women, as managers of the home.[83]

## Between Science and Social Norms

What appears in critical retrospect a mere statistical veneer for a predetermined agenda was vitally important to Morimoto and his contemporaries. Advocates of everyday life reform and the culture life repeatedly sought to root their arguments in quantification, despite the recalcitrance of the middle class as a statistical object. Unlike the *lumpen* aggregate of the slums (who were at the time being intensely studied by the Home Ministry's Social Bureau), middle-class families occupied the same world as that of the researchers themselves, making it both more socially nuanced in their eyes and more private, shielded from the researcher's gaze. Yet deploying numbers asserted the impartiality of the writer and the typicality of the object. In addition to the wider use of social statistics in bureaucracy, Taylorist time-motion studies and such recent extensions of the natural sciences as nutrition research were encouraging the counting, measuring, and surveying of phenomena that had once eluded quantification and were encouraging intellectuals to find means of expressing their ideas in terms of the counted, measured, and surveyed. Waseda University literature professor Hoashi Riichirō, for example, redefined the old problem of sitting on the floor as one of "living efficiency" (*seikatsu nōritsu*) and calculated the cumulative hours, minutes, and seconds lost in an individual's lifetime to the task of sitting down on the floor and standing up again, then multiplied that number by the national population to conclude that this custom cost Japanese a total of eighteen billion hours each generation.[84]

Reform architects in the postwar period similarly began to draw on statistics, finding ways to link their programs for the dwelling to the abstract framework of housing as a social category. Ōkuma Yoshikuni, an architect who had written frequently on house design since the early 1910s, joined the Everyday Life Reform League's Dwelling Reform Committee in 1920. In contrast to his earlier writings, which dealt with the relative merits of Japanese and Western houses and with questions of style, Ōkuma began his 1921 article "The Architecture of the New House, Based on a Contemporary Standard" ("Gendai o hyōjun to shita shin jūtaku no kenchiku") with calculations of the average number of occupants per household and average floor area per person in Tokyo and adjacent districts, proposing that these averages would yield the appropriate starting point for middle-class house reform. On the basis of these calculations, he concluded that a house of 17 *tsubo* (approximately 612 square feet) would be appropriate for a family of five, and one of 23.8 *tsubo* (approximately 857 square feet) for a family of seven. Since municipal statistics represented every type of dwelling, including the rowhouse tenements occupied by most Tokyoites, this average house size was considerably below the scale of what Ōkuma and his colleagues ordinarily designed. In fact, the model house plan Ōkuma went on to propose in the same article, although not large by the standards of his professional peers, was nevertheless considerably larger than the "contemporary standard" he himself had derived statistically from aggregate figures on Tokyo housing.[85]

Displaying a similar propensity for scientific language and in keeping with the *modus operandi* of the social bureaucracy and its advisory organs, the various committees of the Everyday Life Reform League framed their work in the form of what were called "surveys." Newspapers reported that one or the other committee was "presently surveying" the particular aspect of material life it had been assigned to reform.[86] In 1923, the league published a report entitled "Matters Determined by the Everyday Life Reform Surveys" ("Seikatsu kaizen chōsa kettei jikō"), the contents of which were an assembly of all the reform proposals the League had announced in its three years of activity. Neither this report nor the newspaper articles about league activities indicated that the league's survey work had involved systematic observation of any kind. This is not to say that the committees had been slack in their duties. The report compiled information from a variety of sources, and its prescriptions were detailed. But the project at hand was to urge reform, and with regard to the middle-class life that was their target, the reformers were in broad agreement without needing verification from direct study of existing conditions.

Social-scientific language and statistics cloaked a search for norms or for substantial proof of the legitimacy of practices whose position of cultural privilege, either in the order of nations or within the structure of Japanese society, was a foregone conclusion. Statistics provided a rhetoric for talking about society rather than a rigid template for drawing reform plans. In the best tradition of social science, Morimoto Kōkichi acknowledged that his numbers were provisional and that further study would be necessary. Yet it is impossible to accept Morimoto's claim of scientific neutrality because his conception of the efficient "culture life" was a closed logical circuit set in motion by Japan's disparity with the West. Similarly, the "survey" provided a universal frame to particular experiences and expectations, often to the same concerns that had preoccupied the progressive elite of the previous generation.

Postwar discussion of dwellings and everyday life began with the discovery by government and elite intellectuals of urban mass society. Sharing the platform of social policy with reformers from outside government, progressive bureaucrats engaged the state in promoting a program for proper consumption behavior devised for the "middle class" by its self-appointed representatives. The fundamental class affinity between social bureaucrats and these reformers resulted in a social policy that in retrospect may appear curious. It is difficult to understand how the mass social crisis of the rice riots could prompt a campaign to promote the use of chairs, for example, without recognizing the background of the people mediating between these two events. Yet even as they recycled aspects of an old agenda, the reformers of the educated elite were changed by the realization of a larger middle class around them. Responding to the new social and intellectual climate, architects turned their attention toward the issues of urban planning and housing provision. The urban women and men of the Everyday Life Reform League confronted the era of mass society first by attempting the tactics of propaganda in the streets, sending their own youths out among the "Marx boys" and the sandwichmen before retreating into the more secure intellectual milieus of the research group and the monthly journal.

Moreover, in contrast to the particular and personally focused domestic reform models of architects in the first decades of the century, everyday life reform after the war sought universal representations of the problem. Statistics served in this period as a new means to imagine the mass, as well as an expansion of the bounds of science for purposes of self-legitimation. Middle-class models in the new reform vision were believed to be only provisionally middle-class—eventually all of society would meet the same standard. By the same token, many reformers held the conviction that the proper reforms for everyday life would be the same for all humanity. This was particularly evident in the new rhetoric of "culture." Morimoto and many of his contemporaries after the war (including, in a different sense, the political left) had taken a leap of faith toward the ideal of a single world culture, which they believed was in the process of formation (this is hinted, for example, in the fact that Morimoto's journal *Bunka seikatsu kenkyū*, like many other publications of the time, bore an Esperanto subtitle, "La Studado pri la Kultura Vivo"). Morimoto believed that the right forms and practices for modern life could be empirically determined, and that empirical study would reveal them to be predominantly Western.

Still, bourgeois reformers could turn to international standards with greater ease than they could depart from bourgeois interests. A common belief in the legitimacy and importance of modern ideals of the home and the need to make dwellings conform to them defined the constituency for everyday life reform. In the early 1920s, before Reform League programs began to move to the countryside, the old guard of reformers comfortably disregarded the unenlightened masses outside this constituency. But even a narrow bourgeois focus did not ensure consensus. The work of reform among the cultural standard-bearers was complicated by the fact that the class of educated people who shared the values of reform had grown and fragmented. As the newspapers and new magazines like *The Housewife's Companion* provided a voice for new participants in the construction of middle-class identity, the former hierarchy of bourgeois society came under attack, and middle-classness itself became contested ground. Although the ideological bases of reform were shared by a larger sector of society than before, a multitude of actors now claimed a stake in determining its shape.

# 6

# Cosmopolitanism and Anxiety: Consumers of the Culture Life

## The Dream of Cosmopolitan Modernity

In the 1920s, *bunka seikatsu* (culture life) left the hands of reformers and became the name for a dream of cosmopolitan modernity. This dream appealed especially to the new urban residents who entered the growing white-collar workforce during and after the war. Their desire for a life unencumbered by either local traditions or the established distinctions of native and foreign was met by a plethora of new publications and commodities purveyed under the name of *bunka*.

Laden with meanings peculiar to the moment of their emergence, terms like *bunka* and *bunka seikatsu* are difficult to lift from their Taishō context (and difficult to translate into English).[1] In fact, like so many modern mass-market commodities, the terms themselves traced fleeting trajectories, briefly illuminating the popular imaginary before fading into obscurity. Arriving in 1917, *bunka* had run its course by 1926. *Bunka seikatsu* was at its zenith for an even shorter period.[2] Arguably, Morimoto Kōkichi's concept was complicit in its own demise, because it related centrally to consumption practices, which invited its exploitation for commercial purposes and therefore its rapid vulgarization. The mass market's incessant pursuit of the new guaranteed the devolution of *bunka* until it became simply a popular label for shoddy new-fangled things. By the time this point in the cycle had been reached, the market was ready for another term, and found it in *modan* (modern).[3]

All of this was plain to Ōya Sōichi in 1930, when he encapsulated the brief history of the term:

[*Bunka*] is a catchphrase that stood for our consumption ideals. The money that flowed in during the boom of the Great European War years, which vastly increased the consumption (*shōhi seikatsu*) of middle- and upper-class homes in our country, formed the material for receiving the idle philosophy of "culturalism" (*yūkan tetsugaku taru "bunka tetsugaku"*) that happened to emerge at the time in Germany. In time, it brought about the "culture house" and gave birth to a remarkable craze, so that from everyday things for the household to the merchandise that hucksters sold at night-stalls, nothing would sell unless it was capped with the word "culture." But this, too, was just a passing moment, and the serious recession of late has blown the catchphrase away.[4]

Ōya's description leaps between two "cultures": the rarified abstraction of social and aesthetic philosophers and the hackneyed slogan toward which it subsequently degenerated. In between lay the middle-brow culture campaigns of Morimoto and of the Everyday Life Reform League.

*Bunka seikatsu* thus bore the chimerical promises of consumer capitalism. *Bunka*, in the words of Harry Harootunian, "was a sign of excess" that, when prefixed to any commodity, had the power to make it "for a moment not like a commodity."[5] In short, it was an advertising tool, and one with the advantage of a European high-cultural source. The particular product might be of domestic manufacture, but the West was the font of fantasy from which *bunka* drew its surplus. Everyday life amid "culture" commodities, Harootunian writes, was a phantasmagoria "penetrated and shaped by practices and knowledges distant and distinct from those received from an immediate history and culture."[6] Campaigns for reform to this time had been premised on incremental progress toward standards set in the West, but "culture" was ahistorical, since as an idea it spoke the language of universalism, and as a label it implied being up-to-the-minute.

As Morimoto Kōkichi's writing makes clear, the dream of "culture" nevertheless depended equally on the self-reforming ethos that had shaped bourgeois consciousness since the Meiji era. Morimoto's own usage of the term fell somewhere in between the German-influenced abstract ideal and *bunka* as popular icon. Even after the term escaped the institutional bounds of reform discourse, the progressive aura he had given it continued to adhere: "culture" goods were not only "improved" but "improving." This contributed to their surplus of meaning, too—"culture," that is, made a commodity more than a commodity by fetishizing it in a particular way: as a material realization of practical and moral ideals of domesticity advocated since the growth of *katei* discourse in the 1890s.

"It goes without saying that as the level of our culture gradually becomes global (*sekaiteki*), our lifestyle and the style of our architecture naturally become closer to something global," began architect Serizawa Eiji in the introduction to *Dwellings for New Japan* (*Shin Nihon no jūka*; 1924), a collection of house designs in a colorful small volume for nonspecialist readers.[7] Serizawa filled his book with illustrations and photographs of Western interiors, together with his own designs. A welter of similar publications after World War I offered guides to modern living and sold images of "culture houses," the new focus of bourgeois aspiration. Improved graphic publishing techniques and the explosion of consumer culture in the United States gave Japanese books and magazines on the home a new look in the 1920s, filled with illustrations and photographs of consumer goods (see Fig. 6.1). Illustrations of appliances such as refrigerators and toasters now appeared in the pages of girls' school textbooks, and the encyclopedias of domestic advice that had been published since the turn of the twentieth century now incorporated extensive information about new technology. Writers treated technological advances as central to the culture life, making frequent—and frequently vague—references to "science." *Bunka seikatsu no chishiki* (Knowledge for the Culture Life; 1925), a single-volume encyclopedia written in simple language suited to readers with only a primary-school education, opened with moral advice and tales of success reminiscent of the nineteenth-century literature of self-advancement, but followed this with over a hundred pages on electrical devices for the home, particularly radios (broadcasting began in Japan in the year the book was published).[8] The long period of univocal bourgeois exhortation for domestic reform thus gave way to a medley of reformers, designers, and other cultural intermediaries serving readers eager for information on the latest goods.

The resulting proliferation of attractive images only heightened most readers' awareness of the disparity between their own lives and modern domestic models. Radios diffused rapidly in the cities, but new houses and large appliances remained beyond the reach of most salaried workers. "Culture" thus represented both a vision of a cosmopolitan utopia and the aspira-

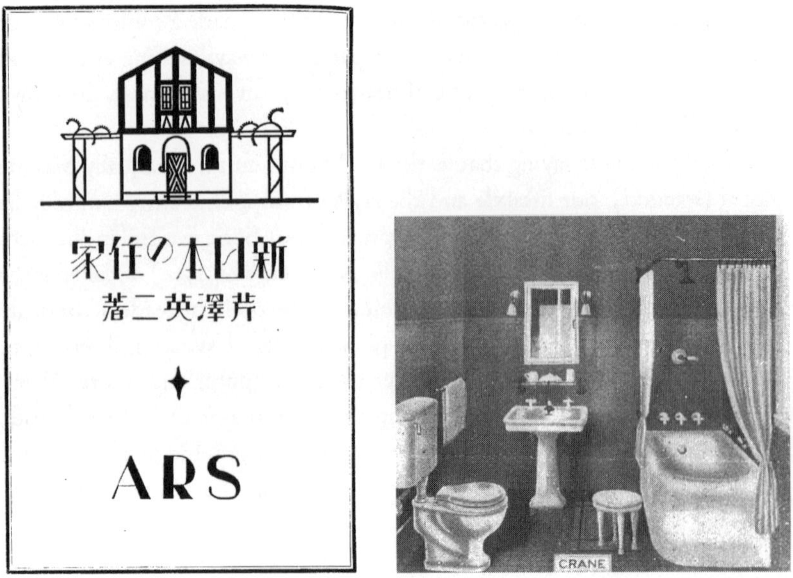


Fig. 6.1 The frontispiece (*left*) and an illustration (*right*) from Serizawa Eiji's *Dwellings for the New Japan* (*Shin Nihon no jūka*, 1924). Serizawa was an architect employed in the Construction Division of the Ministry of Finance. In addition to the author's own plans, the book included photographs and plans from Western architectural sources ranging from model kitchens for an American competition to the German Art Nouveau (*Jugendstil*) interior of a house in Mainz.

tions of a middle class struggling to participate in bourgeois culture. Two contrasting images emerge of the new urbanites in 1920s Japan, one of enthusiastic consumers of the same mass entertainments and commodities that circulated in Western capitals and another of precariously situated white-collar proletarians struggling to secure their social position within domestic society. Various circumstances conspired to help Japanese urbanites after World War I imagine themselves as cosmopolitans in a way few in an earlier generation had sensed themselves to be. Yet if global cultural participation had become easier, class participation was an issue more fraught than ever.

## The Culture Consumer's Cosmopolitanism

The talk of reform and reconstruction that flourished after the end of World War I was given new impetus by the Kantō Earthquake of September 1923, which reduced nearly three-quarters of Tokyo to ashes. The years

Fig. 6.2 Façade of a glass shop in a Secession or rudimentary Art Nouveau style; Ginza, mid-1920s. The temporary structures built for merchants in the Ginza offered ideal material for architectural experiments. Unusual designs suddenly blossomed all along the main avenue, confirming for many in Tokyo that the city was emerging anew, unconstrained by past conventions. Under the belltower at the top, a sign in Esperanto reads "The Bell of Revival" (*Kenchiku shashin ruiju*, reprinted in Fujimori Terunobu et al., *Ushinawareta teito Tōkyō*, 176).

from 1923 until completion of the recovery project in 1931 were a period of rebirth for the capital. In the immediate aftermath of the earthquake, a number of intellectuals publicly rejoiced at the destruction of the city's commercial and working-class downtown, despite the tremendous loss of life incurred, seeing it as a great opportunity to lift the city from its former squalor and transform it into a world capital. Should the model be Paris—or was Tokyo more like London?—the tastemaking elite wondered aloud in the pages of the newspaper *Jiji shinpō*, which solicited their opinions for a series of columns entitled "Architecture and the Re-emergence of a Beautiful Tokyo" that ran for a half-year following the disaster. All called for reconstruction in fireproof materials, and praised buildings such as Frank Lloyd Wright's Imperial Hotel and the city's first reinforced concrete office structure, the Maru Building, both of which had been completed on the verge of the earthquake and had survived it. Some also wrote reviews of the new temporary structures going up in the Ginza commercial district, many of which were decorated with bold "Secession-style" facades (see Fig. 6.2). Planners and other bourgeois intellectuals lamented the powerlessness of the city government to appropriate land for monumental replanning in the face of strong opposition from landlords.[9] The mayor's grandest plans for a new Tokyo were never realized, yet amid broad propaganda efforts to awaken civic pride and cajole Tokyo citizens into cooperating, blocks were regularized, new tree-lined boulevards were built, structures of concrete and glass went up at key intersections downtown, and Tokyo took on some of the appearance of a modern world capital.[10]

Cosmopolitanism, together with a sense of accelerating change catalyzed by expanding audiences, underlay new developments in the arts in the same years. The Japanese avant-garde in the 1920s evolved simultaneously with movements elsewhere in the world, thwarting the tidy classifications established by the Meiji academy.[11] As Suzuki Sadami observes, following talk of reform and reconstruction, "newly emergent" or "new" (*shinkō*) became the key word among artists and critics after the earthquake, in expressions such as "the new art" (*shinkō geijutsu*), "the new literature" (*shinkō bungaku*), "the new cinema" (*shinkō eiga*), and "the new class" (*shinkō kaikyū*). These phrases bespoke the abandonment of a unitary program for national progress and its replacement by a kaleidoscope of ephemeral movements, rising into view and fading again, spilling over one another in rapid cycles of change.[12] Events at the cutting edge of modernist culture played out in the streets of Tokyo, often in close alliance with an increasingly adventurous commercial sector. Indeed, vanguard graphic artists saw the signboards, the building façades, and the streets of the city as their canvas and sought to erase the distinction between commercial and studio art.[13] Since the bold new advertising used cosmopolitan imagery and graphic styles to target middle-class consumers, avant-garde modernism in the arts was closely linked to the middle-brow modernism of the culture life. Both belonged to the broad sea change from elite-controlled modernization premised on linear development to a modernity shaped in the fragmented and fluctuating space of signs, produced and diffused simultaneously and globally.

Even to those unaware of the global context of these artistic developments, Tokyo's cosmopolitanism declared itself through new technology and the messages of international media. Through wire services, cinema, radio, graphic magazines, and other media, broad publics in Tokyo and Osaka witnessed themselves living simultaneously alongside the people of London, Berlin, Paris, and New York.[14] Incorporation and advances in printing technology after World War I made the *Asahi* and *Mainichi* into mass newspapers with circulation in the millions and began an intense rivalry between the two. In 1928, the *Tokyo Asahi* flew in photographs from China of the explosion that killed Chinese nationalist Chang Tso-lin, printing them less than a day after the event. The *Mainichi* responded by importing a French device for wireless photo transmission. By the end of the decade, the pages of major newspapers thus juxtaposed stories and images of other parts of the world and news of domestic society with equal vividness and negligible time lag.[15]

The moving image and sound were breaking the same barriers. American culture rushed in with sensual force in Hollywood films, a flood of images immediately apprehended by the eye.[16] Film was an inherently popular medium. Unlike many Western cultural imports in the Meiji period, its products were not monopolized by a literate elite and not proffered to the public as morally improving. Radio broadcasts, although domestically produced and strictly circumscribed by the Ministry of Communications, blended contemporary Western music and drama with native forms, creating an officially sanctioned modern culture that defied standard dichotomies. When the single national station JOAK began broadcasting in 1925, the music programming was weighted toward Western symphonic music, reflecting the tradition of government-sponsored didacticism in Western high traditions. But the station increasingly gave air time to dance bands, which played foxtrots like the 1928 hit "My Blue Heaven," rewritten with Japanese lyrics. The first dance band to be aired was an amateur group formed by foreigners living in Kobe. Japanese bands included the "Cosmopolitan Novelty Orchestra" and the station's own "Oriental Jazz Band."[17] The station also commonly broadcast performances of the orchestras on visiting international cruise ships. In addition to music that was unambiguously Western in origin, radio listeners also heard "Japanese-Western ensemble" music, a newly invented genre that combined native *nagauta* singing and sometimes native instruments with Western orchestra and was particularly popular as the accompaniment to silent films.[18]

An increasingly hybrid popular culture accompanied the internationalization of media. Theater revues in the 1920s turned away from native historical themes to win new audiences with stories of world travel involving exotic sets and enormous casts. The success of the Takarazuka Girls' Opera

Fig. 6.3 Eclectic profusion of the modern city: the concrete, glass, and neon Tokyo downtown as represented in the stage production of *Tokyo March* (1929).

performance of "Mon Pari" in 1927 was followed by "New York March," "Italiana," "Miss Shanghai," and others (see Figs. 6.3–6.4).[19] "Tokyo March," the best-known popular song of the late 1920s, parodied the sudden spate of imported fashions by using lyrics sprinkled with new loanwords and references to the most recent landmarks of the modern city: *jazu*, *rikyūru* (liqueur), *dansaa*, *Maru biru* (the Maru Building), *rasshu awaa* (rush hour), *shinema* (cinema), and *chikatetsu* (subway). Tied to a film and based on a novel serialized by popular writer Kikuchi Kan in the magazine *Kingu*, the song sold an unprecedented 250,000 records.[20] If listeners were not yet familiar with the new terms when they first heard the song, they learned them from it.

In everyday life, many urbanites could look to their own material circumstances for confirmation that Western modernity was no longer a distant ideal. Modernity became mundane through experiences such as riding the commuter trains, the streetcars, and buses or the new subway (completed in 1927); walking on pavements, working in multistory office buildings and factories built of brick, stone, steel, and concrete, or having trade contact with them; shopping in department stores or along streets lit with electric lights and neon signs; as well as through more personal acts such as wearing items of Western dress (which was universal among employees in offices and large factories and prevalent among students), using electric lights at home, and

Fig. 6.4 The "Egyptian Dance" from the Takarazuka Revue's "Mon Pari" (1927). The dancers' naked limbs are said to have shocked audiences (courtesy Hankyū Ikeda bunko).

using Western cosmetics—or at least washing with soap from a commercial wrapper labeled in Roman letters. These encounters with modern technology and mass-produced commodities directly affected people's bodies as well as their physical relationship to their surroundings.

In areas of everyday life where such changes had not come, it was often felt that "scientific" rationalization demanded them for the next generation. Children were dressed in Western clothes by mothers who continued to wear kimono, for example. Middle-school uniforms provided a precedent, and women's magazines promoted homemade Western children's clothes as more practical. The *Housewife's Companion* frequently printed patterns and sewing instructions for simple frocks and playsuits for small children, emphasizing that they were economical, easy to clean, and allowed the child freedom of movement.[21] Only in dwellings did things seem to lag, creating the sense of urgency for advocates of the culture life, who focused on the home. After the term was coined in 1922, the "culture house" served as a touchstone in the discussion of improving "middle-class" life, and in debates over social inequality among white-collar urbanites. For the consumer public, the disparity between the modernity that accosted them in the mass media and in the streets, on the one hand, and the persistent forms of the houses most of them continued to occupy, on the other, opened a space for the fantasy images of "culture" marketing to do their work.[22]

## Cosmopolitanism and Empire

Along with the ethos of national reform and self-improvement, "culture" in middle-brow and popular discourse retained another feature from the era of civilization and enlightenment, namely, the hierarchical vision of the nations of the world ranked within the imperialist order. The achievement of great power status—"civilization"—in Meiji provided a psychological anchor for the cultural cosmopolitanism of the 1920s. "Culture," despite the universalist claims of the philosophy from which it had emerged, was thus also definable as what the people of the metropole enjoyed and the colonized peoples did not. And although the imperialist underpinnings of *bunka* discourse went unremarked, the fact that so much of what was being promoted came from the West exposed *bunka* to the same nationalist criticism that an earlier era of Civilization and Enlightenment advocates had faced, in which Japan played the victim of imperialism.

For an ethnic Japanese born in the empire after the turn of the century, Japan's status as an imperial power was a birthright, since twentieth-century Japan was a colonizing rather than a semi-colonized country. Although many intellectuals would continue to dwell upon the threat of cultural subjugation to the West, the security of being an imperial citizen licensed a combination of cosmopolitanism and national pride that had not been tenable in the nineteenth century. This consciousness derived not only from the position Japan now enjoyed among the powers, but from the new status for the home islands, and Tokyo in particular, as the metropole of a colonial empire. Apart from news of war, suppression of insurrections, or the attacks of so-called bandits, colonial affairs were not often in the foreground of the metropolitan press, but as recent studies of popular culture have revealed, the empire made its way into metropolitan consciousness in a variety of ways.[23] Taking their cue from the international expositions in which Japan had participated, for example, frequent domestic expositions in Tokyo touted the empire's conquests in colonial pavilions, which displayed imported artifacts and living humans. Colonial exhibits were greatly expanded from the time of the 1914 Tokyo Taishō Exposition. The 1922 Peace Exposition featured a South Seas Pavilion for the islands in Micronesia over which Japan had recently acquired a mandate, as well as a Siberia Pavilion, perhaps in anticipation of some territorial acquisition that might result from the Siberian campaign in which Japanese troops were engaged at the time.[24] Advertisements also trumpeted Tokyo's technological and commercial advances as signs of the country's hegemony in Asia, absorbing at the same time the Western imperialist geography that grouped Japan with other non-European countries in the "Orient." Posters for the subway advertised it as "the only subway in the Orient," and when Mitsukoshi rebuilt in 1914, newspapers announced that the new store was the "largest department store east of the Suez."[25] Well before the war fever of 1931 put the empire in the daily headlines, Tokyoites received images of it, packaged and marketed as a natural component of the city's cosmopolitanism.

Miriam Silverberg has proposed referring to the mass public in prewar Japan as "consumer-subjects" because ideological indoctrination and media censorship circumscribed their role as consumers within their identity as subjects of the emperor system.[26] Being the privileged subjects of empire was the flip side of the same identity, with the opposite (though not contradictory) implication that while knowledge inimical to the emperor-state was closely regulated or suppressed, imperial discourses and the practical reality of empire also created an expanded space for utopian visions and experiments.[27] Although not often made explicit in the discussions of Japan's modernity at the time, it structured popular consciousness at a deep level, just as construction and maintenance of the empire remained unquestioned at the foundation of statecraft even in the most liberal years of Taishō politics and diplomacy.

For the Meiji intelligentsia, the unequal pairing of West and East in eclectic architecture and everyday-life practice had reproduced in miniature the Meiji political world, reflecting the fact of Japan's political inequality with the Western powers. This inequality and its practical homologies no longer ordered the intellectual world in Taishō. Politically, the end of the unequal treaties in 1899, decisive victory over China in 1895, alliance with Great Britain in 1902, and successful conclusion of the war with Russia in 1905 freed the post-Meiji generation from the burden of cultural inferiority borne by earlier nation-minded intellectuals. Fukuzawa Yūkichi had pronounced Japan a semi-civilized nation, only halfway up the ladder. For Fukuzawa in 1885, "escaping Asia" was the only way to ascend further. The generation who came of age in Taishō found the problem at least partially finessed by colonial conquest in Asia. The situation made it easier for intellectuals in the 1920s to regard "the culture life" as a universal value and a right that belonged as naturally to themselves as to the people of other progressive—which was to say, dominant—nations. For liberal political theorists writing during and after World War I, cosmopolitan culture did not conflict with ethnic nationalism. Some interpreted away the growing problem of Korean anticolonial nationalism by defining a Japanese "national people" (*kokumin*) composed of multiple ethnic nations (*minzoku*); others saw the development of "global culture" (*sekai bunka*) as an object reached through the maturation of ethnic nations (*minzoku kokumin*) toward full realization in "state nations" (*kokka kokumin*).[28] In either case, the hegemony of Japan, as a stable state ruling stateless ethnic groups elsewhere in Asia, was reaffirmed and fused with ideals of universal progress overcoming racial conflict. "Culture" in this context provided a universalist justification for hegemony while still recognizing some measure of pluralism. It was in this sense that the term was used when, following the March First movement in 1919, the less draconian policy instituted for colonial administration in Korea, which granted limited freedom to Korean-language media, was called "culture policy" (*bunka seiji*).[29]

At the same time, consumer subjects in cities of the Japanese metropole took pleasure in exotic appropriations from the empire and the global marketplace of "culture." Particularly for those who had not traveled outside Japan, the eclecticism of Tokyo's metropolitan life made it a surrogate Western capital, its diversity the proof of Japan's world status. Just as foreign goods and fashions flowing into the capital established Japan's modernness, people coming from overseas reaffirmed its cosmopolitanism and reminded Tokyoites that they occupied the center of an Asian empire. In this popular imaginary there was less a battle between native tradition and Western modernity than a triumphant Modern, which separated the Japanese race from the history-burdened Chinese and Koreans and from ahistorical primitives elsewhere in Asia.

Kawamura Minato has shown that depictions in popular media of the "native" (*dojin*) or "savage" (*yabanjin*) of Taiwan and Micronesia and of "coolies" on the continent provided the means to confirm that Japan was "civilized." Taiwan's "wild" or "untamed savages" (*seiban*) established themselves gradually in the national imagination through Japanese travelogues and reports on anthropological research, as well as accounts of violent uprisings against Japanese rule that were violently suppressed.[30] In 1920, immediately after Japan received the League of Nations mandate to rule the former German colonies in Micronesia, primary-school readers incorporated a "letter from the Truk Islands," in which it was related that the natives were "not yet very civilized" (*mada yoku hirakete imasen*), but that the children were learning to speak Japanese in newly built schools. Japanese speech was thus established for young readers as the vehicle of a civilizing mission, retroactively conferring the status of an established civilization on Japan.[31] *Nihon chiri fūzoku taikei*, an atlas of the empire published between 1929 and 1932, revealed that there were "savages" being tamed even in the metropole; photographs of smiling, bare-breasted Pacific Islanders on the Bonin (Ogasawara) Islands were reproduced at the back of the "Greater Tokyo" volume, since these islands a thousand kilometers south of the city were administratively part of Tokyo Prefecture.[32]

Civilizational equivalence with the Western powers was the message of a series of cartoons by Taira Michi published in 1928, which portrayed three pairs of "modern girl" tourists from overseas negotiating the complexities of urban Japan (see Fig. 6.5). All these girls belonged in various ways to the category "Japanese," since two came from Taiwan and two from the South Pacific Islands, making them imperial subjects, and the remaining two were portrayed as ethnically Japanese Hawaiians. All were shown wearing Western clothes. Here, then, was another way to incorporate the rest of the world into metropolitan Japan: make them into modern girls and have them come to visit. Imperial status and the technological modernity of the city made it possible to envision Tokyo as a place where exotic primitives came to encounter frightening civilization (and perhaps be civilized by it), while strangely familiar Hawaiians came to confirm that this civilization was no different from what they had "over there" (and perhaps to learn the truth that they really belonged over here). Why should Japan's civilization be any different, after all? The cultural logic sustaining imperial domination placed the Japanese metropole unambiguously on the side of the West. Where the terms of representation could be determined freely, Japanese modern and cosmopolitan modern fused. Imaginary colonial subjects transformed into *moga* demonstrated Japan's modernity at the same time that they made ideal material for satire. The joke depended on the audience's belief that *moga* themselves embodied in caricature the problematic conjunction of the modern and the female, and were therefore inherently objects of fun; and that, at the same time, it was absurd that these primitives could be *moga*.

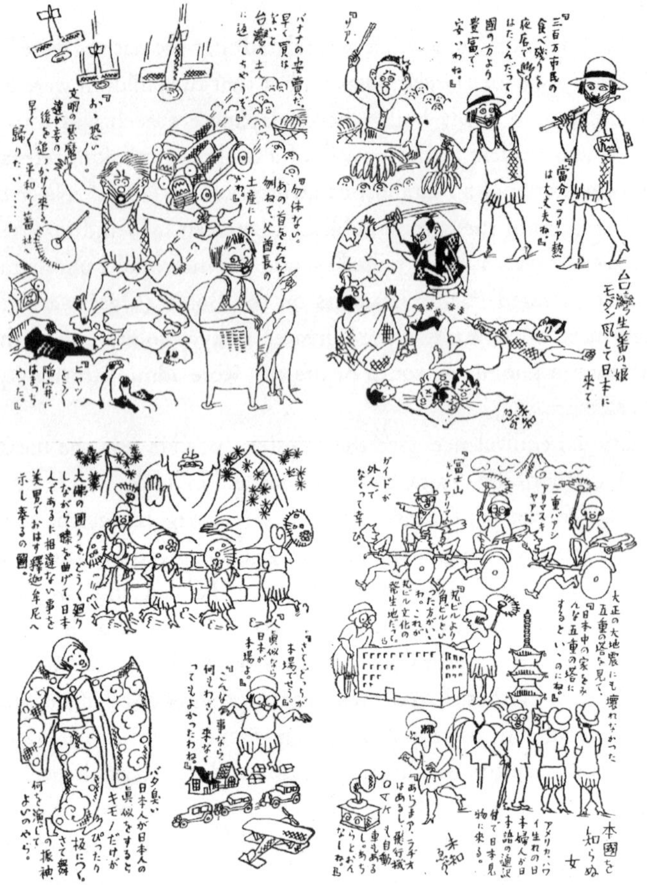


Fig. 6.5 "Wild Taiwanese Savage Girls in Modern Style" (*top*) and "Women Who Don't Know Their Native Land" (*bottom*) (Taira Michi, "Taiwan seiban no musume modan fū shite Nihon ni kite" and "Hongoku o shiranu onna," in *Gendai manga taikan 9: onna no sekai,* 1928, 162–67). The cartoonist manages to fuse imperial and cosmopolitan conceptions of the modern by rendering in caricature the cultural distance between colonized people and the modern metropole while, at the same time, making satiric jabs at the hybrid character of Japanese modernity—particularly at modern girls, its favorite popular icons. The two "wild Taiwanese savage girls" discover the prosperity of the metropole when they see bananas sold cheaper than at home. The one posing stylishly in the rattan chair points toward figures in a samurai drama and says, "What a waste. I'd like to bundle all those severed heads together and bring them home as souvenirs to the chief of the tribe." The visit ends in disaster: frightened by the "devils of civilization," the Taiwanese girls abandon their *moga* suaveté, discard their shoes, and run headlong before menacing automobiles and airplanes. In another cartoon, a pair of "South Pacific savages in Western dress" encounter a similar fate. Meanwhile, two Hawaiian-Japanese modern girls find everything the same as "over there," in the United States. One points at a radio, while the other looks over a landscape of culture houses, automobiles, and an airplane, shrugging in befuddlement and asking: "Well then, which is the original place [*honba*]?" Her companion replies: "When it comes to imitation, Japan is the original place."

If the civilizing process that brought these fictional Japanese subjects and wayward cousins to the metropole required that they arrive dressed as *moga*—Japanese hybrid products of Western modernity—then it was by the same token that Japan represented itself in the colonies through Western architecture and techniques of urban planning, the latter of which, as Koshizawa Akira has demonstrated, were subsequently imported back to the Japanese metropole.[33] In the colonies too, where architects and planners enjoyed free rein, expressions of imperial sovereignty relied on reference to an abstracted concept of modern civilization rather than to any concrete Japanese or European model. The design of colonial cities displayed Japan's power and colonial administrative mastery through architecture that was more Western, and therefore modern, than in the Japanese metropole, and through city plans that exceeded the older European capitals in their rational orderliness.[34]

## The Threat of Cosmopolitanism

Since "culture" bore these potential implications of colonial dominance and subjection, for critics it could equally be associated with the threat of Japan's colonization by Western products. As the market brought *bunka* down from lofty ideals to mundane wants and desires, the culture life thus became a shibboleth in debates over consumption of foreign goods. When the Imperial Diet tried to curb imports by imposing tariffs on 290 items deemed to be luxuries, writers in the journal *Chūō kōron* (Central Review) questioned whether the desire for things such as gramophones, Western clothes, and culture houses should be called extravagant. There are those, wrote Chiba Kameo in the journal, who "immediately criticize as luxurious living what we today call the culture life, or a small-scale version of it, or even an impoverished version that lacks the true meaning of the culture life." The true problem, according to Chiba, was the inequality of distribution; culture houses and the culture life were desirable for all of society but presently enjoyed by a small leisure class. These luxuries should instead be considered necessary to fostering a "positive nation and efficient society."[35]

Reaction against the culture life was a specific case of the generalized anxiety among male intellectuals about modernity and the loss of native tradition, particularly about "Americanism," which frequently connoted uncontrolled consumerism, hedonism, and superficiality.[36] Critics viewed the culture life as an indiscriminate embrace of all things Western, and its proponents as guilty of "West worship" (*seiyō sūhai*) or afflicted with "the Western infection" (*seiyō kabure*). These critics rightly saw that not only nativized hybrids, but directly imported products and fashions were reaching deeper than before into everyday life and popular consciousness. As in all redoubts of cultural nationalism, implicitly the ultimate threat was a racial one. Through dress and cosmetics, the Japanese were making themselves look more Western; it was not difficult for the nationalist mind to extrapolate that they would eventually succumb to the dystopian dream of miscegenation and particularly the taking of native women by foreigners.[37] Tanizaki Jun'ichirō's *A Fool's Love* (*Chijin no ai*; 1924) won notoriety and a huge readership by exploring and satirizing the submerged threats in culture-life cosmopolitanism. Falling in love with a lower-class Japanese girl because of her resemblance to the American screen actress Mary Pickford, Tanizaki's narrator enters a downward spiral of obsession and masochistic subjection. Throughout the novel, Western dancing, Western clothes, and a Western-style "culture house" play key roles in portraying characters debased by craven adulation of everything from the West. At the end, the two live together as husband and wife in name while she openly consorts with several Western lovers.[38]

Although psychological interpretations have had a continuing appeal since then, at the time changing conditions of commodity production and the global mass market were forces at least as powerful in the diffusion of Western fashions and cultural forms as any dilemma of the national psyche. And since many Japanese manufacturers were producing modern goods for both global and local markets, the penetration of Japan by Western capital offers only part of the explanation. Children's dolls and magazine depictions of infants hint at the extent to which images from the West reached into popular consciousness. Because of their closeness to birth and the fact that they are culturally only partly formed (and often less clothed), dolls and representations of infants seem to instantiate the problem of race with a special acuteness. Yet their role as commodities often pre-empts calculation of racial messages. For example, many Japanese children had grown up with imported German and French dolls. As in other markets, Germany lost its dominant position during World War I, to be replaced by the United States, where celluloid dolls were mass-produced at low prices, and then by Japan.

Fig. 6.6 Child with oversized Kewpie doll (photograph by Tanaka Taisuke, early twentieth century) (Edo-Tokyo Museum).

By 1928, Japan was producing over 70 percent of the world's celluloid toys. Most of these toys, like the archetypal and enormously popular "Kewpie" (designed in the United States but manufactured throughout the world) had blue eyes. "Blue-eyed Doll," a popular Japanese song from the mid-1920s, referred to a doll of "American-born celluloid," reflecting the perception of celluloid dolls as American despite the fact that most were then being manufactured domestically. In contrast to the cheap celluloid American or American-style dolls, French dolls were made of soft fabric and known for their elaborate dress. Akiyama Masami, a collector of prewar Japanese children's culture, writes that it became popular among girls and young women in the late 1920s to dress traditional Japanese dolls in French style and recolor their eyes blue.[39] Thus, the successful development of a toy industry that rivaled and ultimately overtook Western producers also served a domestic market for occidental exotica, which eventually became so naturalized that some child consumers actively participated in the hybridization.

In visual media for women, occidental images mixed with, or even supplanted, native ones. While girls played at mothering blue-eyed babies, adult

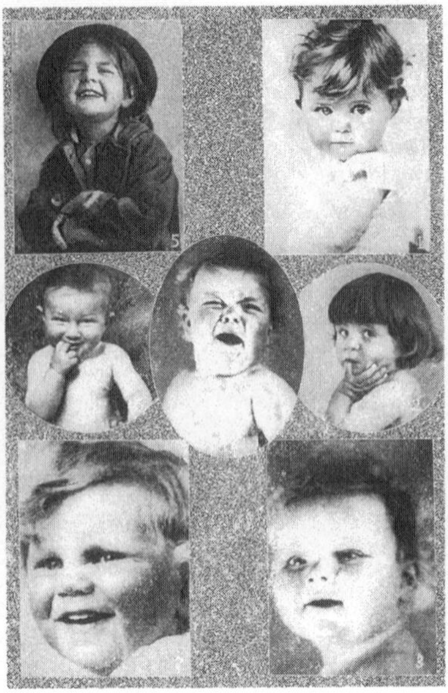

Fig. 6.7 "Children's Expressions"
(from the women's encyclopedia *Arusu fujin kōza*, 1927, vol. 2).

female readers of the women's magazines, domestic management texts, and popular manuals increasingly encountered Western children and mothers in plates published for didactic purposes or purely romantic appeal. Studio photographs of white women embracing infants and children, captioned "love," and "protection," prefaced a collection of lectures on women's health and childrearing published by the art publisher Arusu in 1927. None of the photo captions identified the subjects or the picture's place of origin. Other plates in the same volume included a group of cameos of white babies' and children's faces with playful speculations about their emotions in captions below, and a series showing a naked white infant playing alone, with a rapturous caption that concluded, "A child is the closest divinity to the world of adults, a gift granted [to us] of infinite love and adoration" (see Fig. 6.7).[40] Some publications also featured pictures of Japanese children, but the strain of gushing romanticism that emerged in literature on childhood in the 1920s was more often accompanied by photos of Westerners or images from Western art. This coincidence of discourse, media, and international commerce is in fact the critical point: ideas of romantic innocence and Western children belonged together because they were, in effect, marketed together. To interpret these photographs as evidence of the readers' psychological state risks serious misreading. Mass-market graphic publications commodified exotic children's faces and bodies as they did clothing, houses, and other objects conveying new and imported fashions associated with the culture life. A combination of exotic appeal and privilege as the source of the new gave these images from the West cachet as commodities that pictures of native children lacked.

Yet with the racial nation as their implicit foundation, it was not difficult for critics to condemn the liberal abandon with which everyday life reform advocates and the popular vehicles of *bunka seikatsu* purveyed not only practical commodities but also images of everything Western, including Western bodies. For their part, cultural intermediaries were frequently at pains to emphasize that they were not merely advocating that Japanese imitate Europeans and Americans. Blind adulation of things Western was unpalatable to intellectuals of all beliefs, not only because it suggested a lack of national pride but also because the capacity to discriminate among the material and cultural products of the West and appraise them alongside things native had become an important mark of their social position. With regard to the dwelling, critics addressed "West-worshipping" reforms primarily on aesthetic grounds. Morimoto Kōkichi responded by taking the position that the issue of dwelling reform was not an aesthetic but an economic one, and he advocated a blend of native and Western architectural elements (very similar to that proposed by the Everyday Life Reform League) as best suited to "present economic life."[41]

## Class Anxieties

Many culture consumers also experienced anxiety amid the city's rapid modernization, but their anxiety related more commonly to the uncertainties of class position in a volatile capitalist economy than to the fate of what right-wing activists called the "national essence." After the brief war boom, white-collar workers found themselves in a protracted period of instability. Even as the economy contracted, the universities and higher schools kept producing increasing numbers of graduates. Unemployment grew steadily through the decade and then worsened markedly with the onset of the depression in 1929.[42]

A change of designation for many private higher schools led to increasing overproduction of college graduates after the mid-1920s. Starting incomes at the large firms in the 1920s were ranked according not only to the level of the entering employee's education but also to the school he had attended, creating intense competition to enter the elite universities and high unemployment rates for the glut of university graduates.[43] The cases of failure in this system were especially conspicuous, since a university diploma had almost guaranteed bureaucratic appointment or corporate employment not long before. Ozu Yasujirō's film *Daigaku wa deta keredo* (I Graduated College, But . . . ) appeared in 1929. The title became a popular phrase. Roughly half the graduates from Tokyo's leading universities in 1930 failed to find jobs on graduation, and the figure dropped to 36 percent the following year.[44]

Despite steadily worsening prospects for college graduates, the households of white-collar employees in aggregate consumed more in 1930 than they had a decade earlier. The 1920s were the great era of the household budget survey in Japan. Drawing on surveys conducted in Tokyo and budgets submitted by readers to women's magazines, social historian Terade Kōji has found a marked rise in white-collar living standards between 1919 and 1922, then a general leveling afterward, marking the stabilization of what he regards as the pattern of professional household consumption that persisted until economic high growth in the 1960s. Relative increases in expenditure on food and clothing for 1919, then housing and clothing for 1919–22, followed by social and cultural activities for 1922–27, suggest a growing freedom to spend on items of choice rather than necessity during these years. The steady rise of expenditure in the category surveys labeled "self-cultivation and entertainment" (*shūyō goraku*) further confirms this trend, although the levels are low in absolute terms. The distribution of expenditures that emerged after 1922, according to Terade, is typical of a professional-class nuclear family seeking to remain permanently settled in the city.[45]

The development of a stable consumption pattern did not mean that these households were well-off or economically independent. The women's magazines continued to publish advice on making ends meet through what today seems like penurious scrimp-and-saving, as well as quite meager sample household budgets. Examining family budget surveys for the nation as a whole, economic historian Chimoto Akiko has found that male company employees' incomes only surpassed their actual household expenditures in 1933. Teachers' incomes lagged until 1938. The difference was made up by a combination of income from their spouses, other family members, and other sources (most commonly remittances from parents in the countryside). It is not surprising, then, that along with articles on budgeting, articles on home occupations (*naishoku*), described as "elegant" and "ladylike" but also profitable, continued to be common in the *Housewife's Companion* and other women's journals. Chimoto's findings show that the contribution of spouses to household income was not large—a bare 1–2 percent on average after 1925—but moved up or down following the husband's relative income and expenditure, implying that the spouse's earnings were still being called on when expenditures rose.[46]

Yet for men seeking to climb in the professional world, investment in things Western and expenditure on self-cultivation or socializing were strategically indispensable. To gain company employment, one had to acquire a variety of cultural capital ranging from mastery of etiquette in a Western room to general knowledge about modern technology, world politics, and contemporary art and music.[47] Getting ahead also depended on dressing well (in Western suits), spending liberally on entertainment, and "maintaining a good address."[48]

After World War I, companies constructed a fixed status system based on educational background, placing graduates of the universities and vocational colleges in full staff (*sei shokuin*) positions, secondary-school graduates in auxiliary staff (*jun shokuin*), and primary-school graduates in factory positions.[49] Personal contacts played a large role in hiring, and employers weighted "personality" (*jinkaku*) more heavily than academic performance, in some cases actually preferring candidates with "middling grades" as less likely to be insubordinate. This mode of selection further helped to establish and perpetuate class distinctions among professionals and compelled young men seeking white-collar employment to conform to a narrowly defined "company-man" mold.[50]

The term "salaryman" (*sarariiman*) entered standard parlance in these years, as did *puchiburu*, an abbreviation for "petit bourgeois." Recognizing for the first time the permanence of lower white-collar professional status for the majority of middle-school and college graduates, journalists began speaking of the *sarariiman* as a new social type. While cartoonists lampooned, and novelists and filmmakers made gentle fun of the salarymen (often for salaryman audiences), social critics emphasized their desperation. In the eyes of Ōya Sōichi in 1929, the new consumers, whom he dubbed "the modern class" (*modansō*), represented the "cutting edge of the era," but it was a "narrow, fragile, and feeble" edge. The market value of education, he went on, had plummeted, creating a large "educated propertiless class" (*yūshiki musan kaikyū*).[51] Echoing Ōya, Marxist Aono Suekichi saw the salaryman as lacking a distinct lifestyle of his own, imitating the bourgeoisie as he struggled to avoid falling into the proletariat:

> The proletariat, in the laborers' quarter and in the factory, leads a distinct, collective, tribal life. The bourgeoisie, with its mansions and clubs, at the seashores and in the mountains of their summering and wintering, also have a distinct way of life. The salaryman alone does not possess any typical, conventional lifestyle in that sense. And so, while constantly quivering with fear at the thought of becoming a proletariat, they move closer to the bourgeoisie's lifestyle and try somehow to imitate it.[52]

Alienated from the social realities of their lives yet unable to escape them, Aono's salarymen experienced "disillusionment everywhere they turn." This bleak picture served to slot a new class into the Marxist reading of capitalist society's ills, but as Aono pointed out, the difficulties of urban living at this time were in fact more profound in some ways for white-collar workers than for men on the factory line. Starting salaries even for university graduates were lower than the monthly income of blue-collar workers in lucrative industries like construction.[53] White-collar employees did not yet enjoy the kind of job security that later became characteristic of large Japanese companies and had much greater difficulty than laborers in gaining new employment when laid off.[54] Unions in the 1920s were winning greater job security for blue-collar workers at the larger plants than most office clerks enjoyed. A salaryman union was formed in 1924, but when members first sought recognition from the Japan Federation of Labor Unions (Sōdōmei), they were laughed out of the meeting amid jeers of "What are you talking about?—Capitalists!"[55] Perhaps more significant for the class as a whole, since the white-collar worker's investments in education and lifestyle were greater, so was the need for stable employment.

This combination of limited security with increased spending on durables, education, and leisure makes Ōya's assessment of the new urban class as a "fragile cutting edge" seem apt. Unlike the bourgeoisie, who had long had the freedom to spend as they liked, these new professionals after 1922 would indeed have appeared to be "cutting-edge" consumers, visibly inventing their lifestyle from scratch through the goods they acquired. Yet at the same time, they were not in aggregate saving money, and economic downturns threatened their ability to maintain what they had, which accounts for the appearance of fragility.

White-collar proletarianization was so pronounced that in the 1960s sociologist Ōkōchi Kazuo judged that Japan before World War II had never in fact had a "middle class."[56] Yet, despite the failure of the majority of salaried employees to prosper or to organize politically, there is no question that a distinct salaryman lifestyle emerged in the interwar years and that it was seen by many young men as desirable, just as the role of professional housewife lured women. The appeal for youth in the countryside is suggested by frequent talk in the press of "urban fever" (*tokai netsu*) and confirmed by the proliferation of urban night-schools and correspondence programs during and after World War I. Here working students (called *kūgakusei*, "struggling students") could earn the equivalent of a middle-school diploma, the passport to white-collar employment. Most were from the provinces.[57] Shopkeepers in the city also saw reasons to envy the salaryman lifestyle, since salaried employees were assured a steady income and guaranteed leisure time. Maeda Hajime, author of the novel *Salaryman Story* (*Sarariman monogatari*; 1928), recorded the saying that "earning a salary is like begging—do either for three days and you won't be able to quit." Even more tellingly, a 1933 report on conditions among wage-earners observed that compared to other sources of income, salaried income had "higher social status and respect," and that even aristocrats encouraged their sons to work for a salary rather than enter into business on their own. By this time, it seems, not only did poor rural youth aspire to the life of the white-collar professional, members of the upper class regarded it as a normative model.[58]

For young men as for young women, the lifestyle appeared reasonably respected, low-risk, and clean, as well as assured of a certain amount of leisure time. For men, it included play opportunities in the city's cafes and dance halls. A considerable part of the positive appeal was consumption-based: separation of the man's work from the home made it possible to maintain a tidy suburban house and garden with running water and gas in the kitchen and a few electric appliances, ideally with a Western room containing rattan chairs, a set of one-yen books, a radio or a gramophone, or better still, a piano or organ; a clean change of Japanese clothes in the evening and Western clothes in the morning for the breadwinner, a white *kappōgi* apron and silk kimono for his wife, and Western clothes for the children. Modest as it was, a life composed of such things suggested ease to most Japanese, and offered those who enjoyed it a tangible sense of sharing the bourgeois culture whose achievement had been a national mission for the past generation and more.

## Dream and Reality

During the brief period when *bunka seikatsu* was a ubiquitous catchphrase for cosmopolitan dreams, the true *bunka* was treated both in earnest expressions of aspiration and in parody as somehow never quite achievable; it always lay just out of reach for the common man and woman. The cover of *Tokyo Puck* in May 1922 showed *bunka seikatsu* as a speeding train rushing past a male "Japan," who stood wide-eyed on the platform with bundles on his back labeled "Politics, Economy, Religion, Thought, Family (*katei*)." The caption read: "Japan's anxiety: 'How can I possibly jump onto this ceaselessly moving express train while carrying this baggage [of old customs]?'" (see Fig. 6.8).[59] Progressives perceived the pace of modernity and the totality of the changes it demanded as challenges to the nation and to themselves. This man standing alone on the platform thus stood both for the Japanese nation as striving parvenu in international society and for the individual petit-bourgeois Japanese in domestic society, yearning to share in the bourgeois ideals that the phrase connoted.

The gap between dreams and reality is a standard trope in histories of consumer culture. In a sense, it is a truism—for when does reality ever accord with dreams? Yet there are times when social factors coalesce with particular force to promote the manufacture and consumption of fantasies. The brief efflorescence of "culture" discourse in the early 1920s was one such moment. It also marked the beginning of an incessant dialectic between consumers' dreams and their frustrated reality that is itself an aspect of the modern condition. *Bunka* and *modan* attached themselves to a limitless variety of things, revealing that the pursuit of cosmopolitan modernity was open-ended.

As in the depiction of the culture life as a train racing past a helpless Japan, part of the anxiety attached to modern experience for Taishō urbanites derived precisely from the perception that it emanated from elsewhere. The effect of distance combined with the deluge of images from overseas was to create an ineluctable desire to test one's own surroundings against these

Fig. 6.8 "Japan's anxiety: 'How can I possibly jump onto this ceaselessly moving express train while carrying this baggage [of old customs]?'" The man, whose hat is labeled "Japan," bears "Politics," "Economy," "Religion," "Philosophy," and "Family" (*katei*) on his back as he watches a train labeled "Culture Life" race past the platform (Cartoon by Shimokawa Hekoten, *Tōkyō pakku*, May 1922).

images. The irony of the culture consumers' condition lay not merely in the gap between dreams and reality but in the fact that the popular media conveying images of cosmopolitan modernity established metropolitan Japan's position squarely within it, yet made secure "middle-class" arrival for the empire's consumer-subjects seem ever more distant.

# 7

# Culture Villages: Inscribing Cosmopolitanism in the Landscape

## Summer 1922, a Point of Arrival and a Point of Departure

Images of the kinds of consuming that should occupy modern home life and the kinds of houses to accommodate it crystallized in 1922 in the form of a group of fourteen houses erected for the Peace Memorial Exposition (Heiwa kinen hakurankai) held in the Ueno district of Tokyo that year. The walk-through exhibit, named Culture Village (Bunka mura), became a spectacle of broader public interest than any previous product of domestic reform efforts and a touchstone for debates around domestic ideals (see Fig. 7.1). Although the language of "culture" implied universal values, the architectural solutions offered here in its name were narrowly bourgeois in form. The cosmopolitan ideal of culture thus provided a mask for the continued pursuit of bourgeois ideals.

Culture Village was the result of a petition made to the exposition's planners by the Society of Japanese Architects. A committee of architects led by Tanabe Junkichi announced the society's request to build a group of full-size "reformed houses" (*kairyō jūtaku*) for the benefit of the public. Through the use of the ambiguous phrase *jūtaku mondai,* which could refer to either the deficiencies of the individual house or the broader urban problem of housing provision, the petitioners were able to tie their agenda for the

Fig. 7.1 Aerial sketch of Culture Village at the 1922 Peace Memorial Exposition in Ueno (Takanashi Yūtarō, *Bunka mura no kan'i jūtaku*, 1922).

Japanese bourgeois home to recent trends in social policy in the West. Since World War I, the petition noted, great effort had been devoted to solving the housing problem in Europe and the United States. The growth of industry during the war had caused a shortage of housing in Japan as well. But Japan's housing problem, they explained, was not only one of quantity; it was a fundamental question of lifestyle: "In view of the ill-effects of the double life in our country at present," the petitioners wrote, using the standard phrase of the time for the mix of native and Western dress and house forms, "it is clear that in comparison with the nations of Europe and the United States, our dwelling problem (*waga jūtaku no mondai*) is of yet greater importance." Once exhibition space had been allotted, the committee solicited entries, and fourteen houses, designed according to committee guidelines and described by the society as "practical, simple, and small," were put on display.[1]

The management of Culture Village was closely connected with the Dwelling Reform Committee of the Everyday Life Reform League established two years earlier. The two architects chiefly responsible for presenting the petition, soliciting and selecting entries for the model houses, and managing the village during the exposition were active members of the League. Tanabe Junkichi was vice chairman of the league's Dwelling Reform Committee. Ōkuma Yoshikuni, Tanabe's senior at Tokyo Imperial University and a colleague on the Dwelling Reform Committee, was appointed "headman" (*sonchō*) of the temporary village. The guidelines for architects' submissions required that principal rooms be designed for chairs and encouraged several other features that corresponded to the Reform League model. In addition, both men were members of the Dwelling Reform Society established earlier by domestic economist Misumi Suzuko and builder Hashiguchi Shinsuke, founder of Amerika-ya. Amerika-ya was among the contributors to the exposition's group of model houses, as was the Everyday Life Reform League itself. Thus, to a considerable degree, Culture Village represented the work of the same circle of people who had formed the core of the dwelling reform movement for several years.

For these reformers, the houses at Ueno represented the fruition of two decades of efforts to demonstrate that a general reform of domestic life could be achieved within the means of educated urbanites. Tanabe had presented plans at the exhibition two years earlier to show his audience that a typical rented house of three rooms plus kitchen could be converted for comfortable Western-style living, including functionally divided rooms, chairs, and beds, without increasing its size (see Fig. 5.5).[2] In the same spirit, Culture Village's competition guidelines limited construction costs to 200 yen per *tsubo* and discouraged houses of over 20 *tsubo* in total floor area. Accompanying publications presented detailed accounts of costs, which ranged from 1,980 to 7,500 yen. All the houses were designed for small families. Most of the entrants also emphasized that their designs were for simple living (see Fig. 7.2).[3]

Just as Hashiguchi had failed to persuade the public to abandon *tatami* mats and the efforts of the Everyday Life Reform League had not engendered the revolution in habits League members had anticipated, the immediate impact of Culture Village appears to have been mixed. The houses were available for purchase but found few buyers. In the press, critics and satirists found fault with them on a range of points.[4] On the other hand, the exposition houses enjoyed an audience beyond the Ueno fairgrounds. Two private presses specializing in architecture books published handbook-size collections of photographs, plans, and building specifications for the fourteen houses, and both of these books went through multiple printings in a short time.[5] A similar exhibition in Osaka the same year met with greater success; it gained the collaboration of a local landowner, who sold the houses

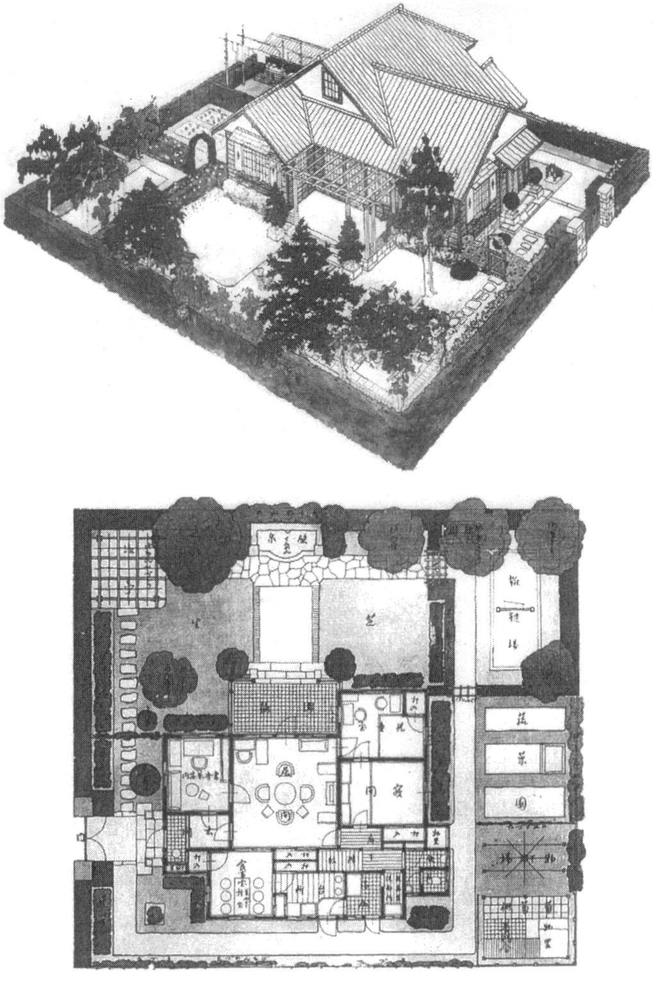

Fig. 7.2 Perspective (*top*) and plan (*bottom*) of the model house designed by the Everyday Life Reform League for Culture Village, 1922 (Seikatsu kaizen dōmeikai, *Jūtaku kagu no kaizen*, 1924). The entrance to the house is from the lower left on the floor plan. The chief planning reforms this house boasted were a central living room (*ima*), a children's room, and a wide porch in place of the usual peripheral corridor (*engawa*). By replacing sitting rooms (*chanoma*) and formal rooms (*zashiki*) furnished with *tatami* mats with a plan centered on a chair-sitting living room, this house rejected the gendered segregation of space that had persisted in house designs until World War I. Although some male visitors thought this too great a sacrifice for the master of the house (noting the small size of the master's study, one critic called the house a "women's world" [*onna tenka*; quoted in Fujiya Yōetsu, "Heiwahaku bunka mura shuppin jūtaku no sehyō ni tsuite," 2364]), the design actually asked greater compromises of the mistress, since it eliminated the rooms where she would ordinarily sew and fold kimono, as well as the space for traditional accoutrements of her authority such as the *nagahibachi*, the brazier at which she made tea and smoked.

省線目白驛より府道を約十丁、驛より文化村迄乗合自動車の便があります、市内電車豫定線停留場より約二丁


Fig. 7.3 "The houses completed or now under construction at [Mejiro] Culture Village appear to be vying with one another in their diverse range of styles. Here's a house with a steeply sloped and pointed high roof, while here is another that is extremely gently sloped and low; here's a tall and buoyant two-story house, while here is a low and cumbrous one reminiscent of the Imperial Hotel. If red tiles symbolize the pre-earthquake days, the green copper roof is a post-earthquake expression. White plastered walls, black creosote-sealed clapboards, window frames painted pure white, brown brick columns—these have been incorporated into the exterior of each structure according to the builder's fancy, attracting the eyes of passersby and stealing the hearts of even the uncouth with an architectural beauty of limitless variety and a rich palette of color" (*Shufu no tomo*, Feb. 1924). Postcard advertising Mejiro Village (courtesy Shinjuku Historical Museum).

with their lots rather than requiring buyers to move them. The Osaka site became a desirable new neighborhood soon after the exhibition closed.[6] The real significance of Culture Village, however, was iconic, for with the presentation of model houses to the fair-going public, the ideals and forms of the bourgeois home entered the mass market. Culture Village was Japan's first model house fair, the forerunner of a phenomenon that became common in subsequent years. Commercial developments borrowed the name, implicating it symbolically in the explosion of suburban development and speculative building that followed. In addition, the term "culture house" was applied to countless houses after the exposition, becoming so popular that it eventually became a symbol of the era itself.

Although the words quickly became marketers' catchphrases, it would be trivializing the sentiments initially aroused by the idea of culture villages and culture houses to imagine them only as marketing ploys. Like the philosophical discussions of *bunka* that preceded it, the new architecture expressed profound desires for a life unencumbered by tradition. It connoted a cosmopolitan modernity that was the common currency of educated urbanites. "How delightful it would be if there really were places in Japan's geography books with this name—no, if there were something possessing both the name and the reality of a 'culture village,'" mused writer Ubukata Toshirō upon visiting the fair in Ueno.[7] Architects and entrepreneurs shared his sentiment and, judging that many others did too, sought to make the most of the idea's market value.

Cultural historians have assumed a natural connection between culture villages, culture houses, and the new middle classes (*shin chūkansō*). They are surely correct that young professionals in the lower strata of the bourgeoisie were the most likely to be attracted by their promise of a cosmopolitan modern lifestyle. Yet in the promotional language of the time, "culture" (*bunka*) was less often conjoined to that earlier keyword of bourgeois ideals, "middling" (*chūryū*), than it was substituted for it. The original petition and official text for Ueno's Culture Village made no reference to class, referring consistently to the houses as "small houses" (*shō jūtaku*) for "the advancement of culture" and pursuit of the "culture life," rather than as middle-class houses (*chūryū jūtaku*), although it was beyond question that they were promoting a bourgeois model. In this sense, like the phrase *jūtaku mondai*, "culture" licensed the promoters to treat the bourgeois dwelling as a national issue. In the same way, suburban developers after Culture Village took advantage of the universal values of modernity signified by *bunka* to further promote bourgeois ideals and to advocate town plans that were more exclusively class-based than anything that had preceded them in Japan.

## Culture in the Landscape

The expanding suburbs of Japanese cities in the 1920s provided a space for experiments in lifestyle and architectural design. Banks, trust companies, and real estate agents (representing a profession that had emerged only at the turn of the twentieth century) sought undeveloped land for housing construction and, using a combination of financial incentives and personal pressure, wrested it from the constraints of long-held tenure. A boom in real estate trading began during World War I. Although the number of lots traded in Tokyo Prefecture dropped precipitately in the economic bust of 1919 and never recovered to the levels of the wartime "land fever," suburban land values continued to rise rapidly, and developers bought larger lots, keeping the total value of trades at the wartime peak until the end of the 1920s.[8]

The planned residential subdivisions sold by large real estate and rail companies formed a patchwork of scattered fragments on the growing city map, but they had a disproportionately large impact on public consciousness because of their novelty and the media attention they commanded. They also left a visible imprint on the city through the power to rename, etching into the land an imagined cosmopolis of "culture villages," "garden cities" (*den'en toshi*), "college parks" (*gakuen*), and neighborhoods called such-and-such "heights," "hills" (*yama, dai*, or *oka*), or "gardens" (*en*), linked by streetcar and rail to the old city.[9] Affixing "culture" or "garden" to a name demarked the site and emphasized that it was not merely an extension of the city. Like a brand-name, it also made the new neighborhood an immediately identifiable commodity. In retrospect, there is some irony in the popular use of "garden" to set new neighborhoods apart from the old city, since Tokyo had always been a city unusually rich in gardens.[10] Architects of the new suburbs in the 1920s, however, were reconceiving not only the townscape, but the relationship between dwellings and their surroundings.

Mejiro Culture Village, sold by Tsutsumi Yasujirō's Hakone Land Company, was the first major development to take its name from the Ueno exposition. Tsutsumi had amassed capital by selling resort property during the war boom. Mejiro was the largest of a half-dozen developments he had begun on former aristocratic estates in and around Tokyo in 1922. The development company provided gas, piped water, underground sewage, and roads lined with supporting walls of the porous local sandstone, *ōya ishi*.[11] There were actually four Mejiro culture villages, all located in the village of Ochiai near Mejiro Station on the Yamanote line, each labeled with a number in the order they were built. The first 39 lots of roughly 100 *tsubo* each went up for sale in June 1922, while the exposition was still in progress in Ueno. Unadvertised, they nevertheless sold within a month. Following this success, Tsutsumi quickly prepared 102 lots on an adjacent site. Culture Village Two went on the market in May 1923. It was from this time that he began to promote the development with the name Culture Village. The first subdivision, which had been called Fudō Garden, adopting a local placename, was now renamed Culture Village One, and the district was promoted in the newspapers with large-format advertisements depicting the new Mejiro houses, the first such advertisements that Tokyoites had seen. The company also printed postcards, bearing a statement in the language of the everyday life reform movement, with references to "the need for reconstruction of Japanese life in all aspects" and "abolition of the double life."[12] Tsutsumi promised additional "cultural facilities" such as underground electric cables, roads suited to automobiles, telephone lines, and a clubhouse. Tennis courts were also planned. In the newspaper advertisements, the site was described as "Mejiro Culture Village, in the zone of intersection between the Musashi Plain, created by god, and the city created by men."[13]

Image outran reality in Tsutsumi's developments. The tennis courts were never built, and the clubhouse, as in Kobayashi Ichizō's Ikeda Muromachi, received so little use that it was sold in 1926 as a private residence.[14] Meanwhile, Tsutsumi transferred his attention to attracting college campuses to locations in more distant suburbs, where he built rail lines and subdivided residential property. Here, bad luck, the world depression, and the long distance of the sites from downtown Tokyo conspired to yield poor initial results. Yet throughout the 1930s the company persisted in promoting the cosmopolitan image of these out-of-the-way suburban new towns. In the village of Ōizumi, located along the Musashino Line northwest of central Tokyo, Tsutsumi planned a "college park city" (*gakuen toshi*) with over 1,000 residential lots, each a generous 300 *tsubo*. A Western-style station building was erected, and the stop named Ōizumi College Park (Ōizumi gakuen) in expectation of the new campus for Tokyo Commercial College. To attract buyers, the company built thirty model houses, each with a distinct design (see Figs. 7.4–7.5). But the college settled on another site, leaving the town in Ōizumi College Park unrealized. The model houses stood alone in the woods and remained largely unoccupied until after World War II.[15] Tsutsumi was somewhat more successful at the next site, called Kunitachi College Town, where the commercial college and a music conservatory established new campuses in 1929. The Hakone Land Company engineer responsible for the plan toured college towns in the West and is said to have used Göttingen, Germany, as a model. Among Kunitachi's selling points

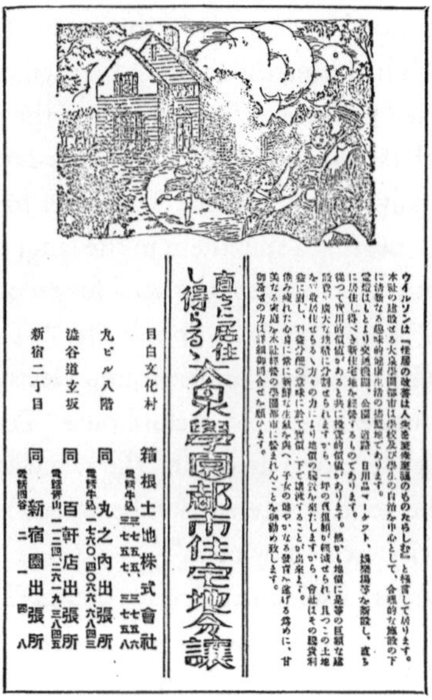


Fig. 7.4 Advertisement in the *Housewife's Companion*: "Ready to Occupy—Lots for Sale in the Residential Subdivisions of Ōizumi College Park City" ("Tadachi ni kyojū shieraruru Ōizumi gakuen toshi jūtakuchi bunjō") (*Shufu no tomo*, Jan. 1925). A father comes home to four waiting children in front of an isolated two-story house. The well-attired, ostensibly Western family and spacious, cultivated garden seem calculated to compensate for the impression Tokyo consumers would get from the new subdivision's location, which was still thoroughly rural. The text below quotes Woodrow Wilson proclaiming that reform of the dwelling brings the greatest happiness in life and informs readers that the new district has rational amenities to provide for a "fresh, tasteful, healthy life."

were three broad radial avenues lined with gingkoes and sycamore trees, laid out to separate pedestrian and vehicle traffic, a feature that was rare not only in the suburbs but in most of the city. Advertisements emphasized the orderliness and scale of the streets. But lot sales began just as the world recession hit. Prices dropped throughout the 1930s, and the town filled slowly. Hostility from local landlords who had sold to Tsutsumi under unfavorable terms created bitterness between old residents and newcomers that outlasted the war. Yet amid failure as a business venture and as a community, Kunitachi in the 1920s and 1930s managed to keep its unusual modern appearance. Early residents of the sparsely populated district remember the efforts of the company to maintain the promised exotic air with recorded music playing continuously in front of the real estate office beside the station, a fountain in

Fig. 7.5 "View of Ōizumi Village" in a photographic survey of Greater Tokyo (*Dai Tōkyō shashin annai*, 1933). "The village farthest from the center of Greater Tokyo. . . . Even if one flies at full speed in the latest model Nash, it takes a full hour to get there. While it is a pure farm village, the eastern section of the village contains Ōizumi College Park, and the Hakone Land Company manages a culture village there, endeavoring to attract urban residents."

the station square, an aviary with pelicans and cranes, and even caged bears, monkeys, and other zoo animals at intersections.[16]

Den'en Chōfu, Tokyo's most famous planned suburb, was another product of cosmopolitan idealism awkwardly conjoined to the dictates of marketing. The entrepreneurs behind this "garden city" promoted their development as a practical realization of the culture life. The sources for the project, beginning with the Garden City idea itself, lay in the West, but Western models were less important as prescriptions for urban planning and management than as visual and sensual spurs to the imaginations of the developers and buyers. Here too, the exotic occident sustained a dreamscape.

Originally called Tamagawadai Garden City (Tamagawadai den'en toshi), the site was developed by Shibusawa Eiichi's Garden City Company, established in 1918. It was one of three suburban subdivisions the company had assembled between ten and thirteen kilometers west of Meguro Station on the Yamanote Line. The doyen of the Meiji business world, Shibusawa was by this time in semi-retirement. He entrusted the planning largely to his son Hideo, giving the "garden city" something of the character of a pet project presented by an indulgent millionaire to his son. In 1919, Hideo was sent on a seven-month world tour to research other garden cities. His itinerary included not only the original garden city in Letchworth, England, founded by Ebenezer Howard's Garden City Association, but planned bourgeois suburbs in five countries. Unlike Letchworth, Tokyo's "garden city" was to be a commercial real estate venture, not an experiment in cooperative town management.[17] The Shibusawas, like the Home Ministry officials who had authored *Den'en toshi* in 1908, had no interest in Howard's financing system, plans for communal ownership, and underlying socialist ideals. The senior Shibusawa's chief interest was in creating conditions for the separation of workplace and home that his experience in the West had led him to believe was a cornerstone of national progress. For the practicalities of management, Kobayashi Ichizō's Hankyū suburbs provided a model closer to home. Kobayashi came to monthly board meetings to advise from 1922 on.[18] Plans for the new suburb proceeded in tandem with the Meguro-Kamata (Mekama) rail line, which was managed as a subsidiary of the Garden City Company. Lots in the first subdivision at Senzoku went on the market in July 1922.[19] Although advertising pamphlets were not printed until 1924, the Shibusawas had no difficulty promoting the project, since the press followed everything they did. Earlier, when Hideo had embarked on his research tour, the *Tokyo Asahi* had reported in detail on the mission and printed a photograph of the young Shibusawa together with wife and children.[20] The rail line was completed early in 1923. In October 1923, one month after the Kantō Earthquake, Tamagawadai Garden City opened its gates to buyers.

Tamagawadai's radial plan with broad concentric rings of curving streets quickly made the new suburb famous (see Fig. 7.6). As Fujimori Terunobu has observed, this plan was as thoroughly impractical as it was unmistakable. Fujimori argues that in light of its impracticality, combined with the fact that the housing development began before the rail line had been built, the Garden City Company cannot be understood as a rational business venture and must rather be seen as rooted in Shibusawa Eiichi's modernizing idealism. The street pattern was "uneconomical from a sales perspective, since it produced only irregular lots," and "inconvenient for street traffic," since it was difficult for pedestrians to orient themselves. The geometric elegance of the plan is fully evident only when seen from the air or in drawings. "Perhaps," Fujimori speculates, "people of the Taishō period felt in this

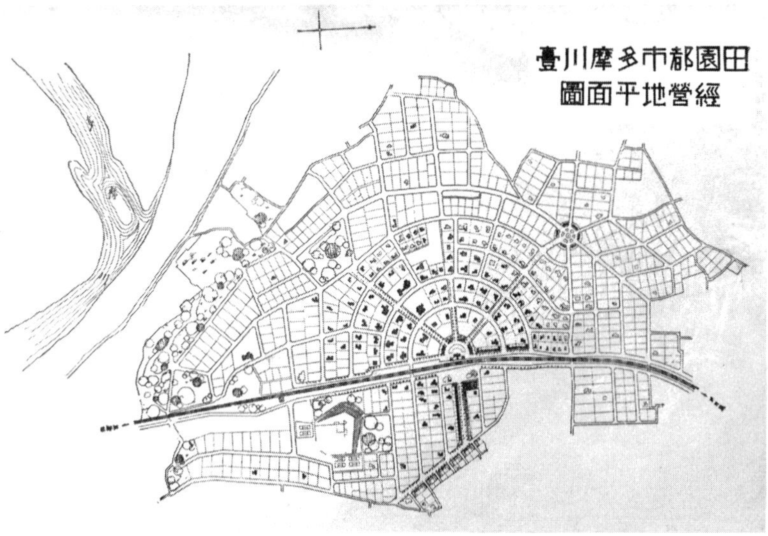


Fig. 7.6 Map of Tamagawadai Garden City, with indication of lots available, 1922 (courtesy Edo-Tokyo Museum).

centrifugality the sense of a Taishō 'self' fulfilled" and found in the self-contained plan the image of a microcosm removed from urban disorder.[21]

The precise semi-circles of this plan also bring to mind the pervasive use of circles in Howard's original diagrams. In the 1902 edition of *Garden Cities of Tomorrow*, Howard offered two hypothetical maps, one of a circular city divided radially into six segments with concentric streets, the other a detail of one section of the Garden City, a sixty-degree wedge sliced from the circle (see Fig. 7.7). Howard stressed that the maps were drawn this way only for convenience of argument, writing that the Garden City "*might be* circular in form" (emphasis added) and noting on the plans in bold print, "NB: A Diagram Only, plan must depend upon site selected."[22] Nevertheless, the conception of a town structured in concentric rings was fundamental to the distribution of functions in Howard's description of the Garden City. Howard gave his circular plans further substantiality by including scale and other concrete geographical indicators. Equally suggestive, the purely schematic first illustration in *Garden Cities of Tomorrow*, which showed "The People" pulled between "Town," "Country" and "Town-Country" under the heading "The Three Magnets," was also drawn as a radial diagram of evenly segmented concentric rings (in this case made up of words), despite the fact

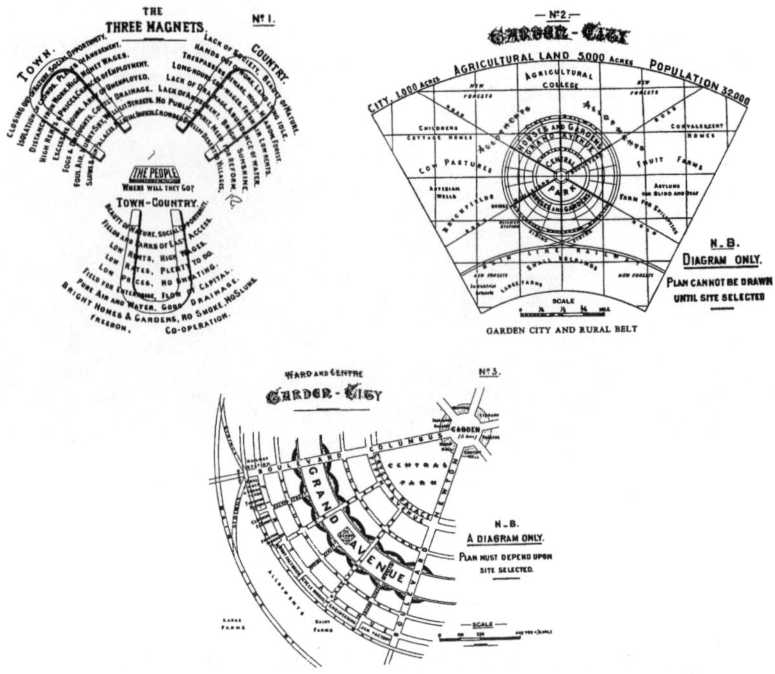


Fig. 7.7 "The Three Magnets" (*top left*), "Garden City and Rural Belt" (*top right*), and "Garden City Ward and Centre" (*bottom*): diagrams from Ebenezer Howard, *Garden Cities of Tomorrow*, 1902.

that this tripartite circular configuration served poorly to make Howard's point, which was that one of the magnets ("Town-Country") represented a place that did not yet exist, but would be more attractive than the other two should it be realized.[23] Howard's repetition of circular forms suggests that they played a powerful—if perhaps unconscious—metaphoric role for him, evoking completeness and harmony. There can be no question that the visual appeal of the highly legible circular diagram aided the global diffusion of the Garden City idea. It also had literal impact on future urban planning.[24] Still, few new towns came as close as did Tamagawadai Garden City to reproducing Howard's conceptual maps faithfully on the ground.

Redrawn in Japanese, Howard's two maps appeared as the first illustrations and the only maps in the Home Ministry's garden city book. Howard's caveat that they were hypothetical was omitted.[25] This book would certainly have been familiar to the planners working for Shibusawa's Garden City Company. Inoue Yūichi, the chief ministry official in the group that authored it, was governor of Tokyo Prefecture from 1915 to 1919, which put him in professional contact with Shibusawa Senior.[26] The book was in its seventh edition in 1913, the year Shibusawa Eiichi began investigating suburban sites for a garden city.[27] In a postwar memoir, however, Shibusawa Hideo claimed that the inspiration for the Tamagawadai half-circle was his own, and came not from Howard's diagrams but from St. Francis Wood, a development in San Francisco he had visited in 1919 after Letchworth and other sites in England, Germany, and the United States. In St. Francis Wood, he found what he described as an *etoile* ("*etowaaru shiki*") road plan, like a miniature of Paris around the Arc de Triomphe. On his return, he instructed architect Yabe Kintarō, a young designer hired away from the Home Ministry to work for the Garden City Company, that he wanted a semi-circular "etoile." The layout appealed to him, Shibusawa recalled, for its "beauty and depth," and the capacity of curved streets to inspire "curiosity and dreams."[28] Yabe, who did the actual rendering, did not follow the plan of St. Francis Wood literally. It is certain, nevertheless, that the choice of this street plan followed the younger Shibusawa's research trip and accorded with his wishes. Part of the inspiration for the unmistakable Tamagawadai crescents thus emerged from the young entrepreneur's visit to the wealthy San Francisco neighborhood combined with his perception of that place mediated through a memory of monumental Paris. The visual and kinesthetic experience of these spaces, so different from any native city, sparked the imagination. For young Shibusawa, who departed on his Western tour with the stated purpose of "seeing the sights,"[29] "the West" was less a source of planning models to be studied and emulated than a treasure trove of exotic images and experiences communicating directly to the senses, much as "the East" often was for European travelers in the same years.

Still, the similarity of the Tamagawadai plan to Howard's hypothetical map remains distinctive. Three broad boulevards radiate from the center, intersecting five semi-circular avenues. Secondary radials project from the second ring out to the fifth. All of this appears to replicate Howard's schema. Although the Japanese garden city possessed none of the social aims and few of the functional features of the English program, it resembled the original diagram more closely than did any of the new towns Howard's vision had parented in England and elsewhere. Company promotional materials included a simplified map that emphasized the radial streets, leaving most of the area outside the semi-circle blank.[30] As Fujimori points out, for those who saw the plan at the time the lots went on sale, the perfect abstraction of the semi-circle was what made Tokyo's "garden city" so striking. Advertising thus returned the semi-circular diagram from the realm of Shibusawa Hideo's actual experience of place to an abstract sign. While this symbolism mirrored the utopian imagery of Howard's original maps and diagrams, the signs did not signify the same things in Japan as they did in England. For the Japanese designers and their projected audience, geometrically regular and monumental Western city plans articulated the order and grandeur of universal civilization and thus held an inherent utopian promise. And although it may have been more the social ideals of Shibusawa Junior and Senior than straightforward business sense that brought about this plan, its iconic character, coupled with the cosmopolitan appeal of the "garden city" label, undoubtedly contributed to its marketing, causing a rise in land values until the area ultimately became one of the city's most exclusive residential districts.[31]

The publications of Tokyo's Garden City Company generally lacked Kobayashi Ichizō's marketing genius and literary flare. The company's first promotional pamphlet began by acknowledging the difference between its garden city and Howard's, explaining that Letchworth was designed to serve factory laborers, whereas Japan's garden city "has in sight a residential area for members of the intellectual class commuting to the great factory called Tokyo." "As a result," the pamphlet continued, "we were naturally compelled to build a smart suburban residential neighborhood with a high standard of living."[32] Sounding faintly like a disclaimer, this introduction makes odd ad copy. It suggests, however, just how important the Western point of reference and legitimation was for the pamphlet's authors, and perhaps for readers as well (see Fig. 7.8).

In the end, the promise of safety provided Tamagawadai its surest advertising claim. The coincidence that Tamagawadai property went on the market just one month after the earthquake, as well as the fact that the Garden City Company happened to have bought comparatively stable ground (none of the forty houses then complete in the earlier development at Senzoku had collapsed), allowed the company to trumpet in the newspapers that the earthquake had "proved" their property to be a "safe zone." Moving there was like "moving from a cinema with no emergency exits into a vast open park," the company proclaimed; "now is the time to establish a safe place to live, the foundation of everything."[33] Yet, useful as the earthquake was to the

Fig. 7.8 "Guide to the Ideal Residential Area" ("Risōteki jūtakuchi annai"), pamphlet published by the Garden City Company, ca. 1922 (courtesy Edo-Tokyo Museum).

Garden City Company's success, it only added to the appeal of an already popular development. The company history records that 80 percent of the Senzoku property sold immediately after its announcement in 1922.[34] Tamagawadai reached this level by 1928. The lure of the western suburbs as the site of an emerging modern lifestyle and the high profile of Shibusawa's "garden city" with its perfect radial plan, a cosmopolitan dream written physically into the landscape, formed a powerful enough "town-country magnet" to attract new buyers without a physical push from the city.

In suburbs where the development was not carried out directly by the railroad or a garden city company, small and mid-size real estate businesses entered to handle the process that transferred farm landholdings onto the market for acquisition by urban consumers.[35] Unlike the railroad capitalists and planners of ideal communities, these brokers remain shadowy presences in the city's history, yet in aggregate they were responsible for the majority of Tokyo's suburban residential development. Their work included property selection and acquisition, parceling of lots and street construction, promotion and sales. The example of realtor Takayama Kisaku reveals that new advertising techniques played a key role in these smaller developments as well. After the earthquake, Takayama bought land in the still-rural Tachikawa and Kita-Tama districts to sell in lots of 1,000 square meters. At the entrance to the estate, he set up a billboard with a painted panorama of the site. In the center, a tower was erected, and ropes extended from it in all directions, festooned with the flags of the world. Takayama's developments attracted lines of visitors, and the technique was soon imitated by others. It became common practice after World War II.[36] In the 1920s, the tower and national flags would have brought to mind the state-sponsored expositions in Ueno or an event at Mitsukoshi. Like Mejiro Culture Village's picture advertisements in the newspapers, the festival atmosphere at Takayama's suburban sites reinvented the commodity. Typically a house for rent was advertised simply with a sign hung in front by the landlord, and the transaction was effected by word-of-mouth or chance discovery. Here, however, housing was no longer what was being marketed. With modest capital but the same need as the rail companies to attract attention to otherwise undistinguished patches of former farmland, real estate developers like Takayama took a page from the book of propaganda techniques used by the state and the department stores and sold suburban land with the rhetoric of cosmopolitan modernity.

The large developers, who continued to manage the neighborhoods they built after they had sold the lots, did more to ensure that subsequent development conformed to the ideal image initially promoted, which was bourgeois and Westernized. The Garden City Company provided loans to buyers following Kobayashi's formula and imposed restrictive covenants (among the country's first), which regulated lot coverage, setbacks, fences, and minimum building cost per *tsubo*, a guarantee of class uniformity that had powerful long-term effects.[37] Company publications further indicated that for the overall visual harmony of the district, homeowners ought to build in Western style and urged them to hire architects. To ensure that at least when visitors alighted at the station they would see a vista of Western-style houses, in Senzoku the company set aside five central blocks as a "Western architecture zone."[38] Together with the station building, the houses on these lots would stand as signs of the suburb's cosmopolitanism, more permanent counterparts to Takayama's flags.

Both the Garden City Company and the Hakone Land Company additionally built houses to order for buyers. A photograph published in 1923 of a house in Mejiro built by the company shows a design with sweeping eaves and narrow horizontal tiles on the walls, suggesting the influence of Frank Lloyd Wright or his Japanese disciple Endō Arata.[39] Mejiro residents later recalled that almost all the houses were "Western." This "Western style" with which suburban developers sought to unify their neighborhoods was not so much the lifestyle of chair-sitting or family-centered living rooms that was the primary concern of everyday life reform advocates, however, as an exterior style, identified by walls, windows, and roof materials.

"Why, it's a miniature Los Angeles!" the advertisements for Mejiro Culture Village had an American visitor exclaiming.[40] Tsutsumi and other suburban developers promoted their product with Western houses and gardens, with advertisements depicting Western families, and here, with the verbal endorsement of a Westerner. It bears noting that the Western point of reference in this case was Los Angeles rather than New York, London, or Paris. California's young metropolis lacked the high cultural status of older Western cities. Meiji state efforts at creating an orderly and monumental cityscape, from the arcades and tree-lined boulevard of the brick-built Ginza in 1872 to the "one-block London" that was the showpiece of the Marunouchi business district in the first decade of the twentieth century, had emulated an older urban "West." In clear contrast, Mejiro found validation in no established canon of Westernism. Los Angeles evoked instead exuberant prosperity and a landscape of eccentrically designed new houses. If Tokyo's new suburbs appeared surprising to Japanese contemporaries, certainly they looked no more bizarre than Los Angeles itself, which was also a cultural hybrid.

Advertisements associating Tokyo suburbs with California or with fictional Western scenes themselves reinscribed the landscape of Tokyo, at least metaphorically. Although modern suburbanites doubtless responded to older local images of the suburbs in Tokyo's Musashi plain, and the decision to move to the suburbs was inevitably based on practical considerations for many, the idea of the suburb and with it the look of the new suburbs now overlapped in consumers' minds with landscapes of single-family houses and gardens in faraway places like California. Building these residential neighborhoods anew, developers were free to play to the culture consumer's imagination.

## Modern Conveniences

In the market after 1922, "culture" stood for practical modern conveniences such as gas fixtures, electrical appliances, and plate-glass windows, as well as more utopian images of the exotic West. Dwelling reform advocates promoted these products in the architectural press and the women's magazines as enthusiastically as the manufacturers themselves. Reformers portrayed modern conveniences as integral to their models of a more enlightened lifestyle, and in the process supplemented them with a dose of fantasy. In their depictions, the culture life was a world not only of greater efficiency, but of bright colors, harmonious communities, and happy families.

In 1924, the informed culture watcher would have known of two "electric homes" built in Tokyo for promotional purposes. The first, built by Waseda graduate and Amerika-ya architect Yamamoto Setsurō to promote his brother Tadaoki's appliance company, was occupied by Tadaoki himself and not open to the public; the second, built in Tamagawadai Garden City not by an appliance manufacturer but by Shibusawa Hideo for his own occupancy, was opened to the public. Both were more like performances of the future possibilities of electrification in the home than strategies for marketing appliances.

When it was built in 1921, Yamamoto's "electric house" in Mejiro cost the extravagant sum of 60,000 yen, including all the electrical equipment. This made it fifteen times the projected cost of a house built according to the sponsors' guidelines at Ueno's Culture Village. Yet the electric house was promoted in *Jūtaku* magazine for its thrift: electrification saved the 35 yen per month one would spend on a maid's wages. Setsurō published several articles about electrical appliances in *Jūtaku*. His brother reported to readers after a year of living in the new house, presenting the monthly costs to demonstrate that electrical appliances for the home were not the extravagance people imagined. He reported that electricity did not provide the most economical source for the large amount of energy required to heat a bath but smaller appliances reduced labor throughout the house at reasonable cost. In addition to using radiating electric heaters, one could quickly ready guests' chairs for a winter visit with electric cushions and footwarmers. Percolators in each room and an electric milk-warmer in the nursery reduced the need for service. Overall, electrification promised to

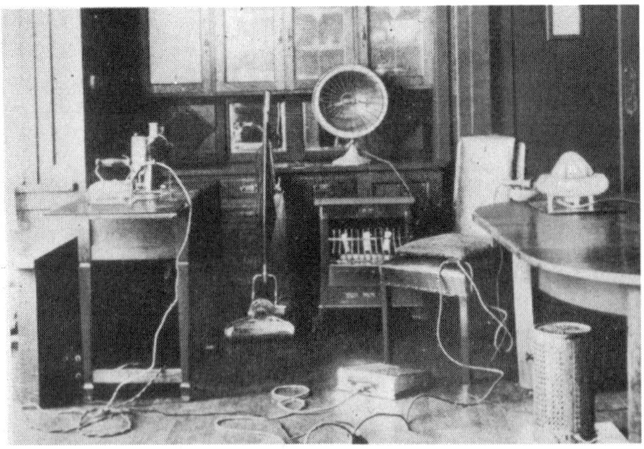

Fig. 7.9 Kitchen of Yamamoto Tadaoki's Electric Home, ca. 1922 (photograph courtesy of Uchida Seizō).

reduce the wasted time that burdened households "economically and in family terms (*kateiteki ni*)," making for a more efficient "culture life" (see Fig. 7.9).[41] For three years after construction, Uchida Seizō relates, the Yamamoto family lived without a maid—an experiment that would have made them anomalous among families of company executives and doubtless came with considerable burdens of its own for female family members in such a large house. In Yamamoto's eyes, it set a good example for his children and demonstrated to visitors and the reading public that electrical appliances would result in both efficient homes and happy families.[42]

Shibusawa Hideo built the second electric house in 1924 and opened it to the public as a promotional event for the new suburb. Admission was free. Between October 12 and October 31, 1924, 12,000 people visited. Amerika-ya, Mitsukoshi Department Store, a manufacturer of plumbing fixtures, two electric companies, and the *Tōkyō nichinichi* newspaper participated in the promotion. The *Tōkyō nichinichi* opened the campaign on October 8 with an article trumpeting the "fantastic house at Garden City bedecked in electricity" and followed several days later with a report written in the form of a dialogue between a couple visiting the house. The couple lingered admiringly on each feature of the house and its setting. They spoke not only of the electric fans, footwarmers, futons, and the kitchen full of gadgets but also of visual details such as the stained glass window in the front door, the "romantic" pink cover on a flower stand, the pale brown chandeliers, the "smiling faces of the cosmos and wild chrysanthemums" outside, and the "cobalt blue"

Fig. 7.10 "Please See the Electric Home of Chōfu," advertising pamphlet for the Garden City Electric Home, 1924. Although the authors declared the house to be a model for a new age in which electricity would replace fire as a source of light, heat, and energy, the house appealed through images of modern cosmopolitan culture generally more than through practical conveniences (courtesy Edo-Tokyo Museum).

sky.[43] As the visiting reporter's literary imagination wandered free of the modern conveniences the house was supposed to be exhibiting, the culture life's fantasy surplus came into play (see Fig. 7.10).

In practical terms, both "electric houses" demonstrated the promise of the electrified future more than the convenience of electric appliances in the present. The element of fantasy invested in the appliances they displayed clearly exceeded their value as labor-saving devices. Yamamoto's report on living in the electric house served his company's interests, and opening Shibusawa's house to the public was good propaganda for the Garden City. Yet in light of the fact that neither publicity effort involved selling anything, both promoters appear to have been at least as concerned to display their personal visions of modern living as they were to assure effective advertising. Like the geometrically planned suburb where one of them was located, they fashioned a dream from the material forms of Western modernity.

## An American Suburban Idyll

Utopian hopes for the culture house and planned suburb emerged again in a design competition held in 1922 for houses at Ōfuna Garden City, a development situated south of Tokyo and built by an organization unrelated to Shibusawa's Garden City Company. Here, immediately following his role in Ueno's Culture Village, Ōkuma Yoshikuni joined five other architects to judge entries. The development company stipulated that houses were to be on lots of 100 *tsubo* with fences and hedges less than four feet high on the street side and under six feet between houses. They also required that the houses be "Western" in external appearance.

What appears at first simply an aesthetic choice was understood very much in practical terms by the competition judges, for whom stipulating a "Western" exterior served to ensure structural modifications to the traditional house form, particularly the use of glass windows and elimination of *engawa* surrounding corridors. The standard vernacular detached house had removable shutters and paper *shōji* doors combined with wood-floored *engawa*, which provided a buffer to protect the *tatami* interior from rain. In warm weather, an entire side of the house could be opened to the garden, and often was, to let air in the house and allow occupants to see the garden. Glass windows with sills above the floor obviated the *engawa* and *shōji*, since they permitted sunlight and views while sealing the interior from the elements. They also gave the house a more closed shell, removing the intermediate space that allowed easy passage between the garden and the interior of the house (see Fig. 7.11). In the houses of many elite peasants, samurai, and their descendants, high fences had been used to screen the house from the street, thereby protecting ornamental gardens and permitting relative privacy for the occupants despite the open structure of the house itself.[44] Working-class rowhouses and smaller farmhouses, on the other hand, went unshielded by fences or hedges, allowing children to come and go between the house, the garden, and the street and neighbors to pay casual visits via the *engawa*.[45]

To bourgeois Japanese who visited wealthy suburbs in the United States and England, the absence of high fences appeared to be evidence of a Western civic-spiritedness lacking in Japan. This civic spirit could be quite elitist in class terms, however. In 1903, Shiga Shigetsura, who had studied architec-

Fig. 7.11 Glass windows sharpen the division of interior and exterior. (*left*) "A Middle-Class House for 2000 Yen" (Shufu no tomo henshūkyoku, *Chūryū jūtaku no mohan sekkei*). (*right*) Edward Sylvester Morse's rendering of a Tokyo house viewed from the rear garden, 1880s (Morse, *Japanese Homes and Theirs Surroundings*, 1886).

ture in Illinois, reported in *Kenchiku zasshi* that private houses in the West were understood as a kind of public property. They were, he wrote, "ornaments of the state" and even "works of charity . . . [since they] decorate the city and please the eyes of the poor."[46] This elitist view prefigured the somewhat more communitarian one of the Everyday Life Reform League, which also took its model from Anglo-American suburbs. The league's garden specialist urged that front gardens be made available to view, asserting that "when houses in the future come to be built with glass windows, it should be little trouble to dispense with the socially divisive (*kakkyoteki*) fences and hedges."[47] Gardens, he further insisted, should be designed for children's play rather than ornament. The reformers' model, reflecting their own class position and concerns, considered only elite tradition, assuming that all Japanese houses had high fences and ornamental gardens and criticizing these as indulgences that indicated the native lack of civic spirit.

The architects judging designs for Ōfuna Garden City followed the view of the league and earlier reform architects and called for fenceless gardens as a community asset. Writing anonymously for the group in the introduction to a compilation of winning entries, one of the judges stressed the aesthetic aspect in particular, noting that high fences made the residential street "like a row of matchboxes, rather than a bright, open-feeling neighborhood." But in this instance more explicitly than in the exhortations of the Daily Life Reform League, fantasies of the exotic West entered to animate the reformers' utopian model. Immediately following the bleak assessment of native "matchboxes," the passage shifted in tone to sketch a vignette of Western domestic bliss:

> A front garden surrounded by low hedges, with flowers blooming in profusion, the grass green as green can be; and on the lawn children play, bathed in sunlight, while father is absorbed in a book on the sofa, mother occasionally rests from her knitting to look out on the children playing—this kind of bright, delightful scene absolutely cannot be gained in a Japanese-style house.

Then reverting to the hortatory register, the writer urged readers to share the sacrifice necessary to achieving a better community: "We have our doubts about attempting to transfer directly to Japan an American-style garden city with hardly any fences at all. [Yet] we feel that at least the front fences ought to be low. We must cast aside the petty desire that people not see inside for the larger merit of living in a bright and pleasant town."[48] Implicit throughout this program for the new community was the bourgeois assumption, so important to proselytizers of domestic ideology, that families must be sequestered and their private apartments hidden. Walled rooms with glass windows would accomplish this, and front gardens would then be available for public display.

In the long run, the introduction of glass windows and this imported suburban ideal had far-reaching effects on Japanese urban culture, as they did everywhere in the world that suburbs of privately built single-family houses and lawns developed. In the Tokugawa period, house structure and ornament had manifested fixed status distinctions. Abolition of these distinctions after the Meiji Restoration had theoretically freed people to occupy whatever sort of house they should want and simultaneously opened the field to speculation about others' social standing and taste. Putting suburban houses and gardens on continuous display, as dwelling reformers demanded, made the aesthetics of the whole a public expression laden with class meaning.

At the same time, the social meanings that had previously connected fences, *engawa*, and landscaped gardens ill-suited to children's play were also genuine: a system of norms had related these things with established habits of life in the old samurai districts of Tokyo. When one resolved to abandon those habits, the fences, gardens, and façades emerged as problems demanding some form of architectural resolution. In the names of both family intimacy and national progress, Meiji reformers had rejected a native mode of dwelling that embodied a strict social hierarchy but that at the same time left broad room for traditional leisure pursuits and unstructured play in its interstices. In its place, they promoted a combination of native and Western dwellings that embodied the bourgeois separation of domestic space from a competitive outside world. The culture village and garden city advocates who came in the wake of the Meiji bourgeois ideologues inherited their idealization of domestic intimacy. They added a notion of comfort that was entangled with fantasy images of Western life and an exaggerated hope for architecture's capacity to give flower to a new family and community.

When the Everyday Life Reform League and the competition judges at Ōfuna Culture Village treated the problem of displaying or concealing houses and their gardens as a contrast in national civic traditions, they suppressed the fact that it also possessed profound class dimensions. Like restrictive covenants—and closely associated with them—the park-like landscape of private lawns unobstructed by garden walls or hedges that had spread over vast areas around cities in the United States beginning in the mid-nineteenth century imposed standards of occupancy and use that guaranteed social homogeneity. The lawn proved to be the great enforcer of bourgeois habits, since it required owners to devote time and money to maintaining the public appearance of their houses and lots for the sake of property values even as it buffered the home from direct contact with the street.[49] Confronting an elite native urban tradition of walled enclosures and evincing no interest either in the rowhouse form or in the housing needs of the working class, promoters of the garden city and the culture village in Japan limited their community aspirations to the low horizon of the American bourgeois suburb. As the Ōfuna judges' idyll of suburban family life suggests, their admiration for this civic tradition had less to do with public objectives for the community than with desire for the private lifestyle at its heart.

## Tokyo's New Suburbanites

While the most renowned developments popularized a vision of suburban arcadia mediated through Western modernity, the majority of Tokyo's new suburbanites moved into unplanned residential neighborhoods scattered in the fields and wooded hills around long-established farming villages.[50] In the 1920s and 1930s, much of suburban Tokyo was converted for housing with minimal infrastructure, as a laissez-faire planning policy regulated only lot lines to guarantee a minimum street width and allowed the streets to form as abutting lots gradually came to be built upon. In areas where even this was not applied, footpaths and embankments between fields became roads through new housing developments.[51]

One result of piecemeal development was a sharp contrast between small peasant farmers and their new white-collar neighbors. This provided a favorite subject for humor in the magazines (see Fig. 7.12). Some popular media also portrayed the new suburbanites as pioneers or presented "culture" as colonizing the capital's hinterland, further underscoring the cultural divide between old and new residents. From the point of view of the old residents of this hinterland, the urban newcomers posed an unprecedented incursion. Most came either from central Tokyo or from other parts of Japan (including the colonies) without any previous connection to local society. Peasants did not alienate their land readily, and the large sums of money involved, as well as the coercive tactics of the rail companies, sparked struggles in the villages between pro- and anti-development factions.[52]

Aristocrats and bourgeois intellectuals had already initiated the south- and westward migration into the Musashi Plain around the turn of the century. A growing cohort of white-collar workers followed them in the 1920s. Using directories of managers working in the Marunouchi business district for 1922, 1926, and 1931, Fujioka Hiroyasu and Imafuji Akira have found that the balance of this population moved in the course of the decade from the fifteen wards of the old city to the surrounding counties and prefectures. In 1922, 59.2 percent listed Tokyo City addresses, compared with 40.1 percent in 1931. The shift was more pronounced among lower-level managers than among board chairmen and company directors. By 1931, only 28.5 percent of men at the head clerk (*kakarichō*) level lived within the fifteen wards. The rest had addresses in the southern and western suburbs.[53] By 1930, the

Fig. 7.12 Cartoonist Okamoto Ippei's Culture Village. Peasants swing hoes in the foreground, as new residents swing golf clubs behind them. "How many places called Culture Village must there be along the suburban rail lines? Imitation German modernism and imitation American bungalows are jumbled together with the thatched roofs. The characteristic of these Western houses is that there's always a Japanese *zashiki* with *shōji* screens squeezed in somewhere" (*Keizai ōrai*, Oct. 1932).

population of Tokyo's five surrounding counties had surpassed that of the central wards, leading to their incorporation into the new Greater Tokyo (Dai Tōkyō) in 1932. Census-takers in 1930 counted 298,000 daily commuters from the surrounding counties, over one-quarter of the total working population resident there.[54]

In less than a decade, these new arrivals transformed the demographic makeup of Tokyo's western suburbs (see Fig. 7.13). The population of the four municipalities of what would become Suginami Ward after the creation of Greater Tokyo rose from 17,366 in 1919 to 143,105 in 1926. Between the 1920 and 1930 censuses, the proportion of Suginami's working population employed in agriculture and fishing dropped from 58.9 percent to 8.3 percent.[55] Until 1919, the average household in this district had over 6.5 members; this had plunged to about 4.5 by 1926. The figure climbed slightly in the years following, stabilizing between 4.5 and 5.0 before World War II.[56] Thus, as the rails made the western suburbs increasingly convenient to

Fig. 7.13 Growth of Tokyo's western suburbs along the Chūō Line near Nakano, 1909, 1926, and 1932. Reproduction of 1:10,000 topographic maps (courtesy Geographical Survey Institute, Japan).

commuters, the Suginami villages witnessed a migration of small nuclear households that quickly overwhelmed the existing peasant population and then settled down to have, on average, two or three offspring. These new households were not very wealthy, by and large. Although a live-in maid was considered one of the standard markers of bourgeois status, the percentage of new suburban households with servants was low. The 1930 census found 4,300 female domestic servants resident in Suginami Ward, at a time when the total number of households in the ward was 28,715, meaning that only one in six or seven households in the ward would have had a live-in maid.

Most new suburbanites occupied houses smaller than the models presented at Ueno. Three-room houses with ten to fifteen *tatami* were the mean among families judged to be "middle-class" (*chūtō kaikyū*) on the basis of occupational criteria in a survey conducted by the Tokyo Prefecture Social Bureau in 1922.[57] Even in the new suburbs that blossomed after this time, housing conditions for the aggregate population appear to have been little better. According to the 1930 census, more households in Suginami Ward lived in houses with three main rooms than with either four or five. Three-room houses were recorded as the most common for households of three, four, five, six, and even seven members.[58] In contrast, the informal 20-*tsubo* limit that Culture Village judges set on design entries for its "small houses" readily permitted a house of five standard-size rooms, and several of the entries exceeded even this.

However small the dwellings, homeownership did accompany the move to the suburbs for an increasing number during the 1920s. At the beginning of the decade, the overwhelming majority of salaried professionals were still living in rented dwellings. The Social Bureau survey of 1922 found that more than 93 percent were renting. Roughly half lived in detached houses, and the rest in rowhouses.[59] In contrast, data from 1932 indicate that homeownership was considerably more common in the suburbs, where many professionals had moved in the intervening decade. In the five suburban counties, just over 20 percent of the "dwelling houses" (which excluded combined shop-houses but included residential tenements) were owner-occupied by this time.[60] The same data for individual neighborhoods (*chō*) immediately west of Shinjuku station, many of which had been converted to bedroom suburbs during the 1920s, reveal owner-occupancy rates consistently higher than 20 percent.[61]

Subsequent writers have treated the earthquake of 1923 as the catalytic event in the process of prewar suburbanization, as if the suburbs had developed because the destruction of the old city drove residents to settle in the relative security of the surrounding hills. This is only a partial truth. Although the balance of the city's population shifted to the suburbs after the earthquake, the growth of industry during the war boom had already attracted newcomers to the city, increasing the pressure on urban real estate and accelerating suburban sprawl, and the same thing was occurring in the Kobe-Osaka area, where no disaster had occurred.[62] The population of the fifteen central wards of Tokyo had already reached a rough plateau by the end of the war, whereas the suburban population climbed steadily.[63] As new stations opened along the suburban train lines, the population took off in one district after another. Suginami-chō, in the heartland of Tokyo's western suburban development, doubled in population in the single year *prior* to the earthquake, immediately following the opening of local stations on the Chūō Line and the installation of street lamps.[64] Nor can we assume that the western suburbs were filled by a direct flow of people from the fifteen wards of the old city. Only 16 percent of the residents of Suginami-chō at the time of the 1930 census had been born in Tokyo's wards, and 58 percent of the residents originated from outside the Tokyo region (Tōkyō-shi and Tōkyō-fu) altogether.[65] It is likely that many of these non-native Tokyoites came to Suginami after first living elsewhere in Tokyo, but the statistic has important social implications nevertheless, since it suggests that the majority of the suburban middle class of this period consisted of comparatively new arrivals to the capital, the children neither of Edo commoners nor of the educated bourgeoisie who had reshaped the city's culture in the Meiji period.

The population of Tokyo roughly doubled between 1900 and 1920, and the white-collar population grew with particular rapidity after World War I. This growth made the professional population of Tokyo not only larger but more socially diverse. Much of the "intellectual class" or "middle class" at whom culture life writing was directed and about whose lives it revolved thus comprised new urbanites, without roots in the city's culture, whose very identity emerged from new patterns of consumption. They were thus more readily disposed to experiment with their lifestyles. The impact of the earthquake on this population was as much on the imagination as on their physical condition, for reconstruction showed the metropolis everywhere starting anew, free from the past.

## Suburban Neighborhood Sketches

It is surprisingly difficult to get a sense of what a simple cross-section of housing for a given area of Tokyo looked like in the 1920s. The destruction of World War II and frequent rebuildings in the years since have left no completely intact neighborhoods from before 1945. As is always the case with an architecture built of perishable materials, the dwellings that have survived tend to be the upper crust of sturdily built, larger structures in the possession of established landowners, and these have often undergone extensive modification. Thanks to the intrepid architect and folklorist Kon Wajirō, however, we are afforded a glimpse of one newly built Taishō suburban neighborhood in snapshot form. In November 1925 in the vicinity of Asagaya Station, which had been built on the Chūō line just four years earlier, Kon led a group that recorded the external appearance of 588 houses as seen from the street, classifying them into "Japanese style," "culture style," and "combined Western and Japanese." In his report of the results, Kon did not specify the criteria for determining the first two but referred to the third as houses with "only the reception room Western" (see Fig. 7.14).

The group also classified houses by roofing material, distinguishing black tile, red tile, thatch, slate, and metal. They found that fully 40 percent of the houses were roofed in metal.[66] Galvanized sheet iron was lighter and cheaper than tile. Its wide use in the newly developed Asagaya suggests that a large part of the first generation of suburban commuter housing was of the simplest possible construction. In contrast, Kon found only 5 percent of the surveyed houses roofed with red tiles, the new type of roofing that was a proverbial attribute of the culture house.

In total, Kon and his assistants classified 20 percent of the Asagaya houses as "culture style." Kon described this number as surprisingly small in light of all the publicity the culture house had received. In retrospect it seems large, however, when one considers that these houses could have been no more than three or four years old, yet already far outnumbered the houses Kon labeled "combined Japanese and Western style," which constituted only 5 percent of the total. The single Western reception room by which Kon identified the combined Japanese and Western style suggests the interior-corridor house that had emerged as the bourgeois model at the end of the Meiji period, although it is impossible to know the plans of these

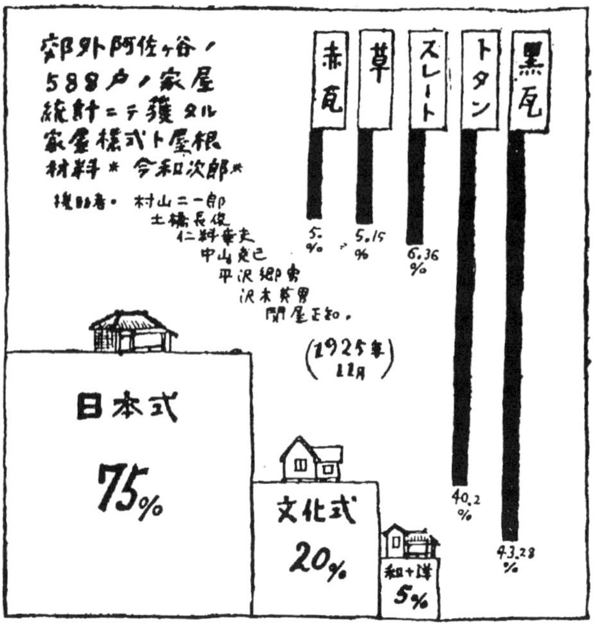


Fig. 7.14 Roofing material and style of façade on 588 houses in Asagaya district, November 1925. From the left, the houses are "Japanese style," "Culture style," and "Japanese + Western" (Kon Wajirō, "Kōgai fūzoku zakkei" [Miscellaneous scenes of suburban manners and customs]; reprinted in idem and Yoshida Kenkichi, *Moderunorojio "Kōgengaku,"* 1930, 115).

houses, since Kon was observing them only from the outside. Whatever precise attributes marked another 20 percent of the houses as "culture style," something other than the windows or gable of a single attached Western room—and therefore distinct from the Meiji reformers' ideal—distinguished them from their neighbors. And regardless of the distinction between the two, as a proportion of the total, these two house types together correspond well with the average percentage of owner-occupiers in the area, suggesting a likely correlation between homeownership and the two new house types.

More observant of social class markers than architectural nuances, Ōya Sōichi explained the "culture house" as distinct precisely by virtue of being owner-occupied:

If you walk the suburbs of Tokyo, everywhere you will find rows of Japanese-Western eclectic half-barracks, made as if from a single mold. The majority of them are rented, while some are "culture houses" built with a seven to three combination of low-interest loans and savings. And most of them, more than being syntheses of Japanese and Western, are Japanese houses of only three rooms, with a "Western room" of 4½ or 6 mats attached, so that from the outside they have a feeling like someone wearing Western clothes and *geta*. They have acquired "Western style," as it were, to about the same degree that the master of the house or his wife speaks English. It goes without saying that the "Western-style" "reception room," is furnished with three-legged rattan chairs and two or three series of one-yen books.

The minimal "culture house" in this sketch captures the degree of Westernization that culture consumers with limited means could achieve. Owner-occupied houses, however modest, were more likely to have distinctive new features than rented houses, since landlords building for rental tended to provide only what was essential. Those who bought or built their own houses when rental was still the more common choice were also more likely to be inclined to experiment with the latest architectural trends. Ōya collapsed Kon's two categories of non-native housing, but like Kon and other observers looking for a way to distinguish the culture house, he picked principally visual cues. Architecture historians focusing on floor plans have emphasized the dominance of the interior-corridor house type in urban housing before World War II and associated the more "Westernized" living room–centered type (*ima chūshin gata*) with the culture house phenomenon. Yet to observers at the time, these distinctions were less evident than the outward appearance of the new houses. The fact that Kon classified houses purely on the basis of their facades is itself a crucial historical lesson of his survey: "culture style" referred most of all to houses that stood out among their neighbors. A decade earlier, before the speculative market in suburban real estate and the cosmopolitan dream of culture had provided the stimuli for new architectural experiments, a survey like Kon's would hardly have been meaningful, if indeed possible.

## Summer 1922: Commodification and Utopia

Contemporary writing about the houses at Ueno Culture Village reveals that despite the promoters' effort to present them as models for rationalizing everyday life, they inspired stronger responses on an aesthetic level. This was true not only among critics who found them too "West-worshipping," but among architecture writers who wrote of them approvingly. "Elegantly designed not to lose a familiar Japanese taste in the facade while being Western inside," wrote a reviewer of the Reform League's house in one of the two handbooks to the village.[67] The other book commented more elaborately: "The facade employs Japanese-type clapboards, and the roof is done in Japanese tile so as not to lose the taste of our country's houses. The roof shows sufficient complexity to feel deeply suggestive (*ganchiku no fukaki o omowase*), with Western-style glass windows distributed in the [composition]. Compensating effectively for the tendency of buildings of this type to fall into shallowness, it reveals a generous (*onsha*) character."[68] This was the irony of Culture Village: the product of efforts to reshape domestic habits and mores shifted at the moment of its materialization from the arena of science and rationalization to the arena of visual aesthetics.

It was a paradox inherent in everyday life reform. Since the home exhibition of 1915, domestic experts had succeeded in refocusing discourse on the home away from bourgeois morality and practice and toward new commodities and consumption. Culture life proponents developed this reconception of everyday life and domesticity yet further, and Culture Village offered a summation in a variety of architectural forms. The result was to objectify the dwelling, making it a commodity or an ensemble of commodities more than an orderly and efficient instrument for producing model families and model national subjects. In the mass market of images, outward visual appeal was the way that commodities distinguished themselves.

Promoters of the culture villages and garden cities after Ueno drew on this new meaning for the dwelling, appealing to the dream content of the commodity. Suburban land made a particularly fertile object for the investment of fantasy since its value was latent; the site itself was empty, so one could inscribe any ideals in it. The people who bought or built themselves culture houses in the new suburbs need not have been lost in irrational fantasy to share the cosmopolitan hopes of progressive architects and suburban entrepreneurs. Many occupied houses that fit the striving petit-bourgeois stereotype Ōya Sōichi belittled, and the cosmopolitanism of their "culture life" was correspondingly humble. But together with the entrepreneurs of cosmopolitan culture, they began transforming the periphery of Tokyo into bedroom communities of white-collar nuclear family households. This first wave of Tokyo suburbanites was lured by an environment and lifestyle quite unlike either the city or the villages of the past and by images of a place with a touch of California.

The strong orientation toward the West, or eastward toward the other side of the Pacific—but really toward a fictional "West"—distinguished Tokyo's planned suburbs of the 1920s. The residential districts built by Kobayashi Ichizō in the Osaka-Kobe area a decade earlier provided a business precedent and a sourcebook of management know-how for the developers of Mejiro and Tamagawadai but not a cultural model. Ikeda Muromachi was laid out on a simple grid of streets no wider than in Japan's old castle towns. Kobayashi sold both lots and houses, and in this sense, his was the more ambitious business venture, but the architectural vocabulary he promoted (which he called "Tokyo style") had none of the eye-catching audacity of the houses built in the Tokyo developments after Culture Village. Tsutsumi and the Shibusawas left most buyers to build for themselves, but in an architectural climate sharply differing from that of Osaka a decade earlier. The developers, and the new consumers of the 1920s who bought their land, were committed to making the "culture life" substantial. Interpreting "culture" variously, the individual builders and architects at Mejiro and Tamagawadai produced an eclectic townscape unlike anything Japan had seen before.

Suburbs before World War I had addressed the desire for a "middle-class home" (*chūryū katei*), a conjugally centered household sustained by the ideologies of family intimacy, hygiene and environmentalism, "simple living," and homeownership. These ideologies persisted in the suburban designs of the 1920s, but they were subsumed to a larger utopianism. Since the suburban entrepreneurs and reform architects now blithely assumed that the "small houses" of their garden cities and culture villages would house *chūryū* families, the universalist idea of "culture" only thinly concealed the further marketing of bourgeois domesticity. Now, however, the object of desire was presented as modern living itself, its cosmopolitanism underscored in concrete gestures from the zoo animals to the electric house, to the *etoile* plan of Tamagawadai Garden City. Kobayashi had taken the imported conception of "home" and marketed it as an object of erotic fantasy. Suburbs after Culture Village spun their fantasies from cosmopolitan modernity.

# 8

# House Design and the Mass Market

"There is hardly a suburban house these days that is not influenced by the so-called culture house," wrote Kon Wajirō in a guide to the city published in 1929. He went on to list typical traits: red roof tiles, glass windows, walls of narrow painted clapboards or cement mortar on the exterior, curtains and rattan furniture in a sunroom inside, and a pergola out front.[1] As Kon realized, the influence was not only stylistic. Although technically unsophisticated structures, the new suburban houses signified a decisive break with past urban culture and with the existing regime of vernacular building.[2] Both the housing market and the building process in Tokyo came to be mediated through new agents and institutions that had not existed before World War I. Where once carpenters and clients had worked out the basic elements of a house and its actual design had derived from the carpenter's fund of building experience, pattern-book writers, architects, and building inspectors intervened, creating a building regime informed by texts and mediated through several levels of authority.

## The Architect as Intermediary

Architects mediated in the new housing market less directly than real estate developers but in a way of greater significance to the multiplication of new house forms. The majority of professional architects worked for construction companies or government offices. Beginning in the 1910s, several also began building small private houses or writing books on house design. Since all but a few houses previously had been built without them, architects seeking to gain residential commissions had to wedge themselves into the existing system of relations between clients and craftsmen or persuade first-time homebuilders that the modern house demanded a professional designer. Architects ultimately secured a role in the production of houses by publishing and consulting on design more than by gaining design commissions themselves. The profession stood in a central position in the mass-marketing of architectural expertise in the 1920s and had the most at stake. Books of plans and design advice poured onto the market from the early 1920s onward. Novelist Hayashi Fumiko later recalled having referred to "close to two hundred" such books when planning her own house in 1939.[3] This number need not have included technically specialized works. Published by women's magazines as well as architecture publishers, house books formed a new popular genre, directed at young architects and builders and perhaps especially at middle-class readers planning—or dreaming of—their own home.

Some sense of the design and working methods of house carpenters before this time can be gained from the media that predated modern architectural education and indirectly from descriptions in the pattern books that altered the process in the 1910s and 1920s. Prior to this time, the only published pattern books for domestic architecture were *hinagatabon*, densely packed compendia of drawings showing standard ornamental elements such as *tokonoma* alcove and shelf combinations or decorative transoms (*ranma*), in elevation without explanatory captions (see Fig. 8.1).[4] Other design ideas and technical know-how were acquired through apprenticeship and on-site building experience. Carpenters usually worked only with a floor plan, drawn on a board in single lines with points indicating posts.[5] The absence of full-wall elevations and other drawings reflects not simply the modularity of Japanese architecture, but the fact that after long apprenticeships, experienced carpenters were able to solve design problems through a vocabulary of formulas from past solutions, in a process of bricolage that has been observed in vernacular building around the world. Some master carpenters considered it a matter of pride not to study plans on site.[6]

Kamata Kenzō, author of a popular text on house design first published in 1918, described the way in which the typical rich amateur went about building a house. First, according to Kamata, the man's wife decided the

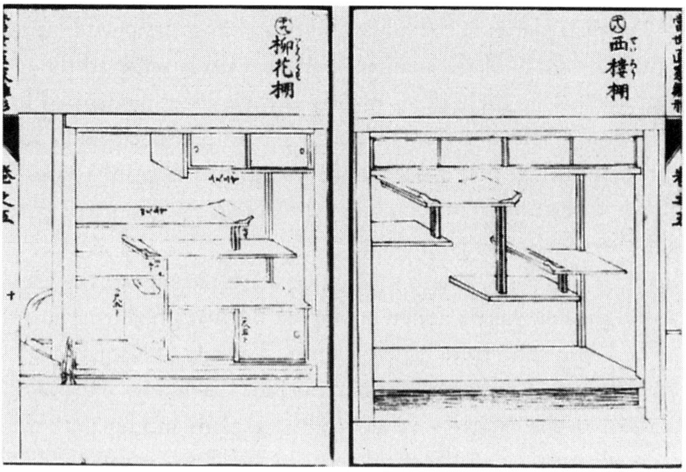


Fig. 8.1 "West Pavilion Shelf" and "Willow Flower Shelf": two pages from the carpenter's pattern book *Tōsei shōka hinagata: tana hinagata no bu 5* (Contemporary Craftsman's Patterns: Shelf Patterns, 1882, vol. 5) by Hirahara Suketsugu. Measurements for irregular pieces are written directly on the drawing.

location of the kitchen, bath, sitting room, and closets. Then the couple asked the carpenter to draw a plan. After having the plan checked by a house diviner, they requested the house at a certain figure, leaving the rest to the carpenter. Although Kamata's description was intended to disparage, we have no reason to believe it grossly inaccurate. It is interesting to note the large role of the mistress of the house in this process. In Kamata's account, her responsibility for the interior functions of the house extended to deciding the layout of functional spaces. This would set the stage for conflict with modern architects, who had their own notions of function. But the objects of Kamata's criticism here were the geomancer and the carpenter, both of whom were allowed to determine matters of house design despite their lack of "scientific knowledge" (*rigaku jō no chishiki*). Kamata urged his readers to hire an architect.[7] Criticisms like this of "leaving things to the carpenter" were standard in the design books. Behind them we can see the perpetuation of a system of vernacular production in which plan elements were determined through negotiation between the craftsman and the client (or his wife) and modified to agree with the diviner's principles of geomancy (popularly known today as *feng shui*). Craftsmen then drew on their experience to design all vertical planes in the house. Since architect-designed houses never took a majority share of the market, architects never achieved the ultimate goal of subordinating these other experts to their direct guidance. However, the diffusion of books like Kamata's among both producers and consumers in the housing market had a clear influence on the design of houses, and as we shall see, architects were soon given the opportunity to participate regularly in the vernacular design process.

In contrast to the carpenter's toolbox of design techniques, the knowledge purveyed in the new house design books was distinguished by claims to universality and derivation from expert sources. The text of Kamata's book, like many others, established a normative model for the family, and championed modifications to the design—"family-centered" plans and separate children's rooms, for example—to fulfill the domestic ideal. Kamata then laid out general principles of taste, stressed the importance of scientific hygiene, and emphasized that without the expertise of an architect, grave errors were likely to be made. Popular pattern books for the builder or potential homeowner thus refocused dwelling design around *katei* ideology. Equally importantly, through drawings, photographs, and the rhetoric of historic and national styles, they introduced visual aesthetics to house building, transforming what had been an essentially practice-based system of production.

For the architect himself, purveying design expertise to the mass public meant veering from the ideal course prescribed by the academy, whose primary aim was to nurture engineers and designers for state buildings. The defections began in the 1910s, when a few graduates of the imperial universities and Waseda University struck out to make careers designing houses and writing about them. Larger numbers graduating from technical schools followed in the 1920s. There were never many independent architects sustaining themselves solely on house designs, but many more took residential commissions and published their designs while holding professional positions in industry, government, or academia.

One of the first of these architects and also one of the field's most prolific writers was Yasuoka Katsuya. Graduating from Tokyo Imperial University's Architecture Department in 1900, Yasuoka proceeded along the top of the elite career track of the time, beginning in the office of Mitsubishi Real Estate under Sone Tatsuzō, who was then carrying out the construction of Tokyo's central business district begun by Englishman Josiah Conder.

From 1913, Yasuoka diverged from the expected path by establishing his own practice and devoting himself to designing private residences. He published his first popular guide, *Risō no jūtaku* (The Ideal House), in 1915. Significantly, it appeared in a series called the Ladies' Home Library. In the preface, Yasuoka pronounced the present native awareness of residential architecture "juvenile" and asserted, in a manner proverbial among Meiji reformers, that "the level of a nation's civilization is apparent at a glance in its architecture, and the nobility or vulgarity of owners' tastes immediately visible in the interior of their homes."[8] Just as tasks had become increasingly divided in industry, he observed, houses today had numerous rooms with special functions. The most challenging issue for contemporary experts was how to harmonize Japanese and Western rooms now that people required Western facilities in their houses.[9] "The house the era demands," Yasuoka told readers, was a Japanese one with two or three Western rooms.[10] He went on to discuss the characteristics of Western houses, using illustrations ostensibly taken from Western architectural and domestic management texts, and then presented his designs of native houses, most of them large and in the "combined Japanese-Western" (*wayō setchū*) arrangement of the late Meiji period, with Western reception rooms. Admonishing female readers to develop their knowledge of architecture, he encouraged them to try drawing plans, since "such things as the construction of the kitchen, its lighting and position in relation to adjacent houses," were "good material for women's study."[11] This encouragement accorded with the perception nurtured by women's educators of the housewife as domestic scientist and maintained the aesthetic aspects of house design as a male architectural concern. Yasuoka went on to publish thirteen more books and collections of drawings in the next twelve years, most of which were filled with houses of his own design.[12]

The combined Japanese-Western house posed a monolithic West against the native, dictating not only distinct materials and construction for each, but a distinct planning system and orthography. The opposition was functional as well as stylistic, as two complete material and cultural systems were embodied in the contrast of kimono and Western clothes, chair-sitting and floor-sitting, sliding paper *shōji* and glass windows. Even the full-fledged Western houses built by the privileged few in Meiji derived their design from an internal necessity: the problem of entertaining visitors wearing Western clothes (particularly Westerners and the emperor) in a setting appropriate to the modes of cultural expression established under the modern state. In the pattern books and the houses of the suburban boom that began during World War I, the dichotomy between West and East became more complex, as the monolithic Westernness of the *yōkan* was replaced by a catalogue of national types from which to borrow. Yasuoka Katsuya's houses reflect this clearly. The collection *Japanized Small Western Houses* (*Nihonka shitaru yōfū shōjūtaku*), first published in 1924, contained designs of houses recently built by the author and described as "seven parts Western and three parts Japanese." Within "Western style," Yasuoka distinguished a range of national and regional styles, including "English," "American country," "Swiss chalet," "contemporary German," "pure German," and "pure French" (see Fig. 8.2).[13] Greater familiarity with trends overseas had enriched the Japanese designer's palette. The eclectic revival in England also encouraged Yasuoka and his contemporaries to master a diversity of styles—which, in the Japanese context, were not revivals at all.

Hashiguchi Shinsuke's residential design firm, Amerika-ya, and the magazine *Jūtaku* became important nodes in the professional network of culture house designers and promoters during the 1920s. Architect Yamamoto Setsurō was among Amerika-ya's chief designers from the time he completed his degree in 1917 until the early 1930s. As a graduate of Waseda University, Yamamoto possessed elite credentials, but from the youngest of the university architecture programs and one outside the imperial system. While designing for Amerika-ya, he also taught "dwelling studies" (*jūkyogaku*) at the Tokyo Women's Higher Normal School (precursor of Ochanomizu University), and wrote for *Jūtaku*, as well as for other architecture and women's magazines.[14] In contrast with Yasuoka, Yamamoto evinced little concern for the canons of style. Nor was he driven by the missionary zeal to reform habits of domestic life that had inspired Hashiguchi in founding the company and magazine. Yamamoto's designs, published in *Jūtaku*, were distinguished by an aesthetic vocabulary that resolved functionally Western interiors with the traditional Japanese technique of exposing posts and beams inside.[15] Previously, the native *tatami* room dressed up as a *yōma* had been a compromise—now, an architect from within the academy but less bound to academic orthodoxy than previous architects made the combination of Western furniture and native construction an aesthetic virtue (see Fig. 8.3). Use of the carpenter's customary method had the added advantage of making the house cheaper to build.

Fig. 8.2 Sketches accompanying Yasuoka Katsuya's plans for "Japanized Small Western Houses": (*top*) contemporary German; and (*bottom*) pure French. Yasuoka's publication of a panoply of styles signaled a new turn in Japanese dwelling design, but Yasuoka himself retained a worldview derived from his nineteenth-century training. Since European knowledge acquired through orthodox channels was still what distinguished the elite architect, his primary concern remained promotion of formally correct European design.

Fig. 8.3 A mixed Japanese-Western style study from Yamamoto Setsurō's sketchbook. Yamamoto's Western interiors used the exposed wood posts and lintels characteristic of Japanese vernacular. His eclecticism went hand in hand with a positive regard for the idiosyncrasies of individual taste. He opposed the comprehensively designed interiors of Frank Lloyd Wright and his Japanese adherents, for example, because they prevented occupants from decorating with furniture of their own choice (Yamamoto Setsurō, *Setsu sensei e nikki*, 162).

In the 1920s *Jūtaku* magazine featured many smaller houses than it had previously. Several competing journals publishing similar designs, all of which began in the late 1910s and early 1920s, used the same blend of proselytizing and marketing that characterized Amerika-ya.[16] At the same time, a larger cohort of architects, most of whom probably never received the commissions necessary to support themselves as residential designers, published designs of houses both built and unbuilt and sought to teach the domestic ideals and architectural fashions of the day by writing explanations in simple language, free of technical information—although often liberally spiced with imported words. Through this moonlighting as popular writers, numbers of architects entered the mass market, joining other writers and entrepreneurs who made a living teaching readers the ingredients of cosmopolitan modernity.

Although many of the pattern books of the 1920s described the houses they depicted as "middle-class" (*chūryū*), the term "culture house" was not class-delimited in an economic sense. The first of a series of photograph collections titled *Culture Houses*, for example, included both the house of a member of the peerage and a row of semi-detached houses for rent in Osaka.[17] In the new architectural literature, a house became a culture house less because it had particular physical characteristics or was identified with a class of consumers than because it was designed according to tenets of domestic ideology, scientific management and hygiene, or following some architectural style, instead of the customary practices of carpenters. This meant that directly or indirectly, it bore the imprint of a trained architect.

## State Institutions and the Mediation of Architects in Vernacular Building

Just as the Taishō culture consumer represents both a new generation, distinct from the bourgeoisie of Meiji, and a greatly expanded educated class, the emergence of cultural intermediaries in the market for architecture and design signaled both a generational shift in these professions and the expansion of their ranks to include individuals of less privileged background. Only five colleges in the country offered degrees in architecture before World War I. Vocational schools were established throughout the country, however, and many of these were recertified as colleges in 1918. They spawned thousands of graduates with expertise derived from Western architectural texts, but without the elite status guaranteed by the universities.[18] Full membership in the Japan Society of Architects was granted only to university graduates. By 1930, the number of associate members, admitted after several years in practice without the university degree, had reached 5,549, or almost three times the number of full members. The society's 1934 directory listed graduates from 133 schools, the great majority of which were technical colleges (*kōgyō gakkō*).[19]

Quite by chance, state regulations on construction created the circumstances for this new cohort of non-elite architects to solidify their position as intermediaries in the building process. The law in question was the Urban Building Law (Shigaichi kenchikubutsu hō), which went into effect together with the Town Planning Law (Toshi keikaku hō) in 1920. These two laws were the product of over a decade of traffic in drafts, reviews, revisions, and amendments between the mayor of Tokyo, the Home Ministry, and the Society of Architects, with the aim of introducing zoning regulations, lot lines for minimum road width, land readjustment procedures for creating uniform blocks, density and height limits, and restrictions for fire safety.[20] Uchida Yoshikazu, a student of Sano Toshikata at Tokyo University, was the key representative of the Society of Architects. He and Sano formed the core of a group working to transform the practice of architecture in Japan from an applied art into a science that combined structural engineering and social policy. Their chief concerns were earthquake- and fire-resistant structures, housing, and urban planning.[21] Eighty-seven meetings held by a Society-appointed Building Law Review Committee (Kenchiku hōki shingi iinkai) under Uchida's direction between 1914 and 1918 transformed plans for a Tokyo municipal building code into a petition for a national law to apply to all urban areas and for the immediate placement of an architectural engineer in the Home Ministry's Police Agency.[22] The law eventually went into effect for the six largest cities and the urbanizing areas around them, referred to as urban planning zones (*toshi keikaku kuiki*).

In order to enforce the law, bylaws stipulated that plans for all new construction be submitted to the police. Since architects knew the police regulations and were trained in drafting, as few carpenters were, this had the effect of creating work for them as representatives for the carpenters or clients (known as *daigannin*, or colloquially *daiganya*, "proxy applicants"). A circuit thus developed linking clients, carpenters, architects, police, the Home Ministry, and the architectural academy. Design and consultation offices sprang up in clusters around police stations, which became a kind of zone for the production of paper between carpenters and the state.[23] If modern design is the abstraction of creative processes that the vernacular builder would work out in concrete material, then it was through this circuit, and through the mediation of young architects in need of work, that modern design insinuated itself into vernacular construction. It is impossible to tell to what extent these professional intermediaries determined the final appearance of most buildings. Usually, clients need only have commissioned them to draft floor plans and occasional structural sections. But the situation clearly created both the opportunity and incentive for them to introduce clients to their own designs or those in the latest pattern books, in order to apply their newly acquired knowledge—and presumably to gain larger commissions. The impact of the law is particularly evident in Osaka, where in the 1920s, design features that bore the stamp of "culture" turned up in *nagaya* rowhouses, which were the dominant dwelling form in new and old neighborhoods. Municipal bylaws there required builders to submit elevations as well as plans and sections for buildings over 50 *tsubo*. A group of three or more rowhouses built under one ridge thus required elevations. Shortly after promulgation of the law, reformed *nagaya* began to appear, first with new

Fig. 8.4 Marks of "culture" in Osaka rowhouses. (*top*) The street façade of four units in a row built early in the twentieth century. (*bottom*) Two semi-detached houses built in the same district in the late 1920s or 1930s. In the new designs, entrances to units project from the façade wall. The round windows, particularly fashionable in the late 1920s, reflect the convenient agreement of native *sukiya* style with Art Deco (Wada Yasuyoshi, "Ōsaka ni okeru kindai toshi jūtaku seiritsu ni kansuru kisoteki kenkyū").

interior layouts and then with separate projecting entries distinguishing each unit from the row; eventually a range of Western- and *sukiya*-influenced façade elements emerged (see Fig. 8.4).[24] In Tokyo, the reach of the law was extended to the new suburbs in stages and finally covered the city and surrounding counties only in 1930. Still, the timing agrees with the expansion of white-collar suburbs and the accompanying march of new architectural styles. In addition, the visually adventurous new pattern books began to proliferate from around the time that the law was established. Some of the architects who wrote these books also published guides to the law.[25]

Put in extreme terms, the implication is that design fashions associated with the visually conspicuous and often-lampooned culture house were in part the child of a building code established in the interest of safe and rational urban development. If so, it would be highly ironic for Uchida and Sano, who staked their careers on demonstrating that architecture had nothing to do with ornament, which Sano called a trivial and feminine concern.[26] But it would not be an entirely surprising result, since state regulation caused analogous accidents elsewhere. The new fire code authored by Uchida catalyzed radical changes in façade design in the post-earthquake reconstruction of Tokyo's commercial districts, where the requirement for fire-resistant facing on wooden structures spawned a Westernesque vernacular that Fujimori Terunobu has dubbed "signboard architecture" (*kanban kenchiku*).[27] The same requirement ultimately had an equally radical impact on the external appearance of detached houses in the suburbs, whose unfinished clapboards were replaced by a cement mortar for fireproofing. Mortar and stucco came to be treated as stylistic elements in the "modern Japanese" (*kindai wafū*) and "Spanish" styles popular in the 1930s.

The law combined with new materials and building techniques to affect the relationship between clients, designers, and carpenters in other ways, with the result of devaluing the aesthetic importance of the carpenter's work. For carpenters, standards of joinery and the type, grain, and finish of woods, left exposed and uncoated, were the marks of a building's quality. Neither of these things had a role in culture house design, where significance lay instead in overall planning and the visual impression of the whole. To make wooden structures more resistant to earthquakes, the Urban Building Law required builders to stiffen joints with metal bolts, diminishing the need for complex joinery. Carpenters maintained old techniques out of pride, but some of their refined, labor-intensive techniques could now be sidestepped to reduce costs. Imported lumber, plywood, paint, paper stencils, and wallpaper made it easier to build an attractive Western-style house that showed few of its structural timbers.[28] American pine began to displace native woods in the Tokyo market after World War I. It cost about half the price. Greatly boosted by the demand for lumber after the earthquake, American imports surpassed the native product in 1925.[29] With cheap imported lumber and paint to hide it, a Western house could now actually be cheaper to build. One writer on culture houses encouraged readers to choose their own lumber in order to avoid being overcharged by carpenters.[30] The combination of these factors not only affected the autonomy of the carpenter on the building site and interrupted old trade ties that had supported vernacular production (which might indeed take advantage of the innocent client) but also created a rift between the tastes of the new client building a house, whose eyes were trained on marks of "culture," and the carpenter, whose craft began with appreciation of the wood itself.

In addition to possessing the knowledge gained from a Western technical education, and the ability to draft plans for official approval, architects thus found a niche in the 1920s because they could be expected to share the tastes of clients building a house for the culture life. *Model Designs of Middle-Class Houses* (*Chūryū jūtaku no mohan sekkei*), one volume in a series of pocket manuals of household information published by the *Housewife's Companion*, warned readers that the old master carpenter asked to build a Western house would be likely to conjure up images of schools and post offices. Young architects, by contrast, "recognize our feelings," making it easier to talk to them. A basic sympathy with bourgeois tastes did not make them any more trustworthy than carpenters, however. The author described the local architects cum builders' representatives as "young men just out of school, who get together with two or three friends and put out a sign advertising design and [construction] supervision, but actually act as something like contractors. . . . Since these young people are usually poor, there is the worry that things will stop progressing in the middle of construction, and they'll wind up abandoning the job. One must be extremely cautious about this."[31] Readers were advised to make specifications as concrete and detailed as possible in dealing with both architects and carpenters and to draw things rather than merely describing them. Drawing was the one means to gain control over the design. The ability to represent something on paper empowered clients in dealing with builders and architects just as it empowered architects in dealing with the law. "In the same way that a meeting (*miai*) or a photograph of the prospective mate (*miai no shashin*) is necessary to a marriage match, in architecture, drawings are master rather than words," the text continued, suggesting as examples that one show with a drawing what height to make the windows or draw a structural plan to show diagonal bracing. The *Housewife's Companion* editors appear to have seen a greater design role for their possibly female readers than Yasuoka Katsuya had earlier allowed readers of the Ladies' Home Library. The two examples they gave are also noteworthy because they deal with vertical planes of the building. Window height would ordinarily have been determined by a carpenter's rule of thumb (when there were windows at all, since traditional houses often had only sliding door panels). Diagonal braces were an earthquake-resistant improvement mandated by the Urban Building Law. Knowing their proper placement and drafting structural plans to illustrate it were aspects of the expertise offered by the architect.

## Sources of Culture House Design

This is not to say that carpenters without formal training could not build culture houses. The knowledge needed to build a version of a California bungalow or add some stucco and painted clapboards to the outside walls of a native dwelling was easily acquired. University-trained architects alone possessed the more arcane knowledge for the design and detailing of large public buildings in orthodox Western academic styles, but credible façade decoration for a small house could be improvised. What distinguished the technical school graduates from traditionally trained carpenters was an approach to building that proceeded from drawings rather than rule of thumb. They had studied both Japanese and Western structures through books and classroom lectures, a method that in its nature rendered building into a process of applying structural and formal principles, translating two-dimensional representations, mathematical formulas, and written language into form and space. The young architect designing houses thus boasted not so much a technical ability unattained by carpenters as a worldly literacy and a conception of architecture and aesthetics shaped outside the bodily practice of building.

The textbooks widely used in technical colleges were conservative, however, and slow to incorporate Western conceptions of architecture as an art. Until the first decade of the twentieth century, the schools aimed primarily to produce engineers and carpenters literate in modern technology, rather than architects versed in an aesthetic canon. The Japanese portion of the curriculum was essentially a rationalized education in native carpentry, in which the use of tools, joinery, and the traditional proportional system—techniques that apprentices would ordinarily learn by what was called "stealing" from the master (*nusumi geiko*) while working alongside him—were studied through texts and classroom instruction. At this stage, ornament in the textbooks came from *hinagatabon*. The standard text before 1904 treated elevations, whose composition would define the visual character of the building, as secondary in importance, and unnecessary for the experienced builder. In the course of two years of instruction, students built a wooden structure with a roof supported by a Western truss. Hands-on experience with this technological improvement held clear priority over visual composition. The new syllabus of 1904 included drafting of the Greek and Roman orders but apparently not with the expectation that students would be applying this knowledge in practice, since the textbooks contained only three plans, for a wood and brick structure, an earthquake-resistant farmhouse, and a "reformed wooden house."[32] Although the curriculum was clearly shifting emphasis from craft to technique, this disjuncture between the purely formal exercise of learning Western academic style and the practical emphasis of the rest of the program reveals that aesthetics were still treated as a matter of convention, not as the basis of creative expression.

Textbooks in the 1920s still emphasized technology over aesthetics but taught a wide range of materials that could be incorporated into new house designs. The 1926 revised version of Ishikawa Katsushi's *Practical Text of Japanese Building Structure* (*Jitsuyō Nihon kaoku kōzō*) included a new final chapter on culture houses, with plans, an elevation, and an exterior perspective of a simple "living-room based" house similar to one of the Ueno model houses.[33] This was the only house the book illustrated in perspective. The text judged the Western floor plan very economical and noted that the house showed Japanese taste in the details. Ishikawa compiled a corresponding text on Western buildings that included information on new materials, fixtures, and construction techniques, as well as interior features such as the construction of a Western stairway, wooden cornices, and three types of coffered ceiling.[34] Thus, while design aesthetics were introduced only sparingly to formal instruction at technical schools, texts like Ishikawa's both endorsed the fusion of native and Western domestic architecture in culture houses and provided concrete instruction on Western elements that could be incorporated into them.

Beyond classroom texts, students seeking knowledge of Western architectural styles could look to a range of other sources, some intended specifically for young men entering the lower ranks of the profession. Members of the university architecture departments lectured to and wrote for technical school students, exposing non-elite architects to the cosmopolitan atmosphere in which their superiors moved. The progressive group of architects researching dwelling form at Waseda University, for example, offered junior colleagues direct encouragement to think stylistically. A lecture on "residential architecture" co-authored by Takeuchi Yoshitarō and Kon Wajirō (both of Waseda) and published in a series of pamphlets by the Imperial Technical Education Association, described six styles of culture house: bungalow, Secession, Spanish Mission, New Dutch, Chicago (Frank Lloyd Wright), and New French, illustrating each with a photograph or sketch.[35] For detailed depiction of Western houses inside and out, the technical school student could turn to a collection of illustrations and photographs, apparently taken from European texts, compiled by students at Waseda under the straightforward title *Materials for Design of Modern Western Houses* (*Kindai seiyō jūtaku sekkei shiryō*)—a kind of printed hand-me-down of architectural information, which contained everything from illustrations of the use of moldings ("Caution: use of a heavy molding causes a white wall to look weak and inappropriate"), to flower boxes, pergolas, breakfast alcoves, and a Murphy "in-a-door-bed." The opening pages showed elevations and a floor plan for a single-story house with a large verandah, presumably designed by one of the Waseda group. The house was small, even smaller than most of the Ueno houses, suggesting the desire of these architects to prove to their readers that Western design was achievable even within the budget and space limits of most petit-bourgeois families.[36]

Another source of design information was *Dai kenchikugaku*, a multivolume encyclopedia of architectural knowledge that served as a resource for textbook writers. The revised version published in 1925 included such visual innovations as color illustrations of art nouveau stained-glass windows, structural details for a spiral staircase, and diagrams explaining the mathematics of perspective and axonometric drawing, as well as the text of the Urban Building Law. The authors of this vast compilation were major figures in the Japanese Society of Architects. Distribution was by special order only, but through the technical colleges these volumes conveyed detailed technical and aesthetic knowledge from the center of modern architectural authority to the broad middle stratum of the design field.[37]

A series of publications called *Kenchiku shashin ruiju* (Compendium of Architectural Photographs) played a special role in diffusing visual images of new architecture to students, designers, carpenters, and clients. Published monthly beginning in 1915, the series continued until late 1943, resulting in a cumulative body of some 13,000 images of contemporary buildings, most in Japan, but many also in the West. Subscribers paid one yen per month to receive the small volumes, each of which was a folder containing a loose bundle of 50 photographs and drawings, printed on heavy paper sheets slightly larger than postcards. Minimal information was provided in captions to the numbered images. As in the carpenter's traditional *hinagatabon*, the mode of communication was almost entirely visual. Volumes were classified by architectural feature or genre, in a manner also reminiscent of *hinagatabon*, so that some sets showed only gates, entries, or guest rooms, and others dealt with banks or apartment houses. Unlike the traditional carpenter's pattern book, however, these images were not drawings of standardized details, but photographic records of existing buildings, including their contents and surroundings (see Fig. 8.5).[38]

The editors compiled five volumes titled *Culture Houses* between 1922 and 1926.[39] These included interior and exterior photographs with a few plans, identified only by the names of owners (occasionally only a family name or initial) and sometimes their designers. No other text was provided. Most but not all of the houses were large, with multiple Western-style rooms. Inside and out, oblique-angle shots were used to bring as much of the house as possible into the frame. Interior shots exhibited a tidy, lived-in intimacy, revealing the occupants' tastes in art and décor as well as the architectural design. In addition to decorative objects, the photographs captured portable stoves and braziers, table lamps, casually tossed cushions, tea utensils, ashtrays, books, letters, slippers, and occasionally mismatched chairs. Service spaces were seldom shown. The human occupants themselves were generally out of sight, although children appeared in a few pictures. As a whole, there was little sign of the careful cropping to eliminate context and emphasize formal effects that would characterize architectural photography after the Modern Movement. Compared to the experiments with abstract composition in high modernist architectural photography (already beginning to appear in Japanese journals such as *Shin kenchiku* [New Architecture] and *Kokusai kenchiku* [International Architecture], both of which began publication in 1925), these were decidedly prosaic images, unpretentious and documentary.[40]

*Kenchiku shashin ruiju*'s significance to the housing market lay in this simple documentary style and convenient format. The comparatively artless photography provided maximum information about the shapes, proportions, ornament, and contents of hundreds of private houses. Individual sheets were convenient to pull out and examine, show to a builder, or perhaps spread out on a desk alongside sheets from other volumes. Advertisements for the series highlighted its universal convenience and accessibility with phrases like "A key for builder and client," and "Friend to the expert, mother to the student, guide to the amateur."[41] The editors used photography as the

Fig. 8.5 Leaves from a photo album of culture houses in the *Kenchiku shashin ruiju* series (Kenchiku shashin ruiju kankōkai, *Kenchiku shashin ruiju dai 4 ki dai 22 kai: bunka jūtaku III*, 1924). The photos provide a tour of the houses, paying as much attention to the occupants' lifestyle as to the architecture.

most expedient medium of communication rather than as a mode of artistic expression. Photographs facilitated conversation with clients. The camera was also the ideal device to assist designers interested in learning the available range of materials and design features or the tastes of the rich.

In addition to native sources of images and ideas for culture house designs, the Western architectural press may have been particularly influential. Its conspicuousness certainly made it a ready object for criticism. In a meeting sponsored by the western Japan branch of the national organization of architects known as the Kenchikushikai, instructors at technical schools in the region heard the organization's complaint that recent students appeared to be designing "new things that make a display of eccentricity," without first doing sufficient "studies" of the traditional "styles" (the loanwords *sutadei* and *sutairu* implying acquisition of the nineteenth-century canon through Western academic methods). The instructors responded that in addition to lacking staff, their institutions lacked the materials for proper style studies, and whereas students in the countries of the West could find examples of the historical styles just by "taking a step outside the city," this was practically impossible in Japan. As a result, "students are inspired by new architecture appearing in the magazines coming recently from foreign countries, particularly German magazines."[42]

Whether the visual material came directly in publications from Europe, or predigested by Japanese architects, students of architecture in the 1920s found no dearth of it. To the distress of some of their teachers and more conservative architects, liberal notions of a universal culture that had emerged in the aftermath of World War I encouraged immediate appropriation from this abundance of sources, and the established hierarchy of expertise no longer bound their choices.

Two house design competitions in the newspapers, the first sponsored by the *Hōchi shinbun* in 1916 and the second by the *Asahi shinbun* in 1929, frame the culture house era and reveal the expansion of the architectural field in the decade after World War I (see Fig. 8.6). The phenomenon of a newspaper-sponsored house design competition itself exemplifies the massification of architectural media taking place. Entries were solicited from the general public, and the circulation of newspapers ensured that winning entries reached a large audience. The sixteen prize winners in the *Asahi* contest were built as a model village in the suburb of Seijō Gakuen and subsequently

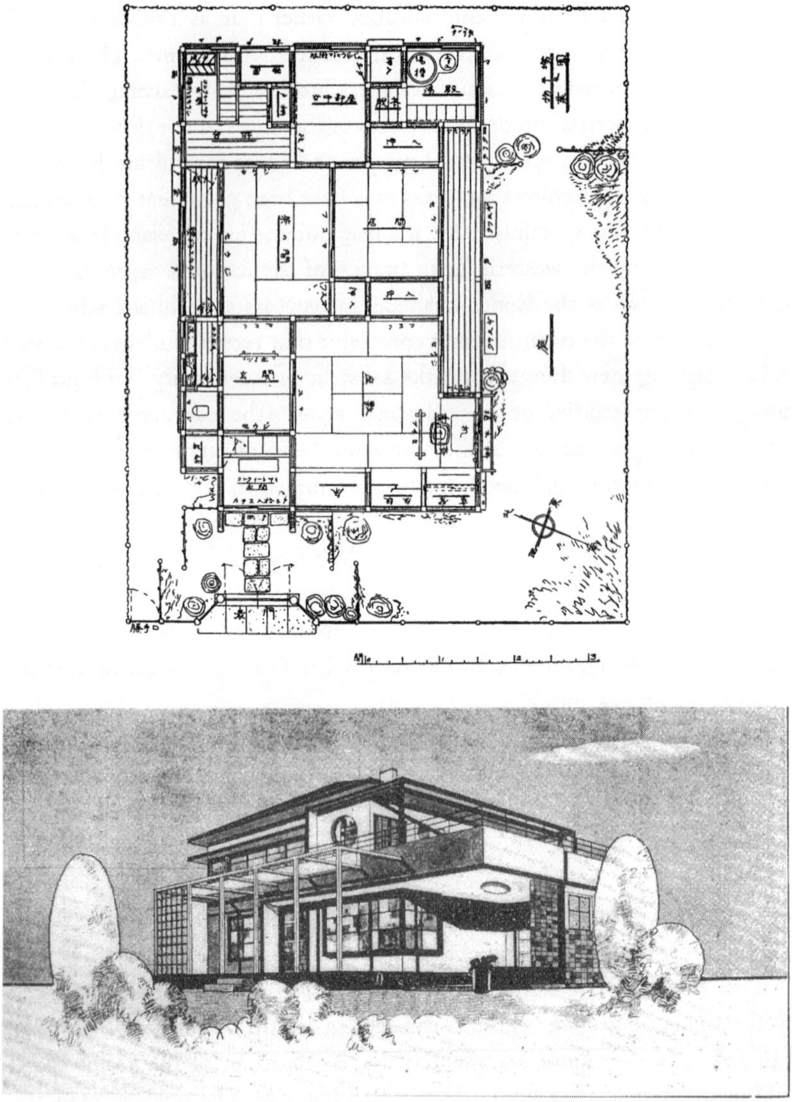

Fig. 8.6 House plans submitted to two newspaper-sponsored competitions framing the culture house era. (*top*) The *Hōchi shinbun* competition of 1916 (Satō Kōichi, *Hōchi shinbun jūka sekkei zuan*, 1916). (*bottom*) The *Asahi shinbun* competition of 1929 (Tonedate Masao, ed., *Asahi jūtaku zuanshū*, 1929).

sold.[43] In both instances, collections of entries were published in book form.[44] In style of visual presentation, however, the two volumes could hardly have contrasted with one another more. The *Hōchi* entries are floor plans in black ink hardline, some including a few site elements, and a small minority including an elevation. In the book compilation, these entries were published anonymously, most without written specifications or descriptions. Many appear to have been drawn by amateurs. The illustrations published by the *Asahi* thirteen years later, by contrast, are unmistakably the work of professionally trained designers. The book is a visually rich collection of color perspectives, section drawings of construction details, cutaway axonometrics, and stylized graphic techniques suggesting Bauhaus and other European influence. The drawings are signed, and the architects provided page-length specifications, as well as discussions of their design intentions.[45] The striking disparity between these two collections eloquently demonstrates the rapid evolution of design education during the intervening decade. With a clarity not seen before, the house designer emerged in the *Asahi* competition of 1929 as a sophisticated manipulator of form and graphic technique, whose designs were both personal expressions and up-to-the-minute responses to the contemporary field of architecture at home and abroad.[46]

## A Native Textual Tradition Responds

The flood of new architectural knowledge into vernacular production ultimately compelled a response from geomancers, who were guardians of the native textual tradition most concerned with house plans. Geomancy derived house form from a different kind of graphic, the house divination plan (*kasōzu*), a type of cosmogram. Although the hegemony of modern architectural discourse was by no means entire, architects impugned the legitimacy of these diagrams and of the diviners' practice. The assault called for new strategies to maintain geomancy's relevance. Forward-looking practitioners judged that their long-term interests lay not merely in preserving the traditional status of their profession but in joining the architects and other intermediaries offering modern expertise to a broad urban audience. There were losses as well as gains in this strategy.

In two general-audience books (written in simple language with syllabary glosses), geomancer Takagi Jō sought to re-establish the legitimacy of house divination by combining geomantic prescriptions with the tenets and rhetoric of contemporary architectural design. Takagi made conspicuous use of transliterated English, plainly seeking to display a cosmopolitanism contrary to what readers would expect. Takagi's books asserted that the purposes of divination were, in fact, the very aims of modern architectural design, although the practice applied only to Japanese houses. Diviners identified the "convenient, hygienic and comfortable aspects, that is architecturally perfect points" in a house, as auspicious, while "architecturally deficient points" were inauspicious.[47]

His first book railed against other geomancers, labeling them phonies who "imitate the ancients" the way street urchins imitated "Eyeballs Matsunosuke," a popular cinema swashbuckler. These geomancers were behind the times, purveyors of "fragmentary dogma" whose principles of divination applied "only to people in regions where culture does not progress." The underlying reason for their failure, according to Takagi, was that they had "no knowledge of the discipline of architecture." In the place of all this false science, he promised to make manifest the principles of divination and to use the "proper reasoning" of architecture.[48] Apart from debunking some superstitions about sites with ghosts or curses, however, the body of the book espoused standard divination practice, relying on yin-yang and Chinese zodiacal principles to demonstrate which house plans were auspicious. Presentation rather than practical content set this work apart from the tradition it represented. Takagi's claim was that the valid principles of geomancy could be induced from observation. In place of the traditional approach, which simply catalogued the effects on occupants' fates that resulted from particular placements of rooms, numbers of *tatami*, or orientations of convex and concave outer walls, Takagi took a case-study approach, describing families who had prospered or been stricken by misfortune because of the plans of their houses, mentioning each occupant's profession as well as the neighborhood of Tokyo where the house was located, and then analyzing the plan in question in order to demonstrate why the occupants' fate had turned for better or worse and to suggest remedies.[49] Of a dozen houses given detailed analysis, two were culture houses of the author's own design, and one was a summer house whose design was based on one built by Amerika-ya in Karuizawa. The text described these plans as auspicious but provided little information about their divination, focusing instead on their practical convenience for modern living. The extreme compactness of the summer house made it difficult to devise a plan that was both convenient and geomantically perfect, the author acknowledged, but this was judged tolerable in light of the fact that the house would be occupied only for short periods.

In the preface to his second compendium, Takagi redirected the energy he had previously devoted to condemning unenlightened geomancers toward defending geomancy from the criticism of architects. To do so, he made a plea for native aesthetics. Geomantic principles created the "mood" of native architecture, he explained. "House divination . . . possesses the conditions for much taste (*tashumi no jōken*) . . . that should be the mother to Japanese architecture," he averred.[50] Many Japanese architects of the time shared Takagi's sentiment for a special native taste that should be preserved in the new design, but few would have given Takagi's science such centrality in it. Of twenty architects who responded to a survey in the journal *Architecture and Society*, only two unequivocally affirmed a belief in house divination. Twelve rejected it, and six reported that they considered it only insofar as it confirmed hygienic principles.[51]

If the spate of publication by architects and others on house design threatened to marginalize geomancy as mere superstition, the question for geomancy experts in the market of architectural expertise was how to divine without appearing to be mere diviners. As in Takagi's justifications, the tradition could be found to agree with modern science or claimed as a source of native architectural beauty. The one remaining choice was to treat it as an object of historical interest, in the manner of Matsudaira Hideaki, a Tokyo City Hall bureaucrat who co-authored a book on divination with an engineer. In the opening words of the book, Matsudaira announced that his main interest in house divination science was for purposes of historical research, "not in order to do so-called readings (*kasōmi*)." In his years of research, he had "discovered some quite interesting common points in the divination principles" espoused by various past experts.[52] The book presented these points, citing their sources. Yet in the end, what he and co-author Honma Gorō had to offer readers was much the same as what Takagi purveyed. Also like Takagi, they presented brief case studies to demonstrate geomantic principles operating in the fates of various buildings' occupants. Since Matsudaira and Honma were not defending their own liveli-

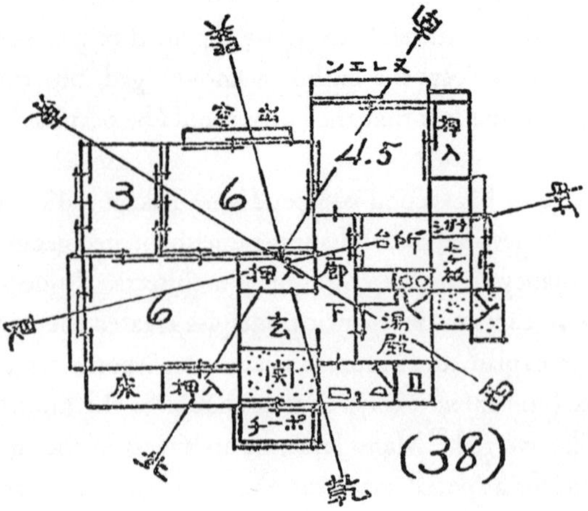


Fig. 8.7 Divination plan for a modern house built by the Dōjunkai Housing Authority (Matsudaira Hideaki and Honma Gorō, *Kasō no hanashi* [House Divination Tales], 1930, 165). Three adjacent rooms numbering six, six, and three mats make the plan inauspicious. The authors' solution is to expand the six-mat room to eight mats, and remove the *tatami* from the three-mat room, converting it into a sunroom.

hood, their readings were more skeptical and tentative, yet nevertheless they sought to show the applicability of divination to a range of sites, including culture houses, farmhouses, the Western-style house where General Nogi Maresuke had committed suicide, and the Tokyo mayor's office. Matsudaira and Honma presented their reading of a house designed by the new semi-public housing authority Dōjunkai that they reported had caused repeated misfortune and found that its ill-aspect could be improved by some minor reconstruction work, including the addition of a sunroom (*sanrūmu*; see Fig. 8.7). Like many "irresponsible ready-built houses," this one had been poorly designed to begin with, the authors explained; "ignoring the taste peculiar to Japanese houses," it was a "house like a box, with no *engawa*, and such a cramped feeling."[53] Dwelling reform advocates had already made the idea of the sunroom popular as a substitute for the narrower traditional *engawa*. As their reference to sunrooms and *engawa* together suggests, the authors did not regard Western-influenced house designs to be inherently bad. The concluding example in the book was a house whose outward appearance was Western while all rooms but one were Japanese. This house, designed by an architect, was called the source of "ten thousand fortunes," because of the architect's combination of "scientific divination" and economical design.[54]

The physical congruence between an auspicious house and a hygienic one was in some cases genuine. Ultimately, however, the aims of geomancy were different from those of modern architectural planning, since the auspicious plan promised to visit prosperity upon the household, rather than to accommodate the occupants in maximum comfort, to increase the efficiency of domestic work, or to conform to modern principles of hygiene. Through the efforts of geomancy's experts and adherents, the two were able to coexist in the market. Geomancers survived, however, by accepting the claim to universality of Western architectural knowledge, thus placing themselves institutionally and intellectually in a subordinate position to architects.

## A Changed Field of Production

Housing and the field of cultural production as a whole after 1922 involved a different set of players and new terms of play. A chain of causes beginning with the wartime boom, followed by the everyday life reform movement, Culture Village, and other media events, influenced by the new planning and building regulations, and all closely tied to growth in the ranks of professionally trained designers, created a broad spectrum of house designs and design books. The rhetoric of reform had changed little, but the range of people advocating it had grown, and everyone engaged in shaping or seeking to change dwelling space now marketed some image of cosmopolitan modernity—or felt compelled to participate in the marketing, since this was now what planning, designing, building, and divining were about. These practices had been removed from the nexus of vernacular production.

The architects whose drafting ability and legal literacy made them indispensable as proxies for builders under the Home Ministry's new regime need not always have determined design outcomes directly. Together with domestic reformers, pattern-book writers, police, and urban planners, they participated in a restructured system of housing production that situated vernacular design in a field of texts, abstract representations, and bureaucratic regulation. Neighborhood carpenters still worked much as they had; they were not swept aside by a new industrial system. Even geomancers preserved their niche. But a mode of production had been born that was governed by the expertise of architects and imbricated within systems of government regulation.

9

# Domestic Modernism

Like the model suburbs, the eclectic house designs of the 1920s represented as much a utopian social vision as an architectural aesthetic, for designers hoped that by re-examining how to dwell they would yield solutions to the social challenges of modernity in everyday life as well as to the conflicts of native and Western in modern culture. As an alternative path in architecture alongside the institutionally organized Modern Movement, which also appeared in Japan in these years, the range of proposals for new dwelling forms constituted what could be termed a "domestic modernism," focused on the private house and the attributes of homeyness, yet distinctly modernist because, like the members of the Modern Movement, its proponents represented themselves as artists and social visionaries responding to the conditions of modernity. Culture house designers also shared with modernists in the avant-garde worlds of contemporary art and architecture a thoroughgoing cosmopolitanism and unceasing pursuit of the new. Where they differed was in the site of their efforts and in their relation to the mass market. Their alternative modernism reinvented the dwelling as a visual object and a personal aesthetic expression and encouraged consumers to make acquisition of a house a creative act of their own.

The standard history of high modernism or the architectural avant-garde in Japanese architecture begins with the secessionist group known as the Bunriha, whose founding manifesto, published in 1920, marks the first time architects in Japan had formed an organized movement proclaiming political and aesthetic aims. They were followed by several other groups, including the explicitly Bauhaus-influenced International Architecture Association

(Nihon intaanashonaru kenchikukai), founded in Kyoto in 1927.[1] High modernists in the Bunriha and the International Architecture Association concerned themselves with the architect's public role and generally remained aloof from the vernacular housing market. Yet high modernists in Japan were not antagonistic to domesticity, unlike their counterparts in Europe, who launched polemics against bourgeois domestic ornament and sentimentality. The material forms of a new, more decorated, and effusive image of home were just taking shape in Japan, and their newness saved them from signifying the stagnant accumulation of bourgeois taste against which European modernists rebelled.[2] Romantic rather than rationalist, Bunriha architects led the way by championing individual creativity above all else. They directed their invective at the general conservatism of the native architectural academy rather than at any particular style of architecture or decoration.[3] Since it was possible in Japan during the 1920s to adopt a modernist position—if not a Bauhaus purist one—without crusading against bourgeois domesticity, a broad arena was opened for architects to formulate a domestic modernism that agreed at least in general spirit with the avant-garde.

The personae and modes of architectural expression of domestic modernism were largely distinct from those of high modernism. Unlike the high modernists, whose positions in the academy (particularly in the imperial universities) permitted them to proclaim their aesthetic ideals free from economic constraints, most domestic modernists were compelled to market themselves. Yet despite the difference of social position and vocabulary, domestic modernists as much as high modernists believed their role was to rebuild everyday life on new models. Indeed, Japan's domestic modernists pioneered the role of architect as social critic and visionary before their elite, European-trained colleagues. Subsequent architecture history has retrospectively privileged the elite movements culminating in international-style modernism, rendering other modernisms inauthentic. Yet, while its radicalism has since been obscured, and its authors have been omitted from the canonical history of architecture, in social terms, the most radical architectural statement of the era was the tiny culture house.

## The Visibility of the Culture House

From the vantage point of Tokyo consumers in the mid-1920s, images of attractive new houses were springing up in so many places that it was as if the dwelling itself had been discovered for the first time. Liberated from the strictures of vernacular production and socially embedded uses, house forms lent themselves to manipulation for visual and spatial effect. Vernacular architectural expression was in no sense suppressed or swept aside in this efflorescence; rather, it was seeded with images, ideas, and techniques. A cycle of constantly changing fashions had begun, in which Western designs provided the raw material.

For architects trained in the university system, finding a blend of native and Western elements that would provide the basis for a viable national identity in architecture had been the concern for over a generation. The sense of nation was changing together with Japan's changing place in the international system, and the global simultaneity of modern media was reshaping the cultural situation daily. The earthquake of 1923 gave this broader cultural crisis an immediate local correlative, a point of departure from which artists and architects imagined that they could reinvent the city. And for the first time there was a broad enough base of consumers, not wealthy but freed from the constraints of family, property, and community, to provide a market for new designs. The culture life propaganda to which they responded came in forms more direct, intimate, tactile, and visually stimulating than any previous efforts to reshape the everyday. This coalescence of developments in cultural production and consumption signaled by the culture life thus bound the national cause of reform to the liberation of personal desire.

New house designs made the detached house suddenly conspicuous not simply by being gaudy or exotic. A critical element of the culture house phenomenon, aptly symbolized in the ur-event of the exposition, was that houses became more visible and more specular objects. This happened in four ways.

First, in the most obvious sense, the houses at Culture Village were for looking at. Ironically, they were not for going into; visitors were allowed to enter the houses only by special invitation.[4] This only made them more purely visual objects (or objects for voyeurism), since the typical fairgoer's experience of them was limited to peering into the doorways and through the windows. Here, for the first time, were detached houses, the quintessentially private architectural form, built expressly for public display (see Fig. 9.1).

Second, graphic styles made the culture house a specular object. The illustrations that filled new architectural pattern books and culture life guides showed not only technical advances but innovations in visual presentation. Authors included perspective sketches and color, stylized freehand

Fig. 9.1 "Culture Village feels like a suburban neighborhood. And the sight of the spectators going from house to house peering into the windows brings to mind people looking at ordinary houses for rent. These young couples wandering around whispering to one another recall a scene one often sees around Nakano or Yoyohata. In this era of vexing housing shortages, you could say that Culture Village is not only an architecture exhibit but a living display of contemporary urban social conditions" (cartoon by Maekawa Senpan, published in *Chūō bijutsu*, May 1922).

elevations, and photographs, where formerly they had made do with only floor plans and an occasional hard-line elevation. Houses were consciously rendered as aesthetic objects, the single-point perspective, especially, giving primacy to vision, creating allure, and embodying the eye of possessive individualism (see Fig. 9.2).[5]

Third, in magazine advertisements and elsewhere in the mass media after the exposition, images of houses became popular symbols, used to evoke both progress and cozy domesticity. The Ajinomoto Company, makers of monosodium glutamate flavoring, advertised their product in the newspapers of late 1922 with a sketch of a steep-roofed half-timber style house and the words "appropriate to the name of Culture" (see Fig. 9.3).[6] Soap companies, soy-sauce manufacturers, a chocolate maker, and other producers of items for home use employed similar images. These were the first advertisements in Japan to exploit the home as a signifier of consumer satisfaction.

Fig. 9.2 New modes of representation: magazine and pattern-book illustrations of houses in the 1920s were both bolder artistically and more calculated to allure. (*left*) Suburban house by Nakanishi Yoshio, *Jūtaku* magazine, 1922. (*right*) "A Simple Small House," from Serizawa Eiji, *Dwellings for a New Japan* (*Shin Nihon no jūka*, 1924). This illustration, the text notes, "is a sketch drawn by the author of a house he would truly recommend to serious house lovers."

Fig. 9.3 Newspaper advertisement for Ajinomoto seasoning, early 1920s. The text reads: "Appropriate to the Name of Culture: a great saving of time and effort; results are extremely delicious and nutritious; effective and economical without compare." As in other advertisements of this period, the exotic Western house embodying "culture" is only obliquely related to the function of the product being marketed.

Fig. 9.4 Culture houses stood out from their surroundings, in contrast to traditional urban detached houses, which were hidden behind walls and hedges. Gables facing the street and second-story windows further distinguished them. (*top*) Street in the former samurai district of Hirosaki, Aomori prefecture (Miyazawa Satoshi, ed., *Nihon no bijutsu: machiya to machinami* [Shibundō, 1980]). (*middle*) New houses built along the Odakyū private rail line in Tokyo (*Nihon chiri taikei, Dai Tōkyō hen*, 1929]). (*bottom*) House of Baron Tokuse Hideo from a collection of culture house photographs (Kenchiku shashin ruiju kankōkai, *Kenchiku shashin ruiju dai 4 ki dai 7 kai: bunka jūtaku 1*, 1923).

Invented by domestic ideologues in the late nineteenth century, the idea of home as a place outside the sphere of market exchange was by this time firmly rooted in popular consciousness. Now it acquired a graphic form, too, permitting advertisers to use it as an icon of essential value whose symbolism purified the commodity.[7]

Finally, culture houses were dwellings rendered visible actually, and physically, since the new houses appearing in suburban neighborhoods of the time were more available to view from nearby streets. Surrounded by low fences rather than high walls and hedges, often two stories where most of their neighbors were one, with gables facing the street side, and dormers or attic windows cut into the gables rather than heavy, unbroken masses of roof tile (as if the eyes of the culture house were set higher on the head than native eyes), culture houses were conspicuous additions to the landscape (see Fig. 9.4).

Despite its failure to establish a universal model for reform, Ueno's Culture Village manifested the dwelling as an object of desire, and in this the exhibition was an undoubted success. For several years afterward, any image of a house that clearly differed from previous vernacular forms could be labeled "culture house." The label and visual presentation announced its novelty—and underscored its commodity status. Quite disparate structures designed by architects, carpenters, and amateurs shared the trait of conspicuous novelty, and as did high modernist buildings, they enjoyed the status of sculpted forms, designed to appeal to the eye.

## Homeownership and Personal Expression

In the eyes of domestic modernist designers and amateurs, the private house now loomed as an opportunity for creative expression of the personal taste and lifestyle of its occupants. Among academy architects, Yamamoto Setsurō exemplifies the emerging romance with the home as the realization of private ideals, as the vessel for possessions of sentimental value, and as an intimate space. In a short essay introducing the regular column he ran in *Jūtaku*, he described this private romance as what had first inspired him to become an architect. The essay began by recalling a visit to his friend K when the two were still students. He found K bent over a floor plan:

"The guest room will have a touch of *sukiya* style with a round window here, I'll put a fireplace in the Western room, and this will be the place for the piano," he explained to me, his eyes glittering. I felt envious that K might have a girlfriend who could play the piano, but more than that I was drawn by the appeal of making an imaginary house. I think this was one of the things that motivated me afterward to become a residential architect, [although at the time] I was interested in biology. . . .

It is quite a fascinating thing to plan and design your own house, even if you don't necessarily build it. [You imagine] "I'd like the study to be like this," or "On the bookshelf let's put that cute doll we saw in the show-window in Ginza," or "On summer evenings let's bring a rattan table with a white tablecloth onto the balcony here and drink English tea together." It provides us an open plain where the imagination has no limits. If you are walking in town and you see a painting of the Madonna, why not picture it decorating the wall of your imaginary house? Naturally, you are free to think of a photograph of a particular scene with Lillian Gish instead. Someday the two of you will probably look into the price of a Westinghouse electric range at the Takada Trading Company. Of course, you don't have to buy it. And what about the site? When you go strolling in the suburbs, or even as you look out the window of a train, why not keep an eye out for a sunny hill slope?[8]

In Yamamoto's eyes the architect's task was to help clients realize these personal dreams. This sense of his own role contrasted sharply with the public-mindedness promoted by the country's architectural institutions. Yamamoto's portrait of domesticity also implied a different understanding of the clients, imagined here as a couple. They are seen building a new house not because the progress of national life or the social norms of the era demand it, but because it permits them to translate their desires into material form. Yamamoto perceived his clients not only as lovers of family intimacy but as people whose lives were shaped by their roles as consumers. In this story, the hypothetical clients' purchases and their dreams of a house for those purchases seem in fact to bind them as a couple. The modern city offers a cornucopia for their desires. In intimate acts of consumption, from buying and bringing home the doll displayed in a show window to consuming the suburban landscape together from the window of a train, they share the pleasure of personal choice.

This pleasure of designing and choosing things was great enough, Yamamoto suggested, that it might in fact be enjoyed entirely in the realm of the imagination. At least for a time—needless to say, Yamamoto did not suppose that suspending oneself in a state of unrequited desire was pleasant indefinitely. His encouragement of a dream life composed of cozy houses filled with sentimental possessions and new consumer durables also served to advertise the design firm for which he worked and the manufacturers of new home products with whom it was affiliated, in preparation for the time when dreaming readers would be ready to spend. Consumers would consummate the romance by becoming homeowners, perhaps choosing a house design from one of *Jūtaku* magazine's compilations, if not calling upon Amerika-ya to build for them.

Yet by elevating the ordinariness and availability of the new domestic style rather than touting their own specialized knowledge, architects like Yamamoto opened the door to amateurs wishing to promote their own designs. The logical extreme of the popularization of Western architectural knowledge was an architectural field in which architects lost their privileged position, where any man could build his own culture house, and enjoy an audience by writing about it. In the women's magazines, homeowners introduced their houses to other readers, or accounts of their experience building and living in houses based on plans earlier published in the same magazine. Articles in the *Housewife's Companion* introduced houses built at low cost, modifications of old houses to produce affordable culture houses, and examples of ways to reuse old lumber, including detailed construction budgets.

One popular article, published in 1926, was by an amateur who had designed his own two-room house and built it for the unusually small sum of 600 yen. This was less than one year's rent for a single room in the famous *Bunka apaatomento*, the country's first Western-style apartment house, built in downtown Tokyo by Morimoto Kōkichi shortly after the earthquake.[9] The author announced proudly that he was enjoying all the luxury of a first-class cabin on a European luxury liner. Readers might imagine that such a small house would look like a shed or garage, he admitted, but his possessed a dignified mien "worthy of the mansions of kings and aristocrats." He had painted the sheet-metal roof dark green and the clapboard walls (the narrow type known as "Nanking clapboards") white. Although it was popular to paint clapboards with only sealant, white paint, he claimed, looked "higher class." Inside, life was entirely Western-style, with beds, chairs, and a Western bath. His family of three occupied this cozy 7.5 *tsubo* (270 square feet) without inconvenience, he reported.

This writer had done some of the construction work himself. It would not be difficult to do all of the carpentry without help of a carpenter if one put the structure together in the American fashion with nails instead of joints, he concluded.[10] The article drew sufficient interest that the editors invited the author back in the following issue to provide further details

Fig. 9.5 "A Culture House for Six Hundred Yen." "Conditions for a culture house: the inevitable red roof, the little bird, radio, slippers, the one or two framed pictures—even clipped from the newspaper is ok—the rattan chairs, the coffee set, and then the one-yen anthology volumes and the bookshelf—this is about enough to qualify for starters, if you happen to be asked by a schoolteacher or on a mental test (*mentaru tesuto*), you're all right if you say that much."

"A particular women's magazine introduced a method for building an inexpensive house of your own design, and ended up whipping up a sensational 600-yen house building fever among the lunchbox-dangling office workers of the metropolis."

. . . "So, here it is built. It's a bit of fun to have a doorbell."

"Well, that's one of the conditions for a culture house, you know."

"Keeping an umbrella up in the house, pretty nifty (*furutte iru ne*). If Master Basho were alive he would be delighted."

"In a neighborhood like this (*basho gara*), you can't say that too loud." (Sogyū, "Roppyaku en no bunka jūtaku," *Kenchiku to shakai*, April 1928, 12).

about furnishing and fixtures.[11] Two years later, it appears to have inspired a satiric cartoon in the Kansai journal *Architecture and Society*, which claimed that "a particular women's magazine" had sparked a "600-yen house sensation" (see Fig. 9.5).[12] Similarly humble and still cheaper examples of amateur design appeared in print elsewhere, emphasizing that even the most minimal shelter could be fashioned to express the ideals of a person of taste.

Since speculative construction of houses for sale rather than for rental was still exceptional in the Tokyo of the 1920s, more owner-occupied culture houses of the kind in the magazines were built to the owners' specifications or to those of an architect than were ready-built. The mass pursuit of home-ownership emerged in Tokyo from this romance with the private home (prefigured in the Hankyū suburbs of Osaka) rather than from widespread valuation of property as a secure investment. Since even wealthy executives and elite bureaucrats had commonly lived in rented houses in late nineteenth-century Tokyo, the owners of modest culture houses were instigating a marked shift in habits through their lifestyle choice.[13] The established bourgeois domestic reformers would have found the new owner-occupied culture houses absurdly small. They hardly placed their owners securely in the propertied class, but culture houses did announce the owners' modern tastes and domestic ideals.

The ideal of owning one's own small house eventually found expression in popular song as well as in the many evocations of domestic coziness in other media. In the Japanese version of the American song "My Blue Heaven," first released in 1928, lyricist Horiuchi Keizō interpolated the words *semai nagara tanoshii wagaya* (small as it is, it's my happy home). The song became a runaway hit (described as the most popular jazz song before World War II), and the phrase entered common parlance.[14]

## The Utopian Everyday

As much as the outward appearance of new houses struck consumers and critics in the 1920s, architects and writers on the house were interested in what was within, as they searched for new, more natural, and comfortable forms with which to clothe domestic life. Culture-house advocates of the early 1920s fashioned utopian ideals from the material of the ordinary. Utopianism colored the content of their proposals for the new domesticity, their polemics against pretension, and the very style of their prose, which was punctuated with short, emphatic pronouncements that mirrored in language the simple style they espoused in architecture. Although it inhabited the same historical moment and sometimes the same texts as the scientific-rationalist language of domestic reform, the utopian language of culture remained recognizably different.

In *A Study of Cultural Houses* (*Bunkateki jūtaku no kenkyū*; 1922), for example, authors Moriguchi Tari and Hayashi Itoko interspersed concrete prescriptions for such things as the height of kitchen sinks and construction of storage space with advice on reforming everyday life delivered in urgent rhetoric that seemed to treat the prosaic aspects of women's domestic life as the stuff of poetry. Part of the book was composed as a series of imaginary letters addressed to "our beloved younger sisters":

> Have you thought of your life in the future? . . . Your future life will not only be keeping the *zashiki* tidy and quietly playing the *koto*. . . . If you, too, love your future life, don't imagine it as some kind of multicolored dream; think of it as something more practical. Then the sprouts of ideal forms of food, clothing, and shelter will emerge. . . . It's true of everything. What doesn't emerge from love for life is neither true reform nor true taste.[15]

Illustrations in *A Study of Cultural Houses* depicted buildings ranging from opulent mansions (Japanese and European) to a converted stable, most unconnected to one another and in unidentified locations, but all far removed from what was within the typical female Japanese reader's experience. Although Moriguchi and Hayashi warned their readers against daydreaming, the entire work was really an invitation to dream, to imagine reconstructing everyday life without social or material limitations.

Particularly when not writing explicitly for a female audience, domestic modernists presented an ideal of everydayness built around the individual spirit rather than the practicalities of housework or social relations. Fujine Daitei's *The Ideal Culture House* (*Risō no bunka jūtaku*; 1923) opened with reflections on the unity of body and soul, explaining that just as true physical beauty emanated from the spirit, beauty in the architecture of the dwelling resulted from an outward extension of the occupant's everyday life. The justly proportioned house, which emerged at a point of equilibrium in this extension, would be "a temple of happy living to rest the noble human spirit."[16] Architect Nose Kyūichirō's pattern book *Improved Houses Buildable on 30 Tsubo* (*Sanjuttsubo de dekiru kairyō jūtaku*; 1924) offered similar thoughts in plainer language and concrete form. Nose accompanied his house plans with paeans to simple living and denunciations of social pretension: "A cultural life is a scientific life. To put it plainly, that means a simple life. To live a simple life, you must live in a simple house. Dancing isn't the only thing that's the culture life. People who play the piano or sing in a chorus aren't the only ones living the culture life."[17] The ultimate destination of this simplification of life was a house of one room: "One large living room is plenty for our daily life," Nose declared, "Just living in a big house is not the culture life."[18] These pronouncements were more theoretical ideals, however, expressions of a pure state in which nothing extraneous compromised the direct fulfillment of the individual's immediate wants, and nothing was adopted for form's sake. Most of Nose's houses were designed to accommodate families and recognized their needs in more conventional terms. The plans printed alongside these passages in the text were for houses of four and five rooms, including children's rooms with little desks. Although his polemic implied that the simple life had no need for piano players, Nose indicated an open wall space in one living room and suggested, "If you make a little money, you can put a piano here."[19] In practical terms, the unpretentious house and lifestyle he was promoting were in no way incompatible with these modest bourgeois appurtenances.

The work of self-trained architect Nishimura Isaku encapsulates the values of domestic modernism with particular clarity (see Fig. 9.6). Starting with his own American bungalow in 1906, and publishing his popular first book, *The Happy House* (*Tanoshiki jūka*), in 1919, Nishimura was also a pioneer, perhaps the first Japanese designer to combine social idealism with an exploration of the artistic possibilities in house design. Family wealth alleviated him of the need to earn a living, making him freer to follow his interests than most house architects. His own experiences occupied an unusually prominent place in his books, more than one of which began with an autobiographical chapter. After his marriage in 1907, Nishimura endeavored to base every aspect of his home life on Anglo-American models of domesticity, taking his information from magazines like *House and Garden* and ordering the necessary goods directly from Montgomery Ward and other mail-order companies overseas. The "Swiss chalet"–style house he built in his native town of Shingū, Wakayama Prefecture, expressed not only his fascination with Western domestic models but his social ideal of a completely transparent, unaffected everyday life centered on personal pleasures. A linked dining room and living room, which Nishimura also called the "conversation room" (*danwashitsu*), dominated the first floor. Around the fireplace at the end of the room, an inglenook was built into a windowed projection on the front side of the house, the inside of which could be seen from the entry. The design was intended to prescribe a more open lifestyle: "One wants to nurture the spirit to live in a house in which a large, cheerful living room has been built in place of an entry vestibule (*genkan*) or hall," he wrote, "where one can

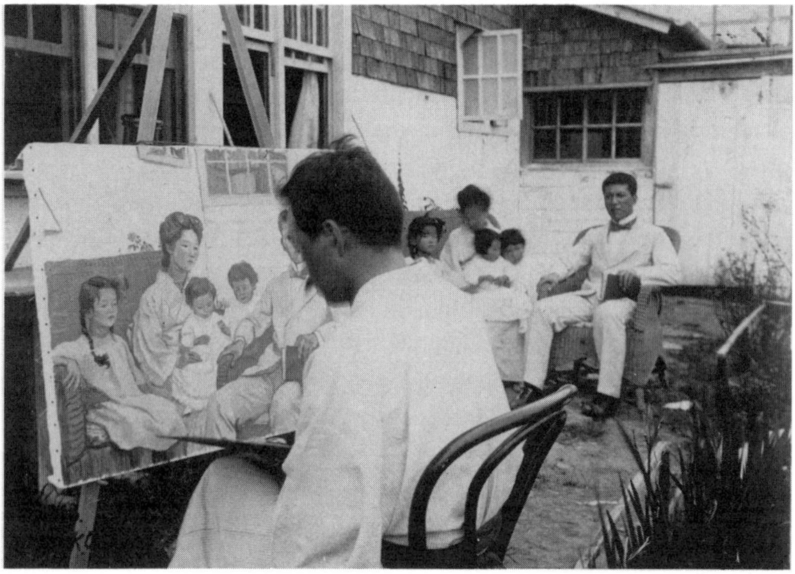

Fig. 9.6 Nishimura Isaku sits with his wife and children for artist Ishii Hakutei's painting *Mr. N and His Family* (*N shi to sono ikka*), in the garden of the family house in Shingū (Mie Prefecture), 1913. This was one of the first family portraits to appear in the Ministry of Education's annual exhibition (*bunten*) (photograph courtesy Bunka gakuin).

look out through the window to see friends coming to visit and greet them with a smile before even getting up."[20] Nishimura also found social import in putting the dining area within sight of guests. Combining the two spaces might be thought a source of inconvenience in the event visitors came when one was eating, he acknowledged, but there ought to be nothing shameful about being seen eating. Civilized people needn't take their meals as if they were "beasts" hiding their prey, he asserted.[21]

As is evident in Nishimura's second book, *Making Art of Life* (*Seikatsu o geijutsu to shite*; 1922), the architect treated his domestic life as a kind of edifying performance, a *Gesamtkunstwerk* encompassing architecture, dress, and food, as well as the collaboration of friends and family as fellow players. It was a performance admired by the many Taishō writers and artists who visited the Nishimura house in Shingū, and the ideals underlying it impressed enough of them to help Nishimura develop a substantial architectural practice, which completed over fifty private houses in Osaka and Tokyo. *The Happy House* also went into multiple printings.[22]

Just as it stood at the logical extreme of culture-house populism, the amateur-built minimal house also lay at the far pole among idealizations of simplicity in everyday living. In a personal essay and practical guide for amateurs written a few months before the earthquake, writer Kanno Kyūichi placed the story of his own tiny suburban home and the parallel story of an artist friend living nearby within Japan's long tradition of rustic hermitage. In Kanno's story, the two meet over drinks one day at a Ginza bar, and the friend confides his longing for a small country retreat, recalling as he does so the itinerancy of famous native poets and the humble dwellings of hermits and tea masters. In a form reminiscent of Kamo no Chōmei's thirteenth-century classic, *An Account of My Hut*, the author then recounts the history of his residence in seven different locations during five years in Tokyo, leading ultimately to his decision to build a house of two rooms—one Japanese and one Western—and no fences in Chiba prefecture, an hour's commute from the city.[23] Here he grows vegetables and "gets in touch with the soil" (*tsuchi ni shitashimu*), which teaches him profound lessons in the meaning of life. Later, his friend follows suit and builds a house nearby. His friend's house is "like a tearoom" on the outside but a "genuine Western house" inside.[24]

In their utopian idyll, the minimal houses of Kanno and his friend surpass the promises of simple living to accomplish what the author proclaims—in the popular phrase of the day—"the transformation of life into art" (*seikatsu no geijutsuka*). A house, his friend tells him, is a work of pure creation greater than the writing of a novel. Indeed, the friend no longer wants to paint as long as he can live each day as he likes in his own house, making life art. To set this idle artist apart from the traditional image of the gentleman in retreat, Kanno points out that his friend's tastes are as eclectic as the design of his house: he occupies some evenings on the *engawa* meditating on the stone Buddha in the garden; on other evenings he loses himself in hymns at the pedal organ. As the two sip cocoa in rattan chairs outdoors and converse, the author teases his friend with the buzzword that had recently come to animate the political journals: "You're quite the bourgeois, aren't you?" (*kimi wa mattaku burujaa da ne*); and the artist allows that he is. The label is an expression of approbation. No matter how ascetic his living conditions, the author reflects, his friend can't be proletarian because he is "rich in his heart." He is a "charming little (*kawaii*) bourgeois."

Fig. 9.7 Cover (*left*) and illustration (*right*) from *The Three-Hundred Yen House* (Kanno Kyūichi, *Sanbyaku en no ie*, 1923). Meditation on the *engawa*, hymns at the pedal organ, and cocoa in rattan chairs in the garden: "You're quite the bourgeois, aren't you?" the author remarks with admiration to his suburban neighbor.

These "little bourgeois" men's utopias differed from the ascetic retreats of earlier generations in another important respect. They were family homes. The artist's wife serves the cocoa. Since Kanno has brought his wife and child to the house in Chiba, all the usual issues of concern to domestic reformers come into play in reduced form, as he touches on questions of kitchen design, childcare, and guest reception. The first third of the book thus seeks to demonstrate that the house the author has designed is sufficient for a pleasant and proper bourgeois lifestyle. Since the author's aim was to achieve this at minimal cost, the book details techniques for cutting corners and reducing the carpenter's bill, including using slats from old beer crates for clapboards. In an ironic play on the hermit's tradition of renouncing worldly affairs, the artist friend has named his house "Hermitage of Yearning for the World" (Seshian). Fitting to the "little bourgeois" lifestyle it embodies, the name of the author's own house, at least in the title of his book, announces its price: "The 300-Yen House" (see Fig. 9.7)[25]

Whether building for themselves or for others, domestic modernist designers treated their houses as prototypes for experiments in living. Unlike

European modernists, however, they did not direct their invective against bourgeois domesticity; on the contrary, that was precisely what they were promoting. The plain language and personal examples of these proselytizing designers expressed a shared mission to show others that the satisfactions of bourgeois living were in fact simple ones, available to all.

The culture house can be called a bourgeois utopia, based on domestic intimacy, personal aesthetic expression, and the sacralized everyday experience of the "simple life." The community circumscribed by this utopia was narrow, but that made it no less utopian, since it was an imaginary place of perfect harmony from which social contradictions were absent. Kanno could rightfully claim that a 300-yen house was "proletarian" in economic terms, but there was no proletariat here—neither the needs of factory laborers nor the urban institutions sustaining the downtown shopkeepers' Tokyo found a place in the culture house fantasy of simple living and suburban leisure.

## Fusing East and West

This kind of idealization of intimacy and ennobling of simple quotidian practices had considerable design implications. To begin with, such ideals demanded that architects reconsider the established distinctions of East and West in interiors, since these had been premised on the formal protocols of Meiji polite society. Among young architects, the new language of design became generally less stiff and more spontaneous, in keeping with the domestic modernist message of liberation from convention. The generation who began publishing designs in the 1920s adopted a hybrid style to replace not only the architectural forms but the discrete Western and Japanese orthography and planning systems that had ruled the day in architectural education. Their plans blended Western and Japanese features in a single loose freehand. The Kansai architect who reported in *Architecture and Society* on the troubling state of technical college education located the source of freehand sketching in specific overseas influences:

> In the past, one used five elements to draw an architectural elevation: the T-square, triangle, compass, spring, and free hand. But when things in the so-called Secession Style appeared, the compass and spring vanished; then some time after the appearance of Mendelsohn's Einstein Laboratory even the straight-edges vanished too, and the extremely bold method came into vogue among students of dealing with everything entirely in freehand.[26]

European avant-garde trends thus licensed young Japanese architects to break with the orthodoxy of their teachers, who had taught them to look to Europe for models in the first place. The borrowing from Europe also became more casual and piecemeal. Strongly linear and angular design motifs associated with the Viennese Secession (by this time long over in its place of origin) were mixed with high gables or mansard roofs and pointed roof ornaments—some of which came from German and Austrian vernacular house design—and the composite was referred to as "German" or "Secession" style interchangeably. Young architects in Japan thus picked up what suited them from media that carried the European avant-gardists' iconoclastic message and designs (along with less radical ones), claiming what they found for the purposes of their own challenge to the academy within Japan.[27]

The ideals, architectural forms, and graphic language of domestic modernism were all in evidence in entries to a competition to design a small house with a floor area of 15–16 *tsubo* (roughly 500–600 square feet) sponsored by the publishers of *Kenchiku shashin ruiju* in 1925–26. In accompanying texts, the winners identified their houses with stylistic labels that intentionally defied past categories, calling them things like "nativized modern," "modern Germanesque," or simply "contemporary style." The first-prize winner announced that his design should be "called by the neologism Japanesque" (*Japanesuku to iu shingo*). The designers' texts emphasized simple living and such simple pleasures of domestic leisure as listening to the sound of insects in the summer or stretching out on a rattan reclining chair. One description led the reader on a tour through the house, beginning with the words "a beautiful white door opens silently" and proceeding in theatrical style to describe the sights and sounds one would encounter within (see Fig. 9.8). Several also evoked romantic imagery to paint the small suburban house as the salaried worker's object of longing, speaking, for example, of every man's "desire . . . for a fulfilled life in the deep green suburbs," where a "goddess of love" awaited him. In their interiors, the designs mixed sliding partitions, swing doors and curtains, chairs and *tatami* mats, abandoning the formulaic distinctions of *yōma* and native *zashiki*. External shapes ranged from low sweeping roofs clearly influenced by the architecture of Frank Lloyd Wright to the more vertical, sharply angular, "German" forms. Freehand rendering predominated among perspective drawings and was common in plans and elevations as well. Dramatic shading, stylized lettering, and

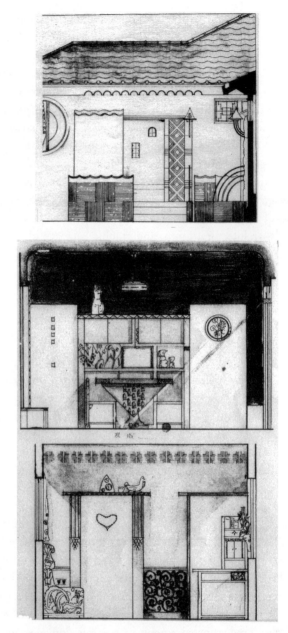

Fig. 9.8 "A beautiful white door opens silently . . . ." Front and interior elevations from a winning entry in the *Kenchiku shashin ruiju* small house competition, 1925.

unusual backgrounds announced the designers' departure from academic architectural conventions as well as their distance from the simple diagrams of amateurs.[28]

## Material Metaphors

In a manner as alien to most senior architects as it was to carpenters, domestic modernists adopted the stance of modern artists in pursuit of novel expression. Yet as much as they sought new architectural idioms unbeholden to the orthodoxy of national styles, they frequently found their hybrid designs identified by observers simply as "Western." Together with the design competition, architectural criticism had become an integral part of the institutions of architecture since the 1910s, and the old accusation of infection with Westernism (*seiyō kabure*) continued to surface in both specialist and popular media. In architecture as in other areas of society, "Americanism" served as a watchword for craven submission to cultural imperialism.[29] Finding new ways to negotiate East and West thus became the focus of artistic expression in houses as much as in public architecture. Nor was it only a matter of visual appearance, since architects who found in the dwelling a site for expressing utopian ideals viewed the questions of domestic comfort and intimacy as fundamentally of a piece with questions of design aesthetics. As each new design positioned itself in relation to what was already built or published and sought to demonstrate an effective cultural synthesis, house form was shaped in an aesthetic dialogue—aesthetic, that is, in the broad sense of concerning the whole of the body's sensory relation to its environment. Although this aesthetic dialogue drew heavily on architectural vocabulary from Europe and the United States, it took place primarily within a field that was local to Japan. In terms of both visual expression and the molding of domestic space, the problem of "Westernness" provided the catalyst for an internal process in which forms emerged from other forms, taking on meaning in relation to them.[30]

The East-West design dynamic led high modernist architects toward increasing abstraction of native architectural forms, as they sought to define a national identity that could inhabit Western modernity.[31] In domestic modernism, it led toward a restless play of forms shaped by the quest for comfort and aesthetic pleasure. If Western forms provided the material both for rationalizing the dwelling around a more intimate domestic life and for creating visual appeal, however, the two motives did not always coincide. In some instances, what was modern in a practical sense failed to communicate modernness, or the right kind of modernness, in its appearance. Culture house design was a matter of negotiating not a set of stable signs and referents but a vocabulary of material metaphors, whose signifying ability depended on context.

In the eyes of many reformist designers in the 1920s, the American bungalow was the most affordable vehicle to modernity. Rejected by the Japanese market when Amerika-ya had first tried to import them before World War I, these small, rectangular, and simply laid-out products of the ready-built housing industry in the United States now provided an affordable model for the Japanese suburban house. There was no question that bungalows could be built at low cost, and a few others even followed Amerika-ya in importing them directly from the United States.[32] In plan, several of the Culture Village houses and many more designs in subsequent pattern books were close to the typical American bungalow, zoned into master bedroom, children's room, bathroom, and kitchen around a large living-dining area. In visual terms, however, the style's affinity to Japanese vernacular dwellings gave the deep-eaved single-story bungalow potentially negative value as symbolic capital. Squat and understated, bungalows lacked the design cachet of grander-looking two-story Western buildings, particularly the German and English styles common among houses of the wealthy built in the 1910s. These houses tended to have steep roofs with little or no eave projection.[33] Even after the architectural academy had tired of the Secession style, the sharply sloped roof continued to have iconic power as a sign of modernity. Chikama Sakichi, author of several collections of house plans, prefaced a volume of designs for rental houses with an exegesis on the "dwelling problem" and the solutions proposed by the Everyday Life Reform League. He then endorsed bungalows as both ideal for the new suburban dwelling and lucrative for the speculator, concluding, "These bungalow-type houses have already been built everywhere in the environs of Tokyo, Yokohama, Osaka, and Kobe, and in the Meguro and Shibuya area of Tokyo they are even available for rent. Their value has been widely recognized."[34] No bungalows were to be found, however, among the twenty-eight houses in Chikama's book. Chikama's Western-style houses had the steep roofs and tall, narrow windows associated with what Japanese called German or Secession style.

The author doubtless recognized that in the pattern book market, the visual rhetoric of new houses was at least as important as their promise to rationalize everyday life, and the Secession elevation was the Western model most likely to catch the eyes of contemporary readers.

Favored models changed quickly, however. If the house designs entered in the 1929 competition sponsored by the *Asahi* newspaper five years after Chikama's book may be taken as a measure, the steep roof had a short life. Only two or three of the eighty-five published designs had the steep roofs that had been common in publications of the early 1920s. Other new features were more in evidence. Elements of Bauhaus modernism and the Art Deco style coincided with features of *sukiya* design, and architects incorporated these instead. Thirty-nine of the published *Asahi* designs had round windows, and roughly the same number featured horizontal window grills and coursing or were rendered so as to accent narrow parallel bands in a manner suggestive of the streamlined Art Deco look.[35]

Broad gabled roofs with projecting eaves recalling California Arts and Crafts designs also emerged as a popular device in the 1929 competition.[36] Nineteen of the published entries had gabled roofs with projecting eaves. Because of their projecting eaves, these gabled roofs were regarded as according with native tradition, although they were new to carpenters, since almost all urban detached houses in Japan had borne hipped or combination hip-and-gable roofs before. The gabled roof design had considerable impact on living conditions. On the one hand, it permitted brighter interiors, since the gable side presented a larger vertical surface in which to cut windows. On the other hand, it also made leaks and wall damage more likely in a typhoon (see Fig. 9.9).[37]

From the late 1920s, particularly in western Japan, the "Spanish style," with white stucco, red semi-circular roof tiles, and round arched windows and entries, had become the new trend. *Supanishu*, as it was usually known, had come not from Spain but from the West Coast of the United States, a fact inscribed in the transliterated English name. It lasted through the 1930s. In 1940, *Kingu* magazine's annual lexicon of words in the news explained its background: "The overseas expansion of the Spaniards caused this style to spread on the American continent as an architecture with a foreign sensibility (*jōcho*). Its Oriental quality (*tōyōteki fūshu*) came to be appreciated by the people of our country, and it is used widely in houses and elsewhere."[38] With

Fig. 9.9 Asahi Model House no. 3, by Ōshima Kazuo (Asahi shinbunsha, ed., *Asahi jūtaku zuan shū*, 1929, 15). Round windows, horizontal coursing, and gabled roofs with projecting eaves were in fashion at the time.

the aesthetic term *jōcho*, this colloquial definition fused the Spanish colonial settlement of the seventeenth century with the twentieth-century American revival of "Spanish style." *Kingu*'s editors thus treated *Supanishu* simultaneously as a fashion and a national architecture, giving it a history, but a blurred one in which agreement with Japanese people's "Oriental" taste made it at least as natural a part of the Japanese landscape as it was of the American one from which it had been imported. Indeed, the editors of *Kingu* could not be faulted for regarding *Supanishu* as something free of history, since Spanish style in California was equally a modern invention. Just as architects had ceased to treat styles as permanently rooted in the soil of particular nations, urban Japanese consumers after World War I, like their counterparts in Los Angeles, were able to accept new styles as their own on the basis of aesthetic appeal rather than rigidly defined national identities (see Fig. 9.10).

One important intermediary in the translation of California "Spanish" style into *Supanishu* was William Merrill Vories, an American. Arriving in Japan in 1905 as a missionary with the YMCA, Vories went on to make a career designing mission buildings and houses and preaching the virtues of

Fig. 9.10 Two examples of *Supanishu* style in the Osaka area. (*top*) The Ōbayashi construction company's entry in the Kansai Dwelling Reform Exposition, built in the Osaka suburb of Sakurai in 1922 (photograph taken in the 1980s; courtesy Aihara Isao). Palm trees, like the two beside the entry to this house, were a popular way to enhance the tropical flavor of the exotic new architecture. (*bottom*) Perspective drawing of an entry to the Healthy Dwelling Design Competition, conducted by the *Ōsaka Mainichi* newspaper in 1929 (Ōsaka Mainichi shinbunsha, ed., *Kenkō jūtaku sekkei zuanshū*, 1930, 32).

American domestic architecture. He built several New England colonial-style houses before turning to Spanish style in 1925, at the height of the Spanish revival in California housing. Between 1925 and 1939, Vories designed a dozen Spanish style houses, most of them mansions and company residences in Kansai. His designs for schools and college campuses were particularly influential.[39] He also published two popular books in Japanese on house design.

In interwar Japan, however, an American without reputation overseas did not enjoy the status that Westerners had had a generation earlier. Indeed, the value of "America" as a cultural marker was increasingly insecure in the 1920s.[40] In addition to the concern many social critics expressed about the baleful effects of Ford automobiles, Hollywood, and other aspects of "Americanism," the United States' 1924 Exclusion Act delivered an insult that even the most ardent internationalist could not disregard. Moreover, architectural expertise was more widely available and the channels bearing information on the latest fashions overseas were broader. Many of Vories's Japanese colleagues looked at the same journals and pattern books as he did, and some had visited California specifically to see new housing. The fact that *Supanishu* took off in Japanese housing almost simultaneously with Spanish style in California reveals that vernacular design no longer depended either on mediation through the rarified field of elite architectural production or on the imprimatur of a foreigner.[41]

Certain shapes and textures belonging to imported architectural styles carried particular expressive weight by virtue of their contrast with what had preceded them in Japan. The gently sloping roofs of the late 1920s reacted against the conspicuous and often-parodied steep roofs of German-influenced houses popular earlier. The solidity and coarse tactility of the stuccoed "Spanish" of the late 1920s and 1930s countered the flatness and shoddy appearance of hastily painted and quickly aging clapboards on culture houses from the 1920s, much as lightweight rattan furniture and light fabrics in the 1910s and 1920s had rebelled again the ponderousness of cushioned and brocaded Meiji *yōkan* interiors.

As with fenced gardens and glass windows, design moves based on Western models provided metaphors for reconceiving everyday life. The steeply sloped roof popular in the early 1920s was an articulate instance of this. Steep roofs and narrow fenestration became a kind of shorthand for the culture house in popular depictions. For architect and Culture Village judge Ōkuma Yoshikuni, the vertical thrust of contemporary designs was a metaphor for the age, confirming a sense that modernity itself was vertically oriented, and that its arrival in the home meant that women, too, were finally becoming modern: "Whereas houses formerly extended horizontally, the so-called culture house extends vertically. Not high up, but upright (*rittaiteki ni*). That women today have awakened upright (*rittaiteki ni*) is related to this vertical (*rittaiteki*) development of the house. Tastes today are all fundamentally vertical (*rittaiteki*)."[42] Ōkuma's synesthetic view of verticality in houses and the "upright" modern woman was predicated on the changes in architecture and everyday practice that had preceded this. The introduction of chairs, first in public places, then in the Western reception rooms and gentlemen's studies of elite houses, and gradually thereafter into the private space of the more progressive new houses, had helped construct a web of associations that tied sitting on the floor, native tradition (or backwardness), and femininity. So the new woman, in Ōkuma's eyes, would express her modernness by standing or sitting in a chair in a "vertical" house. At the same time, the fashion for high roofs and attic rooms to which Ōkuma made oblique reference here was not only metaphoric, but in fact a radical departure from past practice, since second floors had been marginal spaces in most dwellings before. Most houses apart from commercial rowhouses and brothels had been single-story, and where there was a second floor, it was a hidden space one had to climb a ladder-like stair to reach.[43] This sharp contrast made it possible to see "vertical" house design as a metaphor whose material expression had real consequences not only for the ways people dwelled but for the ways that they thought and felt. Like the ideal planned suburban development, the full two-story house represented a liberation of space, promising brightness and openness.

For geomancer Takagi Jō, verticality was the key distinguishing characteristic of Western architecture generally. It also posed the greatest challenge to his Eastern science, which operated by determining what he called "horizontal stability." Takagi regarded most Western architecture, particularly apartment buildings and other multistory structures, as beyond the purview of geomancy, because its stability (which he meant in terms of cosmic energy, not physical structure) was vertical rather than horizontal.[44] The greater attention lavished on elevations in culture house designs thus seemed to signal the end of design principles as they had existed. In both the progressive view of architects like Ōkuma and the more conservative view of the geomancer, verticality functioned as a material metaphor bearing spiritual meaning.

These readings of architectural form were specific to Japan. It is doubtful that German or Viennese architects designing houses with steep roofs and high, narrow windows conceived themselves to be expressing the upward thrust of modernity, let alone creating an architecture that bore forces contrary to the cosmic energy embodied in single-story structures. Meanwhile in English, Australian, and North American suburbs at the same time, the stylistic tropes were moving in the opposite direction, as bungalows presented a model of horizontal living that accorded with the modern sense of home as a place of leisure.[45]

## Native Style

Among modernists, Japaneseness became another stylistic resource rather than a native system of space and practice. What architecture historians today call "modern Japanese style" (*kindai wafū*) had already developed a complete decorative and tectonic vocabulary in the public architecture of the 1890s. The term itself was seldom used, however, until the late 1920s, when architects began to define aesthetic Japaneseness in broader terms and to challenge the use of stock monumental features for Japanizing Western architecture. "Chinese gables" (*karahafu*), the ponderous roofs that had commonly been built over entrances to the mansions of the rich and used to add a native accent to Meiji public buildings were ridiculed as "hearse-style architecture."[46] The wealthy who had built eclectic-style mansions in the days before the culture house vogue were now accused of tasteless vanity for "putting roofs for temples and shrines on Western buildings."[47]

Seeking native traditions more in keeping with modern tastes, architects turned to features of rural houses and the *sukiya* tradition. Tokyo University graduate Horiguchi Sutemi, for example, followed an early-career infatuation with the Austrian Secession and contemporary Dutch architecture by immersing himself in study of *sukiya*, the influence of which emerged clearly in his house designs beginning in the 1920s. In the same years, both Fujii Kōji, who succeeded Takeda Goichi as instructor of "dwelling studies" (*jūtakuron*) at the Kyoto College of Arts and Engineering, and Yamada Jun, who had a private practice in Tokyo, did detailed studies of the relation of Japanese dwellings to climate. Performing these studies on traditionally constructed houses of their own design, they reached the predictable conclusion that native construction was well-adapted to the temperature and humidity range of the central Honshū regions where the architects themselves were living and working.[48] Inside the experimental houses Fujii built on his suburban Kyoto estate, he artfully combined chair-sitting and *tatami* and employed *sukiya* structural features as well as furniture and light fixtures with *sukiya*-inspired designs.[49] Outside, walls had plaster rather than the more common local clapboards and glass windows instead of sliding paper doors.

Fig. 9.11 Chochikukyo, Fujii Kōji's fifth experimental house: (*left*) exterior; (*right*) interior, with *sukiya* details (Koji Fujii, *The Japanese Dwelling-House*, 1930).

The tiled roofs were gabled and more gently sloped than in most vernacular structures (see Fig. 9.11). The appearance was still unmistakably "Japanese," yet distinct from everything around it, since the design had been reached by a circuitous route through formal (which was to say Western) architectural education, a personal mission to demonstrate the scientific validity of an abstractly conceived native tradition, and an exploration of the possibilities of *sukiya* aesthetics as a suitable concrete embodiment of that tradition.

University-trained architects and designers subsequently pursued the quest for a true native architecture by experimenting with materials, proportions, ornament—or the expunging of ornament—and construction techniques or by creating visual effects suggestive of native construction. Some promoted their solutions by writing theoretical tracts on Japanese aesthetics and space. Native dwellings played a special role in this search for tradition, embodying a purely indigenous milieu in which the architectural principles of European modernism seemed already to have existed before modernity.[50]

Tea masters and folklorists prefigured the modernist appropriation of rural house form. The rustic beauty of the unfinished posts, thatched roof, deep eaves, and open hearth of the common Japanese country house had inspired teahouse design over three centuries earlier. A few wealthy Meiji connoisseurs took literally the well-worn metaphor of stylized rusticity and moved actual farmhouses to their urban estates to use for tea gatherings. Cultural historian Kumakura Isao reports that the transplanted country house (*inakaya*) had become something of a fashion among tea men by the Taishō period.[51] Folklorists, meanwhile, reappraised rural houses in romantic terms, connecting their design to simple life ideals. Before his famous

Fig. 9.12 "A Farmer's House Converted to a Middle-Class Home," from *Housewife's Companion Collection of Middle-Class Western and Japanese Houses* (Shufu no tomo henshūkyoku, *Chūryū wayō jūtaku shū*, 1929).

studies of modern life in Tokyo, architect Kon Wajirō had been a pioneer in this field as well. Between 1918 and 1921, when he was still an assistant in the architecture department at Waseda, Kon traveled throughout Japan, making detailed records of construction, setting, material contents, and habits of life in the houses of all classes of people. The product of his travels was *Nihon no minka* (People's Dwellings of Japan), published in 1922, the book that coined and popularized the term *minka* and became the foundational work in a new field of rural house studies.[52] *Minka* for Kon held secrets about how to dwell in the world, an understanding of which would contribute to reforming urban architecture. They were also intrinsically noble and beautiful in his eyes, as he made clear through citations of Ruskin and careful and copious sketches of the houses themselves.[53]

The same recasting of native tradition in aesthetic terms is evident in some of the popular culture house guides of the 1920s, minus the elite intellectual's burden of a sense of national mission (see Fig. 9.12). Contrary to the claims of contemporary critics, culture house designers did not all reject native architectural forms. Pattern books from the 1920s and the 1930s

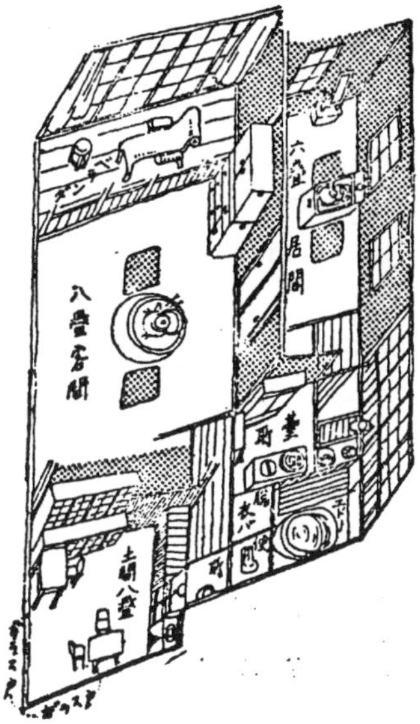

Fig 9.13 "An Ideal Country House for the New Era" from *Housewife's Companion* ("Shin jidai no risōteki den'en jūtaku," *Shufu no tomo* 5, Nov. 1921, 165). Entry to the house is from the bottom left. Note the lounge chair on the veranda at the top. Although architects drew on the rural vernacular for aesthetic purposes, domestic modernist utopianism also inspired writers to condemn many common characteristics of life in large rural houses. The reporter for the *Housewife's Companion* introducing this "ideal country house" of only two *tatami* rooms, an earth-floored room with Western furniture, and a veranda (*berandaa*), argued that large old houses failed "to conform to the daily life [of the new era]," and could not meet demands "to heighten work efficiency." The article then addressed owners of such houses accusingly: "Why don't you pay more attention to [bringing in] sunlight before taking pride in that piece of solid zelkova wood? Before scolding the maid for the way she polishes the floor of that long corridor, isn't it more pressing business to remove the cobwebs in the kitchen? You should know that we have left the era of living for the house (*ie*) and must now progress into the era of building houses for living." The darkness and the cobwebs of large houses, the owners' pride in costly materials and details of construction, along with the hierarchy and conservatism of the house (*ie*) as a social institution rather than merely a domicile here all belong to a portrait of the past that the new urban generation could locate definitively in the provinces. In contrast stood the new urban house: bright, efficient, tasteful, and designed for the small family. Readers of the non-elite *The Housewife's Companion* were more likely to have known the experience of working under the authority of another woman than the experience of ruling over a large rural house. For such women, the opportunity to manage a private house large enough only for the nuclear family could indeed connote liberation.

treated the Japanese vernacular as a style in its own right, finding things to utilize in the traditional farmhouse, now aestheticized as "rustic" and "subdued" or viewed with nostalgia as "possessing a certain quality difficult to part with."[54] This was the same sentiment that inspired Kon's folkhouse research, expressed in more personal terms. Culture house architect Nose Kyūichirō published designs for modified farmhouses in the pages of *Jūtaku*, posing their solidity and rustic charm against the flimsiness of some of the new houses being built at the time. With the sharp visual contrasts created by European-influenced eclectic houses sprouting in the semi-rural landscape of suburban Tokyo, the peasant dwelling could now come into its own as a reaffirmation of the sturdiness of native building. The nostalgic appeal is also understandable in light of the fact that so many Taishō urbanites were new to the city and had therefore spent their childhoods in houses with massive thatched roofs, unfinished timbers, and open hearths. It is nonetheless striking that these architects would freely accommodate features of the native rural house within a cosmopolitan vocabulary of style, for it underscores the vast social distance they had traveled in such a short period of time.

## Universalism and Pastiche

The spate of pattern books published in the early 1920s mixed genres and modes of representation to a surprising degree. The same book that contained European modernist sketches of house exteriors also showed photographs and illustrations of American colonial interiors, native *sukiya*, and contemporary Japanese architects' designs. In addition to expressing the culture life's spirit of universalism, the jumble of images expressed culture's surplus: the diverse range of sketches and photographs presented buildings and interiors to readers as alluring signs of cosmopolitan modernity rather than as models for literal imitation. Chikama Sakichi's book of designs for modest rental houses, for example, opened with a perspective drawing and plans of an unidentified apartment building remote in scale and construction from anything else in the book or in the Japanese housing market of the time.[55]

When contrasted with the formulaic stiffness of the old *yōkan*, the free appropriation of diverse styles suggests that the Tokyoites who built themselves houses in the 1920s were largely liberated from the onus of a sense of cultural inferiority that had burdened bourgeois intellectuals earlier. Although comparisons with the West persisted in writing, revealing that many intellectuals continued to situate Japan in a hierarchically ordered international social space, at least one segment of the popular market appears to have moved beyond such concerns. Popular writing on houses continued to be full of talk of "increasing efficiency" or of the older "family centering" but abandoned the didactic tone and statist goals of everyday life reform. Perhaps most significant, the interiors of small Tokyo houses, most of them still rented, now accommodated a growing mass of furniture, knick-knacks, and modern devices that overflowed the earlier generation's ideal divisions of Western and native space. When Kon Wajirō inventoried the contents of a tiny suburban house of three *tatami* rooms occupied by a Waseda colleague and his wife, he found that the main living area contained a set of rattan chairs and sofa purchased from Mitsukoshi, two tables also from department stores, a gramophone, several framed pictures, and smaller decorative items, in addition to a piano.[56] The combination of rattan chairs, piano, and *tatami* mats constituted a three-piece set that also appeared frequently in pattern books and magazines (see Fig. 9.14). To record clothing and hair fashions along the main street in Ginza the previous year, Kon had drawn up a complex array of classifications under the overarching dichotomy of "Japanese" and "Western." As Miriam Silverberg has observed, there was already considerable hybridity among these categories of dress.[57] The fusion appears complete in Kon's suburban dwelling survey, where he abandoned the distinctions *wa* and *yō* altogether in favor of labeling objects with their prices.

Although culture houses were easily criticized for abandoning native traditions, the overriding concern in culture house design, as in culture life discourse, was the road to modernity rather than the expression of national identity. Culture house designers professed to be searching the world for architectural forms that would be progressively modern while still in harmony with Japanese surroundings, suited to Japanese habits and tastes. Twentieth-century Japan's political position as the first non-European colonial power gave Japanese architects and intellectuals an opportunity to define Japaneseness to some degree in their own terms, at the same time that it left them in a position of anxiety in relation to the still-dominant West. Domestic modernism's pastiche was a product of this anomalous cultural location in the modern world. This pastiche was tinged with utopianism in two senses, as many of its promoters shared faith in the idea of a single world culture, and all of them shared an idealized notion of domestic intimacy.

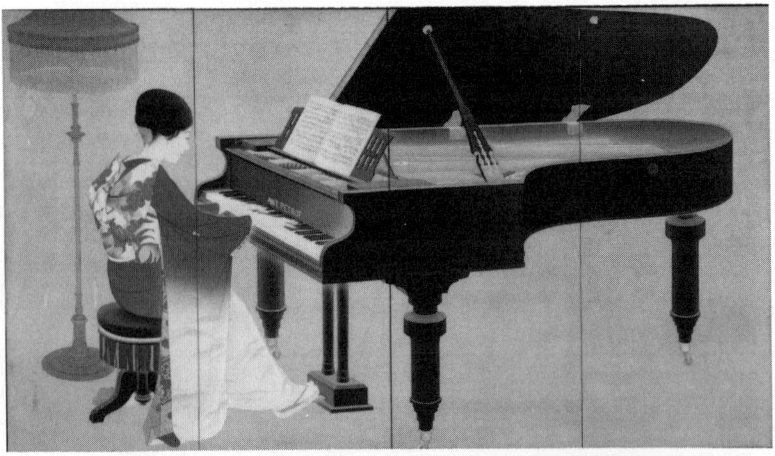

Fig. 9.14 In Japan as in Europe and the United States, the piano became a critical status symbol for bourgeois households, and piano lessons became important marks of good breeding for young women. Upright pianos decorated with tasseled lace covers were enshrined in the parlors of many culture houses. When a boom in piano sales occurred in 1923–24, newspapers noted that the piano was replacing the *koto* as a favorite dowry item for young women of good family. Even if no one could play it, one newspaper also noted, it was becoming a necessary adornment of the "culture life" (Nishihara Minoru, *Piano no tanjō*, 246). (*top*) Nakamura Daizaburō, *Piano* (1926). This *nihonga* style painting of a fashionably dressed young woman at the piano appeared in the Seventh Imperial Exhibition (*teiten*). It inspired a vogue for paintings depicting beautiful daughters of the bourgeoisie engaged in modern pursuits (courtesy Kyoto Municipal Museum of Art). Reception room with upright piano and rattan chairs (*Jūtaku*, June, 1928). Upright pianos at this time ranged in price from 650 to 1,200 yen. Although this put them beyond the means of most households, they appeared frequently in images of modest-sized, new Western-style interiors like this one.

Certainly some part—perhaps a substantial part—of the stylistic experimentation in culture house design took place only on paper. It is impossible to determine how many of the exotic patterns in books were actually built. Vernacular housing is less prone to the vicissitudes of fashion than clothing, since the production cycle is slow and houses are large investments, not easily discarded once bought. Domestic modernism, rather than being governed directly by the economy of fashion, was governed by a meta-economy of style, in which designs spoke to other designs but were only occasionally tested in the market. As long as they were mere images on paper, the production of new designs was cheap, and house styles could indeed be ephemeral commodities in an exchange of signs, unconstrained by the weight of investment in real building. This meta-economy could flourish relatively free of actual construction, since most of the architects writing pattern books were otherwise employed, and the pattern books were much more than collections of design information, they were part of the larger literary production of cosmopolitan fantasy. Nevertheless, the meta-economy of style intersected with the housing market when consumers bought pattern books, and when architects negotiated with carpenters and clients.

We should avoid the temptation to regard domestic modernism and the culture house condescendingly as the superficial copies of an authentic modernism born in the West. For designers, this was a pursuit of comfort and convenience within bounds of the possible and affordable. The mass market surrounded and structured this field of experiment, as consumers responded to the most effective advertisements, and builders picked up the most readily appropriable images and techniques. Pursuit of the ideal of cosmopolitan modernity generated both the compelling need for greater comfort and convenience and an irrational surplus of constantly modulating elements that signified the promise of comfort and convenience.

# 10

# The Culture Life as Contested Space

## The Depreciation of Culture

One aspect of the culture house boom is not easily gleaned from the pattern books. This is the monotony of most new suburban construction. The paradox of the mass market was that it created sameness out of the pursuit of difference. When owners built their own culture houses, it could yield the kind of variety celebrated at Mejiro Culture Village, but the new market also generated speculative housing with the minimum attributes necessary to distinguish the units from the usual run of earlier vernacular buildings. Compared to the unbroken rows of shophouses and tenements that filled the downtowns of the country's large cities at the time, spec-built houses in new districts symbolically asserted some autonomy, if not individuality, merely by the separation of each house from its neighbors and the reorientation of gables toward the street (see Fig. 10.1). Any more variation of form than this, however, put the houses beyond the means of most buyers or renters. In the cheaper suburbs, a mass of consumers in search of something new and slightly different thus encountered rows of identical culture houses hastily erected by local speculative builders with little capital. A cartoon in *Tokyo Puck* showed the middle-class consumer confronting this irony: a drunken officeworker on his way home at night finds himself unable to identify which house in the row is his. "Phooey!" he says, "What's so cultured about these

Fig. 10.1 Rowhouses in Osaka with gables facing the street and projecting entry porches (photograph by Wada Yasuyoshi, in Terauchi Makoto, *Ōsaka no nagaya: kindai in okeru toshi to jūkyo* [INAX Album 7, 1992]).

houses?" (see Fig. 10.2).[1] Cheap, mass-produced new houses were the butt of the joke. Underneath, however, lay a broad anxiety awakened by the fluidity of status in the modern city and the hollowness of the security provided by new houses and goods. Surely the culture life meant something more authentic than mere petit-bourgeois vanity, but when the object of desire turned out to be mass-produced for the desires of countless others, what, after all, did it mean? (see Fig. 10.3) "Culture," signifying both the illusion of a universal measure of value and the desire for what was newest, seemed to be launching everyday life into an endless process of manufactured desires and superficial differences. Contemporary writers of every stripe watched this process with skepticism and dismay. Indeed, satires and criticisms are easier to find in writing on the culture house and culture life than earnest advocacy.

Reflecting critically at the end of the decade, Yanagita Kunio observed that the word "culture" had come to describe everything that people who were still bound by rural custom lacked, regardless of its cheapness or uselessness, and rang so hollow that it had even become an embarrassment for

Fig. 10.2 "Phooey! What's so cultured about these houses?" Cartoon by Miyao Shigeo (*Tōkyō pakku*, Mar. 1923).

city people. Yanagita, unlike Ōya Sōichi, viewed the aspirations of daily life reform, the culture life, and Japanese garden cities with fundamental sympathy but lamented that their potential for the nation as a whole had been weakened because they remained driven by the "impulses" of privileged urbanites and were ultimately opening farm villages to the predations of capital.[2]

In popular journalism, the problem with "culture" often became simply a matter of fashion, which was mercurial. By 1934, any unironic conception of a *true* culture house belonged to history. A handbook of contemporary language published by the best-selling *Kingu* magazine described the culture house as "a past house form in this country, appropriately flavored with Western style to suit modern life." The entry referred to the rows of red- and blue-roofed houses, "looking something like chocolate [boxes]," criticized them as mere "show architecture" that did not consider Japanese people's daily lives, and concluded that because "wretched houses" of this sort had been built everywhere, the phrase no longer had its original sense, now implying rather "a phony Western-infected house" (*seiyō kabure no inchiki*

Fig. 10.3 Kitazawa Rakuten's modern consumers, aboard a boat labeled "The Vanity," endangered by their overreaching desire for new commodities (*Jiji manga*, no. 26 [Aug. 7, 1921]) (courtesy Saitama Municipal Cartoon Art Museum).

*jūtaku*), or "a barrack house disguised with paint" (*penki o nutte gomakashita barakku jūtaku*).[3]

Culture's devaluation had been quick. The depreciation of the rhetorical value of the term started even before the original Culture Village had closed its gates. During and after the Ueno Exposition, writers in the architectural and popular press found things to criticize about every aspect of the model village, some focusing on aesthetic features, others on questions of practicality.[4] The range of criticisms, however, should not be read as evidence that the public rejected new house designs. What was taking place, rather, was a multiplication of publics, public purveyors, and public spokesmen and an escalating competition of taste. As Miriam Silverberg has pointed out, if we resituate the discourse of the 1920s in the media context of the time, it becomes possible to recognize "'Taishō Culture' as constituted by contending cultures." Underlying the contest within bourgeois reform was the larger breakdown of a unitary progressive discourse caused by the participation of a vastly expanded educated class.[5]

The criticism of Culture Village subsequently extended to culture houses in general. Constant shifts of style assured that the latest culture house always had some easily stereotyped external feature. In the early 1920s, the stereotypical motif was a red tile roof. "People think that a Western-style house has to have red tiles to be new," Nishimura Isaku wrote disapprovingly in 1922. "The red tiles called 'French tiles' are too red and uninteresting in shape. The ones I find the most repulsive, and also the ones I see most often, are the cement tiles with some ochre-like pigment applied to the surface." He went on to criticize steep roofs, broad gable boards, and the fashion for painted half-timbers. In a final condemnation, he remarked, "What Japanese think is new is always out-of-date in the West."[6] Nishimura urged readers to throw away their German pattern books (for Nishimura's classification of Western-style houses, see Fig. 10.4).

Indeed, the eager new culture consumers and the culture life as a whole invited parody. But as in the case of the *Asahi* newspaper's ridicule of the elite membership of the Everyday Life Reform League, it was not difficult to criticize a particular group of consumers or advocates while adopting

Fig. 10.4 "Several types of Western-style house" (from Nishimura Isaku, *Sōshoku no enryo* [Restraining Ornament], 1922). The text reads: "(1) A roof called a gambrel roof used widely in the United States; (2) a steep roof of the kind built a lot recently in Japan, with post forms attached to look like half-timbers; (3) the kind of Western house Japanese build; (4) the modern American style, a variation on colonial style; (5) a small house in German style; (6) an American Western bungalow; (7) Chicago style (Wright); (8) contemporary English style; (9) the new type of cottage-style bungalow; (10) pueblo style (adobe), the building style of Southwest American natives."

the same rhetoric of reform. In many criticisms during the 1920s, others' daily life reform or culture life was judged mistaken, and the "true culture life" said to lie elsewhere. Promoters of the culture life thus wrote polemically, posing their models consciously against one another. Viewed as a competitive strategy in the terms of Pierre Bourdieu's sociology of taste, Nishimura's criticism of new house styles articulates the position of the vanguard intellectual finding his monopoly of Western knowledge challenged in the market by the superficial knowledge of parvenus without comparable cultural capital. Pattern-book and magazine writers were quick to adopt features of dominant-class aesthetics and promote them with an enthusiastic tone of consumer liberalism. Responding to the incursion of these new players in the game, more pedigreed tastemakers—both established and avant-garde—sought to shift the ground. Elite architects and writers thus led the way in finding that the culture house idea had "gone too far" or been "poorly executed" by ignorant builders. This became a standard trope in the introductions to books by elite architects, including the architect who had presided over the original Culture Village in 1922.[7]

Criticism of the culture life exposed new anxieties about maintaining bourgeois class boundaries. The targets were various: some writers reviled the vulgarity of the nouveaux riches, others ridiculed the ignorance of the petite bourgeoisie, and yet others championed the stability of native tradition in the countryside against an over-Westernized urban lifestyle. Most of all, however, critics targeted what was eye-catching and easily replicated.[8] Like *katei* for the previous generation, *bunka seikatsu* was an expression of bourgeois aspirations, but more conspicuously than previously, those aspirations were entangled with mass-market representations and competitive claims of class identity.

## House Design as a Field of Cultural Competition

New writers and designers purveying the culture life entered a field of production already occupied by the reform-minded members of the bourgeois elite who had dominated higher education and publishing since the late nineteenth century. A comparatively small group of ideologues had controlled the magazines and other print media through which images of modernity were produced, and also dominated the new cultural professions, from journalism to architecture. Not until the World War I years did major

Fig. 10.5 Cover illustrations of (*left*) Yamada Jun, *For the Person Building a House* (*Ie o tateru hito no tame ni*, 1928); and (*right*) Nose Kyūichirō, *Improved Houses Buildable on 30 Tsubo* (*Sanjuttsubo de dekiru kairyō jūtaku*, 1923]).

magazines represent other voices. The distinction between the older generation of bourgeois proselytizers and new cultural intermediaries, however, was one not only of background but also of motives. Meiji bourgeois proselytizers exhorted their audience in the faith that they acted for the good of the nation but not with the expectation that the class boundaries guaranteeing their own privileged position within it were open to all traffic. Where these people saw a nation in need of guidance, the less privileged new culture life proponents saw a diverse and competitive market.

Within architecture, the competition played out between university-trained architects, most of whom served the needs of the state and the established bourgeoisie, and graduates of technical schools, who tended toward lower civil service positions, employment in construction firms, and private practice. Both published designs for the burgeoning new market. Yamada Jun's *For the Person Building a House* (*Ie o tateru hito no tame ni*; 1928) and Nose Kyūichirō's *Improved Houses Buildable on 30 Tsubo* (see Chapter 9), both written for general audiences, illustrate the contrast between established architect and new cultural intermediary (see Fig. 10.5). They follow a common formula, combining critical pronouncements on the present state of Japanese middle-class housing with the authors' own house designs and simple descriptions, including a minimum of technical information. Both authors promoted their designs as "cultured," and using the common rhetoric of the era, the houses are described as scientific, efficient, and hygienic. At the same time, both defended elements of native Japanese aesthetics. But other aspects of their descriptions and of the designs themselves differ significantly. The writing and drawings of these two architects reveal two sets of strategies in the competition of taste launched by the culture house's liberation from native craft and design conventions.

The social contrast is suggested first in what the two books reveal about their authors. Yamada Jun, we learn from his introduction, was a graduate of Tokyo Imperial University who had completed the proverbial grand tour of Europe and the United States in 1922. *For the Person Building a House* also contains two prefaces praising Yamada's work, the first by Satō Kōichi, professor of architecture at Waseda University. Yamada is a well-documented figure in the history of the Japanese Society of Architects. He established himself in independent practice in 1917 and opened a Tokyo office in the wealthy suburb of Shōtō in 1924.[9] In contrast, little can be gleaned about Nose Kyūichirō from his publications. *Improved Houses* bears no preface by a senior member of the profession, and the author's name appears without indication of degree or title. Judging from the date of Nose's afterword, the book was completed a few months before the Ueno Exposition. At this time, the term "culture house" was not yet in use. Some time before 1926, however, Nose created a Culture House Research Association (Bunka jūtaku kenkyūkai) and published plans in pamphlet form under its name.[10]

Architects took different positions in relation to their readership and to the building trade. Yamada defended the boundaries of the architectural profession, beginning with a condemnation of the general run of culture houses (which by 1928 was formulaic) and including long diatribes against ignorant builders (even describing violent confrontations he had had on construction sites) and against clients who failed to give their architect complete authority over the design. By contrast, Nose was a populist. His invective was saved for people who did not understand that the culture life is the "simple life." Where Yamada emphasized the sanctity of the specialist's role, Nose taught readers to draw their own house plans.

Two distinct culture-house aesthetics emerge from the two texts' illustrations and language and from the house designs themselves. Nose's book contains only sketches, drawn in the stylized, uneven freehand in vogue at the technical colleges; Yamada's includes photographs and hard-line plans, with center lines drawn through fixtures and furniture. Nose's inclusion of sketches conveys a sense of artistic spontaneity that is recognizably modern, departing from the rigidity of typesetting and hard-line drawing in earlier architecture publications. It also suggests to the reader the simplicity of the houses and the ease of designing one's own. Yamada's use of illustrations, and particularly photographs, is also unequivocally modern, but his is the modernity of scientific rationalism, in which the image claims objectivity.

The preferred modifiers in Nose's and Yamada's writing further suggest the different ways the two architects positioned themselves. Nose's aesthetic gives primacy to immediate effects, described with adjectives such as "simple," "cheerful," and "fun" (*kan'i, tanoshii, omoshiroi*). Yamada's aesthetic implies lineage and codification, through adjectives such as "pure" or "authentic" and "harmonious" (*jun, chōwa shita*). Categories of architectural style are vague for Nose, whose designs are generally in an unspecified eclectic style. Yamada's designs are also stylistically eclectic, but the elements of the mix are carefully distinguished. His examples include houses from various parts of Europe, the United States, and Japan, classified by national origin of both the designer and the style employed. Yamada thus demonstrated his expertise as an aesthetic arbiter in the classification of national styles and periods. He found his own aesthetic resolution in a fusion of English gothic revival and "authentic" Japanese style. Yamada's architectural strategies thus reveal the position taken by established intellectuals faced with the challenge of popular imitators. While making proprietary claims on Western knowledge, the source of all that could be vanguard, he spoke at the same time from the comfort of an elite native style already canonized as "authentic," the source of all that could be traditional.[11]

Nose had his own conception of native authenticity, as reflected in his magazine articles promoting the merits of rustic farmhouses. His design for a New Country House published in the *Housewife's Companion* in 1926 used unplastered earth walls and a thatched roof for an "authentic Japanese style" exterior. He encouraged readers to let the external shape of the house follow the style that was common in their region, since regional styles had developed from generations of experience. They had the added merit, he noted, that local carpenters who had never dealt with Western architecture would be able to build them.[12] This regional native aesthetic differed markedly from Yamada's, which was premised not on rustic solidity but on the refined craftsmanship and construction of upper-class urban detached houses, whose roots lay in samurai districts of castle towns.

The designs in Nose's *Improved Houses* call for accents of color, with red roof tiles and painted flowerboxes on the outside and paint and wallpaper inside, in contrast to the traditional grays, browns, and whites of wood, earth, and plaster that Yamada's designs maintain. Flowers in flowerboxes and climbing vines on pergolas are the final accent to Nose's culture houses. Bright, unconcealed, quick to grow, and immediately gratifying, they are the antithesis of the traditionally status-marking Japanese garden adopted by Yamada, which is subtle, hidden from outside view, and gradually cultivated, presupposing commensurate investment in personal cultivation (see Fig. 10.6).[13]

Nose's appropriation of "Western style" in its most readily available, easily reproduced elements recalls Bourdieu's portrait of the petit bourgeois who invests "in the minor forms of legitimate cultural goods," seeking to make "his home and himself look bigger than they are."[14] Put in a less Veblenesque manner, the visual charm of the new, the progressive, and the imported worked most upon those who were least invested in the old, the conservative, and the indigenous and most immediately upon those who lacked, or did not care for, the intellectual's subtler criteria for distinguishing the genuinely avant-garde.

Although an enthusiastic popularizer, Nose was still an architect, whose authority was sustained by his aesthetic discernment in both Western and indigenous design. He drew freely from currently fashionable Western designs, rejecting stylistic orthodoxy, but he also censured the use of low-cost and cheap-looking materials. Most of the designs in *Improved Houses* called for exterior walls of cement, stone, and unpainted narrow clapboards. Nose opposed painted clapboards, because paint tended to peel, and natural wood looked more "elegant" (*yukashiku mieru*). Like Nishimura Isaku, he criticized the use of cement tiles painted red. Central to Nose's aesthetic was a calculated effect of natural accident—a rough stucco finish rather than smooth plaster, foundation walls of irregular bricks and stones, in which it was "essential to mix large and small and various colors," unmatched tiles, uneven spots in the walls, and floorboards of American pine with knots.[15]

Fig. 10.6 Distinct "culture" aesthetics. (*top*) "A New Style of House," from Nose Kyūichirō, *Improved Houses Buildable on 30 Tsubo* (*Sanjuttsubo de dekiru kairyō jūtaku*, 1923). Nose's aesthetic gives primacy to immediate effects, and the style of rendering suggests spontaneity and do-it-yourself simplicity. (*bottom*) "A Japanese-Style Culture House," from Yamada Jun, *For the Person Building a House* (*Ie o tateru hito no tame ni*, 1928). Use of windows instead of sliding doors and surrounding corridors, in addition to the absence of garden walls, mark this as a "culture house."

Intentional rusticity served claims of being up-to-date and true to tradition at the same time—and it was affordable. This, rather than faithful maintenance of native aesthetic traditions or proper application of foreign stylistic canons, ensured that Nose's buildings would not be lumped with the hastily built culture houses of speculators.

## Practical Settings

The houses in these two books contrast even more significantly as settings for social practices, a contrast that suggests the different circumstances of their intended audiences. Yamada's plans have a discrete guest-reception room, usually set next to the *genkan*, with Western furniture. Nose created open plans without guest rooms or dining rooms and asserted: "People who say they need a guest room and dining room understand nothing about the culture life. These are the same people who think that the culture life is just dancing and playing the piano."[16] Such criticisms of conservative standards and the outmoded up-to-dateness reflected in the classic "high-collar" accomplishments, whose acquisition took an investment of time, evoke the denial of class markers that Bourdieu describes as part of the petit-bourgeois' "dream of social flying, a desperate effort to defy the gravity of the social field." In a subtle move against social hierarchy, Nose furnished one corner of the living room with an L-shaped bench and chairs. Such an arrangement would be problematic for the established bourgeois gentleman receiving guests, since it provided no seat of honor (*kamiza*).[17]

Yamada's reception rooms are studied adaptations of European interiors, but the author points out that the furniture has been arranged "with consideration of Japanese customs." This appears to refer to the placement of two armchairs directly facing one another across a small table in front of a mantelpiece, replicating in furniture the positions of host and guest in traditional elite practices of reception, with the mantel as *tokonoma*. Elsewhere in the plan, Yamada situated two linked *tatami* rooms across a corridor from the kitchen and maid's room, following the pattern of the "interior corridor plan," which retained contiguous *tatami* areas (*zashiki*) for private and formal uses. Large *zashiki* were necessary for occasions such as weddings and funerals in the houses of propertied families. Nose's houses have no large contiguous *tatami* spaces, since his presumed client did not carry the obligations of inheritance. In addition, few have maid's rooms (see Fig. 10.7).

Fig. 10.7 Contrasting conceptions of the culture house as practical setting. (*top*) "A Small Single-Story House" (interior), from Nose Kyūichirō, *Improved Houses Buildable on 30 Tsubo* (*Sanjuttsubo de dekiru kairyō jūtaku*, 1923). Thwarting the spatial demands of formal reception, Nose designs a living room with L-shaped fixed seating. (*bottom*) Reception room designed in consideration of Japanese reception customs "without losing the traits of pure Western-style architecture," from Yamada Jun, *For the Person Building a House* (*Ie o tateru hito no tame ni*, 1928). Two armchairs face one another perpendicular to the fireplace, like host and guest in front of a *tokonoma* alcove.

Finally, the houses in these two books differ strikingly in size. House designs in pattern books had been getting steadily smaller as architects came in contact with a broader market after World War I, but some of the houses represented in Nose's book are tiny indeed, competing with the amateur-built minimal dwellings published around the same time (Nose's smallest examples are 9.6 *tsubo*, or about 350 square feet). Although Yamada's work reflects the general trend toward smaller houses, the dwellings he depicts are still well outside the middle range of the housing stock of the time. *For the Person Building a House* includes houses with floor areas over 2,000 square feet among drawings labeled "small houses."[18]

Nose, too, was defending the field from incursions of vulgar taste. For Nose, the offenders were speculative builders constructing cheaper houses with painted clapboards and cement-tile or sheet-metal roofs. When the term "culture house" broke free of its idealistic origins, it was often to these carpenter-built houses that it became attached. Although it makes no mention of cost, *Improved Houses* addresses builders repeatedly with advice on the proper selection and application of new and imported materials, revealing the architect's concern to impose aesthetic standards on new housing. Yet higher standards inevitably had a price, and price was likely to be the first consideration for most people building or buying their first house, as it was for speculative builders.

## Artist, Reformer, Cultural Intermediary

Despite differences in social position, Yamada and Nose shared with the many other architects who moonlighted as writers on the culture life the domestic modernist role of reformers seeking an audience. This set them apart from the small coterie of elite architects who were able to design houses without having to purvey their talent in popular-market books or compromise it to the wishes of clients.[19] Insulated from the mass market by academic position, independent wealth, or assured patronage, the high modernist architect could experiment freely and enjoy the luxury of conceiving his designs as constituting an oeuvre. Fujii Kōji, the seminal designer of "modern Japanese style" dwellings, was rich enough to build his experimental designs on his own property. Frank Lloyd Wright disciple Endō Arata held a long-time association with domestic reformers, but as both an imperial university graduate and student of Wright, he was securely positioned to play the role of high modernist. When he published his house designs in a special issue of Hani Motoko's *Ladies' Companion* magazine in 1924, the houses were presented as a series of formal types and variations, labeled with titles like "Linear Form House," "Variation on the Linear Form House," "House Three-*ken* Wide," "Variation on the Three-*ken* House," "Two Roofed House," and so forth.[20] His architectural knowledge gained directly from a Western source and his patronage assured, Endō treated the designs as a unified sequence of formal experiments rather than a miscellany of discrete efforts constrained by the tastes and needs of different clients. As a result, a distinct and self-conscious personal style—the trait that defined the canonized architects of the twentieth century—clearly differentiated Endō from culture-house designers. The label "culture house" was applied to none of his ouevre.

Yamada Jun, although also a graduate of the Tokyo Imperial University and thus privileged by education as an arbiter of native and Western architectural taste, lacked the cultural capital to play the artist and instead appeared in his writings as a reformer. His designs were constrained by the wishes of clients, resulting in a uniformity that reflected the relatively conservative taste of the established bourgeois men who brought him commissions rather than the unified aesthetic vision of the architect. The simplest evidence that the two men occupied and perceived themselves in distinct social roles is that Endō signed his drawings while Yamada did not. Endō's houses in the *Ladies' Companion* were sketched freehand in stylized frames with legends at the bottom providing the architect's office name, the name of the client, the location of the house, and the date of the drawing. In contrast, the businesslike hard-line drawings and photographs of the designs in Yamada's book were numbered, without location or owner's name. Yamada's clients seem often to have requested anonymity, in contrast to most owners of canonized modern architects' "works."[21] Introducing the houses, Yamada added the caveat that "two or three of these include extreme [modifications] in accordance with requests of clients, so not all are my ideal designs, but in general they may be considered to have applied my principles and research results."[22] Unable to present his work as an autonomous art, Yamada positioned himself instead as a scientist of dwelling form, and treated his houses as contributions to the project of rationalizing Japanese bourgeois life.

If one returns to the drawings of Nose with the same questions in mind, however, the architect appears at first glance to have leaped past elite architect-intermediary Yamada and joined Endō in the position of autonomous artist. Nose not only published stylized freehand drawings but signed and dated them conspicuously in block-lettered English. Clearly he regarded them as artworks. But to the extent that modes of appropriation from the West were a significant measure of position in the cultural field, Nose's choice to write in English (and his occasional lapses of English spelling) give him away. Whereas Endō developed a Japanese orthography based on Frank Lloyd Wright's signature style, Nose lacked the experience to develop so subtle and confident a fusion and was compelled to assume the pose of cosmopolitan artist with the fewer tools at his disposal. Similarly, the word *henka*, which Endō used to mean "variations" on a single planning concept, meant simply "variety" for Nose and other writers in more popular media like the *Housewife's Companion*, where it was a common term for an attractive visual effect.[23] And more significant in career terms, not only could Nose ill afford to build in a unified idiom, it is unclear from his eclectic compilation of designs whether any of the houses in his book were in fact built at all. He may have been doing no more than dreaming up fantasy houses for the consumption of other dreamers. Regardless of how many were actually built, Nose appears to have had no independent practice and only a minor reputation as an architect.

Elite architects, therefore, were not predisposed to be conservative nativists but were invested in demonstrating greater mastery of native as well as Western forms. The minor players, in contrast, were assured artistic freedom by having less to lose. Nose published his house designs in pamphlets printed at his home in Tokyo's western suburbs. His drawings continued to appear in women's magazines. In 1929, he contributed a chapter of instructions on drawing and reading plans to a collection of "middle-class Japanese and Western houses," published by the *Housewife's Companion.*[24] Noborio Gen'ichi, another young architect from the Kansai area endorsed by Takeda Goichi, advertised his own architectural practice in the back of *Everyday Life and House Design (Seikatsu to jūtaku no sekkei*; 1925), a collection of his designs and homespun philosophy. The advertisement announced that the author would design or consult on all types of buildings, parks, and garden cities, specializing particularly in "devising dwellings for the new Japanese life. From European native dwelling style [cottages], single-story bungalows suited to simple living, and other styles, I take things particularly suited to Japanese, meeting our taste, with the idea of enabling a world lifestyle and avoiding falling into the double life."[25] Barred from full membership in the Society of Japanese Architects and limited in their access to bourgeois clients, these entrepreneurial young architects penned their guides to the culture life and purveyed architectural styles freely as means to reach wider audiences.

Discourse and design production around the culture house thus sorts itself into class-based positions roughly along Bourdieuan lines. As small, Western-influenced culture houses became common, architects serving the established bourgeoisie were positioned to become defenders of native tradition. These men claimed mastery of both the native and the imported and defined taste in the proper deployment of each. Their clients already possessed property and often large native dwellings. An avant-garde of designers with reputations based largely on their interpretation of the latest trends in the West championed more cosmopolitan styles and positioned themselves as artists, aloof from the conventional tastes of the bourgeoisie. Similarly, writers and other intellectuals whose cultural capital depended first on Western knowledge criticized the "false" or superficial West of the new Japan (as did Nishimura Isaku and writer Nagai Kafū, who built his own eccentric but "truly Western" house, with no *tatami* on the floor, in 1920).[26] Architects like Nose who lacked elite training or overseas experience sought a petit-bourgeois audience by making what they had acquired of the dominant culture immediately accessible.

Meanwhile, the mass of educated urbanites, who collaborated in producing the culture life only through small acts of consumption, struggled to acquire culture houses and whatever other goods with the features of the dominant-class forms they could afford. Intellectuals and salaried workers whose class position derived solely from white-collar professions and secondary education would have been the primary consumers of the more overtly Western-oriented style and relatively unhierarchical plan of the stereotypical small culture house; small landlords and entrepreneurial capitalists who relied less on the cultural capital of cosmopolitan knowledge would tend to build or acquire the more hierarchically planned and conservative (though still modern) "combined native and Western" houses with the interior corridor and attached *yōma*. Hence, it is not surprising to find that the more radical new culture houses tended to be built in Tokyo's commuter suburbs, and houses built on the more conservative model with the interior corridor plan predominated in older neighborhoods close to where shopkeepers and small business owners continued to reside.

## The Dangerous Seductions of the Culture Life

When the contest over *bunka* is compassed more fully, however, other factors besides class enter. For example, we could call Nose Kyūichirō's promotion of "simple living" making a virtue of necessity, and his criticism of dominant cultural practices evidence of what Bourdieu calls a petit-bourgeois "dream of social flying," yet because the wide practice of single-son inheritance left second and third sons propertiless, many actual occupants of the small culture houses Nose designed may have possessed the same class background and education, or even have come from the same families, as Yamada's wealthier clients. To accommodate such contingencies requires a very fluid model of social class with the potential for innumerable gradations.[27]

The negative image of the culture house purveyed by dominant intellectuals reveals that the occupants of these small houses on the margins of the city were themselves situated on the margins of legitimate culture. But must we regard the "petit-bourgeois" consumer as Bourdieu insists, "in every respect a bourgeois writ small" or could he (or *she*) have been a less totally subjugable subject? There are suggestions that the vanguard among consumers of the culture life was doing more than merely struggling to emulate the lifestyle of the elite without the fancy trappings. If we shift our focus from class to gender, social transgression rather than social climbing emerges at the core of the culture life. In fact, the conjugal ideal that new petit-bourgeois couples pursued in the Tokyo suburbs of the 1920s challenged patriarchal traditions in significant ways.

The issues of cohabitation and the conjugal relationship that had animated *katei* discourse at its outset in the 1880s had ceased to be central in discussions of domesticity by around the time that the Civil Code was enacted in 1898. Late Meiji domestic reformers focused rather on adapting Anglo-American notions of home to the circumstances of native bourgeois households. After World War I, however, these issues returned to haunt official, academic, and popular cultural discourse. In 1919, the Hara Kei government created a Special Investigative Commission on Legal Institutions (Rinji hōsei shingikai) to review the legal status of couples and individuals in relation to the lineage-based family model that had been institutionalized in the 1898 Code. Over the next six years, the commission deliberated such questions as whether parents should retain the right to approve or annul their children's marriages, whether a man's illegitimate children could be introduced into the household without his legal wife's consent, and whether a husband's infidelity could be legal grounds for divorce, as well as questions of maternal authority and women's property rights. On all these issues, the commission proposed compromises, hardly egalitarian, yet nevertheless bringing women some greater measure of rights under civil law. Civil code revision returned official attention to definitions of the household: who could form one, who controlled it, and who had the right to dissolve it. It also aroused new debates in the newspapers and journals over norms of family and household in a society more mobile than that of the 1890s.[28]

In 1926, just as this legal review was coming to a close, sociologist Toda Teizō published his pathbreaking *Research on the Family* (*Kazoku no kenkyū*), based on the national census of 1920. In this book, he sought to determine empirically the relative dominance of extended and nuclear households and to consider what combination was best for the nation, since he judged the "intimate relations" of the family to be paramount to the "stability of national life."[29] Toda believed that Japanese differed from Westerners in their special attachment to family, due to Japan's ancient tradition of life in large families (*dai kazoku seikatsu*).[30] He found, however, that particularly in the major cities, statistics showed a weakening in the capacity of the family, which he concluded was producing a "certain unease" in national life.[31] Toda's effort to extract meaning for the nation from statistical analyses of household composition marked a new phase in the figuring of the domestic unit as a social space. The census itself, Japan's first simultaneous national population count, institutionalized the modern conception of family by mapping a nation of households (*setai*) defined by cohabitation and shared consumption rather than one of houses (*ie, ko*) defined by name or occupational lineage.[32]

Meanwhile, the popular press brimmed with news and debate relating to conjugal matters, lavishing particular attention on romantic love and the scandals it occasionally engendered. In early 1921, the *Tōkyō nichinichi* ran a series in twenty installments featuring the opinions of various luminaries on the subject of "freedom of divorce."[33] Later the same year, the *Asahi* printed a series titled "Modern Views of Love," in which the author championed romantic love as the only full realization of personhood.[34] Highly public elopements animated the debate to an even greater extent. Two famous incidents were so public as to be literally inseparable from their own publication. Both involved letters of annulment written by women to their spouses and printed in full in the newspapers. All the women's magazines printed special issues on these scandals.[35] By posing legal households against households founded on love, they contributed further to the revival of conjugality as a contested subject in the popular imagination.[36]

The conjugal household thus re-emerged as an object of concern, yet this time the term *katei* carried no special rhetorical weight, since it had long since lost its polemical power and been absorbed into normative language. Instead, conjugality came under the sign of the "culture life." To male critics, the culture life represented isolation of the conjugal couple from the extended family, with disturbing social and erotic implications. Here, the very diminutiveness of the small house designs in the women's magazines and in pattern books like Nose's posed a challenge to traditional authority, because they were private spaces conceived for two or at most three. Theoretically, if all young couples were to occupy such houses, traditional patriarchy would lose its site of authority and transmission. Journalist Yumeno Kyūsaku, who came to Tokyo from Kyushu to report on conditions after the earthquake, claimed acerbically that expulsion of old people was a basic condition of the culture life and worried aloud "where Japan [would] end up" if the trend continued. Children would follow, he predicted, and the older and younger generations would be replaced by books and pets, respectively.[37] As this exaggerated forecast makes plain, Yumeno was expressing his alarm partly tongue-in-cheek. His censure of couples pursuing the new lifestyle was genuine, however, and accompanied by a heavy dose of condescension toward new members of the urban middle class.[38]

Fixed walls and lockable doors contributed to male critics' anxiety about the culture house's new domesticity. The first fear was that these things would lead to the liberation of women from the home. With fewer doors to the outside, small Western houses were easier to lock up and leave empty. Writers in the women's magazines stressed the convenience this afforded housewives, who no longer had to stay at home all day to watch the house.[39] The notion of women coming and going from the house as they pleased

Fig. 10.8 "What Is the Culture Life?" postcards, by cartoonist Iizawa Tenyō (early 1920s). The text accompanying the postcard on the right reads: Wife: "Goodbye. You mustn't leave the house while I'm out. If I have visitors, please be sure to receive them politely." Husband: "Come home early." Wife: "Social duties won't allow it. I can come home whenever I like."

disturbed both the norms of the old patriarchal family and the male dominance perpetuated in modern nuclear families, in which it was the husband who enjoyed this freedom while his wife waited at home for him to return. For men to whom the city provided casual erotic opportunities while the suburban home preserved one woman pledged to monogamy, the wife's mobility within the city insinuated a dangerous loss of control (see Fig. 10.8).

Further down the road of erotic speculation lay the prospect that a couple left alone would be swallowed in an abyss of passion. Tanizaki's scandalous and enormously popular novel *A Fool's Love* (*Chijin no ai*, 1924) rendered explicit this unspoken supplement of the conservative male critique by turning the intimate space of the culture house into a setting for female erotic domination. The novel's protagonist Jōji begins his descent by wishing for a "simple life" alone with the young Naomi, free from the traditional furnishings and fixed responsibilities of the Japanese "*katei*" (*katei* here serving as a signifier for conservative domestic norms).[40] The house's lockability takes on added threatening significance in the novel, as Naomi's secret affairs gradually become evident to Jōji through discoveries of locked doors and keys passed to other men. Tanizaki's culture house thus becomes a private space of unlimited erotic possibilities.

Unlike the flexible *tatami*-room floor plan, small house designs with designated functions for rooms confronted the public with physical embodiments of living arrangements. In a *tatami*-floored house, any room could serve as a sleeping chamber, and as a result, no room bore specifically erotic overtones in the manner of the Western bedroom or boudoir. A couple with a Western bedroom possessed a special place for hiding themselves from others, surrounded by fixed walls. The general absence of a native tradition of marking a private space in the home for the conjugal couple only enhanced the eroticism of bedrooms and beds.[41] Most of the houses in culture house guides had at least one room labeled "sleeping chamber," often with paired single beds shown abutting one another on the floor plan, although the interiors of these rooms were rarely shown in illustrations. If this perhaps bespoke reticence, with regard to double beds, whose presence in the room practically announced sexual relations, the erotic resonance, and the taboo, were more certain. When new hotels catering to couples seeking privacy for trysts (precursors of the "love hotels") began to appear in Tokyo in the late 1920s, they advertised three physical features: Western construction, locks on the guest rooms, and double beds. By 1932, the police had banned use of the term "double bed" in advertisements.[42]

Although some popular fiction invented dystopian versions of the culture life, other works deftly resolved erotic anxieties with petit-bourgeois longings. In Goshō Heinosuke's comic film *Madamu to nyōbo* (The Neighbor's Wife and Mine; 1930), a Western-style culture house was contrasted with a humble native one as the site of threatening seductions for the male protagonist, Shibano. The film also played upon the character of the culture house as specular object. In the opening scene, Shibano is seen strolling among the open lots of a sparsely populated suburb where new development is just beginning. He approaches a painter sitting at an easel, studying two houses in the distance. One is a typical rental house of the day, the other a two-story white-stuccoed "Western-style" cottage—the very epitome of "culture." The painter's canvas depicts only the Western house. The role the two houses play in the ensuing story captures the contradictory relationship between the new petit-bourgeois consumer and the culture house. Shibano's family moves into the plainer house, where scenes of typical domesticity unfold. They are disturbed, however, by the woman next door, who is a vampish jazz singer. Her living room has been converted into a rehearsal space, where she and a band of male musicians drink, smoke, and play loudly. Harmony is restored in Shibano's house only after he has plucked up the courage to go next door and confront the alluring woman who has disturbed his domestic peace. As the key scene unfolds, we see him wearing Japanese dress and standing in the entry vestibule of the Western house, trying in vain to swagger, uncertain whether to remove his *geta* clogs. The jazz singer emerges and pulls him aggressively into the house, where he soon succumbs, drinking and dancing with her, and making his wife jealous.[43] Ultimately, it is the song "My Blue Heaven," with its combination of the risqué jazz sound and lyrics exalting domestic happiness, that symbolically unites the realm of untamed desire represented by the culture house and the realm of familial responsibility represented by the protagonist's less glamorous home. In the film's closing scene, Shibano reconciles with his wife as the jazz band next door strikes up the well-known melody and the couple sings along.

## Feminine Taste and the Culture Life Contest

This is not to say that culture houses and the culture life invariably connoted sexual liberation or male fears of female sexuality. Male critics saw the culture life tied to indulgence of private desires in many forms, including the benign petit-bourgeois desire to surround oneself with new goods arranged for pleasant effect. It bears noting that the fantasy initially concocted by Tanizaki's Jōji is one of "playing house," and that the first thing Jōji and Naomi do is to find a culture house and decorate it together. Tanizaki refers to the stage for their pas-de-deux in quotation marks as a "fairy-tale house."[44] The phrase is a quotation in a quite literal sense, since the language common in the home design features of magazines such as the *Housewife's Companion* encouraged fantasy in similar terms. Like Nose's book of improved houses, women's magazines described the new models they proffered as "cozy" (*kojinmari shita*), "comfortable" (*igokochi yoi*), "bright" (*akarui*), and "cheerful" (*tanoshii*). Written for and sometimes by women, articles objectified "home" not merely as the site of childrearing and domestic labor, but as a personal artistic project.

The feminine tastes represented in the *Housewife's Companion* thus challenged gender categories formulated in the course of Meiji modernization, albeit in more subtle ways than Naomi's unbridled promiscuity. Articles on house style and interiors positioned the female consumer-reader beyond the bounds of her established duties as "good-wife wise-mother," and beyond her traditional aesthetic purview, which had been limited to the

Fig. 10.9 "As someone inclined to the study of middle-class houses, I found myself drawn to this irresistibly poetic house." Illustration of a female reporter's dream house near Ōfuna Station in the Tokyo suburbs (*Shufu no tomo*, Dec. 1920).

decoration of her own body for male consumption. Here, through the cultural mediation of the *Housewife's Companion* and other publications, she could look and choose in the male sphere of architecture. The regime of domesticity—domestic hygiene, domestic economy, and all the other rationalizations the Everyday Life Reform League advocated—had assigned women new authority as modern homemakers. The mass-market specularization of the house now licensed women to extend that authority to the aesthetics of the domestic environment.

The *Housewife's Companion* occasionally ran descriptive pieces based on visits to new houses by members of the magazine staff. These presented an opportunity for further exploration of taste in domestic architecture.[45] One early piece of this kind, written in 1920 (before the birth of the neologism "culture house") under the by-line of a woman named Tsuruko, describes a "small Western house" the writer had spied from the train near Ōfuna station, south of Tokyo (see Fig. 10.9).[46] She tells of her encounter with the house almost as if recounting a romantic intrigue, from her first glimpse of it through the train window to the moment she resolves to approach the house and request admittance:

As I passed the spot two or three times a week, I would stare at this house each time until my neck hurt, never tiring of it. Finally, on the fifteenth of last month, a clear autumn day, I alighted at Ōfuna station and, without even knowing whose house it was, went to have it shown to me.[47]

Describing the view of the house from afar, Tsuruko paints a scene of mystery and visual allure:

At dusk, with the setting sun glowing red on the white walls and on the glass of the bay window with flowers in it, a fine wisp of smoke rising from the green chimney, one is impressed with a certain storybook-like poignancy. In the morning . . . the red tiles of the roof are bathed in the brilliant light of the sun, and with the curtains in the window open, the sight of a day about to begin appears beautiful and vivid, as if one were looking at it through a magnifying glass.[48]

The story of discovery itself announces Tsuruko's physical mobility. But more than this, through an intimate verbal tableau, she adopts an unusual role for the "housewife" of the time, pursuing and visually possessing the object of her desire. Of course, there was no taboo explicitly broken in the fantasy, since such domestic images were well within the legitimate bounds of feminine desire. Nevertheless, her voyeuristic and covetous description recalls the language Kobayashi Ichizō had earlier used to eroticize suburban houses and home life for a male audience, and its overt expression by a woman writing for a female audience suggests the new roles emerging in the context of the growing public romance with the private dwelling.

Even the sanctioned, thoroughly feminine pursuit of *shugei* (small handicrafts such as needlepoint, lace, and knitting) was breaking gender boundaries in the culture house. The decorating of formal rooms in the bourgeois house, which consisted mainly of selecting objects for the *tokonoma* alcove and adjacent shelves, had previously been considered a male prerogative.[49] Culture houses presented new spaces and wall surfaces requiring furniture and decoration. Judging from the advertising in the *Housewife's Companion*, most of the magazine's female readership had limited buying power in this market. The items advertised were overwhelmingly small, personal products such as cosmetics and medicines. Food products and some kitchen appliances were also advertised, but not furniture. Instead, the magazine's readers were encouraged to make do with what they could make themselves. As writers on *shugei* sought new applications for the expertise they purveyed, they urged female readers to decorate otherwise spartan interiors with small

Fig. 10.10 "Cool Interior Decorations for Summer" (*Shufu no tomo*, June 1926). The housewife transforms her house for the season with printed fabrics and a woven mat. These soft materials were part of a new feminine vocabulary for domestic interiors. Fittingly, the man of the house is absent from this scene.

items of their own manufacture. The use of fabric to wrap, cover, and drape, combined with the choice of rounder, softer forms of furniture, such as throw cushions and the ubiquitous rattan chair, contributed to a tactile feminization of the home.[50] New domestic crafts overlaid connotations of warmth and softness on the culture life's surface of modern efficiency. "For those who live the culture life, cushions (*kusshon*) are familiar as warm pads (*shitone*) for leisure use," a publication on the use of embroidery and other *shugei* in interior decorating explained, making clear that these alien pieces of décor made a home both homier and more cosmopolitan.[51] In the *Housewife's Companion* of June 1926, an anonymous article on decorating a *zashiki* for summer encouraged readers to sew light printed-cotton curtains to hang in front of the cabinets and traditional *shoin* window, spread two narrow pieces of linen crossing one another over a table, hang a cloth cover over the electric light, and if the *tatami* mats were not new, spread something called "Taiwan Panama" over them. The author of the article may have been a man, but if so, he represented little of the older canon of male taste, treating the room rather as an opportunity for female expression. The accompanying illustration depicted a room occupied by two women in kimono, with a small boy sitting on a rattan chair in the background (see Fig. 10.10).[52]

As the popular press translated the conjunction of women and domesticity into a creative role for women, women joined and sometimes even challenged architects in the search for the ideal dwelling. *Sunday Mainichi*, a weekly news magazine that began publication in 1922, ran a series of articles under the title "Amateur Design" ("Shirōto sekkei"), penned by a self-described housewife named Ono Michiko. Each installment dealt with some problem of dwelling reform, discussing the author's own experience and reviewing the designs of others' houses.[53] Since *Sunday Mainichi* had begun publication with the stated aim to "examine the culture life," a subject that straddled the professions of architect and housewife, it is fitting that this magazine presented what was perhaps the first series of articles on architecture written by a woman. In her first installment, Ono described to readers how the frustrations of living in a poorly designed rented house had led her to think about improving house plans. Drawing houses "ended up becoming my pastime (*dōraku*)," she wrote, using a term predominantly connoting male pleasures.[54] Yet her approach to design reflected a perspective on the house that seldom emerged in the architecture magazines. While writing of house design as a taste and an avocation, she planned for the convenience of the person who had to clean the house and serve the meals. The articles make clear that she was doing most of this work herself. Then after several articles accompanied by plans without Western rooms, Ono wrote a piece that began, "I'm lost," confessing frankly to readers that she felt stuck, unable to solve the problem of reforming the dwelling without switching to chair-sitting. She had had guests to stay and was forced by the experience to recognize the advantage of having a separate dining room with table and chairs, because the person serving the meals could avoid continually getting up from the floor to serve. She had thought that dining rooms were for the rich, she wrote, but now realized that they were actually needed most by "small families, particularly people living without a maid." A dining room with table and chairs did not harmonize with floor-sitting rooms, she believed; hence changing the dining room would compel her to change the rest of the house. Yet she felt attached to a floor-sitting lifestyle. She gave her audience no architectural way out of this quandary but offered instead a criticism of contemporary ways of talking about Westernization:

> Among the various assessments made recently of the new houses, there are people who, in order to ridicule [others], bring up the negative points about occupying Western houses while failing to live in a purely Western manner. I think this sort of thing is thoughtless caviling (*ageashitori*). . . . If we were to worry about every time someone laughed "That's not going to be Western style," or "This is incorrect," any-

one who wanted to build a Western house and live in it would have to go overseas to study the lifestyle—master, mistress, and maid. I think the Japanese lifestyle is not at such an impasse that we need to do anything that foolish.[55]

Ultimately, she concluded, a new type of house would have to be built from the ground up, taking the merits of native experience together with the advantages of what came from elsewhere. In her final article, which followed this one, she took the search for a solution in an entirely different direction, proposing semi-communal living in a house designed for two families who shared an entry, reception room, dining room, bath, and kitchen, so that the housewives could pool their labor.[56] Few architects or women's educators in Japan had explored arrangements for communal living, because most were too deeply invested in the ideology of single-family domesticity to allow such ideas into the discussion of domestic rationalization.[57] Even without this bold solution, Ono's articles emerge from the 1920s discourse of everyday life reform and the culture life as an unusual voice, representing the subjective experience of a woman keeping house without help, feeling the constrictions and inconveniences of contemporary rental housing, and groping for reform solutions in response to practical problems that emerged in her own everyday experience. Even her sense of what taste meant was clearly rooted in practice as much as aesthetics. One can only wonder what different forms of domesticity might have emerged from a truly gender-integrated architectural field.[58]

In the *Ladies' Companion*, an anonymous male architect appraised the house plans submitted by readers in a monthly column started in early 1923. The series ended in September (the month of the Tokyo earthquake) with a long letter from a female reader challenging the architect's recommendations on earlier submissions point by point and offering her own designs.[59] Two decades of instruction in house design at the girls' higher schools, as well as the extensive practical information provided in Hani's magazine, had prepared female readers to respond in this way. In a society where the number of women in public roles of authority was minuscule and the number of women in the architectural academy zero, women like this reader were taking the modern homemaker's mandate in an expanded sense and refashioning a male specialization into their own.

The liberal ethics of new cultural intermediaries permitted a blurring of boundaries between masculine architecture, a modern, Westernizing, and public pursuit, and feminine ornament, considered traditional, native, and private. This kind of transgression did not threaten the social order in the way that a woman's freedom to leave the home did, but it formed part of a general destabilization of the established, homologous categories that had defined domestic interiors as well as public space. For an elite architect like Yamada Jun, the reader of women's magazines, with little legitimate cultural capital of her own, embodied the undiscriminating middle-brow consumer whose emergence threatened the hegemony of rational bourgeois men.[60] Beyond the regimes of hygiene and efficiency or enveloped in the same house with them, here was a domesticity that was playful, indulgent, and, in the eyes of some, transgressive. The culture house was both a place the modern woman could leave and a site for her to remake.

## Everyday Life in Question

One way around the question of whether to read the "culture life" as conforming to predictable class categories or as something more radical is to situate the politics of the home in the larger landscape of everyday practices. Satō Kōichi's preface to Yamada Jun's book spoke of a recent "awakening to daily life (*seikatsu*)." Morimoto Kōkichi and others wrote in a similar vein of making the transition from "survival" (*seizon*) to "living" (*seikatsu*). This *seikatsu* can be understood only as the material life generated by modern capitalism, a world of new commodities. Houses are typically the largest, most durable of commodities. What happens when the most fundamental aspects of the dwelling, as an objectification of daily life, are brought to the surface of consciousness to be made negotiable, exchangeable?

The 1920s in Japan were a period when houses, household goods, and domestic space came to be manipulated politically, not only in the state politics of "housing" but also (indeed, far more extensively) in the social politics of the mass market. Rationalization campaigns like those of the state-sponsored Everyday Life Reform League and Morimoto's Culture Life Research Association attempted to control the entropic power of modernity within the safe locus of the bourgeois home. Contrary to the intentions of the culture life's progenitors, however, the fluidity of identities, the unconstrained pleasures, and the disregard for gender and generational hierarchy made possible by modern mass society began to rear their heads even here. Of course, most petit-bourgeois couples did not live in the decadence of Tanizaki's Naomi and Jōji, and the women decorating their homes according to the helpful hints in the *Housewife's Companion* were hardly fomenting a revolution, but the pleasures of home as a private paradise of romantic love and consumption conflicted with the disciplines of home as a rationalized unit within the state. In a fragmented social space, culture life discourse could not be contained entirely within the normative, as it promised both the exposure of everyday practice to the even light of rationality and the pursuit of secret fantasies in a hidden space of play.

# Conclusion

# Inventing Everyday Life

## The Site of Seikatsu

This book has traced the genealogy of a private sphere of everyday life, or *seikatsu*. The process began with the invention of an abstract space called *hōmu* or *katei*; subsequently, new domestic interiors and shapes in the urban landscape made the abstraction material. Eventually houses themselves were reinvented as objects of fashion and consumer fantasy. The product of this sequence of developments was not a house type but a new sensibility about everyday life and, with it, a new mode of occupying space itself. Even before the growth of the industrial city had repatterned the social reality of bourgeois lives, bourgeois reform discourse had developed the terms for conceiving of an everyday life separate from productive labor and shaped by consumption choices. The linguistic and material vocabulary that took shape beginning in the 1890s was taken for granted by the 1920s, when all talk of everyday life reform (*seikatsu kaizen*) and the culture life (*bunka seikatsu*) assumed that the site of *seikatsu* was the single-family home.

By the 1920s, dwellings in Japan were lodged in the interlocking discourses of domestic science and design aesthetics, and their function was premised on modern bourgeois family ideology. These forces now shaping the domestic environment had been new to Japan in the late nineteenth century. The totalizing discourses of science and aesthetics colonized and recast systems of practical knowledge that had once managed households and built cities. Subsequently, these systems were allowed to survive, but only as subaltern or as relic.[1] The appearance of terms like *katei* (home), *shumi* (taste), *kenchiku* (architecture), *eisei* (hygiene), *nōritsu* (efficiency), and *yōshiki* or *fū* (style), together with the refinement of terms such as *jūtaku* (dwelling-house) and *kagu* (furniture), signified not only the development of codes for modern fields of professional expertise but also a reshaping of the everyday itself, because each of these terms accompanied normative systems that intervened in domains previously configured differently within multiple local traditions. These new structuring principles for dwellings thus built the foundations of modern bourgeois life as much as did the definition of social universals such as labor and leisure.

Whether one views the range of campaigns and outpouring of writing relating to *seikatsu* in the 1920s in terms of the operations of hegemonic power or of small acts of local resistance—that is, the discovery of the private sphere as a final colonization by systems of knowledge in service to the state or as the reverse, a first tentative oppositional move against the state's pervasiveness—depends on where one looks for examples. The "everyday life" of the Everyday Life Reform League, particularly as articulated by Education and Home Ministry bureaucrats, fits naturally within a Foucauldian conception of modern institutions, whose power operates through invisible channels to create docile subjects. Nishimura Isaku's "life as art," on the other hand, although in political terms entirely within the safe confines of bourgeois progressivism, implied through its very flamboyance and explicitly theatrical character that a true modern subjectivity was not to be formed through the silent internalization of collective norms.

In each case that they were used, the words *seikatsu kaizen* and *bunka seikatsu* bore the freight of class positions and dispositions. Bourgeois ideologues beginning with Morimoto Kōkichi wore *bunka* as a cosmopolitan mask for their narrow attention to class-cultural ideals of the consumption-centered household and the homogeneous residential suburb. By treating these things as universal fruits of modernity whose attainment by even a privileged few constituted national progress, they were able to remain comfortably blinkered to actual class conflict and political ferment in a volatile era. Female consumers struggling to better their position through middlebrow media like the *Housewife's Companion* appropriated everyday life reform discourse together with new attitudes toward the home in what can be seen as a form of oppositional re-reading of elite-led Westernization. Male cultural critics, like their counterparts in the West, regarded the liberated female consumer as an embodiment of the dangers of modern mass society. But whereas Western critics associated the threat with the abundance of mass-produced commodities and the loss of authentic craft products, Japanese critics saw the female consumer's liberation together with the promiscuous hybridity of culture houses as threatening the purity of national categories or the loss of their own control over national culture to rootless newcomers to the city, newcomers to the dominant class, newcomers to public discourse, and unauthorized authorities. Attempting to define the politics of specific gestures in this multiparty contest as either complicit or resistant leads quickly into the cul-de-sac of debates over the relative importance of hegemonic structures and individual agency in mass society. What is certain is that the contested nature of *seikatsu* in the 1920s represented a new stage of public discourse, in which top-down reforms and the products of mass culture became equally manipulable commodities.

The concrete "stuff" for the new private life built on consumption practices—the houses themselves, the rattan furniture, the pianos, the accoutrements of Western parlors for receiving guests, the gas cooking appliances for modernized kitchens, and so forth—were an ensemble shaped through constant interaction between discourse, practice, and the material world. Imported discourses of domesticity, for example, initially encountered resistance in the practical reality of multigenerational Japanese households, which still required space for functions of the corporate family, an encounter that resulted in the material form of the interior-corridor plan. Discourses of national style dislodged interiors and domestic objects from contexts of established practice, but the liberation was brief, since in order to survive, new commodities had to be reinsertable into practical settings—either by accommodating themselves to existing practices such as the transmission of wealth in the form of dowry or by acquiring an appearance of naturalness through sensual associations with other goods, such as the association of rattan with *tatami*. Physical things are polysemic, allowing wide latitude for reinterpretation in the actual process of translation between practical contexts. This applied to native material forms such as *tatami* mats and *engawa* or scroll paintings and antiquities, as well as to goods translated through physical importation or imitation of something from overseas. The importation of bungalows, for example, neither served a single ideology nor dictated a particular lifestyle; rather, it provided material for the elaboration of discourse around the home and for experimentation with new modes of domestic practice.

Containing *seikatsu* within the private space of the home affected the commodity nature of the dwelling itself. To say that dwellings were commodified in the Meiji and Taishō eras captures only half of the transformation, however. As Yanagita Kunio observed, there were two vernacular traditions in dwelling, which (in their ideal-typical forms) stood at opposite extremes in relation to market exchange.[2] The large farmhouse was built and maintained by the hands of its occupants and their village neighbors or by local craftsmen. It functioned as one of the most visible and inalienable embodiments of the family's continuity through time. In contrast, the urban commoner's tenement of the Tokugawa period was already a completely exchangeable commodity. People moved frequently between rented lodgings that were almost indistinguishable from one another. Practically every element of their material surroundings was alienable. In fact, all the pieces of the house except the roof and the posts and beams supporting it were commonly rented separately. Many tenement dwellers also rented such household essentials as bedding.

With the advent of the culture house in the 1920s, houses became commodities that promised to be more than commodities, signs shaped to awaken consumer desire. Ironically, this would make them less alienable than the old urban tenement, since full consummation of that desire came in making the house one's own—literally, by purchase rather than rental, and figuratively, by the myriad little investments put into personalizing it, making it "homey." Urban dwellings in the new housing market lost the flexibility that they had previously possessed, becoming heavily inscribed, manipulated, delimited enclosures of space, singularized (as each new house was to be imagined singularly suited to its particular owners) in order to be recommodified in a more differentiated market. From the perspective of the rural house (or its ideological form as an embodiment of corporate continuity), the ephemeral, individuated, and entirely secular new domesticity stood for a disenchanted modernity, devoid of the numinous power that dwelling had once held. From the perspective of the tenement city of anonymous, undifferentiated shelter, on the other hand, it belonged to a world enchanted by the fantasy surplus that lures modern consumers.[3]

## A Domesticity Built of Goods and Practices

In Western historiography, the term "domesticity" has been applied chiefly to the strong family affections that people either genuinely came to feel in the modern age or were exhorted to feel by modern ideologues. The development of the new conception of family has been associated in England and the United States with evangelicalism and other reform movements within Christianity.[4] In Japan, although the initial cues came from Protestant converts, a domestic ideology was able to develop almost without reference to religion. Japanese domesticity was constructed from goods and practices: rituals of family, tasks of housewifery, and programs for childrearing, along with new house designs, furniture, and ornament.

The first generation of bourgeois reformers in the late nineteenth century sought to realize the new domestic morality by inventing rituals and routines for the family, much as the state invented new rituals and routines in order to unify and stabilize the nation. Older rituals of community and the quotidian practices of casual social exchange were remade at the same time. Defining the dwelling around cohabitant family, reformers rejected the complex of social functions that had once intersected in the dwelling interior. In the Western reception room, a space was made for contact with outsiders, and a suitable etiquette, a pastiche of earlier samurai and contemporary Victorian practices, was devised to maintain social distinctions.

One senses in these ritualizations the struggle to anchor a ship that had come unmoored. Although domestic reformers were explicitly inspired by images of Anglo-American family behavior, they acted equally from the sense of a need to reinforce the domestic group against the centrifugal and entropic forces of modern society. Implicitly, new ritual enactments were attempts to embody the configuration of power within the household, yet this itself was in flux. As nuclear-family households and their variants increased in number and social prominence, some of the practices developed in the initial effort to reinvent home would prove more serviceable and take hold, and others would leave only written traces to remind us of the concerns of the early reformers.

Although dwelling reformers in the Meiji period had been content with local modifications in house plans to accommodate these practices and separations, increasingly radical calls for redesigning houses followed. By 1919, some advocates of dwelling reform had come to see the vernacular house *in toto* as an instrument perpetuating an outmoded society. Architects analyzed its parts, finding various culprits, in *engawa* corridors and their shutters, in tatami mats, in the placement of guest rooms, or in the general practice of building on irregular, spread-out single-story plans. This process of analysis, fully developed in the proposals of the Everyday Life Reform League and the model houses at Culture Village, injected the idea of rationalization, or the demand for a manifest functional logic, into dwelling design. The stripped-down functionalist aesthetic just emerging in Europe at the time, later to be referred to as the International Style, was not the dominant result, however. Instead, Japanese architects, builders, and their clients treated all styles, modernist and historicist alike, as comparable merchandise from an international catalogue of design. As design energy was redirected toward resolving the aesthetic conflict of East and West, key components of bourgeois family ideology were tacitly absorbed into the foundations of modern dwelling in the name of rationalization. The family circle that had required ritual articulation in the Meiji home, for example, ceased to be an explicit issue for reform campaigns but was preserved and enshrined in the architecture of reform plans.

The fact that so much of modern domestic ideology in Japan can be seen taking shape through a process of conscious importation and domestic propaganda campaigns accentuates its inherent artificiality. In increasing their emotional and material investment in the home, the people who bought into this domestic ideology made a curious choice; for if they were indeed freer from the bonds of community and family tradition, forming households of their own will, then they presumably had less need to worry about maintenance of a permanent domicile either to pass on to future generations or to honor previous ones. Why, then, should this generation have chosen to find greater meaning than before in the acquisition and decoration of houses, as well as in the elaboration of domestic practices of all kinds?

This investment in domestic permanence is not explicable in terms of the logic of capital alone. Recent feminist scholarship on the family in Japan has emphasized the centrality of the institutions of the nation-state in defining the modern family. Nishikawa Yūko, for example, has inverted the historiographic tradition of treating the modern *katei* as a liberal challenge to the unique Japanese institutions of the *ie* and the emperor-centered "family-state" by asserting that all modern nation-states have been family states, because all seek to reinforce family ideology and exploit it for governance. This is a vital corrective to social theories that had taken little account of gender dynamics within the modern household, but it is less than a full historical explanation, since it still leaves open the question of why such a hegemonic discourse developed largely outside the institutions of the state. Two additional historical factors in the shaping of modern Japanese domestic ideology are relevant here. The first is that the women's journals, girls' higher schools, and reform campaigns that were the primary vehicles for bourgeois domestic ideology sold critical components of class membership. The second—and this aspect emerges more clearly after World War I—is that domestic ideology whetted the appetite of urbanites to enjoy a new mode of consumption, in which choosing and adorning a house became an opportunity for personal expression or a form of play for young couples living on professional incomes and remittances from the countryside.

The institutions of the bourgeois state created the spatial divisions that left the home as a residuum. The state had a clear interest in seeing that this residuum was managed in a way that reproduced loyal and healthy subject-citizens and perpetuated patriarchy. Yet bourgeois women and men were not merely complicit in producing homes for the nation; they were the primary agents of their creation, responsible for making each home a heterogeneous space apart from society. They bought this heterogeneity in goods and articulated it in consumption practices. As institutions outside the house increasingly took over the production of goods and knowledge, families responded to the pressure of ideology—or fulfilled the psychological need—to fashion an autonomous sphere by composing lifestyles from the furniture and fabrics, objets d'art, foodstuffs, appliances, kitchen tools, and gadgets, as well as the models, recipes, and advice available to them on the market.

Arriving in a cultural field where *katei* was already a concept replete with concrete connotations concerning family behavior, domestic labor, taste in interiors, and homeownership, petit-bourgeois "salarymen" and their wives in the 1920s inherited the idea but adjusted it to their social circumstances. They embraced the ideal of the family-centered home but showed less compunction about representing it ritually. New cultural intermediaries pitched their visions of the home to young couples, bringing conjugal romance to the fore among the meanings of private dwelling space. Women in this generation realized all the elements of modern bourgeois housewifery for the first time, as more graduates of the girls' higher schools did their own housework and donned the uniform that marked them as full-time professionals. Alone in the home, without the presence of a maid to reaffirm her privilege, the professional housewife was more likely to ground her class identity in conditions and dispositions that marked her apart from working-class neighbors or peasants in the village from which she had come. Taishō middle-class consumers evinced less concern for questions of national style than the bourgeois tastemakers who had helped establish the department-store culture at the turn of the twentieth century, but they flocked to the department stores and carried home the bourgeois belief that the style and interior decor of a house should express the personality of its occupants, interpreting this with a liberality well beyond the intentions of their cultural mentors. The bourgeois man's desire for a suburban house and lot in his own name, which would form the basis of culture house dreams in the 1920s, had already received its rationale from Kobayashi Ichizō in the previous decade. The cosmopolitan utopianism of the 1920s provided a new role for "the West" and a new relationship to things Western that enhanced this desire and gave it a broader cultural legitimacy. Altogether, the evolution of the home in the mass market of the 1920s made it a place of multiple private pleasures, completing the process of commodification for domestic ideals that had been introduced a generation earlier as a moral armature for national progress.

## Reform Discourse as Cultural Capital

From the 1890s through the 1920s, talk of dwelling reform and the domestic ideals that informed it were restricted to educated urban professionals. Not only did this reform discourse continue until late in the 1920s with hardly an eye to the needs of the peasantry, it largely ignored the old merchant elite and the urban working class. The fact that most of Tokyo was made up of shopkeepers' rowhouses was completely invisible in the programs of the Everyday Life Reform League. Early twentieth-century dwelling reform efforts never represented the mass of people in Japan, or even the majority population of the capital. Even as this limits their significance, it brings into sharper relief the efforts to constitute a class identity that underlay the reform effort.

Reform rhetoric and new domestic practices were a type of cultural capital. Taking meals as a family, with appropriate table manners and conversation, keeping a hygienic kitchen and cooking recipes from a cookbook or the newspaper (apt to involve new equipment such as frying pans or ovens and experimentation with new ingredients), maintaining a Western reception room or an eclectic approximation of one and receiving guests with the proper etiquette, summering away from home, devoting a separate space in the house to children and monitoring their habits—all these things distinguished the bourgeois family. A monopoly of the progressive, cosmopolitan ideas and practices derived from advanced education and the informal media to which education gave access was the foundation of privilege and what distinguished one from the laboring classes of both city and country.

Although city residents had distinguished themselves from countryfolk centuries before bourgeois cultural discourse took shape in the Meiji period, modern conditions inflected the urban-rural divide in new ways. On the one hand, the influx of people of all classes to Tokyo and Osaka meant that a large proportion of urbanites possessed recent memory of a village home. Many of the new middle class of the Taishō era, like the male protagonist Jōji in Tanizaki's novel, had not yet cut the umbilicus linking them to their rural native places. Jōji receives not only money but also domestic labor from the countryside—when he and Naomi set up house, his mother sends a maid to work for them. On the other hand, the discourses of hygiene and eugenics and the general urban bias of everyday life reform sharpened the bourgeois perception of peasant life and customs as barbaric and primitive. In 1910, when Nagatsuka Takashi published *The Soil* (*Tsuchi*), a novel about the travails of a tenant-farming family based on memories of the author's own native village, some urban critics considered the naturalistic descriptions too vile for public consumption. Even as sensitive an intellectual as Natsume Sōseki, who understood the fragility of cosmopolitan Japan more deeply than most of his contemporaries, commended the novel's moral value but could find only terms of horror and revulsion to describe the living conditions and behavior of the peasants in it.[5] The rural family in Murai Gensai's *Shokudōraku* (1904) were objects of ridicule for their ignorance of civilized urban habits and the inefficiency of their domestic customs. To evoke yet greater alarm, Murai portrayed them as threatening racial progress because of their ignorance of the dangers of inbreeding. As with the threat of the lower classes as carriers of epidemic disease, reform discourse in one and the same gesture both presented the bourgeoisie as threatened and reconfirmed readers' bourgeois identities.

At the same time, since the samurai families of the Tokugawa period had not, for the most part, been a landed gentry, Japanese domestic ideologues and suburban builders, unlike their precursors in England and the United States, lacked the comfort of reference to myths of the country seat or rural homestead. Although most members of the new urban classes still had their native place in some farming village, and a few architects adapted aesthetic features from rural houses, bourgeois domesticity in Japan placed the customs and the architecture of the nation's peasant majority in a dark, feudal past. In the 1920s, when new culture houses spread around the outskirts of the city, the cultural antenna still pointed cityward, and from there toward the West.

As the Japanese empire expanded, colonial others added another layer to the urban-rural cultural hierarchy, less visible in metropolitan life but available to be imagined in any form precisely because of the distance that separated Tokyo from the colonies. Imperialism allowed a broader population into the fold of bourgeois culture by placing all ethnic Japanese at least nominally on the dominant side of the barrier between civilization and backwardness. Readers of popular magazines in the 1920s such as the *Housewife's Companion* might feel animosity toward the wealthy native elite, but they shared with them the confidence that the national self-civilizing project had been largely accomplished now that Japanese ruled Pacific islanders and other "savages."

But as long as enlightened domestic habits, together with the houses and furniture necessary to their full realization, were still being promoted as reforms rather than simply transmitted as patrimony, their value as capital was inevitably insecure. Sharing reformism is a paradoxical basis for class identity, since it implies a disposition toward change rather than a stable model to be pursued. With the expansion of secondary education, "middle class" came to signify a stratified series of groups with distinct living standards, experiences, and expectations. In magazines and newspapers after World War I, the lower strata in this expanded bourgeoisie, whose numbers were the greatest, added their voices to a field of discourse that had been controlled by the wealthy. Divided by the material choices available to them, diverse players in the 1910s and 1920s used the common rhetoric of reform to compete over class identity. "Everyday life reform," the "family-based house," and other stock phrases, once they gained currency, were used by everyone, regardless of social position. There was also a consensus that the material contents of everyday life—houses, furniture and other household objects, clothing, and food—needed reforming. Everyday life reform thus constituted a discursive space for different "middle classes" with different agendas, a kind of playing field on which the goals remained the same while the team lineups and game strategies changed.

Contest within the bourgeois cultural project could not reveal itself in choice of house style until houses *had* styles and until more than a small elite could afford to make such choices. The symbolic depreciation of culture houses represents the beginning of this class-based aesthetic taxonomy of houses. The people with the most cultural capital could cheapen "culture" (*bunka*) by portraying culture houses as imitations, reflecting their superior knowledge of Western ways and their access to houses of better construction. But at the same time, the fact that "culture" sold goods reveals the existence of a larger group for whom it had positive connotations. In contrast to countries with stable and emulatable bourgeois or aristocratic traditions, in Japan, the dominant elite of the modern era began its career by rejecting much of the old and embracing reform. The result was that standards of taste were disputable when the middle class expanded. The struggling petite bourgeoisie in this context were apt to be the most willing to embrace exotic house styles, since they had the least traditional capital to part with, making a certain anti-conventionalism the proper convention to follow.

## Cultural Intermediaries

The fact that so much of the dominant culture being repackaged for the Japanese mass market was imported gave a special role to people in a position to explain and translate, opening a broad social space for the people I have called cultural intermediaries. In Western histories of the modern domestic interior, the architects, designers, advertisers, and magazine editors who promoted new lifestyles have often been referred to as arbiters of taste or tastemakers.[6] To describe the propagation of new lifestyles in Japan, the category must be expanded in two ways, first to include people in a wider range of professions and second to recognize that these people were promoting a cultural package that extended beyond fashions in architecture or interior design. The diverse group of experts who contributed to the reform of everyday life and public discourse on the shape of the middle-class house included bureaucrats in several branches of government, politicians, members of the medical profession, educators, novelists, artists, and journalists, in addition to the professions whose primary occupation was designing or marketing things for the home.

There was also a distinct shift in the nature and composition of this group in Japan from the 1890s to the 1920s. Late Meiji cultural intermediaries were more homogeneous in class terms; speaking, writing, and designing from established bourgeois positions in the name of a domestic *mission civilisatrice.* Even when they were discussing dining habits, national goals were never far removed from the private concerns of Meiji proselytizers of bourgeois culture, whose own intellectual development had coincided with the growth of the nation-state. But from the turn of the twentieth century, this group increasingly shared its public with a new sort of progressive intellectual, further removed from elite political circles and more reliant on claims of specific expertise or personal experience. These people made their careers purveying the norms and forms of elite-derived new lifestyles to a growing literate public—particularly a female one—and they were apt to be in the game as much to make a living as to serve the nation. In addition, many of the professions they represented were themselves new and created to fill market niches rather than the needs of the state: residential architect, interior designer, home economist, nutritionist, women's magazine reporter, free-lance writer. Their entry into the field thus reflects an expansion of the channels of cultural production, and their many publications intimate the growth of a large and diffuse middle-brow audience extending far beyond that of the nineteenth-century proselytizers.

Since new institutions and channels of expertise propagated the rhetoric of reform, the shapes it produced reflected the necessities of those institutions and experts. Architects needed problems of design as a space in the cultural field where their expertise held sway. Women's educators, lacking the guarantees of professional authority provided to architecture by the state, had yet greater need to claim a turf of their own. The definition of the field of domestic management in terms of clothing, food, and shelter (*ishokujū*) defined the dwelling as material on which they could operate.

Without recognizing that modes of thought were as much products of new institutions and professions as the other way around, it is difficult to comprehend all the concern generated over the layout of private houses. The issue here was not the dwellings of the working class, management of which had obvious implications for the state and capital, nor technological changes in the mass production of dwellings, which would also be of direct and obvious institutional significance. Rather, it was the reshuffling of spaces in the plans of privately owned or rented single-family houses. The problems addressed revolved around guest reception, decoration, family gatherings, kitchen work, furniture, bodily comportment, and so forth—all matters that would appear of marginal relevance to the master narratives of national development. Yet an array of professionals in architecture, education, and related fields treated these matters as central to the creation of a modern society. Quite apart from the power of Western models in reform discourse or the reality of social changes such as the growth of an educated bourgeois market, the emergence of new professions connected to the issues of dwelling must itself be counted a significant factor behind the public concern over private space. For architects and household management experts, the house plan was an empty stage on which to design and choreograph domestic life. Permutations of the basic set of living and service spaces were explored in endless variation: the sequence, orientation, and adjacency of rooms were made to signify whole philosophies of everyday life.[7] This elaboration mirrored the elaboration of expertise around the dwelling or, to put it more pointedly, was produced of necessity by experts who claimed the dwelling as the object on which their new knowledge could be exercised. The value of these experts' own cultural capital depended on broad social recognition of the importance of reforming the home.

## The Problem of Borrowing

Since the Meiji period Japanese intellectuals have often criticized the heavy reliance of cultural intermediaries on imported texts and images as blind imitation or as evidence of a Westernizing corruption of national culture. It is an appealing response to this brand of purism, which essentializes both Japan and the West, to point to the creative ways in which particular forms were appropriated as Japan progressively joined global trends of fashion and of thought. Yet the appropriations were never made freely. The choice of things Western, which seems at times to transcend all other evaluative criteria, replicated relations of power, since the modes of interpretation available for Japanese to conceive their social and material world were determined by the forces of their political world. For reformers, an internal logic seemed to make each choice of the Western model over the indigenous necessary. Reforming the dwelling from the inside out brought a result that looked "Western style" on the exterior, admitted Tanabe Junkichi of the Everyday Life Reform League, but he explained that his model was not an imitation; it had "come naturally to resemble a Western house."[8] Tanabe may be taken at his word—that "the West" was inescapably present did not mean that everyday life reform was pursued out of an affection for the West or a disaffection with Japan. Nor, conversely, were reform discourses inevitably motivated by nationalism, seeking to promote Japan in the political order by means of cultural emulation. Individual reformers chose class strategies that combined East and West according to their own social capital and cultural competence.

The combination of the unequal treaties imposed on Japan by the Western powers and the rapid modernization program led by the Meiji state in response made Tokyo a kind of satellite or colonial outpost in the global hegemony of European culture, and the modernizing elite of Meiji comparable to colonial administrators, a caste apart from the subaltern masses but also alienated from the European metropole. Many of the new elite were in fact only recent arrivals in domestic high society as well as in international diplomacy, eager to demonstrate their cultural mastery in native contexts on the one hand at the same time that they Westernized themselves for Westerners who were likely to regard them as inferior examples of Westernness on the other.

Thus, even though all the aesthetic articulations of Japaneseness and Westernness were so many moves within a domestic field of class-cultural competition—a "classification struggle," in Bourdieu's words—this field was in turn nested inescapably within an unequally configured international cultural field, in which analogous deployments of codes of taste were made toward the ends of national-cultural competition. Because of Japan's anomalous in-between position in international politics, members of the governing elite and bourgeoisie who dominated at home were, metaphorically speaking, struggling petite bourgeoisie vis-à-vis their European counterparts. If the dynamics of class-cultural competition can be transposed into international terms, Bourdieu's description of the petit-bourgeois social position becomes apposite to the cultural condition of elite Japanese in the era of the unequal treaties:

> Equidistant from the two extreme poles of the field of the social classes, . . . the petit bourgeois are constantly faced with ethical, aesthetic or political dilemmas forcing them to bring the most ordinary operations of existence to the level of consciousness and strategic choice. In order to survive in the world of their aspirations they are condemned to "live beyond their means" and to be constantly attentive and sen-

sitive, hypersensitive, to the slightest signs of the reception given to their self-representation.[9]

Substitute a phrase like "imperial hierarchy" or "international order" for "field of the social classes," and the "two extreme poles" in this transposed reading might be read as the dominated position of colonized peoples and the dominant position of the Western powers. Meiji Japan's political position between these poles circumscribed the cultural positions individual Japanese could choose and determined their valence. Nativism aligned one with the dominated position and cosmopolitanism with the dominant.

The point is not, of course, that the Japanese were as a whole petit bourgeois but that positions within the field of domestic class competition were inflected by Japan's position within the field of international competition.[10] All positions within the domestic social field were thus doubly determined, by their relation to other Japanese and by Japan's position among the powers. A small group of well-traveled and wealthy grande bourgeoisie in Meiji Japan adorned their houses in a free pastiche that appropriated things Eastern and Western with cosmopolitan authority, but most Meiji bourgeois proselytizers looking to Western models could not escape awareness of themselves as occupants of a lower stratum in international society despite being society's elite at home. Members of the Taishō generation with less investment in native traditions were willing to take greater risks. Their adventures moved even further in the direction of abandoning native practice not only because they had less to lose but also because Japan itself had moved, through acquisition of a colonial empire and termination of the unequal treaties, into a more advantageous "class" position among nations.

In Bourdieu's formulation, the petite bourgeoisie relies the most on, and contributes the most to, the media that propagate models for improving the home, because it has abandoned the stable conventions of its social inferiors yet lacks the reserves of actual goods and cultural capital that permit established bourgeois households the luxury of expressing themselves with the material at hand and the confidence of success. Beginning at the end of the nineteenth century, many of Japan's progressive elite followed strategies analogous to Bourdieu's petite bourgeoisie, distinguishing themselves from a conventional past and pursuing new models for an aesthetic in their domestic surroundings that drew on the elements of cosmopolitan culture they could afford. The prominence of cultural intermediaries and the highly public nature of campaigns to modernize the home in late Meiji and Taishō Japan should be seen against this background.

## Consumer Education

By the mid-1920s, new commodities and technology were vying for space in bourgeois houses large and small. With their piano, gramophone, and complete set of Mitsukoshi rattan furniture, as well as an assortment of decorative bric-a-brac, the couple whose belongings Kon Wajirō surveyed in 1926 was spending money in ways unimaginable to people of their social position in an earlier generation and unlikely to have been emulated in contemporary working-class households. They had filled their new home with objects reflecting their personal taste and serving no practical purpose but to enhance their leisure and demonstrate to others their acquisition of *bunka*.

Yet this accumulation of furniture and ephemera did not represent wealth. This couple occupied a house of only 9.75 *tsubo* (roughly 350 square feet), no larger than most working-class tenements. The kitchen had no electrical appliances and only one oil burner for cooking. The disparity between the kitchens and houses shown in magazines and textbooks and what most readers could afford persisted until after the national economic expansion of the 1960s. Ever since the popular *Shokudōraku* had introduced readers to the kitchen of Baron Ōkuma with its imported English oven, images of ideal kitchens had offered glimpses into a bright fictional world where all the reforms necessary for hygiene and efficiency and a rich variety of home cooking were accomplished and the goods to be desired were all in place. In the didactic contexts in which these images were shown, the reform of habits was linked to new goods or houses that few could yet afford. The largest market in Japan, with its highly literate population, was for the most affordable commodity: print. In the United States, where mass consumption was far in advance of Japan for most of the century, it was the manufacturers who were teaching housewives how to be middle-class consumers; in Japan, women were learning more from textbooks, newspapers, and magazines.

The majority of contemporary Japanese think of the modern kitchen as a product of the 1960s, but it had what might be called a long gestation period, since readers of women's magazines and girls' school texts had been looking at images of model kitchens since the turn of the twentieth century. Some had designed their own to submit to magazine competitions or include in public exhibitions. Few households actually possessed the electric appliances that are today associated with the growth of consumerism, but many were exerting themselves to compose the culture life, an image of modernity whose building blocks were new goods. The mentality of consumerism was thus evident in Japan before any revolution in buying power. Japanese consumerism rose from a culture of abundant knowledge rather than a culture of abundance.

For the people who bought or built one, a culture house was likely to have been the first large material investment, long before an automobile, private ownership of which was rare in prewar Japan, and probably unaccompanied by purchase of any electrical appliance larger than a lamp. Since the Meiji Restoration, the forms of Japanese everyday life had been relativized by elite consciousness of Western ways. Yet the question first posed by the newspaper sponsors of the 1915 Home Exhibition—What things shall we have for our everyday life?—transferred the seat of the dilemma from the opposition of an indigenous way and a foreign way of building and living to the uncertain ground of consumer choice. By the mid-1920s, both native and foreign media had immersed the middle classes of Tokyo in a global consumer culture. If a considerable part of their participation was vicarious, the fact that most of the tangible goods were still in the hands only of Westerners simply focused the desires of Japanese consumers more acutely.

## The Settling of Modern Forms

In several respects, not only domestic ideology but the material and practical terms of bourgeois domestic space and everyday life had settled into fixed forms by the 1930s. Socially, it is symbolic that professional housewife status finally became an attainable ideal in the mid-1930s, as men's wages in white-collar occupations reached levels that matched average household expenditure.[11] Already in the mid-1920s, as many women as men were completing secondary education at girls' schools that equipped them for their new role with instruments of the modern science of domestic management. These women carried into the home both new technical knowledge from the classroom and an aesthetic sensibility that reinforced the associations formulated by Meiji-period architects and reformers linking Japanese femininity and traditional architectural space. Thus the full-time professional housewife finally arrived in a secure position, bringing with her habits and tastes that would define the character of middle-class homes for as long as her role itself remained stable.

The art of tea was an important conduit for inculcating native taste as feminine virtue. The modern recasting of tea culture provides a clear example of the process of reconstituting everyday life that was begun in response to the radical dislocation of cultural hierarchies in the Meiji period and completed in the mass culture of the 1920s and 1930s. Threatened with extinction after the Meiji Restoration, tea schools survived partly by claiming the value of tea as etiquette training. Gradually thereafter, tea instruction was incorporated into the etiquette curriculum of girls' higher schools. As the content of women's secondary education was appropriated into mass media in the twentieth century, tea became increasingly associated with female self-cultivation. Tea historian Kumakura Isao estimates that by the 1930s, women predominated at the large annual tea gatherings sponsored by Kyoto temples and the tea schools. This marked the end of its broad sea-change from a male-centered art of practice for a specially designed interior to a female-centered social discipline intended to inculcate manners for application outside the tearoom.[12] Tea continued thereafter to be the great finishing school for women, instilling in them an awareness of their national identity intimately linked to native architectural space and reinforcing the connection between native space and female gender even after women ceased to wear kimono as everyday attire.

Meanwhile, new canons of architectural and interior design aesthetics began in the 1920s to draw upon the *sukiya* tradition associated with tea. Architects thereby resituated *sukiya* in an entirely different frame, making it a sourcebook for nativist architectural aesthetics disconnected from tea or other social practice. This, combined with the massification of tea as native etiquette training and marital asset for women, signified the marginalization of wealthy amateurs of *suki*, for whom tea gatherings, collecting, and interior design had been components of a single aesthetic practice. By the late 1930s, then, the social art of tea, formerly the province of male aficionados, had been dismantled, and its usable elements salvaged for two distinct sets of national-cultural and commercial aims.

In residential architecture, the riot of experimentation in the mid-1920s gave way to a more subdued blend of native and Western idioms in the 1930s. Hybrid Japanese-Western designs like those of Amerika-ya architect Yamamoto Setsurō, which had looked avant-garde in the early 1920s, were standard by the mid-1930s.[13] Although Yamamoto's designs look quite Japanese when compared with the flat roofs and concrete construction of international modernist architecture, it is important to note that the fusion of Japanese and Western styles developed by Yamamoto and others like him was as innovative when it first appeared as were the more strongly European designs. Drawing in part from *sukiya,* which had won the competition for a place within modern constructions of tradition, they had helped to define a new native aesthetic. When this vocabulary was sufficiently naturalized, what had seemed vanguard came to appear traditional. Houses with closed exteriors and a mix of *tatami* and chairs indoors, featuring a number of native aesthetic markers such as exposed wooden posts, round windows, and unglazed roof tiles, came to be the most common style in the pattern books and the suburbs.

Along with the surge of experiments in dwelling form, the waves of cultural reformism targeting the urban middle classes had subsided by the 1930s. The fanfare that had accompanied the Everyday Life Reform campaign in 1920 and Culture Village in 1922, the criticism they suffered, and the subsequent proliferation of new house types under the sign of "culture" seemed already to belong to an earlier era when Yanagita Kunio wrote his classic *Meiji Taishōshi sesōhen* (A Social History of the Meiji and Taishō Eras) in 1931. In a concluding chapter titled "Objectives for the Reform of Everyday Life," Yanagita asserted that the advances of the era were visible in the fact that Japan no longer imitated the West: "The sense has faded that our cultural enterprises (*bunka jigyō*) must look to foreign countries," he wrote, observing that Japanese had matured and become self-reliant.[14] In the "unexpected miscellany of house styles" that blossomed after the 1923 earthquake, Yanagita saw a beneficial element of this process: "Our imagination, which had long been submerged, came to the surface, almost to an indiscriminate degree. We were able to examine the question of comfort in detail, from front and back."[15] Many of the proposals for everyday life reform had been elitist and out of touch with the poor majority of Japanese, Yanagita wrote, yet "it was itself a reform" that people had learned to pursue changes in everyday life through organized campaigns rather than merely individual effort, as it was that women's organizations were given a leading role where "politics directly touches our homes."[16] For better and for worse, these things were indeed legacies of the 1920s.

## Postwar Homes

The ways that house and home evolved after Yanagita's 1931 summation are a story for another book. It would be too facile to leap over national mobilization, war, and seven years of foreign military occupation and claim that subsequent dwellings derived simply from blueprints drawn in the 1920s. Yet it is undeniable that many of the cultural inventions of early twentieth-century bourgeois ideologues lived on and found new incarnations during and after the war. Several recent scholars have pointed to the mid-1970s as a transition more significant than 1945 in the history of private life in Japan. In a lucid study of national demographic trends, Ochiai Emiko describes what she calls the "postwar family system," based on nuclear family ideals, as operating from 1955 to 1975. Nishikawa Yūko, whose focus is on family ideology and the dwelling, proposes an era of *katei* culture beginning in the late Meiji period and ending in the 1970s. As Nishikawa points out, it was around 1975 that the actual circumstances of most Japanese households finally came close to matching the domestic models that had long been proffered to them.[17]

In short, the process of constructing the Japanese bourgeois family continued until the traffic of commodities that manifested it met with a national-level mass society. Demographic trends after the war played a key role in this massification by transforming the nuclear family from popular ideal to reality for a large new generation of Japanese. As Ochiai shows, the baby boom of 1947 to 1949 was followed by a rapid decline in fertility brought about by the liberalization of abortion laws and urbanization of the workforce. By 1955, a highly uniform pattern of two children per couple had emerged. As children of the postwar boom came of marrying age in the 1970s, the number of nuclear family households rose markedly. By 1975, there were twice as many nuclear households as there had been in 1955, giving rise to the perception that the "*ie* system" was on the wane and Japanese society as a whole was "nuclearizing." In fact, statistics reveal that households including non-nuclear kin had not declined at all, meaning that the custom of having one inheriting male cohabit with his parents after marriage, which formed the foundation of the *ie* ideal, was still being maintained and that the increased population of non-inheriting children was responsible for the blossoming of the nuclear family. The members of this baby-boom cohort (known in Japanese as *dankai sedai*, the "lump generation"), because of their numbers and conspicuousness, were a natural target for media attention and marketing. By 1975, the number of nuclear households had reached its zenith. The real conflict between the patriarchal stem *ie* and the nuclear *katei* emerged only after that.[18]

Apart from massification of scale, there were two major structural differences in the later stages of the *katei*'s evolution. First, from the time of the Occupation, the United States became overwhelmingly the dominant model for emulation, partly because of the presence of Americans on Japanese soil and the heavy hand of American administration in shaping postwar Japanese society, but perhaps even more because of the impact of the affluent lifestyle of American families as seen in popular media. Second, in contrast to the years in which bourgeois cultural intermediaries had been a social and political vanguard, from the late 1950s all the structures of the corporate state—large enterprises, government, and financial institutions—aggressively contributed to producing bourgeois families through macro-planning and financing.[19]

As Simon Partner has shown, appliance manufacturers led the postwar resurrection of consumerism under the banner of the "bright life," which bore much the same sense as the "culture life" had in the mass market of the 1920s.[20] As in the Everyday Life Reform campaign of the 1920s, state agencies were again engaged in promoting "rationalization" while encouraging changes of lifestyle that required new goods, although by this time the primary target had shifted to the countryside.[21] Since everyday life reform as a bourgeois class-constituting project had already established a coherent set of norms decades earlier, reform discourse no longer revolved around problems of bourgeois domestic life. The "ill-effects of the double life," for example, once regarded as a matter of critical public moment, faded to invisibility. Ideals of the home as private paradise of consumption and of the home as state-regulated site for the production of subject-citizens dovetailed more readily for the postwar state, since the largest enterprises were now dependent on creating domestic demand for their products.[22]

The consumerism of the 1960s focused on a parade of appliances, but as these things diffused to the entire population in the 1970s, the vanguard of marketing shifted to using images of the home as a place for personal indulgence in order to promote luxury goods. Interior magazines proliferated. Advertisements sketched an idyll of the couple-centered "New Family," in which husband and wife expressed their intimacy through such acts of shared consumption as drinking wine *a deux* and wearing matching colors.[23] For a short period the media spotlight turned on young professional couples with double incomes and more egalitarian relationships. Ochiai observes that the newness of the new family turned out to be a marketing myth, since the real demographic trend was actually toward the realization of what she calls the "modern family" and I call the "modern bourgeois family": a companionate nuclear family maintaining the standard division of labor, its status confirmed in a tastefully appointed private dwelling.[24] The only thing "new" about these families that distinguished them from families in the Tokyo suburbs of the 1920s was their numbers.

The 1970s were unquestionably the years in which homeownership soared, helped by government incentives and corporate lending programs for employees. Low-interest loans brought a tenfold increase in financing for new houses between 1966 and 1971, followed by another fivefold increase in the second half of the decade. The national Public Housing Authority (Jūtaku Kōdan), established in 1955 to provide housing to "urban working families," began building the majority of its units for sale rather than rental in 1977, following the first year in which it faced a shortage of applicants for its rental units.[25] But if owning a home was becoming a national standard, the pressures on the working male to acquire and pay for it had vastly increased, as had the isolation of the professional housewife who maintained it.

And ironically, when the detached suburban house finally became the property of the masses in the late 1970s, the media were suddenly filled with talk of new anxieties about the "collapse of the family." Public attention focused almost obsessively on a handful of shocking domestic homicides, which social critics read as revelations of the hollowness of the home ideal for which so many had strived. Thus, as the bourgeois home was transformed from mass-marketing fantasy to mass-society reality, the producers of bourgeois discourse shifted the ground again, reading alarming trends in the isolation of individuals from the family and families from the urban community just as an earlier generation had expressed alarm over the isolation of nuclear units from the extended family.[26]

Indeed, according to many journalists and social critics, the very first aim of Meiji reformers, to create an intimate family circle, remained an elusive goal. Inheriting a century-old strain of criticism, late-twentieth-century popular media continued to lament the lack of mealtime rituals to confirm the harmony of the cohabitant family in Japan. Setting aside the sociological explanations for this, such as the tendency of postwar white-collar fathers to be overworked and absent, the expressions of despair themselves demonstrate the durability of domestic discourse. To the end of the century, the ever-unattained domestic ideal continued to provide material for utopian longing, in some cases for a model belonging to the imaginary "West" and in other cases for a golden age in the prewar Japanese past when families were supposedly whole and intimate. The same yearning for authentic domestic unity also inspired dystopian parodies.[27]

## Postwar Houses

To a greater or lesser extent, all houses since the culture house have been culture houses, too. "Culture" never designated a specific style or the work of any school of architects; it was, rather, the materialization of a sensibility toward dwelling and the incorporation of dwellings into the sphere of modern design. Its influence has thus extended not only to the shape of houses but to the way they are depicted, talked about, and marketed. Detached houses built since the 1970s have reflected the work of hygienists and scientific managers in the so-called system kitchen, as well as the results of prewar dwelling reform campaigns in the central living room and the child's study room. When the market has been strong, as it was in the 1980s, the newspapers have filled with advertisements for detached houses in a pageant of national styles and hybrids. Critics of the box-shaped, white-paneled American style "shortcake houses" that became popular in these years echoed the derision heaped upon vulgar "culture houses" in the 1920s. The class competition of taste, perhaps the aspect of Taishō bourgeois culture whose legacy was least visible during the long trajectory of postwar economic expansion, resurfaced in these years. Only since the 1970s had many Japanese been able to afford such houses, but when large-scale development began, there was a wealth of past models for both designers and critics to draw upon.

Another significant outcome of the reform campaigns early in the century was the layout scheme used in postwar public housing known as the "nDK plan." This formula, which joined two or more sleeping chambers to a linked open dining-room and kitchen ("DK" standing for "dining kitchen"), derived from the wartime surveys of architect and reformer Nishiyama Uzō. In need of a single spatial principle to apply to the layout of minimal housing units and serve as a "national dwelling" (*kokumin jūtaku*) model, Nishiyama arrived at the principle of separating eating and sleeping space (*shokushin bunri*) as the fundamental criterion for "maintenance of an orderly life."[28] Although

Nishiyama claimed to have derived it empirically, this priority on ensuring a distinct space for taking meals was as much a product of his own disposition toward dwelling, which ultimately traced its roots to the Meiji performance of the family circle. The nDK plan retained *tatami* mats but located meals in the dining-kitchen, which was designed for chairs, since Nishiyama and his colleagues assumed that synchronized family meals required a room of their own, no matter how small the dwelling, and hygienic thought proscribed eating on *tatami* mats that might also be used for sleeping. The dining-kitchen, typically accessed immediately from the entrance to the house, also ended the distinctions of frontstage and backstage in the dwelling, a move that was thinkable now that servants and the older generation had departed. Dwellings on the nDK formula removed all the specialized accommodations that had been made for guests in the past—the enclosed *genkan*, reception room, and *zashiki*.[29] Guest reception of either a casual or formal nature became uncommon, and the home was left an isolated nuclear family cloister.[30]

Meanwhile, the older indigenous elements of the house moved inexorably from the realm of practical necessities to the realm of aesthetic preferences—albeit not all at the same pace. Decorative alcoves and enclosed *genkan* vestibules, which had been almost universal in urban detached houses since their liberation from sumptuary restrictions after the Meiji Restoration, were treated by architects in the early postwar years as pernicious "feudal remnants" and banished from new house designs.[31] In the long term, this made them symbols of self-consciously traditional "Japanese style." *Genkan* in the average run of houses after this were built as small as possible and given single Western-style swing doors in place of paired sliding doors. *Tokonoma* continued to be built in inns and returned to favor as traditional symbols in houses when few other indigenous markers were left. Long *engawa* that allowed occupants to open one or more entire sides of the house to the outdoors disappeared from urban houses with the spread of aluminum sash glass doors in the 1960s, so that the open garden-side corridor, too, became a distinction of "Japanese style" inns and upper-class houses.[32] *Tatami* mats had greater longevity than most Taishō-period progressives would have anticipated. They could finally be removed when men and women stopped wearing kimono (and women stopped sewing them), and the practical, though not the ideological, links between women, kimono, and floor-sitting were broken. In the better class of detached houses, one formal "Japanese room" (*washitsu*), with *tatami* and a *tokonoma* alcove, was retained for reception of occasional guests, its formality accentuated by the contrast with the rest of the house.[33] Today, the dichotomy of chair-sitting and floor-sitting, so important early in the century, seems to have melted into insignificance, but this has occurred largely at the cost of floor-sitting habits. *Seiza*, or "formal sitting," which is considered the proper posture to be adopted when sitting on *tatami* mats, particularly by women, is widely dreaded by contemporary Japanese, and at the same time treated as a minor "traditional accomplishment" akin to, and associated with, making tea in the method of the tea schools.[34]

The narrow normative pattern of the modern mode of dwelling generated a number of related traditionalisms as its mirror. In some Tokyo districts, neighborhood associations managed by the shopkeeping old petite bourgeoisie in the 1980s reinforced traditional practices manifesting neighborhood autonomy and solidarity. As Theodore Bestor's ethnography of one such neighborhood has shown, these shopkeepers were not showing the inherent conservatism of their class but crafting a neo-traditionalist subculture in opposition to the dominant culture of white-collar professionals and the dominant urbanism of office blocks and bedroom suburbs.[35] Municipal offices discovered that aspects of this subculture could then be marketed back to the rest of society and began to promote local festivals and shopping streets in Tokyo's old downtown as tourist attractions.[36] In architecture, the chief traditionalist response to modern bourgeois dwellings was the category of *minka*, or "houses of the people," which originated with Kon Wajirō's surveys in 1919. Kon's rural survey methods and writing had been sustained by a blend of Ruskinian romanticism, left-progressive concern for the lives of the poor, and a folklorist's admiration for all products of peasant ingenuity, new and old. In the process of systematic classification, surveying and preservation under the sponsorship of the Ministry of Education after World War II, these sensibilities were largely lost, and rural houses were museified as part of a national past in complete discontinuity with modernity. The oldest and best-constructed were restored to their earliest known form, to be preserved as emptied (and usually uninhabited) signifiers of vernacular production and the history of everyday life.

Folklorists in the 1930s reversed the two terms in "culture life" to create the neologism *seikatsu bunka* (everyday life culture), stabilizing the term *seikatsu* in a folk world often imagined as timeless and unchanging.[37] This term enjoyed a more robust career in postwar parlance than the earlier *bunka seika-*

*tsu*, reflecting the growing tendency, particularly since the 1970s, to define the nation in terms of cultural uniqueness and the concurrent waning of cosmopolitan utopianism. Dreams of the "culture life" were still very much alive in the first two decades after the war, however. The catchphrase that had signified a goal for the striving middle classes of the 1920s was enshrined in Article 25 of the 1947 Constitution, which guaranteed a "healthy and cultural life" as the right of every Japanese citizen.[38]

Taken in aggregate, the type of house in which most Japanese lived made the complete transition in the course of the century, from an artifact made by the hands of its occupants and surrounding community and built to serve functions of larger communities as much as the family, to a commodity manufactured by corporations, sold and rented by other corporations, and serving isolated nuclear families, whose alienation from the process was complete. An individual migrating to Tokyo from the countryside any time between the 1920s and the 1960s might well have experienced the entire transformation. Bourgeois reform campaigns in the first three decades of the century had made dwelling a matter of consumption, accelerating the demise of the vernacular and casting the mold of the modern.

# Reference Matter

# Notes

For complete author names, titles, and publication information for work cited here by short forms, see the Bibliography, pp. 435–67. A date in parentheses following the title of a Japanese-language work indicates that the work can be found in the "Japanese-Language Primary Sources" section, pp. 435–42, of the Bibliography; those without a date appear in the "Japanese-Language Secondary Sources" section, pp. 443–55.

## Introduction

1. Sack, *Place, Modernity and the Consumer's World*, 3.

2. See, e.g., Csikszentmihalyi and Rochberg-Halton, *The Meaning of Things*; Hummon, "House, Home and Identity in America"; Putnam, "Regimes of Closure," 195–207.

3. See Friedrich Engels's critique of the "petit bourgeios socialism" of Proudhon in *The Housing Question*.

4. For a study that seeks to treat these aspects of Japanese modernity comprehensively, see Ri Takanori, *Hyōshō kūken no kindai*.

5. James L. Huffman, *Creating a Public*, 325. Benedict Anderson's discussion of "print capitalism" is an obvious point of reference for any discussion of reading and national consciousness, although he is by no means alone in stressing its importance.

6. Balibar, "The Nation Form: History and Ideology," in Balibar and Wallerstein, *Race, Nation, Class*, 90.

7. See Narusawa, "Social Order of Modern Japan"; and LeFebvre, *Production of Space*, 91. On parks, see Shirahata, *Kindai toshi kōenshi no kenkyū*.

8. Morse, *Japanese Homes and Their Surroundings*.

9. For related thoughts on the architectural vocabulary of premodern Chinese cities, see Bray, *Technology and Gender*.

10. This has been a central issue in feminist political theory; for lucid discussions, see Okin, "Gender, the Public and the Private"; and Olsen, "The Family and the Market."

11. Ariès, *Centuries of Childhood*.

12. For a provocative study that questions the assumptions of the literature on domesticity from a different angle, see Marcus, *Apartment Stories*.

13. See Ryan, *The Empire of the Mother*, for a critique of the earlier historiography.

14. On home economists and house design, see Wright, *Moralism and the Model Home*, 150–70.

15. Kashiwagi, *Kaji no seijigaku*, 183, 147. See also Wright, *Moralism and the Model Home*; and Dolores Hayden, *The Grand Domestic Revolution*, both of which restrict themselves to the United States. In contrast, Kashiwagi follows the movement's growth through the United States, Germany, and Japan, giving equal attention to each. This contrast with the English-language research seems to reveal the distinct position that Japanese intellectuals have occupied, and continue to occupy, in the modern global economy of knowledge—that is, not as the custodians of a peculiar "borrower culture," since all culture is constructed of borrowed elements, but as marginalized cosmopolitans, far more aware of developments in the West than Western intellectuals are of those in Japan.

16. On Key in Japan, see Miyake, "Kindai Nihon joseishi no saisōzō no tame ni," 94–121. On the protection of motherhood debate, see Rodd, "Yosano Akiko and the Taishō Debate over the 'New Woman,'" 189–200.

17. See Saarikangas, *Model Houses for Model Families*, 53–84.

18. Duben and Behar, *Istanbul Households*, 194–238.

19. Chatterjee, *The Nation and Its Fragments*, 116–34.

20. See Comaroff and Comaroff, "Home-Made Hegemony," 37–74.

21. Brown, "'Fine Arts and Fine People,'" 121–39.

22. Bourdieu, "Social Space and Symbolic Space," 637.

23. De Tocqueville described a town in which citizens distinguished 36 classes, some occupied by only three or four people (cited in Pilbeam, *The Middle Classes in Europe*, 4).

24. For a theoretical formulation of the idea of class as rhetoric, see also G. S. Jones, *Languages of Class*. Furbank, *Unholy Pleasure*, is an eloquent polemic against the idea of class, emphasizing that it is no more than rhetoric. Furbank nevertheless stresses the profundity of the social changes that produced the modern rhetoric of class and offers some valuable insights into the nature of class as what anthropologists would call an "emic category." Wahrman, *Imagining the Middle Class*, takes a

stance similar to that of Furbank in treating the idea of the middle class in the political discourse of nineteenth-century England.

25. See, e.g., Blackbourn and Evans, *The German Bourgeoisie*, xiv–xvi. This is one of several possible overlapping terms, each of which has its own nuance. Some writers have preferred the phrase "professional managerial class" (e.g., Ohmann, *Selling Culture*), but this is an imperfect fit for Meiji Japan, in which corporate structures were only emerging, and academics and self-employed professionals like doctors played a prominent role in shaping class identity. Others adopt Gramsci's encompassing conception of "intellectuals" as a group "whose work is socially defined as being based upon the possession and exercise of knowledge"; see Frow, *Cultural Studies and Cultural Value*, 90. This definition serves well for many of the producers of discourse in these pages but fails to accord with the common self-perceptions of most of the consumers, perhaps especially women.

26. Giddens, *The Class Structure of the Advanced Societies*, 111.

27. Nagatani Ken, "Kindai Nihon ni okeru jōryū kaikyū imeeji no hen'yō." I have drawn upon the insights of this fine essay but do not agree with the author's conclusion that because journalists frequently condemned aristocratic wealth, the upper class in Japan failed to provide a cultural model.

28. The *Ladies' Graphic* (*Fujin gahō*; inaugural issue, 1906) presented photographs of aristocratic households at the front of almost every issue.

29. M. A. Jones, "Children as Treasures," 42–43.

30. Yokoyama Gennosuke, *Meiji fugōshi* (1910), 107.

31. M. A. Jones, "Children as Treasures," 42.

32. See Minami, *Taishō bunka*.

33. With the exception of *puchiburu*, these labels are all occupationally based and therefore androcentric.

34. "The Japanese Middle-Class House," 13.

35. Hobsbawm, *The Age of Empire*, 180.

36. See Habermas, *The Structural Transformation of the Public Sphere*, 30, 36–37.

37. Gluck, *Japan's Modern Myths*, 9–10.

38. Moral discourse on everyday domestic practice was by no means invented by these Meiji ideologues. Late Tokugawa nativist scholar Hirata Atsutane, for example, built a theory of national identity on the foundation of everyday practices, including such domestic matters as eating customs (see Harootunian, *Things Seen and Unseen*).

39. Bourdieu (*Distinction*, 325, 360–66) restricts the term to marginal members of the intelligentsia whose economic insecurity compels them to sell whatever expertise they can. I have used it in a broader sense, to include anyone putting elite knowledge on the popular market.

40. Miller, *Material Culture and Mass Consumption*, 69–82.

41. A point also made by David Bromfield with respect to Perth, Australia, and Arjun Appadurai with respect to most of the world (for Bromfield, see Morris, "Metamorphoses at Sydney Tower," 385; Appadurai, *Modernity at Large*, 9).

42. Similar claims have been made even for England; see Richards, *The Commodity Culture of Victorian England*. The traditional view in Western historiography, however, has been to assume that cheap mass-produced goods form the foundation of all consumer cultures.

43. Minami, *Taishō bunka*, 187.

44. Newspapers and publishers of general-interest books had begun building mass markets earlier (Richter, "Marketing the Word").

45. Soseki, "Civilization and Modern-Day Japan," 273.

46. See Garon, "Rethinking Modernization and Modernity in Japanese History"; and idem, *Molding Japanese Minds*.

47. For the various new restrictions on public behavior contained in the "Ishiki kaii jōrei" of 1873 and for racial reform, see Ogi Shinzō, "Kaisetsu I," in Ogi et al., *Nihon kindai shisō taikei 23: fūzoku, sei*, 466–69, 471.

48. Ibid., 470.

49. See, e.g., Dohi, "Edo kara Tōkyō e no toshi ōpun supeesu no hen'yō."

50. Garon, *Molding Japanese Minds*, 231–33.

51. Ibid., 7, 17.

52. See the essays in Nishikawa and Matsumiya Hideharu, *Bakumatsu Meijiki no kokumin kokka keisei to bunka hen'yō*, a landmark publication in this new historiography of the nation-state.

53. Garon, *Molding Japanese Minds*, 20.

54. Ibid., 175–77.

## Chapter 1

1. There is a large literature on the *ie*, or family system. For a review of writings in English, see Uno, "Questioning Patrilineality."

2. Kano Masanao, *Senzen "ie" no shisō*, 51.

3. On the dual emergence of the *ie* and *katei*, see Nishikawa Yūko, "Sumai no hensen to 'katei' no seiritsu"; and idem, "The Changing Forms of Dwellings and the Establishment of the *Katei* (Home) in Modern Japan." I have drawn a number of insights for this discussion of the concept of *katei* and Meiji domestic space generally from Nishikawa's work.

4. Ueki Emori, "Nihonjin, ie no shisō," *Doyō shinbun*, Sept. 9, 1886; reprinted in idem, *Katei kaikaku, fujin kaihōron* (1971), 43–46.

5. "Shasetsu: Nihon no kazoku dai 1: ikka no waraku danran," *Jogaku zasshi*, no. 96 (Feb. 11, 1888), 1–4; "Nihon no kazoku, dai 2: Nihon ni kōfuku naru kazoku sukunashi," *Jogaku zasshi*, no. 97 (Feb. 18, 1888), 1–4.

6. Ueki Emori, "Shifu wa kyūko to bekkyo subeshi," *Kokumin no tomo*, no. 33 (Nov. 2, 1888); reprinted in idem, *Katei kaikaku, fujinron* (1971), 367–79.

7. Uchimura Kanzō, "Kurisuchan *hōmu*," *Jogaku zasshi*, no. 125 (Sept. 1, 1888): 4–8.

8. See Iwamoto Yoshiharu, "Tōzai jogaku hikan, 1," *Jogaku zasshi*, no. 403 (Oct. 27, 1894): 10–11; and the discussion of Iwamoto's shift in Yamamoto Toshiko, "Kindai Nihon ni okeru 'katei kyōiku' ishiki."

9. Ezawa Teruaki, *Wagaya kenpō* (1908).

10. *Katei*, strictly speaking, was only a quasi-neologism in the 1880s, since the combination of characters had been used occasionally before. They appear in the titles of a few Tokugawa moral texts. Between 1876 and 1877, Fukuzawa Yukichi published a magazine called *Katei sōdan*. Although its title may have been influential in spreading use of the term among Meiji intellectuals, *katei* seldom appeared elsewhere in this magazine, and the word's meaning was not discussed. *Katei* does not appear as an entry in dictionaries until the turn of the century; see Nakazawa Yōko, "*Katei*, uchi, kanai, *hōmu*." For a comprehensive survey of *katei* discourse in six Meiji journals, see Muta, "Images of the Family in Meiji Periodicals."

11. In contrast to *Katei zasshi*, *Jogaku zasshi* was as much about women as for them. Despite its central role in framing the Japanese home idea, prior to the 1890s its pages were dominated by fiction and Christian homilies rather than practical information or advice specifically targeted at women. A review of the field in the second issue of *Katei zasshi* classified *Jogaku zasshi* as a magazine for "woman-like men" (*joseiteki danshi*) (Nagahara Kazuko, "Heiminshugi no fujinron," 63).

12. Ōmura Jintarō, "Nihon no katei" (Aug. 1905); reprinted in idem, *Kyōiku sōsho*, 193–94.

13. "Jogaku sekai shūki zōkan: shakai hyaku seikatsu," *Jogaku sekai* 4, no. 12 (Sept. 15, 1904): 144. This characterization of Japanese society as already dominated by the "middle class" at the turn of the twentieth century would have surprised advocates on both sides of the 1970s debate on Japan as a "middle-class society." But since the fundamental disagreement in the 1970s was over who constituted the middle class, this odd statistic from 1904 serves as a reminder of the arbitrariness of "middle" as an objective category. For the middle-class society debate, see articles by Murakami Yasusuke, Kishimoto Shigenobu, and Tominaga Ken'ichi in *Japan Interpreter: A Quarterly Journal of Social and Political Ideas* 12, no. 1 (Winter 1978): 1–11. European political economists like Adam Smith and Emile Guizot also distinguished the "productive" middle from the "unproductive classes" (Bauman, *Memories of Class*, 37).

14. Kishimoto Ryūko, "Ōsaka shōka no katei," in "Jogaku sekai shūki zōkan: shakai hyaku seikatsu," 65–72.

15. "Kaigun shikan no seikatsu," in ibid., 85–96.

16. Ueki, "Shifu wa kyūko to bekkyo subeshi," in idem, *Katei kaikaku, fujinron* (1971), 378.

17. Reprinted in *Tōkyō-shi shikō shigai hen* 3, vol. 80 (1988): 410–42.

18. "Hibachi no hotori," *Jogaku zasshi*, no. 435 (Feb. 10, 1897): 5.

19. Itagaki Taisuke, "Fūzoku kairyō iken" (1903), 450–52. "Katei ongaku" became a central preoccupation of music magazines in the 1910s (see Hosokawa Shūhei, forthcoming).

20. Minyūsha, *Katei no waraku*, 98–101.

21. Manpuku Naokiyo, *Kokutei kyōkasho ni mietaru kaji kyōju shiryō* (1906), 77–78. In the 1890s, the term *sawakai*, which may be a translation of the English "tea party," also came to refer to political cliques in the Imperial Diet. In addition to promoting tea gatherings, the morals texts showed other signs of a reconception of family relations in this period. Muta Kazue ("Nihon kindaika to kazoku," 78–83) has shown that the textbook illustrations accompanying passages on filial piety and indebtedness to one's parents came to suggest affective bonds between parents and children in the 1890s and 1900s. In early illustrations children were shown bowing to their parents from outside a room, whereas in later illustrations they shared a common space. By 1911, primary-school morals textbooks included an illustration labeled *katei no tanoshimi* depicting grandparents, parents, and children gathered around a dinner table.

22. Ōhama Tetsuya, "'Risō no katei to genjitsu," 34.

23. Matsuura Masayasu, "Shufu no maki," in Dai Nihon kasei gakkai, *Katei no shiori: Fujin bunko* (1909), 267.

24. Chokei Dōjin, *Katei no kairaku* (1902), 4–7, 47–49. The paraphrase I have given here intentionally retains the causative verb forms of the original Japanese, which specify for each act one party giving a command and another receiving it.

25. Yanagita Kunio, *Meiji Taishōshi sesōhen* (1931), 79.

26. On dinner-table conversations, see M. A. Jones, "Children as Treasures," 58–60.

27. Examples from personal memoirs may be found in Yoshida Noboru, "Jiden ni yoru katei kyōiku no kenkyū," 256–57. The diary kept by Kobayashi Nobuko, wife of an executive in the Ōkura trading company, records her husband's return after the family mealtime on most days and mentions deliveries of food for her husband. When the family ate together, she made special note of it (Kobayashi Shigeki, *Meiji no Tōkyō seikatsu* [1991]). This book prints the diary interspersed with commentary by the diarist's son.

28. Sakai Toshihiko, *Katei no shin fūmi* (1901–2), 51.

29. Ibid.

30. For example, Koizumi Kazuko, *Kagu to shitsunai ishō no bunkashi*, 318. The modern shift from individual trays to a common table is intriguing from a compara-

tive perspective, since it appears to be a reverse of the process that occurred in Europe and the United States, where the refinement of table manners and increased variety of household goods brought the replacement of a common pot with individual dishes (Bushman, *Refinement of America*). Pollution taboos and strict rules of distribution are possible reasons for the widespread use of separate utensils by each household member in Japan before the twentieth century. Shared one-pot dishes such as *sukiyaki* and *yosenabe* were a new phenomenon when women's magazines began to promote them in the Taishō period (Kumakura Isao, "Enkyo to shite no shokutaku").

31. Zushi Shōichirō, *Ie* (1907), 289–92.

32. Described as a traditional virtue: Inouye, *Home Life in Tokyo*, 63–64; criticized as unhygienic: Ito Sakon, *Katei eisei kōwa*, 123.

33. Inoue Tadashi, "Shokutaku seikatsu shi no ryōteki bunseki," in Ishige Naomichi et al., *Gendai Nihon ni okeru katei to shokutaku*, 79, 115–18.

34. The three-member household depicted in Natsume Soseki's *Mon* provides one such example. Husband and wife eat together at a small table, and the maid has a separate tray and utensils.

35. The etymology of the name is uncertain, but some association is probable with the restaurants serving foreigners in Japanese treaty ports, known as "chabuya," a word deriving either from an onomatopoeia for food and drink or from the Anglicized Cantonese "chop suey" (Ishige Naomichi, "Shokutaku bunkaron," in Ishige et al., *Gendai Nihon ni okeru katei to shokutaku*, 24–25).

36. Nōshōmushō, Sanrinkyoku, *Mokuzai no kōgeiteki riyō*, 323–25; Inoue Tadashi, "Shokutaku seikatsushi no chōsa to bunseki," in Ishige Naomichi et al., *Gendai Nihon ni okeru katei to shokutaku*, 70.

37. See the correspondence course text "Tsūshin kyōju: Joshi kaseigaku" (Tsūshin kōgikai, 1889); reprinted in Tanaka Chitako and Tanaka Hatsuo, *Kaseigaku bunken shūsei zokuhen*, 65.

38. Cited in Nakagawa Kiyoshi, *Nihon no toshi kasō*, 137. Koizumi Kazuko (*Daidokoro dōgu imamukashi*, 25) suggests that the *chabudai* was adopted more quickly in working-class households because they tended to be more egalitarian.

39. See Inoue Tadashi, "Shokutaku seikatsu shi no ryōteki bunseki," in Ishige Naomichi et al., *Gendai Nihon ni okeru katei to shokutaku*, 72–74, for the range of factors that emerged from interviews.

40. Kōda Rohan, "Kaoku" (1897).

41. Tsuchiya Gensaku, *Kaoku kairyōdan* (1898), 2, 90–125 *passim*.

42. T.A., "Nihon kaoku kairyōdan ni tsuite," *Kenchiku zasshi*, no. 142 (Oct. 1898): 321.

43. Uchida Seizō, *Nihon no kindai jūtaku*, 16–23. The term "Western building" (*yōkan*) stood for a congeries of Japanese perceptions of "the West" and knowledge

from the anglocentric Meiji architectural education. The essential features that contemporaries agreed to be "Western" were solid walls with unexposed posts, tall door and window frames, and mat-less floors with chairs and tables.

44. Kitada Kyūichi, "Wayō setchū jūka," *Kenchiku zasshi*, no. 144 (Dec. 1898): 377–79.

45. The word "privacy" had appeared once previously in *Kenchiku zasshi*, intriguingly translated as *okumaritaru koto*, "being deeply recessed" (Uchida Seizō, "Meijiki no jūtaku kairyō ni mirareru puraibashii no ishiki ni tsuite").

46. Shiga Shigetsura, "Jūka (Kairyō no hōshin ni tsuite)," *Kenchiku zasshi*, nos. 194, 196, 199, 201, 202; Tsukamoto Yasushi, "Jūka no hanashi," *Kenchiku zasshi*, no. 199; Yahashi Kenkichi, "Honpō ni okeru kaoku kairyōdan," *Kenchiku zasshi*, no. 203.

47. The Meiji state created no public housing authority and, unlike the shogunate and *han* governments, imposed little regulation on house construction.

48. Monbushō, Gakumukyoku, *Shōgakkō kyōin jūtaku zuan* (1908), 8

49. The *nakarōka* plan as a type was first defined in Kimura Norikuni, "Nihon kindai toshi dokuritsu jūtaku yōshiki."

50. Aoki Masao and his students champion the thesis that the interior-corridor plan evolved through carpenters' responses to modern family needs (Aoki Masao et al., "Chūryū jūtaku no heimen kōsei ni kansuru kenkyū").

51. Particularly the plans of Australian houses introduced in *Kenchiku zasshi* in 1908.

52. Both Aoki and Kimura make use of the designs from pattern books, magazines, and public competitions but ignore the significance of these new media themselves.

53. Ōkawa Naomi, *Sumai no jinruigaku*, 178. Aoki traces the origins of this pattern to lower samurai houses, but Ōkawa asserts that the two linked rooms facing onto the garden are more characteristic of farmhouses.

54. For an interesting discussion of the gradual removal of funerary practices from the family and community in Tokyo, see Murakami Kōkyo, "Taishōki Tōkyō ni okeru sōsō girei no henka to kindaika."

55. Dai Nihon kasei gakkai, *Katei no shiori* (1909), 299.

56. Tsukamoto Hamako, *Shinpen kaji kyōhon*, 2: 145.

57. For a comparative study of gift-giving practices in Japan with an extensive survey of the anthropological literature, see Itō Mikiharu, *Zōyo kōkan no jinruigaku*; see also Befu, "Gift-Giving in Modernizing Japan." Kobayashi Nobuko's diary describes frequent drop-in visits at a socially well-connected bourgeois household at the turn of the century (the surviving portion was written in 1898–99). The custom of paying respects with small gifts was so pervasive and taken for granted, in fact, that at one point she recorded that a person no one in the house knew appeared at the door, perhaps by accident, and proffered a calling card, a box of red-bean rice,

and twenty-five *sen* worth of gift certificates for bonito flakes, which were duly accepted. The person disappeared before his mistake was recognized (Kobayashi Shigeki, *Meiji no Tōkyō seikatsu* [1991], 96).

58. Ōkawa Naomi, *Sumai no jinruigaku*, 170–71.

59. Yanagita Kunio, *Meiji Taishōshi sesōhen* (1931), 88. *Dei* was one of many regional terms for a large front room, typically wood-floored and facing the earth-floor space.

60. Ibid., 89.

61. Actual practice varied. Despite the implication in this criticism that people were sacrificing comfort to preserve their "best rooms," some families used the room as a bedroom on ordinary nights. Inouye (*Home Life in Tokyo*, 51) refers to this room as the "parlor" and indicates that families without a separate bedchamber slept in it.

62. Takahashi Bunjirō, *Shōgaku onna reishiki kunkai* (1882), is an early illustrated text of this kind.

63. See Kumakura Isao, *Bunka to shite no manaa*, 125–57.

64. For examples from magazines of the late Meiji period, see Aoki Masao et al., "Chūryū jūtaku no heimen kōsei ni kansuru kenkyū, 1," 89.

65. Ogasawara Seimu interview, "Raikyaku ni tai suru reigi," *Katei jogaku kōgi* 9 (Mar. 10, 1907): 80.

66. Quoted in Bushman, *Refinement of America*, 270.

67. See Koyama Shizuko, "'The Good Wife and Wise Mother' Ideology in Post–World War I Japan," 49–50.

## Chapter 2

1. For a succinct theoretical statement in Japanese, see Ueno Chizuko, *Shihonsei to kaji rōdō*.

2. Hirota Masaki, "Raifu saikuru no shoruikei," 263; Kawamura Kunimitsu, *Otome no inori*, 204–23.

3. Tsunemi Ikuo, *Kateika kyōikushi*, 120–21, 126.

4. Ibid. In 1995, *kateika* became mandatory for both sexes in junior high school.

5. "Kaisetsu: Kobayashi Yoshinori, 'Kōsei futsū kasei shōgaku,'" in Tanaka Chitako and Tanaka Hatsuo, *Kaseigaku bunken shūsei zokuhen: Meijiki I*.

6. Itō Yōjirō, *E iri nichiyō kaji yōhō: tsūzoku keizai* (1886), 22–23.

7. A seminal article by Sharon H. Nolte and Sally Ann Hastings, "The Meiji State's Policy Toward Women, 1890–1910," contrasts the ideological position of women in Meiji Japan and Victorian America by proposing a "cult of productivity" in place of the American "cult of domesticity." These textbooks confirm Nolte and Hastings's thesis with regard to Japan, since the books portray the house as a productive enterprise to which the housewife was expected to contribute. However, the greater difference between the domestic literature in nineteenth-century Japan and

the United States related to the meanings given to house and family rather than to the role given women within them. American writers like Catharine Beecher stressed the mistress's productive role as a household manager and repeatedly urged their readers to handle more housework themselves. Although many Victorian men described woman as the "weaker sex," domestic economy writers in the United States and England did not regard women as weak or passive any more than did their Japanese counterparts.

8. Tanaka Chitako and Tanaka Hatsuo, "Kaisetsu: seidoshiteki Meiji kasei kyōiku shōshi," in Tanaka and Tanaka, *Kaseigaku bunken shūsei zokuhen, Meijiki VIII*, 6–7.

9. Statistics from Koyama Shizuko, *Ryōsai kenbo to iu kihan*, 98; and Ōhama Tetsuya, *Ōe Sumi sensei*, 101–3.

10. Gokan Kikuno and Sakata Shizuko, *Kaji kyōkasho* (1898); reprinted in Tanaka Chitako and Tanaka Hatsuo, *Kaseigaku bunken shūsei zokuhen: Meijiki VIII*, 3–4. Tsukamoto Hamako, *Shinpen kaji kyōhon*, 1: 2–3.

11. See, e.g., Gokan and Sakata, *Kaji kyōkasho*, in Tanaka Chitako and Tanaka Hatsuo, *Kaseigaku bunken shūsei zokuhen: Meijiki VIII*, 4. The same language dominated arguments for the importance of the housewife's role in the *katei* columns and magazines; e.g., Iwamoto Yoshiharu, "Katei wa kokka nari," *Taiyō* 2, no. 5 (1896): 145–48.

12. Tsunemi, *Kateika kyōikushi*, 29.

13. *Katei no tomo* 1, no. 3 (Apr. 1903): 82; 2, no. 6 (Sept. 1904): 181.

14. See Imai Yasuko, "The Emergence of the Japanese *Shufu*."

15. Kano Masanao, *Senzen 'ie' no shisō*, 117–18.

16. This attitude toward young brides in farming households persisted into the 1970s. Simon Partner (*Assembled in Japan*, 142, 181–82) notes that it posed an obstacle to the diffusion of appliances in the postwar years, since the older generation saw no reason to spend money in order to save the labor of young women.

17. Kano Masanao, *Senzen 'ie' no shisō*, 127.

18. "Daidokoro raboratorii," *Jogaku zasshi*, no. 515 (Aug. 31, 1901): 20–21.

19. Inouye, *Home Life in Tokyo*, 159–61.

20. "Katei ni okeru shujin to jochū to no shin kankei" and "Jochū ran," *Fujin sekai* 4, no. 6 (May 1909): 102–5. The column continued irregularly afterward.

21. Tsuboi Hirofumi, "Seikatsu bunka to josei," 21.

22. Yamaguchi Masatomo, *Daidokoro kūkangaku*, 388.

23. Ishibashi Chūwa, *Shobutsu seihō myōjutsu kihō* (1886), 216–17.

24. Miyake Yonekichi, "Bungaku hakase Naka Michiyo-kun den"; quoted in Tsunemi Ikuo, *Kateika kyōikushi* 132–33. Naka hired the proprietress of a restaurant to give the classes. The proprietress in this passage, apparently written before 1920, is called *ryōriten no shufu*, "the mistress of a restaurant." Since the word *shufu* subse-

quently narrowed to refer only to housewives, in later Japanese she would have to be called *fujin keieisha* (lady manager) or *onna shujin* (female master).

25. Kosuge Keiko, *Nippon daidokoro bunkashi*, 87–88; quoted material on 88.

26. For a discussion of the most famous of the Meiji cooking schools, see Cwiertka, "Minekichi Akabori and His Role in the Development of Modern Japanese Cuisine," 68–80.

27. Kosuge Keiko, *Nippon daidokoro bunkashi*, 90–91. See also Yamakawa, *Women of the Mito Domain*, 60–61.

28. Aoki Sukekiyo, "Kaji keizaikun" (1881); reprinted in Tanaka Chitako and Tanaka Hatsuo, *Kaseigaku bunken shūsei zokuhen: Meijiki I*, 232–35.

29. See, e.g., Sakata Shizuko and Gokan Kikuno, *Kōtō jogakkōyō kaji kyōkasho* (1912), 2nd ed., 1: 72–73 (charts), 95–96; Tsukamoto Hamako, *Shinpen kaji kyōhon*, 44–52.

30. Handa Tatsuko, "Taishōki no kateika kyōiku," 84.

31. Kondō Kōzō, *Shinpen kaji kyōkasho* (1930), 1: 193.

32. Food-related questions made up two to three times more of the examination material than any other subject on tests given between 1912 and 1924 (Ōmoto Moichirō, *Bunken kaji gōkaku shishin* [1925], 27).

33. See Tanaka Satoshi, *Eisei tenrankai no yokubō*, for a discussion of these threats to the home in the context of Ministry of Education exhibitions on hygiene.

34. Amano Seisai, *Daidokoro kairyō* (1907), 1–3. The Tenpō period (1830–43) was proverbial for the feudal past and for anything out of date.

35. Ibid., 12.

36. Comings and goings in the kitchen of a small family house with one maid are described in Natsume Soseki's novel *I Am a Cat*, written in 1905. The house in the novel is modeled on one in which the author himself lived. See Takahashi Akiko and Baba Masako, *Daidokoro no hanashi*, 52–56, for a discussion of Soseki's kitchen.

37. Amano Seisai, *Daidokoro kairyō* (1907), 78, 118, 180, 187, 196, 200–202.

38. Ibid., 10–11, 42, 76, 99.

39. Ibid., 123–24. On Kitazato, see Bartholomew, *Formation of Science in Japan*.

40. Amano Seisai, *Daidokoro kairyō* (1907), 54–57. Efforts like this to promote practices of purification in the home came at a time of heightened anxiety about promiscuous mixing in urban and national space as well. Bubonic plague had caused a panic when it came to Japan through the port of Kobe in 1899. This precipitated a flurry of municipal regulations concerning public hygiene. In Tokyo, a citywide cleaning campaign was ordered, and hygiene inspectors accompanied by policemen went from house to house posting certificates of inspection on doors and gates (see Yamashita Shigetami, "Tōkyōshi sōjihō jikkō no keikyō," *Fūzoku gahō*, no. 202 [Jan. 10, 1900]: 11–13). In the same year foreigners had been allowed residence in internal areas of Japan beyond the designated treaty ports. "Mixed residence" (*naichi zakkyo*)

was a subject of heated controversy and was seen by its opponents as a threat to territorial and ethnic unity.

41. Ōmoto Moichirō, *Bunken kaji gōkaku shishin* (1925), 4–26 *passim*.

42. Ochiai Shigeru, *Arau bunka shiwa*, 148, 172, 177. Industrial uses account for part of this rapid expansion during World War I, but Japanese households were also increasing their consumption. Sales of one major brand for household use rose between 20 and 40 percent annually in the same seven years. On soap marketing, see Rubinfien, "Commodity to National Brand"; for Kaō brand sales figures, see ibid., 402–3.

43. Amano Seisai, *Daidokoro kairyō* (1907), 118.

44. Ibid., 203.

45. "Sakurada fujin no kaji seiri," *Fujin gahō*, no. 45 (Apr. 1918).

46. "Oryōri," in ibid.

47. Yanagita Kunio, *Meiji Taishōshi sesōhen* (1931), 11.

48. Yamaguchi Masatomo, "Gasutō kara ōbun made," in Nakane Kimirō et al., *Gasutō kara ōbun made*, 163.

49. Satō Kenji, "Meiji kokka to katei ideorogii," 84–91. My analysis of *Shokudōraku* relies substantially on Satō's essay.

50. As a vehicle for domestic ideology, *Shokudōraku* offers an interesting comparison to Hannah More's evangelist novel *Coelebs In Search of a Wife*, published in England roughly one century earlier. In the Japanese tale of culinary evangelism, kitchen expertise takes the place of Christian virtue as the overriding qualification for the model wife. For a discussion of *Coelebs in Search of a Wife* (originally published in 1808), see Hall, "The Early Formation of Victorian Domestic Ideology," 9–14.

51. Satō Kenji, "Meiji kokka to katei ideorogii," 91.

52. Murai Gensai, *Zōho chūshaku Shokudōraku* (1903–4), "Haru no maki," 180.

53. Ibid., "Natsu no maki," 238–39.

54. Ibid., 244–45.

55. Ibid., "Haru no maki," 191–93, 200–202.

56. Ibid., 209.

57. Yamaguchi Masatomo, *Daidokoro kūkangaku*, 374–76.

58. Murai Gensai, *Zōho chūshaku Shokudōraku* (1903–4), "Natsu no maki," 254.

59. Kosuge Keiko, *Nippon daidokoro bunkashi*, 63.

60. Yamaguchi Masatomo, "Gasutō kara ōbun made," in Nakane Kimirō et al., *Gasutō kara ōbun made*, 203–5.

61. Kosuge Keiko, *Nippon daidokoro bunkashi*, 62, 69.

62. Sugita Kōichi, "Daidokoro no henka to chōri e no eikyō," in Yamaguchi Masatomo and Ishige Naomichi, *Katei no shokuji kūkan*, 58. The oil-stove advertisement reportedly began in 1905.

63. Kosuge Keiko, *Nippon daidokoro bunkashi*, 63; Ezura Tsuguto, "Shomin jūkyo no hensen to gasu setsubi," in Nakane Kimirō et al., *Gasutō kara ōbun made*, 136.

64. Kosuge Keiko, *Nippon daidokoro bunkashi*, 64–65.

65. Ōmoto Moichirō, *Bunken kaji gōkaku shishin* (1925), 5.

66. "Nenryō no keizaiteki kenkyū," *Fujin no tomo*, Jan. 1912; quoted in Kosuge Keiko, *Nippon daidokoro bunkashi*, 66–67.

67. The maid who squandered a week's worth of gas by keeping the stove burning continuously was also following the usual practice in wood- or coal-burning kitchens, where one fire was kept smoldering as long as possible to provide a source from which to ignite coal for cooking and heating elsewhere, as well as to keep the kitchen warm.

68. Murai Gensai, *Zōho chūshaku Shokudōraku* (1903–4), "Haru no maki," 181.

69. Household governance and economics overlapped in suggestive ways in late Tokugawa and early Meiji writing and translation on the subject of economy. A *bakumatsu*-period English dictionary translated the word *economy* as *kaji suru* (performing domestic matters). Fukuzawa Yukichi, who was well attuned to money matters, was among the first translators to advocate translating "economy" in English scholarly works as *keizaigaku* but offered a gloss that reveals how grounded in the everyday the concept remained in his mind: "*Keizaigaku* is the study of wealth. . . . Therefore, *keizaigaku* is the means of correctly ordering the constructive rules that exist between people and things (*hito to mono no aida ni sonsuru zōka no teisoku*)" (quoted in Suzuki Shūji, *Bunmei no kotoba*, 77).

70. Fujita Hisamichi, "Kaji keizairon" in Tanaka Chitako and Tanaka Hatsuo, *Kaseigaku bunken shūsei zokuhen: Meijiki I*, 260.

71. Ibid., 276.

72. I have relied on the third edition: Hani Motoko, *Katei no tomo kakeibo* (1906). Other categories of expenditure in this volume are education, furniture, clothing, dwelling, recreation, personal cultivation, occupation, special, and emergency expenses. The "Hani Motoko Account Book" is widely known in Japan and continues to be published annually in much the same format.

73. "Katei nōritsu zōshin gō," *Fujin no tomo*, Mar. 1917. In 1931, the operative term was "rationalization." Hani's school sponsored a "Rationalization of Home Life Exhibition" and the magazine again published a special issue; see "Katei seikatsu gōrika gō," *Fujin no tomo* 25, no. 12 (Dec. 1931). "Industrial rationalization" had been proclaimed a priority of state policy by the Hamaguchi Cabinet in 1929. The rhetoric of domestic reform in the twentieth century thus mutated through adoption of the language of industry. On Taylorism in Japan, see Tsutsui, *Manufacturing Ideology*.

74. Edo no aru machi Ueno, Yanesen kenkyūkai, *Shinpen Yanesen roji jiten*, 171–72.

75. "Kaoku kairyōan," *Katei no tomo* 1, no. 3 (Apr. 1903): 70. It merits noting that men in many traditional crafts in Japan continue to work sitting on the floor, as do

seamstresses making kimono. Floor-sitting has been banished from the kitchen, however.

76. "Kateiyō ryōridai," *Fujin no tomo* 8, no. 7 (July 1914), 0-2 (advertisement). For a discussion of this worktable, see Kosuge Keiko, *Nippon daidokoro bunkashi*, 182–84.

77. Yamaguchi Masatomo, "Gasutō kara ōbun made," in Nakane Kimirō et al., *Gasutō kara ōbun made*, 172 (photograph).

78. Yamada Kikusui, "Dōsa keizai no ue kara kufū shita daidokoro," *Fujin no tomo katei nōritsu zōshin gō* (Mar. 1917): 109.

79. Uchida Seizō, *Amerikaya shōhin jūtaku*: 90–91. Christine Frederick was advocating the same kind of application of Taylorist thinking to kitchens in the United States at this time. It is unclear whether Misumi and others in Japan had read her work, which seems not to have been available in Japanese until the 1930s. Since Frederick's influence in Europe is documented, however, her ideas may have come to Japan indirectly.

80. "Anka de tateta benrina ie," *Shufu no tomo*, Mar. 1917: 35–39. In May, the magazine reported that it had received a particularly enthusiastic response to this article from readers.

81. Sakata Shizuko and Gokan Kikuno, *Kōtō jogakkōyō kaji kyōkasho* (1912), 2nd ed., 1: 14–15 illustrations.

82. See, e.g., Yoshimura Chizu, *Jitchi ōyō kaji kyōkasho* (1919), 1: 11; Ōe Sumiko, *Ōyō kaji kyōkasho*, 1: 15; Ishizawa Yoshimaro, *Kaji shin kyōkasho* (1926), 1: 22–23.

83. See, e.g., Kondō Kōzō, *Shinpen kaji kyōkasho* (1930), 1: 86.

84. Quoted in Kosuge Keiko, *Nippon daidokoro bunkashi*, 193–94.

85. "Daidokoro ima mukashi 1: Hajimete miru benrina mono ni azen," *Asahi shinbun*, Aug. 23, 1994.

86. Suzuki Yuriko, "Juka josei no seikatsu," 133–51. Baishi was the mother of historian Rai Sanyō.

87. For analysis of the role of citizen groups in the promotion of state reform agendas, see Garon, "Rethinking Modernization and Modernity in Japanese History"; and idem, *Molding Japanese Minds*.

## Chapter 3

1. Jinno Yuki, *Shumi no tanjō*, 7–9.

2. Tsubouchi Shōyō, "Shumi," *Shumi* 1:1 (June, 1906): 1.

3. Hatsuda Tōru, *Hyakkaten no tanjō*, 60, 66–69. The advertisement is quoted from the *Jiji shinpō*, Jan. 2, 1905.

4. Seidensticker, *High City, Low City*, 109.

5. There is a growing body of research on Mitsukoshi. In English, see Aso, "New Illusions"; and Moeran, "The Birth of the Japanese Department Store." See Enami Shigeyuki and Mitsuhashi Toshiaki, *Saiminkutsu to hakuranka*, 372–79, for a provoca-

tive analysis of the epistemology of consumer desire in the context of department store growth during this period.

6. "Shumi hakkō no shushi," *Shumi* 1, no. 1 (June 1906): 3.

7. Hatsuda Tōru, *Hyakkaten no tanjō*, 88–90.

8. Eagleton, *Ideology of the Aesthetic*, 23.

9. Guth, *Art, Tea and Industry*, 91–93.

10. Sugimoto Buntarō, *Zukai Nihon zashiki no kazarikata* (1912), 2–8.

11. Sugimoto Buntarō, *Nihon jūtaku shitsunai sōshoku hō* (1910), 1–14.

12. Ibid., 105.

13. Sugimoto Buntarō, *Zukai Nihon zashiki no kazarikata* (1912), 156.

14. Matsuura Masayasu, "Shufu no maki," in Dai Nihon kasei gakkai, *Katei no shiori* (1909), 242. The operative term in this and similar cautionary writing was *kanka*, which meant something like "influence," with specifically moral connotations.

15. Sugimoto Buntarō, *Zukai Nihon zashiki no kazarikata* (1912), 23.

16. Sakata Shizuko and Gokan Kikuno, *Joshi sahōsho* (1906), 27–35.

17. For an example of decorating advice that demonstrates both Sugimoto's approach, giving conventional prescriptions for the formally correct guest room, and a Victorian stress on the moral influence of decoration in rooms for daily use, see Hoshino Shinnosuke, "Shitsunai sōshoku no hanashi," *Fujin no tomo* 1, no. 10 (Nov. 1908), 294–97; 2no. 3 (Mar. 1909), 113–14.

18. Shimoda Utako, *Kaji yōketsu* (1899), 263, 269. Almost identical language can be found in many other nineteenth-century texts.

19. Ibid.

20. Sakata Shizuko and Gokan Kikuno, *Joshi sahōsho* (1906), 64; Kondō Masakazu, *Kasei hōten* (1906), 98, 112.

21. See, e.g., "Isu ni yoru kokoroe" (How to sit in a chair), in Iwase Matsuko, *Wayō shoreishiki annai* (1905), 84–85.

22. Sugimoto Buntarō, *Nihon jūtaku shitsunai sōshoku hō* (1910), 54; Shimoda Utako, *Kaji yōketsu* (1899), 262.

23. Shimoda Utako, *Kaji yōketsu* (1899), 269.

24. Kondō Masakazu, "Kōtō kanri no seikatsu," in *Jogaku sekai shūki zōkan: shakai hyaku seikatsu* (1904), 56, 64. This author would appear to be the same Kondō Masakazu who wrote *Kasei hōten* cited in Fig. 3.3 of this chapter. He bears the title of lecturer in an institution of etiquette instruction (*reihō kōshūkai shihan*).

25. Sugimoto Buntarō, *Nihon jūtaku shitsunai sōshoku hō* (1910), 173–74.

26. *Fujin gahō teiki zōkan: shitsunai sōshoku* (1906). For further discussion of these interiors, see Sand, "Was Meiji Taste in Interiors 'Orientalist'?" The formal mantelpiece display was not of strictly Japanese invention. Writing in 1885, Edward Morse (*Japanese Homes and Their Surroundings*, 136) had criticized the same rigid symmetry in the decoration of American mantelpieces, contrasting it with the

asymmetry of Japanese interiors. Thus, there were clear Victorian precedents for the formal treatment that mantelpieces received in Japan. Morse's Arts and Crafts taste encouraged him to caricature his own countrymen's habits, however. By the time that these photographs were published in the *Ladies' Graphic*, the Arts and Crafts had contributed to a general simplification and loosening of the rigidity of Victorian parlor decoration. On American interiors, see Halttunen, "From Parlor to Living Room," 157–90. On the popularization of American Arts and Crafts, see Wright, *Moralism and the Model Home*, 126–32.

27. Quoted in Koizumi Kazuko, "Kagu," in Ōta Hirotarō, *Jūtaku kindaishi*, 212.

28. Jinno Yuki, *Shumi no tanjō*, 95–102.

29. This mode of division has since become a stock device for the Japanesque interiors of public buildings demanding signs of national or "traditional" taste, such as wedding banquet halls, although "weaponry" has disappeared from the decorator's vocabulary since World War II.

30. Iwaya Sazanami, *Pari no bettenchi* (1908); quoted in Jinno Yuki, *Shumi no tanjō*, 102.

31. Hatsuda Tōru, *Hyakkaten no tanjō*, 157.

32. Jinno Yuki, *Shumi no tanjō*, 90–91.

33. Quoted in Hatsuda Tōru, "Meiji, Taishōki ni okeru Mitsukoshi no kagu to shitsunai sōshoku," 1421.

34. Shimoda Utako, *Fujin jōshiki no yōsei*, 269.

35. Nakatani Norihito, *Kokugaku, Meiji, kenchikuka*, 34.

36. Fujimori Terunobu, *Nihon no kindai kenchiku*, 1: 214.

37. On the question of defining national identity in Meiji buildings, see Jonathan Reynolds, "Japan's Imperial Diet Building and the Construction of a National Identity," *Art Journal* 5, no. 3 (1996): 538–47.

38. For further analysis of the separation of function and aesthetics that was part of the lesson learned by Meiji architects from English eclecticism, see Nakatani Norihito, *Kokugaku, Meiji, kenchikuka*, 57–64. As Suzuki Hiroyuki pithily remarks, the eclectic revival in England "made style into an overcoat" (quoted in ibid., 61).

39. Kinoshita Naoyuki, *Bijutsu to iu misemono*, 21, 24.

40. Itō Chūta, "Aakitekuchūru no hongi o ron shite sono yakuji o sentei shi waga zōka gakkai no kaimei o nozomu," *Kenchiku zasshi* 87 (1894); reprinted in Fujimori Terunobu, *Nihon kindai shisō taikei 19: toshi, kenchiku*, 406. See also Kashiwagi Hiroshi, *Kindai Nihon no sangyō dezain shisō*, 57–58. Part of what Itō took issue with in the term *zōka* was that it contained the Chinese character for "house." The character did not refer strictly to dwelling architecture, however, since in terms such as *kaoku*, it could mean any form of built shelter. Itō asserted that tombs, memorials, and religious architecture were not *kaoku*. *Kaoku* continued to be used in some public documents as a designation that included nonresidential buildings for some decades

afterward, however. Today, *kaoku* and the Chinese character for "house" refer only to dwelling houses. It is also interesting to note what went on Itō's list of non-*kaoku* architecture in light of the time that this article was published. Itō included first memorials and triumphal gates, the quintessential built expressions of the modern imperial state. This was the high period of monumental construction among the European powers. Japan's first triumphal gate would be built the following year to celebrate the victory in the Sino-Japanese War and the achievement of empire status. Itō also described the construction of temple halls and pagodas as "managed" by architects. In fact, no academy-trained Japanese architect had played any direct role in Buddhist or Shinto building projects before Itō himself, with the assistance of master carpenter Kigo Kiyoyoshi, designed the historical re-creation of Heian Shrine, which was completed the year after this article was published; see Cherie Wendelken, "Tectonics of Japanese Style."

41. Fujimori Terunobu, *Nihon no kindai kenchiku*, 2: 12–13.

42. Nishiyama Uzō, *Nihon no sumai*, 2: 27.

43. Fujimori Terunobu, *Nihon no kindai kenchiku*. See also Don Choi, "Educating the Architect in Meiji Japan."

44. For instances of this ping-ponging of design motifs, see *Japan and Britain*.

45. Quoted in Hasegawa Takashi, *Toshi kairō*, 124.

46. Fujimori Terunobu, *Nihon no kindai kenchiku*, 2: 32–35.

47. Uchida Seizō, *Nihon no kindai jūtaku*, 47–49.

48. Fujimori Terunobu, *Nihon no kindai kenchiku*, 2: 8

49. Edward Morse, unquestionably the most careful Western observer of Japanese dwelling architecture in the nineteenth century, recorded many examples of *sukiya* style and was well aware of the large influence of tea aesthetics on the houses he saw. *Japanese Homes and Their Surroundings* nevertheless imparted the strong impression that the rusticated style of interior of which the author was fond represented the ordinary run of house construction. In fact, it was the province of a coterie of literati and wealthy men in retirement. There may well have been some popularization of *sukiya*-style features in residential building (and inns) during the nineteenth century, but *sukiya* was still far from being typical. The owners of the houses Morse saw, where indicated, were men such as "an antiquarian," or "a famous potter in Kioto"; in other words, men who were likely to be intimate with the cultural rules of *suki*. The *tatami* rooms he sketched were all guest rooms or tearooms, the rooms that would best exhibit *sukiya* style.

50. Ishida Jun'ichirō, "Takeda Goichi," 36–37.

51. This assessment is based on a list of works in Hakubutsukan Meiji mura, *Takeda Goichi*; and clients' biographies in the who's-who guide *Jinji kōshinroku*, 1936.

52. Uchida Seizō, *Nihon no kindai jūtaku*, 49–51.

53. Fujimori, *Nihon no kindai kenchiku*, 2: 35–36, 155.

54. Begun in 1898, the Viennese Secession was already over as a formal movement by 1903, when the last issue of the journal *Ver Sacrum* was published. On revolutionary movements in architecture around the turn of the twentieth century, see Frampton, *Modern Architecture*, 42–83. On the Viennese Secession in architecture, see Schorske, *Fin de Siecle Vienna*, 79–95; and Shedel, "Art and Identity." Aesthetic movements did not carry their politics intact even across borders within Europe, as Schorske (303–4 and 304 note) points out with regard to Art Nouveau and early modernism generally in England, France, and Austria.

55. Hatsuda Tōru, *Hyakkaten no tanjō*, 158.

56. Uchida Seizō, *Amerikaya shōhin jūtaku*, 35–38.

57. For a provocative discussion of furniture and interiors in the age of mass production in the United States, see Miles Orvell, *The Real Thing*, esp. chap. 2, "A Hieroglyphic World."

58. Koizumi Kazuko, *Wa kagu*, 155–56.

59. The chests and other articles in a woman's dowry could be elegantly ornamented, although outside the aristocracy they tended to be made of unlacquered wood. The quality of materials and the detail work were finely gauged to display family wealth within the bounds of local customs and sumptuary regulations.

60. On dowries in general, particularly regional variations, see Koizumi Kazuko, *Tansu*, 252–64. Describing what he regarded as typical of the "middle class" in 1910, Jūkichi Inouye (*Home Life in Tokyo*, 181) gave a list similar to that given here, adding "various utensils needed for tea-making and flower-arrangement, a koto, and work-boxes, and sometimes even kitchen utensils." The flower-arrangement and tea utensils, along with the koto (a thirteen-string musical instrument), were the tools of the ladylike accomplishments expected of young women of the educated elite before marriage.

61. The *Minshū kanrei ruiju*, surveys of local legal practices compiled in the 1870s for preparation of the Civil Code, describe a wide range of dowry customs. One strong commonality was that the use of land or cash for dowry was hemmed in with regulations and taboos. There is the suggestion here of an old association of women with material property and men with land and cash; see John Henry Wigmore, *Law and Justice in Tokugawa Japan*, pt. VII: "Persons: Civil Customary Law."

62. Koizumi Kazuko, *Tansu*, 258.

63. Advertisements for dowry chests made by Tokyo cabinetmakers appeared in *Jikō* 3, no. 9 (Aug. 1903) and elsewhere. The lavish dowry prepared for Fumiko, daughter of publishing magnate Ōhashi Shintarō, is illustrated in ten photographs along with a cameo of the bride and groom under the title "Tōten nite chōsei shitaru gokonrei chōdo," in *Mitsukoshi* 2, no. 8 (Aug. 1912): 6–7.

64. Koizumi Kazuko, *Tansu*, 193–99.

65. Fujii Kenjirō, "Seiyō no shitsunai sōshoku to Nihon no shitsunai sōshoku," *Shumi* 2, no. 11 (Nov. 1907): 103, 104.

66. Ibid., 105. The writer omitted mention of the Japanese popular art of the woodblock print, which was not regarded as part of the field of art by most connoisseurs of this period.

67. Suzuna Sei, "Keisaku o atsumetaru kaigashitsu," *Jikō* 6, no. 3 (Mar. 1908): 4.

68. Ibid. Paintings were also reproduced in *Jikō* 6, no. 1 (Jan. 1908) and 6, no. 2 (Feb. 1908). Like the Art Department itself, the descriptive language here mixes native and Western idioms in what is ultimately a Western-derived mode of critical contextualization. Art criticism in Meiji took shape in close relation to the international expositions. For analysis of the positions shaping the critical field in its initial stage, see Ōkuma Toshiyuki, "Meijiki ikō no bijutsu hihyō ron I."

69. Quoted in Hatsuda Tōru, *Hyakkaten no tanjō*, 146.

70. Kaneko Seikichi, *Nihon jūtaku kenchiku zuan hyakushu* (1913). The plan without an alcove was for a one-room house.

71. Quoted in Hatsuda Tōru, *Hyakkaten no tanjō*, 147.

72. Kinoshita, Naoyuki, *Bijutsu to iu misemono*, 272.

73. *Yomiuri shinbun*, *Tōkyō nichinichi shinbun*, *Yorozu chōhō*, and *Chūgai shōgyō shinpō*; all quoted in *Mitsukoshi*, 2, no. 6 (June 1912): 2–5.

74. "Mitsukoshi no yōga tenrankai," *Mitsukoshi* 2, no. 13 (Dec. 1912): 3–8.

75. For a theoretical discussion of middle-brow culture, see Bourdieu, *Field of Cultural Production*, 125–31.

76. Minami Hiroshi, *Taishō bunka*, 51.

77. Although native dowry pieces could be described as *kagu*, they were kept discrete from Western furniture. A booklet of photographs (*Mitsukoshi shashinchō* [n.d.]) showing the store interior around 1915 includes pictures of a "Japanese Furniture Department" and a "Western-Style Interior Decoration Department." The Japanese furniture is grouped and stacked in sets, each of which could constitute one dowry, with *tansu*, mirror and toilet-box, sewing box, and a tea-shelf. No *nagamochi* are shown. This may reflect the fact that they were falling out of use in urban households. The preface to this booklet indicates that it was published to commemorate the opening of the store's new building in October 1914.

78. See Sand, "Bungalows and Culture Houses."

79. *Mitsukoshi*, 1, no. 5, 48–49; 1, no. 9, 55; 1, no. 11, 33.

80. "Gubijinsō," "Nowake," and "Sanshirō"; quoted in Kayano Yatsuka, *Kindai Nihon dezain bunkashi*, 229.

81. "Kenshō kagu zuan chinretsukai," *Mitsukoshi* 3, no. 6 (June 1913), 3–4.

82. Ōkuma Yoshikuni, "Sesesshon shiki no ryūkō o mite," *Kenchiku sekai* 8, no. 4 (Apr. 1914): 6.

83. Ibid., 6–7; Oka Chiyoji, "Sesesshon no yūgi," *Kenchiku gahō* 7, no. 7 (July 1916): 25–27; "Aki no kita sesesshon shiki," *Kenchiku sekai* 10, no. 3 (Mar. 1916). For a rough recapitulation of the debate, see Itō Chūta, "Sesesshon no kaiko," *Kenchiku shinchō* 9, no. 6 (June 1928).

84. Jinno Yuki, *Shumi no tanjō*, 109. Hayashi himself felt that among European styles, Louis XVI best suited Japan.

85. Quoted in Hatsuda Tōru, *Hyakkaten no tanjō*, 161–62.

## Chapter 4

1. Hara Takeshi, *"Minto" Ōsaka tai "teito" Tōkyō*, 21–27, 66–69. Tramlines were distinguished by the fact that they ran on public thoroughfares rather than land privately owned by the company. The director of the Hanshin railroad created a precedent by receiving the license for a line of which only 5 out of 30 kilometers ran on city streets. For the politics of national rail development, see Erickson, *Sound of the Whistle*.

2. In addition to Hara Takeshi, *"Minto" Ōsaka tai "teito" Tōkyō*, see also Tsuganesawa Toshihiro, *Takarazuka senryaku*; and the essays in "Hanshinkan modanizumu" ten jikkō iinkai, *Hanshinkan modanizumu*.

3. Founded in 1907 as the Minō-Arima Electric Tramline (Minō Arima denki kidō) and then renamed Minō Electric Tramline, the rail line became Hanshin kyūkō dentetsu (Osaka-Kobe rapid railroad), or Hankyū, in 1918.

4. Tsuganesawa Toshihiro, *Takarazuka senryaku*, 28–29.

5. Ibid., 45. For a historical and anthropological exploration of the revue, see Robertson, *Takarazuka*.

6. Inose Naoki, *Mikado no shōzō*, 163.

7. "Kōgai seikatsu no fukuin: wazuka jū ni en no geppu de kaeru hatenkō no kōgai jūtaku to tochi," *Sanyō suitai*, 1, no. 1 (July 1913): 4–5.

8. Shūkan Asahi, *Nedanshi nenpyō*, 51.

9. Kondō Masakazu, "Kōtō kanri no seikatsu," in *Jogaku shūki zōkan: shakai hyaku seikatsu* (1904), 64.

10. Ōsakashi toshi jūtakushi henshū iinkai, *Machi ni sumau*, 176. This study cites an edict issued by the Osaka *machi bugyō* office in 1793.

11. Ibid., 180–81.

12. Quoted in Nakagawa Osamu, *Jūzei toshi*, 162.

13. Ibid., 190–191.

14. Advertisements in *Sanyō suitai* 1, no. 1 (July 1913), 6; reproduced in Keihanshin kyūkō dentetsu kabushiki gaisha, *Keihanshin kyūkō dentetsu gojūnenshi*, 119.

15. Gamachi Norio, "Fudōsan torihiki no hensen katei," 97.

16. Writing in 1919, journalist Hasegawa Nyozekan claimed that the suburban boom in Osaka was led by young men who came to the city from elsewhere and dis-

covered to their frustration that there were no lodgings for "student-style gentlemen" (*gakuseifū no shinshi*) of the kind found in the Hongō district of Tokyo (quoted in Nakagawa Osamu, *Jūzei toshi*, 144–45).

17. Ibid., 150; see p. 151 for a photograph.

18. Quoted in Suzuki Yūichirō, "'Kōgai seikatsu' kara 'den'en toshi' e," 86.

19. "Ikanaru tochi o erabu beki ka, ikanaru kaoku ni sumu beki ka" (1910); reproduced in Keihanshin kyūkō dentetsu kabushiki gaisha, *Keihanshin kyūkō dentetsu gojūnenshi*, 118–20.

20. "Sakurai no hanjikan," *Sanyō suitai* 1, no. 1 (July 1913): 9.

21. M.T. fujin dan, "Kodomo no tame ni kōgai e," *Sanyō suitai*, 3, no. 9 (May 1916): 18–19.

22. Both Tsuganesawa Toshihiro (*Takarazuka senryaku*) and Hara Takeshi (*"Minto" Ōsaka tai "teito" Tōkyō*) use the term, as do Sugiyama Mitsunobu and Yoshimi Shun'ya ("Kindai Nihon ni okeru yūtopia undō to jaanarizumu"). These authors may have been influenced by Robert Fishman's study of suburbs in England and the United States, *Bourgeois Utopias*.

23. Kobayashi Ichizō, *Itsuō jijoden* (1952), 182.

24. "Ikanaru tochi o erabu beki ka ikanaru kaoku ni sumu beki ka" (1909); reproduced in Yoshiwara Masayuki, *Hanshin kyūkō dentetsu nijūgonenshi*, "Tochi jūtaku keiei no gansō," 3–4. This company history reproduces a different portion of the original pamphlet from that found in Keihanshin kyūkō dentetsu kabushiki gaisha, *Keihanshin kyūkō dentetsu gojūnenshi*.

25. Natsume Soseki, *I Am a Cat*, 215.

26. I borrow the notion of environmental thinking, or environmentalism, from a study by Nicholas Green (*The Spectacle of Nature*) of the connections between urban discourse and the commodification of landscape in France.

27. See Jannetta, *Epidemics and Mortality in Early Modern Japan*, 188–207. Jannetta examines data from before the Meiji period to explain what had shielded Japanese populations from many of these epidemics.

28. Kano Masanao, "Korera, minshū, eisei gyōsei," 267.

29. Anbo Norio, *Minato Kōbe, korera, pesuto, suramu*, 141. This is a detailed study of the biases underlying hygiene and urban policy, as well as of the role of newspapers in exacerbating them.

30. Narita Ryūichi, "Kindai toshi to minshū," 27.

31. Quoted in Yasujima Hiroyuki and Soshiroda Akira, *Nihon bessōshi nōto*, 46–47.

32. Ogi Shinzō et al., *Edo Tōkyōgaku jiten*, 798, 860. An English translation of *Hototogisu* was published as *Nami-ko: A Realistic Novel*, trans. Sakae Shioya and E. F. Edgett (Tokyo: Yurakusha, 1905).

33. Tsuganesawa Toshihiro, *Takarazuka senryaku*, 82.

34. Oda Yasunori, *Toshi kōgai no keisei.*

35. Nakagawa Osamu, *Jūzei toshi*, 148.

36. Maeda Ai, *Toshi kūkan no naka no bungaku*, 187–89. The quotation (189) is from Nagayo Sensai, often called the father of modern hygiene in Japan.

37. Satō Kenji, "Toshi shakaigaku no shakaishi," 170. For reference to the first city-planning efforts in Osaka, see Anbo Norio, *Minato Kōbe, korera, pesuto, suramu*, 176–77.

38. See Maeda Ai, *Toshi kūkan no naka no bungaku*, 184–93; Satō Kenji, "Toshi shakaigaku no shakaishi," 151–227.

39. For examples, see Sōgō kenkyū kaihatsu kikō, *Shinbun ni miru shakai shihon seibi no rekishiteki hensen*, 267–74.

40. Dodd, "An Embracing Vision." Yokoi's articles were later reprinted in a volume entitled *Tokai to inaka* (The city and the countryside). Yokoi was also an early exponent of the agrarianist philosophy of *nōhonshugi*. For Yokoi's writings on agriculture and political economy, see Vlastos, "Agrarianism Without Tradition"; and Havens, *Farm and Nation in Prewar Japan*.

41. See Ishizuka Hiromichi, "Shakai byōri to shite no densenbyō," in idem, *Nihon kindai toshiron*.

42. Narita Ryūichi, "Kindai toshi to minshū," 24.

43. Abe Isoo, *Ōyō shisei ron* (1908), 4–5.

44. Johnston, *The Modern Epidemic*, 223.

45. Quoted in Sōgō kenkyū kaihatsu kikō, *Shinbun ni miru shakai shihon seibi no rekishiteki hensen*, 268.

46. Satō Kenji, *Fūkei no seisan, fūkei no kaihō*, 153.

47. "Shigai kyojū no susume" (A Recommendation to Live Outside the City); cited in Nakagawa Osamu, *Jūzei toshi*, 155.

48. Ono Takahiro, "Kenkōchi no raifusutairu o kizuita igakushatachi," in "Hanshinkan modanizumu" ten jikkō iinkai, *Hanshinkan modanizumu*, 110–14.

49. *Kōgai seikatsu*, no. 2 (Mar. 1, 1908): 2; no. 31 (Apr. 15, 1909): 2. This is not the same *Kōgai seikatsu* as the later Hanshin magazine of the same title.

50. "Ōsaka wa sekai ichi no kekkaku byōchi," *Sanyō suitai*, no. 6 (Dec. 1912): 9–10.

51. For an examination of the early reception of the idea of the Garden City in Japan, see Watanabe Shun'ichi, *"Toshi keikaku" no tanjō*, 41–59; and idem, "The Japanese Garden City," in Ward, *The Garden City*, 69–87.

52. There is a large literature on this subject. On painting, see Aoki Shigeru, *Shizen o utsusu*; on literature, Karatani Kōjin's provocative and controversial chapter "Discovery of Landscape" in idem, *Origins of Modern Japanese Literature*; and Dodd, "An Embracing Vision." On the popularization of written sketches from life, see Takahashi Osamu, "Sakubun kyōiku no disukūru," 257–86. For a sustained analysis

of the concept of nature in modern Japanese thought, see Thomas, *Reconfiguring Modernity*.

53. On Roka's relationship with Tolstoy, see Kominz, "Pilgrimage to Tolstoy."

54. Yasujima Hiroyuki and Soshiroda Akira, *Nihon bessōshi nōto*, 245–46.

55. Quoted in Tsuganesawa Toshihiro, *Takarazuka senryaku*, 149–50.

56. "Okamachi e!! Okamachi e!!" *Sanyō suitai*, special issue: "Jūtaku keiei" (Aug. 1917): 6.

57. "Ikanaru tochi o erabu beki ka ikanaru kaoku ni sumu beki ka" (1910); reproduced in Keihanshin kyūkō dentetsu kabushiki gaisha, *Keihanshin kyūkō dentetsu gojūnenshi*, 119.

58. For details of development east of the Sumida, see Kōtō-ku, *Kōtō kushi*, 1: 406–21.

59. For a discussion of the political and social implications of the "culture of play," see Harootunian, "Late Tokugawa Culture and Thought," 53–63.

60. Miyamoto Mataji, *Ōsaka*, 148–49.

61. On condemnations of the culture of play, see Saeki Junko, "'Bunmei kaika' no 'asobi.'"

62. Yasujima Hiroyuki and Soshiroda Akira, *Nihon bessōshi nōto*, 241–51.

63. Kawazoe Noboru, "Bessō to ryō," in Ogi Shinzō et al., *Edo Tōkyōgaku jiten*, 124–25.

64. An analogous point is made by Ohmann with regard to the marketing of American suburbs: "The ideology of domesticity in its earliest incarnation was primarily woman-defined, and it had at its center a cultural institution, the family. The suburban ideal of the same era was largely male-defined, and had at its center a physical space, the residential suburb" (*Selling Culture*, 136).

65. Tsuganesawa Toshihiro, *Takarazuka senryaku*, 39–40. Tsuganesawa suggests that Kobayashi's own children may have influenced his company's strategy in this period.

66. "Risō no jūtaku," *Sanyō suitai* 2, no. 1 (July 1914): 12; "Ikeda shin shigai: kenshō tōsen kaoku no rakusei," *Sanyō suitai* 1, no. 7 (Mar. 1914): 8–10.

67. Kobayashi Ichizō, *Itsuō jijoden* (1952), 220. The other significant contrast was with the professional female performers who had preceded the troupe in Takarazuka. In the eyes of Kobayashi and his contemporaries, geisha performance and the girls' opera occupied opposite poles of the moral-cultural spectrum, but it is not easy to describe precisely what defined the distance between them. The dances geisha traditionally performed were not overtly sexual. The girls of the new opera troupe would have been only slightly younger than some of their geisha predecessors. The differences must be sought in the new value placed on childhood innocence and female virginity in the Meiji period and the accompanying stigmatization within progressive society of geisha as "professional women," as well as in the discrediting of all

forms of performance associated with the prostitution quarters. For further discussion of *shōjo*, see Robertson, *Takarazuka*. For the formation of new norms of feminine chastity, see Muta Kazue, *Senryaku to shite no kazoku*, 138–46.

68. Shimizu Shōjirō, "Ranchon taimu," *Sanyō suitai* 2, no. 1 (July 1914): 10–11.

69. "Boku no jūtaku," *Sanyō suitai* 1, no. 6 (Dec. 1913): 4–5.

70. "Sakurai no hanjikan," *Sanyō suitai* 1, no. 1 (July 1913): 7–8. Unconscious erotic innuendo might easily be read into the description of the boy in this landscape as well.

71. "Machiyoi," *Sanyō suitai* 1, no. 3 (Sept. 1913), 6–7. The bedroom suburb's erotic overdetermination would be exploited again in a genre of soft-core pornography films made in the 1960s known as "housing-estate wife" (*danchi zuma*) films. The same combination of anxiety and titillation for the male imagination seems to have been present from the outset.

72. "Shintaku monogatari," *Sanyō suitai* 1, no. 2 (Aug. 1913). The same story ran again in July 1915.

73. Shimizu Shōjirō, "Shimai," *Sanyō suitai* 2, no. 3 (Sept. 1914): 8–9.

74. Abe Isoo, *Shakai mondai gairon* (1921), 635–36.

75. *Kadokawa Nihonshi jiten*, 26.

76. Campbell, *The Romantic Ethic and the Spirit of Modern Consumerism*, 89.

## Chapter 5

1. Gordon, *Labor and Imperial Democracy in Prewar Japan*. For the rice riots, see Lewis, *Rioters and Citizens*.

2. Ōya Sōichi, "Bundan girudo no kaitaiki" (1926); quoted in Maeda Ai, *Kindai dokusha no seiritsu*, 212.

3. Miki Satoko, "Meiji kindai fujin zasshi no kiseki," in Kindai josei bunkashi kenkyūkai, ed., *Fujin zasshi no yoake* (Daikūsha, 1989); cited in Kawamura Kunimitsu, *Otome no inori*, 25–29. According to Kawamura, a new women's magazine became the best-seller every few years. *Jogaku sekai* (Girls' School World), founded 1901, was the first industry leader, with a distribution of 70,000–80,000. By 1911, *Jogaku sekai*, which explicitly targeted girls' higher school students and alumni, had been displaced by *Fujin sekai* (Ladies' World), which was soon surpassed by the magazine *Fujokai* (Women's World), before *Shufu no tomo* (The Housewife's Companion) claimed the premier position it would retain through the 1920s.

4. Maeda Ai, *Kindai dokusha no seiritsu*, 216–17.

5. See Maeda Ai, *Kindai dokusha no seiritsu*, on the generational lag in popular fiction during the same years.

6. Uchida Seizō, *Amerika-ya shōhin jūtaku*, 85–86.

7. *Kokumin shinbun*, Mar. 16, 1915, quoted in ibid., 86.

8. Kokumin shinbunsha, *Risō no katei* (1915), 1–12.

9. See also Uchida Seizō, *Nihon no kindai jūtaku*, 76–78.

10. Kokumin shinbunsha, *Risō no katei* (1915), 113–14, 112 (facing page).

11. Ibid., 128. For a discussion of similar ideological uses of rice, see Ohnuki-Tierney, *Rice as Self*, esp. 105–8.

12. Hashiguchi later recalled that he had been surprised to discover in Seattle that rich and poor alike inhabited "Western houses" (*yōkan*) (Uchida Seizō, *Amerika-ya shōhin jūtaku*, 27).

13. Ibid., 35, 43.

14. Uchida Seizō, *Amerika-ya shōhin jūtaku*, 41, 90–92.

15. "Jūtaku kairyōkai shuisho," *Jūtaku* 1, no. 1 (Aug. 1916), 11. Winning such lofty patronage was an impressive achievement in light of the fact that Hashiguchi and Misumi lacked Tokutomi Sohō's newspaper and political connections.

16. *Jūtaku*, 1, no. 1 (July 1916): 10.

17. Popular in the sense that it appealed to a general audience, as indicated by the fact that words in Chinese characters were printed with syllabary glosses for easier reading. The magazine's circulation is not known. Uchida reports that a readers' questionnaire run in 1916 received 2,709 responses. It seems safe to assume that the total readership would have been substantially greater.

18. Nitobe Inazō, "Nihon no jūtaku ni taisuru watakushi no chūmon," *Jūtaku* 2, no. 1 (Jan. 1917): 6–7.

19. Abe Isoo, "Watakushi ga yōkan jūtaku ni sunda riyū," *Jūtaku* 2, no. 2 (Feb. 1917): 6–7.

20. Ozaki Yukio, "Sansō seikatsu," *Jūtaku* 2, no. 6 (June 1917): 8.

21. For a thorough discussion, see Kinmonth, *The Self-Made Man in Meiji Japanese Thought*, 277–325.

22. *How to Live Inexpensively*, a popular book by a doctor and nutritionist published in the same year as the exhibition, focused on the living difficulties of "mental workers" (*seishinteki rōdōsha*) and taught ways to maximize caloric intake while saving on food costs; see Nukada Yutaka, *Anka seikatsu hō*.

23. Tōkyōto, *Tōkyō hyakunenshi*, 4: 61. The actual annual figures before the 1920 census are problematic, but presuming that counting methods were the same, rates of increase between years prior to 1920 should be fairly reliable.

24. Honma Yoshihito, *Gendai toshi jūtaku seisaku*, 384.

25. Narita Ryūichi, "1920 nendai zenhan no shakuyanin undō," 56.

26. Forty-two associations were formed in Tokyo. By 1930, the number of associations in Tokyo was up to 293, with a total membership of 3,094 (Honma Yoshihito, *Gendai toshi jūtaku seisaku*, 355).

27. Ibid., 358 (chart).

28. The original request, committee members' comments, and final report are reprinted in Watanabe Shun'ichi et al., *Senzen no jūtaku seisaku no hensen ni kansuru*

*chōsa*, 7: 34–37. Tokyo municipal police statistics on buildings also began distinguishing "dwelling houses" from "commercial houses" in 1917.

29. Honma Yoshihito, *Gendai toshi jūtaku seisaku*, 350–51.

30. Ibid., 363–64.

31. "Hakkan no ji," *Kansai kenchiku kyōkai zasshi* 1, no. 1 (Sept. 1917): 1. The journal's name was changed to *Kenchiku to shakai* (Architecture and Society) in January 1920.

32. On Seki Hajime, see Hanes, *The City as Subject*.

33. Subsequently published in book form: Ogawa Ichitarō, *Jūtaku mondai* (1919).

34. The first comprehensive housing report, based on a survey conducted in Osaka in 1920, tabulated the location of houses with relation to the street, orientation, presence or absence of dampness below floorboards, number of stories, whether or not the dwelling was free-standing, presence or absence of a kitchen and toilet for private use, number of rooms, number of *tatami* mats per occupant, ceiling height, volume of air per person (measured in multiples of a standard naval ship cabin), rent, presence or absence of a key deposit and advance rent payment, and average percentage of income paid in rent. The report also stated that the assessment of whether or not dwellings in Osaka were "castles for the happy family" was among the survey's objectives. Official housing surveys continued to pay more attention to lower income groups. This survey was conducted for the households of 7,847 factory workers and 1,274 primary-school teachers (see Yoshino Hideki, "Taishōki no jūtaku chōsa," 189–92).

35. Motono Seigo, "Jūtaku kenchiku no kaizō," *Kansai kenchiku kyōkai zasshi* 1, no. 2 (Oct. 1917): 26–33. It is interesting to see in this essay hints of the language of international modernism several years prior to the founding of the Bauhaus.

36. Katsuno Sōichirō, "Jūtaku kaizō, 1," *Kansai kenchiku kyōkai zasshi* 2, no. 10 (Oct. 1919): 30–35.

37. Yasuoka Katsuya, "Kongo no toshi jūtaku," *Kenchiku zasshi*, no. 390 (June 1919): 24–29. Sixty *tsubo* was more than double the average house size for even the highest income bracket in the Social Bureau's middle-class housing survey, but not far from the size of houses introduced in *Kenchiku zasshi* since the 1890s.

38. Tanabe Junkichi, "Jūtaku ni taisuru wareware no taido," *Kenchiku zasshi* 390 (June 1919): 30–33.

39. Katsuno Sōichirō, "Jūtaku kaizō, 1," *Kansai kenchiku kyōkai zasshi* 2, no. 10 (Oct. 1919): 33

40. See the introduction to Kano Masanao, *Taishō demokurashii no teiryū*.

41. Garon, *The State and Labor in Modern Japan*, 77–78, 83–85. The word "social" had originally been avoided because Prime Minister Terauchi felt it had subversive connotations.

42. Kobayashi Yoshihiro, "Taishōki ni okeru shakai kyōiku seisaku no shin tenkai," 311–13. The term *kyōka* implies a combination of "educating" and "civilizing." For further discussion, see Garon, *Molding Japanese Minds*, 7. "Moral suasion" is Garon's translation.

43. For discussion of the Local Improvement Movement, see Pyle, "The Technology of Japanese Nationalism: the Local Improvement Movement."

44. Tanahashi Gentarō, "Seikatsu kaizen undō" (1927), 5. Tanahashi later cited this clause as an "excellent stimulus" to the development of the Everyday Life Reform Movement. Directives issued by the Ministry of Education in summer 1919 made similar calls for the promotion of diligence and the use of substitute grains in the wake of the rice riots. For a discussion of the background to the Everyday Life Reform Movement, see Nakajima Kuni, "Taishōki ni okeru 'seikatsu kaizen undō.'"

45. Norisugi Kaju, "Seikatsu kaizen no igi," *Shakai kyōiku kōenshū*, 1.

46. Quoted in Chino Yōichi, *Kindai Nihon fujin kyōikushi*, 184.

47. Everyday life reform later came to include campaigns to promote "buying Japanese" to reduce dependence on imports, but national trade was not among the issues in the initial years of the Everyday Life Reform League. One example of this later interpretation of everyday life reform is Ōsaka shōkō kaigisho, *Ishokujū ni kansuru seikatsu kaizen sangyō kaizen* (1931).

48. "Ni man no senden bira: Kaetsu Kōko ga sōshikikan de seikatsu kaizen no tame ni daifuntō," *Tōkyō Asahi shinbun*, Jan. 25, 1920: 5. The *Tōkyō Asahi* reported on the exhibition and the activities of the Reform League six times between late October 1919 and the end of January 1920. Two of the articles allude to the slogan "Better Life," and one glosses the name Seikatsu kaizen dōmeikai in English as "Better Life Union," but since this translation does not appear in the surviving materials of the organization, it seems unlikely that it was much used. "Everyday Life Reform League," I believe, better reflects the character of the organization.

49. Nakajima Kuni, "Taishōki ni okeru 'seikatsu kaizen undō,'" 69. The name was changed in Osaka to Everyday life Reconstruction Exhibition (Seikatsu kaizō tenrankai), and some exhibits were added.

50. Uchida Seizō, *Nihon no kindai jūtaku*, 94. On hygiene exhibitions, see Tanaka Satoshi, *Eisei tenrankai no yokubō*.

51. "Kaizen no senden ga jisseikatsu e no hibiki: kōka mada mada usui," *Tōkyō Asahi shinbun*, Dec. 27, 1920: 5.

52. "Ni man no senden bira," *Tōkyō Asahi shinbun*, Jan. 25, 1920.

53. Chino Yōichi, *Kindai Nihon fujin kyōikushi*, 193.

54. Isono Satomi, "Seikatsu kaizen dōmeikai ni kansuru ikkōsatsu," 136. For rural reform campaigns in the 1930s and 1940s, see Itagaki Kuniko, *Shōwa senzen, senchūki no nōson seikatsu*. For the similar campaigns after the war, see Garon, *Molding Japanese Minds*. As Sheldon Garon has shown, urban women would participate enthusiasti-

cally when the campaign could be interpreted as being in their interest. This may have been increasingly the case in the war years, when the state had greater presence in everyday life. See Garon, "Luxury Is the Enemy."

55. "Kono mama de wa muigi da to shinshin ni fuhei no koe—shinnenkai de kaiin no fuhei ga ichiji ni haretsu shita: Seikatsu kaizen dōmeikai no uchimaku," *Tōkyō Asahi shinbun*, Jan. 20, 1921: 5.

56. "Seikatsu kaizen ni bōfu made ohikiai: nani mo yose kare mo hai se to kibō hyakude no chōbi no kai," *Tōkyō Asahi shinbun*, Dec. 21, 1921: 5. The contrasting article did not champion the plight of day-laborers, who were portrayed as accustomed to their poverty. The newspaper seems to have overstepped the bounds of acceptability with this satire of the Reform League, since an apology was printed in some editions two days later.

57. On critical images of the upper class in the journals, see Mizutani Ken, "Kindai Nihon ni okeru jōryū kaikyū imeeji no hen'yō."

58. Hasegawa Tokunosuke, *Tōkyō no takuchi keiseishi*, 96.

59. Ibid., 96–103.

60. Seikatsu kaizen dōmeikai, *Jūtaku kaizen no hōshin* (1920).

61. "Seikatsu kaizen dōmei katsudō: chūsan seikatsu no kōjō ni tsutomu," *Tōkyō Asahi shinbun*, June 28, 1921.

62. "Den'en seikatsu ni teki suru wayō setchū no jūtaku," *Yomiuri shinbun*, May 1, 1921; reprinted in *Shinbun shūroku Taishōshi*, 9: 161.

63. *Asahi shinbun*, Sept. 17, 1921: 5; Sept. 18, 1921: 4; Sept. 20: 6; Oct. 17: 2.

64. *Kaizō*, *kaizen*, and *kairyō* have distinct nuances, but these three terms were used interchangeably in press treatment of everyday life reform.

65. "Kagu shinseihin chinretsukai," *Mitsukoshi* 11, no. 11 (Nov. 1921), 33.

66. The Matsuzakaya department store, for example, advertised an exhibit organized "under the guidance of the Everyday Life Reform League" that displayed reformed clothing for children, the Seikatsu kaizen dōmeikai shidō joji kairyōfuku tenrankai, in October 1920 (advertisement reprinted in *Shinbun shūroku Taishōshi*, 8: 484).

67. *Fujinkai*, special issue: "Shinnen tokubetsu shin seikatsu," Jan. 1920.

68. "Seikatsu kaizō wa nani yori chakushu subeki ka," *Fujin no tomo*, special issue: "Seikatsu kaizō," Oct. 1919: 16–31; "Kaizō no kyū o yō suru mono wa nani ka," *Fujin kōron* 4, no. 10 (Oct. 1919): 62–73. *Fujin no tomo* published seventy-three responses, sixteen of them from women. Of the total, thirty-seven referred to reforms and used rhetoric that would later appear in the proposals of the Everyday Life Reform League. *Fujin kōron* published forty-seven responses, three from women. Eighteen of them were close to later Reform League rhetoric. Two writers declared apartment buildings necessary to everyday life reform. One demand made by a few respondents that did not resurface in the proposals of the Everyday Life Reform League was for

collectivization of kitchen work. Ten years later, *Fujin no tomo* promoted a design for a four-dwelling unit with a common kitchen, but it appears that few architects were sympathetic to such ideas in 1920.

69. "Wagaya no seikatsu kaizō," *Fujinkai*, special issue: "Shin seikatsu," Jan. 1920: 63–73.

70. Byakuran, "Hōkyū ishokusha no katei kara," *Fujin kōron*, special issue: "Ningen kaizō," 5, no. 4 (1920): 93–94.

71. "Konponteki ni seikatsu o kairyō shite ōi ni seikō su," *Shufu no tomo*, "warai no peeji," 3, no. 12 (Dec. 1919): 148–49. Cypress wood (*hinoki*) was more costly than cryptomeria (*sugi*).

72. "Seikatsu kairyō seikō keiken," *Shufu no tomo* 3, no. 12 (Dec. 1919): 36–46.

73. The word "culture" (*bunka*) was already ponderously overdetermined in philosophical discourse when Morimoto began writing of the culture life. Take, for example, the following early expression of "culturalism" (*bunkashugi*): "When we have purified the collection of values possessed in the history of humanity, and led the linear process of sublimation (*kōshō*) to its extreme, as we stand at that limit, a so-called cultural value is one that can serve as the object of all the efforts of our human history. The metaphysical effort, as it were, to seek the substantial realization of a cultural value of this kind, possessing in theory a universal appropriateness, I will here refer to as "culturalism" (*bunkashugi*)" (Sayuda Kiichirō, "Bunkashugi no ronri," *Reimeikai kōenshū dai isshū*, Mar. 1919; reprinted in Kano Masanao, *Nihon kindai shisō taikei* 34, 5). The essay quoted here also speaks of *bunka seikatsu*, revealing that Morimoto Kōkichi did not coin the term. The role of Morimoto's Bunka seikatsu kenkyūkai, however, was to bring it down to the mundane level of material standards of living. Only after this could "culture" enter the popular lexicon as the tangible object of desire that would soon diffuse in the form of "culture pots," "culture knives," and "culture houses." Harry Harootunian compares the Japanese *bunka* in this period to the contemporary German *kultur* (Silberman and Harootunian, *Japan in Crisis*). See also Kitaoji Takashi, "'Bunka' no poritikkusu I."

74. Nakamura Tatsutarō, "Kenchiku to bunka seikatsu: kaikai no ji," *Kenchiku zasshi* 35, no. 416 (May 1921): 291.

75. Miyake Yūjirō (Setsurei), "Kaizō no teido," *Fujin no tomo*, special issue: "Seikatsu kaizō," Oct. 1919: 11–15; idem, "Bunka seikatsu," *Fujin no tomo*, special issue: "Bunka seikatsu," Jan. 1921: 14–17.

76. Terade Kōji, *Seikatsu bunkaron e no shōtai*, 92–93. Both publications were monthly.

77. Morimoto Kōkichi, "Bunka seikatsu kenkyū ni tsuite," *Bunka seikatsu kenkyū* 1, no. 1 (May 1920): 3–4.

78. Morimoto Kōkichi, *Seikatsu mondai* (1920), 40–41.

79. Harada Katsuhiro, "Seikatsu kaizen undō no shito," 154.

80. Ibid., 156. The surveys are described in Morimoto Kōkichi, *Seikatsu mondai* (1920), 364–65.

81. Morimoto Kōkichi, *Horobiyuku kaikyū* (The Decaying Class; 1924), 293–94.

82. Ibid., 228.

83. Ibid., 209–10; Morimoto Kōkichi, "Bunka seikatsu kenkyū ni tsuite," *Bunka seikatsu kenkyū* 1, no. 1 (May 1920): 11–12, 15.

84. Hoashi Riichirō, *Bunka seikatsu to ningen kaizō* (1922), 280.

85. Ōkuma Yoshikuni, "Gendai o hyōjun to shita shin jūtaku no kenchiku" (1921); reprinted in *Kenchiku nijū kō* (1923), 38–40. The plan showed a single-story dwelling of 31 *tsubo* (approximately 1,116 square feet). The article did not specify the number of occupants for this house, but with only three rooms suited to serve as sleeping places and no servants' quarters, it cannot have been designed to accommodate the average household of roughly nine persons that would occupy a house of this size according to the architect's own calculations.

86. "Shinseimen o hiraku kaizen dōmei no kyōgi," *Tōkyō Asahi shinbun*, Nov. 30, 1921; "Mazu ryokan no kaizen: jūtaku sekkei mo muryō de yaru," *Tōkyō Asahi shinbun*, Mar. 13, 1923.

## Chapter 6

1. The modifier *bunka* in *bunka seikatsu* could alternatively be translated "cultured" or "cultural." Each of these has certain deficiencies: the suggestion of self-cultivation in the word "cultured" makes it too narrow, and the anthropological overtones of "cultural" risk obscuring the universalist (nonrelativist) ideals in *bunka*. I have chosen simply "culture" because it retains more of the sense of the original word's role as a floating signifier for a whole congeries of contemporary ideals. An English phrase like "modern living" perhaps captures more of the flavor of what was conjured by *bunka seikatsu* in the 1920s.

2. I am speaking here of their popularity as advertising slogans. *Bunka, bunka seikatsu,* and *seikatsu kaizen* lived on in the language and acquired new numinous power in the years after World War II.

3. For a useful analysis of the devolution of these terms, see Kitaōji Takashi, "'Bunka' no poritikkusu."

4. Quoted in ibid., 76.

5. Harootunian, "Overcome by Modernity."

6. Harootunian, *History's Disquiet*, 64. The West as a source of fantasy in twentieth-century Asia has been explored by others. For discussion of the uses of the West among Shanghai intellectuals, see Lee, *Shanghai Modern*. Lee stresses that the Chinese in Shanghai appropriated freely from the West rather than being hobbled by a colonial mentality: "The Chinese writers' fervent espousal of Occidental exoticism . . . turned Western culture itself into an 'other' in the process of constructing

their own modern imaginary" (309). Mitziko Sawada's *Tokyo Life, New York Dreams,* examines the hopes for cultural integration and transcendence invested in immigration to the United States.

7. Serizawa Eiji, *Shin Nihon no jūka* (1924), 1.

8. Hirano Shōsen, *Bunka seikatsu no chishiki* (1925). The material emphasis of this work also recalls earlier work like Fukuzawa Yūkichi's *Seiyō jijō* (Conditions in the West; 1866). Now, however, the things introduced were presumed to be as much a part of native Japanese culture.

9. Reprinted in book form as Jiji shinpōsha, *Atarashii Tōkyō to kenchiku no hanashi* (1924).

10. For a positive reappraisal of Tokyo's post-earthquake reconstruction, see Koshizawa Akira, *Tōkyō no toshi keikaku,* 2–86.

11. On the Taishō artistic avant-garde, see Weisenfeld, *Mavo.*

12. Suzuki Sadami, *Modan toshi no hyōgen,* 127.

13. Weisenfeld, "Japanese Modernism and Consumerism," 75–98.

14. The cosmopolitan awareness I am describing here should be understood as distinct from the political internationalism of Taishō liberal thinkers, which is also commonly referred to as cosmopolitan. Experiencing Tokyo or Osaka as sites of the modern world and imagining them in a common space with Western cities did not in itself dictate a political position with regard to international relations, since this simultaneity of experience proved equally compatible with political isolation and ultranationalism in the 1930s.

15. Minami Hiroshi, *Taishō bunka,* 258. For an overview of new media and urban modernity in 1920s Tokyo, see Harootunian, *Overcome by Modernity,* chap. 1.

16. Harootunian, *History's Disquiet,* 115–16; Minami Hiroshi et al., *Shōwa bunka,* 66–68.

17. On jazz in prewar Japan, see Atkins, *Blue Nippon,* 45–126.

18. Takeyama Akiko, "Rajio bangumi ni miru modanizumu."

19. Itō Toshiharu, "Nihon no 1920 nendai," 188.

20. Minami Hiroshi, *Shōwa bunka,* 472. The Ginza line opened in 1928.

21. Ueda Yasuo, "Josei zasshi ga mita modanizumu," 116–17. At least this aspect of the everyday life reform movement's blueprint for the future appears to have been readily endorsed by most contemporary urbanites. Walking through residential neighborhoods between Nakano and Kōenji stations for one hour on March 29, 1926, Kon Wajirō (or possibly a certain Arai-kun, his student) recorded seeing 12 boys and 21 girls in Japanese dress, as compared to 35 boys and 33 girls in Western dress ("Kōgai fūzoku zakkei," in Kon Wajirō and Yoshida Kenkichi, *Moderunorojio* [1930], 121). Minami Hiroshi et al. (*Shōwa bunka,* 92) claim that by the end of the Taishō period in 1926, all schoolchildren were wearing Western clothes. They do not provide clear evidence, however.

22. For Watsuji Tetsurō writing in 1930s, continuities in the form of Japanese houses would signify a vital anachronism challenging universal modernity; see Harootunian, *Overcome by Modernity*, 265–67.

23. For a provocative discussion of several vignettes of prewar and wartime culture in the context of colonialism, see Silverberg, "Remembering Pearl Harbor." For recent monographic studies that treat the role of the empire in metropolitan consciousness, see Young, *Japan's Total Empire*; and Robertson, *Takarazuka*. Both of these works focus on the empire in the 1930s and 1940s. Mark Peattie's "Japanese Attitudes Toward Colonialism" (in Peattie, Myers, and Duus, *The Japanese Colonial Empire*) provides a valuable survey of academic and political debates surrounding colonial management. A seminal collection of essays in Japanese on colonialism and Japanese culture is Ōe Shinobu et al., *Iwanami kōza kindai Nihon to shokuminchi 7*. Until the 1990s, colonialism was usually omitted from the social and cultural history of prewar Japan or bracketed within discussion of military expansionism. The three volumes on Taishō culture, Shōwa culture, and Japanese modernism by Minami Hiroshi et al. treat the politics of Japanese aggression and the role of an increasingly jingoistic press during the war but make no mention of the colonies in the context of popular culture.

24. Yoshimi Shun'ya, *Hakurankai no seijigaku*, 212–14.

25. "Tōyō yuiitsu no chikatetsudō," posters reproduced in Tōkyō kokuritsu kindai bijutsukan, *Sugiura Hisui ten*, 27, 28; newspapers cited in Hatsuda, *Hyakkaten no tanjō*, 101.

26. Silverberg, "Constructing a New Cultural History of Prewar Japan," 127.

27. For discussion of fantasies about Manchuria, see Young, *Japan's Total Empire*, 334–51.

28. Doak, "Culture, Ethnicity and the State in Early Twentieth-Century Japan," 190–92.

29. The Chinese character compound *bunka* is itself old, and this aspect of colonial policy admittedly need not have depended on the importation of German concepts of *kultur* or the subsequent fashion for the word.

30. Kawamura Minato, "Taishū orientarizumu to Ajia ninshiki," 107–36. For Japanese colonial anthropology, see the essays in van Bremen and Shimizu, *Anthropology and Colonialism in Asia and Oceania*.

31. Quoted in Kawamura Minato, "Taishū orientarizumu to Ajia ninshiki," 111–12. On accounts of the 1930 Musha Incident, the most significant confrontation between Taiwanese indigenes and their Japanese rulers, see Ching, "Savage Constructions and Civility Making."

32. Nakama Teruhisa, *Nihon chiri fūzoku taikei 2* (1929–32).

33. Koshizawa Akira, *Manshūkoku no shuto keikaku*, 220–57. Several state-sponsored sightseeing visits to Tokyo by actual parties of colonial subjects had been

conducted prior to this cartoon depiction of colonial *moga;* see Ching, "Savage Constructions and Civility Making," 795–96.

34. Colonial architecture historian Nishizawa Yasuhiko ("Shihai no kan to min," 516–17) points out that this was true of company housing built in the colonies as well, which was generally more Westernized and of a far higher standard than housing for families of comparable status would have been at home. Nishizawa adduces three reasons for this: the need to create incentives to attract professionals to colonial jobs, the need to display imperial power to subject populations and parity to Westerners through architecture, and the fact that most colonial company housing was built in new districts, where the architecture was conspicuous and called on to set a standard for future construction.

35. Chiba Kameo, "Kindaijin no seikatsu shinjō to shashi zeitaku no igi" (1924).

36. For discussion of intellectual critiques of *Amerikanizumu* spanning the interwar period with particular focus on statements made at the 1942 conference on "overcoming the modern" (*kindai no chōkoku*), see Harootunian, *Overcome by Modernity*, 47–65. The various senses in which the term *Amerikanizumu* was used specifically during the 1910s and 1920s are discussed in Henry D. Smith II, "From Wilsonian Democracy to *Modan* Life."

37. Citing an article in the *Tōkyō Asahi shinbun*, Minami Hiroshi (*Taishō bunka*, 369) relates the reactionary tactics of a group of sixty youths who broke into a Western ball at the Imperial Hotel in 1924. Chanting Chinese poetry, they performed a sword dance. They then unfurled a banner bearing a warning, in English, to their Japanese countrymen to consider the threatened position of the Japanese people.

38. Translated into English by Anthony H. Chambers as *Naomi*. Tanizaki himself was a master at manipulating native and Western cultural forms, and his satirical novel was anything but a reactionary anti-Westernizing polemic. For an analysis, see Ito, *Visions of Desire*, 77–100.

39. Akiyama Masami, *Shōjotachi no Shōwashi*, 160–68. Akiyama is the founder of Shōwa shōnen shōjo bungakukan, a museum of twentieth-century Japanese children's toys and literature.

40. *Arusu fujin kōza* (1927), vol. 2: plates.

41. Morimoto Kōkichi, *Seikatsu mondai* (1920), 384–85.

42. For a thorough treatment of white-collar male education and employment conditions during this period, see Kinmonth, *The Self-Made Man in Meiji Japanese Thought*, 277–325.

43. Iwamoto Michiya, "Sarariiman," 281.

44. The survey, conducted in 1930 by the Education Bureau (Gakumukyoku) of Tokyo Prefecture, yielded the following percentages of graduates employed: Tokyo Imperial University, 61 percent; Tokyo Commercial College, 58 percent; Waseda

University, 34 percent; Keiō University, 40 percent; Chūō University, 55 percent (see Kamata Isao, *Gekkyūtori hakusho*, 26; Kinmonth, *The Self-Made Man in Meiji Japanese Thought*, 294).

45. Terade Kōji, *Seikatsu bunkaron e no shōtai*, 184–201; see also idem, "Taishōki ni okeru shokuin seikatsu no tenkai."

46. Chimoto Akiko, "Nihon ni okeru seibetsu yakuwari bungyō no keisei," 220–225. Chimoto also notes that since family members of public servants were not permitted to have jobs in commerce, lower-level bureaucrats and teachers tended to be more dependent on remittances from the countryside than men at equivalent salaries in the private sector, whose wives could take whatever work they liked and contribute openly to the family income.

47. Kinmonth, *The Self-Made Man in Meiji Japanese Thought* (305, 309), cites a 1934 job placement guide that described "how to sit properly, to eat cakes, and to drink tea during a visit" and referred to employment examination problems on Marconi, Hindenburg, "symphonic jazz," and Picasso, as well as "benevolent government" and "cosmopolitanism."

48. Ibid., 316–17.

49. Ichihara Hiroshi, "Howaito karaa no shakai keizaishi," 140.

50. Kinmonth, *The Self-Made Man in Meiji Japanese Thought*, 304–5, 311.

51. Ōya Sōichi, "Modansō to modansō" (1929); reprinted in idem, *Ōya Sōichi zenshū* (1981), 2: 5–6.

52. Aono Suekichi, "The Salaryman's Time of Terror" (*Sarariiman kyōfu jidai*, 1930), trans. Kimberly Gould, in Gould, "The Origins of the Salaryman," sect. II, 5.

53. Kinmonth, *The Self-Made Man in Meiji Japanese Thought*, 316.

54. Ibid., 288.

55. Gould, "The Origins of the Salaryman." 19–20, 28. This informative thesis is supplemented by translations of several classic essays concerning the salaryman.

56. Ōkōchi Kazuo, *Nihonteki chūsan kaikyū* (1960), 89.

57. Ōkado Masakatsu, "Nōson kara toshi e," 174–94.

58. Ichihara Hiroshi, "Howaito karaa no shakai keizaishi," 140.

59. *Tōkyō pakku*, 15, no. 5 (May 1922).

## Chapter 7

1. Takanashi Yūtarō, *Bunka mura no kan'i jūtaku* (1922), 3. For analysis of related issues of class and national agendas in British housing after World War I, see Orbach, *Homes for Heroes*.

2. Tanabe Junkichi, "Jūtaku kaizen no konpon hōshin," in Seikatsu kaizen dōmeikai, *Monbushō kōshūkai* (1922), 102–4.

3. Takanashi Yūtarō, *Bunka mura no kan'i jūtaku* (1922), 6–12.

4. Fujiya Yōetsu, "Heiwahaku bunka mura shuppin jūtaku no sehyō ni tsuite."

5. The other collection is Takahashi Jin, *Bunka mura jūtaku sekkei zusetsu* (1922). The Suzuki shoten volume went through four printings in less than two months during the exposition. The Kōyōsha volume was in its seventh printing in 1925. For a thorough study of Culture Village, see Uchida Seizō, "Jūtaku tenjijō no genfūkei to shite no 'bunka mura,'" 352–69; and idem, "Kenchiku gakkai no katsudō kara mita Taishō 11 nen kaisai no heiwa kinin Tōkyō hakurankai bunka mura ni kansuru ikkōsatsu."

6. Yasuda Takashi, "Minoo, Sakuragaoka no jūtaku kaizō hakurankai," 33–39.

7. Ubukata Toshirō, "Mado kara mita bunka mura" (1922), 75.

8. Gamachi Norio, "Fudōsan torihiki no hensen katei."

9. Kobayashi Ichizō had called his Osaka suburbs simply "new districts" (*shin shigai*), and the earliest planned residential suburb in Tokyo, Sakura Shinmachi, followed this pattern.

10. See Kawazoe Noboru, *Tōkyō no genfūkei.*

11. Noda Masaho and Nakajima Akiko, *Mejiro bunka mura,* 34, 38–39.

12. Ibid., 64–65.

13. Ibid., 85. "Culture village" was used as a formal and informal appellation for planned developments elsewhere in the country as well. A group of suburban houses built in 1921 by a small homeowners' union in Fukuoka, for example, came to be known by neighbors as Culture Village (Miyamoto Masaaki and Kawakami Yoshiaki, "Noma bunka mura no kensetsu keii"). Kansai architect Yoshimura Seitarō built a Culture Village in the Kōbe area in 1924 (Yamagata Masaaki, *Vōrizu no jūtaku,* 225). If one includes popular appellations, there were probably many more than have been studied by architecture historians.

14. Fujiya Yōetsu, "Tsutsumi Yasujirō no jūtakuchi keiei dai ichi gō," 164–65.

15. Matsui Haruko, "Hakone tochi no Ōizumi, Kodaira, Kunitachi no kōgai jūtakuchi kaihatsu," 222. One thousand lots is my conservative estimate based on the total area of the development, which Matsui records as 500,000 *tsubo.*

16. Ibid., 227–28.

17. For further discussion of Den'en Chōfu's background and planning, see Oshima, "The Japanese Garden City."

18. Inose Naoki, *Tochi no shinwa,* 32.

19. Ōsaka Akira, "Senzoku den'en toshi wa kieta ka," 176.

20. Inose Naoki, *Tochi no shinwa,* 12.

21. Fujimori Terunobu, "Den'en Chōfu tanjōki," in Yamaguchi Hiroshi, *Kōgai jūtakuchi no keifu,* 192, 200.

22. Howard, *Garden Cities of Tomorrow,* 51, 53.

23. Ibid., 46.

24. For applications of the Garden City idea in several countries, see Ward, *The Garden City*. Howard's diagram of the three magnets appears in German, French, Russian, and Japanese on p. 195, but the Japanese diagram appears recent.

25. The authors discussed the specific features of Howard's circular plan, comparing it with a grid plan by Sennett and a grid intersected by two diagonals proposed by Buckingham. They concluded that Buckingham's was to be preferred from the perspective of ventilation, but that this ought not to be a major issue in a semi-rural setting (Naimushō, Chihōkyoku yūshi, *Den'en toshi*, 27–30).

26. Inose Naoki, *Tochi no shinwa*, 346.

27. Ibid., 360, 355–59. Hata Yaeimon and Kōno Mitsuji, two protégés of politician Ozaki Yukio, first approached Shibusawa around 1911 with the idea of building a garden city. These men had spent the previous decade developing land and housing for Japanese residents in Korea, but overinvestment and a slack colonial market after the Russo-Japanese War compelled them to return to Tokyo. Inokashira was originally considered for the project, but at some time between 1913 and 1918, Shibusawa decided to buy larger tracts further from the city.

28. Quoted in Fujimori Terunobu, "Den'en Chōfu tanjōki," in Yamaguchi Hiroshi, *Kōgai jūtakuchi no keifu*, 200–201; see also Inose Naoki, *Tochi no shinwa*, 17.

29. Inose Naoki, *Tochi no shinwa*, 12.

30. Reproduced in Fujiya Yōetsu, "Yume ni kieta Ōfuna den'en toshi kōsō," 83.

31. The plan can be traced further in two mountain resorts, one developed by Shibusawa Hideo, the other by Karuizawa developer Nozawa Genjirō. The formal geometry was even less well-suited to the site in these cases (Yasujima Hiroyuki and Soshiroda Akira, *Nihon bessōshi nōto*, 272).

32. Quoted in Inose Naoki, *Tochi no shinwa*, 20.

33. Quoted in ibid., 27.

34. Ibid., 103.

35. The legal framework for conversion of farmland was provided by land readjustment laws that enabled unions of landholders to reapportion lots following minimum guidelines set by the Home Ministry and municipal offices. Most followed the Farmland Readjustment Act (Kōchi seiri hō) of 1909, which was intended to encourage rationalization for agricultural uses rather than conversion for housing; see Ishida Yorifusa, *Nihon kindai toshi keikaku no hyakunen*; and Iwami Ryōtarō, *Tochi kukaku seiri no kenkyū*. On the specific issue of landlords' application of the Farmland Readjustment Act for housing subdivisions, see Ikehata Hiroyuki and Fujioka Hiroyasu, "Tōkyōshi kōgai ni okeru kōchi seiri hō no takuchi kaihatsu ni tsuite."

36. Fudōsan gyōkai enkakushi hensan iinkai, *Fudōsan gyōkai enkakushi*, 127–29.

37. Ōsaka Akira ("Senzoku den'en toshi wa kieta ka," 179) records the following occupational breakdown for the 267 buyers in Senzoku (76 percent of the total) whose occupations could be determined from a register compiled in 1926: company

employees (*kaishain*) 23.9 percent; company executives (*kaisha jūyaku*) 22.4 percent; government bureaucrats (*kanri*) 22.0 percent; military men 11.9 percent; self-employed 7.8 percent; doctors 5.2 percent; free-lance workers 2.9 percent; other 3.3 percent.

38. Ibid., 182–83.

39. Fujiya Yōetsu, "Tsutsumi Yasujirō no jūtakuchi keiei dai ichi gō," 167–69.

40. Noda Masaho and Nakajima Akiko, *Mejiro bunka mura*, 106–7, 85.

41. Yamamoto Tadaoki, "Denki jūtaku yori (dai isshin)," *Jūtaku* 8, no. 3 (Mar. 1923): 25–29.

42. Uchida Seizō, *Nihon no kindai jūtaku*, 157–62. Uchida quotes a memoir by Yamamoto in which he reflects that one reason he wished to replace the maids' labor with electrical appliances was that it was "not educational" to let children learn the habit of giving orders to the maids.

43. Inose Naoki, *Tochi no shinwa*, 109–11.

44. Rapoport, *House Form and Culture*, presents this in elegant schematic form.

45. For further discussion of traditional uses of the *engawa* and reform architects' negative opinions of them, see Sand, "House and Home in Modern Japan," chap. 6.

46. Shiga Shigetsura, "Jūka (kairyō no hōshin ni tsuite)," *Kenchiku zasshi*, no. 194 (Feb. 1903): 38–39. Shiga related that he had first heard the idea that displaying one's house was a form of charity from an American woman. He repeated it apparently without cynicism, appraising the words "extremely tasteful."

47. Seikatsu kaizen dōmeikai, *Jūtaku kagu no kaizen* (1924), 112.

48. Ōfuna den'en toshi kabushiki gaisha, *Den'en jūtaku zushū* (1922), preface p. 2.

49. On lawns, see Fishman, *Bourgeois Utopias*, 146–48; and Jackson, *Crabgrass Frontier*, 54–61.

50. See Suzuki Hiroyuki, *Toshi e*, for an examination of the different forms of suburban development; and Hasegawa Tokunosuke, *Tōkyō no takuchi keiseishi*, for statistics on conversion of farming to housing land, and case studies.

51. Ishida Yorifusa, *Nihon kindai toshi keikaku no hyakunen*, 139–42.

52. Tokutomi Roka portrayed this confrontation in the novel *Mimizu no tawagoto* (An Earthworm's Ramblings, 1913). Similar stories of battles appear in the histories compiled by the suburban ward offices; see, e.g., Mori Yasuki, *Suginami fūdoki*.

53. Fujioka Hiroyasu and Imafuji Akira, "'Marunouchi shinshiroku.'" None of the Marunouchi managers lived in the low-lying northern and eastern counties of Minami Adachi and Minami Katsushika, revealing the sharply divided social geography of the city's expansion.

54. Figures from Hasegawa Tokunosuke, *Tōkyō no takuchi keiseishi*, 154. According to 1930 census figures tabulated in Ebato Akira, *Tōkyō no chiiki kenkyū*, 15, the total working population of the suburban counties subsequently incorporated into Greater Tokyo was 1,135,539. This would make commuters into the central wards

26.2 percent of the working population. For a comprehensive discussion of population movement in the capital, see Tōkyōto, *Tōkyō hyakunen shi*, 4: 69–76.

55. Figures from Ebato Akira, *Tōkyō no chiiki kenkyū*, 12–15.

56. Calculations based on tables in Suginami kuyakusho, *Suginami kushi* (Suginami kuyakusho, 1955), 1247–57.

57. Tōkyōfu, Shakaika, *Tōkyōshi oyobi kinsetsu chōson chūtō kaikyū jūtaku chōsa* (1923), 21. Judging from the average numbers of *tatami*, it appears likely that the surveyors excluded kitchens and other service spaces from their room count. The occupational groups surveyed were primary-school teachers, government bureaucrats, company employees, bank employees, newspaper employees, middle-school teachers, railroad employees, public servants, skilled factory workers, policemen, and others.

58. Figures from Tōkyō shiyakusho, *Shisei tōkei genpyō* (1930), tables, 106–7. Although the tables are not specific, it appears that kitchens, toilets, baths, and entry vestibules were excluded from the number of "rooms" (*shitsu*) in these surveys.

59. Tōkyōfu, Shakaika, *Tōkyōshi oyobi kinsetsu chōson chūtō kaikyū jūtaku chōsa* (1923), figures from 11 (text), 39 (tables).

60. This figure included the large tenement districts in the industrial periphery to the east of the city, where owner-occupancy rates were low.

61. Calculated from statistical tables in Tōkyōfu, Gakumubu, Shakaika, *Tōkyōfu gogun ni okeru kaoku chintai jijō chōsa* (1932), 13, 20, 23–24. The owner-occupancy rates for Toyotama-gun, where much of the new development along the Chūō and Yamanote lines near Shinjuku station was taking place, are as follows:

| | |
|---|---|
| Nakano-chō | 23 percent |
| Nogata-chō | 33 percent |
| Wadabori-chō | 43 percent |
| Suginami-chō | 36 percent |
| Ōkubo-chō | 22 percent |
| Totsuka-chō | 20 percent |
| Yodobashi-chō | 17 percent |
| Yoyohata-chō | 23 percent |
| Sendagaya-chō | 20 percent |
| Shibuya-chō | 23 percent |
| Ochiai-chō | 31 percent |

62. *Tōkyō shiiki kakuchō shi* (Tōkyō shiyakusho, 1934); cited in Inose Naoki, *Tochi no shinwa*, 22–23.

63. Graph in Ebato Akira, *Tōkyō no chiiki kenkyū*, 18.

64. Mori Yasuki, *Suginami fūdoki*, 2 88, 247–248.

65. Figures from Suginami kyōdoshi kai, *Suginami-ku no rekishi*, 109.

66. Kon Wajirō, "Kōgai fūzoku zakkei," reprinted in Kon Wajirō and Yoshida Kenkichi, *Moderunorojio* (1930), 115.

67. Takanashi Yūtarō. *Bunka mura no kan'i jūtaku* (1922), 41.

68. Ibid., 78. The critic's admiration for a complex roof form derives from the massing of elite native dwellings, as opposed not only to the box shape of many Western houses but also to native rowhouses and farmhouses. By treating this massing as a key characteristic of Japanese design, architects and critics thus reinterpreted the vernacular standards for elite houses as expressions of national taste.

## Chapter 8

1. Kon Wajirō, *Shinpan dai Tōkyō annai* (1929), 2: 153.

2. The term "vernacular" is distinct from "traditional." Vernacular knowledge emerges from local conditions and thus contrasts with national traditions as much as with international modernity. Local vernaculars also persist in many forms, despite the increasing domination of national and universal systems of cultural production. On the characteristics of the vernacular, both in language and in everyday life practices, see Ivan Illich's provocative anthropological essay, *Gender*. Illich's romantic antimodernism leads him to an essentialist position on gender difference, but his evocation of vernaculars as systems of knowledge and practice remain vivid. See also Hubka, "Just Folks Designing."

3. Hayashi Fumiko, "Ie o tsukuru ni atatte" (n.d.). An independent woman writer building her own house was something radically new itself, of course.

4. The earliest *hinagatabon*, which date from the Muromachi period (14th–16th centuries), showed the proper configuration of *tatami* mats for different ceremonial situations. Manuals of similar format were printed in the Tokugawa period, with separate books illustrating designs for staggered shelves, sliding door panels, transoms, *tokonoma* alcoves and *shoin* windows, and ceilings. From the mid-nineteenth century, these books began to show combinations of *tokonoma*, shelves, and *shoin*, thereby popularizing a more informal style of *shoin zashiki* with obvious *sukiya* influence; see Okamoto Mariko and Naitō Akira, "Daiku gijutsusho 'hinagatabon' ni tsuite" 323–57.

5. For the history of these carpenters' plans, see Hamashima Shōji, "Sashizu to tate chiwarizu ni tsuite"; see also Kawakami Mitsugu, *Kenchiku sashizu o yomu*.

6. On carpenters' disdain for studying plans, see Inaba Shingo, *Machi daiku*, 83. On vernacular architecture and bricolage generally, see Hubka, "Just Folks Designing," 426–32. For the seminal formulation of the contrast between the craftsman's "bricolage" and the technician's scientific knowledge, see Levi-Strauss, *The Savage Mind*, 1–33.

7. Kamata Kenzō, *Sen'en ika de dekiru risō no jūtaku* (1922), 56.

8. Yasuoka Katsuya, *Risō no jūtaku* (1915), preface.

9. Ibid., 18–19.

10. Ibid., 40.

11. Ibid., 56.

12. Uchida Seizō, *Nihon no kindai jūtaku*, 135.

13. Yasuoka Katsuya, *Nihonka shitaru yōfū shō jūtaku* (1924). Yasuoka published a companion volume of "Westernized Small Japanese Houses" in which the proportions were reversed; see *Ōbeika shitaru Nihon shō jūtaku* (1925).

14. Uchida Seizō, *Nihon no kindai jūtaku*, 148–172.

15. Ibid., 163–66.

16. For a discussion of *Jūtaku* magazine, see Uchida Seizō, *Amerika-ya shōhin jūtaku*. Two similar magazines are *Shin jūtaku*, which began publication in 1920, and *Ie no shirube*, published from 1921. Some of *Jūtaku*'s contemporaries are no longer to be found in libraries. Culture house architect and writer Nose Kyūichirō (*Bunka jūtaku zuan hyakushu* [1926], hanrei) listed the journals *Seikatsu to jūtaku*, *Jūtaku kenkyū*, *Kenchiku no fukyū*, *Heimin kenchiku*, *Kōji gahō*, *Ie*, *Teien*, and *Chūō kenchiku* among places where his designs had been published. None of these is preserved in the National Diet Library.

17. Kenchiku shashin ruiju kankōkai, *Kenchiku shashin ruiju dai 4 ki dai 7 kai* (1924).

18. Nihon kenchiku gakkai, *Kindai Nihon kenchikugaku hattatsushi*, table p. 1942.

19. Nihon kenchiku gakkai, *Nihon kenchiku gakkai jūsho seimei roku* (1930); idem, *Shōwa 9 nen kenchiku gakkai kaiin seimei jūsho roku* (1934). The list includes the five imperial universities, as well as colleges and vocational schools in the colonies and nineteen institutions outside the empire. Since there was no licensing or accreditation system at this time, only vocational college diplomas or university degrees in architecture distinguished architects from amateurs.

20. For a basic explanation of the two laws, together with some critical assessment of their impact on urban planning, see Ishida Yorifusa, *Nihon kindai toshi keikaku no hyakunen*, 125–43.

21. Fujimori Terunobu, *Nihon no kindai kenchiku*, 2: 125–26.

22. Watanabe Shun'ichi, *"Toshi keikaku" no tanjō*, 116–18.

23. I am indebted to Gregory Clancey for this way of looking at state regulation of construction.

24. Osaka-based architecture historian Wada Yasuyoshi has done a unique study of the change in Osaka rowhouse design during this period, drawing upon interviews and extensive site surveys. I am grateful to him for sharing his work with me, and for acting as my guide through surviving prewar neighborhoods in Osaka. See Wada Yasuyoshi, "Ōsaka ni okeru kindai toshi jūtaku seiritsu ni kansuru kisoteki kenkyū."

25. For example, Suzukawa Magosaburō, *Dare ni mo wakaru shigaichi kenchikubutsu hō zukai* (An Illustrated Guide Anyone Will Understand to the Urban Building Law; 1924). Several pattern books after 1920 included the law in an appendix.

26. Ōmi Sakai and Hori Isao, *Nihon no kenchiku*, 92.

27. Fujimori Terunobu, *Nihon no kindai kenchiku*, 2: 133–35. For further discussion of the Urban Building Law's influence on vernacular architecture in Tokyo, see Ezura Tsuguto, "Kindai Tōkyō ni okeru shomin jūkyo no hatten ni kansuru kenkyū," 64–75. For a charmingly illustrated and entertaining essay on *kanban kenchiku*, see Fujimori Terunobu (text) and Masuda Akihisa (photographs), *Kanban kenchiku*.

28. On joinery and new materials, see Sakamoto Isao, *Nihon no mokuzō jūtaku no 100 nen*, 113–14, 117–20, 138–39.

29. Figures for the years 1923–28 are given in Kon Wajirō, *Shinpan dai Tōkyō annai* (1929), 1: 157. American pine was associated with cheap culture houses. It was also widely disdained because it tended to sweat; a significant instance in which the West was a source of inferior rather than high-status goods. Playing on this reputation, a scene in the novel *Culture Village Comedy* described new homeowners finding their backs glued to the exposed posts in their culture houses. "Culture houses bear none of the blame for this sort of mess. It's only because Japanese don't know how to use Western houses," the narrator comments wryly; see Sasaki Kuni, "Bunka mura no kigeki" (1926), 369.

30. Kanno Kyūichi, *Sanbyaku en no ie* (1923), 17–19.

31. Shufu no tomo henshūkyoku, *Chūryū jūtaku no mohan sekkei* (1927), 22.

32. Shimizu Keiichi, "Meijiki ni okeru shotō, chūtō kenchiku kyōiku no shiteki kenkyū," 37–40.

33. Ishikawa Katsushi, *Kaitei jitsuyō Nihon kaoku kōzō*, 174–77. The house at Ueno that Ishikawa's culture house most closely resembles is the design by Zenitaka Sakutarō, "Kazoku hon'i no shumi no kōgai muki jūtaku" (A family-oriented tasteful house for the suburbs); reproduced in Takahashi Jin, *Bunka mura jūtaku sekkei zusetsu* (1922), 58–62.

34. Ishikawa Katsushi, *Jitsuyō seiyō kaoku kōzō*.

35. Takeuchi Yoshitarō and Kon Wajirō, "Jūtaku kenchiku" (n.d.). This pamphlet lacks further publication information, but the contents place it between 1924 and 1928.

36. Waseda daigaku, Kenchiku gakka, Jūtaku kenkyūshitsu, eds., *Kindai seiyō jūtaku sekkei shiryō* (1924), table of contents, 1–2.

37. Mitsuhashi Shirō et al., *Dai kenchikugaku* (1925). For discussion of the first edition, which was published between 1904 and 1908, see Ōmi Sakai and Hori Isao, *Nihon no kenchiku*, 97–100.

38. Fujimori Terunobu et al., *Ushinawareta teito Tōkyō*, 4–5, 336–37. This book reprints a selection of photographs from the series.

39. The period during which volumes were printed under the title *Bunka jūtaku* is a fair gauge of the term's longevity in architectural circles. After 1925, comparable collections of new house designs bore names such as "Houses for the New Era" and "New Houses in Oriental Taste" instead.

40. On black-and-white photography and modernist houses, see Oshima, "Towards a Vision of the Real"; and idem, "Media and Modernity in the Work of Yamada Mamoru"; see also Colomina, *Privacy and Publicity*. Although these culture house images, like the photographs Colomina discusses of Viennese buildings, clearly contributed to the transformation of architecture into mass media product, and although the manner of their presentation abstracts them, they are, to my eye at least, far less stagy.

41. Quoted in Fujimori Terunobu et al., *Ushinawareta teito Tōkyō*, 5.

42. Watanabe Setsu, 'Genzai no kenchiku kyōiku hōshin ni tsuite,' *Kenchiku to shakai* 9, no. 12 (Dec. 1926): 15–16. An analogous complaint with regard to women's education was registered by Waseda architecture professor Satō Kōichi earlier the same year. Satō wrote that teachers in the regional women's higher schools had been "infected by recent fancy Western-style (*haikara*) magazines" and were teaching unnecessary things in their instruction on dwellings. Satō urged that women's school instruction focus attention on the fundamental issues of shelter and the maintenance of the home; see Satō Kōichi, "Chihō kōtō jogakkō ni okeru 'jū' no kyōiku ni tsuite," *Kenchiku to shakai* 9, no. 3 (Mar. 1926), 7–8.

43. Sakai Ken'ichi, "Seijō, Tamagawa gakuen jūtakuchi," 244–48.

44. Satō Kōichi, *Hōchi shinbun jūka sekkei zuan* (1916); Tonedate Masao, *Asahi jūtaku zuanshū* (1929). The *Hōchi* collection was still in print, in its 16th edition, as late as 1928.

45. The newspaper offered 2,300 yen for the first prize and received 500 entries. Of these, 85 were published (Tonedate Masao, *Asahi jūtaku zuanshū* [1929], preface).

46. House competitions generally provided an opportunity for newly minted architects to gain recognition. An earlier competition held for Ōfuna Garden City in 1922 had received 300 entries.

47. Takagi Jō, *Kasō hōten* (1928), 3.

48. Takagi Jō, *Kasō hōkan zensho* (1924), 6, 8, 7, 10.

49. The author's emphasis on what he regarded as empirical demonstration is evident in the book's subtitle, *jitchi keiken*, or "actual site-tested."

50. Takagi Jō, *Kasō hōten* (1928), 24.

51. "Wagaya o tateru ni wa, 1," *Kenchiku to shakai* 9, no. 11 (Nov. 1925): 174–79.

52. Matsudaira Hideaki and Honma Gorō, *Kasō no hanashi* (1930), 1.

53. Ibid., 164–67.

54. Ibid., 217–22.

## Chapter 9

1. Reynolds, *Maekawa Kunio and the Emergence of Japanese Modernist Architecture*, 21–35. For an account of several architectural movements in the 1920s, see Inagaki Eizō, *Nihon no kindai kenchiku*, 2: 291–325.

2. On the antidomesticity of European modernism in art and architecture, see Christopher Reed, "Introduction," in idem, *Not at Home*, 7–17.

3. Inagaki Eizō, *Nihon no kindai kenchiku*, 2: 302–3.

4. Uchida Seizō, "Jūtaku tenjijō no genfūkei to shite no 'bunka mura,'" 359; Saitō Sakai, "Tōkyō hakurankai mimono ki," *Shufu no tomo*, May 1922, 143. This article observed that the Culture Village's "closed-country policy" (*sakokushugi*) obscured the promotional value of the houses.

5. The phrase is from MacPherson, *The Political Theory of Possessive Individualism*.

6. Reprinted in *Shinbun shūroku Taishōshi*, 10: 518.

7. Jean Baudrillard speaks of the emergence of a "market of signs" when the commodity "finds its symbolism" outside capitalist exchange (see Gail Faurschou, "Obsolescence and Desire," 239–40).

8. Yamamoto Setsurō, 'Kūsō no jūtaku' (1924), quoted in idem, *Setsu sensei e nikki* (1993), 192–193. On Yamamoto, see also Uchida Seizō, *Nihon no kindai jūtaku*, 148–72.

9. Based on figures in Honma Yoshihito, *Sangyō no Shōwashi*, 83–84.

10. Meiwa Seishū, "Ōshū kōro no tokubetsushitsu yori benrina nana tsubo han no ie o tateta keiken," *Shufu no tomo* 10, no. 4 (Apr. 1926): 89–92.

11. Nawa Kiyosu, "Kane o kakezu ni benri o shu to shita saishō jūtaku no setsubi to kagu," *Shufu no tomo* 10, no. 5 (May 1926): 122–26.

12. Sogyū, "Roppyaku en no bunka jūtaku," *Kenchiku to shakai* 11, no. 4 (Apr. 1928): 12.

13. Property owners remained in the minority among the aggregate of suburban households until the postwar era of "my-homeism." That homeownership in the era of the culture house was more a lifestyle choice than an economic one is suggested in a negative sense by the fact that houses were actually more affordable in relation to real wages in the 1920s and 1930s than they were in the 1960s, yet most white-collar Tokyoites before World War II rented. Only in the 1960s did homeownership become the norm for the majority, aided considerably by state incentives and financing by large enterprises for their employees. See Waswo, *Housing in Postwar Japan*, 50–51, 92–95. For an account strongly critical of state promotion of homeownership, see Shioda Maruo, *Sumai no sengoshi*, esp. 63–71.

14. The phrase *tanoshii nagara . . .* appears to be a translation of the English "be it ever so humble . . . ," but these words do not appear in the English lyrics of the original song.

15. Moriguchi Tari and Hayashi Itoko, *Bunkateki jūtaku no kenkyū* (1922), 20, 23. It is noteworthy that this book was co-authored by a man and a woman, both of whom the preface describes as amateurs. Women's writing on the culture house is discussed further below.

16. Fujine Daitei, *Risō no bunka jūtaku* (1923), 3–6.

17. Nose Kyūichirō, *Sanjuttsubo de dekiru kairyō jūtaku* (1923), 41.

18. Ibid., 50.

19. Ibid., 43.

20. Quoted in Katō Yuri, *Taishō yume no sekkeika*, 91.

21. Nishimura Isaku, *Tanoshiki jūka* (1919), 39.

22. For an insightful analysis of Nishimura's career and life philosophy, see Katō Yuri, *Taishō yume no sekkeika*; for further on his architectural designs, including a list of known works, see Tanaka Shūji, *Nishimura Isaku no tanoshiki jūka*.

23. Punning on the title of a famous collection of Zen *kōan*, the author pronounces himself an adherent of the "gateless" philosophy (*mumonkanshugi*); Kanno Kyūichi, *Sanbyaku en no ie* (1923), 16.

24. Ibid., *furoku* 3–5, 24–32, 33, 17. First published in June 1923, this book was in its ninth printing in early September and tenth revised edition by September 25. The earthquake appears to have helped sales.

25. Ibid., *furoku* 15 and 19, 13–14, 13.

26. Watanabe Setsu, "Genzai no kenchiku kyōiku hōshin ni tsuite," *Kenchiku to shakai* 9, no. 12 (Dec. 1926): 15–16. Einstein Tower, completed in Potsdam, Germany, in 1921, attracted wide international attention for its streamlined and curved forms; see Oshima, "Hijiribashi: Spanning Time and Crossing Place."

27. As noted earlier, the Secession style had influenced furniture, interiors, and graphic design over a decade earlier. Although the original movement had ended, the term continued to be used in Japan for the wider range of architecture emerging in the 1920s that showed the influence of styles from Germany and Austria.

28. Kenchiku shashin ruiju kankōkai, *Kenchiku shashin ruiju dai 5 ki dai 21 kai* (1926). For the winning entrants' descriptions, 1: 1–4.

29. Architect Endō Arata wrote in 1921, for example, that Japanese ought to feel shame calling it "everyday life reform" to import ready-built houses from the United States; see his "Kenchiku wa rittai to shite toriatsukawaneba naranu—apaatomento hausu no sekkei ni atatte," *Katei shūhō* no. 617 (June 1921); reprinted in Endō Arata seitan hyakunen kinen jigyō iinkai, *Kenchikuka Endō Arata sakuhinshū* (1991), 9.

30. I derive the notion of style as an aesthetic dialogue loosely from Anne Hollander's interpretation of European fashion in *Sex and Suits*.

31. See Reynolds, *Maekawa Kunio and the Emergence of Japanese Modernist Architecture*, 196–221. For discussion of the work of several Japanese modernists in the 1930s and their negotiations of the problem of national style, see also Stewart, *The Making of a Modern Japanese Architecture*, 124–46. Ethnic Japanese were not the only architects working in Japan concerned with defining Japaneseness. Czech-American architect Antonin Raymond was an important figure among these modernists.

32. See Uchida, *Nihon no kindai jūtaku*, 168.

33. Examples of such houses are conspicuous in Kenchiku shashin ruiju kankōkai, *Kenchiku shashin ruiju dai 1 ki dai 2 kai* (1915), vol. 1, which features exterior photographs of houses in the Tokyo area and perspective sketches of houses from unidentified Western sources.

34. Chikama Sakichi, *Kashiya kenchiku zuan oyobi rimawari no keisan* (1924), 40.

35. Asahi shinbunsha, *Asahi jūtaku zuan shū* (1929). The preponderance of round windows has been noted in Kayano Yatsuka, *Kindai Nihon dezain bunkashi*, 440. Kayano's book is a rich resource for modern design history. Closer to home than the work of European modernist architects, Shiensō, a celebrated residential design by Horiguchi Sutemi, completed in 1926, had large round windows. On this building, see Reynolds, "The Bunriha and the Problem of 'Tradition,'" 239–42.

36. The California Arts and Crafts house, in turn, is usually considered to have been particularly strongly influenced by Japanese vernacular architecture in its use of natural wood and exposed framing.

37. I am indebted to architect Fukuhama Yoshihiro for this information.

38. Suda Tadao, *Shingo shin mondai hayawakari* (1940), 196.

39. On Vories's designs and career in Japan, see Yamagata Masaaki, *Vōrizu no jūtaku*.

40. The case of Antonin Raymond is suggestive in this connection. Raymond was Czech, but when he opened his Tokyo office in 1922, the sign he hung out read, in English: "American Architectural Office." This choice of a name contrasted Raymond's office tellingly with the older Amerika-ya, which not only used Japanese syllabary but bore the suffix *-ya* for shop, giving the business a pronouncedly commercial "downtown" cast, in keeping with its location in the old furniture district. But although the English language continued to be a useful status marker, Raymond appears to have judged otherwise with regard to the label "American." In 1928, he changed the firm's name simply to "Antonin Raymond, AIA" (Ken Oshima, pers. comm.). Amerika-ya persisted under its increasingly unfashionable name until it was required to change it in 1941 (Uchida Seizō, *Amerika-ya shōhin jūtaku*, 239).

41. According to Vincent Scully, the Spanish Revival or California Mission style began with the San Diego Exposition of 1914. Scully regards it as representing the final decadence of a creative American vernacular tradition into "eclectic pastiche" (*The Shingle Style and the Stick Style*, 157n). Yamagata Masaaki (*Vōrizu no jūtaku*, 103–

11) writes that Spanish Colonial Revival style became popular in California cities from around 1925. He is probably referring to the beginning of Spanish-style buildings on a mass scale, in towns like Pasadena. Subtle distinctions existed between the Spanish and the Spanish Mission styles, but neither Vories nor other architects in Japan maintained them.

42. Ōkuma Yoshikuni, *Kenchiku nijū kō* (1923), 60–61.

43. For a fascinating analysis of the meanings connected to second floors in Meiji fiction, see Maeda Ai, "Nikai no geshuku," in idem, *Toshi kūkan no naka no bungaku*, 250–77.

44. Takagi Jō, *Kasō hōten* (1928), 16.

45. King, *The Bungalow*, 113.

46. Hatsuda Tōru, "Kindai wafū kenchiku nyūmon," in Muramatsu Teijirō and Ōmi Sakae, *Kindai wafū kenchiku*, 26–27. *Karahafu* were condemned not as Chinese imports but as outmoded ornament. In fact, the *karahafu* design was Japanese. William Coaldrake (*Architecture and Authority in Japan*, 232) notes that foreign architects working in Japan continued to favor the *karahafu* as an "Oriental" feature while Japanese architects rejected it.

47. Fujine Daitei, *Risō no bunka jūtaku* (1923), 7.

48. For discussion of Fujii and Yamada, together with excellent photographs of Fujii's Chochikukyo, see Fujiya Yōetsu, "Jūtaku sakka no shin wafū," in Hatsuda Tōru et al., *Kindai wafū kenchiku*. On Fujii, see also Wendelken, "The Culture of Tea and Modern Japanese Architecture in the Interwar Years."

49. Onobayashi Hiroki, "Ōyamazaki no Kōetsu," 56. Between 1920 and 1927, Fujii built four experimental dwellings, after which he published detailed plans and photographs of a fifth in two lavish Japanese folios and a more modest English volume titled *The Japanese Dwelling House*. As Uchida Seizō remarks of Fujii's scientific approach, "although he called it scientific, it was meticulously prepared from the outset to assert the correctness of his own preferred 'Japanese style'" (*Nihon no kindai jūtaku*, 209). Wendelken ("The Culture of Tea and Modern Japanese Architecture in the Interwar Years") writes of the accompanying text in the Japanese folios, "An extreme rhetoric of scientific functionalism presented the houses as the product of rational inquiry and therefore intrinsically modern."

50. On the language of native style in modernist house design, see Wendelken, "The Culture of Tea and Modern Japanese Architecture in the Interwar Years"; and idem, "Pan-Asianism and the Pure Japanese Thing."

51. Kumakura Isao, *Kindai sukisha no chanoyu*, 203. Kumakura also describes a gathering in 1895 at Muian, which was probably the first of these farmhouses-turned-retreat. The wall of the cow stall served as a *tokonoma*, where a scroll was hung bearing the single character *oni* (demon). Guests sat around a large open hearth, where they cooked their own duck and soba noodles (ibid., 77–78). This

suggests an interpretation of rusticity divergent from the earlier tradition of *wabi cha*, or rustic tea. On Meiji tea connoisseurs, see also Guth, *Art, Tea and Industry*.

52. See Wendelken-Mortensen, "Living with the Past."

53. Kon Wajirō, *Nihon no minka* (1922), 34–35.

54. Shufu no tomosha, "Hyakushōya o kaizō shita chūryū jūtaku," in idem, *Chūryū wayō jūtaku*, 64. Some architects, like the tea aficionados, had admired rural houses earlier. Yasuoka Katsuya included a photograph of a thatched Japanese farmhouse in *Risō no jūtaku* (1915), noting that the "the harmony of the naturally built roof with surrounding conditions gives rise to a kind of aesthetic sense (*biteki kannen o okosaseru mono de aru*)" (p. 22).

55. Chikama Sakichi, *Kashiya kenchiku zuan oyobi rimawari no keisan* (1924), 48.

56. Kon Wajirō, "Shin katei no shinamono chōsa" (1926); reprinted in idem and Yoshida Kenkichi, *Moderunorojio* (1930), 164–65.

57. Silverberg, "Constructing the Japanese Ethnography of Modernity," *Journal of Asian Studies* 51:1 (February, 1992), 39.

## Chapter 10

1. "Che! Nani ga bunka jūtaku dee!" *Tōkyō pakku*, 16, no. 3 (Mar. 1923): 10.

2. Yanagita Kunio, *Toshi to nōson* (1929), 92.

3. Suda Tadao, *Shingo shin chishiki tsuki jōshiki jiten* (1934), 205–6.

4. Fujiya Yōetsu, "Heiwahaku bunka mura shuppin jūtaku no sehyō ni tsuite."

5. Silverberg, *Changing Song*, 227.

6. Nishimura Isaku, "Shin jūka no gaikan," in idem, *Sōshoku no enryo* (1922), 68–69, 72.

7. Ōkuma Yoshikuni, "Sōsetsu," in Jiji shinpōsha, *Ie o sumiyoku suru hō* (1927), 6.

8. These positions are well represented in the Kansai journal *Architecture and Society*. See, e.g., Minami Shin, "Hi bunka jūtaku" *Kenchiku to shakai* 10, no. 1 (Jan. 1927): 61–62.

9. The most detailed account of Yamada's career is Uchida Seizō, "Setagaya ni miru jūtaku sakka: Yamada Jun"; see also idem, *Nihon no kindai jūtaku*, 210–23.

10. *Bunka jūtaku zuan hyakushū* (1926) was a compilation of these pamphlets. Nose's name is almost entirely absent from the institutional history. The members directory of the Society of Architects for 1934 listed him as graduate of Hyōgo Prefectural Technical College, employed in the Ministry of Finance's Construction Division. He is known also to have worked briefly at Amerika-ya in the 1920s. In addition, he published frequently in *Jūtaku* and other architecture magazines, as well as writing for *Shufu no tomo* publications (both books and the magazine). The name *Bunka jūtaku kenkyūkai* appears together with Nose's name in *Shufu no tomo* as well.

11. Yasuoka Katsuya, whose cultural position was close to Yamada's although he built more Western-style houses, specifically advocated European over American

sources for designs because they harmonized better with native architecture, while he excoriated bungalows as "uncultured" (*hibunkateki*) and "ridiculous" (*Nihonka shitaru yōfū shōjūtaku*, preface [1924]).

12. Nose Kyūichirō, "Atarashii den'en jūtaku no sekkeizu," *Shufu no tomo* 10, no. 7 (July 1926): *kuchie*. Since Nose's first book of plans does not include similar farmhouse designs, it is possible that Kon's *Nihon no minka* (1922), which appeared in the same year, or subsequent works by Nishimura Isaku encouraged Nose to turn renewed attention to farmhouses. Nose's country house design, along with his design for an urban culture house, were redrawn and presented with cost estimates and new explanatory text in Shufu no tomo henshūkyoku, *Chūryū jūtaku no mohan sekkei* (1927).

13. Ironically, Yamada does not illustrate Japanese gardens of which he approves, instead accompanying photographs of his houses with critical remarks about gardeners hired by his clients who spoil the visual effect of the architecture. The implication is that the house and garden ought to be a self-contained artistic whole, composed under the direction of the architect.

14. Bourdieu, *Distinction*, 321.

15. This taste recalls Gustav Stickley's arts-and-crafts bungalows.

16. Nose, *Sanjuttsubo de dekiru kairyō jūtaku* (1923), 50.

17. Social reformers at the turn of the twentieth century had used seating arrangements and the shape of the table to embody horizontal social relations. A group called the Band of Idealists gathered in 1902 at a T-shaped table "set without any formal seating order or ranking." Nose's designs adopted this progressive reformers' antihierarchical practice and marketed it for the first time. See Ambaras, "Social Knowledge, Cultural Capital."

18. A house size of 2,000 square feet is substantially larger than the average for any occupational category listed in a survey of "middle-class" housing conducted by the Tokyo Prefecture Social Bureau in 1922. The survey included bank professionals making over 300 yen per month (see Tōkyōfu, Shakaika, *Tōkyōshi oyobi kinsetsu chōson chūtō kaikyū jūtaku chōsa* [1923], 45 [chart]).

19. The opposition between establishment architects and newcomers was not absolute. Senior architects like Satō Kōichi and Ōkuma Yoshikuni supported some culture house designers of the younger generation who were not university graduates. Takeda Goichi wrote a preface for a later collection of Nose's house plans, for example.

20. Endō Arata, "Tokubetsu furoku: Jūtaku shōhin jū go shu," *Fujin no tomo*, May 1924: 2–37 (separately paginated).

21. Yasuoka Katsuya took the even greater precaution of omitting photographs and site measurements in deference to the desires of clients in his *Nihonka shitaru yōfū shōjūtaku* (1924); see the preface to this work.

22. Yamada Jun, *Ie o tateru hito no tame ni* (1928), 258.

23. E.g., Nose Kyūichirō, *Sanjuttsubu de dekiru kairyō jūtaku* (1923), 103; Shufu no tomo henshūkyoku, *Chūryū jūtaku no mohan sekkei* (1927), pl. 4.

24. Shufu no tomo henshūkyoku, *Chūryū wayō jūtaku shū* (1929).

25. Noborio Gen'ichi, *Seikatsu to jūtaku no sekkei* (1925), back matter.

26. Seidensticker, *Kafū the Scribbler*, 99. Seidensticker notes that the house appears "undistinguished" in surviving pictures, despite Kafū's reputation for a refined sense of Western aesthetics. Judging only from Kafū's painting (reproduced in Seidensticker), it has more the character of a carpenter-designed Meiji *yōkan* than the latest in *bunka jūtaku*. Kafū's Western taste may have been somewhat antiquated, but he nevertheless had lived in the West and read widely in Western literature, giving him a privileged position from which to ridicule the superficiality of others' Western knowledge.

27. This is, in fact, the kind of model Bourdieu appears ultimately to adopt in *Distinction*, although he seeks to demonstrate that every class fraction can be defined on the basis of empirical criteria. Bourdieu's ability to correlate cultural traits with social positions may reflect an unusually fixed cultural hierarchy in France at the time of his study. Mary Douglas suggests that this makes the model itself peculiarly French. Taishō Japan lacked the stable class definitions that Bourdieu seems to be claiming for modern France, but I believe his conception of cultural production as shaped by competition among people with different social and cultural capital retains value as a model for interpreting discursive positions in a cultural field like the Taishō housing market, where birth and property, along with formal and informal education, inflected individual moves.

28. Nagy, "'How Shall We Live?'" 189–219.

29. Kano Masanao, *Senzen 'ie' no shisō*, 113; Toda Teizō, *Kazoku no kenkyū* (1926), 335. Sociologists of the family usually distinguish the "stem family household," in which multiple generations may cohabit but only one child from each generation stays past marriage, which is the typical Japanese pattern, from extended family households, which may include several adult siblings. Since Toda did not make the distinction and it is unimportant to the present context, I have chosen to use the more familiar term "extended family" to refer to anything larger than a nuclear family.

30. Toda Teizō, *Kazoku no kenkyū* (1926), 281–82.

31. Ibid., 373–374.

32. Kano Masanao, *Senzen 'ie' no shisō*, 114.

33. Kawashima Yasuyoshi, *Fujin katei ran kotohajime*, 183.

34. Oka Mitsuo, *Fujin zasshi jaanarizumu*, 135.

35. Kawashima Yasuyoshi, *Fujin katei ran kotohajime*, 137.

36. One final issue relating to the proper composition of households, and the most controversial one from the point of view of the state, was birth control. Margaret Sanger visited Japan in 1922 but was prevented by the authorities from lecturing. *Kaizō* magazine published summaries of her writing, and the subject was debated widely. Even the relatively apolitical *Housewife's Companion* suffered censorship and threats from a right-wing organization for publishing articles on the subject (see Kawashima Yasuyoshi, *Fujin katei ran kotohajime*, 142–51).

37. Yumeno Kyūsaku, "Gaitō kara mita shin Tōkyō no rimen" (1924).

38. Yumeno (ibid., 134–40) referred to people he was targeting in this satire as "lunchbox-toters of the middle class and above" (*chūryū ijō no koshiben*) and proposed punningly that culture for these people meant cheap bourgeois taste (*bunka wa buruka*).

39. This is mentioned, e.g., in "Anka de tateta benrina ie," *Shufu no tomo* 1, no. 1 (Mar. 1917): 36.

40. Tanizaki Jun'ichirō, *Chijin no ai* (1985), 10.

41. The enclosed sleeping chamber called *nando* in some farmhouses of the seventeenth and eighteenth centuries could be seen as an exception to this, but this room was also used for grain storage, childbirth, illness, and death (Ōkawa Naomi, *Sumai no jinruigaku*, 148–49).

42. Inoue Shōichi, *Ai no kūkan*, 224–25.

43. On the threat of liberated women in the 1920s, see Silverberg, *Changing Song*.

44. See Gerbert, "Space and Aesthetic Imagination in Some Taishō Writings," 70–90, for a discussion of fantasies of enclosed space in Tanizaki's *Naomi* and other works of Taishō fiction; Gerbert notes that several authors referred to their fictional interior settings as "fairylands."

45. Almost all writers on architecture in the *Housewife's Companion* were men, at least when the author was identified. The magazine did have female reporters, however (Shufu no tomosha, *Shufu no tomo sha no gojūnen*, 174).

46. Tsuruko, "Shumi to jitsuyō o kaneru chiisana yōkan," *Shufu no tomo*, Dec. 1920: 126–27. The author was probably Matsuda Tsuruko (Tsuruji), the magazine's first female reporter (Shufu no tomosha, *Shufu no tomo no gojūnen*, 65, 88). This is the same Ōfuna where a garden city would be planned two years later.

47. This was also the first example of the accidental encounter and unannounced visit, a device used several times subsequently in the *Housewife's Companion*. Articles began with the reporter's discovering a particularly attractive house and resolving to go straight to the door. The reporter would then describe the first reaction of the master or mistress of the house, who eventually consented to a tour. Some of these articles were accompanied by construction budgets and interior perspective sketches.

48. Tsuruko, "Shumi to jitsuyō o kaneru chiisana yōkan," *Shufu no tomo*, Dec. 1920: 126.

49. See Sand, "Was Meiji Taste in Interiors Orientalist?" 648–49.

50. The association of textile production and women can be found in almost all cultures since Neolithic times. I do not mean to claim that pliability, softness, and roundness are intrinsically female characteristics, however. Rather, *shugei*'s feminization of the domestic interior functioned through terms provided by a Western discourse of femininity that construed them as such. This aesthetic development cannot be subsumed solely to either gender or national-cultural polarities—the different cultural variables constantly articulate with one another.

51. "Nagaisu no kusshon," *Arusu fujin kōza* (1927), vol. 2, plates.

52. "Ippen shita natsu no shitsunai sōshoku," *Shufu no tomo* 10, no. 6 (June 1926): 33. The magazine's *shugei* advice for women was dominated by men. When a *shugei* competition was sponsored at *Shufu no tomo* headquarters in 1923, for example, entries were judged by an all-male panel (Shufu no tomosha, *Shufu no tomo sha no gojūnen*, 110–11).

53. Ono Michiko, "Shirōto sekkei," *Sandee Mainichi* 1, nos. 1–11 (Apr. 2–June 11, 1922).

54. Ono Michiko, "Shirōto sekkei: Shō jūtaku no kenkyū," *Sandee Mainichi* 1, no. 1 (Apr. 2, 1922): 8. The word *dōraku* suggests indulgence or dilettantism. In verb form and with the suffix *-mono*, it takes on connotations explicitly related to male debauchery.

55. Ono Michiko, "Shirōto sekkei: Watashi wa mayotte imasu, isu to zabuton no fuchōwa," *Sandee Mainichi* (May 21, 1922): 8.

56. Ono Michiko, "Shirōto sekkei: Ni kazoku kyōdō no jūtaku," *Sandee Mainichi* (June 11, 1922): 8.

57. This stands in contrast to the North American feminists whose ideas Dolores Hayden has examined in *The Grand Domestic Revolution*. Hani Motoko published plans for a four-family communal house in 1930, but I am not aware of earlier examples in Japan.

58. Involvement of both women and men in architecture has only recently begun to yield fundamental reconceptions of domesticity in Japan. See in particular the dialogues between feminist sociologist Ueno Chizuko and architect Yamamoto Riken in Ueno Chizuko, *Kazoku o ireru hako, kazoku o koeru hako* (Heibonsha, 2002), 132–55.

59. Mitsuko, "Shichigatsu gō keisai no sekkei o hyō su," in "Jūtaku mondō," *Fujin no tomo*, Sept. 1923: 113–22.

60. I borrow this interpretation from scholars in other contexts. The analysis by Janice Radway ("On the Gender of the Middlebrow Consumer and the Threat of the Culturally Fraudulent Female") of critics' attitudes toward middle-brow cultural institutions like the Book-of-the-Month Club makes an analogous point for the literary field. See also Huyssen, *After the Great Divide*. Nishikawa Yūko ("Otoko no ie,

onna no ie," 623) notes the same point with regard to male Japanese architects in the postwar period.

## Conclusion

1. For a theoretical discussion of the marginalization of practical knowledge, see Certeau, *The Practice of Everyday Life*, esp. 68–72.

2. Yanagita Kunio, *Meiji Taishōshi sesōhen* (1931), 70–72.

3. As Walter Benjamin observed of what he called the "urban phantasmagoria" of the modern marketplace, what was new was not commodification itself but the transformation of commodities into signs, no longer determined by either use value or exchange value (Buck-Morss, *The Dialectics of Seeing*, 81–82).

4. See, e.g., Hall, "The Early Formation of Victorian Domestic Ideology," 9–14; idem, "The Sweet Delights of Home"; and Stone, *The Family, Sex and Marriage in England*.

5. Ann Waswo, "Translator's introduction," in Nagatsuka, *The Soil*, xvi. Nagatsuka, too, was seeing rural conditions with the eyes of an urbanized intellectual. His novel therefore was not a simple record of rural conditions. It was clearly intended to be a sympathetic portrait, yet the narrative also frequently dwells on examples of unenlightened behavior, particularly peasants' ignorance of hygiene.

6. See, e.g., Leora Auslander's sophisticated study of French furniture, *Taste and Power: Furnishing Modern France*; or Karen Haltunnen's classic article on the American living room, "From Parlor to Living Room."

7. This preoccupation with the nuances of house plan reached its zenith in the wartime work of Nishiyama Uzō, who developed the discipline of *jūtaku keikaku*, or dwelling planning, preserved in postwar Japanese architecture departments. It has also dominated more recent analysis of the history of the dwelling, not without considerable fruit. For the genealogy of the system of house planning around southern orientations, see Uchida, "The Issue of Southern Exposure in the Development of Modern Japanese Housing." For thorough analyses of modern single-family dwelling forms entirely in terms of planning permutations, see Kimura Norikuni, "Nihon kindai toshi dokuritsu jūtaku"; and Aoki Masao, "Chūryū jūtaku no heimen kōsei."

8. "Jūtaku kaizen no konpon hōshin," in Seikatsu kaizen dōmeikai, *Monbushō kōshūkai* (1922), 104.

9. Bourdieu, *Distinction*, 345.

10. Radical intellectual Takahashi Kamekichi would argue in the 1930s that Japan was a "proletarian nation" (see Hoston, "Marxism and Japanese Expansionism").

11. Chimoto Akiko, "Nihon ni okeru seibetsu yakuwari bungyō no keisei," 220–25.

12. Kumakura Isao, *Bunka to shite no manaa*, 125–36; see also idem, "Kindai no chanoyu," 84–85, 223.

13. Fujimori Terunobu in Yoshimura Junzō, Ikeda Takeo, Fujimori Terunobu, and Uchida Seizō, "Jūtaku sakka no kusawake, Yamamoto Setsurō o kataru," in Yamamoto Setsurō, *Setsu sensei nikki* (1993), 207.

14. Yanagita Kunio, *Meiji Taishōshi sesōhen* (1931), 335. This concluding chapter, so different in tone from the nostalgic narrative preceding it, seems rarely to have been noted by Yanagita scholars.

15. Ibid., 69.

16. Ibid., 339.

17. Nishikawa Yūko, "Otoko no ie, onna no ie," 628.

18. Ochiai, *The Japanese Family System in Transition*, 38–45, 60–61.

19. Miura Atsushi, *"Kazoku" to "kōfuku" no sengoshi.*

20. Partner, *Assembled in Japan*, 137–92 *passim.*

21. Home extension officers, initially trained by U.S. Occupation authorities and sent throughout the Japanese countryside by the Ministry of Agriculture in the 1950s, 1960s, and 1970s, carried forward the mission to reform kitchens for hygiene and efficiency. By the fourth postwar decade, the task was largely accomplished, thanks most of all to the increased affluence that permitted farm households to install gas, running water, stainless steel counters, and refrigerators. Local government offices still maintain a desk for a female home extension officer trained by the Ministry of Agriculture, who is known as an "everyday life improvement promoter" (*seikatsu kairyō fukyūin*). The focus of her work has shifted, however, toward regional culture boosterist activities such as assisting women's volunteer groups to develop new products for the tourist market.

22. Partner, *Assembled in Japan*, 184–85.

23. Miura Atsushi, *"Kazoku" to "kōfuku" no sengoshi*, 14–16.

24. Ochiai, *The Japanese Family System in Transition*, 104–11.

25. Miura Atsushi, *"Kazoku" to "kōfuku" no sengoshi*, 139; Nishikawa Yūko, "Otoko no ie, onna no ie," 628.

26. This is not to say that the alienated youth, soured marriages, and the dwindling importance of kin support networks lamented by social critics since the late 1970s are fictional. The new emphasis, however, shows that the mass media had ceased to be the unequivocal promoters of bourgeois domesticity that they had been during the years that it was a goal yet to be achieved by the majority of the nation.

27. For an example of the golden-age utopian version of prewar domesticity, see Honma Chieko, *Chichi no iru shokutaku*. One of the best-known dystopian images of home in popular media of the same era is the film *Kazoku geemu* (Family game, directed by Morita Yoshimitsu; 1983). The family in this film dine together but seated in line facing the camera, in an ironic spatial antithesis to the circle promoted by *katei* ideologues.

28. Funo Shūji, "Nishiyama Uzō ron josetsu III," 116.

29. Nishikawa Yūko, "Otoko no ie, onna no ie," 621.

30. Receiving guests at home had in fact become so uncommon that appliance manufacturer Matsushita ran advertisements in 1958 urging consumers to invite guests into their homes more often (presumably with the aim of increasing opportunities for "keeping-up-with-the-Joneses" comparisons) (see Partner, *Assembled in Japan*, 155–56). Although the context and the social meaning of the message differed, juxtaposed with the rhetoric of late Meiji reformers, who were anxious that their audience make greater efforts to preserve the family circle by keeping guests at a distance, this campaign shows a case in which domestic propaganda had come full circle in a half-century.

31. The classic expression of this was architect Hamaguchi Miho's influential 1949 work *The Feudalism of Japanese Houses* (*Nihon jūtaku no hōkensei*); see Ōkawa Naomi, *Sumai no jinruigaku*, 195.

32. *Nihon mokuzō jūtaku no 100 nen*, 192.

33. For an analysis of the long evolution toward the single *washitsu*, see Ōkawa Naomi, *Sumai no jinruigaku*, 163–92.

34. On the modern history of floor-sitting and chairs in Japan, see Sawada Tomoko, *Yukaza, isuza*.

35. Bestor, *Neighborhood Tokyo*, 261–65.

36. See Bestor, "The Shitamachi Revival."

37. On *seikatsu bunka* and philosophies of the folk, see Harootunian, *Overcome by Modernity*, 292–357; and Brandt, "The Folk-Craft Movement in Early Showa Japan, 1925–1945."

38. The Japanese text of Article 25 reads: "Subete no kokumin wa, kenkō de bunkateki na saitei gendo no seikatsu o itonamu kenri o yūsuru." According to Inoue Kyoko (*MacArthur's Japanese Constitution*, 91), the "aspirational clause" about a "healthy and cultured life" was added by Japanese participants in the drafting process.

# Bibliography

Unless otherwise noted, the place of publication for Japanese-language works is Tokyo.

## Japanese-Language Primary Sources

Abe Isoo. *Ōyō shisei ron*. Hidaka yūrindō, 1908.

———. *Shakai mondai gairon*. Waseda daigaku shuppanbu, 1921.

Amano Kaoru (Seisai). *Daidokoro kairyō: katei hōten*. Hakubunkan, 1907.

———. *Katei nichijō no jikken*. Jitsugyō no Nihonsha, 1908.

*Arusu fujin kōza*. 3 vols. Arusu, 1927.

Asahi shinbunsha, ed. *Asahi jūtaku zuan shū*. Tokyo, Osaka: Asahi shinbunsha, 1929.

———. *Jitsuyō kagaku Asahi katei sōsho: Jū no maki*. Tokyo, Osaka: Asahi shinbunsha, 1930.

———. *Jūtaku kairyō no shomondai*. Asahi shinbunsha, 1930.

———. *Katei keizai no kaizen: seikatsu o raku ni suru hō*. Asahi shinbunsha, 1929.

Bungaku dōshikai, ed. *Ie no takara*. Kōseikan, 1895.

Bunka kenkyūkai, ed. *Bunka jūtaku no kenkyū*. Bunka panfuretto, 15. Bunka kenkyūkai, 1923.

Chiba Kameo. "Kindaijin no seikatsu shinjō to shashi zeitaku no igi." *Chūō kōron* 39, no. 9 (Aug. 1924): 56–63.

Chikama Sakichi. *Kashiya kenchiku zuan oyobi rimawari no keisan*. 1922. 4th ed. Suzuki shoten, 1924.

Chokei Dōjin. *Kasei ippan*. Katei zensho, 10. Osaka: Shōbundō, 1901.

———. *Katei no kairaku*. Katei zensho, 11. Osaka: Shōbundō, 1902.

Dai Nihon kasei gakkai, ed. *Katei no shiori*. *Fujin bunko*. Dai Nihon kasei gakkai, 1909.

Endō Arata seitan hyakunen kinen jigyō iinkai, ed. *Kenchikuka Endō Arata sakuhinshū*. Chūō kōron bijutsu shuppan, 1991.
Endō Oto. *Wayō kenchiku sekkei zue*. Ōkura shoin, 1914.
Ezawa Teruaki. *Wagaya kenpō: Katei soshiki hōkan*. Shinseidō, 1908.
Fujii Kōji. *Nihon no jūtaku*. Iwanami shoten, 1928.
Fujine Daitei. *Risō no bunka jūtaku*. Arusu, 1923.
*Fujin gahō dai 2 nen dai 3 gō teiki zōkan: shitsunai sōshoku*. Feb. 15, 1906.
Fujin no tomosha. "Katei seikatsu gōrika tenrankai." In *Jiyū gakuen no rekishi: Zōshigaya jidai*, 278–85. Fujin no tomosha, 1988.
Fukuda Masujirō. *Katei komon*. Seikōkan, 1903.
*Gendai manga taikan 9: onna no sekai*. Chūō bijutsusha, 1928.
Gonda Yasunosuke. "Rōdōsha oyobi shōgaku hōkyū seikatsusha no kakei jōtai hikaku" (1926). In *Seikatsu koten sōsho 7: kakei chōsa to seikatsu kenkyū*, ed. Chūbachi Masayoshi. Kōseikan, 1971.
Gotōken Sensai, ed. *Katei bunko: joshi reigi sahō*. Kōseikan, 1906.
Hamaguchi Miho. *Nihon jūtaku no hōkensei*. Sagami shobō, 1949.
Hani Motoko, ed. *Katei jogaku kōgi*. 1909– .
———. *Katei no tomo kakeibo*. Naigai shuppan kyōkai, 1906.
Hayashi Fumiko. "Ie o tsukuru ni atatte." Reprinted in "Hayashi Fumiko kinenkan" (pamphlet). Tōkyōto Shinjuku kuritsu Hayashi Fumiko kinenkan.
Hirano Shōsen. *Bunka seikatsu no chishiki*. Yūeisha shuppanbu, 1925.
Hoashi Riichirō. *Bunka seikatsu to ningen kaizō*. 6th ed. Hakubunkan, 1922.
Hoshino Tetsuo. *Jūtaku mondai*. Kinbara shoten, 1925.
Inoue Hanjirō. *Tsūzoku kaoku kairyō kenchikuhō*. Hakubunkan, 1902.
Inoue Hideko. *Gendai kaji kyōkasho*. 4th rev. ed. Bunkōsha, 1928.
———. *Katei kanri*. Bunkōsha, 1925.
———. *Saishin kaji teiyō*. Meguro shoten, 1925.
———. *Yomeiri sōsho: kasei hen*. Jitsugyō no Nihonsha, 1929.
Ishibashi Chūwa. *Shobutsu seihō myōjutsu kihō: banmin no jitsueki*. Osaka: Terai Yosaburō, 1886.
Ishikawa Katsushi. *Jitsuyō seiyō kaoku kōzō*. Dai Nihon kōgyō gakkai, 1926.
———. *Kaitei jitsuyō Nihon kaoku kōzō*. Rev. 10th ed. Dai Nihon kōgyō gakkai, 1926.
Ishizawa Yoshimaro. *Kaji shin kyōkasho*. 2 vols. 11th rev. ed. Shūseidō, 1926.
Itagaki Taisuke. "Chūryū no katei to jiyū no seishin (1909)." In *Itagaki Taisuke zenshū*, ed. Itagaki Morimasa, 557–58. Hara shobō, 1969.
———. "Fūzoku kairyō iken (1903)." In *Itagaki Taisuke zenshū*, ed. Itagaki Morimasa, 427–54. Hara shobō, 1969.
———. "Katei no kairyō." In *Itagaki Taisuke zenshū*, ed. Itagaki Morimasa, 501–16. Hara shobō, 1969.

Itō Chūta. "Jūtaku." In *Risō no katei*, ed. Kokumin shinbunsha, 113–28. Minyūsha, 1915.
Ito Sakon. *Katei eisei kōwa*. Kinshi hōryūdō, 1909.
Itō Yōjirō. *E iri nichiyō kaji yōhō: tsūzoku keizai*. 1886. 21st ed. Nagoya: Gyokujundō, 1903.
Iwase Matsuko. *Wayō shoreishiki annai*. Daigakukan, 1905.
Jiji shinpōsha, ed. *Atarashii Tōkyō to kenchiku no hanashi*. Jiji shinpōsha, 1924.
———. *Ie o sumiyoku suru hō*. Jiji shinpōsha, 1927.
*Jogaku sekai dai 4 kan dai 12 gō shūki zōkan: shakai hyaku seikatsu*. Sept. 15, 1904.
Jūtaku kairyōkai, comp. and ed. *Shō jūtaku shū*. Jūtaku kairyōkai, 1925.
"Jūtaku mondai to Nihon kenchiku no shōrai." *Kokka gakkai zasshi* 33, no. 9 (1919).
Kaetsu Kōko. *Katei bunko: kasei kōwa*. Fujin bunko kankōkai, 1916.
Kai Hisako. *Seikatsu kaizen keitōteki kasei kōwa*. 2 vols. Bunka tosho kankōkai, 1922.
Kamata Kenzō. *Sen'en ika de dekiru risō no jūtaku*. 13th rev. ed. Suzuki shoten, 1922.
Kaneko Seikichi. *Nihon jūtaku kenchiku zuan hyakushu*. Kenchiku shoin, 1913.
Kanno Kyūichi. *Sanbyaku en no ie: bunka jūtaku*. Morimoto shoin, 1923.
Kano Yūkichi. *Gendai jūtaku kenchikuron*. Tenjinsha, 1930.
Katei keizai kenkyūkai, ed. *Kaji kyōkasho*. Rev. ed. Teikoku shoin, 1924.
Kawakubo Tokuzō. *Katei o chūshin to suru seikatsu no kaizō*. Kibun shoin, 1921.
Kenchiku sekaisha, ed. *Jūtaku kenchiku*. 1916.
Kenchiku shashin ruiju kankōkai, ed. *Kenchiku shashin ruiju dai 1 ki dai 2 kai: jūtaku no gaikan 1*. Kōyōsha, 1915.
———. *Kenchiku shashin ruiju dai 3 ki dai 20 shū: bessō kenchiku kan ni*. Kōyōsha 1922.
———. *Kenchiku shashin ruiju dai 4 ki dai 7 kai—dai 6 ki dai 7 kai: bunka jūtaku* (5 vols.). Kōyōsha 1924.
———. *Kenchiku shashin ruiju dai 5 ki dai 21 kai: jū go roku tsubo no shō jūtaku*. 3 vols. Kōyōsha, 1926.
Kikuchi Shūichirō. *Shirōto ni wakaru sumigokochi yoki jūtaku to teien*. Nimatsudō, 1924.
Kikuchi Yūhō. "Watashi no tateta watashi no jūtaku." *Shin katei* 3 (May 1918): 16–24.
Kobayashi Ichizō. *Itsuō jijoden: seishun soshite Hankyū o kataru*. 1952. Hankyū dentetsu kabushiki gaisha, 1979.
Kobayashi Shigeki. *Meiji no Tōkyō seikatsu: josei no kaita Meiji no nikki*. Kadokawa sensho, 1991.
Kōda Rohan. "Kaoku." 1897. In *Rohan zenshū 29: Zuihitsu 1*, 89–94. Iwanami shoten, 1954.
Kogure Tadakazu. *Jūtaku to kenchiku*. Dai Nihon hyakka zenshū. Seibundō, 1928.
Kokumin shinbunsha, ed. *Risō no katei*. Minyūsha, 1915.
Kon Wajirō. *Nihon no minka*. 1922. Iwanami bunko, 1989.
———. *Shinpan dai Tōkyō annai*. 1929. Chikuma shobō, 2001.

Kon Wajirō and Yoshida Kenkichi. *Moderunorojio "Kōgengaku."* 1930. Facsimile ed. Gakuyō shobō, 1986.

Kondō Kōzō. *Shinpen kaji kyōkasho.* 2 vols. 4th rev. ed. Kōfūkan, 1930.

Kondō Masakazu, ed. *Kasei hōten.* Tōyōsha, 1906.

———. *Shinsen kaji mondō.* Hakubunkan, 1905.

Maeda Shōin. *Kinsei jūtaku.* Daihōkan, 1923.

Manpuku Naokiyo. *Kokutei kyōkasho ni mietaru kaji kyōju shiryō.* Hōbunkan, 1906.

Matsudaira Hideaki and Honma Gorō. *Kasō no hanashi.* Tōgensha, 1930.

Minyūsha, ed. *Katei no waraku.* Katei sōsho, 1. 1894.

———. *Katei rizai.* Minyūsha katei sōsho gōgai. Minyūsha, 1895.

———. *Kasei seiri.* Katei sōsho, 7. Minyūsha, 1894.

Mitsuhashi Shirō et al. *Dai kenchikugaku.* 4 vols. Ōkura shoten, 1925.

*Mitsukoshi shashinchō: The Illustrated Mitsukoshi Store.* Pamphlet. N.p., n.d. Copy at United States Library of Congress (MLCSJ 89/01536).

Miura Motohide. *Risōteki jūtaku no madori.* Satō shuppan, 1920.

Miwada Masako. *Shin katei kun.* Katei hyakka zensho 1. Hakubunkan, 1907.

Monbushō. *Kōtō shōgaku rika kaji kyōkasho.* Nihon shoseki kabushiki gaisha, 1915.

Monbushō. Gakumukyoku, ed. and comp. *Shōgakkō kyōin jūtaku zuan (tsuki kenchiku shiyōsho gaiyō).* Kokumin kyōikusha, 1908.

Mori Tomokichi, ed. *Nihon jūtaku shashin zufu.* 1912.

Moriguchi Tari and Hayashi Itoko. *Bunkateki jūtaku no kenkyū.* Arusu, 1922.

Morimoto Kōkichi. *Horobiyuku kaikyū.* Dōbunkan, 1924.

———. *Seikatsu mondai.* Dōbunkan, 1920. Reprinted in *Kaseigaku seikatsugaku kenkyū kiso bunkenshū,* vol. 4. Daikūsha, 1988.

———. "Seikatsu yōshiki no shinka yori mitaru shin jūtaku." *Taiyō* 31 (June 1925): 13–15.

Murai Gensai. *Gejo dokuhon e iri.* Hakubunkan, 1903.

———. *Zōho chūshaku Shokudōraku.* 4 vols. Hōchisha shuppanbu, 1903–4.

Naimushō. Chihōkyoku yūshi, ed. *Den'en toshi.* Hakubunkan, 1908.

Nakama Teruhisa, ed. *Nihon chiri fūzoku taikei 2: Dai Tōkyō hen.* Shinkōsha, 1929–32.

Nakamura Kan. "Jūtaku no kaizen ni tsuite," ed. Seikatsu kaizen dōmeikai. In *Kongo no katei seikatsu,* 301–23. Hōbunkan, 1931.

Naya Matsuzō. *Keizai hon'i no jūtaku.* Suzuki shoten, 1920.

———. *Sanzen en ika de dekiru shumi no jūtaku.* Rev. 7th ed. Suzuki shoten, 1924.

Nihon joshi daigakkō. Kasei kenkyūbu, ed. *Jūtaku kairyō to kenchiku zairyō.* Bunkōsha, 1926.

Nihon kenchiku gakkai. *Nihon kenchiku gakkai jūsho seimei roku.* 1930.

———. *Shōwa 9 nen kenchiku gakkai kaiin seimei jūsho roku.* 1934.

Nishimura Isaku. *Seikatsu o geijutsu to shite.* Minbunsha, 1922.

———. *Sōshoku no enryo.* Bunka seikatsu kenkyūkai, 1922.

———. *Tanoshiki jūka.* 3rd ed. Keiseisha shoten, 1919.
Noborio Gen'ichi. *Seikatsu to jūtaku no sekkei.* Geiensha, 1925.
Nose Kyūichirō. *Bunka jūtaku zuan hyakushū.* Bunka jūtaku kenkyūkai, 1926.
———. *Sanjuttsubo de dekiru kairyō jūtaku.* Kōyōsha, 1923.
Nōshōmushō. Sanrinkyoku, ed. *Mokuzai no kōgeiteki riyō.* Dai Nihon sanrinkai, 1912.
Nukada Yutaka. *Anka seikatsu hō.* Seikyōsha, 1915.
Ōe Sumiko. *Nyōbō, seppō, teppō: sanbō shugi.* Hōbunkan, 1911.
———. *Ōyō kaji kyōkasho.* 2 vols. Rev. 6th ed. Hōbunkan, 1925.
Ōfuna den'en toshi kabushiki gaisha, ed. *Den'en jūtaku zushū.* Ōfuna den'en toshi kabushiki gaisha, 1922.
Ogawa Ichitarō. *Dai toshi.* Shimin sōsho, 1923.
———. *Jūtaku mondai.* Umezu shoten, 1919.
Ōhashi Sōtarō, ed. *Nichiyō hyakka zensho dai hachi hen: jūkyo to engei.* Hakubunkan, 1896.
Ōkōchi Kazuo. *Nihonteki chūsan kaikyū.* Bungei shunjūsha, 1960.
Ōkuma Yoshikuni. *Kenchiku nijū kō.* Suzuki shoten, 1923.
———. *Shumi no kenchiku kōwa.* Suzuki shoten, 1921.
Ōmoto Moichirō. *Bunken kaji gōkaku shishin.* Bunkōsha, 1925.
Ōmura Jintarō. *Kyōiku sōwa: Kodomo to katei.* Dōbunkan, 1907.
Ōno Miyuki. *Sumigokochi yoki wayō setchū.* Kōyōsha, 1924.
Ōsaka Mainichi shinbunsha, ed. *Kenkō jūtaku sekkei zuanshū.* Ōkura shoten, 1930.
Ōsaka shōkō kaigisho, ed. *Ishokujū ni kansuru seikatsu kaizen sangyō kaizen.* Osaka, 1931.
Ōya Sōichi. *Ōya Sōichi zenshū.* Sōyōsha, 1981.
Sakai Toshihiko, *Katei no shin fūmi.* 1901–2. Reprinted in *Sakai Toshihiko zenshū dai 3 kan.* Hōritsu bunkasha, 1971.
Sakata Shizuko and Gokan Kikuno. *Joshi sahōsho: gishiki no bu.* Meguro shobō, 1906.
———. *Kaitei kinsei kaji kyōkasho.* 2 vols. 6th rev. ed. Meguro shoten, 1927.
———. *Kōtō jogakkōyō kaji kyōkasho.* Meguro shoten and Narumidō shoten, 1911, 1917.
———. *Kōtō jogakkōyō kaji kyōkasho.* 2 vols. 2nd ed. Meguro shoten, 1912.
Sano Toshikata. *Jūtakuron.* Bunka seikatsu kenkyūkai, 1925.
Sasaki Kichisaburō. *Katei kairyō to katei kyōiku.* Meguro shoten, 1917.
Sasaki Kuni. "Bunka mura no kigeki." 1926. In *Sasaki Kuni zenshū,* 349–97. Kōdansha, 1980.
———. "Fūfu hyakumensō." 1929. In *Sasaki Kuni zenshū,* 5–100. Kōdansha, 1980.
Satō Kōichi, ed. *Hōchi shinbun jūka sekkei zuan.* Ōkura shoten, 1916.
Seikatsu kaizen dōmeikai, ed. *Jūtaku kagu no kaizen.* Seikatsu kaizen dōmeikai, 1924.
———. *Jūtaku kaizen no hōshin.* 1920.
———. *Kongo no katei seikatsu.* Hōbunkan, 1931.
———. *Monbushō kōshūkai: seikatsu kaizen no kenkyū.* Dai Nihon tosho, 1922.

———. *Seikatsu kaizen chōsa kettei jikō*. Seikatsu kaizen dōmeikai, 1923.
Seki Hajime. *Bunka to jūtaku mondai*. Osaka: privately printed, 1921.
———. *Jūtaku mondai to toshi keikaku*. Kyoto: Kōbundō, 1923.
Serizawa Eiji. *Shin Nihon no jūka*. Arusu, 1924.
Shiga Shigetaka. *Nihon fūkeiron*. 1894. Iwanami bunko, 1937.
Shimoda Utako. *Fujin jōshiki no yōsei*. Jitsugyō no Nihonsha, 1910.
———. *Kaji yōketsu*. Katei bunko, 7. Hakubunkan, 1899.
Shufu no tomo henshūkyoku, ed. *Chūryū jūtaku no mohan sekkei*. Shufu no tomo jitsuyō hyakka sōsho, 28. Shufu no tomo sha, 1927.
———. *Chūryū wayō jūtaku shū*. Shufu no tomo sha, 1929.
———. *Daidokoro oyobi yudono no sekkei*. Shufu no tomo sha, 1929.
———. *Mohan jūtaku 29 shu: benrina ie no shinchikushū*. Shufu no tomo, 1936.
Soeda Hisaichi. *Ikka no kiso*. Daigakukan, 1914.
———. "Katei no keizai." In Seikatsu kaizen dōmeikai, ed., *Monbushō kōshūkai: seikatsu kaizen no kenkyū*. Dai Nihon tosho, 1922.
Suda Tadao. *Shingo shin chishiki tsuki jōshiki jiten*. Dai Nihon yūben kōdansha, 1934.
———. *Shingo shin mondai hayawakari (kingu dai jukkan dai ichi gō shinnen gō furoku)*. Dai Nihon yūben kōdansha, 1940.
Sugimoto Buntarō. *Nihon jūtaku shitsunai sōshoku hō*. Kenchiku shoin, 1910.
———. *Zukai Nihon zashiki no kazarikata*. Kenchiku shoin, 1912.
Suzukawa Magosaburō. *Dare ni mo wakaru shigaichi kenchikubutsu hō zukai*. Kenchiku shoin, 1924.
Takagi Jō. *Kasō hōkan zensho: jitchi keiken*. 1924. 2nd ed. Shunkōdō, 1931.
———. *Kasō hōten*. Banrikaku shobō, 1928.
Takahashi Bunjirō, ed. *Shōgaku onna reishiki kunkai*. Takahashi Heizaburō, 1882.
Takahashi Jin, ed. *Bunka mura jūtaku sekkei zusetsu: heiwa kinen Tōkyō hakurankai shuppin*. Suzuki shoten, 1922.
Takanashi Yūtarō. *Bunka mura no kan'i jūtaku*. Kōyōsha, 1922.
Takeda Goichi and Matsumoto Gihachi. *Saishin wayō jūtaku bessō kenchikuhō (zōteiban)*. Sekizenkan, 1923 (1920).
Takeshima Shigeo. *Mohan kyōiku: wagaya no shin katei*. Hōbunkan, 1905.
Takeuchi Yoshitarō and Kon Wajirō. "Jūtaku kenchiku." Pamphlet. Teikoku kōgyō kyōikukai, n.d.
Tamura Kō. "Jūtaku kairyō mondai." *Tōkyō Asahi shinbun*, Jan. 8 and 10, 1922.
Tanahashi Gentarō. "Seikatsu kaizen undō." In Hasegawa Yoshinobu, *Shakai seisaku taikei dai 9 kan*, 1–143 (separately paginated). Daitō shuppansha, 1927.
Tanaka Shirosaemon. *Risō no jūtaku*. Katei bunko. Fujin bunko kankōkai, 1915.
Tanizaki Jun'ichirō. *Chijin no ai*. 81st ed. Shinchō bunko, 1985.
Toda Teizō. *Kazoku no kenkyū*. Kōbundō, 1926.

Tōkyōfu. Gakumubu. Shakaika. *Tōkyōfu gogun ni okeru kaoku chintai jijō chōsa.* Tōkyōfu, 1932.
Tōkyōfu. Shakaika. *Tōkyōshi oyobi kinsetsu chōson chūtō kaikyū jūtaku chōsa.* Tōkyōfu, 1923.
Tōkyōshi. Shakaikyoku. *Tōkyōshi jūtaku chōsa.* 1931.
*Tōkyōshi shikō shigai hen 3*, vol. 80. 1988.
Tōkyō shiyakusho. *Shisei tōkei genpyō (shin shibu hen).* 1930.
Tonedate Masao, ed. *Asahi jūtaku zuanshū.* Asahi shinbunsha, 1929.
———. *Jūtaku kairyō no shomondai.* Asahi shinbunsha, 1930.
Tōyō keizai shinpō. *Nihon bōeki seiran.* Tōyō keizai shinpōsha, 1935.
Tsuboko Hisao. *Gohyakuen kara gosen'en made no wayō jūtaku oyobi nagaya zuanshū.* Suzuki shoten, 1926.
Tsuchiya Gensaku. *Kaoku kairyōdan.* Jiji shinpōsha, 1898.
Tsukamoto Hamako. *Shinpen kaji kyōhon.* 2 vols. Kinkōdō shoseki kabushiki gaisha, 1903.
Ubukata Toshirō. "Mado kara mita bunka mura." *Chūō kōron* 37, no. 5 (May 1922): 75–76.
Ueki Emori. *Katei kaikaku, fujin kaihōron.* Ed. Sotozaki Mitsuhiro. Heibunsha, 1971.
Uno Ryōken. *Katei hōkan.* Chūseidō, 1915.
Uramori Fumi. *Shintei kaji kyōkasho.* Meguro shoten, 1918.
Waseda daigaku. Kenchiku gakka. Jūtaku kenkyūshitsu, ed. *Kindai seiyō jūtaku sekkei shiryō.* Kōyōsha, 1924.
Watanabe Chikuin. *Meiji no katei.* Maekawa bun'eikaku, 1904.
Yamada Inako and Shinnō Masaki. *Jissen kaseihō.* Shūeidō, 1901.
Yamada Jun. *Ie o tateru hito no tame ni.* Shibundō, 1928.
Yamada Taichirō. *Risō no nōson.* Shōkabō, 1905.
Yamagata Kahō. *Nichijō seikatsu: ishokujū.* Jitsugyō no Nihonsha, 1907.
Yamamoto Setsurō. *Setsu sensei e nikki.* Ed. Uchida Seizō. Sumai no toshokan shuppankyoku, 1993.
Yamanaka Setsuji. *Bunka seikatsu to sono jūtaku.* Teikoku kenchiku kyōkai, 1925.
Yanagita Kunio. *Meiji Taishōshi sesōhen.* 1931. Heibonsha Tōyō bunko, 1967.
———. *Toshi to nōson.* Asahi jōshiki kōza, 6. Asahi shinbunsha, 1929.
Yasuoka Katsuya. *Nihonka shitaru yōfū shōjūtaku.* Suzuki shoten, 1924.
———. *Ōbeika shitaru Nihon shōjūtaku.*
———. Suzuki shoten, 1925. *Risō no jūtaku.* Katei bunko. Fujin bunko kankōkai, 1915.
———. *Shōjūtaku no yōfū sōshoku.* Suzuki shoten, 1925.
———. *Wafū o shu to suru setchū shōjūtaku.* Suzuki shoten, 1927.
———. *Yōfū o shu to suru setchū shōjūtaku.* Suzuki shoten, 1927.
Yokoyama Gennosuke. *Meiji fugōshi.* 1910. Reprinted: Gendai kyōyō bunko, 1989.

Yokoyama Shin. *Zukai hon'i shin jūka no sekkei*. Arusu, 1923.
Yoshida Zenzō. *Kairyō Nihon kaoku kōzō*. Dai Nihon kōgyō gakkai, 1922.
Yoshimura Chizu. *Jitchi ōyō kaji kyōkasho*. 2 vols. 6th rev. ed. Tōkyō kaiseikan, 1919.
Yoshiwara Yonejirō. *Wayō jūtaku kenchiku zushū tsuki kaoku shozōsaku hinagata*. Kenchiku shoin, 1910.
Yumeno Kyūsaku. "Gaitō kara mita shin Tōkyō no rimen." 1924. Reprinted in *Yumeno Kyūsaku zenshū 2*. Chikuma bunko, 1992.
Zushi Shōichirō. *Ie*. Keieisha, 1907.

## Periodicals

*Bunka seikatsu kenkyū*. 1920.
*Fujin gahō*. 1905.
*Fujin kōron*. 1916.
*Fujin sekai*. 1906.
*Jikō (Mitsukoshi)*. 1903.
*Jogaku zasshi*. 1885.
*Jūtaku*. 1916.
*Kan'i seikatsu*. 1906.
*Kansai kenchiku kyōkai zasshi (Kenchiku to shakai)*. 1917.
*Katei no tomo (Fujin no tomo)*. 1903.
*Katei zasshi*. 1892.
*Katei zasshi*. 1903.
*Kenchiku zasshi*. 1887.
*Sandee mainichi*. 1922.
*Sanyō suitai*. 1912.
*Seikatsu*. 1913.
*Shufu no tomo*. 1917.
*Shumi*. 1906.
*Tōkyō pakku*. 1905.

## Primary Source Collections

Fujimori Terunobu, ed. *Nihon kindai shisō taikei 19: toshi, kenchiku*. Iwanami shoten, 1990.
Fujimori Terunobu, Hatsuda Tōru, Fujioka Hiroyasu, eds. *Ushinawareta teito Tōkyō: Taishō, Shōwa no machi to sumai*. Kashiwa shobō, 1991.
Kano Masanao, ed. *Nihon kindai shisō taikei 34: Taishō shisōshū II*. Chikuma shobō, 1977.
Ogi Shinzō, Kumakura Isao, and Ueno Chizuko, eds. *Nihon kindai shisō taikei 23: Fūzoku, sei*. Iwanami shoten, 1990.

*Shinbun shūroku Taishōshi.* Taishō shuppan, 1978.

Sōgō kenkyū kaihatsu kikō (NIRA), ed. *Shinbun ni miru shakai shihon seibi no rekishiteki hensen: Meiji, Taishō ki.* Nihon keizai hyōronsha, 1989.

Tanaka Chitako and Tanaka Hatsuo, eds. *Kaseigaku bunken shūsei.* 11 vols. Watanabe shoten, 1976.

Yamamuro Tokuko, ed. *20 seiki shotō: Josei e no messeeji.* Domesu shuppan, 1991.

## Japanese-Language Secondary Sources

Akiyama Masami. *Shōjotachi no Shōwashi.* Shinchōsha, 1992.

Anbo Norio. *Minato Kōbe, korera, pesuto, suramu: shakaiteki sabetsu keiseishi no kenkyū.* Gakugei shuppansha, 1989.

Aoki Masao et al. "Chūryū jūtaku no heimen kōsei ni kansuru kenkyū 1–3." *Jūtaku kenchiku kenkyūjohō* 10 (1983), 85–95; 11 (1984), 69–84; 12 (1985), 111–26.

———. "Meiji ikō no jū yōshiki no henka, hatten ni kansuru ikkōsatsu." *Jūtaku kenchiku kenkyūjohō* 12 (1985).

Aoki Shigeru. *Shizen o utsusu: Higashi no sansuiga, nishi no fūkeiga, suisaiga.* Iwanami shoten, 1996.

Aoyama Nao. *Meiji jogakkō no kenkyū.* Keiō tsūshin, 1970.

Arichi Tōru. "Kindai Nihon ni okeru minshū no kazokukan: Meiji shonen kara Nisshin sensō made." In *Kazoku, seisaku to hō 7: kindai Nihon no kazokukan,* ed. Fukushima Masao. Tōkyō daigaku shuppankai, 1976.

Aruga Kizaemon. *Ie.* Chibundō, 1972.

———. *Sonraku seikatsu.* Kokuritsu shoin, 1948.

Bunka kagaku kōtō kenkyūin. Toshi bunka kagaku sentaa, ed. *Toshi, kūkan, kenchiku no konkyo o saguru: kūkan no sonzairon e.* Tobishima kensetsu kabushiki gaisha, Kaihatsu jigyōbu, 1991.

Chimoto Akiko. "Nihon ni okeru seibetsu yakuwari bungyō no keisei: kakei chōsa o tōshite." In *Seido to shite no onna: sei, san, kazoku no hikaku shakaishi,* ed. Ogino Miho. Heibonsha, 1990.

Chino Yōichi. *Kindai Nihon fujin kyōikushi: taiseinai fujin dantai no keisei katei o chūshin ni.* Domesu shuppan, 1979.

Dohi Masato. "Edo kara Tōkyō e no toshi ōpun supeesu no hen'yō." *Zōengaku* (Kyōto daigaku, Nōgakubu, Zōengaku kenkyūshitsu), Mar. 1994.

Edo no aru machi Ueno, Yanesen kenkyūkai. *Shinpen Yanesen roji jiten.* Sumai no toshokan shuppankyoku, 1995.

Ebato Akira. *Tōkyō no chiiki kenkyū.* Daimeisha, 1987.

Enami Shigeyuki and Mitsuhashi Toshiaki. *Saiminkutsu to hakurankai.* JICC shuppankyoku, 1989.

Ezura Tsuguto. "Kindai Tōkyō ni okeru shomin jūkyo no hatten ni kansuru kenkyū: Chūō-ku, Bunkyō-ku ni okeru jissoku chōsa o chūshin ni." Ph.D. diss., Chiba University, 1991.

Fudōsan gyōkai enkakushi hensan iinkai, ed. *Fudōsan gyōkai enkakushi*. Tōkyōto takuchi tatemono torihiki gyō kyōkai, 1975.

Fujimori Terunobu. *Nihon no kindai kenchiku*. 2 vols. Iwanami shinsho, 1993.

Fujimori Terunobu and Masuda Akihisa. *Kanban kenchiku*. Sanseidō, 1988.

Fujioka Hiroyasu, ed. *Atarashii jūtaku o motomete: kindai no jūtaku o tsukutta kenchiku-katachi*. KBI shuppan, 1992.

Fujioka Hiroyasu and Imafuji Akira. "'Marunouchi shinshiroku' Taishō 11 nenban, Taishō 15 nenban, Shōwa 6 nenban ni keisai sareta kōkyū shain no kyojūchi bunpu ni mirareru tokuchō: Taishō makki kara Shōwa shoki ni okeru Tōkyō no chūsan kaikyū no kyojūchi ni kansuru kenkyū." *Nihon kenchiku gakkai keikakukei ronbunshū* 470 (Apr. 1995): 235–42.

Fujioka Hiroyasu and Ishii Takahiro. "Meiji makki kara Shōwa senzen ni okeru 'jūtaku zushū' ni tsuite: shuppan no haikei to wayō ni tai suru taido." *Nihon kenchiku gakkai taikai gakujutsu kōen kōgaishū* 9029 (Oct. 1990): 787.

Fujiya Yōetsu. "Heiwahaku bunka mura shuppin jūtaku no sehyō ni tsuite." *Nihon kenchiku gakkai taikai gakujutsu kōen kōgaishū*, Oct. 1982: 2363–64.

———. "Tsutsumi Yasujirō no jūtakuchi keiei dai ichi gō: Mejiro bunka mura." In *Kōgai jūtakuchi no keifu*, ed. Yamaguchi Hiroshi. Kajima shuppankai, 1987.

———. "Yume ni kieta Ōfuna den'en toshi kōsō." In *Ginza modan to toshi ishō*, ed. Fujimori Terunobu and Ueda Minoru. Shiseidō kigyō bunkabu, 1993.

Fukushima Masao, ed. *Kazoku, seisaku to hō 6: Kindai Nihon no kazoku seisaku to hō*. Tōkyō daigaku shuppan, 1984.

Funo Shūji. "Nishiyama Uzō ron josetsu III: 'Kokumin jūkyo ronkō' o yomu." *Kenchiku bunka*, Dec. 1994: 113–18.

Gamachi Norio. "Fudōsan torihiki no hensen katei." In *Toshi saikaihatsu: fudōsan torihiki to hō (Tochi mondai sōsho 11)*, ed. Nihon tochi hō gakkai, 92–129. Yūhikaku, 1979.

Habuka Hisao and Hirai Kiyoshi. "Bakumatsu Bichū Matsuyamahan ni okeru oie chū yashiki sadame hō." *Nihon kenchiku gakkai keikakukei ronbun hōkokushū*, no. 415 (Sept. 1990): 121–27.

Hakubutsukan Meiji mura, *Takeda Goichi: Hito to sakuhin*. Nagoya tetsudō kabushiki gaisha, 1987.

Hamashima Shōji. "Sashizu to tate chiwarizu ni tsuite." In *Kozu ni miru Nihon no kenchiku*, ed. Kokuritsu rekishi minzoku hakubutsukan, 168–78. Kokuritsu rekishi minzoku hakubutsukan, 1989.

Handa Tatsuko. "Taishōki no kateika kyōiku." In *Taishō no joshi kyōiku*, ed. Nihon joshi daigaku, Joshi kyōiku kenkyūjo, 74–106. Kokudosha, 1975.

"Hanshinkan modanizumu" ten jikkō iinkai, ed. *Hanshinkan modanizumu*. Enkōsha, 1997.

Hara Takeshi. *"Minto" Ōsaka tai "teito" Tōkyō*. Kōdansha sensho mechie, 1998.

Harada Katsuhiro. "Seikatsu kaizen undō no shito: Morimoto Kōkichi." In *Kindai Nihon no seikatsu kenkyū*, ed. Seikatsu kenkyū dōjinkai. Kōseikan, 1982.

Hasegawa Takashi. *Toshi kairō: aruiwa kenchiku no chūseishugi*. Sagami shobō, 1975.

Hasegawa Tokunosuke. *Tōkyō no takuchi keiseishi: "Yamanote" no seishin*. Sumai no toshokan shuppankyoku, 1988.

Hatsuda Tōru. *Hyakkaten no tanjō: Meiji Taishō Shōwa no toshi bunka o enshutsu shita hyakkaten to kankōba no kindaishi*. Sanseidō sensho, 1993.

———. "Meiji, Taishōki ni okeru Mitsukoshi no kagu to shitsunai sōshoku." *Nihon kenchiku gakkai taikai gakujutsu kōen kōgaishū (Kantō)*, Sept. 1993: 1421–22.

Hatsuda Tōru, Ōkawa Mitsuo, and Fujiya Yōetsu. *Kindai wafū kenchiku, I: dentō o koeta sekai*. Kenchiku chishiki, 1998.

Hirai Kiyoshi. "Jūtakushi no tachiba kara: danran no ba to shite no chanoma o chūshin to suru sumai o minaosō." *Jūtaku kenchiku kenkyūjohō*, no. 12 (1985): 3–12.

Hirota Masaki. "Raifu saikuru no shoruikei." In *Nihon josei seikatsushi 4: kindai*, ed. Joseishi sōgō kenkyūkai, 247–85. Tōkyō daigaku shuppan, 1990.

Honma Chieko. *Chichi no iru shokutaku*. Bungei shunjū, 1987.

Honma Yoshihito. *Gendai toshi jūtaku seisaku*. Sanseidō, 1984.

———. *Naimushō jūtaku seisaku no kyōkun*. Ochanomizu shobō, 1988.

———. *Sangyō no Shōwashi 5: jūtaku*. Nihon keizai hyōronsha, 1987.

Horie Shun'ichi. "Meiji makki kara Taishō shoki no 'kindaiteki kazokuzō': fujin zasshi kara mita 'Yamanote seikatsu' no kenkyū." *Nihon minzokugaku* 186 (May 1991): 39–73.

Hosokawa Shūhei, forthcoming.

Ichihara Hiroshi. "Howaito karaa no shakai keizaishi." In *Kingendai Nihon no shin shiten: keizaishi kara no apurōchi*, ed. Nakamura Masanori. Yoshikawa kōbunkan, 2000.

Ikehata Hiroyuki and Fujioka Hiroyasu. "Tōkyōshi kōgai ni okeru kōchi seiri hō no takuchi kaihatsu ni tsuite." *Nihon kenchiku gakkai keikakukei ronbunshū* 518 (Apr. 1999), 269–76.

Inaba Keiko. "Abe sama no tsukutta gakusha machi Nishikatachō." In *Kōgai jūtakuchi no keifu*, ed. Yamaguchi Hiroshi, 48–60. Kajima shuppankai, 1987.

Inaba Shingo. *Machi daiku*. Heibonsha, 1957.

Inagaki Eizō. *Nihon no kindai kenchiku: sono seiritsu katei*. 2 vols. Kajima shuppankai SD sensho, 1979.

Inose Naoki. *Tochi no shinwa: Tōkyū ōkoku no tanjō*. Shōgakkan raiburarii, 1992.

Inoue Shōichi. *Ai no kūkan*. Kadokawa sensho, 1999.

Ishida Jun'ichirō. "Takeda Goichi." In *Atarashii jūtaku o motomete: kindai no jūtaku o tsukutta kenchikukatachi*, ed. Fujioka Hiroyasu. Osaka: KBI shuppan, 1992.

Ishida Takeshi. "'Ie' oyobi katei no seijiteki kinō: 'seijiteki shakaika' no shiten kara mita renzokusei to henka." In *Kazoku: seisaku to hō, I: sōron*, ed. Fukushima Masao, 311–59. Tōkyō daigaku shuppan, 1975.

Ishida Yorifusa. *Nihon kindai toshi keikaku no hyakunen*. Jichitai kenkyūsha, 1987.

Ishige Naomichi et al. *Gendai Nihon ni okeru katei to shokutaku, meimeizen kara chabudai e*. Kokuritsu minzokugaku hakubutsukan kenkyū hōkoku bessatsu, no. 16. Kokuritsu minzokugaku hakubutsukan, 1991.

Ishizuka Hiromichi. *Nihon kindai toshiron, Tōkyō: 1868–1923*. Tōkyō daigaku shuppankai, 1991.

Isoda Kōichi. *Rokumeikan no keifu*. In *Isoda Kōichi chosakushū 5*. Ozawa shoten, 1991.

Isono Satomi. "Seikatsu kaizen dōmeikai ni kansuru ikkōsatsu: setsuritsu to katsudō naiyō ni kansuru kenkyū." In *Gakuen*, ed. Nihon joshi daigaku, Kindai bunka kenkyūjo. Nihon joshi daigaku, Kindai bunka kenkyūjo, 1993.

Itagaki Kuniko. *Shōwa senzen, senchūki no nōson seikatsu: zasshi "ie no hikari" ni miru*. Sanryō shobō, 1992.

Itō Mikiharu. *Zōyo kōkan no jinruigaku*. Chikuma shobō, 1995.

Itō Toshiharu. "Nihon no 1920 nendai: Tōkyō o chūshin to suru toshi taishū bunka no tenkai." In *Toshi taishū bunka no seiritsu: gendai bunka no genkei 1920 nendai*, ed. Hirai Tadashi et al. Yūhikaku sensho, 1983.

Iwami Ryōtarō. *Tochi kukaku seiri no kenkyū*. Jichitai kenkyūsha, 1978.

Iwamoto Michiya. "Sarariiman." In *Nihonjin no kurashi: 20 seiki seikatsu hakubutsukan*, ed. Kashiwagi Hiroshi, Kobayashi Tadao, and Suzuki Kazuyoshi. Kōdansha, 2000.

Jinnai Hidenobu. *Tōkyō no kūkan jinruigaku*. Chikuma shobō, 1985.

Jinno Yuki. *Shumi no tanjō: hyakkaten ga tsukutta teisuto*. Keisō shobō, 1994.

*Kabushiki gaisha Mitsukoshi 85 nen no kiroku*. Kabushiki gaisha Mitsukoshi, 1990.

*Kadokawa Nihonshi jiten*. Kadokawa shoten, 1966.

Kamata Isao. *Gekkyūtori hakusho*. Kōwadō, 1959.

Kanazawa Toshio, Nishiyama Uzō, et al. *Jūtaku mondai kōza 1: gendai jūkyoron*. Yūzankaku, 1971.

Kaneko Akio. "'Katei shōsetsu' to yomu koto no teikoku." In *Media, hyōshō, ideorogii: Meiji sanjū nendai no bunka kenkyū*, ed. Komori Yōichi, Kōno Kensuke, and Takahashi Osamu, 131–57. Ozawa shoten, 1997.

Kano Masanao. "Korera, minshū, eisei gyōsei." In *Shūkan Asahi hyakka Nihon no rekishi 97: korera sōdō*, 260–66. Asahi shinbunsha, 1988.

———. *Senzen "ie" no shisō*. Sōbunsha, 1983.

———. *Taishō demokurashii no teiryū: 'dozokuteki' seishin e no kaiki*. NHK bukkusu, 1973.

Kashiwagi Hiroshi. *Kaji no seijigaku*. Seidosha, 1995.

———. *Kindai Nihon no sangyō dezain shisō*. Shōbunsha, 1979.

———. *Shōzō no naka no kenryoku*. Heibonsha imeeji riidingu sōsho. Heibonsha, 1987.

Katagi Atsushi, Fujiya Yōetsu, and Kadono Yoshihiro, eds. *Kindai Nihon no kōgai jūtakuchi*. Kajima shuppankai, 2000.

Katakura Hisako. *Edo jūtaku jijō*. Tōkyōto toshi kiyō, no. 34. 1990.

Katō Kōji. *Meiji Taishō no garasu*. Kōgei shuppan, 1976.

Katō Yuri. *Taishō yume no sekkeika: Nishimura Isaku to bunka gakuin*. Asahi sensho. 1990.

Kawahara Kazue. "Dōshin no jidai: Taishōki 'dōshinshugi' o megutte." *Soshioroji* 36 (Feb. 1992): 53–70.

———. *Kodomoken no kindai*. Chūkō shinsho, 1998.

Kawakami Mitsugu. *Kenchiku sashizu o yomu*. Chūō kōron bijutsu shuppan, 1988.

Kawamura Kunimitsu. *Otome no inori: kindai josei imeeji no tanjō*. Kiinokuniya, 1993.

Kawamura Minato. "Taishū orientarizumu to Ajia ninshiki." In *Iwanami kōza kindai Nihon to shokuminchi 7: Bunka no naka no shokuminchi*. Iwanami shoten, 1993.

Kawashima Yasuyoshi. *Fujin katei ran kotohajime*. Seiabō, 1996.

Kawazoe Noboru. *Tōkyō no genfūkei: toshi to den'en no kōryū*. NHK bukkusu, 1979.

Kayano Yatsuka. *Kindai Nihon no dezain bunkashi, 1868–1926*. Fuirumu aato sha, 1992.

Keihanshin kyūkō dentetsu kabushiki gaisha, ed. *Keihanshin kyūkō dentetsu gojūnenshi*. Osaka: Keihanshin kyūkō dentetsu kabushiki gaisha, 1959.

Kimura Kyōko. "Fujin zasshi no jōhō kūkan to josei taishū dokushasō no seiritsu: kindai Nihon ni okeru shufu yakuwari no keisei to no kanren de." *Shisō*, no. 812 (Feb. 1992): 231–52.

Kimura Norikuni. "Nihon kindai toshi dokuritsu jūtaku yōshiki no seiritsu to tenkai ni kansuru shiteki kenkyū." Ph.D. diss., Tokyo University. 1959.

Kinoshita Hiromi. "Kindai fujin, kateiron no tenkai." *Rekishi hyōron* 446 (June 1987): 72–89.

Kinoshita Naoyuki. *Bijutsu to iu misemono*. Heibonsha imeeji riidingu sōsho. Heibonsha, 1993.

Kitaōji Takashi. "'Bunka' no poritikkusu I: Taishō 'bunkashugi' o megutte." *Jōkyō dai ni ki*, Oct. 1996: 66–81.

Kobayashi Teruyuki. *Kindai Nihon no katei to kyōiku*. Sugiyama shoten, 1982.

Kobayashi Yoshihiro. "Taishōki ni okeru shakai kyōiku seisaku no shintenkai: seikatsu kaizen undō o chūshin ni." In *Kōza Nihon kyōikushi 3: Kindai II*, ed. Kōza Nihon kyōikushi henshū iinkai, 308–31. Daiichi hōki shuppan, 1984.

Koizumi Kazuko. *Daidokoro dōgu imamukashi*. Heibonsha, 1994.

———. *Dōgu ga kataru seikatsushi*. Asahi sensho. 1989.

———. *Kagu to shitsunai ishō no bunkashi*. Hōsei daigaku shuppankyoku, 1979.

———. *Tansu.* Mono to ningen no bunkashi, no. 46. Hōsei daigaku shuppankyoku, 1982.

———. *Wa kagu.* Nihon bijutsu, 50. Shōgakkan, 1977.

Koshizawa Akira. *Manshūkoku no shuto keikaku.* Nihon keizai hyōronsha, 1988.

———. *Tōkyō no toshi keikaku.* Iwanami shoten, 1991.

———. *Tōkyō toshi keikaku monogatari.* Nihon keizai hyōronsha, 1991.

Kosuge Keiko. *Nippon daidokoro bunkashi.* Yūzankaku, 1991.

Kōtō-ku, ed. *Kōtō kushi,* vol. 1. 1997.

Koyama Shizuko. "'Katei kyōiku' no tōjō: kōkyōiku ni okeru 'haha' no hakken." In *Kihan to shite no bunka: bunka sōgō no kindaika,* 242–67. Heibonsha, 1990.

———. *Ryōsai kenbo to iu kihan.* Keisō shobō, 1991.

Kumakura Isao. *Bunka to shite no manaa.* Iwanami shoten, 1999.

———. "Enkyo to shite no shokutaku." In *Gendai Nihon bunka ni okeru dentō to henyō 9: Shōwa no sesōshi,* ed. Ishige Naomichi, 29–46. Domesu shuppan, 1993.

———. "Kindai no chanoyu." In *Sadō shūkin 6: Kindai no chanoyu,* ed. Chiga Shirō. Shōgakkan, 1985.

———. *Kindai sukisha no chanoyu.* Kawahara shoten, 1997.

Kurosawa Takashi et al. *Jūtaku no gyakusetsu dai 3 shū: Nichijō e, kindai jūkyo no naiteki kōzō.* Reonarudo no hikōki shuppankai, 1977.

Machida Reiko. "Toshi jūtaku ni okeru kaji rōdō no jū kūkanteki jōken no hensen: Meiji kōki—Taishō makki." *Nihon kenchiku gakkai keikakukei ronbun hōkokushū,* no. 363 (May 1986): 168–75.

Maeda Ai. *Kindai dokusha no seiritsu.* Yūseidō shuppan, 1973.

———. *Toshi kūkan no naka no bungaku.* Chikuma shobō, 1982.

Matsui Haruko. "Hakone tochi no Ōizumi, Kodaira, Kunitachi no kōgai jūtakuchi kaihatsu." In *Kōgai jūtakuchi no keifu,* ed. Yamaguchi Hiroshi. Kajima shuppankai, 1987.

Matsunari Yoshie et al. *Nihon no sarariiman.* Aoki shoten, 1957.

Matsuyama Iwao. *Maboroshi no interia.* Sakuhinsha, 1985.

Minami Hiroshi, ed. *Nihon modanizumu no kenkyū: shisō, seikatsu, bunka.* Bureen shuppan, 1982.

———. *Taishō bunka.* Keisō shobō, 1965.

Minami Hiroshi et al. *Shōwa bunka.* Keisō shobō, 1987.

Miura Atsushi. *"Kazoku" to "kōfuku" no sengoshi: kōgai no yume to jitsugen.* Kōdansha, 1999.

Miyake Yoshiko. "Kindai Nihon joseishi no saisōzō no tame ni: tekisuto no yomikae." In *Kanagawa daigaku hyōron sōsho,* vol. 4, *Shakai no hekken,* 63–128. Ochanomizu shobō, 1994.

Miyamoto Masaaki and Kawakami Yoshiaki. "Noma bunka mura no kensetsu keii." *Nihon kenchiku gakkai taikai gakujutsu kōen kōgaishū,* no. 9040 (Oct. 1982): 2365–66.

Miyamoto Mataji. *Ōsaka*. Chibundō, 1966.

Miyata Noboru. *Onna no reiryoku to ie no kami: Nihon no minzoku shūkyō*. Jinbun shoin, 1983.

Mizutani Ken. "Kindai Nihon ni okeru jōryū kaikyū imeeji no hen'yō: Meiji kōki kara Taishōki ni okeru zasshi media no bunseki." *Shisō*, no. 812 (Feb. 1992): 193–210.

Mori Yasuki. *Suginami fūdoki*. Suginami kyōdoshi kai, 1977.

Murakami Kōkyo. "Taishōki Tōkyō ni okeru sōsō girei no henka to kindaika." *Shūkyō kenkyū*, June 1990: 37–61.

Muramatsu Teijirō and Ōmi Sakae, eds. *Kindai wafū kenchiku*. Kajima shuppankai, 1988.

Muta Kazue. "Meijiki sōgō zasshi ni miru kazokuzō: 'katei' no tōjō to sono paradokkusu." *Shakaigaku hyōron* 41, no. 1 (1990): 12–25.

———. "Nihon kindaika to kazoku: Meijiki 'kazoku kokkakan' saikō." In *"Kindai Nihon" no rekishi shakaigaku*, ed. Tsutsui Kiyotada, 67–93. 1990.

———. *Senryaku to shite no kazoku: kindai Nihon no kokumin kokka keisei to josei*. Shin-yōsha, 1996.

———. "Senryaku to shite no onna: Meiji, Taishō no 'onna no gensetsu' o megutte." *Shisō* 812 (Feb. 1992): 211–29.

Nagahara Kazuko. "Heiminshugi no fujinron: 'Kokumin no tomo' to 'Katei zasshi' ni tsuite." *Rekishi hyōron* 311 (Mar. 1976): 59–76.

Nagahara Keiji and Yamaguchi Keiji, eds. *Kōza Nihon gijutsu no shakaishi 7: kenchiku*. Nihon hyōronsha, 1983.

Nagatani Ken. "Kindai Nihon ni okeru jōryū kaikyū imeeji no henyō." *Shisō*, no. 812 (Feb. 1992): 193–210.

Naitō Akira. *Edo to Edojō*. SD sensho, 1966.

Nakagawa Kiyoshi. *Nihon no toshi kasō*. Keisō shobō, 1985.

Nakagawa Osamu. *Jūzei toshi*. Sumai no toshokan shuppankyoku, 1990.

Nakajima Kuni. "Taishōki ni okeru 'seikatsu kaizen undō.'" *Shirin* 15 (Oct. 1974): 54–63.

Nakane Kimirō, Ezura Tsuguto, and Yamaguchi Masatomo. *Gasutō kara Ōbun made: Gasu no bunkashi*. Kajima shuppan, 1983.

Nakatani Norihito. *Kokugaku, Meiji, kenchikuka*. Ranteisha, 1993.

Nakauchi Toshio. "Kazoku to kazoku no okonau kyōiku: Nihon, 17 seiki–20 seiki." *Hitotsubashi ronshō* 97 (Apr. 1987): 55–80.

Nakauchi Toshio et al. *Kyōiku: tanjō to shūen (sōsho umu, sodateru, oshieru—tokumei no kyōikushi 1)*. Fujiwara shoten, 1990.

Nakazawa Yōko. "Katei, uchi, kanai, hōmu." In *Kōza Nihongo no goi dai 9 kan: goshi I*, ed. Satō Kiyoji, 222–27. Meiji shoin, 1983.

Narita Ryūichi. "Eisei kankyō no henka no naka no josei to joseikan." In *Nihon josei seikatsushi*, vol. 4, *Kindai*, ed. Joseishi sōgō kenkyūkai, 89–124. Tōkyō daigaku shuppankai, 1990.

———. "Kindai toshi to minshū." In *Kindai Nihon no kiseki: Toshi to minshū*. ed. idem, 1–56. Yoshikawa kōbunkan, 1993.

———. "1920 nendai zenhan no shakuyanin undō: shakuyanin dōmei o chūshin ni." *Nihon rekishi* 394 (Mar. 1981): 54–72.

———. "Toshi, eisei, josei." In *Toshi, kūkan, kenchiku no konkyo o saguru: kūkan no sonzairon e*, ed. Bunka kagaku kōtō kenkyūin, Toshi bunka kagaku sentaa, 432–65. Tobishima kensetsu kabushiki gaisha kaihatsu jigyōbu, 1991.

Nihon hōsō shuppan kyōkai, ed. *"Hōsō bunka" shi ni miru Shōwa hōsōshi*. Nihon hōsō shuppan kyōkai, 1990.

*Nihon joseishi dai 4 kan: kindai*, 89–124. Tōkyō daigaku shuppankai, 1982.

Nihon kenchiku gakkai, ed. *Kindai Nihon kenchikugaku hattatsushi*. Maruzen, 1972.

*Nihon kindai kyōikushi jiten*. Heibonsha, 1971.

Nihon tōkei kenkyūjo. *Waga kuni tōkei chōsa no taikei: kakei chōsa no hattatsu (Gyōsei kanrichō itaku chōsa hōkoku)*. 1959.

Nishihara Minoru. *Piano no tanjō: gakki no mukō ni kindai ga mieru*. Kōdansha, 1995.

Nishikawa Nagao. "Nihongata kokumin kokka no keisei: hikakushiteki kanten kara." In *Bakumatsu Meijiki no kokumin kokka keisei to bunka henyō*, ed. Nishikawa Nagao and Matsumiya Hideharu, 3–42. Shinyōsha, 1995.

Nishikawa Nagao and Matsumiya Hideharu, eds. *Bakumatsu Meijiki no kokumin kokka keisei to bunka henyō*. Shinyōsha, 1995.

Nishikawa Yūko. "Otoko no ie, onna no oe, seibetsu no nai heya: zoku sumai no hensen to 'katei' no seiritsu." In *Jendaa no Nihonshi 2: shutai to hyōgen, shigoto to seikatsu*, ed. Wakita Haruko and S. B. Hanley, 609–43. Tōkyō daigaku shuppankai, 1995.

———. *Shakuya to mochiie no bungakushi: "watashi" no utsuwa no monogatari*. Sanseidō, 1998.

———. "Sumai no hensen to 'katei' no seiritsu." In *Nihon josei seikatsushi 4: kindai*, ed. Joseishi sōgō kenkyūkai, 1–50. Tōkyō daigaku shuppankai, 1990.

Nishiyama Uzō. *Nihon no sumai*. 3 vols. Keisō shobō, 1976.

Nishizawa Yasuhiko et al. "Kaigai: kokusaku gaisha no jūtaku seisaku." In *Kindai Nihon no kōgai jūtakuchi*, ed. Katagi Atsushi, Fujiya Yōetsu, and Kadono Yoshihiro, 516–69. Kajima shuppankai, 2000.

Noda Masaho and Nakajima Akiko, eds. *Mejiro bunka mura*. Nihon keizai hyōronsha, 1991.

Ochiai Shigeru. *Arau bunka shiwa*. Kaō sekken kabushiki gaisha, 1973.

Oda Yasunori. *Toshi kōgai no keisei: Kindai Ōsaka no seichō to seikatsu kankyō*. Sekai shisōsha, 1987.

Ōe Shinobu et al. *Iwanami kōza kindai Nihon to shokuminchi 7: bunka no naka no shokuminchi*. Iwanami shoten, 1993.
Ogi Shinzō et al., eds. *Edo Tōkyōgaku jiten*. Sanseidō, 1987.
Ōhama Tetsuya, *Ōe Sumi sensei*. Tōkyō kasei gakuin kōenkai, 1978.
———. "Risō no katei to genjitsu." In *Gendai shomin seikatsu no genkei. Shūkan Asahi hyakka Nihon no rekishi*, no. 112, *Kindai II*. June 12, 1988.
Ōhama Tetsuya and Kumakura Isao. *Kindai Nihon no seikatsu to shakai*. Hōsō daigaku kyōiku shinkōkai, 1989.
Oka Mitsuo. *Fujin zasshi jaanarizumu*. Gendai jaanarizumu shuppankai, 1981.
Okada Yoshirō. *Meiji kaireki: "toki" no bunmei kaika*. Taishūkan shoten, 1994.
Ōkado Masakatsu. "Nōson kara toshi e: seishōnen no idō to 'kūgaku,' 'dokugaku.'" In *Kindai Nihon no kiseki 9: Toshi to minshū*, ed. Narita Ryūichi. Yoshikawa kōbunkan, 1993.
Okamoto Mariko, ed. *Nihon kenchiku koten soshō*, vol. 5, *Kinsei kenchikusho—zashiki hinagata*. Dairyūdō, 1985.
Okamoto Mariko and Naitō Akira. "Daiku gijutsusho 'hinagatabon' ni tsuite." In *Kinsei kenchiku no seisan soshiki to gijutsu*, ed. Kawakami Mitsugu, 323–57. Chūō kōron bijutsu shuppan, 1984.
Ōkawa Naomi. *Sumai no jinruigaku: Nihon shomin jūkyo saikō*. Heibonsha imeeji riidingu sōsho. Heibonsha, 1986.
Ōkuma Toshiyuki. "Meijiki ikō no bijutsu hihyō ron I: Nihon kindai bijutsu hihyōshi kōchiku no tame ni." *Sannomaru shōzōkan nenpō kiyō* 3 (Apr. 1996–Mar. 1997): 46–55.
Ōmi Sakai and Hori Isao. *Nihon no kenchiku, Meiji, Taishō, Shōwa 10: Nihon no modanizumu*. Sanseidō, 1981.
Onobayashi Hiroki. "Ōyamazaki no Kōetsu." *Shin kenchiku 11 gatsu rinji zōkan: Shōwa jūtakushi, Shin kenchiku* 51, no. 13 (Nov. 1976): 50–57.
Ōsaka Akira. "Senzoku den'en toshi wa kieta ka." In *Kōgai jūtakuchi no keifu*, ed. Yamaguchi Hiroshi, 175–90. Kajima shuppankai, 1987.
Ōsakashi toshi jūtakushi hensan iinkai. *Machi ni sumau: Ōsaka toshi jūtakushi*. Osaka: Heibonsha, 1989.
Ōshima Tatehiko. *Sōji no minzoku*. Miyai shoten, 1984.
Ōta Hirotarō. *Jūtaku kindaishi: jūtaku to kagu*. Yūzankaku shuppan, 1969.
Ōta-ku kyōiku iinkai, ed. *Ōta-ku no bunkazai 27: Ōta-ku no kindai kenchiku, jūtakuhen 1, 2*. Ōta-ku kyōiku iinkai, 1992.
Ozawa Takeshi, *Bakumatsu Meiji no shashin*. Chikuma shobō Chikuma gakugei bunko, 1997.
Ri Takanori. *Hyōshō kūkan no kindai: Meiji "Nihon" no media hensei*. Shinyōsha, 1996.
Saeki Junko. "'Bunmei kaika' no 'asobi.'" *Nihon no bigaku* 15 (1990): 185–202.
———. *Sōkan Nihon no bungaku 16: bunmei kaika to josei*. Shintensha, 1991.

———. *Yūjo no bunkashi*. Chūkō shinsho, 1987.

Saitō Tsuyoshi. *Meiji no kotoba: higashi kara nishi e no kakehashi*. Kōdansha, 1977.

Sakai Ken'ichi. "Seijō, Tamagawa gakuen jūtakuchi." In *Kōgai jūtakuchi no keifu: Tōkyō no den'en yūtopia*, ed. Yamaguchi Hiroshi, 237–60. Kajima shuppankai, 1987.

Sakamoto Isao, ed. *Nihon no mokuzō jūtaku no 100 nen*. Shadan hōjin Nihon mokuzō jūtaku sangyō kyōkai, 2001.

Satō Kenji. *Fūkei no seisan, fūkei no kaihō: media no arukeorojii*. Kōdansha, 1994.

———. "Meiji kokka to katei ideorogii." In *Shiriizu henbō suru kazoku 1: kazoku no shakaishi*, ed. Ueno Chizuko, Tsurumi Shunsuke, et al., 78–96. Iwanami shoten, 1991.

———. "Toshi shakaigaku no shakaishi: hōhō bunseki kara no mondai teiki." In *Toshi shakaigaku no furontia 1: kōzō, kūkan, hōhō*, ed. Kurasawa Susumu and Machimura Takashi, 151–215. Nihon hyōronsha, 1992.

Satō Kiyoji, ed. *Kōza Nihongo no goi dai 10 kan goshi II*. Meiji shoin, 1983.

Satō Shigeru. *Shūgō jūtaku danchi no hensen: Tōkyō no kōkyō jūtaku to machizukuri*. Kajima shuppankai, 1989.

Sawada Tomoko. *Yukaza, isuza: kikyo yōshiki ni miru Nihon jūtaku no interia shi*. Sumai no toshokan shuppankyoku, 1995.

Sawayama Mikako. "Kindaiteki hahaoya zō no keisei ni tsuite no ikkōsatsu: 1890–1900 nendai ni okeru ikujiron no tenkai." *Rekishi hyōron* 443 (Mar. 1987): 63–81.

———. "Kosodate ni okeru otoko to onna." In *Nihon josei seikatsushi 4: kindai*, ed. Joseishi sōgō kenkyūkai, 125–62. Tōkyō daigaku shuppankai, 1990.

———. "Kyōiku kazoku no seiritsu." In Nakauchi Toshio et al., *Kyōiku: tanjō to shūen*, 108–31. Fujiwara shoten, 1990.

Senuma Shigeki. "Katei shōsetsu no tenkai." In *Meiji bungaku zenshū 93: Meiji katei shōsetsushū*, 421–30. Chikuma shobō, 1969.

Setagaya-ku kyōiku iinkai, ed. *Setagaya no kindai kenchiku dai isshū: jūtakukei chōsa risuto*. Setagaya-ku kyōiku iinkai, 1987.

Shimizu Isao. *Manga ni egakareta Meiji Taishō Shōwa*. Kyōikusha, 1988.

Shimizu Keiichi. "Meijiki ni okeru shotō, chūtō kenchiku kyōiku no shiteki kenkyū." Ph.D. diss., Tokyo University, 1982.

Shinozuka Shōji. *Tochi shoyūken to gendai: rekishi kara no tenbō*. NHK bukkusu, 1974.

Shioda Maruo. *Sumai no sengoshi: Nihon no jūtaku mondai*. Saimaru shuppan, 1975.

Shirahata Yōzaburō. *Kindai toshi kōenshi no kenkyū: ōka no keifu*. Shibunkaku, 1995.

Shishido Makoto. *Karuizawa bessōshi: hishochi hyakunen no ayumi*. Sumai no toshokan shuppankyoku, 1987.

Shufu no tomosha, ed. *Shufu no tomo sha no gojūnen*. Shufu no tomosha, 1969.

Shūkan Asahi, ed. *Nedanshi nenpyō: Meiji, Taishō, Shōwa*. Asahi shinbunsha, 1988.

Suginami kuyakusho, ed. *Suginami kushi*. Suginami kuyakusho, 1955.

Suginami kyōdoshi kai. *Suginami-ku no rekishi*. Meicho shuppan, 1978.

Sugiyama Mitsunobu and Yoshimi Shun'ya. "Kindai Nihon ni okeru yūtopia undō to jaanarizumu." *Tōkyō daigaku shinbun kenkyūjo kiyō*, no. 41 (1990): 89–152.

Suzuki Hiroyuki. *Toshi e*. Chūō kōronsha, 1999.

Suzuki Sadami. *Modan toshi no hyōgen: jiko, gensō, josei*. Hakuchisha, 1992.

Suzuki Shūji. *Bunmei no kotoba*. Bunka hyōron shuppan, 1981.

Suzuki Yūichirō. "'Kōgai seikatsu' kara 'den'en toshi' e: Meiji makki Ōsaka Tenga chaya ni okeru kōgai jūtakuchi no keisei." *Nihon rekishi*, no. 606 (Nov. 1998).

Suzuki Yuriko. "Juka josei no seikatsu: Rai Baishi no shigoto to shussan, ikuji." In *Nihon no kinsei 15: Josei no kinsei*, ed. Hayashi Reiko, 129–66. Chūō kōronsha, 1993.

Takahashi Akiko and Baba Masako. *Daidokoro no hanashi: monogatari mono no kenchikushi*. Kajima shuppan, 1986.

Takahashi Osamu. "Sakubun kyōiku no diskuuru: 'nichijō no hakken to shaseibun.'" In Komori Yōichi, Kōno Kensuke, Takahashi Osamu, et al., *Media, hyōshō, ideorogii: Meiji sanjūnendai no bunka kenkyū*, 257–87. Ozawa shoten, 1997.

Takeda Nobuaki. *"Koshitsu" to "manazashi": Kikufuji hoteru kara miru Taishō kūkan*. Kōdansha, 1995.

Takeda Yonekichi. *Kenchiku konjaku*. Jitsugyō no Nihonsha, 1948.

Takeyama Akiko. "Rajio bangumi ni miru modanizumu." In *Nihon modanizumu no kenkyū: shisō, seikatsu, bunka*, ed. Minami Hiroshi, 231–48. Bureen shuppan, 1982.

Taki Kōji. *Ikirareta ie*. Tabata shoten, 1976.

———. *Tennō no shōzō*. Iwanami shoten, 1988.

Tanaka Satoshi. *Eisei tenrankai no yokubō*. Seiyasha, 1994.

Tanaka Shūji. *Nishimura Isaku no tanoshiki jūka: Taishō demokurashii no sumai*. Haru shobō, 2001.

Terade Kōji. *Seikatsu bunkaron e no shōtai*. Kōbundō, 1994.

———. "Taishōki ni okeru shokuin seikatsu no tenkai." In *Seikatsugaku*, 7: 34–74. Domesu shuppan, 1982.

Tōkyō kokuritsu kindai bijutsukan. *Sugiura Hisui ten: toshi seikatsu no dezainaa*. Tōkyō kokuritsu kindai bijutsukan, 2000.

Tōkyōto, ed. *Tōkyō hyakunenshi*. 7 vols. Tōkyōto, 1979–80.

Tsuboi Hirofumi. "Jūkyo to genkankaku." In *Nihon minzoku bunka taikei dai 10 kan: ie to josei, kurashi no bunkashi*, 183–222. Shōgakkan, 1985.

———. "Seikatsu bunka to josei." In *Nihon minzoku bunka taikei 10: ie to josei*, 7–28. Shōgakkan, 1985.

Tsuganesawa Toshihiro. *Takarazuka senryaku: Kobayashi Ichizō no seikatsu bunkaron*. Kōdansha gendai shinsho, 1991.

Tsunemi Ikuo. *Kateika kyōikushi*. Kōseika, 1959.

Uchida Seizō. *Amerika-ya shōhin jūtaku: "yōfū jūtaku kaitakushi."* Sumai no toshokan shuppankyoku, 1987.

———. "Jūtaku kairyō undō ni tsuite." In *Kindai shomin seikatsushi 6: shokujū*, ed. Minami Hiroshi, 558–67. San'ichi shobō, 1987.

———. "Jūtaku tenjijō no genfūkei to shite no 'bunka mura': Taishō 11 nen kaisai no heiwa kinen Tōkyō hakurankai bunka mura no sehyō ni tsuite." In *Kenchiku-shi no mawari butai: jidai to dezain o kataru*, ed. Nishi Kazuo. Shōkokusha, 1999.

———. "Kenchiku gakkai no katsudō kara mita Taishō 11 nen kaisai no heiwa kinen Tōkyō hakurankai bunka mura ni kansuru ikkōsatsu." *Nihon kenchiku gakkai keikaku kei ronbunshū*, Mar. 2000: 1–8.

———. "Meijiki no jūtaku kairyō ni mirareru puraibashii no ishiki ni tsuite." *Nihon kenchiku gakkai taikai gakujutsu kōen kōgaishū (Kantō)*, no. 8088 (Oct. 1975): 1565–66.

———. *Nihon no kindai jūtaku*. Kajima shuppankai, 1992.

———. "Setagaya ni miru jūtaku sakka: Yamada Jun." In *Setagaya no kindai fūkei gai-shi*, ed. Setagaya jūtakushi kenkyūkai, 97–129. Setagaya-ku, Kenchikubu, 1991.

Ueda Yasuo. "Josei zasshi ga mita modanizumu." In *Nihon modanizumu no kenkyū*, ed. Minami Hiroshi, 115–140. Bureen shuppan, 1982.

Ueno Chizuko. *Kindai kazoku no seiritsu to shūen*. Iwanami shoten, 1994.

———. *Shihonsei to kaji rōdō: Marukusushugi feminizumu no mondai kōsei*. Kainuisha Monado bukkusu, 1985.

Ueno Chizuko, Ochiai Emiko, et al. *Iwanami kōza gendai no shakaigaku dai 19 kan: "kazoku" no shakaigaku*. Iwanami shoten, 1996.

Unno Hiroshi. *Modan toshi Tōkyō: Nihon no 1920 nendai*. Chūkō bunko, 1983.

Uno Masamichi. "Meijiki ni okeru setai gainen no tōjō katei." *Kazokushi kenkyū* 4 (1981): 38–64.

Ushioda Shōji. "Edo Tōkyō nenjū gyōji no kindaika no shosō: hyakunin isshu to hina o chūshin ni." *Nihon minzokugaku*, no. 192 (Nov. 1992): 90–104.

Wada Yasuyoshi. "Ōsaka ni okeru kindai toshi jūtaku seiritsu ni kansuru kisoteki kenkyū." Ph.D. diss., Ōsaka kōgyō daigaku, 1998.

Watanabe Shun'ichi. *"Toshi keikaku" no tanjō: kokusai hikaku kara mita Nihon kindai toshi keikaku*. Kashiwa shobō, 1993.

Watanabe Shun'ichi et al. *Senzen no jūtaku seisaku no hensen ni kansuru chōsa*. 8 vols. Nihon jūtaku sōgō sentaa, 1980–88.

Yamagata Masaaki. *Vōrizu no jūtaku:"dendō" sareta amerikan sutairu*. Sumai no toshokan shuppankyoku, 1988.

Yamaguchi Hiroshi, ed. *Kōgai jūtakuchi no keifu: Tōkyō no den'en yūtopia*. Kajima shuppankai, 1987.

Yamaguchi Masatomo. *Daidokoro kūkangaku: sono genten to mirai*. Kenchiku chishiki, 1987.

Yamaguchi Masatomo and Ishige Naomichi, eds. *Shoku no bunka fōramu: Katei no shokuji kūkan*. Domesu shuppan, 1989.

Yamamoto Toshiko. "Kindai Nihon ni okeru 'katei kyōiku' ishiki no shutsugen to tenkai: 'ikka danran' zō no keisei o tegakari ni." Ph.D. diss., Tokyo University, 1988.

Yasuda Takashi. "Minoo, Sakuragaoka no jūtaku kaizō hakurankai: sono rekishiteki imi to igi." In Nishiyama Uzō et al., *Taishō "jūtaku kaizō hakurankai" no yume*, 33–39. INAX Booklet, 1988.

Yasujima Hiroyuki and Soshiroda Akira. *Nihon bessōshi nōto*. Sumai no toshokan shuppankyoku, 1991.

Yomiuri kōkokusha shashi hensanshitsu, ed. *Annai kōkoku hyakunenshi*. Dabiddosha, 1970.

Yoshida Noboru. "Jiden ni yoru katei kyōiku no kenkyū." In *Noma kyōiku kenkyūjo kiyō dai 10 shū: katei kankyō no kyōiku ni oyobosu eikyō*, 245–81. Kōdansha, 1953.

Yoshimi Shun'ya. *Hakurankai no seijigaku: manazashi no kindai*. Chūkō shinsho, 1992.

———. *Toshi no doramaturugii: Tōkyō, sakariba no shakaishi*. Kōbundō, 1987.

Yoshino Hideki. "Meijiki no jūtaku chōsa: kindaika no inga." In *Kindai Nihon shakai chōsashi I*, ed. Kawai Takeo. Keiō tsūshin, 1989.

———. "Taishōki no jūtaku chōsa: kyūsai shisō no genkai to 'sumai' no shōhinka." In *Kindai Nihon shakai chōsa shi II*, ed. Kawai Takeo, 177–211. Keiō tsūshin, 1991.

Yoshiwara Masayuki, ed. *Hanshin kyūkō dentetsu nijūgonenshi*. Osaka: Hanshin kyūkō dentetsu kabushiki gaisha, 1932.

## English-Language Sources

Ambaras, David. "Social Knowledge, Cultural Capital, and the New Middle Class in Japan, 1895–1912." *Journal of Japanese Studies* 24, no. 1 (1998): 1–33.

Anderson, Benedict. *Imagined Communities*. Rev. ed. London and New York: Verso, 1991.

Appadurai, Arjun. *Modernity at Large: Cultural Dimensions of Globalization*. Minneapolis: University of Minnesota Press, 1996.

Ariès, Philippe. *Centuries of Childhood: A Social History of Family Life*. Trans. Robert Baldick. New York: Random House, 1962.

Aso, Noriko. "New Illusions: The Emergence of a Discourse on Traditional Japanese Arts and Crafts, 1868–1945." Ph.D. diss., University of Chicago, 1997.

Atkins, E. Taylor. *Blue Nippon: Authenticating Jazz in Japan*. Durham, N.C.: Duke University Press, 2001.

Auslander, Leora. *Taste and Power: Furnishing Modern France*. Berkeley: University of California Press, 1996.

Balibar, Etienne, and Immanuel Wallerstein. *Race, Nation, Class: Ambiguous Identities*. London and New York: Verso, 1991.

Barthes, Roland. *The Fashion System*. Trans. Matthew Ward and Richard Howard. Berkeley: University of California Press, 1990.

Bartholomew, James R. *The Formation of Science in Japan: Building a Research Tradition.* New Haven: Yale University Press, 1989.

Baudrillard, Jean. *The System of Objects.* Trans. James Benedict. London and New York: Verso, 1996.

Bauman, Zygmunt. *Memories of Class: The Pre-History and After-Life of Class.* London: Routledge & Kegan Paul, 1982.

Beecher, Catharine, and Harriet Beecher Stowe. *The American Woman's Home, or Principles of Domestic Science.* 1869. Reprinted—Hartford, Calif.: Stowe-Day Foundation, 1975.

Befu, Harumi. "Gift-Giving in Modernizing Japan." *Monumenta Nipponica* 23, no. 3/4 (1968): 445–56.

Bestor, Theodore. *Neighborhood Tokyo.* Stanford: Stanford University Press, 1989.

———. "The Shitamachi Revival." *Transactions of the Asiatic Society of Japan,* 4th series, vol. 5 (1990): 71–86.

Blackbourn, David, and Richard Evans, eds. *The German Bourgeoisie: Essays on the Social History of the German Middle Class from the Late Eighteenth Century to the Early Twentieth Century.* London: Routledge, 1993.

Blanton, Richard E. *Houses and Households: A Comparative Study.* New York and London: Plenum Press, 1994.

Bourdier, Jean-Paul. "Reading Tradition." In *Dwellings, Settlements and Tradition: Cross-Cultural Perspectives,* ed. Jean-Paul Bourdier and Nezar Alsayyad, 35–52. London, Eng., and Lanham, Md.: International Association for the Study of Traditional Environments and University Press of America, 1989.

Bourdieu, Pierre. *Distinction: A Social Critique of the Judgement of Taste.* Trans. Richard Nice. Cambridge, Mass.: Harvard University Press, 1984.

———. *The Field of Cultural Production: Essays on Art and Literature.* New York: Columbia University Press, 1993.

———. *Outline of a Theory of Practice.* Trans. Richard Nice. Cambridge, Eng.: Cambridge University Press, 1977.

———. "Social Space and Symbolic Space: Introduction to a Japanese Reading of *Distinction.*" Trans. Gisele Spiro. *Poetics Today* 12, no. 4 (Winter 1991): 627–38.

Brandt, Lisbeth Kim. "The Folk-Craft Movement in Early Showa Japan, 1925–1945." Ph.D. diss., Columbia University, 1996.

Bray, Francesca. *Technology and Gender: Fabrics of Power in Late Imperial China.* Berkeley: University of California Press, 1997.

Brown, Jane Converse. "'Fine Arts and Fine People': The Japanese Taste in the American Home, 1876–1916." In *Making the American Home: Middle-Class Women and Domestic Material Culture, 1840–1940,* ed. Marilyn Ferris Motz and Pat Browne, 121–39. Bowling Green, Ohio: Bowling Green State University Popular Press, 1988.

Buck-Morss, Susan. *The Dialectics of Seeing: Walter Benjamin and the Arcades Project.* Cambridge. Mass.: MIT Press, 1993.

Burnett, John. *A Social History of Housing, 1815–1985.* 2nd ed. London and New York: Methuen, 1986.

Bushman, Richard. *The Refinement of America: Persons, Houses, Cities.* New York: Knopf, 1992.

Campbell, Colin. *The Romantic Ethic and the Spirit of Modern Consumerism.* Basil Blackwell, 1987.

Certeau, Michel de. *The Practice of Everyday Life.* Trans. Steven Rendall. Berkeley: University of California Press, 1984.

Chatterjee, Partha. *The Nation and Its Fragments.* Princeton: Princeton University Press, 1993.

Chimoto Akiko. "The Birth of the Full-Time Housewife in the Japanese Worker's Household as Seen Through Family Budget Surveys." *U.S.-Japan Women's Journal English Supplement,* no. 8 (1995): 37–63.

Ching, Leo. "Savage Constructions and Civility Making: The Musha Incident and Aboriginal Representations in Colonial Taiwan." *positions: east asia cultures critique* 8, no. 3 (Winter 2000): 795–818.

Clifford, James. "On *Orientalism.*" In *The Predicament of Culture: Twentieth-Century Ethnography, Literature, and Art,* 255–276. Cambridge, Mass.: Harvard University Press, 1988.

Choi, Don. "Educating the Architect in Meiji Japan." In *Architecture and Modern Japan,* ed. Henry D. Smith II, forthcoming.

Coaldrake, William. *Architecture and Authority in Japan.* London: Routledge, 1996.

———. "Edo Architecture and Tokugawa Law." *Monumenta Nipponica* 36, no. 3 (Autumn 1981): 235–84.

Colomina, Beatriz. *Privacy and Publicity: Modern Architecture as Mass Media.* MIT Press, 1994.

Comaroff, Jean, and John L. Comaroff. "Home-Made Hegemony: Modernity, Domesticity, and Colonialism in South Africa." In *African Encounters with Domesticity,* ed. Karen Tranberg Hansen. New Brunswick, N.J.: Rutgers University Press, 1992.

Creese, Walter L. *The Search for Environment: The Garden City, Before and After.* New Haven: Yale University Press, 1966.

Csikszentmihalyi, Mihaly, and Eugene Rochberg-Halton. *The Meaning of Things: Domestic Symbols and the Self.* New York: Cambridge University Press, 1981.

Cwiertka, Katarzyna. "Minekichi Akabori and His Role in the Development of Modern Japanese Cuisine." In *Cooks and Other People: Proceedings of the Oxford Symposium on Food and Cookery, 1995,* ed. Harlan Walker. Devon, Eng.: Prospect Books, 1996.

Doak, Kevin. "Culture, Ethnicity and the State in Early Twentieth-Century Japan." In *Japan's Competing Modernities: Issues in Culture and Democracy, 1900–1930*, ed. Sharon A. Minichiello, 181–205. Honolulu: University of Hawaii Press, 1998.

Dodd, Stephen. "An Embracing Vision: Representations of the Countryside in Early Twentieth-Century Japanese Literature." Ph.D. diss., Columbia University, 1993.

Duben, Alan, and Cem Behar. *Istanbul Households: Marriage, Family and Fertility, 1880–1940*. Cambridge, Eng.: Cambridge University Press, 1991.

Eagleton, Terry. *The Ideology of the Aesthetic*. Oxford: Blackwell Publishers, 1990.

Engels, Friedrich. *The Housing Question*. 1872. Reprinted—Moscow: Progress Publishers, 1970.

Ericson, Steven J. *The Sound of the Whistle: Railroads and the State in Meiji Japan*. Cambridge, Mass.: Harvard University Press, 1996.

Ewen, Stuart. *All Consuming Images: The Politics of Style in Contemporary Culture*. New York: Basic Books, 1988.

Faurschou, Gail. "Obsolescence and Desire: Fashion and the Commodity Form." In *Postmodernism: Philosophy and the Arts*, ed. Hugh Silverman, 234–59. Routledge, 1990.

Fishman, Robert. *Bourgeois Utopias: The Rise and Fall of Suburbia*. New York: Basic Books, 1987.

Forty, Adrian. *Objects of Desire*. New York: Pantheon Books, 1986.

Frampton, Kenneth. *Modern Architecture: A Critical History*. Rev. ed. London: Thames and Hudson, 1985.

Frow, John. *Cultural Studies and Cultural Value*. Oxford: Oxford University Press, 1995.

Fujii, Koji. *The Japanese Dwelling-House*. Tokyo, Japan: Meiji shobo, 1930.

Fujitani, Takashi. *Splendid Monarchy*. Berkeley: University of California Press, 1996.

Furbank, P. N. *Unholy Pleasure: or the Idea of Social Class*. Oxford: Oxford University Press, 1985.

Garon, Sheldon. "Luxury Is the Enemy: Mobilizing Savings and Popularizing Thrift in Wartime Japan." *Journal of Japanese Studies* 26, no. 1 (2000): 41–78.

———. *Molding Japanese Minds: The State in Everyday Life*. Princeton: Princeton University Press, 1997.

———. "Rethinking Modernization and Modernity in Japanese History: A Focus on State-Society Relations," *Journal of Asian Studies* 53, no. 2 (May 1994): 346–66.

———. *The State and Labor in Modern Japan*. Berkeley: University of California Press, 1987.

———. "Women's Groups and the Japanese State: Contending Approaches to Political Integration, 1890–1945." *Journal of Japanese Studies* 19, no. 1 (Winter 1993): 5–41.

Gerbert, Elaine. "Space and Aesthetic Imagination in Some Taishō Writings." In *Japan's Competing Modernities: Issues in Culture and Democracy, 1900–1930*, ed. Sharon A. Minichiello, 70–90. Honolulu: University of Hawai'i Press, 1998.

Giddens, Anthony. *The Class Structure of the Advanced Societies*. London: Hutchinson, 1973.

Gluck, Carol. *Japan's Modern Myths: Ideology in the Late Meiji Period*. Princeton: Princeton University Press, 1985.

Goffman, Erving. *The Presentation of Self in Everyday Life*. Rev. ed. New York: Anchor Books, 1959.

Gordon, Andrew. *Labor and Imperial Democracy in Prewar Japan*. Berkeley: University of California Press, 1991.

———. "Managing the Japanese Household: The New Life Movement in Postwar Japan." *Social Politics*, Summer 1997: 245–83.

Gould, Kimberly L. "The Origins of the Salaryman." Master's thesis, Columbia University, 1990.

Green, Nicholas. *The Spectacle of Nature: Landscape and Bourgeois Culture in Nineteenth-Century France*. Manchester: Manchester University Press, 1990.

Guth, Christine M. E. *Art, Tea and Industry: Masuda Takashi and the Mitsui Circle*. Princeton: Princeton University Press, 1993.

Habermas, Jurgen. *The Structural Transformation of the Public Sphere: An Inquiry into a Category of Bourgeois Society*. Trans. Thomas Burger and Frederick Lawrence. Cambridge, Mass.: MIT Press, 1989.

Hall, Catherine. "The Early Formation of Victorian Domestic Ideology." In *Fit Work for Women*, ed. Sandra Burman, 15–32. New York: St. Martin's Press, 1979.

———. "The Sweet Delights of Home." In *The History of Private Life IV: From the Fires of the Revolution to the Great War*, ed. Michelle Perrot, 47–93. Cambridge, Mass.: Harvard University Press, 1990.

Halttunen, Karen. "From Parlor to Living Room: Domestic Space, Interior Decoration, and the Culture of Personality." In *Consuming Visions: Accumulation and Display of Goods in America, 1880–1920*, ed. Simon J. Bronner, 157–89. Winterthur, Del.: Winterthur Museum, 1989.

Hanes, Jeffrey Eldon. *The City as Subject: Seki Hajime and the Reinvention of Modern Osaka*. Berkeley : University of California Press, 2002.

Hanley, Susan. *Everyday Things in Premodern Japan: The Hidden Legacy of Material Culture*. Berkeley: University of California Press, 1997.

Harootunian, Harry. *History's Disquiet: Modernity, Cultural Practice, and the Question of Everyday Life*. New York: Columbia University Press, 2000.

———. "Late Tokugawa Culture and Thought." *Cambridge History of Japan*, vol. 5, *The Nineteenth Century*. Reprinted in *The Emergence of Meiji Japan*, ed. Marius B. Jansen, 53–143. Cambridge, Eng.: Cambridge University Press, 1995.

———. "Overcome by Modernity." Paper presented at Georgetown University, April 3, 2000.

———. *Overcome by Modernity: History, Culture, and Community in Interwar Japan.* Princeton: Princeton University Press, 2000.

———. *Things Seen and Unseen: Discourse and Ideology in Tokugawa Nativism.* Chicago: University of Chicago Press, 1988.

Havens, Thomas R. H. *Farm and Nation in Prewar Japan.* Princeton: Princeton University Press, 1974.

Hayden, Dolores. *The Grand Domestic Revolution: A History of Feminist Designs for American Homes, Neighborhoods, and Cities.* Cambridge, Mass.: MIT Press, 1981.

Heidegger, Martin. "Building Dwelling Thinking." In *Poetry, Language and Thought,* trans. Albert Hofstadter. New York: Harper and Row, 1971.

Hobsbawm, Eric. *The Age of Empire, 1875–1914.* New York: Vintage Books, 1989.

Hollander, Anne. *Sex and Suits: The Evolution of Modern Dress.* New York: Kodansha America, 1995.

Hoston, Germaine. "Marxism and Japanese Expansionism: Takahashi Kamekichi and the Theory of Petty Imperialism." *Journal of Japanese Studies* 10, no. 1 (Winter 1984): 1–30.

Howard, Ebenezer. *Garden Cities of Tomorrow,* ed. F. J. Osborn. Cambridge, Mass.: M.I.T. Press, 1965.

Hubka, Thomas. "Just Folks Designing: Vernacular Designers and the Generation of Form." In *Common Places: Readings in American Vernacular Architecture,* ed. Dell Upton and John Michael Vlach, 426–32. Athens: University of Georgia Press, 1986.

Huffman, James L. *Creating a Public: People and Press in Meiji Japan.* Honolulu: University of Hawaii Press, 1997.

Hummon, David. "House, Home and Identity in America." In *Housing, Culture and Design: A Comparative Perspective,* ed. Setha M. Low and Erve Chambers, 207–28. Philadelphia: University of Pennsylvania Press, 1989.

Huyssen, Andreas. *After the Great Divide: Modernism, Mass Culture, Postmodernism.* Bloomington: Indiana University Press, 1986.

Illich, Ivan. *Gender.* New York: Pantheon Books, 1982.

Imai Yasuko. "The Emergence of the Japanese *Shufu*: Why a *Shufu* Is More Than a Housewife." *U.S.-Japan Women's Journal* 6 (1994): 44–65.

Inoue, Kyoko. *MacArthur's Japanese Constitution: A Linguistic and Cultural Study of Its Making.* Chicago: University of Chicago Press, 1991.

Inouye, Jūkichi. *Home Life in Tokyo.* 1910. Reprinted—London: Routledge and Kegan Paul, 1985.

Iriye, Akira. *Cultural Internationalism and the World Order.* Baltimore: Johns Hopkins University Press, 1997.

Ito, Ken K. *Visions of Desire: Tanizaki's Fictional Worlds.* Stanford: Stanford University Press, 1991.

Jackson, Kenneth T. *Crabgrass Frontier: The Suburbanization of the United States.* Oxford: Oxford University Press, 1985.

Jannetta, Ann Bowman. *Epidemics and Mortality in Early Modern Japan.* Princeton: Princeton University Press, 1987.

*Japan and Britain: An Aesthetic Dialogue, 1850–1930.* London: Barbican Art Gallery, 1991.

"The Japanese Middle-Class House." *Architectural Review* 37, no. 1 (Jan. 1915): 13–15.

Johnston, William. *The Modern Epidemic: A History of Tuberculosis in Japan.* Cambridge, Mass.: Harvard University Press, 1995.

Jones, Gareth Stedman. *Languages of Class: Studies in English Working Class History, 1832–1982.* Cambridge, Eng.: Cambridge University Press, 1983.

Jones, Mark Alan. "Children as Treasures: Childhood and the Middle Class in Early Twentieth-Century Japan." Ph.D. diss., Columbia University, 2001.

Karatani Kōjin. *Origins of Modern Japanese Literature.* Trans. and ed. Brett de Bary. Durham, N.C.: Duke University Press, 1993.

King, Anthony D. *The Bungalow.* London: Routledge and Kegan Paul, 1981.

Kinmonth, Earl. *The Self-Made Man in Meiji Japanese Thought: From Samurai to Salaryman.* Berkeley: University of California Press, 1981.

Kominz, Laurence. "Pilgrimage to Tolstoy: Tokutomi Roka's Junrei Kikō." *Monumenta Nipponica* 41, no. 1 (Spring 1986): 51–101.

Koyama Shizuko. "'The Good Wife and Wise Mother' Ideology in Post–World War I Japan." *U.S.-Japan Women's Journal* 7 (1994): 31–52.

Kuroishi, Izumi. "Kon Wajirō: A Quest for the Architecture as a Container for Everyday Life." Ph.D. diss., University of Pennsylvania, 1998.

Lancaster, Clay. "The American Bungalow." In *Common Places: Readings in American Vernacular Architecture,* ed. Dell Upton and John Michael Vlach, 79–106. Athens: University of Georgia Press, 1986.

Lee, Leo Ou-Fan. *Shanghai Modern: The Flowering of a New Urban Culture in China, 1930–1945.* Cambridge, Mass.: Harvard University Press, 1999.

Lefbvre, Henri. *Critique of Everyday Life.* Trans. John Moore. London and New York: Verso, 1991.

———. *The Production of Space.* Trans. Donald Nicholson-Smith. Oxford, Eng., and Cambridge, Mass.: Blackwell, 1991.

Levi-Strauss, Claude. *The Savage Mind.* Chicago: University of Chicago Press, 1966.

Lewis, Michael. *Rioters and Citizens: Mass Protest in Imperial Japan.* Berkeley: University of California Press, 1990.

MacPherson, C. B. *The Political Theory of Possessive Individualism: Hobbes to Locke.* London: Oxford University Press, 1962.

Marcus, Sharon. *Apartment Stories: City and Home in Nineteenth-Century Paris and London*. Berkeley: University of California Press, 1999.

Miller, Daniel. *Material Culture and Mass Consumption*. Oxford, Eng., and Cambridge, Mass.: Blackwell, 1987.

Moeran, Brian. "The Birth of the Japanese Department Store." In *Asian Department Stores*, ed. Kerrie L. MacPherson, 141–76. Honolulu: University of Hawaii Press, 1998.

Morris, Meaghan. "Metamorphoses at Sydney Tower." In *Space and Place: Theories of Identity and Location*, ed. Erica Carter, James Donald, and Judith Squires, 379–96. London: Lawrence and Wishart, 1993.

Morse, Edward Sylvester. *Japanese Homes and Their Surroundings*. 1886. Reprinted—New York: Dover Publications, 1961.

Muta Kazue. "Images of the Family in Meiji Periodicals: The Paradox Underlying the Emergence of the 'Home.'" *U.S.-Japan Women's Journal English Supplement*, no. 7 (1994): 53–71.

Nagatsuka Takashi. *The Soil*. Trans. Ann Waswo. Berkeley: University of California Press, 1993.

Nagy, Margit Maria. "'How Shall We Live?': Social Change, the Family Institution and Feminism in Prewar Japan." Ph.D. diss., University of Washington, 1981.

Narusawa Akira. "The Social Order of Modern Japan." Trans. Timothy S. George. In *The Political Economy of Japanese Society I: Contemporary Japanese Society*, forthcoming.

Natsume Soseki. *I Am a Cat*. Trans. Katsue Shibata and Motonari Kai. Tokyo: Kenkyūsha, 1961.

Nishikawa Yūko. "The Changing Form of Dwellings and the Establishment of the *Katei* (Home) in Modern Japan." *U.S.-Japan Women's Journal English Supplement*, no. 8 (1995): 3–36.

———. "The Modern Japanese Family System: Unique or Universal?" Trans. Sakai Minako and Gavan McCormack. In *Multicultural Japan: Paleolithic to Postmodern*, ed. Donald Denoon et al., 224–32. Cambridge, Eng.: Cambridge University Press, 1996.

Nolte, Sharon H., and Sally Ann Hastings. "The Meiji State's Policy Toward Women, 1890–1910." In *Recreating Japanese Women, 1600–1945*, ed. Gail Lee Bernstein, pp. 151–74. University of California Press, 1991.

Nyström-Hamilton, Louise. *Ellen Key: Her Life and Work*. Trans. A. E. B. Fries. New York and London: G. P. Putnam and Sons, 1913.

Ochiai Emiko. *The Japanese Family System in Transition: A Sociological Analysis of Family Change in Postwar Japan*. Trans. Geraldine Harcourt. LTCB International Library Foundation, 1994.

Ohmann, Richard. *Selling Culture: Magazines, Markets and Class at the Turn of the Century*. London and New York: Verso, 1996.

Ohnuki-Tierney, Emiko. *Rice as Self: Japanese Identities Through Time*. Princeton: Princeton University Press, 1993.

Okada, Richard. "'Landscape' and the Nation-state: A Reading of *Nihon fūkei ron*." In *New Directions in the Study of Meiji Japan*, ed. Helen Hardacre with Adam Kern, 90–107. Leiden and New York: Brill, 1997.

Okin, Susan Moller. "Gender, the Public and the Private." In *Political Theory Today*, ed. David Held, 67–90. Stanford: Stanford University Press, 1991.

Olsen, Frances E. "The Family and the Market: A Study of Ideology and Legal Reform." *Harvard Law Review*, no. 96 (1983): 1497–578.

Orbach, Laurence. F. *Homes for Heroes: A Study of the Evolution of British Public Housing, 1915–1921*. London: Seeley, 1977.

Orvell, Miles. *The Real Thing: Imitation and Authenticity in American Culture, 1880–1940*. Chapel Hill: University of North Carolina Press, 1989.

Oshima, Ken Tadashi. "Hijiribashi: Spanning Time and Crossing Place." Paper delivered at the Annual Conference of the Association for Asian Studies, Apr. 2002.

———. "The Japanese Garden City: The Case of Denenchofu." *Journal of the Society of Architecture Historians* 55, no. 2 (June 1996): 140–51.

———. "Media and Modernity in the Work of Yamada Mamoru." In *Architecture and Modern Japan*, edited by Henry D. Smith II. Forthcoming.

———. "Towards a Vision of the Real." *a+u*, special issue, Mar. 2000: 6–17.

Ota, Ryokichi. *Tadataka Inoo: The Japanese Land-Surveyor*. Trans. Kazue Sugimura. Tokyo: Iwanami shoten, 1932.

Partner, Simon. *Assembled in Japan: Electrical Goods and the Making of the Japanese Consumer*. Berkeley: University of California Press, 1999.

Peattie, Mark, and Ramon Myers. *The Japanese Colonial Empire, 1895–1945*. Princeton: Princeton University Press, 1984.

Pilbeam, Pamela. *The Middle Classes in Europe, 1789–1914: France, Germany, Italy, and Russia*. London: Macmillan Education, 1990.

Putnam, Tim. "Regimes of Closure: The Representation of Cultural Process in Domestic Consumption." In *Consuming Technologies: Media and Information in Domestic Spaces*, ed. Roger Silverstone and Eric Hirsch, 195–207. London and New York: Routledge, 1992.

Pyle, Kenneth B. "The Technology of Japanese Nationalism: The Local Improvement Movement, 1900–1918." *Journal of Asian Studies* 23, no. 1 (Nov. 1973): 51–65.

Radway, Janice. "On the Gender of the Middlebrow Consumer and the Threat of the Culturally Fraudulent Female." *South Atlantic Quarterly* 93, no. 4 (Fall 1994): 871–93.

Ragsdale, Kathryn. "Marriage, the Newspaper Business, and the Nation-State: Ideology in the Late Meiji Serialized *Katei Shōsetsu.*" *Journal of Japanese Studies* 24, no. 2 (1998): 229–55.

Rapoport, Amos. *House Form and Culture.* Englewood Cliffs, N.J.: Prentice-Hall, 1969.

Reed, Christopher, ed. *Not at Home: The Suppression of Domesticity in Modern Art and Architecture.* London: Thames and Hudson, 1996.

Reynolds, Jonathan. "The Bunriha and the Problem of 'Tradition' for Modernist Architecture in Japan, 1920–1928." In *Japan's Competing Modernities: Issues in Culture and Democracy, 1900–1930,* ed. Sharon Minichiello, 228–46. Honolulu: University of Hawaii Press, 1998.

———. *Maekawa Kunio and the Emergence of Japanese Modernist Architecture.* Berkeley: University of California Press, 2001.

Richards, Thomas. *The Commodity Culture of Victorian England: Advertising and Spectacle, 1851–1914.* Stanford: Stanford University Press, 1990.

Richter, Giles. "Marketing the Word: Publishing Entrepreneurs in Meiji Japan, 1870–1912." Ph.D. diss., Columbia University, 1999.

Robertson, Jennifer. *Takarazuka: Sexual Politics and Popular Culture in Modern Japan.* Berkeley: University of California, 1998.

Rodd, Laurel Rasplica. "Yosano Akiko and the Taishō Debate over the 'New Woman.'" In *Recreating Japanese Women, 1600–1945,* ed. Gail Lee Bernstein, 175–98. Berkeley: University of California Press, 1991.

Rubinfien, Louisa. "Commodity to National Brand: Manufacturers, Merchants, and the Development of the Consumer Market in Interwar Japan." Ph.D. diss., Harvard University, 1995.

Ryan, Mary P. *The Empire of the Mother: American Writing About Domesticity, 1830–1860.* Binghamton, N.Y.: Harrington Park Press, 1985.

Rykwert, Joseph. *On Adam's House in Paradise: The Idea of the Primitive Hut in Architecture History.* Cambridge, Mass.: MIT Press, 1981.

Saarikangas, Kirsi. *Model Houses for Model Families: Gender, Ideology and the Modern Dwelling.* Trans. Philip Landon and Tomi Snellman. Helsinki: Societas Historica Fennica, 1993.

Sack, Robert David. *Place, Modernity and the Consumer's World: A Relational Framework for Geographical Analysis.* Baltimore: Johns Hopkins University Press, 1992.

Sand, Jordan. "House and Home in Modern Japan," Ph.D. diss., Columbia University, 1996.

———. "Was Meiji Taste in Interiors 'Orientalist'?" *positions: east asia cultures critique* 8, no. 3 (Winter 2000): 637–73.

Sawada, Mitziko. *Tokyo Life, New York Dreams: Urban Japanese Visions of America, 1890–1924.* Berkeley: University of California Press, 1996.

Schorske, Carl. *Fin de Siecle Vienna: Politics and Culture*. Vintage Books, 1981.
Scully, Vincent. *The Shingle Style and the Stick Style: Architecture and Design from Downing to the Origins of Wright*. Rev. ed. New Haven: Yale University Press, 1971.
Seidensticker, Edward. *High City, Low City: Tokyo from Edo to the Earthquake*. Rutland, Vt.: Charles Tuttle and Co., 1983.
———. *Kafū the Scribbler: The Life and Writings of Nagai Kafū, 1879–1959*. Stanford: Stanford University Press, 1965.
Shedel, James. "Art and Identity: The Wiener Secession, 1897–1938." In *Secession: Permanence of an Idea*, ed. Eleonora Louis. Ostfildern: Verlag Gerd Hatje, 1997.
Shi, David. *The Simple Life: Plain Living and High Thinking in American Culture*. New York: Oxford University Press, 1985.
Silberman, Bernard, and H. D. Harootunian, eds. *Japan in Crisis: Essays in Taishō Democracy*. Princeton University Press, 1974.
Silverberg, Miriam. *Changing Song: The Marxist Manifestos of Nakano Shigeharu*. Princeton: Princeton University Press, 1990.
———. "Constructing a New Cultural History of Prewar Japan." In *Japan in the World*, ed. Masao Miyoshi and H. D. Harootunian. Durham, N.C.: Duke University Press, 1993.
———. "Constructing the Japanese Ethnography of Modernity." *Journal of Asian Studies* 51, no. 1 (Feb. 1992): 30–54.
———. "Remembering Pearl Harbor, Forgetting Charlie Chaplin, and the Case of the Disappearing Western Woman: A Picture Story." *positions: east asia culture critique* 1, no. 1 (1993): 24–76.
Smith, Henry Dewitt II. "From Wilsonian Democracy to Modan Life: Changing Japanese Conceptions of Americanism, 1916–1931." Paper prepared for the Bi-National Conference on Japanese-American Relations from World War I to the Manchurian Incident, sponsored by the Social Science Research Council, Kauai, Hawaii, Jan. 5–9, 1976.
———. *Japan's First Student Radicals*. Cambridge, Mass.: Harvard University Press, 1972.
Stewart, David B. *The Making of a Modern Japanese Architecture: 1868 to the Present*. Tokyo and New York: Kodansha International, 1987.
Stoler, Ann Laura. *Race and the Education of Desire: Foucault's History of Sexuality and the Colonial Order of Things*. Durham, N.C.: Duke University Press, 1995.
Stone, Lawrence. *The Family, Sex and Marriage in England, 1500–1800*. London: Weidenfeld and Nicholson, 1977.
Tanizaki Jun'ichirō. *Naomi*. Trans. Anthony H. Chambers. San Francisco: North Point Press, 1990.
Tansman, Alan. "Isoda Kōichi's 'The Dilemma of Domestic Sensibilities': An Introduction," *Journal of Japanese Studies* 21, no. 1 (Winter 1995): 35–64.

Thomas, Julia Adeney. *Reconfiguring Modernity: Concepts of Nature in Japanese Political Ideology*. Berkeley: University of California Press, 2002.

Tipton, Elise, and John Clark, eds. *Being Modern in Japan: Culture and Society from the 1910's to the 1930's*. Honolulu: Australian Humanities Research Foundation and University of Hawaii Press, 2000.

Tsutsui, William M. *Manufacturing Ideology: Scientific Management in Twentieth-Century Japan*. Princeton: Princeton University Press, 1998.

Uchida Seizō. "The Issue of Southern Exposure in the Development of Modern Japanese Housing." In *Architecture and Modern Japan*, ed. Henry D. Smith II. Forthcoming.

Uno, Kathleen. "Questioning Patrilineality: On Western Studies of the Japanese *Ie*." *positions: east asia cultures critique* 4, no. 3 (Winter 1996): 569–94.

van Bremen, Jan, and Akitoshi Shimizu, eds. *Anthropology and Colonialism in Asia and Oceania*. Richmond, Eng.: Curzon Press, 1999.

Vaporis, Constantine. *Breaking Barriers*. Cambridge, Mass.: Harvard University Press, 1994.

Vlastos, Stephen. "Agrarianism Without Tradition: The Radical Critique of Prewar Japanese Modernity." In *Mirror of Modernity: Invented Traditions of Modern Japan*, ed. Stephen Vlastos. Berkeley: University of California Press, 1998.

Vlastos, Stephen, ed. *Mirror of Modernity: Invented Traditions in Modern Japan*. Berkeley, California: University of California Press, 1998.

Vogel, Ezra. *Japan's New Middle Class: The Salary Man and His Family in a Tokyo Suburb*. 2nd ed. Berkeley, California: University of California Press, 1971.

Wahrman, Dror. *Imagining the Middle Class: The Political Representation of Class in Britain, 1780–1840*. Cambridge, Eng., and New York: Cambridge University Press, 1995.

Ward, Stephen V., ed. *The Garden City: Past, Present and Future*. London: E & F Spon, 1992.

Waswo, Ann. *Housing in Postwar Japan: A Social History*. London: Routledge, 2002.

Weisenfeld, Gennifer. "Designing After Disaster: Barrack Decoration and the Great Kanto Earthquake." *Japanese Studies* 18, no. 3 (Dec. 1998), 229–46.

———. "Japanese Modernism and Consumerism: Forging the New Artistic Field of '*Shōgyō bijutsu*' (Commercial Art)." In *Being Modern in Japan: Culture and Society from the 1910's to the 1930's*, ed. Elise K. Tipton and John Clark. Honolulu: Australian Humanities Research Foundation and University of Hawai'i Press, 2000.

———. *Mavo: Japanese Artists and the Avant-Garde, 1905–1931*. Berkeley: University of California Press, 2002.

Wendelken[-Mortensen], Cherie. "The Culture of Tea and Modern Japanese Architecture in the Interwar Years." In *Architecture and Modern Japan*, ed. Henry D. Smith II, forthcoming.

———. "Living with the Past: Preservation and Development in Japanese Architecture and Town Planning." Ph.D. diss., Massachusetts Institute of Technology, 1994.

———. "Pan-Asianism and the Pure Japanese Thing: Japanese Identity and Architecture in the Late 1930's." *positions: east asia cultures critique* 8, no. 3 (Winter 2000): 819–28.

———. "The Tectonics of Japanese Style: Architect and Carpenter in the Late Meiji Period." *Art Journal* 55, no. 3 (Fall 1996): 28–37.

Wigmore, John Henry. *Law and Justice in Tokugawa Japan.* Tokyo: University of Tokyo Press, 1967–86.

Wolff, Janet. *The Social Production of Art.* 2nd ed. New York: NYU Press, 1993.

Wright, Gwendolyn. *Building the Dream: A Social History of Housing in America.* MIT Press, 1981.

———. *Moralism and the Model Home: Domestic Architecture and Cultural Conflict in Chicago, 1873–1913.* Chicago: University of Chicago Press, 1980.

Yamakawa Kikue. *Women of the Mito Domain: Recollections of Samurai Family Life.* Trans. Kate Wildman Nakai. University of Tokyo Press, 1992.

Yoshimi Shun'ya. "The Evolution of Mass Events in Prewar Japan." *Senri Ethnological Studies* 40 (1995): 85–99.

Young, Louise. *Japan's Total Empire.* Berkeley: University of California Press, 1998.

# Index

## *Harvard East Asian Monographs*
(* out-of-print)

*1. Liang Fang-chung, *The Single-Whip Method of Taxation in China*

*2 Harold C. Hinton, *The Grain Tribute System of China, 1845–1911*

3. Ellsworth C. Carlson, *The Kaiping Mines, 1877–1912*

*4. Chao Kuo-chün, *Agrarian Policies of Mainland China: A Documentary Study, 1949–1956*

*5. Edgar Snow, *Random Notes on Red China, 1936–1945*

*6. Edwin George Beal, Jr., *The Origin of Likin, 1835–1864*

7. Chao Kuo-chün, *Economic Planning and Organization in Mainland China: A Documentary Study, 1949–1957*

*8. John K. Fairbank, *Ching Documents: An Introductory Syllabus*

*9. Helen Yin and Yi-chang Yin, *Economic Statistics of Mainland China, 1949–1957*

*10. Wolfgang Franke, *The Reform and Abolition of the Traditional Chinese Examination System*

11. Albert Feuerwerker and S. Cheng, *Chinese Communist Studies of Modern Chinese History*

12. C. John Stanley, *Late Ching Finance: Hu Kuang-yung as an Innovator*

13. S. M. Meng, *The Tsungli Yamen: Its Organization and Functions*

*14. Ssu-yü Teng, *Historiography of the Taiping Rebellion*

15. Chun-Jo Liu, *Controversies in Modern Chinese Intellectual History: An Analytic Bibliography of Periodical Articles, Mainly of the May Fourth and Post–May Fourth Era*

*16. Edward J. M. Rhoads, *The Chinese Red Army, 1927–1963: An Annotated Bibliography*

17. Andrew J. Nathan, *A History of the China International Famine Relief Commission*

*18. Frank H. H. King (ed.) and Prescott Clarke, *A Research Guide to China-Coast Newspapers, 1822–1911*

19. Ellis Joffe, *Party and Army: Professionalism and Political Control in the Chinese Officer Corps, 1949–1964*

*20. Toshio G. Tsukahira, *Feudal Control in Tokugawa Japan: The Sankin Kōtai System*

21. Kwang-Ching Liu, ed., *American Missionaries in China: Papers from Harvard Seminars*

22. George Moseley, *A Sino-Soviet Cultural Frontier: The Ili Kazakh Autonomous Chou*

23. Carl F. Nathan, *Plague Prevention and Politics in Manchuria, 1910–1931*
*24. Adrian Arthur Bennett, *John Fryer: The Introduction of Western Science and Technology into Nineteenth-Century China*
25. Donald J. Friedman, *The Road from Isolation: The Campaign of the American Committee for Non-Participation in Japanese Aggression, 1938–1941*
*26. Edward LeFevour, *Western Enterprise in Late Ching China: A Selective Survey of Jardine, Matheson and Company's Operations, 1842–1895*
27. Charles Neuhauser, *Third World Politics: China and the Afro-Asian People's Solidarity Organization, 1957–1967*
28. Kungtu C. Sun, assisted by Ralph W. Huenemann, *The Economic Development of Manchuria in the First Half of the Twentieth Century*
*29. Shahid Javed Burki, *A Study of Chinese Communes, 1965*
30. John Carter Vincent, *The Extraterritorial System in China: Final Phase*
31. Madeleine Chi, *China Diplomacy, 1914–1918*
*32. Clifton Jackson Phillips, *Protestant America and the Pagan World: The First Half Century of the American Board of Commissioners for Foreign Missions, 1810–1860*
33. James Pusey, *Wu Han: Attacking the Present through the Past*
34. Ying-wan Cheng, *Postal Communication in China and Its Modernization, 1860–1896*
35. Tuvia Blumenthal, *Saving in Postwar Japan*
36. Peter Frost, *The Bakumatsu Currency Crisis*
37. Stephen C. Lockwood, *Augustine Heard and Company, 1858–1862*
38. Robert R. Campbell, *James Duncan Campbell: A Memoir by His Son*
39. Jerome Alan Cohen, ed., *The Dynamics of China's Foreign Relations*
40. V. V. Vishnyakova-Akimova, *Two Years in Revolutionary China, 1925–1927*, tr. Steven L. Levine
*41. Meron Medzini, *French Policy in Japan during the Closing Years of the Tokugawa Regime*
42. Ezra Vogel, Margie Sargent, Vivienne B. Shue, Thomas Jay Mathews, and Deborah S. Davis, *The Cultural Revolution in the Provinces*
*43. Sidney A. Forsythe, *An American Missionary Community in China, 1895–1905*
*44. Benjamin I. Schwartz, ed., *Reflections on the May Fourth Movement.: A Symposium*
*45. Ching Young Choe, *The Rule of the Taewŏngun, 1864–1873: Restoration in Yi Korea*
46. W. P. J. Hall, *A Bibliographical Guide to Japanese Research on the Chinese Economy, 1958–1970*
47. Jack J. Gerson, *Horatio Nelson Lay and Sino-British Relations, 1854–1864*
48. Paul Richard Bohr, *Famine and the Missionary: Timothy Richard as Relief Administrator and Advocate of National Reform*
49. Endymion Wilkinson, *The History of Imperial China: A Research Guide*
50. Britten Dean, *China and Great Britain: The Diplomacy of Commercial Relations, 1860–1864*
51. Ellsworth C. Carlson, *The Foochow Missionaries, 1847–1880*

52. Yeh-chien Wang, *An Estimate of the Land-Tax Collection in China, 1753 and 1908*
53. Richard M. Pfeffer, *Understanding Business Contracts in China, 1949–1963*
54. Han-sheng Chuan and Richard Kraus, *Mid-Ching Rice Markets and Trade: An Essay in Price History*
55. Ranbir Vohra, *Lao She and the Chinese Revolution*
56. Liang-lin Hsiao, *China's Foreign Trade Statistics, 1864–1949*
*57. Lee-hsia Hsu Ting, *Government Control of the Press in Modern China, 1900–1949*
58. Edward W. Wagner, *The Literati Purges: Political Conflict in Early Yi Korea*
*59. Joungwon A. Kim, *Divided Korea: The Politics of Development, 1945–1972*
*60. Noriko Kamachi, John K. Fairbank, and Chūzō Ichiko, *Japanese Studies of Modern China Since 1953: A Bibliographical Guide to Historical and Social-Science Research on the Nineteenth and Twentieth Centuries, Supplementary Volume for 1953–1969*
61. Donald A. Gibbs and Yun-chen Li, *A Bibliography of Studies and Translations of Modern Chinese Literature, 1918–1942*
62. Robert H. Silin, *Leadership and Values: The Organization of Large-Scale Taiwanese Enterprises*
63. David Pong, *A Critical Guide to the Kwangtung Provincial Archives Deposited at the Public Record Office of London*
*64. Fred W. Drake, *China Charts the World: Hsu Chi-yü and His Geography of 1848*
*65. William A. Brown and Urgrunge Onon, translators and annotators, *History of the Mongolian People's Republic*
66. Edward L. Farmer, *Early Ming Government: The Evolution of Dual Capitals*
*67. Ralph C. Croizier, *Koxinga and Chinese Nationalism: History, Myth, and the Hero*
*68. William J. Tyler, tr., *The Psychological World of Natsume Sōseki*, by Doi Takeo
69. Eric Widmer, *The Russian Ecclesiastical Mission in Peking during the Eighteenth Century*
*70. Charlton M. Lewis, *Prologue to the Chinese Revolution: The Transformation of Ideas and Institutions in Hunan Province, 1891–1907*
71. Preston Torbert, *The Ching Imperial Household Department: A Study of Its Organization and Principal Functions, 1662–1796*
72. Paul A. Cohen and John E. Schrecker, eds., *Reform in Nineteenth-Century China*
73. Jon Sigurdson, *Rural Industrialism in China*
74. Kang Chao, *The Development of Cotton Textile Production in China*
75. Valentin Rabe, *The Home Base of American China Missions, 1880–1920*
*76. Sarasin Viraphol, *Tribute and Profit: Sino-Siamese Trade, 1652–1853*
77. Ch'i-ch'ing Hsiao, *The Military Establishment of the Yuan Dynasty*
78. Meishi Tsai, *Contemporary Chinese Novels and Short Stories, 1949–1974: An Annotated Bibliography*
*79. Wellington K. K. Chan, *Merchants, Mandarins and Modern Enterprise in Late Ching China*

80. Endymion Wilkinson, *Landlord and Labor in Late Imperial China: Case Studies from Shandong by Jing Su and Luo Lun*
*81. Barry Keenan, *The Dewey Experiment in China: Educational Reform and Political Power in the Early Republic*
*82. George A. Hayden, *Crime and Punishment in Medieval Chinese Drama: Three Judge Pao Plays*
*83. Sang-Chul Suh, *Growth and Structural Changes in the Korean Economy, 1910–1940*
84. J. W. Dower, *Empire and Aftermath: Yoshida Shigeru and the Japanese Experience, 1878–1954*
85. Martin Collcutt, *Five Mountains: The Rinzai Zen Monastic Institution in Medieval Japan*
86. Kwang Suk Kim and Michael Roemer, *Growth and Structural Transformation*
87. Anne O. Krueger, *The Developmental Role of the Foreign Sector and Aid*
*88. Edwin S. Mills and Byung-Nak Song, *Urbanization and Urban Problems*
89. Sung Hwan Ban, Pal Yong Moon, and Dwight H. Perkins, *Rural Development*
*90. Noel F. McGinn, Donald R. Snodgrass, Yung Bong Kim, Shin-Bok Kim, and Quee-Young Kim, *Education and Development in Korea*
91. Leroy P. Jones and Il SaKong, *Government, Business, and Entrepreneurship in Economic Development: The Korean Case*
92. Edward S. Mason, Dwight H. Perkins, Kwang Suk Kim, David C. Cole, Mahn Je Kim et al., *The Economic and Social Modernization of the Republic of Korea*
93. Robert Repetto, Tai Hwan Kwon, Son-Ung Kim, Dae Young Kim, John E. Sloboda, and Peter J. Donaldson, *Economic Development, Population Policy, and Demographic Transition in the Republic of Korea*
94. Parks M. Coble, Jr., *The Shanghai Capitalists and the Nationalist Government, 1927–1937*
95. Noriko Kamachi, *Reform in China: Huang Tsun-hsien and the Japanese Model*
96. Richard Wich, *Sino-Soviet Crisis Politics: A Study of Political Change and Communication*
97. Lillian M. Li, *China's Silk Trade: Traditional Industry in the Modern World, 1842–1937*
98. R. David Arkush, *Fei Xiaotong and Sociology in Revolutionary China*
*99. Kenneth Alan Grossberg, *Japan's Renaissance: The Politics of the Muromachi Bakufu*
100. James Reeve Pusey, *China and Charles Darwin*
101. Hoyt Cleveland Tillman, *Utilitarian Confucianism: Chen Liang's Challenge to Chu Hsi*
102. Thomas A. Stanley, *Ōsugi Sakae, Anarchist in Taishō Japan: The Creativity of the Ego*
103. Jonathan K. Ocko, *Bureaucratic Reform in Provincial China: Ting Jih-ch'ang in Restoration Kiangsu, 1867–1870*
104. James Reed, *The Missionary Mind and American East Asia Policy, 1911–1915*
105. Neil L. Waters, *Japan's Local Pragmatists: The Transition from Bakumatsu to Meiji in the Kawasaki Region*
106. David C. Cole and Yung Chul Park, *Financial Development in Korea, 1945–1978*

107. Roy Bahl, Chuk Kyo Kim, and Chong Kee Park, *Public Finances during the Korean Modernization Process*
108. William D. Wray, *Mitsubishi and the N.Y.K, 1870–1914: Business Strategy in the Japanese Shipping Industry*
109. Ralph William Huenemann, *The Dragon and the Iron Horse: The Economics of Railroads in China, 1876–1937*
110. Benjamin A. Elman, *From Philosophy to Philology: Intellectual and Social Aspects of Change in Late Imperial China*
111. Jane Kate Leonard, *Wei Yüan and China's Rediscovery of the Maritime World*
112. Luke S. K. Kwong, *A Mosaic of the Hundred Days:. Personalities, Politics, and Ideas of 1898*
113. John E. Wills, Jr., *Embassies and Illusions: Dutch and Portuguese Envoys to K'ang-hsi, 1666–1687*
114. Joshua A. Fogel, *Politics and Sinology: The Case of Naitō Konan (1866–1934)*
*115. Jeffrey C. Kinkley, ed., *After Mao: Chinese Literature and Society, 1978– 1981*
116. C. Andrew Gerstle, *Circles of Fantasy: Convention in the Plays of Chikamatsu*
117. Andrew Gordon, *The Evolution of Labor Relations in Japan: Heavy Industry, 1853–1955*
*118. Daniel K. Gardner, *Chu Hsi and the "Ta Hsueh": Neo-Confucian Reflection on the Confucian Canon*
119. Christine Guth Kanda, *Shinzō: Hachiman Imagery and Its Development*
*120. Robert Borgen, *Sugawara no Michizane and the Early Heian Court*
121. Chang-tai Hung, *Going to the People: Chinese Intellectual and Folk Literature, 1918–1937*
* 122. Michael A. Cusumano, *The Japanese Automobile Industry: Technology and Management at Nissan and Toyota*
123. Richard von Glahn, *The Country of Streams and Grottoes: Expansion, Settlement, and the Civilizing of the Sichuan Frontier in Song Times*
124. Steven D. Carter, *The Road to Komatsubara: A Classical Reading of the Renga Hyakuin*
125. Katherine F. Bruner, John K. Fairbank, and Richard T. Smith, *Entering China's Service: Robert Hart's Journals, 1854–1863*
126. Bob Tadashi Wakabayashi, *Anti-Foreignism and Western Learning in Early-Modern Japan: The "New Theses" of 1825*
127. Atsuko Hirai, *Individualism and Socialism: The Life and Thought of Kawai Eijirō (1891–1944)*
128. Ellen Widmer, *The Margins of Utopia: "Shui-hu hou-chuan" and the Literature of Ming Loyalism*
129. R. Kent Guy, *The Emperor's Four Treasuries: Scholars and the State in the Late Chien-lung Era*
130. Peter C. Perdue, *Exhausting the Earth: State and Peasant in Hunan, 1500–1850*
131. Susan Chan Egan, *A Latterday Confucian: Reminiscences of William Hung (1893–1980)*
132. James T. C. Liu, *China Turning Inward: Intellectual-Political Changes in the Early Twelfth Century*

133. Paul A. Cohen, *Between Tradition and Modernity: Wang T'ao and Reform in Late Ching China*
134. Kate Wildman Nakai, *Shogunal Politics: Arai Hakuseki and the Premises of Tokugawa Rule*
135. Parks M. Coble, *Facing Japan: Chinese Politics and Japanese Imperialism, 1931–1937*
136. Jon L. Saari, *Legacies of Childhood: Growing Up Chinese in a Time of Crisis, 1890–1920*
137. Susan Downing Videen, *Tales of Heichū*
138. Heinz Morioka and Miyoko Sasaki, *Rakugo: The Popular Narrative Art of Japan*
139. Joshua A. Fogel, *Nakae Ushikichi in China: The Mourning of Spirit*
140. Alexander Barton Woodside, *Vietnam and the Chinese Model.: A Comparative Study of Vietnamese and Chinese Government in the First Half of the Nineteenth Century*
141. George Elison, *Deus Destroyed: The Image of Christianity in Early Modern Japan*
142. William D. Wray, ed., *Managing Industrial Enterprise: Cases from Japan's Prewar Experience*
143. T'ung-tsu Ch'ü, *Local Government in China under the Ching*
144. Marie Anchordoguy, *Computers, Inc.: Japan's Challenge to IBM*
145. Barbara Molony, *Technology and Investment: The Prewar Japanese Chemical Industry*
146. Mary Elizabeth Berry, *Hideyoshi*
147. Laura E. Hein, *Fueling Growth: The Energy Revolution and Economic Policy in Postwar Japan*
148. Wen-hsin Yeh, *The Alienated Academy: Culture and Politics in Republican China, 1919–1937*
149. Dru C. Gladney, *Muslim Chinese: Ethnic Nationalism in the People's Republic*
150. Merle Goldman and Paul A. Cohen, eds., *Ideas Across Cultures: Essays on Chinese Thought in Honor of Benjamin L Schwartz*
151. James Polachek, *The Inner Opium War*
152. Gail Lee Bernstein, *Japanese Marxist: A Portrait of Kawakami Hajime, 1879–1946*
153. Lloyd E. Eastman, *The Abortive Revolution: China under Nationalist Rule, 1927–1937*
154. Mark Mason, *American Multinationals and Japan: The Political Economy of Japanese Capital Controls, 1899–1980*
155. Richard J. Smith, John K. Fairbank, and Katherine F. Bruner, *Robert Hart and China's Early Modernization: His Journals, 1863–1866*
156. George J. Tanabe, Jr., *Myōe the Dreamkeeper: Fantasy and Knowledge in Kamakura Buddhism*
157. William Wayne Farris, *Heavenly Warriors: The Evolution of Japan's Military, 500–1300*
158. Yu-ming Shaw, *An American Missionary in China: John Leighton Stuart and Chinese-American Relations*
159. James B. Palais, *Politics and Policy in Traditional Korea*
160. Douglas Reynolds, *China, 1898–1912: The Xinzheng Revolution and Japan*
161. Roger R. Thompson, *China's Local Councils in the Age of Constitutional Reform, 1898-1911*
162. William Johnston, *The Modern Epidemic: History of Tuberculosis in Japan*

163. Constantine Nomikos Vaporis, *Breaking Barriers: Travel and the State in Early Modern Japan*
164. Irmela Hijiya-Kirschnereit, *Rituals of Self-Revelation: Shishōsetsu as Literary Genre and Socio-Cultural Phenomenon*
165. James C. Baxter, *The Meiji Unification through the Lens of Ishikawa Prefecture*
166. Thomas R. H. Havens, *Architects of Affluence: The Tsutsumi Family and the Seibu-Saison Enterprises in Twentieth-Century Japan*
167. Anthony Hood Chambers, *The Secret Window: Ideal Worlds in Tanizaki's Fiction*
168. Steven J. Ericson, *The Sound of the Whistle: Railroads and the State in Meiji Japan*
169. Andrew Edmund Goble, *Kenmu: Go-Daigo's Revolution*
170. Denise Potrzeba Lett, *In Pursuit of Status: The Making of South Korea's "New" Urban Middle Class*
171. Mimi Hall Yiengpruksawan, *Hiraizumi: Buddhist Art and Regional Politics in Twelfth-Century Japan*
172. Charles Shirō Inouye, *The Similitude of Blossoms: A Critical Biography of Izumi Kyōka (1873–1939), Japanese Novelist and Playwright*
173. Aviad E. Raz, *Riding the Black Ship: Japan and Tokyo Disneyland*
174. Deborah J. Milly, *Poverty, Equality, and Growth: The Politics of Economic Need in Postwar Japan*
175. See Heng Teow, *Japan's Cultural Policy Toward China, 1918–1931: A Comparative Perspective*
176. Michael A. Fuller, *An Introduction to Literary Chinese*
177. Frederick R. Dickinson, *War and National Reinvention: Japan in the Great War, 1914–1919*
178. John Solt, *Shredding the Tapestry of Meaning: The Poetry and Poetics of Kitasono Katue (1902–1978)*
179. Edward Pratt, *Japan's Protoindustrial Elite: The Economic Foundations of the Gōnō*
180. Atsuko Sakaki, *Recontextualizing Texts: Narrative Performance in Modern Japanese Fiction*
181. Soon-Won Park, *Colonial Industrialization and Labor in Korea: The Onoda Cement Factory*
182. JaHyun Kim Haboush and Martina Deuchler, *Culture and the State in Late Chosŏn Korea*
183. John W. Chaffee, *Branches of Heaven: A History of the Imperial Clan of Sung China*
184. Gi-Wook Shin and Michael Robinson, eds., *Colonial Modernity in Korea*
185. Nam-lin Hur, *Prayer and Play in Late Tokugawa Japan: Asakusa Sensōji and Edo Society*
186. Kristin Stapleton, *Civilizing Chengdu: Chinese Urban Reform, 1895–1937*
187. Hyung Il Pai, *Constructing "Korean" Origins: A Critical Review of Archaeology, Historiography, and Racial Myth in Korean State-Formation Theories*
188. Brian D. Ruppert, *Jewel in the Ashes: Buddha Relics and Power in Early Medieval Japan*
189. Susan Daruvala, *Zhou Zuoren and an Alternative Chinese Response to Modernity*

190. James Z. Lee, *The Political Economy of a Frontier: Southwest China, 1250–1850*
191. Kerry Smith, *A Time of Crisis: Japan, the Great Depression, and Rural Revitalization*
192. Michael Lewis, *Becoming Apart: National Power and Local Politics in Toyama, 1868–1945*
193. William C. Kirby, Man-houng Lin, James Chin Shih, and David A. Pietz, eds., *State and Economy in Republican China: A Handbook for Scholars*
194. Timothy S. George, *Minamata: Pollution and the Struggle for Democracy in Postwar Japan*
195. Billy K. L. So, *Prosperity, Region, and Institutions in Maritime China: The South Fukien Pattern, 946–1368*
196. Yoshihisa Tak Matsusaka, *The Making of Japanese Manchuria, 1904–1932*
197. Maram Epstein, *Competing Discourses: Orthodoxy, Authenticity, and Engendered Meanings in Late Imperial Chinese Fiction*
198. Curtis J. Milhaupt, J. Mark Ramseyer, and Michael K. Young, eds. and comps., *Japanese Law in Context: Readings in Society, the Economy, and Politics*
199. Haruo Iguchi, *Unfinished Business: Ayukawa Yoshisuke and U.S.-Japan Relations, 1937–1953*
200. Scott Pearce, Audrey Spiro, and Patricia Ebrey, *Culture and Power in the Reconstitution of the Chinese Realm, 200–600*
201. Terry Kawashima, *Writing Margins: The Textual Construction of Gender in Heian and Kamakura Japan*
202. Martin W. Huang, *Desire and Fictional Narrative in Late Imperial China*
203. Robert S. Ross and Jiang Changbin, eds., *Re-examining the Cold War: U.S.-China Diplomacy, 1954–1973*
204. Guanhua Wang, *In Search of Justice: The 1905–1906 Chinese Anti-American Boycott*
205. David Schaberg, *A Patterned Past: Form and Thought in Early Chinese Historiography*
206. Christine Yano, *Tears of Longing: Nostalgia and the Nation in Japanese Popular Song*
207. Milena Doleželová-Velingerová and Oldřich Král, with Graham Sanders, eds., *The Appropriation of Cultural Capital: China's May Fourth Project*
208. Robert N. Huey, *The Making of 'Shinkokinshū'*
209. Lee Butler, *Emperor and Aristocracy in Japan, 1467–1680: Resilience and Renewal*
210. Suzanne Ogden, *Inklings of Democracy in China*
211. Kenneth J. Ruoff, *The People's Emperor: Democracy and the Japanese Monarchy, 1945–1995*
212. Haun Saussy, *Great Walls of Discourse and Other Adventures in Cultural China*
213. Aviad E. Raz, *Emotions at Work: Normative Control, Organizations, and Culture in Japan and America*
214. Rebecca E. Karl and Peter Zarrow, eds., *Rethinking the 1898 Reform Period: Political and Cultural Change in Late Qing China*
215. Kevin O'Rourke, *The Book of Korean Shijo*
216. Ezra F. Vogel, Yuan Ming, and Tanaka Akihiko, *The Golden Age of the U.S.-China-Japan Triangle, 1972–1989*

217. Thomas A Wilson, ed., *On Sacred Grounds: Culture, Society, Politics, and the Formation of the Cult of Confucius*
218. Donald S. Sutton, *Steps of Perfection: Exorcistic Performers and Chinese Religion in Twentieth-Century Taiwan*
219. Daqing Yang, *Technology of Empire: Telecommunications and Japanese Imperialism, 1930–1945*
220. Qianshen Bai, *Fu Shan's World: The Transformation of Chinese Calligraphy in the Seventeenth Century*
221. Paul Jakov Smith and Richard von Glahn, eds., *The Song-Yuan-Ming Transition in Chinese History*
222. Rania Huntington, *Alien Kind: Foxes and Late Imperial Chinese Narrative*
223. Jordan Sand, *House and Home in Modern Japan: Architecture, Domestic Space, and Bourgeois Culture, 1880–1930*